Patterns for College Writing

A Rhetorical Reader and Guide

Sixth Edition

Patterns for College Writing

A Rhetorical Reader and Guide

Sixth Edition

LAURIE G. KIRSZNER
Philadelphia College of Pharmacy and Science

STEPHEN R. MANDELL
Drexel University

St. Martin's Press   New York

Senior editor: Karen Allanson
Development editor: John Elliott
Manager, publishing services: Emily Berleth
Publishing services associate: Kalea Chapman
Project management: Omega Publishing Services, Inc.
Cover design: David Bamford
Cover painting: Matisse, *Panneau au Masque,* 1947. Courtesy of the Museum of
          Decorative Arts, Denmark. © 1994 Succession H. Matisse, A.R.S./NY.

For information, write:
St. Martin's Press, Inc.
175 Fifth Avenue
New York, NY 10010

ISBN: 0-312-10113-9

Acknowledgments
Acknowledgments and copyrights are continued at the back of the book on pages
695–97, which constitute an extension of the copyright page.

Maya Angelou, "Finishing School." From *I Know Why the Caged Bird Sings.* Copyright © 1969 by
    Maya Angelou. Reprinted with the permission of Random House, Inc.
Judy Brady, "I Want a Wife." From *Ms.,* 1970. Copyright © 1970 by Judy Syfers. Reprinted with
    the permission of the author.
José Antonio Burciaga, "Tortillas." From *Weedee Peepo* (Edinburg, TX: Pan American University
    Press, 1988). Reprinted with the permission of the publishers.
Bruce Catton, "Grant and Lee: A Study in Contrasts." From *The American Story,* edited by Earl
    Schenk Miers. Copyright United States Capitol Historical Society. Reprinted by permission. All
    rights reserved.
Sandra Cisneros, "Only Daughter." From *Glamour,* November 1990. Copyright © 1990 by The
    Conde Nast Publications, Inc. Reprinted with the permission of the publishers.
Norman Cousins, "Who Killed Benny Paret?" From *Present Tense.* Copyright © 1967 by Norman
    Cousins. Reprinted with the permission of Eleanor Cousins.
Joan Didion, "Salvador." From *Salvador* (New York: Simon & Schuster, 1983). Copyright © 1983
    by Joan Didion. Reprinted with the permission of the author.
Barbara Dority, "The PC Speech Police." From *The Humanist,* March/April 1992. Copyright ©
    1992. Reprinted with the permission of the American Humanist Association.
Michael Dorris, "Why Mr. Ed Still Talks Good Horse Sense." From *TV Guide,* May 28/June 3,
    1988. Copyright © 1988 by News America Publications Inc. Reprinted with the permission of
    TV Guide.
Lars Eighner, "On Dumpster Diving." From *Travels with Lizbeth.* Originally published in *The
    Threepenny Review,* Fall 1991. Copyright © 1991, 1993 by Lars Eighner. Reprinted with the
    permission of St. Martin's Press.

For Peter Phelps (1936–1990), with thanks

Preface

In preparing the sixth edition of *Patterns for College Writing,* we have made many changes large and small, but our original purpose and approach remain the same. As always, our main concern is practical: to help students prepare for writing assignments not only in the English classroom but in their other college courses. Our approach combines precept and example: Discussions of writing procedure and rhetorical pattern are immediately illustrated by one or more annotated student papers and then followed by a series of professionally written pieces for analysis and discussion in the classroom.

Many instructors have found that in a single volume *Patterns* answers their needs both for a writing textbook and for an anthology— with the extra benefit that the two complement each other. We are confident that these instructors will find the sixth edition significantly improved in both aspects—its discussions fuller and clearer, its readings more varied and more interesting. The many other instructors who have used *Patterns* mainly as an anthology will find the sixth edition still very manageable for that purpose and considerably strengthened by the new selections.

NEW TO THE SIXTH EDITION

Approximately half of the readings are new to this edition, including seven new student essays. In this edition we have retained the selections that our colleagues felt were most useful to their students and that our own students enjoyed the most. We have replaced other, less favored, readings with fresh, timely selections that will interest students—for example, Amy Wang's "The Same Difference," Michael Dorris's "Why Mr. Ed Still Talks Good Horse Sense," Garry Trudeau's "Anatomy of a Joke," Deborah Tannen's "Sex, Lies, and Conversation," Al Gore's "Ships in the Desert," and José Antonio Burciaga's "Tortillas."

Major changes have been made in the Argumentation chapter, which now includes a brief treatment of Toulmin logic and three sets of paired essays taking opposing positions on issues related to campus life: multicultural education, speech codes, and affirmative action. In addition, to show students that an issue can have more than two sides, the chapter now includes a collection of four essays presenting various points of view on the topic of date rape. With this expanded treatment of argument and thirteen readings, this chapter can be used as a mini-argument reader as well.

Collaborative activities have been added at the end of each chapter. These new activities provide an opportunity for students to work in small groups to generate ideas and discover connections.

A new section at the end of the book, "Essays for Further Reading: Combining the Patterns," includes a professional essay and a student essay that successfully combine a number of different patterns of development. Both essays are annotated to illustrate the use of multiple rhetorical patterns within a single piece of writing.

FEATURES OF *PATTERNS FOR COLLEGE WRITING*

As before, we lead off this edition with "Introduction: Reading to Write," which gives students an overview of critical reading, particularly in relation to the selections and apparatus in *Patterns.* Using a short piece by Henry Louis Gates, Jr., as a model, the introduction demonstrates ways of reading a selection critically and how to highlight and annotate in preparation for class discussion and writing.

The book's first chapter remains a comprehensive treatment of the writing process, which we have carefully revised in response to suggestions from users of previous editions. This chapter, which functions as a "mini-rhetoric," includes extensive advice on strategies for planning, writing, and revising, including brainstorming, clustering, journal writing, and editing. Here we explain to students how they can move confidently through the process of invention by understanding their assignment; recognizing the limits set by a paper's length, purpose, audience, and occasion, as well as by their own knowledge; narrowing a subject to a workable topic; generating ideas through various invention techniques; and formulating a thesis. The chapter goes on to discuss arrangement, analyzing the parts of the essay in some detail. Finally, we consider drafting and revising, illustrating our discussion with a preliminary draft of a student essay followed by its two successive revisions, all accompanied by unusually thorough analysis.

Chapters 2–10 of *Patterns for College Writing* discuss and illustrate the patterns of development that students will use in their college writing assignments: narration, description, exemplification, process, cause and effect, comparison and contrast, classification and division, definition, and argumentation. Each chapter begins with a comprehensive introduction that first presents a paragraph-length example of the pattern to be discussed, then defines and illustrates the pattern, and finally provides a thorough analysis of one or more annotated student papers to show how the chapter's concepts can be applied to particular college writing situations. The commentary that follows each student essay includes a "Focus on Revision" section designed to reinforce the concept that writing is an ongoing process. Each chapter introduction has been revised in the interests of greater completeness and clarity.

Each chapter then goes on to illustrate the pattern more fully with reading selections, diverse in subject, style, and cultural perspective, by professional writers. As in the fifth edition, each chapter (except Argumentation) includes a short story or poem as well as essays. Like the student examples in the introductions, the essays are not intended to be imitated (though they may serve as stimuli for student writing). Rather, they are designed to suggest possibilities for arranging material and developing ideas.

As before, each essay is followed by four types of questions designed to help students measure their comprehension of the essay's content, their understanding of the author's purpose and audience, their recognition of the stylistic and structural techniques used to shape the essay, and their sensitivity to the nuances of word choice and figurative language. In addition, each essay is accompanied by a suggestion for a "Journal Entry," a brief, informal response to the essay's ideas. As in previous editions, with every selection we include a "Writing Workshop" of suggestions for full-length student writing assignments. Many of these ask students to respond to a specific situation and to consider a specific audience and purpose, thus making their assignments not only more concrete but also more interesting. Finally, each essay is followed by the popular "Thematic

Connections" feature, which suggests other works in the text that are thematically related to the selection.

The stories and poems in the text are also accompanied by apparatus. Three "Thinking about Literature" questions following each literary work encourage students to respond to the work's ideas as well as to its structure, a "Journal Entry" suggestion offers a provocative short writing assignment, and the "Thematic Connections" feature identifies thematic links between essays and works of imaginative literature.

At the end of each chapter is a comprehensive list of writing topics, some of which ask students to make connections among several selections in the chapter. Following this list is a "Collaborative Activity," a feature new to the sixth edition. The book's final section, "Essays for Further Reading: Combining the Patterns," is also new to this edition. As before, the book concludes with a helpful glossary of terms.

In this sixth edition, we have continued to adhere to our original approach, as defined in the book's first five editions. We hope that by offering interesting and accessible reading selections, by fully analyzing student writing that represents many academic disciplines, by stressing the importance of purpose and audience in our questions and assignments, and by presenting writing as a flexible, individualized process, we may encourage students to approach college writing not as a chore but as a challenge. We continue to be guided by what our own students have taught us: When writing is presented as a skill that can be learned and applied to assignments in many fields, students will work to master that skill.

ACKNOWLEDGMENTS

As always, friends, colleagues, students, and family all helped this project along. Of particular value were the responses to a questionnaire sent to users of the fifth edition, and we thank each of the instructors who responded so frankly and helpfully: Martin Achatz, Western Michigan University; Christopher Baker, Lamar University; Joy R. Davis, Bessemer State Technical College; Herman K. Dotson, Seminole Junior College; Shirley Rader Felt, Southern California College; James P. Galas, San Diego City College; Charles Hill, Gadsden State Community College; Barbara Huval, Lamar

University–Port Arthur; Conception L. Magana, Garden City Community College; Diana Malouf, Northern Michigan University; Jerry Olson, Middlesex County College; Janet Kay Porter, Leeward Community College; Gene Pouncy, El Centro College; Martha A. Saunders, West Georgia College; Mary Etta Scott, Avila College; Terence J. Sheridan, Massasoit Community College; Pamela Stathes, Southwestern College; Vivian Thomlinson, Cameron University; J. K. Van Dover, Lincoln University; and Delmar C. Wilcox, Western New England College.

We are also grateful to the following colleagues, who provided useful commentary on various drafts of this new edition: Barbara Carr, Stephen F. Austin State University; Duane Hawkinson, St. Cloud State University and Hutchinson Community College; Bill M. Stiffler, Harford Community College; and Barbara Stout, Montgomery College, Rockville Campus.

Special thanks go to Mark Gallaher—a true professional and a valued friend—for revising the Instructor's Manual for this edition.

Through six editions of *Patterns for College Writing,* we have enjoyed a wonderful working relationship with St. Martin's Press. We have always found the editorial and production staff to be efficient, cooperative, and generous with their time and advice. During our work on this edition, we benefited from the thoughtful comments and careful attention to detail of John Elliott, Development Editor, and from the helpful advice of Karen Allanson, Senior English Editor. We are also grateful to Emily Berleth, Manager of Publishing Services, and Richard Wright of Omega Publishing Services for their work in overseeing the book's production. Having people like these around has made our work a lot easier and a lot more pleasant.

We are fortunate to have enjoyed our own nineteen-year collaboration; we know how rare a successful partnership like ours is. We also know how lucky we are to have our families—Mark, Adam, and Rebecca Kirszner and Demi, David, and Sarah Mandell—to help us keep in touch with the things that really matter.

Laurie G. Kirszner
Stephen R. Mandell

Contents

2. NARRATION   63

5. PROCESS   233

6.   CAUSE AND EFFECT   283

my sex of having cornered the world's pleasures. I think something like my bafflement has been felt by other boys (and by girls as well) who grew up in dirt-poor farm country, in mining country, in black ghettos, in Hispanic barrios, in the shadows of factories, in Third World nations—any place where the fate of men is as grim and bleak as the fate of women."

9. DEFINITION   487

10. ARGUMENTATION   533

almost always meant 'Never.' We must come to see, with one of our distinguished jurists, that 'justice too long delayed is justice denied.'"

Thematic Guide to the Contents

Arranged by Subject

EDUCATION

SPORTS AND ENTERTAINMENT

HISTORY AND POLITICS

SCIENCE AND TECHNOLOGY

LANGUAGE AND LITERATURE

ETHICS, JUSTICE, AND RELIGION

GENDER

Introduction:
Reading to Write

On a purely practical level, you will read the selections collected in this text in order to answer study questions and prepare for class discussions. More importantly, however, you will read to evaluate the ideas of others, to form judgments, and, ultimately, to develop original points of view. By introducing you to new ideas and new ways of thinking about familiar concepts, reading prepares you to respond critically to the ideas of others and develop ideas of your own. Because it enables you to formulate informed opinions and judgments, to exchange ideas with others in conversation, to ask and answer questions, and to develop ideas that can be explored in writing, reading is a vital part of your education.

READING CRITICALLY

Reading is a two-way street. Readers are presented with a writer's ideas, but they also bring their own responses and interpretations to what they read. After all, readers have different national, ethnic, racial, and geographic backgrounds and different kinds of knowledge and experiences; as a result, they may react differently to a given essay or story and may interpret it somewhat differently. For example, urban readers may miss the point of an essay about a childhood experience that demonstrates the enriching powers of the wilderness. However, such readers may also have had experiences that enable them to spot bias in or challenge the assumptions of the essay. Readers from an economically and ethnically homogeneous suburban neighborhood may have great difficulty understanding a story about class conflict, but such readers may also approach it with greater objectivity than readers who are struggling with such issues on a personal level.

These differences in reactions do not mean that any interpretation at all is acceptable, that an essay or story or poem may mean whatever a reader wants it to mean. A reader must make sure he or she is not distorting the writer's words, overlooking (or ignoring) significant details, or reading irrelevant information into an essay or story. What is important is not that all readers agree on a particular interpretation, but that each reader carefully and responsibly develop an interpretation that can be supported by the content of the work.

The study questions that accompany the readings in this text encourage you to question writers' ideas. Although some of the questions—particularly those listed under "Comprehension"—will call for fairly straightforward factual responses, other questions—particularly those designated "Journal Entry"—are designed to elicit more complex responses that reflect your individual reaction to the selection.

READING ACTIVELY

When you read a work in this text that you expect to discuss in class (and perhaps to write about), you should read it carefully—and you should read it more than once.

Before You Read

Before you read, look over a selection to get a general overview. If a selection has a headnote, begin by reading it. Next, skim the selection to get a general sense of the order and emphasis of the writer's ideas. As you read, look carefully at the title and at any internal headings, and note the use of bold-face type, italics, and the like. Pay special attention to the introductory and concluding paragraphs, where a writer is likely to make (and reiterate) key points.

As You Read

As you read, ask yourself questions like the following:

What is the writer's general subject?
What is the writer's main point?
What goal does the writer hope to accomplish?
What kind of audience is the writer addressing?

Do you agree with the writer's ideas?

Does the writer seem biased?

Do you have any knowledge that could challenge the writer's ideas?

Is any information missing?

Are any sequential or logical links missing?

Can you identify themes or ideas that you recall from other works you have read?

Can you identify parallels with your own experience?

HIGHLIGHTING AND ANNOTATING

As you read and reread, be sure to record in writing your reactions to the selection. These written notations will help you to understand the writer's ideas and your own thinking about those ideas.

Every reader develops a different system of recording such responses, but many readers use a combination of **highlighting** and **annotating.** When you *highlight,* you mark the text with symbols. You might, for example, underline important ideas, box key terms, number a series of related points, circle an unfamiliar word (or place a question mark beside it), draw vertical lines in the margin beside a particularly interesting passage, draw arrows to connect related points, or place asterisks next to discussions of the work's central issues or themes.

When you *annotate*, you carry on a conversation with the text, making marginal notes that might, among other things, ask questions, suggest possible parallels with other reading selections or with your own experiences, argue with the writer's points, comment on the writer's style, or define unfamiliar terms and concepts. Here too your goal is to better understand what you are reading, and the process of writing down your responses will help you to achieve this goal.

The paragraph that follows, excerpted from Maya Angelou's "Finishing School" (p.78), illustrates the method of highlighting and annotating described above.

Date written?

why does she mention this?

Recently a white woman from Texas, who would quickly describe herself as a liberal, asked me about my hometown. When I told her that in Stamps my grandmother had owned the only Negro general merchandise store since the turn of the century, she exclaimed, "Why, you were a

Serious or sarcastic?

What are these values?

Also true of boys? In North as well as South? True today?

debutante." Ridiculous and even ludicrous. But Negro girls in small Southern towns, whether poverty-stricken or just munching along on a few of life's necessities, were given as extensive and irrelevant preparations for adulthood as rich white girls shown in magazines. Admittedly the training was not the same. While white girls learned to waltz and sit gracefully with a tea cup balanced on their knees, we were lagging behind, learning the mid-Victorian values with very little money to indulge them. . . .

READING THE SELECTIONS IN THIS BOOK

The selection that follows, "What's in a Name?" by Henry Louis Gates, Jr., is typical of those collected in this text. It is preceded by a headnote that provides information about the author's life and career. The essay and the headnote are meant to be read carefully and highlighted and annotated selectively.

"WHAT'S IN A NAME?"

Henry Louis Gates, Jr.

Henry Louis Gates, Jr., was born in 1950 in Keyser, West Virginia. He graduated from Yale University in 1973 and earned his doctorate from Cambridge University in 1979. He has taught at Yale, Cornell, and Duke universities and is currently the W.E.B. DuBois Professor of the Humanities and chair of the Afro-American Studies Department at Harvard University. Gates has edited many publications of the works of black writers as well as numerous books of literary criticism. He is the author of Figures in Black: Words, Signs, and the Racial Self *(1987);* The Signifying Monkey: A Theory of Afro-American Literary Criticism *(1988), which won an American Book Award in 1989;* Loose Canons: Notes on the Culture Wars *(1992); and* Colored People *(1994). Gates advocates a broader representation of non-European cultures in the basic university curriculum and works to establish a strong community of black students and scholars. In this selection, originally published in the journal* Dissent *in 1989, Gates recalls an incident from his childhood that contributed to his understanding of the significance of race in his society.*

The question of color takes up much space in these pages, but the question of color, especially in this country, operates to hide the graver questions of the self.
—James Baldwin, 1961

. . . blood, darky, Tar Baby, Kaffir, shine . . . moor, blackamoor, Jim Crow, spook . . . quadroon, meriney, red bone, high yellow . . . Mammy, porch monkey, home, homeboy, George . . . spearchucker, schwarze, Leroy, Smokey . . . mouli, buck. Ethiopian, brother, sistah. . . .
—Trey Ellis, 1989

I had forgotten the incident completely, until I read Trey Ellis's 1
essay, "Remember My Name," in a recent issue of the *Village Voice* (June 13, 1989). But there, in the middle of an extended italicized list of the by-names of "the race" ("the race" or "our people" being the terms my parents used in polite or reverential discourse, "jigaboo" or "nigger" more commonly used in anger, jest, or pure disgust) it was: "George." Now the events of that very brief exchange return to mind so vividly that I wonder why I had forgotten it.

My father and I were walking home at dusk from his second job.   2
He "moonlighted" as a janitor in the evenings for the telephone
company. Every day but Saturday, he would come home at 3:30 from
his regular job at the paper mill, wash up, eat supper, then at 4:30
head downtown to his second job. He used to make jokes frequently
about a union official who moonlighted. I never got the joke, but he
and his friends thought it was hilarious. All I knew was that my
family always ate well, that my brother and I had new clothes to
wear, and that all of the white people in Piedmont, West Virginia,
treated my parents with an odd mixture of resentment and respect
that even we understood at the time had something directly to do
with a small but certain measure of financial security.

He had left a little early that evening because I was with him and   3
I had to be in bed early. I could not have been more than five or six,
and we had stopped off at the Cut-Rate Drug Store (where no black
person in town but my father could sit down to eat, and eat off real
plates with real silverware) so that I could buy some caramel ice
cream, two scoops in a wafer cone, please, which I was busy licking
when Mr. Wilson walked by.

Mr. Wilson was a very quiet man, whose stony, brooding, silent   4
manner seemed designed to scare off any overtures of friendship,
even from white people. He was Irish, as was one-third of our village
(another third being Italian), the more affluent among whom sent
their children to "Catholic School" across the bridge in Maryland. He
had white straight hair, like my Uncle Joe, whom he uncannily
resembled, and he carried a black worn metal lunch pail, the kind
that Riley carried on the television show. My father always spoke to
him, and for reasons that we never did understand, he always spoke
to my father.

"Hello, Mr. Wilson," I heard my father say.   5

"Hello, George."   6

I stopped licking my ice cream cone, and asked my Dad in a loud   7
voice why Mr. Wilson had called him "George."

"Doesn't he know your name, Daddy? Why don't you tell him your   8
name? Your name isn't George."

For a moment I tried to think of who Mr. Wilson was mixing Pop   9
up with. But we didn't have any Georges among the colored people
in Piedmont; nor were there colored Georges living in the neighbor-
ing towns and working at the mill.

"Tell him your name, Daddy."   10

"He knows my name, boy," my father said after a long pause. "He   11
calls all colored people George."

A long silence ensued. It was "one of those things," as my Mom   12
would put it. Even then, that early, I knew when I was in the
presence of "one of those things," one of those things that provided a
glimpse, through a rent curtain, at another world that we could not
affect but that affected us. There would be a painful moment of
silence, and you would wait for it to give way to a discussion of a
black superstar such as Sugar Ray or Jackie Robinson.

"Nobody hits better in a clutch than Jackie Robinson."   13

"That's right. Nobody."   14

I never again looked Mr. Wilson in the eye.   15

RESPONDING TO READING SELECTIONS

Once you have read a selection carefully and recorded your initial
reactions to it in writing, you should be well prepared to respond to
specific questions about it. The study questions that follow each
essay in Chapters 2 through 10 of this text are intended to guide you
through the rest of the reading process and to help you think critically about what you are reading. These questions begin by testing
your comprehension of what you are reading. They go on to raise
more analytical issues about the writer's purpose and the options he
or she has chosen, and then they ask you to make connections between the selection and your own opinions or personal experiences.
Five types of study questions follow each essay:

Comprehension questions help you to measure your understanding of what the writer is saying.
Purpose and Audience questions ask you to consider why, and for
   whom, each selection was written and to examine the implications of the writer's choices in view of a particular purpose
   or intended audience.
Style and Structure questions encourage you to examine the decisions the writer has made about elements like arrangement
   of ideas, paragraphing, sentence structure, word choice, and
   imagery.
Vocabulary Projects ask you to define certain words, to consider
   the connotations of others, and to examine the writer's reasons for selecting particular words or patterns of diction.
Journal Entry questions ask you to respond informally to what
   you read and to speculate freely about related ideas—perhaps
   exploring ethical issues raised by the selection or offering your

opinions about the writer's actions or statements. Briefer, less polished, and less structured than full-length essays, journal entries allow you to respond critically to a reading selection. Sometimes they can also serve as sources of ideas for more formal kinds of writing.

Following these sets of questions are two additional features:

Writing Workshop assignments ask you to write essays structured according to the pattern of development explained and illustrated in the chapter.

Thematic Connections suggest other readings in this book that explore themes like those in the selection and will therefore enhance your understanding or appreciation of it.

The story or poem that is the final selection in each chapter is followed by *Thinking about Literature* questions, a *Journal Entry,* and *Thematic Connections.* Finally, at the end of each chapter, *Writing Assignments* offer additional practice in writing essays structured according to a particular pattern of development, and a *Collaborative Activity* suggests an idea for a group project.

Following are some examples of study questions and possible responses, as well as a Writing Workshop assignment and Thematic Connections, for "'What's in a Name?'" (pages 5–7). The numbers in parentheses following quotations refer to the paragraphs in which the quotations appear.

COMPREHENSION

1. *In paragraph 1 Gates wonders why he forgot about the exchange between his father and Mr. Wilson. Why do you think he forgot about it?* Gates may have forgotten about the incident simply because it was something that happened a long time ago, or because incidents like this one were commonplace when he was a child. Alternatively, he may *not* have forgotten the exchange between his father and Mr. Wilson but rather pushed it out of his mind because he found it so painful (after all, he says he was never again able to look Mr. Wilson in the eye).

2. *How was the social status of Gates's family different from that of other black families in Piedmont, West Virginia? How does Gates account for this difference?* Gates's family is different from other African-American families in town in that they are treated with "an odd mixture of resentment and respect" (2) by whites. Although other blacks

are not permitted to eat at the drug store, Mr. Gates is. Gates attributes this social status to his family's "small but certain measure of financial security" (2). Even so, when Mr. Wilson insults Mr. Gates, the privileged status of the Gates family is exposed as false.

3. *What does Gates mean when he says, "It was 'one of those things,' as my Mom would put it" (12)?* Gates's comment seems to indicate that the family is used to being slighted, and perhaps even insulted, by whites, but that they have learned to see such mistreatment as routine. In context, the word *things* in paragraph 12 refers to the kind of incident that gives Gates and his family a glimpse of the way the white world operates.

4. *Why does Gates's family turn to discussions of "black superstars" after a "painful moment of silence" such as the one he describes?* Although Gates does not explain the family's behavior, we can infer that they speak of African-American heroes like prizefighter Sugar Ray Robinson and baseball player Jackie Robinson to make themselves feel better. In effect, such discussions are intended to balance the negative images of blacks created by incidents such as the one Gates describes and to bolster the low self-esteem they feel as a result. These heroes seem to have won the respect denied to the Gates family; to mention them is to participate vicariously in their glory.

5. *Why do you think Gates "never again looked Mr. Wilson in the eye" (15)?* Gates may have felt that Mr. Wilson was somehow the enemy, not to be trusted, because he had insulted Gates's father. Or he may have been ashamed to look him in the eye because he believed his father should have insisted on being addressed properly.

PURPOSE AND AUDIENCE

1. *What do you think motivated Gates to introduce his narrative with the two quotations he selects? How do you suppose he expected his audience to react to them? How do you react?* Gates begins with two quotations by black writers, written nearly 30 years apart. Baldwin's words seem to suggest that, in the United States, "the question of color" is a barrier to understanding "the graver questions of the self." That is, the label "black" or "white" may mask more significant characteristics or issues. Ellis's list of names (many pejorative) for African Americans illustrates the specific process by which epithets can be used to dehumanize people—can, in effect, rob a person of his or her "self." This issue of the discrepancy between the name and what lies behind the name is central to Gates's essay. In one sense, then, he begins with these two quotations because they are relevant to the issues he will go on to discuss. More specifically, he is using the two quotations— particularly Ellis's string of unpleasant names—to arouse interest in

his topic and provide an intellectual and emotional context for the piece to follow. He may also be intending to create a sense of discomfort in his white readers and perhaps anger in his black readers. How you react depends on the attitudes about race (and perhaps about language) you bring to the text.

2. *What is the point of Gates's narrative? That is, why does he recount the incident?* It is difficult to isolate any one specific "point" this narrative makes. Certainly Gates wishes to make readers aware of the awkward, and potentially dangerous, position of his father (and, by extension, of other blacks) in a small southern town in the 1950s. He is also making a point about how names help to shape people's perceptions and actions: As long as Mr. Wilson can call all black men "George," he can continue to see them as insignificant and treat them as inferiors. The title of the piece, however, does suggest that the way names shape perceptions is the writer's main point.

3. *The title of this selection, which Gates places in quotation marks, is an allusion to Act 2, Scene 2 of Shakespeare's* Romeo and Juliet, *where Juliet says, "What's in a name? That which we call a rose / By any other name would smell as sweet." Why do you think Gates chose this title? Does he expect his audience to recognize the quotation?* Although Gates could not have been certain that all members of his audience would be able to identify the allusion to *Romeo and Juliet*, he could be reasonably sure that if they did, the reference would enhance their understanding of the selection. In Shakespeare's play the two lovers are kept apart essentially because of their names: She is a Capulet and he is a Montague, and the two families are involved in a bitter feud. In the speech from which Gates takes the title quotation, Juliet questions the logic of such a restriction. In her view, what a person is called should not determine how he or she is regarded—and this, of course, is one of Gates's points as well. (Interestingly, when Mr. Wilson calls Mr. Gates "George," it *does* make a difference; in this sense the allusion is ironic.) Even if readers are not able to identify the allusion, however, the title's quotation still serves to preview the selection's focus on names.

STYLE AND STRUCTURE

1. *Does paragraph 1 add something vital to the narrative, or would it make sense without the introduction? Could a different kind of introduction work as well?* Gates's first paragraph supplies the context in which the incident is to be read—that is, it makes clear that Mr. Wilson's calling Mr. Gates "George" is not an isolated incident but rather part of a pattern of behavior that allows those in positions of power to mistreat those they classify as inferior. For this reason, it is

an effective introduction. While the narrative would make sense without it, its full impact would probably not be as great. Still, Gates could have begun differently. For example, he could have started with the incident itself (paragraph 2) and interjected his comments about the significance of names later in the piece. He could also have begun with the exchange of dialogue in paragraphs 5 through 11 and then moved to the current paragraph 1 to supply the incident's context.

2. *What does the use of dialogue contribute to the narrative? Would the selection have a different impact without dialogue? Explain.* Gates is five or six years old when the incident he describes occurs, and the dialogue helps to establish the child's spontaneity and innocence. It also reveals his father's quiet acceptance of the situation. In short, the dialogue is a valuable addition to the piece because it creates two characters, one innocent and one resigned to the world's injustices, both of whom stand in contrast to the voice of the adult narrator: wise, worldly, but also angry and perhaps ashamed, the voice of a man who has reaped the benefits of the sacrifices made by men like Mr. Gates.

3. *Why do you think Gates supplies the specific details he chooses in paragraphs 2 and 3? In paragraph 4? Is all this information necessary?* The details Gates provides in paragraphs 2 and 3 help to establish the status of the Gates family in Piedmont; because readers have this information, the fact that the Gateses are ultimately disregarded and discounted by whites emerges as deeply ironic. The information in paragraph 4 also contributes to this irony. Here we learn that Mr. Wilson is not liked by many whites, that he looks like Gates's Uncle Joe, and that he carries a workingman's lunch box—in other words, that he has no particular status in the town apart from that conferred by the color of his skin.

VOCABULARY PROJECTS

1. *Define each of the following words as it is used in this selection.*
   by-names (1)—nicknames
   measure (2)—extent or degree
   uncannily (4)—strangely
   rent (12)—torn
   ensued (12)—followed

2. *Consider the connotations of the words* colored *and* black, *both of which are used by Gates to refer to African Americans. What different associations does each have? Why does Gates use both—for example,* colored *in paragraph 9 and* black *in paragraph 12? What is your response to the father's use of the term* boy *in paragraph 11?* In the 1950s, when the incident Gates describes took place, the term *colored* was still widely used, along with *Negro,* to designate people of African

descent. In the 1960s the terms *Afro-American* and *black* replaced the earlier names, with *black* emerging as the preferred term and remaining dominant through the 1980s. Today, while *black* is still preferred by many, others prefer *African American*. (According to a 1990 survey conducted by the Joint Center for Political and Economic Studies, 72 percent of black Americans prefer the term *black*, 15 percent favor *African American,* 3 percent prefer *Afro-American,* and 2 percent *Negro.*) The term *colored*, because it is the oldest designation, may seem old-fashioned and even racist today; *black*, which connoted a certain degree of militancy in the 1960s, is probably perceived today by most people as a neutral term. Gates uses both words because he is speaking from two time periods. In paragraph 9, recreating the thoughts and words of a child in a 1950s Southern town, he uses the term *colored*; in paragraph 12 the adult Gates, commenting in 1989 on the incident, uses *black*. The substitution of *African American* for the older terms might give the narrative a more contemporary flavor, but it might also seem awkward or forced, particularly in paragraph 9. As far as the term *boy* is concerned, different readers are apt to have different responses. Although the father's use of the term can be seen as affectionate, it can also be seen as derisive in this context since it echoes the bigot's use of *boy* for all black males, regardless of age or accomplishments.

JOURNAL ENTRY

Do you think Gates's parents should have used experiences like the one described in "'What's in a Name?'" to educate him about the family's social status in the community? Why do you think they chose instead to dismiss such incidents as "one of those things"? Your responses to these questions will reflect your own opinions and judgments, based on your background and experiences as well as on your interpretation of the reading selection.

WRITING WORKSHOP

Write about a time when you, like Gates's father, could have spoken out in protest but chose not to. Would you have made the same decision today? By the time you approach the Writing Workshop questions, you have read an essay carefully, highlighted and annotated it, responded to study questions about it, discussed it in class, and perhaps considered its relationship to other essays in the text. Often your next step will be to write an essay in response to one of the Writing Workshop questions. Chapter 1 follows Laura Bobnak, a freshman composition student, through the process of writing such an essay.

THEMATIC CONNECTIONS

- *"Finishing School" (p. 78)*
- *"Sexism in English: A 1990s Update" (p. 441)*

As you read and think about the reading selections in this text, you should begin to see thematic links among them. Such parallels can add to your interest and understanding of the work on which you are focusing as well as give you ideas for group discussion and for writing. For example, Maya Angelou's "Finishing School," another autobiographical essay by an African-American writer, has many points of similarity with Gates's. Both essays describe the uneasy position of a black child expected to adhere to the white world's unfair code of behavior, and both deal squarely with the issue of the importance of being called by one's rightful name. In fact, paragraph 26 of "Finishing School" offers some very helpful insights into the problem Gates examines.

A less obvious, but equally valid, thematic link exists between "'What's in a Name?'" and Alleen Pace Nilsen's "Sexism in English: A 1990s Update," which also considers the dangers of using language to separate and demean a group of people. In the process of thinking about Gates's narrative, discussing it in class, or preparing to write an essay on a related topic (such as those listed under Writing Workshop), you might find it extremely useful to consider (or reconsider) Angelou's or Nilsen's essay.

The Thematic Connections suggested in the text identify two or more related reading selections; you should look for others as well.

1

The Writing Process

Every selection in this book is the result of a struggle between a writer and his or her material. If the writer's struggle is successful, the finished work is welded together without a seam, and the reader has no sense of the frustration the writer experienced while hunting for the right word or rearranging ideas. Writing is no easy business, and even a professional writer can have a very difficult time. Still, although no simple formula for good writing exists, some approaches to writing are easier and more productive than others.

At this point you may be asking yourself, "So what? What has this got to do with me? I'm not a professional writer." True enough, but during the next few years you will be doing a good deal of writing. Throughout your college career, you will need to write midterms, final exams, lab reports, and short essays. In your professional life you may have to write progress reports, proposals, business correspondence, memos, and résumés. As diverse as these assignments seem, they have something in common: They can be made easier if you are familiar with the **writing process**—the procedure experienced writers follow to produce a finished piece of writing.

In general, the writing process has three stages. During *invention,* also called *prewriting,* you decide what you will write about and gather information to support or explain what you want to say. During the next stage, *arrangement,* you decide how you are going to organize your ideas. And finally, during *drafting and revision,* you write your essay, progressing through several drafts as you reconsider ideas and refine style and structure.

Although these neatly defined stages make discussing the writing process easier, they do not reflect the way people actually write. Ideas do not always flow easily from the pen or computer keys, and the central point you may set out to develop is not always reflected in the essay you ultimately write. Often writing progresses in fits and starts, with ideas occurring unexpectedly or not at all. In fact, much good writing evolves out of a writer's getting stuck or being confused and continuing to work until ideas begin to take shape on the page or on the screen.

Because writing can be such an erratic process, it also does not simply progress in a linear fashion, with one stage ending before another begins. In fact, the three stages overlap. Most writers engage in invention, arrangement, and drafting and revision simultaneously—finding ideas, considering possible methods of organization, and looking for the right words all at the same time. In addition, no two writers approach the writing process in exactly the same way. Some people outline; others do not. Some take elaborate notes during the prewriting stage; others keep track of everything in their heads.

The writing process that we discuss throughout this book illustrates the many choices writers may make at various stages of composition. But regardless of the different ways writers have of approaching the writing process, one thing is certain: The more you write, the better acquainted you will become with your personal writing process and with ways to modify it to suit various writing tasks. The rest of this chapter will help you to define your needs as a writer and to understand the options available as you approach writing assignments both in and out of college.

STAGE ONE: INVENTION

Although **invention,** or **prewriting,** is an important part of the writing process, many people ignore this stage, either because they underestimate the importance of preparation or because they simply do not know how to plan to write. In college and afterward, when you are given a writing assignment, you may be tempted to plunge into a first draft immediately. Before writing, however, you should take the time to consider the assignment, explore your subject, and decide what you wish to say about it.

Understanding the Assignment

Almost everything you write in college will begin as an *assignment.* Some assignments will be direct and easy to understand:

Write about an experience that changed your life.
Discuss the procedure you used in synthesizing ammonia.

But others will be difficult and complex:

> According to Wayne Booth, point of view is central to the understanding of modern fiction. In a short essay discuss how Henry James uses point of view in *The Turn of the Screw*.

Therefore, before beginning to write, you need to understand what you are being asked to do. If the assignment is a written question, read it carefully several times, and underline its key ideas. If the assignment is read aloud by your instructor, be sure to copy it accurately. (A missed word can make quite a difference.) Whatever the case, do not be afraid to ask your instructor for clarification if you are confused. Remember that an essay, no matter how well written, will be unacceptable if it does not fulfill the assignment.

Setting Limits

Once you are certain you understand the assignment, consider its length, purpose, audience, and occasion and your own knowledge of the subject. Each of these considerations helps to determine what you will say about your subject and thus simplifies your writing task.

Length. Often your instructor will specify an approximate length for a paper, or your writing situation will determine how much you can write. Your word or page limit has a direct bearing on your paper's focus. For example, you would need a narrower topic for a two- or three-page essay than for a ten-page paper. Similarly, during an hour exam you could not discuss a question as thoroughly as you might in a paper prepared over several days.

If your instructor sets no length, consider how other aspects of the assignment might indirectly determine length. A summary of a chapter or an article, for instance, should be much shorter than the original, whereas an analysis of a poem usually will be longer than the poem itself. If you are uncertain about the appropriate length of your paper, discuss ideas for the paper with your instructor.

Purpose. Your **purpose** sets another limit to what you say and also helps you to decide how you say it. For example, if you were to write to a prospective employer about a summer job, you would emphasize different aspects of college life from those you would stress in a letter to a friend. In the first case, you would want to persuade the reader to hire you. To do so you might include your grade-point average or a list of the relevant courses you took. In the second case, you would want to inform and perhaps entertain. To accomplish these aims you might share anecdotes about dorm life or describe one of your favorite instructors. In both cases, your purpose would help determine what information you need to evoke a particular response in your audience.

In general, you can classify your purpose for writing according to your relationship to the audience. For example, your purpose can be to express personal feelings or impressions to your readers. *Expressive* writing includes diaries, personal letters, journals, and often narrative and descriptive essays as well. Your purpose can also be to inform readers about something. *Informative* writing includes much of the writing that you do in college. Essay examinations, lab reports, book reports, expository essays, and some research papers are primarily informative. Finally, your purpose can be to persuade readers to think or act in a certain way. *Persuasive* writing includes editorials, argumentative essays, and many other essays and research papers.

In addition to these general purposes, you can have a number of more specific purposes. For example, in addition to informing, you may also want to analyze, entertain, hypothesize, assess, summarize, question, report, recommend, suggest, evaluate, describe, recount, request, or instruct. Suppose that you wrote a report on the incidence of AIDS in your community. Your general purpose might be to *inform* readers of the situation, but you might also want to *assess* the progression of the disease and to *instruct* readers how to avoid contracting the virus that causes it.

Audience. To be effective, your essay should be written with a particular **audience** in mind. An audience can be an *individual*—your instructor, for example—or it can be a *group,* like your classmates or coworkers. Your essay could address a *specialized* audience, like a group of medical doctors or economists, or a *general* or *universal* audience whose members share no particular common ground, like the readers of a newspaper or news magazine.

When you write most college essays, the audience is your instructor, and the purpose is to demonstrate your mastery of the subject matter, your reasoning ability, and your competence as a writer. Other audiences may include classmates, professional colleagues, and members of a community. Considering the age and sex of your audience, its political and religious values, its social and educational level, and its interest in your subject may help you to define it. Certainly your approach in a report about the spread of AIDS in a community would depend on the report's audience. For example, a report written for teenagers at a local high school would be very different from one addressing a civic group or the city council—or the parents of those teenagers.

Often you may find that your audience is just too diverse to be categorized. In such cases, many writers imagine a universal audience and write for it, making points that they think will appeal to many different readers. Sometimes writers try to think of one typical individual in the audience—perhaps a person they know—so that they can imagine writing to someone specific. At other times writers solve this problem by identifying a common denominator, a role that characterizes the entire audience. For example, when a report on toy safety asserts, "Now is the time for concerned consumers to demand that dangerous toys be removed from the market," it automatically casts its audience in the role of concerned consumers.

Once you have defined your audience, you have to determine how much or how little its members know about your subject. In addition, you should decide how much background information your readers need before they will be able to understand the discussion. Are they highly informed? If so, you will make your points directly. Are they relatively uninformed? If this is the case, you will have to include definitions of key terms, background information, and summaries of basic research. Keep in mind that even an expert in one field will need background information in an area with which he or she is unfamiliar. If, for example, you were writing an essay analyzing the characters in Joseph Conrad's *Heart of Darkness,* you could assume that the literature instructor who assigned the novel was familiar with it and would not need a plot summary. However, in an essay for your history instructor that used *Heart of Darkness* to illustrate the evils of European colonialism in nineteenth-century Africa, you would need to include some plot summary. Even though your history instructor knows a lot about colonialism in Africa, she may not be familiar with the details of Conrad's novel.

Occasion. The occasion for academic writing can be either a classroom writing exercise or an at-home assignment. Although these situations may seem artificial, they are valuable practice for writing you do outside of college. Like these assignments, each writing task you do outside of college requires a special approach that suits the occasion. A memo to your coworkers, for instance, might be informal and more limited in scope than a report to your company's president. A notice about a meeting, sent to your fellow beer-can collectors, might be strictly informational, whereas a letter to your senator about preserving a local historical landmark would be persuasive as well as informational. Similarly, when you are preparing a classroom exercise, remember that college writing should use precise diction and correct grammar and spelling. Keep in mind, however, that there are different kinds of classes, each with different occasions for writing. A response suitable for a psychology class or a history class might not be acceptable for an English class, just as a satisfactory answer on a quiz might be insufficient on a midterm.

Knowledge.   Obviously, what you know (and do not know) about a subject limits what you can say about it. Before writing about any subject, you should ask yourself the following questions:

What do I know about the subject?
What do I need to find out?
What do I think about the subject?

Different writing situations require different kinds of knowledge. A personal essay may draw on your own experiences and observations; a term paper will require you to gain new knowledge through research. Although your experience riding city buses might be sufficient for an impromptu essay in composition class, you will need to research the subject of public transportation for an urban sociology paper. Sometimes you will be able to increase your knowledge about a topic easily because of your strong background in the general subject. At other times, when a general subject is unfamiliar to you, you will need to select a topic particularly carefully so that you do not get out of your depth. In many cases, the amount of time you are given to do the assignment and its page limit will guide you as you consider what you already know and what you need to learn before you can write knowledgeably.

Checklist for Setting Limits

Length
* Has your instructor stipulated a length?
* Does your writing situation suggest a length?

Purpose
* Is your general purpose to express personal feelings? To inform? To persuade?
* In addition to your general purpose, do you have any more specific purposes?
* Does your assignment provide any guidelines concerning purpose?

Audience
- Is your audience a group or an individual?
- Are you going to address a specialized or a general audience?
- Should you take into consideration the audience's age, gender, education, biases, or political or social values?
- Should you cast your audience in a particular role?
- How much can you assume your audience knows about your subject? How much interest does the audience have in the subject?

Occasion
- Are you writing a classroom exercise or an at-home assignment?
- Are you addressing a situation outside the academic setting?
- What special approaches does your occasion require?

Knowledge
- What do you know about your subject?
- What do you need to find out?
- What are your opinions about your subject?

EXERCISES

1. Decide if the following topics are appropriate for the stated limits. Write a few sentences to explain why each topic is or is not acceptable.
   a. A *two-to three-page paper*: A history of the American Civil Liberties Union in Louisiana
   b. A *two-hour final exam*: The role of France and Germany in the American Revolutionary War
   c. A *one-hour in-class essay*: An interpretation of Andy Warhol's painting of Campbell's Soup cans
   d. A *letter to your college newspaper*: A discussion of your school's investment practices

2. Make a list of the different audiences to whom you speak or write in your daily life. (Consider all the different types of people you see regularly, such as your family, your roommate, your instructor, your boss, your friends, and so on.)
   a. Do you speak or write to each in the same way and about the same things? If not, how do your approaches to these people differ?
   b. Name some subjects that would interest some of these people but not others. How do you account for these differences?
   c. Choose a subject, such as your composition class or local politics, and describe how you would speak or write to each audience about it.

Moving from Subject to Topic

Once you have considered the limits of your assignment, you need to narrow your subject to a workable topic. Many writing assignments begin as broad areas of interest or concern. These *general subjects* always need to be narrowed or limited to specific *topics* that can be reasonably discussed within the limits of the assignment. For example, a subject like DNA recombinant research is interesting, but it is too vast to write about for any college assignment except in a general way. You need to narrow such a subject to a topic that can be covered within the time and space available.

Subject	*Topic*
DNA recombinant research	One outcome of DNA recombinant research
Herman Melville's *Billy Budd*	Billy Budd as a Christ figure
Constitutional law	One result of the Miranda ruling
Personal computers	The uses of personal computers in elementary education

As these examples illustrate, a topic does more than narrow a general subject. A topic also defines the manner in which you will treat a subject.

To narrow a general subject, you need to discover the topics it suggests. Do not make the mistake of skipping this stage of the writing process, hoping that a topic will suddenly come to you. Not only will you waste time with this haphazard approach, but you also may fail to realize the potential of your subject. Instead, you can use any of various techniques—*questions for probing, freewriting, brainstorming, journal writing, clustering*—to help you narrow your subject and generate ideas. In the following sections each of these methods of invention is presented and illustrated as a tool for use at a particular stage in the writing process, but remember that most of them can be helpful at almost any stage. Like most other writers, you will probably discover by trial and error which of them work best for you.

Focusing on a Topic: Questions for Probing

You probe your subject by asking a series of questions about it. These questions are useful because they reflect ways in which your mind operates: finding similarities and differences, for instance, or dividing a whole into its parts. By running through the list of questions, you can probe your subject systematically. Of course, not all questions will work for every subject. Still, any question may elicit many different answers, and each answer is a possible topic for your essay.

What happened?
When did it happen?
Where did it happen?
Who did it?
What does it look like?
What are its characteristics?
What impressions does it make?
What are some typical cases or examples of it?
How did it happen?
What makes it work?
How is it made?
Why did it happen?
What caused it?
What does it cause?
What are its effects?
How is it related to something else?
How is it like other things?
How is it different from other things?
What are its parts or types?
How can its parts or types be separated or grouped?
Do its parts or types fit into a logical order?
Into what categories can its parts or types be arranged?
On what basis can it be categorized?
How can it be defined?
How does it resemble other members of its class?
How does it differ from other members of its class?
What are its limits?

When applied to a particular subject, some of these questions can yield many workable topics—some you might never have considered had you not asked the questions. By applying this approach to a general subject, such as "the Brooklyn Bridge," you can generate more ideas and topics than you need:

What happened? A short history of the Brooklyn Bridge
What does it look like? A description of the Brooklyn Bridge
How is it made? The construction of the Brooklyn Bridge

What are its effects? The impact of the Brooklyn Bridge on
American writers

How does it differ from other members of its class? Innovations in
the design of the Brooklyn Bridge

At this point in the writing process, you mainly want to explore
possible topics, and the more ideas you have, the wider your choice.
So write down all the topics you think of. You can even repeat the
process of probing several times to uncover topics that are still more
limited. Once you have generated many topics, eliminate those that
do not interest you or that go too far beyond your knowledge or are
too complex or too simple to fit the limits of the assignment. When
you have discarded these less promising ideas, you should still have
several left. You can select from these possible topics the one that
best suits your paper's length, purpose, audience, and occasion as
well as your knowledge of the subject. (If you are writing on a
computer, you can store your questions in a file that you can look at
every time you have a new topic to probe.)

EXERCISES

1. Indicate whether the following are general subjects or topics that are
   suitably narrow for a short essay. Be prepared to explain your decisions.
   a. An argument for gun control
   b. A comparison of salaries for professional basketball and football
      players
   c. Rap music
   d. Two creation stories in the Book of Genesis
   e. Canadian and U.S. health-care systems
   f. The Haber process for the fixation of atmospheric nitrogen
   g. Political satire on *Saturday Night Live*
   h. The advantages of term over whole life insurance
   i. Video game violence
   j. An analysis of beer commercials
   k. Gender roles

2. Choose two of the following subjects, and generate topics from each by
   using as many of the questions for probing as you can. (Assume that
   the essay you are preparing is due in one week for your English class
   and that it should be about 750 words long.)
   a. Television commercials
   b. Personal computers
   c. MTV
   d. Affirmative action

   e. Substance abuse
   f. Scientific experimentation on animals
   g. Styles of clothing
   h. Date rape
   i. Motorcycles
   j. Talk radio
   k. Diets
   l. Adolescence
  m. Grading
   n. The homeless
   o. Sex education

Starting to Write: Freewriting

You can use **freewriting** at any stage of the writing process—to help you narrow your subject, generate information, or find a thesis. If you have time, it is a particularly useful way to get yourself to relax and start writing about a topic. For a fixed period, perhaps five or ten minutes, just write down *without stopping* everything that comes to mind. Try to focus on the topic, but do not worry if your ideas seem to wander off in other directions. The object of freewriting is to let your ideas flow. Often your best ideas will come to you as a result of unexpected connections that you make as you write. When you freewrite, you should not pay attention to spelling, grammar, or punctuation. Your goal is to get your ideas down on paper so you can react to them. If you find that you have nothing to say, write down anything until ideas begin to emerge—and in time they will. The secret is to *keep writing*.

After completing your freewriting, read it and look for ideas that you can use in your essay. Some writers underline ideas they think they might explore in their essays. These ideas may become supporting information for the writing topic, or they could become subjects for other freewriting exercises. For example, if after reading your freewriting you find a promising idea, you can freewrite again, using your new idea as your focus. This process of writing more and more narrowly focused freewriting exercises—called **looping**—can yield a great deal of useful information and can help you arrive at a workable topic. In fact, many writers freewrite a whole draft of an essay *before* they do a more structured version. In this way, they concentrate on ideas and do not become bogged down in the more formal aspects of writing.

If you do your freewriting on a computer, you may find that staring at your own words can cause you to go blank or to lose your spontaneity. A possible solution to these problems is to turn down the brightness until the screen becomes dark and then freewrite. This technique allows you to block out distracting elements and to concentrate on your ideas. Once you finish freewriting, turn up the brightness and see what you have. If you have expressed an interesting idea, you can move it onto a new page and freewrite again.

A STUDENT WRITER: FREEWRITING

After reading Henry Louis Gates, Jr.'s "'What's in a Name?'" (p. 5), Laura Bobnak, a student in a composition class, chose to write an essay in response to this Writing Workshop question:

> "Write about a time when you, like Gates's father, could have spoken out in protest but chose not to. Would you have made the same decision today?"

Here is a ten-minute freewriting exercise that she did in response to the assignment:

> Write for ten minutes . . . ten minutes . . . at 9 o'clock in the morning—she must be kidding—Just what I want to do in the morning—If you can't think of something to say just write about anything. Right! Time to get this over with—An experience—should have talked—I can think of plenty of times I should have kept quiet! I should have brought coffee to class. I wonder what the person next to me is writing about. That reminds me. Next to me. Jeff Servin in chemistry. The time I saw him cheating. I was mad but I didn't do anything. I studied so hard and all he did was cheat. I was so mad. Nobody else seemed to care either. What's the difference between now and then? It's only a year and a half. . . . Honor code? Maturity? A lot of people cheated in high school. I bet I could write about this—Before and after, etc. My attitude then and now.

After some initial floundering, Laura arrived at an idea that could be the basis for her essay. Although Laura's discussion of the incident still had to be developed, her freewriting had helped her discover a possible topic for her essay.

EXERCISES

1. Assume that you were asked to write a short in-class essay for your composition class. Do a ten-minute freewriting exercise on one of the following subjects. Do not stop; keep writing until you focus on a narrowed topic.

a. Exercise
b. Movies
c. Baseball
d. Music
e. Books
f. Jobs

2. Read what you have just written, and decide on a topic you might be able to write about in a short essay. Freewrite about this topic for another ten minutes to generate ideas that you could use in your essay. Underline the ideas that seem most useful.

Finding Something to Say: Brainstorming

After you have decided on a topic, you still have to find something to say about it. **Brainstorming** is a method of invention that can help you to do this. Like freewriting, brainstorming is a method of free association for generating ideas. You can brainstorm in a group, exchanging ideas with several students in your composition class and writing down the useful ideas that come up. Or, you can brainstorm individually, quickly writing down every fact, idea, or association you can think of that relates to your topic. Your notes might include words, phrases, statements, questions, or even drawings or diagrams. Jot them down in whatever order you think of them, allowing your thoughts to wander freely. Some of the items may be inspired by your class notes; others may be ideas you got from reading or from talking with friends. Still other items may be ideas you have begun to wonder about, points you thought of while working toward your topic, or thoughts that spontaneously occur to you as you brainstorm.

A STUDENT WRITER: BRAINSTORMING

After freewriting, Laura Bobnak had decided to write about a time when she saw someone cheating and did not speak out. In order to narrow her topic further and to find something to say, she made the brainstorming notes on page 28.

Laura obviously had plenty of ideas. After reading her brainstorming notes several times, she decided that she could concentrate on the differences between her attitude in high school and her current attitude. She knew that she could write a lot about this idea and that she could relate it to the assignment. In addition, she felt confident that her topic would be interesting both to her instructor and to the other students in the class.

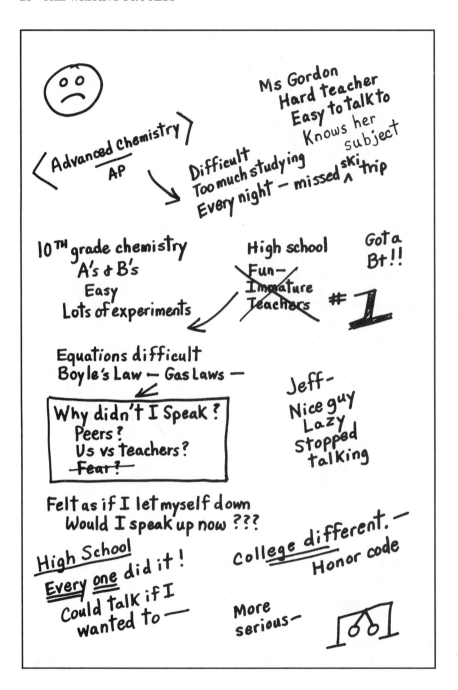

Brainstorming Notes

Exploring Your Reactions: Journal Writing

Once you decide on a topic and gather ideas to write about, you can explore some of the ideas in a journal entry. In fact, **journal writing** can be a useful source of ideas at any stage of the writing process. Many writers routinely keep a journal, jotting down experiences or exploring ideas they may want to use when they write. Sometimes they write journal entries in response to their reading or experiences even when they have no particular writing project in mind. Often these journal entries are the kernels from which longer pieces of writing develop. Your instructor may ask you to keep such a writing journal, or you may decide to keep a journal on your own. In either case, you will find that your journal entries are likely to be more narrowly focused than freewriting or brainstorming, perhaps examining a single section of a reading selection or even one particular statement. Sometimes you will write in your journal in response to a specific question or assignment, like the ones in this text designated "Journal Entry." This kind of assignment can help you start thinking about a reading selection you may later discuss in class or write about.

A STUDENT WRITER: JOURNAL WRITING

The journal entry Laura Bobnak wrote after she decided on a topic for her paper appears below. In this entry she explores one idea from her brainstorming notes—her college's honor code.

> At orientation the dean of students talked about the college's honor code. She said something about how we were a community of scholars who were here for a common purpose—to take part in an intellectual dialogue. According to her, the purpose of the honor code is to make sure this dialogue continues uninterrupted. This idea sounded dumb at first, but now it makes sense. If I saw someone cheating, I'd tell the instructor. First, though, I'd ask the *student* to go to the instructor. I don't see this as "telling" or "squealing." We're all here to get an education, and we should be able to assume everyone is being honest and fair.

Although this journal entry is much narrower than the topic Laura would eventually write about, it focuses on an issue relevant to her paper. Even though Laura did not include much of this entry in her paper, it did help her clarify her ideas about the issue she would be writing about.

Grouping Ideas: Clustering

Once you have generated some ideas for writing, you need to group ideas that belong together. Doing so enables you to discover, for example, the connections that exist among the items on a brainstorming list. **Clustering** is a way of visually arranging your ideas so that you can tell at a glance where ideas belong and where you need to generate more information. Although you can use clustering simply to generate ideas, it is especially useful for identifying major points and seeing how the various ideas you have come up with fit together. (Clustering can also help you to narrow your paper's subject to suit its length. If you find that your cluster diagram is too detailed for your paper, you can write about just one branch of the cluster.)

Begin clustering by writing your topic in the middle of a sheet of paper. After circling it, surround it with the words and phrases that identify the major points you intend to discuss. (You can get ideas from your brainstorming notes and from your freewriting.) Circle these words and phrases and connect them to the topic in the center. Next, arrange other clusters of ideas relating to each major point and draw lines connecting them to the appropriate point. By dividing and subdividing your points, getting more specific as you move outward from the center of the page, you identify the facts, details, examples, and opinions that illustrate and expand your main points.

A STUDENT WRITER: CLUSTERING

Because Laura Bobnak was not particularly visually oriented, she chose not to use this method of grouping her ideas. If she had, however, her cluster diagram might have looked like the one below.

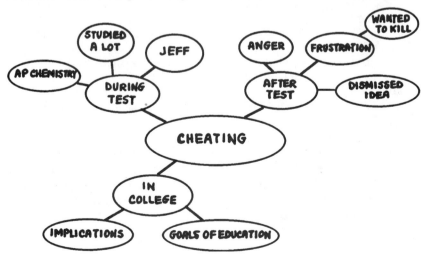

Grouping Ideas: Making an Informal Outline

As an alternative or followup to clustering, you can organize your notes from brainstorming or other invention techniques into an *informal outline*. Quite often an informal outline is just a list of your major points, perhaps presented in some tentative order; sometimes, however, it will include some supporting details or suggest a pattern of development. Informal outlines do not specify all the major divisions and subdivisions of your paper or indicate the relative importance of your ideas; they simply suggest the shape of your emerging essay.

A STUDENT WRITER: MAKING AN INFORMAL OUTLINE

The following outline shows how Laura Bobnak grouped her ideas.

During test
Advanced placement chemistry
Studied a lot
Saw Jeff cheating

After test
Got angry
Wanted to tell
Dismissed idea

In college
Implications of cheating
Goals of education

EXERCISE

Suppose that your English composition instructor has given you the following list of subjects and told you to select one for a short essay, due in two days. Prepare one of these subjects following the procedures for invention just discussed. First, apply the questions for probing. Next, do five minutes of freewriting on the three topics that are most appealing. Then, pick the most promising topic developed from your subject and brainstorm about it. Finally, select the ideas that you would use if you were actually writing the paper, and either cluster ideas or group them into an informal outline.
  a. Grandparents
  b. Drinking on campus
  c. Gay rights
  d. Divorce

e. Equal pay for equal work
f. Fast-food restaurants
g. Financial aid to college students
h. Athletes and drugs
i. Campus security
j. Television comedy

Formulating a Thesis

Once you have decided what your essay is going to discuss, your next job is to formulate a thesis. Your **thesis** is the main idea of your essay, the central point the essay supports.

The word *thesis* at one time denoted an argumentative statement, one that took a firm stand on an issue. But the definition of *thesis* has broadened considerably over the years. Now, the term is commonly used to identify the main idea of an essay whether or not it is argumentative. In this sense, every essay has a thesis.

No fixed rules determine when you formulate your thesis; the decision depends on such variables as the scope and difficulty of your assignment, your knowledge of the subject, and your own method of writing. Sometimes, when you know a lot about the subject, you may formulate a thesis before doing any invention activities like probing your subject or brainstorming. At other times you may wait until you have a chance to review all your material and draw it together into a single statement that indicates your position on the topic. Occasionally, your assignment may specify a thesis by telling you to take a particular position on a given topic. Whatever the case, you should arrive at a tentative thesis before you begin to write the first draft.

As you write, you will continue to discover new ideas and will probably move in directions that you did not anticipate when you formulated this thesis. Still, because your tentative thesis gives you guidance and purpose, it is essential at the initial stages of writing. As you draft your essay, make certain that you review the points you make in light of your thesis and revise the thesis or your support as necessary.

Stating Your Thesis.   Usually you will want to include a one-sentence statement of your thesis in your essay. An effective thesis statement clearly expresses your essay's main idea. Thus, it does more than just present your topic; it indicates what you will say about your topic, and it signals how you will approach your material.

The following thesis statement, from the essay "Grant and Lee: A Study in Contrasts," by Bruce Catton (p. 371), clearly communicates the main idea the writer will support.

> They [Grant and Lee] were two strong men, these oddly different generals, and they represented the strengths of two conflicting currents that, through them, had come into final collision.

This statement indicates that the essay will compare and contrast Grant and Lee; more specifically, it reveals that Catton's approach to his material will be to present the two Civil War generals as symbols of two historical currents that were also in opposition. If it had been less fully developed—for example, had Catton said, "Grant and Lee were quite different from each other"—it would have communicated just the essay's title, and it would have failed to signal the essay's purpose—or its real subject—to his readers.

Your thesis evolves from your purpose, and it is an expression of that purpose. Whether your purpose is to evaluate or analyze or simply to describe or recount, your thesis statement communicates that purpose to your readers. In general terms, your purpose may be to express personal feelings, to present information in a straightforward manner, or to persuade. Accordingly, your thesis can be *expressive,* conveying a mood or impression; it can be *informative,* perhaps listing the major points you will discuss or presenting an objective overview of the essay to follow; or it can be *persuasive,* taking a strong stand or outlining the position you will argue.

Each of the three thesis statements below expresses a different purpose:

> The city's homeless families live in heartbreaking surroundings. (Purpose—to express feelings)

> The plight of the homeless has become so serious that it is a major priority for many city governments. (Purpose—to inform)

> The only responsible reaction to the crisis at hand is to renovate abandoned city housing to provide suitable shelter for homeless families. (Purpose—to persuade)

Whether your thesis statement is expressive, informative, or persuasive, it is always more than a title, an announcement of your intent, or a statement of fact. A descriptive title is useful because it orients your reader, but it is seldom detailed enough to reveal much about your essay's purpose or direction. An announcement of your intent can reveal more, but it is stylistically distracting. Finally, a statement of fact—for instance, a historical or scientific fact or a statistic—is typically a dead end and therefore cannot be developed into an essay. A statement like "Alaska became a state in 1959" or "Tuberculosis is highly contagious" or "The population of Greece is about 10 million" provides your essay with no direction. However, a

ent or opinion in response to a fact *can* be an effective thesis—
tance, "The continuing threat of tuberculosis, particularly in
the inner cities, suggests it is necessary to administer more frequent
diagnostic tests among high-risk populations."

To gain an appreciation of the differences among titles, announce-
ments, statements of fact, and thesis statements, compare the statements in each of the following groups:

Title:	The 55-Mile-Per-Hour Speed Limit: Pro and Con
Announcement:	I will examine the pros and cons of doing away with the 55-mile-per-hour speed limit on major highways.
Statement of Fact:	Most states have now increased the speed limit from 55 to 65 miles per hour.
Thesis Statement:	The federal government should withhold highway funds from any state that decides to increase the speed limit from 55 to 65 miles per hour.

Title:	Orwell's "A Hanging"
Announcement:	This paper will discuss George Orwell's attitude toward the death penalty in his essay "A Hanging."
Statement of Fact:	In his essay Orwell describes a hanging that he witnessed in Burma.
Thesis Statement:	In "A Hanging" George Orwell shows that capital punishment is not only unpleasant but immoral.

Title:	Speaking Out
Announcement:	This essay will discuss a time when I could have spoken out but did not.
Statement of Fact:	Once I saw someone cheating and did not speak out.
Thesis Statement:	As I look back on the situation, I wonder why I kept silent and what would have happened had I acted.

To communicate your essay's main idea, an effective thesis statement—often a single sentence—should be clearly and specifically
worded. Also, it should speak for itself: It is not necessary to say,
"My thesis is that . . ." or "The thesis of this paper is. . . ." The thesis
statement should be pertinent to the rest of the essay, giving an
accurate indication of what follows and not misleading readers
about the essay's direction, emphasis, content, or point of view. Vague
language, confusing abstractions, irrelevant details, and overly complex terminology have no place in a thesis statement. Keep in mind,
too, that your thesis statement should not make promises that your
essay is not going to keep. If you are going to discuss just the effects
of a new immigration law, do not emphasize in your thesis statement
the sequence of events that led to the law's passage.

Naturally your thesis statement cannot include every point you will discuss in your paper. Still, it should be specific enough to indicate the direction in which your essay is going and the scope of your discussion. The statement "The new immigration law has failed to stem the tide of illegal immigrants" does not give your essay much focus. Which immigration law will you be examining? Which illegal immigrants?

The following sentence fulfills the requirements for an effective thesis statement. It clearly indicates what the writer is going to discuss, and it establishes a specific direction and purpose for the essay.

> Because it fails to take into account the economic causes of illegal immigration, the 1986 immigration law is an inadequate solution to the problem of illegal immigration from Mexico into the United States.

Implying a Thesis. Although every essay should have a clear sense of purpose, not every kind of writing requires an explicitly stated thesis. Sometimes a thesis may only be *implied*. Like an explicitly stated thesis, an implied thesis conveys an essay's purpose, but it does not directly state the purpose. Instead, the purpose is suggested by the selection and arrangement of the essay's points. Although using an implied thesis requires that a writer plan and organize carefully, many professional writers whose essays are included in this book prefer this option because an implied thesis is more subtle than a stated thesis. The advantages of an implied thesis are especially apparent in narratives, descriptions, and some arguments, where an explicit thesis would seem heavy-handed or arbitrary. In most college writing, however, you should state your thesis explicitly to avoid any risk of being misunderstood or of allowing the organization of your essay to go astray.

A STUDENT WRITER: FORMULATING A THESIS

After experimenting with different ways of arranging her ideas for her essay, Laura Bobnak was eventually able to sum them up in a one-sentence tentative thesis: "As I look back on the situation, I wonder why I kept silent and what would have happened had I acted."

EXERCISES

1. Assess the strengths and weaknesses of the following as thesis statements, paying particular attention to the question of which would most effectively establish the direction of an essay.

a. Myths and society.
b. Myths serve an important function in society.
c. Contrary to popular assumptions, myths are more than fairy stories; they are tales that express the underlying attitudes a society has toward important issues.
d. Today, almost two marriages in four will end in divorce.
e. Skiing, a popular sport for millions, is a major cause of winter injuries.
f. If certain reforms are not instituted immediately, our company will be bankrupt within two years.
g. Early childhood is an important period.
h. By using the proper techniques, parents can significantly improve the learning capabilities of their preschool children.
i. Fiction can be used to criticize society.
j. Fiction, in the hands of an able writer, can be a powerful tool for social reform.

2. Rewrite the following factual statements to make them effective thesis statements. Make sure that each thesis statement is a clearly and specifically worded sentence.
   a. A number of hospitals have refused to admit patients without health insurance because they feel that such patients do not have the resources to pay their bills.
   b. Several recent Supreme Court decisions say that art that contains a sexual theme is not pornographic.
   c. Many women earn less money than men, in part because they drop out of the work force during their child-rearing years.
   d. People who watch television more than five hours a day tend to think the world is more violent than people who watch less than two hours of television daily.
   e. In recent years the rate of suicide among teenagers—especially middle- and upper-middle-class teenagers—has risen dramatically.

3. Read the following sentences adapted from *Broca's Brain* by Carl Sagan. Then, formulate a one-sentence thesis statement that draws together the points that Sagan makes about robots.
   a. Robots, especially robots in space, have received derogatory notices in the press.
   b. Each human being is a superbly constructed, astonishingly compact, self-ambulatory computer—capable on occasion of independent decision making and real control of his or her environment.
   c. If we do send human beings to exotic environments, we must also send along food, air, water, waste recycling, amenities for entertainment, and companions.
   d. By comparison, machines require no elaborate life-support systems, no entertainment, and no companionship, and we do not feel any strong ethical prohibitions against sending machines on one-way, or suicide, missions.

   e. Even exceptionally simple computers—those that can be wired by a bright ten-year-old—can be wired to play perfect tic-tac-toe.

   f. With this . . . set of examples of the state of development of machine intelligence, I think it is clear that a major effort over the next decade could produce much more sophisticated examples.

   g. We appear to be on the verge of developing a wide variety of intelligent machines capable of performing tasks too dangerous, too expensive, too onerous or too boring for human beings.

   h. The main obstacle seems to be a very human problem, the quiet feeling that there is something threatening or "inhuman" about machines.

   i. But in many respects our survival as a species depends on our transcending such primitive chauvinisms.

   j. There is nothing inhuman about an intelligent machine; it is indeed an expression of all those superb intellectual capabilities that only human beings . . . now possess.

4. For three of the following general subjects and topics, go through as many steps as you need to formulate effective thesis statements.
   a. The importance of your family
   b. Japan
   c. Credit cards
   d. Finding a summer job
   e. One thing you would change about your life
   f. The rain forests
   g. Academic standards for college athletes
   h. The image of women in television commercials
   i. The sub-minimum wage for teenage workers
   j. Plagiarism

STAGE TWO: ARRANGEMENT

Each of the tasks discussed so far represents a series of choices you have to make about your topic and your material. Now, before actually beginning to write, you have another choice to make: how to arrange your material into an essay. This extremely important choice determines how clear and convincing your essay will be and how your audience will react to it.

Sometimes deciding how to arrange your ideas will be easy because the assignment specifies a particular pattern of development. This may often be the case in a composition class, where the instructor may assign, say, a descriptive or a narrative essay. Also, certain assignments or examination questions suggest how your material should be structured. Probably no one except an English composition instructor will say to you, "Write a narrative," but you will have assignments that begin, "Give an account of. . . ." or "Tell about. . . ." Likewise, few teachers will explicitly assign a process essay, but they will do so indirectly when they ask you to explain how something works. Similarly, an examination question might ask you to trace the circumstances leading up to an event. If you are perceptive, you will realize that this question calls for either a narrative or a cause-and-effect answer. The important thing is to recognize the clues that such assignments give, or those you find in your topic or thesis, and to structure your essay accordingly.

One clue to the emerging structure of your essay may be found in the questions that proved most helpful when you probed your subject. For example, if questions like "What happened?" and "When did it happen?" suggested the most useful material, you might consider structuring your paper as a narrative. The list that follows links various questions to the patterns of development they suggest:

What happened?
When did it happen?
Where did it happen?
Who did it?
} Narration

What does it look like?
What are its characteristics?
What impression does it make?
} Description

What are some typical cases or examples of it?
} Exemplification

How did it happen?
What makes it work?
How is it made?
} Process

Why did it happen?
What caused it?
What does it cause?
What are its effects?
How is it related to something else?
} Cause and Effect

How is it like other things?
How is it different from other things?
} Comparison and Contrast

What are its parts or types?
How can its parts or types be
separated or grouped?
Do its parts or types fit into a
logical order? } Classification and Division
Into what categories can its
parts or types be arranged?
On what basis can it be categorized?

What is it?
How does it resemble other
members of its class? } Definition
How does it differ from other
members of its class?
What are its limits?

Notice that the terms in the right-hand column—narration, description, and so on—identify some useful patterns of development that
can help order your ideas. Chapters 2 through 9 explain and illustrate these patterns.

Constructing a Formal Outline

Once you have arranged your ideas into an informal outline,
formulated a thesis, and identified an emerging pattern of development, you may want to construct a *formal outline* for your essay.
Whereas informal outlines are preliminary lists that simply remind
the writer which points to make in which order, formal outlines are
detailed, multilevel constructions. The complexity of your assignment will determine how complete an outline you need. For short
papers, informal outlines like the ones included in Chapters 2–10
are usually sufficient. For a longer, more complex essay, however,
you may need to prepare a formal outline.

Your outline should follow certain conventions of numbering,
indentation, and punctuation to map out your paper's body paragraphs. Group main headings under Roman numerals (I, II, III, IV,
etc.) flush with the left-hand margin. Indent subheadings under the
first word of the heading above. Use capital letters for major points
and numbers for subtopics, and capitalize the first letter of the first
word of both topics and subtopics. Make your outline as simple as
possible, avoiding overly complex divisions of ideas. Many of the

outlines you do will probably not go beyond a third-level heading (1, 2, 3, etc.).

Thesis statement: _____

_____

I. _____
  A. _____
    1. _____
    2. _____
      a. _____
      b. _____
  B. _____
II. _____

The headings in your outline can be either topics or complete sentences ("Advantages and disadvantages" or "The advantages of advanced placement chemistry outweigh the disadvantages"). In either case, all headings and subheadings at the same level should be stated in parallel terms. If Roman numeral I is a noun, II, III, and IV should also be. In addition, each heading must contain at least two subdivisions. You cannot have a *1* without a *2* or an *a* without a *b*.

To construct an outline, review your thesis and all the points compiled during prewriting. As you examine this material, you will see that some points seem more important than others. Write down the points from your informal outline, and group the points from your brainstorming notes or cluster diagram as subheadings under the appropriate headings. When you revise, make sure that each point supports your thesis. Points that do not should be reworded or discarded entirely. In addition, make certain that your outline follows the proper format. (If you use a computer to outline, you can easily add or rearrange the ideas with which you are working. Do not delete points, however, until you are sure that you do not need them.)

A STUDENT WRITER: CONSTRUCTING A FORMAL OUTLINE

The outline Laura Bobnak constructed follows the format discussed above. Notice that the following outline focuses on the body of her paper and does not include the introduction or conclusion—these are usually developed after you have drafted the body. (Compare this formal outline with the informal outline on p. 31 in which Laura simply grouped her brainstorming notes under three general headings.)

Speaking Out

Thesis statement: As I look back on the situation, I wonder why I kept silent and what would have happened had I acted.

  I. The incident
     A. Taking test
     B. Witnessing cheating
     C. Reacting
        1. Anger
        2. Dismissal
 II. Reasons for keeping silent
     A. Other students' attitudes
     B. My fears
III. Current opinion of cheating
     A. Effects of cheating on education
        1. Undercuts the process
        2. Unfair to teachers
     B. Effects of cheating on students

This outline enabled Laura to order her points so that they supported her thesis. As she went on to draft her essay, it served as a useful guide to remind her to arrange and support her points so that the contrast between her present and former attitudes toward cheating is clear.

Understanding the Parts of the Essay

No matter what pattern of development you use, an essay should have a beginning, a middle, and an end—that is, an *introduction,* a *body,* and a *conclusion.*

The Introduction.   The **introduction** of your essay, usually one paragraph and rarely more than two, introduces your subject, engages your readers' interest, and often states your thesis. In so short a space, however, there is no room for an in-depth discussion of your topic.

You can introduce an essay and engage your readers' interest in the following ways:

1. You can give some *background information* and then move directly to your thesis. This approach works well when you know that the audience is already interested in your topic and that you can therefore come directly to the point. It is especially useful for exams, where there is no need or time for subtlety.

With inflation slowing down, many companies have understandably lowered prices, and the oil industry should be no exception. Consequently, fair-minded individuals begin wondering whether the relatively high price of home heating oil is justified given the economic climate. It makes sense, therefore, for us to start examining the pricing policies of the major American oil companies.

(economics take-home exam)

2. You can introduce an essay with a *definition* of a relevant term or concept. (Keep in mind, however, that the "According to *Webster's Dictionary* . . ." formula is overused and trite.) This technique is especially useful for research papers or examinations where the meaning of a specific term is crucial.

Democracy is a form of government in which the ultimate authority is vested in and exercised by the people. This may be so in theory, but recent city elections have caused much concern for the future of democracy here. Extensive voting-machine irregularities and ghost voting have seriously jeopardized people's faith in the democratic process.

(political science paper)

3. You can begin your essay with an *anecdote* or *story* that leads into or prepares readers for your thesis.

Upon meeting the famous author James Joyce, a young student stammered, "May I kiss the hand that wrote *Ulysses?*" "No!" said Joyce. "It did a lot of other things, too." As this exchange shows, Joyce was an individual who valued humor. This tendency is also present in his final work, *Finnegans Wake,* where comedy is used to comment on the human condition.

(English literature paper)

4. You can begin with a *question.*

What was it like to live through the holocaust? Elie Wiesel, in *One Generation After,* answers this question by presenting a series of accounts about individuals who found themselves thrust into Nazi death camps. As he does so, he challenges some of the assumptions we hold in our somewhat smug and highly materialistic society.

(sociology book report)

5. You can also begin with a *quotation.* If it is well chosen, it can interest your audience in reading further.

"The rich are different," said F. Scott Fitzgerald more than fifty years ago. Apparently, they still are. As any examination of the tax laws shows, the wealthy receive many more benefits than do the middle class or the poor.

(business law essay)

No matter which method you select, your introduction should be consistent in tone and approach with the rest of your essay. If it is not, it can misrepresent your intentions and even destroy your credibility. (For this reason, the introduction is often the last part of a rough draft to be written.) A technical report, for instance, should have an introduction that reflects the formality and seriousness of the occasion. The introduction to an autobiographical essay or a personal letter, on the other hand, may have an informal and relaxed tone.

The Body Paragraphs. The middle section, or body, of your essay supports and expands your thesis. The body paragraphs present the detail that convinces your audience that your thesis is reasonable. To do their job, body paragraphs should be *unified, coherent,* and *well developed.*

Body paragraphs should be unified. A paragraph has **unity** when every sentence directly relates to the main idea of the paragraph. Sometimes the main idea of a paragraph is stated in a **topic sentence.** Like a thesis, a topic sentence acts as a guidepost, making it easy for readers to follow your discussion. Although where you place a topic sentence depends on your purpose and your subject, beginning writers often make it the first sentence of a paragraph.

At other times, the main idea of a paragraph is *implied* by the sentences in the paragraph. Professional writers frequently use this technique because they believe that in some situations—especially narratives and descriptions—a topic sentence can seem forced or awkward. Many beginning writers, however, find it helpful to use topic sentences. Topic sentences not only emphasize the ideas that you are discussing in each paragraph, but they also keep you on track by reflecting the major divisions of your outline.

Whatever strategy you use, remember that each sentence in a paragraph should be consistent with your purpose and should develop the main idea of the paragraph. If the sentences in a paragraph do not do these things, the paragraph will lack unity. In the following excerpt from a student essay, notice how the topic sentence unifies the paragraph by summarizing its main idea:

Built on the Acropolis overlooking the city of Athens in the fifth century B.C., the Parthenon illustrates the limitations of Greek architecture. As a temple of the gods, it was supposed to represent heavenly or divine perfection. However, although at first glance its structure seems to be perfect, on closer examination it becomes clear that it is a static, two-dimensional object. As long as you stand in the center of any of its four sides to look at it, its form will appear to be perfect. The strong Doric columns seem to be equally spaced, one next to another, along all four of its sides. But if you take a step to the right or left, the Parthenon's symmetry is destroyed.

The explicit topic sentence, located at the beginning of the paragraph, enables readers to grasp the writer's point immediately. The examples that follow all relate to that point. The whole paragraph is therefore focused and unified.

Body paragraphs should be coherent. A paragraph is coherent if it is composed of sentences that are smoothly and logically connected to one another. **Coherence** can be achieved through three devices. First, you can repeat key words to carry concepts from one sentence to another and to echo important terms. Second, you can use pronouns to refer to key nouns in previous sentences. Finally, you can use **transitions,** words or expressions that show chronological sequence (*then, next, after that*); cause and effect (*as a result, therefore*); addition (*first, second, and, furthermore*); comparison (*similarly*); and contrast (*but, however, still, nevertheless*). These strategies for connecting sentences—which you can also use to connect paragraphs within an essay—spell out for your readers the exact relationships among your ideas. The following paragraph, from George Orwell's "Shooting an Elephant" (p. 96), uses all three techniques to achieve coherence:

> I got up. The Burmans were already racing past me across the mud. It was obvious that the elephant would never rise again, but he was not dead. He was breathing very rhythmically with long rattling gasps, his great mound of a side painfully rising and falling. His mouth was wide open—I could see far down into the caverns of pale pink throat. I waited a long time for him to die, but his breathing did not weaken. Finally I fired my two remaining shots into the spot where I thought his heart must be. The thick blood welled out of him like red velvet, but still he did not die. His body did not even jerk when the shots hit him, the tortured breathing continued without a pause. He was dying, very slowly and in great agony, but in some world remote from me where not even a bullet could damage him further. I felt that I had got to put an end to that dreadful noise. It seemed dreadful to see the great beast lying there, powerless to move and yet powerless to die, and not even be able to finish him. I sent back for my small rifle and poured shot after shot into his heart and down his throat. They seemed to make no impression. The tortured gasps continued as steadily as the ticking of a clock.

In this paragraph Orwell keeps his narrative coherent by using transitional expressions (*already, finally, when the shots hit him*) to signal the passing of time. He uses pronouns (*he, his*) in nearly every sentence to refer back to the elephant, the topic of his paragraph. Finally, he repeats key words like *shot* and *die* (and its variants *dead* and *dying*) to link the paragraph's sentences together. The result is a coherent, cohesive whole.

Body paragraphs should be well developed. A paragraph is well developed if it contains the examples, facts, and discussions readers need to understand its main idea. If a paragraph is not adequately developed, your readers will feel that they have been given only a partial picture of your subject. Just how much information you need depends on your audience, your purpose, and the claims you make in your topic sentence.

Should you find that you need more information in a paragraph, you can consult the brainstorming notes created during your pre-writing. If your notes do not provide enough material to develop your main idea sufficiently, you can freewrite or brainstorm again, review your notes, talk with friends and instructors, read more about your topic, or go to the library and do some research. Your assignment and your topic will determine the kind and amount of information you need. The following paragraph by a student writer presents a good deal of concrete information to support the statement made in the topic sentence:

> Just look at how males have been taught that extravagance is a positive characteristic. Scrooge, the main character of Dickens's *A Christmas Carol,* is portrayed as an evil man until he is rehabilitated—meaning that he gives up his miserly ways and freely distributes gifts and money on Christmas day. This behavior, of course, is rewarded when people change their opinions about him and decide that perhaps he isn't such a bad person after all. Diamond Jim Brady is another interesting example. This individual was a financier who was known for his extravagant taste in women and food. In any given night, he would consume enough food to feed at least ten of the many poor who roamed the streets of late nineteenth-century New York. Yet, despite his selfishness and infantile self-gratification, Diamond Jim Brady's name has become synonymous with the good life.

This student writer provides two examples to support her claim that society teaches males that extravagance is a positive attribute. Her literary and historical examples are complete, carefully chosen, and effectively presented.

In addition to making sure that your body paragraphs are unified, coherent, and well developed, you need to arrange your paragraphs according to the pattern of development you have chosen. For instance, an essay in which you discuss the causes of Hitler's defeat in Russia could be organized according to a *cause-and-effect* pattern:

Introduction: Thesis Statement
Body
    Cause 1:   The Russian winter
    Cause 2:   The opening of a second front
    Cause 3:   The problem of logistics
    Cause 4:   Hitler's refusal to take advice
Conclusion

A lab report on the synthesis of aspirin could be organized like this, following a *process* pattern of development:

Introduction: Thesis Statement
Body
    Step 1:   Mix 5 g. of salicylic acid, 10 ml. of acetic anhydride, and 1–2 ml. of sulphuric acid.
    Step 2:   Wait for the mixture to cool.
    Step 3:   Add 50 ml. of water and collect on a Büchner filter.
    Step 4:   Dry the residue.
    Step 5:   Recrystallize the aspirin from benzene.
Conclusion

These and other patterns of development will be outlined and analyzed in detail throughout the rest of this book.

The Conclusion. Readers remember best what they read last, and so your **conclusion** is extremely important. Always end your essay in a way that reinforces your thesis and your purpose.

Like your introduction, your conclusion should be brief. In a short essay, it can be as brief as one sentence and most often is no longer than a paragraph. Regardless of its length, however, your conclusion should be consistent with the content of your essay. Therefore, it should not introduce new points or material that you have not discussed earlier. Frequently, a conclusion will end an essay by restating the thesis. Like thesis statements, effective conclusions need no announcement, and you should avoid beginning your conclusion with the artificial phrase *In conclusion.*

Conclusions can be as challenging to construct as introductions. Here are several ways to conclude an essay:

1. You can conclude your essay by reviewing your main points and *restating your thesis.*

> Rotation of crops provided several benefits. It enriched soil by giving it a rest; it enabled farmers to vary their production; and it ended the cycle of "boom or bust" that had characterized the prewar South's economy when cotton was the primary crop. Of course, this innovation did not solve all the economic problems of the postwar South, but it did lay the groundwork for the healthy economy this region enjoys today.
>
> (history exam)

2. You can end a discussion of a problem by *recommending a course of action.*

> While there is still time, American engineering has to reassess its priorities. We no longer have the luxury of exotic and wasteful experiments in design for purely aesthetic reasons. Instead, we need technology grounded in common sense and economic feasibility. That the proposed space station seems to have few practical applications illustrates how far we have strayed from old-fashioned common sense and ingenuity.
>
> (engineering ethics report)

3. You can conclude with a *prediction.* Be careful, however, that your prediction follows logically from the points you have made in the essay. The conclusion is not the place to make new points or change direction.

> It is too late to save parts of the great swamps in northern Florida, but it is not too late to preserve the Everglades in the southern part of the state. With intelligent planning and an end of the dam building program by the Army Corps of Engineers, we will be able to halt the destruction of what Native Americans called the "Timeless Swamp."
>
> (environmental science essay)

4. You can also end with a *quotation.* If selected carefully, it can add weight to an already strong essay.

> In *Walden,* Henry David Thoreau said, "The mass of men lead lives of quiet desperation." This sentiment is reinforced by a drive through the Hill District of our city. Perhaps the work of the men and women who run the health clinic on Jefferson Street cannot totally change this situation, but it can give us hope to know that some people, at least, are working for the betterment of us all.
>
> (public health essay)

STAGE THREE: DRAFTING AND REVISION

After you decide on a tentative thesis and arrangement for your ideas, you can draft and revise your essay. Keep in mind that even as you carry out these activities, you may have to generate more material and revise your thesis and organization.

Writing Your First Draft

The purpose of your first draft is to get your ideas down on paper so you can react to them. While writing your draft, you may discover new directions for your essay. If a new idea occurs to you, follow it through. Some of your best writing will come from unexpected turns or accidents. You should think of the first draft as an expression of the ideas you have been gathering about your topic. For this reason, don't let worries about correctness or word choice interfere with the flow of your ideas. All you want to do is keep your momentum until you finish the draft. Later, when you write the second or third draft, you can polish your style, and then you can go on to edit for grammar, punctuation, and mechanics.

Revising Your Essay

Remember that revision is not something to do after your paper is finished. It is a continuing process during which you consider the logic and clarity of your ideas as well as their effective and correct expression. Thus, revision is not simply a matter of proofreading or editing, of crossing out one word and substituting another or correcting errors in spelling and punctuation; it means reexamining and rethinking what you have written (re-vision). In fact, you may even find yourself adding and deleting extensively, reordering whole sentences or paragraphs as you reconsider what you want to communicate to your audience. Revision can take a lot of time, so do not be discouraged if you have to go through three or four drafts of your essay before you think it is ready to hand in.

After you have written your first draft, put it aside for several hours or even a day or two if you can. This "cooling-off" period enables you to distance yourself from your essay so that you can read it more objectively when you return to it. When you read it again, you can begin to revise.

How you revise—what specific strategies you decide to use—depends on your own preference, your instructor's directions, and the time available. Like the rest of the writing process, revision varies from student to student and from assignment to assignment.

Revising with a Checklist. If you have time, you can start your revising by using the following checklist or adapting it to your own writing process.

Revision Checklist

• **Thesis statement.** Is it clear and specific? Does it indicate the direction your essay will take? Is it consistent with the body of your essay? If you departed from your essay's original direction or emphasis while you were writing, you will need either to revise the thesis statement so that it accurately sums up the ideas and information contained in the body or to remove from the body any sections unrelated to the thesis statement—or to revise them so that they *are* relevant.

• **Body.** Are the body paragraphs unified? Coherent? Well developed? If not, you might have to add more facts or examples or smoother transitions. Do the points you make in these paragraphs support your thesis? Does the essay have a clear pattern of development?

• **Introduction and conclusion.** Are they appropriate for your material, your audience, and your purpose? Are they interesting? Do they reinforce your thesis?

• **Sentences.** Are they effective? Interesting? Varied in length and structure? Are there any sentences that should be deleted or moved?

• **Words.** Should you make any substitutions?

• **Title.** Responsible for your readers' first impression of your essay, your title should arouse their interest in what you will be saying. Usually, single-word titles ("Love") and cute ones ("The Cheery Cheerleader") do little to draw readers into your essay. To be effective, a title should reflect your purpose and your tone. The essays in this book illustrate a number of types of titles you can use.

Type	*Model*
Unusual topic	"Why Mr. Ed Still Talks Good Horse Sense"
Question	"Who Killed Benny Paret?"
Topic + question	"The Civil Rights Movement: What Good Was It?"
Controversy	"Let's Tell the Story of All America's Cultures"
Topic + controversy	"Television: The Plug-In Drug"

Revising with an Outline.   If you do not have time to consult a detailed checklist, you can check the logic of your essay's structure by making a *review outline.* Either an informal outline or a formal one can show you whether you have omitted any important points. An outline can also show you whether your essay follows the pattern of development you have chosen. Finally, an outline can clarify the relationship between your thesis and your support paragraphs.

Revising with a Peer Critique.   Another revision strategy you might find helpful is seeking a *peer critique*—in other words, asking a friend to read your essay and comment on it. Sometimes a peer critique can be quite formal. An instructor may require students to exchange papers and evaluate their classmates' work according to certain standards, perhaps by completing a form. Often, however, a peer critique is informal. Even if your friend is unfamiliar with your topic, he or she can still tell you honestly whether you are getting your point across—and maybe even advise you on how to communicate more effectively. (Remember, though, that your critic should be only your reader, not your ghostwriter.)

Guidelines for Peer Critiques

1. Be positive. Remember your purpose is to help other students improve their essays.
2. Begin by emphasizing the good points about what you have read. Make sure you mention one or two things that the writer has done particularly well.
3. Offer concrete suggestions about what the writer could do better. Vague words like "good" or "bad" provide little guidance.
4. If you are doing a critique orally, make sure you interact with the writer as you read. Ask questions, listen to responses, and explain your comments.

5. When possible, write down your comments—either on a form your instructor provides or in the margins of the paper.

Revising on a Computer.   If you revise on a computer, you can add, delete, and move information quickly and effortlessly. Still, some writers have difficulty revising on a computer because most screens show only a portion of a page, and so the connections between ideas are hard to see and to keep track of. Therefore, many writers find that they have an easier time revising on a hard copy of their essay, making their changes on paper and then entering them into the computer.

A STUDENT WRITER: REVISING A FIRST DRAFT

Here is the first draft of Laura Bobnak's essay.

When I was in high school, I had an experience like the one Henry Louis Gates talks about in his essay. It was then that I saw a close friend of mine cheat in chemistry class. As I look back on the situation, I wonder why I kept silent and what would have happened had I acted.   1

The incident I am going to describe took place during the final examination for my advanced placement chemistry class. I had studied hard for it, but even so, I found the test difficult. As I struggled to balance a particularly difficult equation, I noticed that my friend Jeff Servin, who was sitting across from me, was acting strangely. I noticed that he was copying material from a paper. After watching him for a while, I dismissed the incident and got back to my test.   2

After the test was over, I began to think about what I had seen. The more I thought about it the angrier I got. It seemed unfair that I had struggled for weeks to memorize formulas and equations while all Jeff had done was to copy them onto a cheat sheet. For a moment I considered going to the teacher, but I quickly dismissed this idea. After all, cheating was something everybody did. Besides, I was afraid if I told on Jeff, my friends would stop talking to me.   3

Now that I am in college I see the situation differently. I find it hard to believe that I could ever have been so calm about cheating. Cheating is certainly something that students should not take for   4 granted. It undercuts the educational process and is unfair to teachers and to the majority of students who spend their time studying.

If I could go back to high school and relive the experience, I now know that I would have gone to the teacher. Naturally Jeff would have been angry at me, but at least I would have known I had the courage to do the right thing. 5

After writing this rough draft, Laura put it aside for a few hours and then reread it. Later, Laura's instructor divided the class into small groups and had them read and write critiques of each other's papers. As a result of her own reading and three written critiques, Laura was able to focus on a number of areas that needed revision.

The Introduction. Laura realized that she would have to present more detail in her introduction. The students in her peer group said that her introduction was dull and that it did little to draw them into the essay. In addition, they said that they did not think the thesis statement addressed the second half of the assignment—to explain whether or not she would have acted differently today.

Keeping these comments in mind Laura rewrote her introduction. First, she created a context for her discussion by more specifically linking her story to Gates's essay. Next, she decided to postpone mentioning her subject—cheating—until later in the paper, hoping that this strategy would stimulate the curiosity of her readers and make them want to read further. Finally, she revised her thesis statement to reflect the specific wording of the assignment.

The Body Paragraphs. The students in her peer group also indicated to Laura that she needed to expand her body paragraphs. Although she thought that most of her readers would be familiar with courses like advanced placement chemistry, the questions several students asked made her realize that her assumption was incorrect. One student suggested she add more detail to her descriptions to help readers put themselves in her place. Finally, some students in her group thought that she should expand the paragraph in which she described her reaction to the cheating. They wondered what the other students in the class had thought about the incident. Did they know? Did they care? Laura's classmates were curious, and they thought other readers would be too.

Before revising the body paragraphs, Laura did some brainstorming to think of additional ideas to include. She decided to describe the difficulty of advanced placement chemistry and the pressure that all the students in the class felt. She also decided to summarize discussions she had had with several of her classmates after the test. In addition, she wanted to explain in more detail her present views on cheating. She felt that the paragraph in which she presented these ideas did not contrast clearly enough with the paragraphs that dealt with her high school experiences.

To make sure that her sentences led smoothly into one another, Laura added transitional words and phrases whenever she could and rewrote entire sentences when necessary, signaling the progression of her thoughts by adding words and phrases like *therefore, for this reason, for example,* and *as a result.* In addition, Laura tried to repeat key words from sentence to sentence so that important concepts would be reinforced.

The Conclusion. Laura's biggest concern as she revised was to make sure her readers would see the connection between her essay and the assignment. To make this connection clear, she decided to mention in her conclusion a specific effect the incident had on her: its impact on her friendship with Jeff. Laura also decided to link her reactions to those of Henry Louis Gates, Jr.: Like him, she had been upset by the actions of someone she knew. Employing this strategy, she was able to bring her essay full circle and develop an idea she had alluded to in her introduction. By rewriting her conclusion, Laura reinforced her thesis statement and provided closure to her essay.

A STUDENT WRITER: REVISING A SECOND DRAFT

The following draft incorporates Laura's revisions as well as some preliminary editing of punctuation and grammar.

SPEAKING OUT

In his essay " 'What's in a Name?' " Henry Louis Gates, Jr. recalls an   1
incident from his past in which his father did not speak up. Perhaps he kept
silent because he was afraid or because he knew that nothing he said or did
would change the situation in Piedmont, West Virginia. Although I have never
encountered the kind of prejudice Gates describes, I did have an experience in

high school where, like Gates's father, I could have spoken up but did not. As I now look back on the situation, I know I would not have made the same decision today.

The incident I am going to describe took place during the final 2 examination in my advanced placement chemistry class. The course was very demanding and required hours of studying every night. Every day after school, I would meet with several students and outline chapters and answer homework questions. Sometimes we would even work on weekends. We would often ask ourselves whether we had gotten in over our heads. As the semester dragged on, it became clear to me, as well as to the other students in the class, that passing the course was not something we could take for granted. Test after test came back with grades that were well below the "A's" and "B's" I was used to getting in the regular chemistry course I took in tenth grade. By the time we were ready to take the final exam, most of us were worried that we would fail the course--despite the teacher's assurances that she would mark on a curve.

The final examination for advanced placement chemistry was given on a 3 Friday morning from nine to twelve o'clock. As I struggled to balance a particularly complex equation, I noticed that the person sitting across from me was acting strangely. At first I thought I was imagining things, but as I stared I saw Jeff Servin, my friend and study partner, fumbling with his test booklet. About a minute passed before I realized that he was copying material from a paper he had taped inside the cuff of his shirt. After a short time, I dismissed the incident and finished my test.

Surprisingly, when I mentioned the incident to others in the class, they all 4 knew what Jeff had done. The more I thought about Jeff's actions, the angrier I got. It seemed unfair that I had struggled for weeks to memorize formulas and equations while all Jeff had done was to copy them onto a cheat sheet. For a moment I considered going to the teacher, but I quickly dismissed this idea. Cheating was nothing new to me or to the others in the school. Many of my classmates cheated at one time or another. Most of us saw school as a war between us and the teachers, and cheating was just another weapon in our arsenal. The worst crime I could commit would be to turn Jeff in. As far as I was concerned, I had no choice. I fell in line with the values of my high school classmates and dismissed the incident as "no big deal."

I find it hard to believe that I could ever have been so complacent about cheating. The issues that were simple in high school now seem complex. I now ask questions that never would have occurred to me in high school. Interestingly, Jeff and I are no longer very close. Whenever I see him I have the same reaction Henry Louis Gates, Jr. had when he met Mr. Wilson after he had insulted his father--I have a hard time looking him in the eye.

Laura could see that her second draft was stronger than her first. But after reading and analyzing it, she decided on a number of ways in which her draft could be improved.

The Title. Laura's original title was only a working title, and now she wanted one that would create interest and draw readers into her essay. She knew, however, that a humorous, cute, or "catchy" title would undermine the seriousness of her essay. After rejecting a number of possibilities, she decided on "The Price of Silence." Not only was this title thought-provoking, but also it was descriptive; thus, it prepared readers for what was to follow in the essay.

The Introduction. Although Laura was basically satisfied with her introduction, she identified one problem. She realized that she had incorrectly assumed that everyone reading her essay would be familiar with Gates's essay. By adding material that defined the problems Gates's father faced, she could accommodate readers who did not know or remember Gates's comments.

The Body Paragraphs. After reading her first body paragraph, Laura thought that she could sharpen its focus. She decided to delete the first sentence of the paragraph because it seemed too conversational. In addition, she deleted several other sentences that she thought gave too much detail about how difficult advanced placement chemistry was. After all, cheating—not advanced placement chemistry—was the subject of her paper. If she included this kind of detail, she ran the risk of distracting or confusing readers with an irrelevant discussion.

In her second body paragraph, Laura saw that her first and second sentences did not seem to be linked together, and she realized that a short discussion of her reaction to the test itself would connect these two ideas. She also decided to add transitional words and phrases to the last part of the paragraph to clarify the sequence of events she described. Phrases like *at first, about a minute passed,* and *after a short time* would help her readers follow her discussion.

Laura thought that the third body paragraph was her best, but even so, she felt that she needed to add some material. After reading the paragraph several times, she decided to expand her discussion of the students' reactions to cheating. More information—perhaps a quotation—would help her strengthen her assertion that cheating was condoned by the students in her class.

The Conclusion.   Laura realized her conclusion began by mentioning her present attitude toward cheating and then suddenly shifted to the effect cheating had on her relationship with Jeff. To remedy this situation, Laura decided to take her discussion about her current view of cheating out of her conclusion and put it in a separate paragraph. By doing this, Laura would now be able to focus her conclusion on the effect cheating had on both Jeff and her. This strategy would not only enable Laura to present her views about cheating in more detail, but it would also help her to end her essay forcefully.

A STUDENT WRITER: PREPARING A FINAL DRAFT

Based on her analysis, Laura revised and edited her draft and handed in this final version of her essay.

THE PRICE OF SILENCE

Introduction (provides background)   In his essay " 'What's in a Name?' " Henry Louis   1
Gates, Jr. recalls an incident from his past in which his father encountered prejudice and did not speak up. Perhaps he kept silent because he was afraid or because he knew that nothing he said or did would change the racial situation in Piedmont, West Virginia. Although I have never encountered the kind of prejudice Gates describes, I did have an experience in high school where, like Gates's father, I could have spoken out but did not. As I think back on the

Thesis statement situation, I realize that I have outgrown the immaturity and lack of confidence that made me keep silent.

Narrative begins In my senior year in high school I, along with fifteen other students, took advanced placement chemistry. The course was very demanding and required hours of studying every night. As the semester dragged on, it became clear to me, as well as to the other students in the class, that passing the course was not something we could take for granted. Test after test came back with grades that were well below the "A's" and "B's" I was used to getting in the regular chemistry course I had taken in tenth grade. By the time we were ready to take the final exam, most of us were worried that we would fail the course--despite the teacher's assurances that she would mark on a curve.

Key incident occurs The final examination for advanced placement chemistry was given on a Friday morning between nine o'clock and noon. I had studied all that week, but even so, I found the test difficult. I knew the material, but I had a hard time answering the long questions that the teacher asked. As I struggled to balance a particularly complex equation, I noticed that the person sitting across from me was acting strangely. At first I thought I was imagining things, but as I stared I saw Jeff Servin, my friend and study partner, fumbling with his test booklet. About a minute passed before I realized that he was copying material from a paper he had taped to the inside of his shirt cuff. After a short time, I stopped watching him and finished my test.

Narrative continues: reactions to the incident It was not until after the test that I began thinking about what I had seen. Surprisingly, when I mentioned the incident to others in the class, they all knew what Jeff had done. Some even thought that Jeff's actions were justified. "After all," one student said, "the test was hard." But the more I thought about Jeff's actions, the angrier I got. It

2

3

4

seemed unfair that I had struggled for weeks to memorize formulas and equations while all Jeff had done was copy them onto a cheat sheet. For a moment I considered going to the teacher, but I quickly dismissed this idea. Cheating was nothing new to me or to the others in the school. Many of my classmates cheated at one time or another. Most of us saw school as a war between us and the teachers, and cheating was just another weapon in our arsenal. The worst crime I could commit would be to turn Jeff in. As far as I

Narrative ends

was concerned, I had no choice. I fell in line with the values of my high school classmates and dismissed the incident as "no big deal."

Analysis of key incident

Now that I am in college, however, I see the situation   5 differently. I find it hard to believe that I could ever have been so complacent about cheating. The issues that were simple in high school now seem complex--especially in light of the honor code that I follow in college. I now ask questions that never would have occurred to me in high school. What, for example, are the implications of cheating? What would happen to the educational system if cheating became the norm? What are my obligations to all those who are involved in education? Aren't teachers and students interested in achieving a common goal? The answers to these questions give me a sense of the far-reaching effects of my failure to act. If confronted with the same situation today, I know I would speak out regardless of the consequences.

Conclusion (aftermath of incident)

Interestingly, Jeff and I are no longer very close.   6 Whenever I see him I have the same reaction Henry Louis Gates, Jr. had when he met Mr. Wilson after he had insulted his father--I have a hard time looking him in the eye. Jeff Servin is a first-year student at the state university and, like me, was given credit for chemistry. I feel certain that not

Reinforcement of thesis

only did I fail myself by not turning him in, but also that I failed him. I gave in to peer pressure instead of doing what I knew to be the right thing. The worst that would have happened to Jeff had I spoken up is that he would have had to repeat chemistry in summer school. By doing so, he would have proven to himself that he could, like the rest of us in the class, pass on his own. In the long run, this knowledge would have served him better than the knowledge that he could cheat whenever he faced a difficult situation.

Each draft of Laura's essay enabled her to sharpen the focus of her discussion. In the process, she clarified her own thoughts about her subject and reached some new and interesting conclusions. Although much of her paper is narrative, it also contains a contrast between Laura's current ideas about cheating and the ideas she had in high school. Perhaps the major weakness of Laura's paper is that she could have explained the reasons behind her current ideas about cheating more fully. Even so, her paper gives a straightforward account of the incident and analyzes its significance without lapsing into clichés or simplistic moralizing. Especially effective is Laura's conclusion, in which she examines the effects of cheating. By placing this material at the end of her discussion, she makes sure that her readers will not lose sight of the implications of her experience. By ending her conclusion with a forceful statement of her position, she ensures that her major point will stay with her audience after they have finished reading.

A Note on Editing

When you finish revising your essay, it is tempting to hand it in to your instructor and breathe a sigh of relief. This is one temptation you should resist. You still have to edit your paper to correct many of the small problems that remain even after you revise. When you edit, you put the finishing touches on your essay. You correct misspellings, check punctuation, search for grammatical inaccuracies, look at your paper's format, and consider any other surface features that might weaken its message or undermine your credibility. Editing is your last chance to make sure your paper says what you want it to.

A computer can be especially useful in editing. By using the global *find* and *replace* commands, you can change overused words and check punctuation. Spell checkers will locate misspelled words in your paper, and text analysis programs can scan for grammatical errors, sexist language, jargon, and wordy or vague expressions. (You should ask your instructor's permission before you use such programs.)

Of course, you could spend literally hours checking your essay for every possible error, but this approach would be time-consuming and impractical. As you edit, keep in mind that certain errors occur more frequently than others. By concentrating on these errors, and by keeping a record of the specific errors that you make most often, you will be able to edit your essays quickly and efficiently.

The following checklist calls your attention to many of the most common errors. Consult a handbook of grammar and usage for detailed discussion of these errors.

Editing Checklist

• **Subject-verb agreement.**   Do all your verbs agree in number with their subjects? Remember that singular subjects take singular verbs and plural subjects take plural verbs.

• **Clear pronoun reference.**   Do pronouns that refer back to specific nouns do so clearly? Be especially careful of unclear references involving *this*. To avoid this problem, always follow *this* with a word that clarifies the reference—*this problem, this event,* and so on.

• **Punctuation.**   Are any commas misplaced, missing, or unnecessary? Remember to use commas before coordinating conjunctions (*and, but,* etc.) in compound sentences.

• **Misspelled words and typos.**   Proofread for spelling even if you have run a computer spell check. Also be on the lookout for mistakes in capitalization, as well as for improper spacing and omitted letters.

• **Commonly confused words.**   Be alert for words that are often confused with each other. Remember, for example, that *it's* is a contraction meaning *it is,* and *its* is the possessive form of *it.*

• **Sentence fragments.**   Does each group of words punctuated as a sentence have a subject and a verb? Does it make sense on its own, without being attached to another sentence?

• **Comma splices.**   Is a comma alone used to connect two independent clauses? If so, correct this problem by adding the appropriate coordinating conjunction (*and, but,* etc.), changing the comma to a semicolon, or making the clauses into separate sentences.

• **Inconsistencies.**   Are you consistent in expressing yourself throughout your paper? For example, do not shift from the present to the past tense unless your meaning requires you to do so.

• **Manuscript form.**   Have you followed your instructor's guidelines? In addition, make sure that your essay is neat and clearly printed.

Each of the reading selections in the chapters that follow is organized around one dominant pattern of development. It is not at all unusual, however, to find more than one pattern used in a single work (see Essays for Further Reading: Combining the Patterns, p. 659). In any event, these patterns are not to be imitated blindly but should be adapted to your subject, your audience, and your writing occasion.

2

Narration

WHAT IS NARRATION?

Narration tells a story by presenting events in an orderly, logical sequence. In the following paragraph from her memoir *I Know Why the Caged Bird Sings,* Maya Angelou recalls her high-school graduation.

Narrative presents events in orderly sequence

Topic sentence

The school band struck up a march and all classes filed in as had been rehearsed. We stood in front of our seats, as assigned, and on a signal from the choir director, we sat. No sooner had this been accomplished than the band started to play the national anthem. We rose again and sang the song, after which we recited the pledge of allegiance. We remained standing for a brief minute before the choir director and the principal signaled to us, rather desperately I thought, to take our seats. The command was so unusual that our carefully rehearsed and smooth-running machine was thrown off. For a full minute we fumbled for our chairs and bumped into each other awkwardly. Habits change or solidify under pressure, so in our state of nervous tension we had been ready to follow our usual assembly pattern: the American national anthem, then the pledge of allegiance, then the song every Black person I knew called the Negro National Anthem. All done in the same key, with the same passion and most often standing on the same foot.

Narration can be the dominant pattern in history, biography, autobiography, essays, and works of fiction and narrative poetry as well as in less formal writing, such as personal letters and entries in diaries and journals. Narration is also an essential part of casual conversation, and it underlies folk and fairy tales and radio and television news reports. In short, any time you "tell what happened," you are using narration.

Although a narrative may simply recount events or create a particular mood or impression, in college writing narration is more likely to present a sequence of events in order to support a thesis. For instance, in a narrative essay about your first date, your purpose may be to show your readers that dating is a bizarre and often unpleasant ritual. Accordingly, you do not simply "tell the story" of your date. Rather, you select and arrange details of the evening to show your readers *why* dating is bizarre and unpleasant. As in any other kind of essay, you may state your thesis explicitly ("My experiences with dating have convinced me that this ritual should be abandoned entirely"), or you may imply your thesis through the selection and arrangement of events.

Narrative passages may appear in an essay that is not primarily a narrative. In an argumentative essay in support of stricter gun-control legislation, for example, you may devote one or two paragraphs to a story of a child accidently killed by a handgun. In this chapter, however, we focus on narration as the dominant pattern of a piece of writing. During your college career, you will have many assignments that call for such writing. In an English composition class, for instance, you may be asked to write about an experience that was important to your development as an adult; on a European history exam, you may need to relate the events that led to Napoleon's defeat at the Battle of Waterloo; in a technical writing class, you may be asked to write a letter of complaint summarizing in detail a company's negligent actions. In each of these situations (as well as in case studies for business management classes, reports for criminal justice classes, and many additional assignments), the piece of writing has a structure that is primarily narrative, and the narrative is presented to support a thesis.

The skills you develop in narrative writing will also help you in other kinds of writing. A process essay, such as an account of a laboratory experiment, is like a narrative in that it outlines a series of steps in chronological order; a cause-and-effect essay, such as your answer on an economics midterm that directs you to analyze the events that led to the Great Depression, also resembles narrative in that it traces a sequence of events. A process essay, however, presents events to explain how to do something, and a cause-and-effect essay presents them to explain how they are related. (Process essays and cause-and-effect essays are dealt with in chapters 5 and 6, respectively.) Still, writing process and cause-and-effect essays will be easier if you master narration.

Including Enough Detail

Narratives, like other types of writing, need rich, specific detail if they are to be convincing. Each detail should help to create a picture for the reader; even exact times, dates, and geographical locations can be helpful. Look, for example, at the following excerpt from the essay "My Mother Never Worked," which appears later in this chapter.

> In the winter she sewed night after night, endlessly, begging cast-off clothing from relatives, ripping apart coats, dresses, blouses, and trousers to remake them to fit her four daughters and son. Every morning and every evening she milked cows, fed pigs and calves, cared for chickens, picked eggs, cooked meals, washed dishes, scrubbed floors, and tended and loved her children. In the spring she planted a garden once more, dragging pails of water to nourish and sustain the vegetables for the family. In 1936 she lost a baby in her sixth month.

In this excerpt the list of details gives the narrative authenticity and makes it convincing. The central figure in the narrative is a busy, productive woman, and readers know this because they are presented with an exhaustive catalog of her activities.

Varying Sentence Structure

When narratives present a long series of events, all the sentences can begin to sound alike: "She sewed dresses. . . . She milked cows. . . . She fed pigs. . . . She fed calves. . . . She cared for chickens. . . ." Such a predictable string of sentences may affect your readers as a ride down a monotonous stretch of highway would. You can eliminate this monotony by varying your sentence structure— for instance, by using a variety of different sentence openings or by combining simple sentences: "In the winter she sewed night after night, endlessly. . . . Every morning and every evening she milked cows, fed pigs and calves, cared for chickens. . . ."

Maintaining Clear Narrative Order

Many narratives present events in exactly the order in which they occurred, moving from beginning to end, from first event to last. Whether or not you follow a strict **chronological order** depends on the purpose of your narrative. If you are writing a straightforward account of a historical event or listing a series of poor management practices, you will probably want to move from beginning to end. In personal experience essays or fictional narratives, however, you may engage your reader's interest by beginning with an event from the middle of your story, or even from the end, and then presenting the events that led up to it. You may also begin in the present and then use one or more *flashbacks,* shifts into the past, to tell your story.

Using Verb Tenses. Verb tense is extremely important in writing that recounts events in a fixed order because tenses show the temporal relationships of actions—earlier, simultaneous, later. When you write a narrative, you must be especially careful to keep verb tense consistent and accurate so your readers can follow the time sequence. Naturally, you must shift tenses to reflect an actual time shift in your narrative. For instance, convention requires that you use present tense when discussing works of literature ("When Hamlet's mother *marries* his uncle . . ."), but a flashback to an earlier point in the story calls for a shift from present to past tense ("Before their marriage, Hamlet *was* . . ."). Nevertheless, it is important to avoid unwarranted shifts in verb tense because they will make your narrative confusing.

Using Transitions. Transitions—connecting words or phrases—help link events in time, thereby enabling narratives to flow smoothly. Without them, narratives would lack coherence, and readers would be unsure of the correct sequence of events. Transitions can indicate to readers the order in which events in a narrative occur, and they also signal shifts in time. Transitions commonly used for these purposes in narrative writing include *first, second, next, then, later, at the same time, meanwhile, immediately, soon, before, earlier, after, afterwards, now,* and *finally.* In addition to these transitions, specific time markers—such as *three years later, in 1927, after two hours,* and *on January 3*—indicate how much time has passed between events.

STRUCTURING A NARRATIVE ESSAY

Like other essays, narratives have an introduction, a body, and a conclusion. If it is explicitly stated, your essay's thesis will, in most cases, appear in the *introduction.* The *body* of your essay will recount the series of events that makes up your narrative, following a clear and orderly plan. Finally, the *conclusion* will give your reader the sense that your story is complete, perhaps by restating your thesis.

Suppose you are assigned a short history paper about the Battle of Waterloo. You plan to support the thesis that if Napoleon had kept more troops in reserve, he might have defeated the British troops under Wellington. Based on this thesis, you decide that the best way to organize your paper is to present the five major phases of the battle in strict chronological sequence. An informal outline of your essay might look like this:

Introduction:	Thesis statement—Had Napoleon kept more troops in reserve, he might have broken Wellington's line with another infantry attack and thus reversed the outcome of the battle of Waterloo.
Phase one of the battle:	Napoleon attacks the Château of Hougoumont.
Phase two of the battle:	The French infantry attacks the British lines.
Phase three of the battle:	The French cavalry stages a series of charges against the British lines that had not been attacked before. Napoleon commits his reserves.
Phase four of the battle:	The French capture La Haye Sainte, their first success of the day but an advantage which Napoleon, having committed troops elsewhere, cannot maintain without reserves.
Phase five of the battle:	The French infantry is decisively defeated by the combined thrust of the British infantry and the remaining British cavalry.
Conclusion:	Restatement of thesis; summary of key points.

By discussing the five phases of the battle in chronological order, you clearly demonstrate the validity of your thesis. As you turn your informal outline into a historical narrative, exact details, dates, times, and geographical locations are extremely important. Without them, your assertions are open to question. In addition, to keep your readers aware of the order in which the events of the battle took place, you must select appropriate transitional words and phrases carefully and pay special attention to verb tenses.

A STUDENT WRITER: NARRATION

The following essay is typical of the informal narrative writing many students are asked to do in English composition classes. It was written by Tiffany Forte in response to the assignment "Write an essay about a goal or dream you had when you were a child."

MY FIELD OF DREAMS

Introduction   When I was young, I was told that when I grew up I   1
could be anything I wanted to be, and I always took for
granted that this was true. I knew exactly what I was going
to be, and I would spend hours dreaming about how
wonderful my life would be when I grew up. One day,
Thesis   though, when I did grow up, I realized that things had not
statement   turned out the way I had always expected they would.

Narrative   When I was little, I never played with baby dolls or   2
begins   Barbies. I wasn't like other little girls; I was a tomboy. I was
the only girl in the neighborhood where I lived, so I always
played with boys. We would play army or football or (my
favorite) baseball.

Almost every summer afternoon, all the boys in my   3
neighborhood and I would meet by the big oak tree to get a
baseball game going. Surprisingly, I was always one of the
first to be picked for a team. I was very fast, and (for my
size) I could hit the ball far. I loved baseball more than
anything, and I wouldn't miss a game for the world.

My dad played baseball too, and every Friday night I   4
would go to the field with my mother to watch him play. It
was just like the big leagues, with lots of people, a snack
bar, and lights that shone so high and bright you could see
them a mile away. I loved to go to my dad's games. When
all the other kids would wander off and play, I would sit and
cheer on my dad and his team. My attention was focused on
the field, and my heart would jump with every pitch.

Even more exciting than my dad's games were the   5
major league games. The Phillies were my favorite team,
and I always looked forward to watching them on television.
My dad would make popcorn, and we would sit and watch

in anticipation of a Phillies victory. We would go wild, yelling and screaming at all the big plays. When the Phillies would win, I would be so excited I couldn't sleep; when they would lose, I would go to bed angry just like my dad.

Key experience introduced (¶s 6–7)

6   It was when my dad took me to my first major league baseball game that I decided I wanted to be a major league baseball player. The excitement began when we pulled into the parking lot of Veterans Stadium. There were thousands of cars. As we walked from the car to the stadium, my dad told me to hold on to his hand and not to let go no matter what. When we gave the man our tickets and entered the stadium, I understood why. There were mobs of people everywhere. They were walking around the stadium and standing in long lines for hot dogs, beer, and souvenirs. It was the most wonderful thing I had ever seen. When we got to our seats, I looked down at the tiny baseball diamond below me and felt as if I were on top of the world.

7   The cheering of the crowd, the singing, and the chants were almost more than I could stand. I was bursting with enthusiasm. Then, in the bottom of the eighth inning, with the score tied and two outs, Mike Schmidt came up to bat and hit the game-winning home run. The crowd went crazy. Everyone in the whole stadium was standing, and I found myself yelling and screaming along with everyone else. When Mike Schmidt came out of the dugout to receive his standing ovation, I felt a lump in my throat and butterflies in my stomach. He was everyone's hero that night, and I could only imagine the pride he must have felt. I slept the whole way home and dreamed of what it would be like to be the hero of the game.

Narrative resumes

8   The next day, when I met with the boys at the oak tree, I told them that when I grew up, I was going to be a major

league baseball player. They all laughed at me and said I could never be a baseball player because I was a girl. I told them that they were all wrong, and that I would show them.

Analysis of childhood experiences   In the years to follow I played girls' softball in a   9 competitive fast-pitch league, and I was very good. I always wanted to play baseball with the boys, but there were no mixed leagues. After a few years, I realized that the boys from the oak tree were right: I was never going to be a major league baseball player. I realized that what I had been told when I was younger wasn't the whole truth. What no one had bothered to tell me was that I could be anything I wanted to be--as long as it was something that was appropriate for a girl to do.

Conclusion   In time, I would get over the loss of my dream. I found   10 new dreams, acceptable for a young woman, and I moved on to other things. Still, every time I watch a baseball game and someone hits a home run, I get those same butterflies in my stomach and think, for just a minute, about what could have been.

Points for Special Attention

Introduction.   Tiffany's introduction is very straightforward, yet it arouses reader interest by setting up a contrast between what she expected and what actually happened. Her optimistic expectation—that she could be anything she wanted to be—is contradicted by her thesis, encouraging readers to read on to discover how things turned out, and why.

Thesis.   Tiffany's assignment was simply to write about a goal or dream she had when she was a child, but her instructor made it clear that she expected the essay to have an explicitly stated thesis that made a point about the goal or dream described in the essay. Tiffany knew she wanted to write about her passion for baseball, but she also knew that just listing a series of events would not fulfill the assignment. Her thesis statement—"One day, though, when I did grow up, I realized that things had not turned out the way I had always expected they would"—puts her memories in context, using them to draw a general conclusion about the gap between dreams and reality.

Structure. The body of Tiffany's essay traces the development of her involvement with baseball: Playing with the neighborhood boys, watching her father's games, watching baseball on television, and, finally, seeing her first major league game. Each body paragraph introduces a different aspect of her experience with the game, culminating in the vividly described Phillies game. The balance of the essay (paragraphs 8–10) presents the aftermath of that game, Tiffany's brief overview of her later years in baseball, and, finally, her conclusion.

Detail. Personal narratives like Tiffany's are especially dependent on detail because the writers want readers to see and hear and feel what they did. To present an accurate picture of the experiences and reactions she describes, Tiffany includes all the significant sights and sounds she can remember: the big oak tree, the lights on the field, the popcorn, the excited cheers, the food and souvenir stands, the crowds, and so on. She also names Mike Schmidt ("everyone's hero"), his team, and the stadium in which she saw him play. Despite all the details she includes, though, she omits a few vital ones—in particular, how old she was at each stage of her essay.

Sentence Variety. Tiffany's varied sentences help to keep her readers interested. In paragraph 4, for example, she varies sentence length and opening strategies and includes transitions that make the logical and sequential relationships between sentences clear:

> My dad played baseball too, and every Friday night I would go to the field with my mother to watch him play. It was just like the big leagues, with lots of people, a snack bar, and lights that shone so high and bright you could see them a mile away. I loved to go to my dad's games. When all the other kids would wander off and play, I would sit and cheer on my dad and his team. My attention was focused on the field, and my heart would jump with every pitch.

In an earlier draft, a string of choppy, disconnected sentences, all beginning with the subject, made her paragraph monotonous:

> My dad played baseball too. I went to the field with my mother every Friday night to watch him play. It was just like the big leagues.

There were lots of people and a snack bar. The lights shone so high and bright you could see them a mile away. I loved to go to my dad's games. All the other kids would wander off and play. I could sit and cheer on my dad and his team. My attention was focused on the field. My heart would jump with every pitch.

Verb Tense. Maintaining clear chronological order is very important in narrative writing, where unwarranted shifts in verb tenses can confuse readers. Knowing this, Tiffany is careful to avoid unnecessary tense shifts. In her conclusion, she shifts from past to present tense, but this shift is both necessary and clear. Elsewhere she uses *would* to identify events that recurred regularly. For example, in paragraph 5 she says, "My dad *would* make popcorn" rather than "My dad *made* popcorn," which would suggest that he did so only once.

Transitions. Tiffany's skillful use of transitional words and expressions moves her readers smoothly through her essay. In addition to transitional words like *when* and *then,* she uses specific time markers like "When I was little," "Almost every summer afternoon," "every Friday night," "The excitement began when," "As we walked," "The next day," "In the years to follow," and "After a few years" to advance the narrative and carry her readers along.

Focus on Revision. Tiffany could strengthen her essay by adding some dialogue. For example, in paragraph 8 she could quote the boys' taunts and her own reply. In addition, she could expand paragraph 9, giving a more detailed overview of her most recent experiences with baseball. Finally, she could edit to eliminate **clichés** (overused expressions), substituting fresher, more original language for phrases like "I felt a lump in my throat and butterflies in my stomach" and "I felt as if I were on top of the world."

The selections that follow illustrate some of the many possibilities open to writers of narratives.

ONLY DAUGHTER

Sandra Cisneros

Sandra Cisneros was born in Chicago in 1954 to a Mexican father and a Chicana mother who took the family back to Mexico City regularly. Cisneros attended the University of Iowa's Writer's Workshop and has taught at California State University in Chico. She is the author of three books: The House on Mango Street *(1983), a collection of interlocking short stories that is sometimes classified as a novel;* My Wicked Wicked Ways *(1987), a collection of poetry; and a collection of stories entitled* Woman Hollering Creek *(1991). Cisneros writes about a Latino culture and world that she believes is very different from the world of many of her potential readers. In the autobiographical "Only Daughter," which was published in* Glamour *in 1990, she tells the story of the isolation and alienation she experienced as the only daughter in a family of six sons.*

Once, several years ago, when I was just starting out my writing career, I was asked to write my own contributor's note for an anthology I was part of. I wrote: "I am the only daughter in a family of six sons. *That* explains everything." 1

Well, I've thought about that ever since, and yes, it explains a lot to me, but for the reader's sake I should have written: "I am the only daughter in a *Mexican* family of six sons." Or even: "I am the only daughter of a Mexican father and a Mexican-American mother." Or: "I am the only daughter of a working-class family of nine." All of these had everything to do with who I am today. 2

I was/am the only daughter and *only* a daughter. Being an only daughter in a family of six sons forced me by circumstance to spend a lot of time by myself because my brothers felt it beneath them to play with a *girl* in public. But that aloneness, that loneliness, was good for a would-be writer—it allowed me time to think and think, to imagine, to read and prepare myself. 3

Being only a daughter for my father meant my destiny would lead me to become someone's wife. That's what he believed. But when I was in the fifth grade and shared my plans for college with him, I was sure he understood. I remember my father saying, "*Que bueno, ni'ja,* that's good." That meant a lot to me, especially since my brothers thought the idea hilarious. What I didn't realize was that my father thought college was good for girls—good for finding a 4

73

husband. After four years in college and two more in graduate school, and still no husband, my father shakes his head even now and says I wasted all that education.

In retrospect, I'm lucky my father believed daughters were meant for husbands. It meant it didn't matter if I majored in something silly like English. After all, I'd find a nice professional eventually, right? This allowed me the liberty to putter about embroidering my little poems and stories without my father interrupting with so much as a "What's that you're writing?" 5

But the truth is, I wanted him to interrupt. I wanted my father to understand what it was I was scribbling, to introduce me as "My only daughter, the writer." Not as "This is only my daughter. She teaches." *Es maestra*—teacher. Not even *profesora*. 6

In a sense, everything I have ever written has been for him, to win his approval even though I know my father can't read English words, even though my father's only reading includes the brown-ink *Esto* sports magazines from Mexico City and the bloody *¡Alarma!* magazines that feature yet another sighting of *La Virgen de Guadalupe* on a tortilla or a wife's revenge on her philandering husband by bashing his skull in with a *molcajete* (a kitchen mortar made of volcanic rock). Or the *fotonovelas,* the little picture paperbacks with tragedy and trauma erupting from the characters' mouths in bubbles. 7

My father represents, then, the public majority. A public who is uninterested in reading, and yet one whom I am writing about and for, and privately trying to woo. 8

When we were growing up in Chicago, we moved a lot because of my father. He suffered bouts of nostalgia. Then we'd have to let go our flat, store the furniture with mother's relatives, load the station wagon with baggage and bologna sandwiches and head south. To Mexico City. 9

We came back, of course. To yet another Chicago flat, another Chicago neighborhood, another Catholic school. Each time, my father would seek out the parish priest in order to get a tuition break, and complain or boast: "I have seven sons." 10

He meant *siete hijos,* seven children, but he translated it as "sons." "I have seven sons." To anyone who would listen. The Sears Roebuck employee who sold us the washing machine. The short-order cook where my father ate his ham-and-eggs breakfasts. "I have seven sons." As if he deserved a medal from the state. 11

My papa. He didn't mean anything by that mistranslation, I'm sure. But somehow I could feel myself being erased. I'd tug my father's sleeve and whisper: "Not seven sons. Six! and *one daughter.*" 12

When my oldest brother graduated from medical school, he 13 fulfilled my father's dream that we study hard and use this—our heads, instead of this—our hands. Even now my father's hands are thick and yellow, stubbed by a history of hammer and nails and twine and coils and springs. "Use this," my father said, tapping his head, "and not this," showing us those hands. He always looked tired when he said it.

Wasn't college an investment? And hadn't I spent all those years 14 in college? And if I didn't marry, what was it all for? Why would anyone go to college and then choose to be poor? Especially someone who had always been poor.

Last year, after ten years of writing professionally, the financial 15 rewards started to trickle in. My second National Endowment for the Arts Fellowship. A guest professorship at the University of California, Berkeley. My book, which sold to a major New York publishing house.

At Christmas, I flew home to Chicago. The house was throbbing, 16 same as always; hot *tamales* and sweet *tamales* hissing in my mother's pressure cooker, and everybody—my mother, six brothers, wives, babies, aunts, cousins—talking too loud and at the same time, like in a Fellini film, because that's just how we are.

I went upstairs to my father's room. One of my stories had just 17 been translated into Spanish and published in an anthology of Chicano writing, and I wanted to show it to him. Ever since he recovered from a stroke two years ago, my father likes to spend his leisure hours horizontally. And that's how I found him, watching a Pedro Infante movie on Galavisión and eating rice pudding.

There was a glass filmed with milk on the bedside table. There 18 were several vials of pills and balled Kleenex. And on the floor, one black sock and a plastic urinal that I didn't want to look at but looked at anyway. Pedro Infante was about to burst into song, and my father was laughing.

I'm not sure if it was because my story was translated into 19 Spanish, or because it was published in Mexico, or perhaps because the story dealt with Tepeyac, the *colonia* my father was raised in and the house he grew up in, but at any rate, my father punched the mute button on his remote control and read my story.

I sat on the bed next to my father and waited. He read it very 20 slowly. As if he were reading each line over and over. He laughed at all the right places and read lines he liked out loud. He pointed and asked questions: "Is this So-and-so?" "Yes," I said. He kept reading.

When he was finally finished, after what seemed like hours, my 21 father looked up and asked: "Where can we get more copies of this for the relatives?"

Of all the wonderful things that happened to me last year, that 22 was the most wonderful.

COMPREHENSION

1. What does Cisneros mean when she says her being an only daughter in a family of six sons "explains everything" (1)?

2. What distinction does Cisneros make in paragraphs 2 and 3 between being "the only daughter" and being "only a daughter"?

3. What advantages does Cisneros see in being the only daughter? In being "only a daughter"?

4. Why does her father think she has wasted her education? What is her reaction to his opinion?

5. Why was her father's reaction to her story the most wonderful thing that happened to Cisneros that year?

PURPOSE AND AUDIENCE

1. Although Cisneros chooses to use many Spanish words in her essay, in most cases she defines or explains these words. What does this decision tell you about her purpose and audience?

2. What is Cisneros's thesis? What incidents and details support her point?

3. Do you think Cisneros aims to convey to her audience a sympathetic or a critical impression of her father? Explain.

STYLE AND STRUCTURE

1. "Only Daughter" is not a single continuous narrative but a series of brief related episodes. Where does Cisneros interrupt the narrative to comment on or analyze events? What does this strategy accomplish?

2. Are the episodes presented in chronological order? Explain.

3. What transitional expressions does Cisneros use to introduce new episodes?

4. Cisneros quotes her father several times. What do we learn about him from his words?

5. Why does Cisneros devote so much space to describing her father in paragraphs 16–18? How does this portrait compare with the one she presents in paragraphs 9–11?

VOCABULARY PROJECTS

1. Define each of the following words as it is used in this selection.

   embroidering (5)   stubbed (13)

2. What is the difference in connotation between *sons* and *children*? Between *teacher* and *professor*? Do you think these distinctions are as significant as Cisneros seems to think they are?

JOURNAL ENTRY

In what sense do the number and gender(s) of your siblings "explain everything" about who you are today?

WRITING WORKSHOP

1. Write a narrative essay consisting of a series of related episodes that show how you gradually gained your parents' approval and respect.

2. In "Only Daughter," Cisneros traces the development of her identity as an adult, a female, and a writer. Write a narrative essay in which you trace the development of your own personal or professional identity.

THEMATIC CONNECTIONS

- "My Field of Dreams" (p. 68)
- "Suicide Note" (p. 347)
- "The Men We Carry in Our Minds" (p. 435)

FINISHING SCHOOL

Maya Angelou

Maya Angelou was born Marguerita Johnson in 1928 in St. Louis and grew up in Stamps, Arkansas. Angelou has had a highly diverse career as a writer, political activist, and performing artist. She served as northern coordinator for the Southern Christian Leadership Conference, the civil rights group organized by Martin Luther King, Jr., and she lived abroad for many years, working as a journalist in Egypt and Ghana. Trained as a dancer, she has appeared in theatrical and musical productions and a television drama and has also written for film and television. Angelou is the author of several autobiographical volumes, including I Know Why the Caged Bird Sings *(1970), a memoir of her childhood, and most recently* Wouldn't Take Nothing for My Journey Now *(1993). Her early volumes of poetry are published together in* Poems: Maya Angelou *(1986); her most recent volumes are* I Shall Not Be Moved *(1990) and* On the Pulse of Morning *(1993), a long poem she composed and read for the inauguration of Bill Clinton as President of the United States. She currently teaches at Wake Forest University. In "Finishing School," a chapter from* I Know Why the Caged Bird Sings, *Angelou explores a theme she returns to often: her inability to understand the ways of the whites in her hometown and their inability to understand her.*

Recently a white woman from Texas, who would quickly describe 1
herself as a liberal, asked me about my hometown. When I told her
that in Stamps my grandmother had owned the only Negro general
merchandise store since the turn of the century, she exclaimed,
"Why, you were a debutante." Ridiculous and even ludicrous. But
Negro girls in small Southern towns, whether poverty-stricken or
just munching along on a few of life's necessities, were given as
extensive and irrelevant preparations for adulthood as rich white
girls shown in magazines. Admittedly the training was not the
same. While white girls learned to waltz and sit gracefully with a tea
cup balanced on their knees, we were lagging behind, learning the
mid-Victorian values with very little money to indulge them. . . .

We were required to embroider and I had trunkfuls of colorful 2
dishtowels, pillowcases, runners and handkerchiefs to my credit. I
mastered the art of crocheting and tatting, and there was a life-

time's supply of dainty doilies that would never be used in sacheted dresser drawers. It went without saying that all girls could iron and wash, but the finer touches around the home, like setting a table with real silver, baking roasts and cooking vegetables without meat, had to be learned elsewhere. Usually at the source of those habits. During my tenth year, a white woman's kitchen became my finishing school.

Mrs. Viola Cullinan was a plump woman who lived in a three-bedroom house somewhere behind the post office. She was singularly unattractive until she smiled, and then the lines around her eyes and mouth which made her look perpetually dirty disappeared, and her face looked like the mask of an impish elf. She usually rested her smile until late afternoon when her women friends dropped in and Miss Glory, the cook, served them cold drinks on the closed-in porch.

The exactness of her house was inhuman. This glass went here and only here. That cup had its place and it was an act of impudent rebellion to place it anywhere else. At twelve o'clock the table was set. At 12:15 Mrs. Cullinan sat down to dinner (whether her husband had arrived or not). At 12:16 Miss Glory brought out the food.

It took me a week to learn the difference between a salad plate, a bread plate and a dessert plate.

Mrs. Cullinan kept up the tradition of her wealthy parents. She was from Virginia. Miss Glory, who was a descendant of slaves that had worked for the Cullinans, told me her history. She had married beneath her (according to Miss Glory). Her husband's family hadn't had their money very long and what they had "didn't 'mount to much."

As ugly as she was, I thought privately, she was lucky to get a husband above or beneath her station. But Miss Glory wouldn't let me say a thing against her mistress. She was very patient with me, however, over the housework. She explained the dishware, silverware and servants' bells. The large round bowl in which soup was served wasn't a soup bowl, it was a tureen. There were goblets, sherbet glasses, ice-cream glasses, wine glasses, green glass coffee cups with matching saucers, and water glasses. I had a glass to drink from, and it sat with Miss Glory's on a separate shelf from the others. Soup spoons, gravy boat, butter knives, salad forks and carving platter were additions to my vocabulary and in fact almost represented a new language. I was fascinated with the novelty, with the fluttering Mrs. Cullinan and her Alice-in-Wonderland house.

Her husband remains, in my memory, undefined. I lumped him with all the other white men that I had ever seen and tried not to see.

On our way home one evening, Miss Glory told me that Mrs. 9
Cullinan couldn't have children. She said that she was too delicate-
boned. It was hard to imagine bones at all under those layers of fat.
Miss Glory went on to say that the doctor had taken out all her lady
organs. I reasoned that a pig's organs included the lungs, heart and
liver, so if Mrs. Cullinan was walking around without those essentials, it explained why she drank alcohol out of unmarked bottles.
She was keeping herself embalmed.

When I spoke to Bailey about it, he agreed that I was right, but he 10
also informed me that Mr. Cullinan had two daughters by a colored
lady and that I knew them very well. He added that the girls were
the spitting image of their father. I was unable to remember what he
looked like, although I had just left him a few hours before, but I
thought of the Coleman girls. They were very light-skinned and
certainly didn't look very much like their mother (no one ever
mentioned Mr. Coleman).

My pity for Mrs. Cullinan preceded me the next morning like the 11
Cheshire cat's smile. Those girls, who could have been her daughters, were beautiful. They didn't have to straighten their hair. Even
when they were caught in the rain, their braids still hung down
straight like tamed snakes. Their mouths were pouty little cupid's
bows. Mrs. Cullinan didn't know what she missed. Or maybe she
did. Poor Mrs. Cullinan.

For weeks after, I arrived early, left late and tried very hard to 12
make up for her barrenness. If she had her own children, she
wouldn't have had to ask me to run a thousand errands from her
back door to the back door of her friends. Poor old Mrs. Cullinan.

Then one evening Miss Glory told me to serve the ladies on the 13
porch. After I set the tray down and turned toward the kitchen, one
of the women asked, "What's your name, girl?" It was the speckled-
faced one. Mrs. Cullinan said, "She doesn't talk much. Her name's
Margaret."

Is she dumb?" 14

"No. As I understand it, she can talk when she wants to but she's 15
usually quiet as a little mouse. Aren't you, Margaret?"

I smiled at her. Poor thing. No organs and couldn't even pronounce 16
my name correctly.

"She's a sweet little thing, though." 17

"Well, that may be, but the name's too long. I'd never bother 18
myself. I'd call her Mary if I was you."

I fumed into the kitchen. That horrible woman would never have 19
the chance to call me Mary because if I was starving I'd never work
for her. . . .

That evening I decided to write a poem on being white, fat, old 20
and without children. It was going to be a tragic ballad. I would have
to watch her carefully to capture the essence of her loneliness and
pain.

The very next day, she called me by the wrong name. Miss Glory 21
and I were washing up the lunch dishes when Mrs. Cullinan came to
the doorway. "Mary?"

Miss Glory asked, "Who?" 22

Mrs. Cullinan, sagging a little, knew and I knew. "I want Mary to 23
go down to Mrs. Randall's and take her some soup. She's not been
feeling well for a few days."

Miss Glory's face was a wonder to see. "You mean Margaret, 24
ma'am. Her name's Margaret."

"That's too long. She's Mary from now on. Heat that soup from last 25
night and put it in the china tureen and, Mary, I want you to carry
it carefully."

Every person I knew had a hellish horror of being "called out of his 26
name." It was a dangerous practice to call a Negro anything that
could be loosely construed as insulting because of the centuries of
their having been called niggers, jigs, dinges, blackbirds, crows,
boots and spooks.

Miss Glory had a fleeting second of feeling sorry for me. Then as 27
she handed me the hot tureen she said, "Don't mind, don't pay that
no mind. Sticks and stones may break your bones, but words . . . You
know, I been working for her for twenty years."

She held the back door open for me. "Twenty years. I wasn't much 28
older than you. My name used to be Hallelujah. That's what Ma
named me, but my mistress give me 'Glory,' and it stuck. I likes it
better too."

I was in the little path that ran behind the houses when Miss 29
Glory shouted, "It's shorter too."

For a few seconds it was a tossup over whether I would laugh 30
(imagine being named Hallelujah) or cry (imagine letting some white
woman rename you for her convenience). My anger saved me from
either outburst. I had to quit the job, but the problem was going
to be how to do it. Momma wouldn't allow me to quit for just any
reason.

"She's a peach. That woman is a real peach." Mrs. Randall's maid 31
was talking as she took the soup from me, and I wondered what her
name used to be and what she answered to now.

For a week I looked into Mrs. Cullinan's face as she called me 32
Mary. She ignored my coming late and leaving early. Miss Glory was
a little annoyed because I had begun to leave egg yolk on the dishes

and wasn't putting much heart in polishing the silver. I hoped that she would complain to our boss, but she didn't.

Then Bailey solved my dilemma. He had me describe the contents of the cupboard and the particular plates she liked best. Her favorite piece was a casserole shaped like a fish and the green glass coffee cups. I kept his instructions in mind, so on the next day when Miss Glory was hanging out clothes and I had again been told to serve the old biddies on the porch, I dropped the empty serving tray. When I heard Mrs. Cullinan scream, "Mary!" I picked up the casserole and two of the green glass cups in readiness. As she rounded the kitchen door I let them fall on the tiled floor. 33

I could never absolutely describe to Bailey what happened next, because each time I got to the part where she fell on the floor and screwed up her ugly face to cry, we burst out laughing. She actually wobbled around on the floor and picked up shards of the cups and cried, "Oh, Momma. Oh, dear Gawd. It's Mamma's china from Virginia. Oh, Momma, I sorry." 34

Miss Glory came running in from the yard and the women from the porch crowded around. Miss Glory was almost as broken up as her mistress. "You mean to say she broke our Virginia dishes? What we gone do?" 35

Mrs. Cullinan cried louder. "That clumsy nigger. Clumsy little black nigger." 36

Old speckled-face leaned down and asked, "Who did it, Viola? Was it Mary? Who did it?" 37

Everything was happening so fast I can't remember whether her action preceded her words, but I know that Mrs. Cullinan said, "Her name's Margaret, goddamn it, her name's Margaret." And she threw a wedge of broken plate at me. It could have been the hysteria which put her aim off, but the flying crockery caught Miss Glory right over her ear and she started screaming. 38

I left the front door wide open so all the neighbors could hear. 39

Mrs. Cullinan was right about one thing. My name wasn't Mary. 40

COMPREHENSION

1. What is Angelou required to do in the white woman's kitchen? Why are these tasks so important to Mrs. Cullinan?

2. Why does Angelou feel sorry for Mrs. Cullinan at first? When does her attitude change? Why?

3. Why does Mrs. Cullinan's friend recommend that Angelou be called "Mary"? Why does this upset Angelou so deeply?

4. When Angelou decides she wants to quit, she realizes she cannot quit "for just any reason." How does Bailey help her resolve her dilemma?

5. What does Angelou actually learn through her experience? That is, in what sense does the kitchen really serve as a finishing school?

PURPOSE AND AUDIENCE

1. Is Angelou writing for Southerners, blacks, whites, or a general audience? Point to specific details to support your answer.

2. Angelou begins her narrative by summarizing a discussion between herself and a white woman. What is her purpose in doing this?

3. What is Angelou's thesis?

STYLE AND STRUCTURE

1. What image does the phrase *finishing school* usually suggest? How is the use of this phrase ironic in view of its meaning in this selection?

2. How does Angelou signal the passage of time in this narrative? Identify some transitional phrases that show the passage of time.

3. How does the use of dialogue highlight the contrast between the black and the white characters? In what way does this contrast strengthen the narrative?

4. What details does Angelou use to describe Mrs. Cullinan and her home to the reader? How does this detailed description help advance the narrative?

VOCABULARY PROJECTS

1. Define each of the following words as it is used in this selection.

tatting (2)	pouty (11)	dilemma (33)
sacheted (2)	barrenness (12)	shards (34)
impudent (4)	ballad (20)	
embalmed (9)	construed (26)	

2. According to your dictionary, what is the difference in meaning between *ridiculous* and *ludicrous* (1)? Between *soup bowl* and *tureen* (7)? What is the effect of Angelou's distinctions?

3. Try substituting an equivalent word for each of the following, paying careful attention to the context of each in the narrative.

perpetually (3)   station (7)   biddies (33)
exactness (4)   peach (31)

Does Angelou's original choice seem most effective in all cases? Explain.

JOURNAL ENTRY

Have you ever received any training or education that you considered to be "extensive and irrelevant preparation for adulthood" (1)? Do you now see any value in such preparation?

WRITING WORKSHOP

1. Think about a time in your life when an adult in a position of authority treated you unjustly. How did you react? Write a narrative essay in which you recount the situation and your responses.

2. Have you ever had an experience in which you were the victim of name calling—or in which you found yourself doing the name calling? Summarize the incident, including dialogue and description designed to help your readers understand your motivations and reactions.

3. Write a narrative essay in which you retell an incident from a work of fiction—specifically, an incident that serves as a character's initiation into adulthood. In your essay, explain how the experience helped the character to grow up.

THEMATIC CONNECTIONS

- "Midnight" (p. 186)
- "The Civil Rights Movement: What Good Was It?" (p. 315)
- "Revelation" (p. 466)

MY MOTHER NEVER WORKED

Donna Smith-Yackel

Although this essay, which was first published in Women: A Journal of Liberation *in 1975, draws on personal experience, it makes a pointed statement about what society thinks of "women's work." According to federal law, a woman who is a homemaker is entitled to Social Security benefits only through the earnings of her husband. Therefore, a homemaker who becomes disabled receives no disability benefits, and her husband and children are allowed no survivors' benefits if she should die. Although this law has been challenged in the courts, a woman who does not work for wages outside the home is still not entitled to Social Security benefits in her own right. Without explicitly stating her thesis, Donna Smith-Yackel comments on this situation in her narrative.*

"Social Security Office." (The voice answering the telephone sounds very self-assured.) 1

"I'm calling about . . . I . . . my mother just died . . . I was told to call you and see about a . . . death-benefit check, I think they call it . . ." 2

"I see. Was your mother on Social Security? How old was she?" 3

"Yes . . . she was seventy-eight. . . ." 4

"Do you know her number?" 5

"No . . . I, ah . . . don't you have a record?" 6

"Certainly. I'll look it up. Her name?" 7

"Smith. Martha Smith. Or maybe she used Martha Ruth Smith? . . . Sometimes she used her maiden name . . . Martha Jerabek Smith." 8

"If you'd care to hold on, I'll check our records—it'll be a few minutes." 9

"Yes. . . ." 10

Her love letters—to and from Daddy—were in an old box, tied with ribbons and stiff, rigid-with-age leather thongs: 1918 through 1920; hers written on stationery from the general store she had worked in full-time and managed, single-handed, after her graduation from high school in 1913; and his, at first, on YMCA or Soldiers and Sailors Club stationery dispensed to the fighting men of World War I. He wooed her thoroughly and persistently by mail, and though she reciprocated all his feelings for her, she dreaded marriage. . . . 11

"It's so hard for me to decide when to have my wedding day—   12
that's all I've thought about these last two days. I have told you
dozens of times that I won't be afraid of married life, but when it
comes down to setting the date and then picturing myself a married
woman with half a dozen or more kids to look after, it just makes me
sick. . . . I am weeping right now—I hope that some day I can look
back and say how foolish I was to dread it all."

They married in February, 1921, and began farming. Their first   13
baby, a daughter, was born in January, 1922, when my mother was
26 years old. The second baby, a son, was born in March, 1923. They
were renting farms; my father, besides working his own fields, also
was a hired man for two other farmers. They had no capital initially,
and had to gain it slowly, working from dawn until midnight every
day. My town-bred mother learned to set hens and raise chickens,
feed pigs, milk cows, plant and harvest a garden, and can every fruit
and vegetable she could scrounge. She carried water nearly a
quarter of a mile from the well to fill her wash boilers in order to do
her laundry on a scrub board. She learned to shuck grain, feed
threshers, shock and husk corn, feed corn pickers. In September,
1925, the third baby came, and in June, 1927, the fourth child—both
daughters. In 1930, my parents had enough money to buy their own
farm, and that March they moved all their livestock and belongings
themselves, 55 miles over rutted, muddy roads.

In the summer of 1930 my mother and her two eldest children   14
reclaimed a 40-acre field from Canadian thistles, by chopping them
all out with a hoe. In the other fields, when the oats and flax began
to head out, the green and blue of the crops were hidden by the
bright yellow of wild mustard. My mother walked the fields day
after day, pulling each mustard plant. She raised a new flock of baby
chicks—500—and she spaded up, planted, hoed, and harvested a
half-acre garden.

During the next spring their hogs caught cholera and died. No   15
cash that fall.

And in the next year the drought hit. My mother and father   16
trudged from the well to the chickens, the well to the calf pasture,
the well to the barn, and from the well to the garden. The sun came
out hot and bright, endlessly, day after day. The crops shriveled and
died. They harvested half the corn, and ground the other half, stalks
and all, and fed it to the cattle as fodder. With the price at four cents
a bushel for the harvested crop, they couldn't afford to haul it into
town. They burned it in the furnace for fuel that winter.

In 1934, in February, when the dust was still so thick in the   17
Minnesota air that my parents couldn't always see from the house to

the barn, their fifth child—a fourth daughter—was born. My father hunted rabbits daily, and my mother stewed them, fried them, canned them, and wished out loud that she could taste hamburger once more. In the fall the shotgun brought prairie chickens, ducks, pheasant, and grouse. My mother plucked each bird, carefully reserving the breast feathers for pillows.

18   In the winter she sewed night after night, endlessly, begging cast-off clothing from relatives, ripping apart coats, dresses, blouses, and trousers to remake them to fit her four daughters and son. Every morning and every evening she milked cows, fed pigs, and calves, cared for chickens, picked eggs, cooked meals, washed dishes, scrubbed floors, and tended and loved her children. In the spring she planted a garden once more, dragging pails of water to nourish and sustain the vegetables for the family. In 1936 she lost a baby in her sixth month.

19   In 1937 her fifth daughter was born. She was 42 years old. In 1939 a second son, and in 1941 her eighth child—and third son.

20   But the war had come, and prosperity of a sort. The herd of cattle had grown to 30 head; she still milked morning and evening. Her garden was more than a half acre—the rains had come, and by now the Rural Electricity Administration and indoor plumbing. Still she sewed—dresses and jackets for the children, housedresses and aprons for herself, weekly patching of jeans, overalls, and denim shirts. She still made pillows, using feathers she had plucked, and quilts every year—intricate patterns as well as patchwork, stitched as well as tied—all necessary bedding for her family. Every scrap of cloth too small to be used in quilts was carefully saved and painstakingly sewed together in strips to make rugs. She still went out in the fields to help with the haying whenever there was a threat of rain.

21   In 1959 my mother's last child graduated from high school. A year later the cows were sold. She still raised chickens and ducks, plucked feathers, made pillows, baked her own bread, and every year made a new quilt—now for a married child or for a grandchild. And her garden, that huge, undying symbol of sustenance, was as large and cared for as in all the years before. The canning, and now freezing, continued.

22   In 1969, on a June afternoon, mother and father started out for town so that she could buy sugar to make rhubarb jam for a daughter who lived in Texas. The car crashed into a ditch. She was paralyzed from the waist down.

23   In 1970 her husband, my father, died. My mother struggled to regain some competence and dignity and order in her life. At the rehabilitation institute, where they gave her physical therapy and

trained her to live usefully in a wheelchair, the therapist told me: "She did fifteen pushups today—fifteen! She's almost seventy-five years old! I've never known a woman so strong!"

From her wheelchair she canned pickles, baked bread, ironed clothes, wrote dozens of letters weekly to her friends and her "half dozen or more kids," and made three patchwork housecoats and one quilt. She made balls and balls of carpet rags—enough for five rugs. And kept all her love letters. 24

"I think I've found your mother's records—Martha Ruth Smith; married to Ben F. Smith? 25

"Yes, that's right." 26

"Well, I see that she was getting a widow's pension. . . ." 27

"Yes, that's right." 28

"Well, your mother isn't entitled to our $255 death benefit." 29

"Not entitled! But why?" 30

The voice on the telephone explains patiently: 31

"Well, you see—your mother never worked." 32

COMPREHENSION

1. Why wasn't Martha Smith eligible for a death benefit?

2. What kind of work did Martha Smith do while her children were growing up? List some of the chores she performed.

3. How does the government define *work*?

PURPOSE AND AUDIENCE

1. What is the essay's thesis? Why is it never explicitly stated?

2. This essay appeared in *Ms.* magazine and other publications whose audiences are sympathetic to feminist goals. Could it just as easily have appeared in a magazine whose audience was not? Explain.

3. The author mentions relatively little about her father in this essay. How can you account for this?

STYLE AND STRUCTURE

1. Is the title effective? If so, why? If not, can you suggest an alternative?

2. The author could have outlined her mother's life without framing it with the telephone conversation. Why do you think she includes this frame?

3. What strategies does the author use to indicate the passing of time in her narrative?

4. This narrative piles details one on top of another almost like a list. Why does the author list so many details?

5. In paragraphs 20 and 21, what is accomplished by the repetition of the word *still*?

VOCABULARY PROJECTS

1. Define each of the following words as it is used in this selection.

   scrounge (13)   rutted (13)   intricate (2)
   shuck (13)   reclaimed (14)   sustenance (21)
   shock (13)   flax (14)
   husk (13)   fodder (16)

2. Try substituting equivalent words for those italicized in the sentence below:

   He *wooed* her *thoroughly* and *persistently* by mail, and though she *reciprocated* all his feeling for her, she *dreaded* marriage . . . (11).

   How do your substitutions change the sentence's meaning?

3. Throughout her narrative, the author uses very concrete, specific verbs. Review her choice of verbs, particularly in paragraphs 13–24, and comment on how such verbs serve the essay's purpose.

JOURNAL ENTRY

Do you believe homemakers should be entitled to Social Security death benefits? Explain your reasoning.

WRITING WORKSHOP

1. If you can, interview one of your parents or grandparents (or another person you know who might remind you of Donna Smith-Yackel's mother) about his or her work, and write a chronological narrative based on what you learn. Include a thesis that your narrative can support.

2. Write Martha Smith's obituary as it might have appeared in her hometown newspaper. If you are not familiar with the form of an obituary, read a few in your local paper.

3. Write a narrative account of the worst job you ever had. Include a thesis that expresses your negative feelings.

THEMATIC CONNECTIONS

- "Midnight" (p. 186)
- "The Men We Carry in Our Minds" (p. 435)
- "I Want a Wife" (p. 503)
- "The Company Man" (p. 507)

38 WHO SAW MURDER DIDN'T CALL THE POLICE

Martin Gansberg

*Martin Gansberg, a native of Brooklyn, New York, was born in 1920
and was on the staff of the New York Times for about forty years. He
has also taught at Fairleigh Dickinson University and written for
numerous magazines. The following article was written for the
Times two weeks after the murder it recounts, which shocked the
entire country and has been the subject of countless articles and
editorials, as well as a television movie. The murder of Kitty
Genovese is still cited today as an example of public indifference,
and Gansberg's article is frequently reprinted. Its thesis, though not
explicitly stated, retains its power.*

For more than half an hour 38 respectable, law-abiding citizens in   1
Queens watched a killer stalk and stab a woman in three separate
attacks in Kew Gardens.

Twice their chatter and the sudden glow of their bedroom lights   2
interrupted him and frightened him off. Each time he returned,
sought her out, and stabbed her again. Not one person telephoned
the police during the assault; one witness called after the woman
was dead.

That was two weeks ago today.   3

Still shocked is Assistant Chief Inspector Frederick M. Lussen,   4
in charge of the borough's detectives and a veteran of 25 years of
homicide investigations. He can give a matter-of-fact recitation on
many murders. But the Kew Gardens slaying baffles him—not
because it is a murder, but because the "good people" failed to call
the police.

"As we have reconstructed the crime," he said, "the assailant had   5
three chances to kill this woman during a 35-minute period. He
returned twice to complete the job. If we had been called when he
first attacked, the woman might not be dead now."

This is what the police say happened beginning at 3:20 A.M. in the   6
staid, middle-class, tree-lined Austin Street area:

Twenty-eight-year-old Catherine Genovese, who was called Kitty   7
by almost everyone in the neighborhood, was returning home from
her job as manager of a bar in Hollis. She parked her red Fiat in a

lot adjacent to the Kew Gardens Long Island Rail Road Station, facing Mowbray Place. Like many residents of the neighborhood, she had parked there day after day since her arrival from Connecticut a year ago, although the railroad frowns on the practice.

She turned off the lights of her car, locked the door, and started to walk the 100 feet to the entrance of her apartment at 82–70 Austin Street, which is in a Tudor building, with stores in the first floor and apartments on the second. 8

The entrance to the apartment is in the rear of the building because the front is rented to retail stores. At night the quiet neighborhood is shrouded in the slumbering darkness that marks most residential areas. 9

Miss Genovese noticed a man at the far end of the lot, near a seven-story apartment house at 82–40 Austin Street. She halted. Then, nervously, she headed up Austin Street toward Lefferts Boulevard, where there is a call box to the 102nd Police Precinct in nearby Richmond Hill. 10

She got as far as a street light in front of a bookstore before the man grabbed her. She screamed. Lights went on in the 10-story apartment house at 82–67 Austin Street, which faces the bookstore. Windows slid open and voices punctuated the early-morning stillness. 11

Miss Genovese screamed: "Oh, my God, he stabbed me! Please help me! Please help me!" 12

From one of the upper windows in the apartment house, a man called down: "Let that girl alone!" 13

The assailant looked up at him, shrugged, and walked down Austin Street toward a white sedan parked a short distance away. Miss Genovese struggled to her feet. 14

Lights went out. The killer returned to Miss Genovese, now trying to make her way around the side of the building by the parking lot to get to her apartment. The assailant stabbed her again. 15

"I'm dying!" she shrieked. "I'm dying!" 16

Windows were opened again, and lights went on in many apartments. The assailant got into his car and drove away. Miss Genovese staggered to her feet. A city bus, O–10, the Lefferts Boulevard line to Kennedy International Airport, passed. It was 3:35 A.M. 17

The assailant returned. By then, Miss Genovese had crawled to the back of the building, where the freshly painted brown doors to the apartment house held out hope for safety. The killer tried the first door; she wasn't there. At the second door, 82–62 Austin Street, he saw her slumped on the floor at the foot of the stairs. He stabbed her a third time—fatally. 18

It was 3:50 by the time the police received their first call, from a   19
man who was a neighbor of Miss Genovese. In two minutes they were
at the scene. The neighbor, a 70-year-old woman, and another woman
were the only persons on the street. Nobody else came forward.

The man explained that he had called the police after much delib-   20
eration. He had phoned a friend in Nassau County for advice and
then he had crossed the roof of the building to the apartment of the
elderly woman to get her to make the call.

"I didn't want to get involved," he sheepishly told police.   21

Six days later, the police arrested Winston Moseley, a 29-year-old   22
business machine operator, and charged him with homicide. Moseley had no previous record. He is married, has two children and
owns a home at 133–19 Sutter Avenue, South Ozone Park, Queens.
On Wednesday, a court committed him to Kings County Hospital for
psychiatric observation.

When questioned by the police, Moseley also said that he had slain   23
Mrs. Annie May Johnson, 24, of 146–12 133d Avenue, Jamaica, on
Feb. 29 and Barbara Kralik, 15, of 174–17 140th Avenue, Springfield
Gardens, last July. In the Kralik case, the police are holding Alvin L.
Mitchell, who is said to have confessed that slaying.

The police stressed how simple it would have been to have gotten   24
in touch with them. "A phone call," said one of the detectives, "would
have done it." The police may be reached by dialing "O" for operator
or SPring 7–3100.

Today witnesses from the neighborhood, which is made up of   25
one-family homes in the $35,000 to $60,000 range with the exception
of the two apartment houses near the railroad station, find it
difficult to explain why they didn't call the police.

A housewife, knowingly if quite casually, said, "We thought it was   26
a lovers' quarrel." A husband and wife both said, "Frankly, we were
afraid." They seemed aware of the fact that events might have been
different. A distraught woman, wiping her hands in her apron, said,
"I didn't want my husband to get involved."

One couple, now willing to talk about that night, said they heard   27
the first screams. The husband looked thoughtfully at the bookstore
where the killer first grabbed Miss Genovese.

"We went to the window to see what was happening," he said, "but   28
the light from our bedroom made it difficult to see the street." The
wife, still apprehensive, added: "I put out the light and we were able
to see better."

Asked why they hadn't called the police, she shrugged and replied: 29
"I don't know."

A man peeked out from a slight opening in the doorway to his 30
apartment and rattled off an account of the killer's second attack.
Why hadn't he called the police at the time? "I was tired," he said
without emotion. "I went back to bed."

It was 4:25 A.M. when the ambulance arrived to take the body of 31
Miss Genovese. It drove off. "Then," a solemn police detective said,
"the people came out."

COMPREHENSION

1. How much time elapsed between when Kitty Genovese was first
   stabbed and when the people finally came out?

2. What excuses did the neighbors make for not having come to Kitty
   Genovese's aid?

PURPOSE AND AUDIENCE

1. This article appeared in 1964. What effect was it intended to have on
   its audience? Do you think it has the same impact today, or has its
   impact changed or diminished?

2. What is the article's main idea? Why does Gansberg imply his thesis
   rather than stating it explicitly?

3. What is Gansberg's purpose in describing the Austin Street area as
   "staid, middle-class, tree-lined"?

4. Why does Gansberg provide the police department phone number in
   his article?

STYLE AND STRUCTURE

1. The author is very precise in this article, especially in his references
   to time, addresses, and ages. Why?

2. The objective newspaper style is dominant in this article, and yet the
   author's anger shows through. Point to words and phrases that reveal
   his attitude toward his material.

3. Because this article was originally set in the narrow columns of a
   newspaper, there are many short paragraphs. Would it be more effective if some of these brief paragraphs were combined? If so, why? If
   not, why not? Give examples to support your answer.

4. Examine the dialogue. Does it strengthen the author's presentation?
   Would the article be more compelling without dialogue? Explain.

5. This article does not have a formal conclusion; nevertheless, the last paragraph sums up the author's attitude. How?

VOCABULARY PROJECTS

1. Define each of the following words as it is used in this selection.

stalk (1)	adjacent (7)	distraught (26)
baffles (4)	punctuated (11)	apprehensive (28)
staid (6)	sheepishly (21)	

2. The word "assailant" appears frequently in this article. Why is it used so often? What impact is this repetition likely to have on the reader? What other word could be used?

JOURNAL ENTRY

In a similar situation, would you call the police? What factors might influence your decision?

WRITING WORKSHOP

1. In your own words, write a ten-sentence summary of the article. Try to reflect the author's order and emphasis as well as his ideas.

2. Rewrite the article as if it were a diary entry of one of the thirty-eight people who watched the murder. Outline what you saw, and explain why you decided not to call for help.

3. If you have ever been involved in or witnessed a situation where someone was in trouble, write a narrative essay about the incident. If people failed to help the person in trouble, explain why you think no one acted. If people did act, tell how. Be sure to account for your own actions.

THEMATIC CONNECTIONS

- "Salvador" (p. 128)
- "Samuel" (p. 226)
- "Who Killed Benny Paret?" (p. 298)

SHOOTING AN ELEPHANT

George Orwell

George Orwell (1903–1950) was born Eric Blair in Bengal, India, where his father was a British civil servant. Instead of going to a university, Orwell joined the Imperial Police in Burma (now Myanmar), where he remained for the next five years. His sense of guilt about British colonialism and his role as its defender led Orwell to leave Burma to live and write in Paris and London. Wishing to learn about the life of the poor first hand, Orwell struggled to survive on his income from menial jobs. He wrote about his experiences in his first book, Down and Out in Paris and London *(1933). His other books include* The Road to Wigan Pier *(1937), about the lives of unemployed coal miners and factory workers in the north of England;* Homage to Catalonia *(1938), about his experiences fighting in the Spanish Civil War in 1936 and 1937; and* Animal Farm *(1945) and* 1984 *(1949), novels portraying the dangers of totalitarianism. Orwell also wrote many essays as well as articles for the left-wing British journal* Tribune *and other periodicals; his nonfiction writings are published in four volumes entitled* Collected Essays, Journalism and Letters *(1968). "Shooting an Elephant," set in Burma, relates an incident that clarified for Orwell the nature of British rule.*

In Moulmein, in Lower Burma, I was hated by large numbers of people—the only time in my life that I have been important enough for this to happen to me. I was sub-divisional police officer of the town, and in an aimless, petty kind of way anti-European feeling was very bitter. No one had the guts to raise a riot, but if a European woman went through the bazaars alone somebody would probably spit betel juice over her dress. As a police officer I was an obvious target and was baited whenever it seemed safe to do so. When a nimble Burman tripped me up on the football field and the referee (another Burman) looked the other way, the crowd yelled with hideous laughter. This happened more than once. In the end the sneering yellow faces of young men that met me everywhere, the insults hooted after me when I was at a safe distance, got badly on my nerves. The young Buddhist priests were the worst of all. There were several thousands of them in the town and none of them seemed to have anything to do except stand on street corners and jeer at Europeans.

All this was perplexing and upsetting. For at that time I had al- 2 ready made up my mind that imperialism was an evil thing and the sooner I chucked up my job and got out of it the better. Theoretically—and secretly, of course—I was all for the Burmese and all against their oppressors, the British. As for the job I was doing, I hated it more bitterly than I can perhaps make clear. In a job like that you see the dirty work of Empire at close quarters. The wretched prisoners huddling in the stinking cages of the lockups, the grey, cowed faces of the long-term convicts, the scarred buttocks of the men who had been flogged with bamboos—all these oppressed me with an intolerable sense of guilt. But I could get nothing into perspective. I was young and ill-educated and I had had to think out my problems in the utter silence that is imposed on every Englishman in the East. I did not even know that the British Empire is dying, still less did I know that it is a great deal better than the younger empires that are going to supplant it.* All I knew was that I was stuck between my hatred of the empire I served and my rage against the evil-spirited little beasts who tried to make my job impossible. With one part of my mind I thought of the British Raj as an unbreakable tyranny, as something clamped down, in *saecula saeculorum,*** upon the will of prostrate peoples; with another part I thought that the greatest joy in the world would be to drive a bayonet into a Buddhist priest's guts. Feelings like these are the normal byproducts of imperialism; ask any Anglo-Indian official, if you can catch him off duty.

One day something happened which in a roundabout way was 3 enlightening. It was a tiny incident in itself, but it gave me a better glimpse than I had had before of the real nature of imperialism—the real motives for which despotic governments act. Early one morning the sub-inspector at a police station the other end of the town rang me up on the phone and said that an elephant was ravaging the bazaar. Would I please come and do something about it? I did not know what I could do, but I wanted to see what was happening and I got on to a pony and started out. I took my rifle, an old .44 Winchester and much too small to kill an elephant, but I thought the noise might be useful *in terrorem.* Various Burmans stopped me on the way and told me about the elephant's doings. It was not, of course, a wild elephant, but a tame one which had gone "must."*** It had been chained up, as tame elephants always are when their

*EDS. NOTE—Orwell was writing in 1936, when Hitler and Stalin were in power and World War II was only three years away.
**EDS. NOTE—from time immemorial. *Raj:* sovereignty.
***EDS. NOTE—that is, gone into an uncontrollable frenzy.

attack of "must" is due, but on the previous night it had broken its chain and escaped. Its mahout, the only person who could manage it when it was in that state, had set out in pursuit, but had taken the wrong direction and was now twelve hours' journey away, and in the morning the elephant had suddenly reappeared in the town. The Burmese population had no weapons and were quite helpless against it. It had already destroyed somebody's bamboo hut, killed a cow and raided some fruit-stalls and devoured the stock; also it had met the municipal rubbish van and, when the driver jumped out and took to his heels, had turned the van over and inflicted violences upon it.

The Burmese sub-inspector and some Indian constables were wait- 4
ing for me in the quarter where the elephant had been seen. It was a very poor quarter, a labyrinth of squalid bamboo huts, thatched with palm-leaf, winding all over a steep hillside. I remember that it was a cloudy, stuffy morning at the beginning of the rains. We began questioning people as to where the elephant had gone, and, as usual, failed to get any definite information. That is invariably the case in the East; a story always sounds clear enough at a distance, but the nearer you get to the scene of events the vaguer it becomes. Some of the people said that the elephant had gone in one direction, some said that he had gone in another, some professed not even to have heard of an elephant. I had almost made up my mind that the whole story was a pack of lies, when we heard yells a little distance away. There was a loud, scandalized cry of "Go away, child! Go away this instant!" and an old woman with a switch in her hand came round the corner of a hut, violently shooing away a crowd of naked children. Some more women followed, clicking their tongues and exclaiming; evidently there was something that the children ought not to have seen. I rounded the hut and saw a man's dead body sprawling in the mud. He was an Indian, a black Dravidian coolie, almost naked, and he could not have been dead many minutes. The people said that the elephant had come suddenly upon him round the corner of the hut, caught him with its trunk, put its foot on his back and ground him into the earth. This was the rainy season and the ground was soft, and his face had scored a trench a foot deep and a couple of yards long. He was lying on his belly with arms crucified and head sharply twisted to one side. His face was coated with mud, the eyes wide open, the teeth bared and grinning with an expression of unendurable agony. (Never tell me, by the way, that the dead look peaceful. Most of the corpses I have seen looked devilish.) The friction of the great beast's foot had stripped the skin from his back as neatly as one skins a rabbit. As soon as I saw the dead man I sent an

orderly to a friend's house nearby to borrow an elephant rifle. I had already sent back the pony, not wanting it to go mad with fright and throw me if it smelled the elephant.

The orderly came back in a few minutes with a rifle and five 5 cartridges, and meanwhile some Burmans had arrived and told us that the elephant was in the paddy fields below, only a few hundred yards away. As I started forward practically the whole population of the quarter flocked out of the houses and followed me. They had seen the rifle and were all shouting excitedly that I was going to shoot the elephant. They had not shown much interest in the elephant when he was merely ravaging their homes, but it was different now that he was going to be shot. It was a bit of fun to them, as it would be to an English crowd; besides they wanted the meat. It made me vaguely uneasy. I had no intention of shooting the elephant—I had merely sent for the rifle to defend myself if necessary—and it is always unnerving to have a crowd following you. I marched down the hill, looking and feeling a fool, with the rifle over my shoulder and an ever-growing army of people jostling at my heels. At the bottom, when you got away from the huts, there was a metalled road and beyond that a miry waste of paddy fields a thousand yards across, not yet ploughed but soggy from the first rains and dotted with coarse grass. The elephant was standing eight yards from the road, his left side towards us. He took not the slightest notice of the crowd's approach. He was tearing up bunches of grass, beating them against his knees to clean them and stuffing them into his mouth.

I had halted on the road. As soon as I saw the elephant I knew 6 with perfect certainty that I ought not to shoot him. It is a serious matter to shoot a working elephant—it is comparable to destroying a huge and costly piece of machinery—and obviously one ought not to do it if it can possibly be avoided. And at that distance, peacefully eating, the elephant looked no more dangerous than a cow. I thought then and I think now that his attack of "must" was already passing off; in which case he would merely wander harmlessly about until the mahout came back and caught him. Moreover, I did not in the least want to shoot him. I decided that I would watch him for a little while to make sure that he did not turn savage again, and then go home.

But at that moment I glanced round at the crowd that had 7 followed me. It was an immense crowd, two thousand at the least and growing every minute. It blocked the road for a long distance on either side. I looked at the sea of yellow faces above the garish clothes—faces all happy and excited over this bit of fun, all certain that the elephant was going to be shot. They were watching me as they would watch a conjurer about to perform a trick. They did not like me, but with the magical rifle in my hands I was momentarily worth watching. And suddenly I realized that I should have to shoot the elephant after all. The people expected it of me and I had got to do it; I could feel their two thousand wills pressing me forward, irresistibly. And it was at this moment, as I stood there with the rifle in my hands, that I first grasped the hollowness, the futility of the white man's dominion in the East. Here was I, the white man with his gun, standing in front of the unarmed native crowd—seemingly the leading actor of the piece; but in reality I was only an absurd puppet pushed to and fro by the will of those yellow faces behind. I perceived in this moment that when the white man turns tyrant it is his own freedom that he destroys. He becomes a sort of hollow, posing dummy, the conventionalized figure of a sahib. For it is the condition of his rule that he shall spend his life in trying to impress the "natives," and so in every crisis he has got to do what the "natives" expect of him. He wears a mask, and his face grows to fit it. I had got to shoot the elephant. I had committed myself to doing it when I sent for the rifle. A sahib has got to act like a sahib; he has got to appear resolute, to know his own mind and do definite things. To come all that way, rifle in hand, with two thousand people marching at my heels, and then to trail feebly away, having done nothing—no, that was impossible. The crowd would laugh at me. And my whole life, every white man's life in the East, was one long struggle not to be laughed at.

But I did not want to shoot the elephant. I watched him beating 8 his bunch of grass against his knees, with the preoccupied grandmotherly air that elephants have. It seemed to me that it would be murder to shoot him. At that age I was not squeamish about killing animals, but I had never shot an elephant and never wanted to. (Somehow it always seems worse to kill a *large* animal.) Besides, there was the beast's owner to be considered. Alive, the elephant was worth at least a hundred pounds; dead, he would only be worth the value of his tusks, five pounds, possibly. But I had got to act quickly. I turned to some experienced-looking Burmans who had been there when we arrived, and asked them how the elephant had been behaving. They all said the same thing: he took no notice of you if you left him alone, but he might charge if you went too close to him.

It was perfectly clear to me what I ought to do. I ought to walk up 9 to within, say, twenty-five yards of the elephant and test his behavior. If he charged I could shoot, if he took no notice of me it would be safe to leave him until the mahout came back. But also I knew that I was going to do no such thing. I was a poor shot with a rifle and the ground was soft mud into which one would sink at every step. If the elephant charged and I missed him, I should have about as much chance as a toad under a steam-roller. But even then I was not thinking particularly of my own skin, only of the watchful yellow faces behind. For at that moment, with the crowd watching me, I was not afraid in the ordinary sense, as I would have been if I had been alone. A white man mustn't be frightened in front of "natives"; and so, in general, he isn't frightened. The sole thought in my mind was that if anything went wrong those two thousand Burmans would see me pursued, caught, trampled on and reduced to a grinning corpse like that Indian up the hill. And if that happened it was quite probable that some of them would laugh. That would never do. There was only one alternative. I shoved the cartridges into the magazine and lay down on the road to get a better aim.

The crowd grew very still, and a deep, low, happy sigh, as of people   10
who see the theatre curtain go up at last, breathed from innumerable throats. They were going to have their bit of fun after all. The rifle was a beautiful German thing with cross-hair sights. I did not then know that in shooting an elephant one would shoot to cut an imaginary bar running from ear-hole to ear-hole. I ought, therefore, as the elephant was sideways on, to have aimed straight at his ear-hole; actually I aimed several inches in front of this, thinking the brain would be further forward.

When I pulled the trigger I did not hear the bang or feel the kick—   11
one never does when a shot goes home—but I heard the devilish roar of glee that went up from the crowd. In that instant, in too short a time, one would have thought, even for the bullet to get there, a mysterious, terrible change had come over the elephant. He neither stirred nor fell, but every line on his body had altered. He looked suddenly stricken, shrunken, immensely old, as though the frightful impact of the bullet had paralyzed him without knocking him down. At last, after what seemed a long time—it might have been five seconds, I dare say—he sagged flabbily to his knees. His mouth slobbered. An enormous senility seemed to have settled upon him. One could have imagined him thousands of years old. I fired again into the same spot. At the second shot he did not collapse but climbed with desperate slowness to his feet and stood weakly upright, with legs sagging and head drooping. I fired a third time. That was the shot that did for him. You could see the agony of it jolt his whole body and knock the last remnant of strength from his legs. But in falling he seemed for a moment to rise, for as his hind legs collapsed beneath him he seemed to tower upwards like a huge rock toppling, his trunk reaching skywards like a tree. He trumpeted, for

the first and only time. And then down he came, his belly towards me, with a crash that seemed to shake the ground even where I lay.

I got up. The Burmans were already racing past me across the mud. It was obvious that the elephant would never rise again, but he was not dead. He was breathing very rhythmically with long rattling gasps, his great mound of a side painfully rising and falling. His mouth was wide open—I could see far down into the caverns of pale pink throat. I waited a long time for him to die, but his breathing did not weaken. Finally I fired my two remaining shots into the spot where I thought his heart must be. The thick blood welled out of him like red velvet, but still he did not die. His body did not even jerk when the shots hit him, the tortured breathing continued without a pause. He was dying, very slowly and in great agony, but in some world remote from me where not even a bullet could damage him further. I felt that I had got to put an end to that dreadful noise. It seemed dreadful to see the great beast lying there, powerless to move and yet powerless to die, and not even to be able to finish him. I sent back for my small rifle and poured shot after shot into his heart and down his throat. They seemed to make no impression. The tortured gasps continued as steadily as the ticking of a clock. 12

In the end I could not stand it any longer and went away. I heard later that it took him half an hour to die. Burmans were bringing dahs* and baskets even before I left, and I was told they had stripped his body almost to the bones by the afternoon. 13

Afterwards, of course, there were endless discussions about the shooting of the elephant. The owner was furious, but he was only an Indian and could do nothing. Besides, legally I had done the right thing, for a mad elephant has to be killed, like a mad dog, if its owner fails to control it. Among the Europeans opinion was divided. The older men said I was right, the younger men said it was a damn shame to shoot an elephant for killing a coolie, because an elephant was worth more than any damn Coringhee coolie. And afterwards I was very glad that the coolie had been killed; it put me legally in the right and it gave me a sufficient pretext for shooting the elephant. I often wondered whether any of the others grasped that I had done it solely to avoid looking a fool. 14

COMPREHENSION

1. Why was Orwell "hated by large numbers of people" in Burma? Why did he have mixed feelings toward the Burmese people?

*EDS. NOTE—heavy knives.

2. Why did the local officials want something done about the elephant? Why did the crowd want Orwell to shoot the elephant?

3. Why did Orwell finally decide to kill the elephant? What made him hesitate at first?

4. Why does Orwell say at the end that he was glad the coolie had been killed?

PURPOSE AND AUDIENCE

1. One of Orwell's purposes in telling his story is to show how it gave him a glimpse of "the real nature of imperialism." How does the story illustrate this?

2. Do you think Orwell wrote this essay to inform or to persuade his audience? How did Orwell expect his audience to react to his ideas? How can you tell?

3. What is the essay's thesis?

STYLE AND STRUCTURE

1. What is the function of Orwell's first paragraph? Where does the introduction end and the narrative itself begin?

2. The essay includes almost no dialogue. Why do you think Orwell's voice as narrator is the only one the reader hears? Is this a strength or a weakness? Explain.

3. Why does Orwell devote so much attention to the elephant's misery (paragraphs 11 and 12)?

4. Orwell's essay includes a number of editorial comments inserted into his text between parentheses or pairs of dashes. How would you characterize these comments? Why are they set off from the text?

5. Compare the following passages: "Some of the people said that the elephant had gone in one direction, some said that he had gone in another . . ." (4); "Among the Europeans opinion was divided. The older men said I was right, the younger men said it was a damn shame to shoot an elephant . . ." (14). How do these passages reinforce the theme expressed in paragraph 2 ("All I knew was that I was stuck between my hatred of the empire I served and my rage against the evil-spirited little beasts . . .")? Can you find other examples that reinforce this theme?

VOCABULARY PROJECTS

1. Define each of the following words as it is used in this selection.

   baited (1)   despotic (3)   conjurer (7)
   perplexing (2)   labyrinth (4)   dominion (7)
   oppressors (2)   squalid (4)   magazine (9)
   lockups (2)   professed (4)   cross-hair (10)
   flogged (2)   ravaging (5)   remnant (11)
   supplant (2)   miry (5)   trumpeted (11)
   prostrate (2)   garish (7)   pretext (14)

2. Use your dictionary to help you determine the origins as well as the definitions of these words:

   coolie (4)   paddy (5)   mahout (6)   sahib (7)

3. Because Orwell is British, he frequently uses words or expressions that an American writer would not be likely to use. Substitute a contemporary American word or phrase for each of the following, making sure it is appropriate in Orwell's context.

   raise a riot (1)   rubbish van (3)   a bit of fun (5)
   rang me up (3)   inflicted violences (3)   I dare say (11)

   Do any other expressions need "translating" for a contemporary American audience?

JOURNAL ENTRY

Do you think Orwell is a coward? Do you think he is a racist? Explain your feelings.

WRITING WORKSHOP

1. Orwell says that even though he hated British imperialism and sympathized with the Burmese people, he found himself a puppet of the system. Write a narrative essay about a time when you had to do something that went against your beliefs or convictions.

2. Orwell's experience taught him something not only about himself but also about something beyond himself—the way imperialism worked. Write a narrative essay that reveals how an incident in your life taught you something about some larger social or political force as well as about yourself.

3. Write an objective, factual newspaper article recounting the events Orwell describes.

THEMATIC CONNECTIONS

- "On Seeing England for the First Time" (p. 146)
- "The Arab World" (p. 382)
- "The Untouchable" (p. 494)

THE OPEN WINDOW

Saki (H. H. Munro)

*Hector Hugh Munro, who took the pen name Saki, was born in 1870
in Akyab, Burma (now Myanmar), the son of an officer in the
British military police. Following his mother's death when Munro
was not yet two years old, he was sent to England to be raised by his
aunts. In 1893 Munro himself joined the military police in Burma,
but he was forced to leave after a year because of ill health. He then
worked in London as a writer for the* Westminster Gazette, *the*
Bystander, *the* Daily Express, *and the* Morning Post, *for which he
was a foreign correspondent for six years in the Balkans, Russia,
and Paris. Munro enlisted in the army at the beginning of World
War I and was killed in November 1916 by a German sniper during
a British attack on Beaumont-Hamel in France. Although he also
wrote political sketches and plays, he is best known for his humorous, often cynical fiction, including the novel* The Unbearable
Bassington *(1912) and the short stories collected in* The Westminster Alice *(1902),* Reginald in Russia *(1910), and* Beasts and
Super-Beasts *(1914), among other volumes. In "The Open Window,"
from* Beasts and Super-Beasts, *Munro tells the story of a man's
disturbing visit to the home of an excessively imaginative young
girl.*

"My aunt will be down presently, Mr. Nuttel," said a very self-possessed young lady of fifteen; "in the meantime you must try and put up with me."

Framton Nuttel endeavoured to say the correct something which should duly flatter the niece of the moment without unduly discounting the aunt that was to come. Privately he doubted more than ever whether these formal visits on a succession of total strangers would do much towards helping the nerve cure which he was supposed to be undergoing.

"I know how it will be," his sister had said when he was preparing to migrate to this rural retreat; "you will bury yourself down there and not speak to a living soul, and your nerves will be worse than ever from moping. I shall just give you letters of introduction to all the people I know there. Some of them, as far as I can remember, were quite nice."

Framton wondered whether Mrs. Sappleton, the lady to whom he   4
was presenting one of the letters of introduction, came into the nice
division.

"Do you know many of the people round here?" asked the niece,   5
when she judged that they had had sufficient silent communion.

"Hardly a soul," said Framton. "My sister was staying here, at the   6
rectory, you know, some four years ago, and she gave me letters of
introduction to some of the people here."

He made the last statement in a tone of distinct regret.   7

"Then you know practically nothing about my aunt?" pursued the   8
self-possessed young lady.

"Only her name and address," admitted the caller. He was   9
wondering whether Mrs. Sappleton was in the married or widowed
state. An undefinable something about the room seemed to suggest
masculine habitation.

"Her great tragedy happened just three years ago," said the child;   10
"that would be since your sister's time."

"Her tragedy?" asked Framton; somehow in this restful country   11
spot tragedies seemed out of place.

"You may wonder why we keep that window wide open on an   12
October afternoon," said the niece, indicating a large French window
that opened on to a lawn.

"It is quite warm for the time of the year," said Framton; "but has   13
that window got anything to do with the tragedy?"

"Out through that window, three years ago to a day, her husband   14
and her two young brothers went off for their day's shooting. They
never came back. In crossing the moor to their favourite snipe-
shooting ground they were all three engulfed in a treacherous piece
of bog. It had been that dreadful wet summer, you know, and places
that were safe in other years gave way suddenly without warning.
Their bodies were never recovered. That was the dreadful part of it."
Here the child's voice lost its self-possessed note and became
falteringly human. "Poor aunt always thinks that they will come
back, some day, they and the little brown spaniel that was lost with
them, and walk in at that window just as they used to do. That is
why the window is kept open every evening till it is quite dusk. Poor
dear aunt, she has often told me how they went out, her husband
with his white waterproof coat over his arm, and Ronnie, her
youngest brother, singing, 'Bertie, why do you bound?' as he always
did to tease her, because she said it got on her nerves. Do you know,
sometimes on still, quiet evenings like this, I almost get a creepy
feeling that they will all walk in through that window—"

She broke off with a little shudder. It was a relief to Framton when 15
the aunt bustled into the room with a whirl of apologies for being
late in making her appearance.

"I hope Vera has been amusing you?" she said. 16

"She has been very interesting," said Framton. 17

"I hope you don't mind the open window," said Mrs. Sappleton 18
briskly; "my husband and brothers will be home directly from
shooting, and they always come in this way. They've been out for
snipe in the marshes today, so they'll make a fine mess over my poor
carpets. So like you men-folk, isn't it?"

She rattled on cheerfully about the shooting and the scarcity of 19
birds, and the prospects for duck in the winter. To Framton it was all
purely horrible. He made a desperate but only partially successful
effort to turn the talk on to a less ghastly topic; he was conscious
that his hostess was giving him only a fragment of her attention,
and her eyes were constantly straying past him to the open window
and the lawn beyond. It was certainly an unfortunate coincidence
that he should have paid his visit on this tragic anniversary.

"The doctors agree in ordering me complete rest, an absence of 20
mental excitement, and avoidance of anything in the nature of
violent physical exercise," announced Framton, who laboured under
the tolerably wide-spread delusion that total strangers and chance
acquaintances are hungry for the least detail of one's ailments and
infirmities, their cause and cure. "On the matter of diet they are not
so much in agreement," he continued.

"No?" said Mrs. Sappleton, in a voice which only replaced a yawn 21
at the last moment. Then she suddenly brightened into alert attention—but not to what Framton was saying.

"Here they are at last!" she cried. "Just in time for tea, and don't 22
they look as if they were muddy up to the eyes!"

Framton shivered slightly and turned towards the niece with a 23
look intended to convey sympathetic comprehension. The child was
staring out through the open window with dazed horror in her eyes.
In a chill shock of nameless fear Framton swung round in his seat
and looked in the same direction.

In the deepening twilight three figures were walking across the 24
lawn towards the window; they all carried guns under their arms,
and one of them was additionally burdened with a white coat hung
over his shoulders. A tired brown spaniel kept close at their heels.
Noiselessly they neared the house, and then a hoarse young voice
chanted out of the dusk: "I said, Bertie, why do you bound?"

Framton grabbed wildly at his stick and hat; the hall-door, the 25
gravel-drive, and the front gate were dimly noted stages in his

headlong retreat. A cyclist coming along the road had to run into the hedge to avoid imminent collision.

"Here we are, my dear," said the bearer of the white mackintosh, coming in through the window; "fairly muddy, but most of it's dry. Who was that who bolted out as we came up?"   26

"A most extraordinary man, a Mr. Nuttel," said Mrs. Sappleton;   27
"could only talk about his illness, and dashed off without a word of good-bye or apology when you arrived. One would think he had seen a ghost."

"I expect it was the spaniel," said the niece calmly; "he told me he   28
had a horror of dogs. He was once hunted into a cemetery some-where on the banks of the Ganges by a pack of pariah dogs, and had to spend the night in a newly dug grave with the creatures snarling and grinning and foaming just above him. Enough to make any one lose their nerve."

Romance at short notice was her specialty.   29

THINKING ABOUT LITERATURE

1. Why is it essential that the story Vera tells Mr. Nuttel be extremely detailed?

2. How does the dialogue included in "The Open Window" characterize Mrs. Sappleton, Mr. Nuttel, and Vera? Give specific examples to support your answer.

3. Why is each of these details important to "The Open Window"?
    a. Mr. Nuttel is recovering from a nervous breakdown.
    b. Mr. Nuttel knows almost nothing about Mrs. Sappleton.
    c. Vera is "a very self-possessed young lady."
    d. The window is open.

    How would the story be different without each of these details?

JOURNAL ENTRY

Explain the meaning of the story's last line (paragraph 29). In what sense does it serve as a thesis statement for the story? How would the story be different if this "thesis" appeared earlier?

THEMATIC CONNECTIONS

- "The Spider and the Wasp" (p. 251)
- "The Ways We Lie" (p. 455)

WRITING ASSIGNMENTS FOR NARRATION

1. Trace the path you expect to follow to establish yourself in your chosen profession, considering possible obstacles you may face and how you expect to deal with them. Include a thesis that conveys the importance of your goals.

2. Write a personal narrative in which you look back from some point in the far future on your own life as you hope it will be seen by others. Use third person if you like, and write your own obituary; or, assess your life in the form of a letter to your great-grandchildren.

3. Write a news article recounting in objective terms the events described in "The Open Window" or "My Mother Never Worked." Include a descriptive headline.

4. Write a historical narrative tracing the roots of your family or your hometown or community. Be sure to include the kind of specific details—including dialogue and description of people and places—used by Cisneros and Angelou.

5. Write an account of one of these "firsts": Your first date; your first serious argument with your parents; your first experience with physical violence or danger; your first extended stay away from home; your first encounter with someone whose culture was very different from your own; your first experience with the serious illness or death of a close friend or relative. Make sure your essay includes a thesis that your narrative can support.

6. George Orwell and Martin Gansberg both deal with the consequences of failing to act. Write an essay or story in which you recount what would have happened if Orwell had *not* shot the elephant or if one of the eyewitnesses *had* called the police right away.

7. Maya Angelou's "finishing school" was Mrs. Cullinan's kitchen. What institution served as your finishing school? What did you learn there, and how did this knowledge serve you later?

8. Write a short narrative summarizing a class, a short story, a television show, a conversation, a fable or fairy tale, or a narrative poem. Include as many details as you can.

9. Write a narrative about a time when you were an outsider, isolated because of social, intellectual, or ethnic differences between you and others. Did you resolve the problems your isolation created? Explain. (If you like, you may refer to the Angelou or Orwell essays.)

10. Imagine a meeting between any two characters in this chapter's reading selections. Using dialogue as well as narrative, write an account of this meeting.

COLLABORATIVE ACTIVITY FOR NARRATION

Working with a group of students of about your own age, write a history of your television-viewing habits. Begin by working individually to list all your most-watched television shows in chronological order, beginning as far back as you can remember. Then, compile a single list that reflects a consensus of the group's preferences, perhaps choosing one or two representative programs for each stage of your life (preschool, elementary school, and so on). Have a different student write a paragraph on each stage, describing the chosen programs in as much detail as possible. Finally, combine the individual paragraphs to create a narrative essay that traces the group's changing tastes in television shows. Be sure to include a thesis statement that expresses what the preferences you identify reveal about your generation's development.

3

Description

WHAT IS DESCRIPTION?

You use **description** whenever you want to convey to readers the physical characteristics of a person, place, or thing. Description relies on the five senses—sight, hearing, taste, touch, and smell—to convey experience to readers. In the following paragraph from "Knoxville: Summer 1915," for example, James Agee uses sight, sound, and touch to recreate a scene for an audience that is unfamiliar with it.

Topic sentence	It is not of games children play in the evening that I want to speak now, it is of a contemporaneous atmosphere that has little to do with them; that of fathers and
Description using sight	families, each in his space of lawn, his shirt fishlike pale in the unnatural light and his face nearly anonymous, hosing their lawns. The hoses were attached to spigots that stood out of the brick foundations of the houses. The nozzles were variously set but usually so there was a long sweet
Description using touch	stream of spray, the nozzle wet in the hand, the water trickling the right forearm and the peeled-back cuff, and the water whishing out a long loose and low-curved cone,
Description using sound	and so gentle a sound. First an insane noise of violence in the nozzle, then the still irregular sound of adjustment, then the smoothing into steadiness and a pitch as accurately tuned to the size and style of stream as any violin.

So many qualities of sound out of one hose: so many choral differences out of those several hoses that were in earshot. Out of any one hose, the almost dead silence of the release, and the short still arch of the separate big drops, silent as a held breath, and the only noise the flattering noise on leaves and the slapped grass at the fall of each big drop. That, and the intense hiss with the intense stream; that, and the same intensity not growing less but growing more quiet and delicate with the turn of the nozzle, up to that extreme tender whisper when the water was just a wide bell of film.

Before we make judgments about the world, before we compare or contrast or classify our experiences, we describe. Scientists describe their observations whenever they conduct experiments, and you describe whenever you write a paper. In a comparison-and-contrast essay, for example, you may describe the performance of two cars to show that one is superior to the other. In an argumentative essay, you may describe a fish kill in a local river to show that factory pollution is a problem. Through description, you introduce your view of the world to your readers. If your readers come to understand or share your view, they are more likely to accept your conclusions and judgments. Therefore, in almost every essay you write, knowing how to write effective description is important.

A narrative essay presents a series of events; it tells a story. A descriptive essay tells what something looks like or what it feels like, sounds like, smells like, or tastes like. Description can also go beyond personal sense impressions. Novelists can create imaginary landscapes, historians can paint word pictures of historical figures, and scientists can describe physical phenomena they have never seen. When you write description, you use language to create a vivid impression for your reader. As mentioned in Chapter 2, a good narrative may depend heavily on descriptive details. A narrative, however, always presents events in time, in some sort of chronological order, whereas a description usually presents things in spatial rather than temporal order.

In this chapter, we focus on descriptive writing as a strategy for a whole essay. Writers of descriptive essays often use an implied thesis when they describe a person, place, or thing. This technique allows them to convey the essay's **dominant impression**—the mood or quality that is emphasized in the piece of writing—subtly through the selection and arrangement of details. When they use description to support an idea or assertion, however, many writers prefer to use an explicitly stated thesis. This strategy eliminates ambiguity by letting readers see immediately what point the writer is making— for example, "The sculptures that adorn Philadelphia's City Hall are a catalog of nineteenth-century artistic styles." Whether you state or imply your thesis, the details of your descriptive essay must work together to create a single dominant impression. In many cases your thesis may simply be the statement of the dominant impression;

sometimes, however, your thesis may go further and make a point about the dominant impression.

Objective and Subjective Descriptions

Descriptions can be objective or subjective. In an **objective description,** you focus on the object itself rather than on your personal reactions to it. Your purpose is to convey a precise, literal picture of your subject. Many writing situations require exact descriptions of apparatus or conditions, and in these cases your goal is to construct as accurate and unemotional a picture as possible for your audience. A biologist describing what he sees through a microscope and a historian describing a Civil War battlefield would both write objectively. The biologist would not, for instance, say how exciting his observations were, nor would the historian say how disappointed she was at the outcome of the battle. Newspaper reporters also try to achieve this impersonal objectivity, and so do writers of technical reports, scientific papers, and certain types of business correspondence. Of course, objectivity is an ideal that writers strive for but never achieve. In fact, even in selecting some details and leaving out others, writers are making personal decisions.

In the following descriptive passage, Thomas Marc Parrott aims for objectivity by giving his readers all the factual information they need to visualize Shakespeare's theater:

> When James Burbage built the Theatre in 1576 he naturally designed it along the lines of inn-yards in which he had been accustomed to play. The building had two entrances—one in front for the audience; one in the rear for actors, musicians, and the personnel of the theatre. Inside the building a rectangular platform projected far out into what was called "the yard"—we know the stage of the Fortune ran halfway across the "yard," some twenty-seven and a half feet.

Note that Parrott is not interested in responding to or evaluating the environment he describes. Instead, he chooses words that convey sizes, shapes, and distances. His use of adjectives such as *two* and *rectangular* reflects this intent. Only one word in the paragraph—*naturally*—suggests an opinion.

In contrast to objective description, **subjective description** discloses your personal impression of or your emotional responses to what you see and tries to get your readers to share them. These responses are not necessarily expressed directly, through a straightforward statement of your opinion or perspective. Often they are revealed indirectly, through your choice of words and phrasing. If an English composition assignment asked that you describe a place of special meaning to you, you could convey your subjective reaction to your topic by selecting and emphasizing details that showed your feelings about the place. For example, you could write a subjective description of your room by focusing on particular objects—your desk, your window, and your bookshelves—and conveying the associations these things bring back to you. Thus, your desk could be a "warm brown rectangle of wood whose surface contains the scratched impressions of a thousand school assignments."

A subjective or impressionistic description should convey not just a factual record of sights and sounds but also their meaning or significance. For example, if you objectively described a fire, you might include its temperature, its duration, and its scope. In addition to these quantifiable details you might describe, as accurately as possible, the fire's color, movement, and intensity. If you subjectively described the fire, however, you would include more than these unbiased observations about it. Through your choice of language and your phrasing, you would try to recreate for your audience a sense of how the fire made you feel: your reactions to the crackling noise, to the dense smoke, to the sudden destruction.

In the following passage, notice how Mark Twain subjectively describes the Mississippi River:

> I still kept in mind a certain wonderful sunset which I witnessed when steamboating was new to me. A broad expanse of the river was turned to blood; in the middle distance the red hue brightened into gold, through which a solitary log came floating, black and conspicuous; in one place a long, slanting mark lay sparkling upon the water; in another the surface was broken by boiling, tumbling rings, that were as many-tinted as an opal.

In this passage, Twain uses words that convey emotions—*wonderful*—and comparisons that suggest great value—*gold, opal*—to convey his feelings to the reader. By focusing on details like the red color, the solitary log "black and conspicuous," and the "boiling, tumbling rings," he shares with his readers his unique perception of sunset on the river.

Neither objective nor subjective description exists independently. Objective descriptions almost always contain some subjective elements, and subjective descriptions need some objective elements to convey a sense of reality. The skillful writer adjusts the balance between objectivity and subjectivity to suit the topic, thesis, audience, purpose, and occasion of an essay.

Objective and Subjective Language

As the passages above by Parrott and Twain illustrate, both objective and subjective descriptions depend on specific and concrete words to appeal to a reader's senses. But the two kinds of descriptions use different kinds of language. Objective descriptions rely on precise, factual language that presents a writer's observations without conveying his or her attitude toward the subject. These kinds of descriptions rely on words and phrases so unambiguous that many readers can agree on the accuracy of the observations. Subjective descriptions, on the other hand, generally rely on richer and more suggestive language. They are more likely to rely on the **connotations** of words, their emotional associations, than on their **denotations,** or more direct meanings. They may deliberately provoke the individual reader's imagination with striking phrases or vivid comparisons. For example, a subjective description might compare the behavior of a peacock spreading its feathers to that of a pet Siamese cat posturing and posing, thus evoking a lively image in the reader's mind.

Although both kinds of description may use comparisons to convey impressions to the reader, subjective descriptions rely more on elaborate or imaginative comparisons. When you write subjective descriptions, you can compare two similar things, using the familiar parakeet to describe the unfamiliar peacock. Or you can find similarities between things that are dissimilar, such as the peacock and the cat, and provide a fresh view of both. Such special comparisons are known as **figures of speech.** Three of the most common are *simile, metaphor,* and *personification.*

A **simile** uses *like* or *as* to compare two dissimilar things. These comparisons occur frequently in everyday speech—for example, when someone claims to be "happy as a clam," "free as a bird," or "hungry as a bear." As a rule, however, you should avoid overused expressions like these in your writing. Effective writers constantly strive to use original similes. In his short story "A & P," for example, John Updike uses a striking simile when he likens people going through the checkout aisle of a supermarket to balls dropping down a slot in a pinball machine.

A **metaphor** compares two dissimilar things without using *like* or *as.* Instead of saying that something is like something else, a metaphor says that it *is* something else. Twain uses a metaphor when he says, "A broad expanse of the river was turned to blood."

Personification endows animals or objects with the qualities of human beings. If you say that the wind whispered or that an engine died, you are using personification.

In addition to these figures of speech, writers of subjective descriptions can also use allusions to enrich their writing. An **allusion** is a reference to a person, place, event, or quotation that the writer expects readers to recognize. In "Letter from Birmingham Jail" (p. 562), for example, Martin Luther King, Jr. frequently alludes to biblical passages and proverbs with which he expects his audience of clergy to be familiar.

Your purpose and audience determine whether you should use predominantly objective or subjective description. An assignment that specifically asks for reactions calls for a subjective description. In contrast, however, legal, medical, technical, business, and scientific writing assignments frequently require objective descriptions. In such contexts, your purpose is primarily to give your audience factual information about your subject. (Even in these areas, of course, you may use figurative language. Scientists routinely use such language to describe an unfamiliar object or concept to an audience. In their pioneering article on the structure of DNA, for example, James Watson and Francis Crick use a simile when they say that a molecule of DNA looks like two spiral staircases winding around each other.)

Selection of Detail

Sometimes inexperienced writers load their descriptions with empty words like *nice, great, terrific,* or *awful,* substituting their own reactions to an object for the qualities of the object itself. To produce an effective description, however, you must do more than just *say* something is wonderful—you must use details that evoke this reaction in a reader, as Twain does with the sunset. Twain does in fact use the word *wonderful* at the beginning of his description, but he then goes on to supply many concrete details that make the scene he describes vivid and specific.

All good descriptive writing, whether objective or subjective, relies heavily on specific details that enable readers to imagine what you are describing. Your aim is not simply to *tell* your readers what something looks like but to *show* them. Every person, place, or thing has its special characteristics, and you must use your powers of observation to detect them. You then must select the concrete words that will convey your dominant impression, that will enable your readers to experience imaginatively what you describe. Do not be satisfied with "He looked angry" when you can say, "His face flushed, and one corner of his mouth twitched as he tried to control his anger." What is the difference? In the first case, you simply identify the man's emotional state. In the second, you describe his appearance by providing enough detail so that readers can tell not only that he was angry but also how he revealed the intensity of his anger.

Of course, you could have provided even more detail by noting the man's beard or his wrinkles or any number of other features. However, not all details are equally useful or desirable, and you should take care to include only those that contribute to the dominant impression you wish to create. Thus, in describing a man's face to show how angry he was, you would probably not describe the shape of his nose or the color of his hair. (After all, a person's hair color does not change when he or she gets angry.) In fact, the number of details you use is less important than their quality and appropriateness. To avoid a seemingly endless list of details that blur the focus of your essay, you must select and use only those details relevant to your purpose.

Factors like the level, background, and knowledge of your audience also influence the kind of detail you include. For example, a description of a DNA molecule written for first-year college students would contain more basic details than a description written for junior biology majors. In addition, the more advanced description would contain details—the sequence of amino acid groups, for instance—that would be inappropriate for first-year students.

STRUCTURING A DESCRIPTIVE ESSAY

When you write a descriptive essay, you begin with notes that record randomly organized details, which you then arrange in a way that supports your thesis and communicates your dominant impression. As you consider how to arrange your details, you have a number of options. For example, you can move from a specific description of an object to a general description of other things around it. Or you can reverse this order, beginning with the general and proceeding to the specific. You can progress from the least important feature to the most important one. You can also move from the smallest to the largest item or from the least unusual to the most unusual detail. You can present the details of your description in a straightforward spatial order, moving from left to right or right to left, from top to bottom or bottom to top. Finally, you can combine organizing schemes, using different schemes in different parts of the essay. The particular strategy you choose depends on the dominant impression you want to convey, your thesis, and your purpose and audience.

Suppose your English composition instructor has asked you to write a short essay describing a person, place, or thing. After thinking about the assignment for a day or two, you decide to write an objective description of the Air and Space Museum in Washington, D.C. because you have visited it recently and many details are fresh in your mind. The museum is large and has many different exhibits, so you know you will not be able to describe them all. Therefore, you decide to concentrate on one, the heavier-than-air flight exhibit, and you choose as the topic for your essay the particular display that you remember most vividly: Charles Lindbergh's airplane, *The Spirit of St. Louis.* You brainstorm to recall all the details you can, and when you read over your notes, you realize that the organizing scheme of your essay could reflect your actual experience in the museum. You decide to present the details of the airplane in the order in which your eye took them in, from front to rear. The dominant impression you wish to create is how small and fragile *The Spirit of St. Louis* appears, and your thesis is the statement that communicates this impression. An informal outline for your essay might look like this:

Introduction:	Thesis statement—It is startling that a plane as small as *The Spirit of St. Louis* could fly across the Atlantic.
Front of plane:	Single engine, tiny cockpit
Middle of plane:	Short wing span, extra gas tanks
Rear of plane:	Limited cargo space filled with more gas tanks
Conclusion:	Restatement of thesis; summary of key points

STUDENT WRITERS: DESCRIPTION

Each of the following student essays illustrates the principles of effective description. The first one, by Joseph Tessari, is an objective description of the light microscope. The second, by Mary Lim, is a subjective description of a place in Burma (now Myanmar).

THE LIGHT MICROSCOPE

Introduction   The simple light microscope is widely used in the   1
scientific community. The basic function of the microscope
is to view objects or biological specimens that would
otherwise be invisible to the naked eye. Light microscopes
come in a variety of shapes and sizes, with different degrees
of magnification and complexity. Most microscopes,
however, are made of metal or plastic (primarily metal) and

Thesis statement

stand approximately ten to thirteen inches tall. A description of the microscope's design illustrates its function.

Description of stand

A simple light microscope consists of several integrated parts (see attached diagram). The largest piece is the stand. The base of the stand, which is wishbone-shaped, rests on the tabletop. A vertical section approximately nine inches tall extends out of the base and is shaped like a question mark.

2

Description of optic tube

At the end of the vertical piece of the stand is the black metal optic tube, a vertical cylinder approximately three to four inches long. One entire side of this tube is attached to the stand, so that the tube sits in front of the stand when the microscope is viewed from the front.

3

Description of eyepiece

Sitting directly on top of this tube is a cylindrical eyepiece. The eyepiece, slightly smaller in diameter than the optic tube, is approximately two inches long. The top of the eyepiece is fitted with a clear glass lens called the fixed lens.

4

Description of coarse and fine adjust- ment knobs

On the stand, adjacent to the point where it meets the optic tube, are two coarse adjustment knobs--one on each side of the microscope. When rotated, these knobs raise and lower the optic tube. This raising and lowering of the tube focuses the image of the object being viewed. Two fine adjustment knobs at the bottom of the stand permit finer adjustments in focus. These knobs are especially useful at high magnifications where smaller adjustments are needed.

5

Description of objective lenses

Attached to the bottom of the optic tube is a rotating disk that contains two small silver objective lenses spaced one hundred eighty degrees apart. These lenses have different magnification powers. When an objective lens is in place, the eyepiece, optic tube, and objective lens fall in a vertical line.

6

Description of viewing stage

Directly below the objective lens, attached to the bend in the question mark of the vertical stand, is the viewing stage, a square horizontal plate with a small circular hole in the center. This circular hole is approximately the same

7

diameter as the objective lens and falls along the same vertical line. On either side of the hole are metal clips that hold a glass slide or a specimen plate in place.

Description of mirror

A few inches below the viewing stage is a small circular mirror. This mirror can pivot around a horizontal axis and is attached to the stand by a Y-shaped clamp. When the mirror is moved, light is reflected up through the hole in the viewing stage and into the objective lens, optic tube, and eyepiece.   8

Conclusion

The simple light microscope has been an extremely useful biological tool for many years. It has helped scientists gain a better understanding of human anatomy and physiology as well as a number of diseases. With modern technology, new and more complex instruments, such as the electron microscope, have been developed. Still, the light microscope remains an important tool for both students and serious researchers.   9

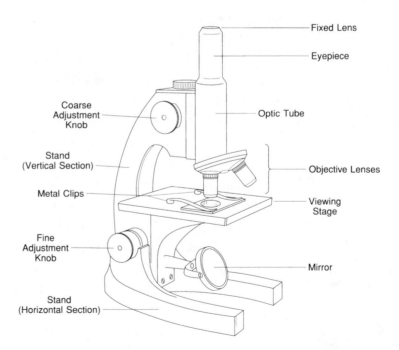

Fixed Lens

Eyepiece

Coarse Adjustment Knob

Optic Tube

Stand (Vertical Section)

Objective Lenses

Metal Clips

Viewing Stage

Fine Adjustment Knob

Mirror

Stand (Horizontal Section)

Points for Special Attention

Objective Description.   Joseph Tessari, a toxicology major, wrote this paper as an exercise for a class in scientific writing. His assignment was to write a detailed, factual description of an instrument, mechanism, or piece of apparatus or equipment used in his study of his major field. Because he is writing an objective description, he does not react subjectively to the microscope or point out its strengths and weaknesses. Instead, he describes the microscope's physical features. Joseph's thesis statement emphasizes his purpose and conveys his straightforward intention to his readers.

Objective Language.   Because his essay is written for a class in scientific writing, Joseph keeps his objective description technical. His factual, concrete language concentrates on the size, shape, and composition of each part and on each part's physical relationship to the other parts and to the whole. He does not use subjective language or elaborate figures of speech.

Structure.   Joseph chooses to describe the microscope piece by piece. He starts at the bottom of the microscope with its largest part—the stand. He next directs the reader's attention upward from the optic tube to the eyepiece and then downward past the coarse adjustment knobs to the bottom of the optic tube (where the objective lens is located) and down to the viewing stage and the mirror. In his introduction, Joseph comments on the microscope's purpose and general appearance; in his conclusion, he summarizes the microscope's historical significance and briefly considers its future.

Selection of Detail.   Joseph's assignment identified his target audience as a group of well-educated nonscientists. He was told he could assume that his readers would know generally what a microscope looked like but that he would have to describe the individual components in some detail.

Diagram.   Joseph knew that describing the relationships among the parts of the microscope would not be easy. In fact, his initial attempts to do so produced sentences like "When viewed from the side, the objective lens makes a forty-five degree angle with the front of the optic tube and is higher in front of the microscope than in back." In order to avoid complicated and tedious passages of description like this, which would just confuse readers, Joseph included a diagram. Not only does the diagram present the parts of the microscope in relationship to one another, but it also depicts certain parts—like the objective lenses—that are difficult to visualize. Notice that the diagram is clearly drawn and labeled.

Focus on Revision. In addition to deleting wordy sentences, Joseph could go on to eliminate many of the phrases that describe the shape of the various parts of the microscope. The labeled diagram eliminates the need for phrases such as "Y-shaped clamp" and "a small circular mirror": Because viewers can see these structures, there is no need to describe them in precise detail.

Unlike "The Light Microscope," Mary Lim's essay uses subjective description so that readers can share, as well as understand, her experience.

THE VALLEY OF WINDMILLS

Introduction

In my native country of Burma (which is now called Myanmar), strange happenings and exotic scenery are not unusual. For Burma is a mysterious land that in some areas seems to have been ignored by time. Mountains stand jutting their rocky peaks into the clouds as they have for thousands of years. Jungles are so dense with exotic vegetation that human beings or large animals cannot even enter. But one of the most fascinating areas in Burma is the

Description (identifying the scene)

Valley of Windmills, nestled between the tall mountains near the fertile and beautiful city of Taungaleik. In this valley there is beautiful and breathtaking scenery, but there are also old, massive, and gloomy structures that can disturb a person deeply.

Description (moving toward the valley)

The road to Taungaleik twists out of the coastal flatlands into those heaps of slag, shale, and limestone that are the Tennesserim Mountains in the southern part of Burma. The air grows rarer and cooler, and stones become grayer, the highway a little more precarious at its edges until

Description (immediate view)

ahead, standing in ghostly sentinel across the lip of a pass, is a line of squat forms. They straddle the road and stand at

1

2

intervals up hillsides on either side. Are they boulders? Are they fortifications? Are they broken wooden crosses on graves in an abandoned cemetery?

Description (more distant view)

These dark figures are windmills standing in the misty   3 atmosphere. They are immensely old and distinctly evil, some merely turrets, some with remnants of arms hanging derelict from their snouts, and most of them covered with dark green moss. Their decayed but still massive forms seem to turn and sneer at visitors. Down the pass on the other side is a circular green plateau that lies like an arena below, where there are still more windmills. Massed in the plain behind them, as far as the eye can see, in every field, above every hut, stand ten thousand iron windmills, silent and sailless. They seem to await only a call from a watchman to clank, whirr, flap, and groan into action. Visitors suddenly feel cold. Perhaps it is a sense of loneliness, the cool air, the desolation, or the weirdness of the arcane windmills--but something chills them.

Description (windmills contrasted with city)

As you stand at the lip of the valley, contrasts rush as if   4 to overwhelm you. Beyond, glittering on the mountainside like a solitary jewel, is Taungaleik in the territory once occupied by the Portuguese. Below, on rolling hillsides, are the dark windmills, still enveloped in morning mist. These ancient windmills can remind you of the impermanence of life and the mystery that still surrounds these hills. In an odd way, the scene in the valley can disturb you, but it also can give you an insight into the contrasts that seem to define our lives here in my country.

Conclusion (thesis statement)

Points for Special Attention

Subjective Description. One of the first things readers notice when they read Mary's essay is her use of vivid details. The road to Taungaleik is described in specific terms: It twists "out of the coastal flatlands" into the mountains, which are "heaps of slag, shale, and limestone." The iron windmills are decayed and stand "silent and sailless" on a green plateau that "lies like an arena." Using language in this way, Mary creates her dominant impression of the Valley of Windmills as dark, mysterious, and disquieting. The point of her essay—the thesis—is stated in the last paragraph: The Valley of Windmills embodies the contrasts that characterize life in Burma.

Subjective Language and Figures of Speech. Mary conveys the sense of foreboding she felt by describing the windmills in several different ways. Upon first introducing them, she questions whether these "squat forms" are "boulders," "fortifications," or "broken wooden crosses," each of which has a menacing connotation. After telling the reader what they are, she personifies the windmills by describing them as dark, evil, sneering figures with "arms hanging derelict." She sees them as ghostly sentinels awaiting a call from a watchman to spring into action. Through this figure of speech, Mary masterfully recreates the unearthly quality of the scene she witnessed.

Structure. Mary's purpose in writing this paper was to give her readers the sensation of actually being in the Valley of Windmills. She uses an organizing scheme that takes readers along the road to Taungaleik, up into the Tennesserim Mountains, and finally to the pass where the windmills wait. From the perspective of the lip of the valley, she describes the details closest to her and then those farther away, as if following the movement of her eyes. She ends by bringing her readers back to the lip of the valley, contrasting Taungaleik "glittering on the mountainside" with the windmills "enveloped in morning mist." Through her description, she builds up to her thesis about the nature of life in her country. She withholds the explicit statement of her main point until her last paragraph, when readers have been fully prepared for it.

Focus on Revision. Mary's thesis about life in Burma could use more support. Although her description is quite powerful, it does not really convey the contrasts she alludes to in her conclusion. Another paragraph in which Mary discusses something about her life, perhaps her reasons for visiting the windmills, could help supply this missing information. She could, for example, tell her readers that right after her return from the valley, she found out that a friend had been accidentally shot by border guards, and that it was this event that caused her to see the windmills in the light she describes. Such information would explain the somber mood of the passage as well as underscore the ideas presented in the conclusion.

The following selections illustrate different types and uses of description. As you read them, pay particular attention to the difference between objective and subjective description.

SALVADOR

Joan Didion

Joan Didion was born in 1934 in Sacramento, California. She graduated from the University of California at Berkeley in 1956 and worked as an editor at Vogue *and a columnist for* The Saturday Evening Post, Life, The National Review, *and* Esquire. *She is now a regular contributor to* The New York Review of Books *and* The New Yorker. *Didion's essays, for which she is best known, have been collected in* Slouching Towards Bethlehem *(1968),* The White Album *(1979),* Essays and Conversations *(1984), and* After Henry *(1992). She has also written four novels,* Run River *(1963),* Play It As It Lays *(1970),* A Book of Common Prayer *(1977), and* Democracy *(1984) and two works of nonfiction,* Salvador *(1983), an account of her journey to El Salvador in 1982, and* Miami *(1987), about Cuban exiles in Florida. In addition, she has collaborated on several screenplays with her husband, John Gregory Dunne. The following selection is from* Salvador, *a book that portrays a country engulfed by the fear and violence of civil war. Here Didion presents her initial impressions of El Salvador and focuses on the "mechanism of terror" that she sees operating everywhere in the capital city of San Salvador.*

The three-year-old El Salvador International Airport is glassy and white, splendidly isolated, conceived during the waning of the Molina "National Transformation" as convenient less to the capital (San Salvador is forty miles away, until recently a drive of several hours) than to a central hallucination of the Molina and Romero regimes, the projected beach resorts, the Hyatt, the Pacific Paradise, tennis, golf, water-skiing, condos, *Costa del Sol;* the visionary invention of a tourist industry in yet another republic where the leading natural cause of death is gastrointestinal infection. In the general absence of tourists these hotels have since been abandoned, ghost resorts on the empty Pacific beaches, and to land at this airport built to service them is to plunge directly into a state in which no ground is solid, no depth of field reliable, no perception so definite that it might not dissolve into its reverse.

The only logic is that of acquiescence. Immigration is negotiated in a thicket of automatic weapons, but by whose authority the weapons are brandished (Army or National Guard or National Police or Customs Police or Treasury Police or one of a continuing proliferation of other shadowy and overlapping forces) is a blurred point. Eye contact is avoided. Documents are scrutinized upside down. Once clear of the airport, on the new highway that slices through green hills rendered phosphorescent by the cloud cover of the tropical rainy season, one sees mainly underfed cattle and mongrel dogs and armored vehicles, vans and trucks and Cherokee Chiefs fitted with reinforced steel and bulletproof Plexiglas an inch thick. Such vehicles are a fixed feature of local life, and are popularly associated with disappearance and death. There was the Cherokee Chief seen following the Dutch television crew killed in Chalatenango province in March of 1982. There was the red Toyota three-quarter-ton pickup sighted near the van driven by the four American Catholic workers on the night they were killed in 1980. There were, in the late spring and summer of 1982, the three Toyota panel trucks, one yellow, one blue, and one green, none bearing plates, reported present at each of the mass detentions (a "dentention" is another fixed feature of local life, and often precedes a "disappearance") in the Amatepec district of San Salvador. These are the details—the models and colors of armored vehicles, the makes and calibers of weapons, the particular methods of dismemberment and decapitation used in particular instances—on which the visitor to Salvador learns immediately to concentrate, to the exclusion of past or future concerns, as in a prolonged amnesiac fugue.

Terror is the given of the place. Black-and-white police cars cruise   3
in pairs, each with the barrel of a rifle extruding from an open window. Roadblocks materialize at random, soldiers fanning out from trucks and taking positions, fingers always on triggers, safeties clicking on and off. Aim is taken as if to pass the time. Every morning *El Diario de Hoy* and *La Prensa Gráfica* carry cautionary stories. *"Una madre y sus dos hijos fueron asesinados con arma cortante (corvo) por ocho sujetos desconocidos el lunes en la noche"*: A mother and her two sons hacked to death in their beds by eight *desconocidos,* unknown men. The same morning's paper: the unidentified body of a young man, strangled, found on the shoulder of a road. Same morning, different story: the unidentified bodies of three young men, found on another road, their faces partially destroyed by bayonets, one face carved to represent a cross.

It is largely from these reports in the newspapers that the United   4
States embassy compiles its body counts, which are transmitted to Washington in a weekly dispatch referred to by embassy people as "the grimgram." These counts are presented in a kind of tortured code that fails to obscure what is taken for granted in El Salvador,

that government forces do most of the killing. In a January 15 1982 memo to Washington, for example, the embassy issued a "guarded" breakdown on its count of 6,909 "reported" political murders between September 16 1980 and September 15 1981. Of these 6,909, according to the memo, 922 were "believed committed by security forces," 952 "believed committed by leftist terrorists," 136 "believed committed by rightist terrorists," and 4,889 "committed by unknown assailants," the famous *desconocidos* favored by those San Salvador newspapers still publishing. (The figures actually add up not to 6,909 but to 6,899, leaving ten in a kind of official limbo.) The memo continued:

> "The uncertainty involved here can be seen in the fact that responsibility cannot be fixed in the majority of cases. We note, however, that it is generally believed in El Salvador that a large number of unexplained killings are carried out by the security forces, officially or unofficially. The Embassy is aware of dramatic claims that have been made by one interest group or another in which the security forces figure as the primary agents of murder here. El Salvador's tangled web of attack and vengeance, traditional criminal violence and political mayhem make this an impossible charge to sustain. In saying this, however, we make no attempt to lighten the responsibility for the deaths of many hundreds, and perhaps thousands, which can be attributed to the security forces. . . ."

The body count kept by what is generally referred to in San Salvador as "the Human Rights Commission" is higher than the embassy's, and documented periodically by a photographer who goes out looking for bodies. These bodies he photographs are often broken into unnatural positions, and the faces to which the bodies are attached (when they are attached) are equally unnatural, sometimes unrecognizable as human faces, obliterated by acid or beaten to a mash of misplaced ears and teeth or slashed ear to ear and invaded by insects. *"Encontrado en Antiguo Cuscatlán el dia 25 de Marzo 1982: camison de dormir celeste,"* the typed caption reads on one photograph: found in Antiguo Cuscatlán March 25 1982 wearing a sky-blue nightshirt. The captions are laconic. Found in Soyapango May 21 1982. Found in Mejicanos June 11 1982. Found at El Playón May 30 1982, white shirt, purple pants, black shoes.

The photograph accompanying that last caption shows a body with no eyes, because the vultures got to it before the photographer did. There is a special kind of practical information that the visitor to El Salvador acquires immediately, the way visitors to other places acquire information about the currency rates, the hours for the museums. In El Salvador one learns that vultures go first for the soft tissue, for the eyes, the exposed genitalia, the open mouth. One learns that an open mouth can be used to make a specific point, can be stuffed with something emblematic; stuffed, say, with a penis, or, if the point has to do with land title, stuffed with some of the dirt in question. One learns that hair deteriorates less rapidly than flesh, and that a skull surrounded by a perfect corona of hair is a not uncommon sight in the body dumps.

All forensic photographs induce in the viewer a certain protective numbness, but dissociation is more difficult here. In the first place these are not, technically, "forensic" photographs, since the evidence they document will never be presented in a court of law. In the second place the disfigurement is too routine. The locations are too near, the dates too recent. There is the presence of the relatives of the disappeared: the women who sit every day in this cramped office on the grounds of the archdiocese, waiting to look at the spiral-bound photo albums in which the photographs are kept. These albums have plastic covers bearing soft-focus color photographs of young Americans in dating situations (strolling through autumn foliage on one album, recumbent in a field of daisies on another), and the women, looking for the bodies of their husbands and brothers and sisters and children, pass them from hand to hand without comment or expression.

> "One of the more shadowy elements of the violent scene here [is] the death squad. Existence of these groups has long been disputed, but not by many Salvadorans. . . . Who constitutes the death squads is yet another difficult question. We do not believe that these squads exist as permanent formations but rather as ad hoc vigilante groups that coalesce according to perceived need. Membership is also uncertain, but in addition to civilians we believe that both on- and off-duty members of the security forces are participants. This was unofficially confirmed by right-wing spokesman Maj. Roberto D'Aubuisson who stated in an interview in early 1981 that security force members utilize the guise of the death squad when a potentially embarrassing or odious task needs to be performed."

> *From the confidential but later declassified January 15, 1982 memo previously cited, drafted for the State Department by the political section at the embassy in San Salvador.*

The dead and pieces of the dead turn up in El Salvador everywhere, every day, as taken for granted as in a nightmare, or a horror movie. Vultures of course suggest the presence of a body. A knot of children on the street suggests the presence of a body. Bodies turn up in the brush of vacant lots, in the garbage thrown down ravines in the richest districts, in public rest rooms, in bus stations. Some are dropped in Lake Ilopango, a few miles east of the city, and wash up near the lakeside cottages and clubs frequented by what remains in San Salvador of the sporting bourgeoisie. Some still turn up at El Playón, the lunar lava field of rotting human flesh visible at one time or another on every television screen in America but characterized in June of 1982 in the *El Salvador News Gazette,* an English-language weekly edited by an American named Mario Rosenthal, as an "uncorroborated story . . . dredged up from the files of leftist propaganda." Others turn up at Puerta del Diablo, above Parque Balboa, a national *Turicentro* described as recently as the April–July 1982 issue of *Aboard TACA,* the magazine provided passengers on the national airline of El Salvador, as "offering excellent subjects for color photography."

I drove up to Puerta del Diablo one morning in June of 1982, past 9
the Casa Presidencial and the camouflaged watch towers and heavy concentrations of troops and arms south of town, on up a narrow road narrowed further by landslides and deep crevices in the roadbed, a drive so insistently premonitory that after a while I began to hope that I would pass Puerta del Diablo without knowing it, just miss it, write it off, turn around and go back. There was however no way of missing it. Puerta del Diablo is a "view site" in an older and distinctly literary tradition, nature as lesson, an immense cleft rock through which half of El Salvador seems framed, a site so romantic and "mystical," so theatrically sacrificial in aspect, that it might be a cosmic parody of nineteenth-century landscape painting. The place presents itself as pathetic fallacy: the sky "broods," the stones "weep," a constant seepage of water weighting the ferns and moss. The foliage is thick and slick with moisture. The only sound is a steady buzz, I believe of cicadas.

Body dumps are seen in El Salvador as a kind of visitors' must-do, 10
difficult but worth the detour. "Of course you have seen El Playón," an aide to President Alvaro Magaña said to me one day, and proceeded to discuss the site geologically, as evidence of the country's geothermal resources. He made no mention of the bodies. I was unsure if he was sounding me out or simply found the geothermal aspect of overriding interest. One difference between El Playón and Puerta del Diablo is that most bodies at El Playón appear to have been killed somewhere else, and then dumped; at Puerta del Diablo the executions are believed to occur in place, at the top, and the bodies

thrown over. Sometimes reporters will speak of wanting to spend the night at Puerta del Diablo, in order to document the actual execution, but at the time I was in Salvador no one had.

The aftermath, the daylight aspect, is well documented. "Nothing 11 fresh today, I hear," an embassy officer said when I mentioned that I had visited Puerta del Diablo. "Were there any on top?" someone else asked. "There were supposed to have been three on top yesterday." The point about whether or not there had been any on top was that usually it was necessary to go down to see bodies. The way down is hard. Slabs of stone, slippery with moss, are set into the vertiginous cliff, and it is down this cliff that one begins the descent to the bodies, or what is left of the bodies, pecked and maggoty masses of flesh, bone, hair. On some days there have been helicopters circling, tracking those making the descent. Other days there have been militia at the top, in the clearing where the road seems to run out, but on the morning I was there the only people on top were a man and a woman and three small children, who played in the wet grass while the woman started and stopped a Toyota pickup. She appeared to be learning how to drive. She drove forward and then back toward the edge, apparently following the man's signals, over and over again.

We did not speak, and it was only later, down the mountain and 12 back in the land of the provisionally living, that it occurred to me that there was a definite question about why a man and a woman might choose a well-known body dump for a driving lesson. This was one of a number of occasions, during the two weeks my husband and I spent in El Salvador, on which I came to understand, in a way I had not understood before, the exact mechanism of terror.

COMPREHENSION

1. What does Didion mean in paragraph 2 when she says that the only logic in El Salvador is "that of acquiescence"?

2. According to Didion, who does most of the killing in El Salvador? What evidence does she present to support this assertion?

3. What special kind of practical information do visitors to El Salvador acquire immediately?

4. What is the "exact mechanism of terror" that Didion mentions in her conclusion?

PURPOSE AND AUDIENCE

1. What dominant impression does Didion create with her description of El Salvador? What does she hope to achieve by including graphic descriptions of atrocities?

2. In paragraph 7 Didion includes the text of a memo drafted by the American embassy in San Salvador. What is her purpose for doing so?

3. Does Didion state her thesis explicitly, or does she imply it? Explain why she chose the strategy she did.

4. Is Didion addressing an audience that she believes knows a lot or a little about conditions in El Salvador? Explain your answer.

STYLE AND STRUCTURE

1. Why does Didion begin with a description of the El Salvador International Airport?

2. Explain what Didion means at the end of paragraph 2 when she says that a visitor immediately learns to concentrate on certain brutal details "to the exclusion of past or future concerns, *as in a prolonged amnesiac fugue.*"

3. Throughout this selection, Didion alternates objective commentary (supported by evidence) with subjective description. What does she achieve with this strategy?

4. Explain Didion's use of the language of a travel guide in paragraph 10, when she describes body dumps as "a kind of visitors' must-do, difficult but worth the detour."

5. In her conclusion, does Didion simply summarize the ideas that she has presented, or does she expand on those ideas? Explain.

VOCABULARY PROJECTS

1. Define each of the following words as it is used in this selection.

   acquiescence (2)   amnesiac (2)   vigilante (7)
   brandished (2)   fugue (2)   bourgeoisie (8)
   dismemberment (2)   obliterated (5)   uncorroborated (8)
   decapitation (2)   laconic (5)   vertiginous (11)

2. Throughout this selection, Didion uses Spanish words and phrases. After identifying these words and phrases, determine why Didion includes them and how she conveys their meaning to her readers.

JOURNAL ENTRY

What message does the situation Didion describes in El Salvador have for those of us who live in the United States? For example, could the drug or gang culture in American inner cities generate "the logic of horror" for people in some neighborhoods?

WRITING WORKSHOP

1. Write an essay in which you describe a place that was frightening to you. As Didion does, vary your subjective account with objective description.

2. Assume that you are a Salvadoran, and write a letter to a relative who lives in the United States, describing conditions in your country. Use information from Didion's essay and from an article that you find in the library that describes conditions in El Salvador in 1982. Include a strong, explicit thesis statement.

3. Go to your college library and consult *The New York Times Index* or *The Readers' Guide to Periodical Literature* to find articles that describe present conditions in El Salvador. Then, write a description of life in El Salvador today.

THEMATIC CONNECTIONS

- "Shooting an Elephant" (p. 96)
- "The Lottery" (p. 272)
- The Declaration of Independence (p. 556)

THE MYSTERY OF
MICKEY MOUSE

John Updike

John Updike was born in 1932 in Shillington, Pennsylvania. After graduating from Harvard University in 1954, he attended the Ruskin School of Drawing and Fine Arts in England for a year and then worked for several years as a staff writer for The New Yorker *magazine, to which he has continued to contribute poems, short stories, essays, and book reviews. Updike is the author of numerous books of poetry, fiction, and criticism. His most recent works include* Collected Poems 1953–1993 *(1993); the short-story collection* Trust Me *(1987); a memoir,* Self-Consciousness *(1989); the essay collections* Just Looking *(1989) and* Odd Jobs *(1991); and two novels,* Memories of the Ford Administration *(1992) and* Brazil *(1994). Updike received Pulitzer Prizes for* Rabbit Is Rich *(1981) and* Rabbit at Rest *(1990), the last two of four novels that chronicle the changes in American society from the 1950s through the 1980s as reflected in the life of a man of Updike's generation. "The Mystery of Mickey Mouse" originally appeared in the magazine* Art & Antiques *in 1991 and was also published as the introduction to* The Art of Mickey Mouse *(1991), a collection of artists' interpretations of the famous cartoon character. In this essay Updike describes Mickey's transformations from his creation in 1927 to his current incarnation in the Walt Disney theme parks.*

It's all in the ears. When Mickey Mouse was born, in 1927, the world of early cartoon animation was filled with two-legged zoomorphic humanoids, whose strange half-black faces were distinguished one from another chiefly by the ears. Felix the Cat had pointed triangular ears and Oswald the Rabbit—Walt Disney's first successful cartoon creation, which he abandoned when his New York distributor, Charles Mintz, attempted to swindle him—had long floppy ears, with a few notches in the end to suggest fur. Disney's Oswald films, and the Alice animations that preceded them, had mice in them, with linear limbs, wiry tails, and ears that are oblong, not yet round. On the way back to California from New York by train, having left Oswald enmeshed for good in the machinations of Mr. Mintz, Walt and his wife Lillian invented another character based—

1

the genesis legend claims—on the tame field mice that used to wander into Disney's old studio in Kansas City. His first thought was to call the mouse Mortimer; Lillian proposed instead the less pretentious name Mickey. Somewhere between Chicago and Los Angeles, the young couple concocted the plot of Mickey's first cartoon short, *Plane Crazy,* costarring Minnie and capitalizing on 1927's Lindbergh craze*. The next short produced by Disney's fledgling studio—which included, besides himself and Lillian, his brother Roy and his old Kansas City associate Ub Iwerks—was *Gallopin' Gaucho,* and introduced a fat and wicked cat who did not yet wear the prosthesis that would give him his name of Pegleg Pete. The third short, *Steamboat Willie,* incorporated that brand-new novelty a sound track, and was released first, in 1928. Mickey Mouse entered history, as the most persistent and pervasive figment of American popular culture in this century.

His ears are two solid black circles, no matter the angle at which 2 he holds his head. Three-dimensional images of Mickey Mouse—toy dolls, or the papier-mâché heads the grotesque Disneyland Mickeys wear—make us uneasy, since the ears inevitably exist edgewise as well as frontally. These ears properly belong not to three-dimensional space but to an ideal realm of notation, of symbolization, of cartoon resilience and indestructibility. In drawings, when Mickey is in profile, one ear is at the back of his head like a spherical ponytail, or like a secondary bubble in a computer-generated Mandelbrot set. We accept it, as we accepted Li'l Abner's hair always being parted on the side facing the viewer. A surreal optical consistency is part of the cartoon world, halfway between our world and the plane of pure signs, of alphabets and trademarks.

In the sixty-four years since Mickey Mouse's image was promul- 3 gated, the ears, though a bit more organically irregular and flexible than the classic 1930s appendages, have not been essentially modified. Many other modifications have, however, overtaken that first crude carton, born of an era of starker stylizations. White gloves, like the gloves worn in minstrel shows, appeared after those first, to cover the black hands. The infantile bare chest and shorts with two buttons were phased out in the forties. The eyes have undergone a number of changes, most drastically in the late thirties, when, some historians mistakenly claim, they acquired pupils. Not so: the old eyes, the black oblongs that acquired a nick of reflection in the sides, *were* the pupils; the eye whites filled the entire space beneath

---

*EDS. NOTE—The American aviator Charles Lindbergh (1902–1974) received worldwide acclaim for making the first solo nonstop transatlantic flight in 1927.

Mickey's cap of black, its widow's peak marking the division between these enormous oculi. This can be seen clearly in the face of the classic Minnie; when she bats her eyelids, their lashed shades cover over the full width of what might be thought to be her brow. But all the old animated animals were built this way from Felix the Cat on; Felix had lower lids, and the Mickey of *Plane Crazy* also. So it was an evolutionary misstep that, beginning in 1938, replaced the shiny black pupils with entire oval eyes, containing pupils of their own. No such mutation has overtaken Pluto, Goofy, or Donald Duck. The change brought Mickey closer to us humans, but also took away something of his vitality, his alertness, his bugeyed cartoon readiness for adventure. It made him less abstract, less iconic, more merely cute and dwarfish. The original Mickey, as he scuttles and bounces through those early animated shorts, was angular and wiry, with much of the impudence and desperation of a true rodent. He was gradually rounded to the proportions of a child, a regression sealed by his fifties manifestation as the genius of the children's television show *The Mickey Mouse Club,* with its live Mouseketeers. Most of the artists who depict Mickey today, though too young to have grown up, as I did, with his old form, have instinctively reverted to it; it is the barechested basic Mickey, with his yellow shoes and oval buttons on his shorts, who is the icon, beside whom his modified later version is a mere mousy trousered pipsqueak.

His first, iconic manifestation had something of Chaplin to it; he was the little guy, just over the border of the respectable. His circular ears, like two minimal cents, bespeak the smallest economic unit, the overlookable democratic man. His name has passed into the language as a byword for the small, the weak—a "Mickey Mouse operation" means an undercapitalized company or minor surgery. Children of my generation—wearing our Mickey Mouse watches, prying pennies from our Mickey Mouse piggy banks (I won one in a third-grade spelling bee, my first intellectual triumph), following his running combat with Pegleg Pete in the daily funnies, going to the local movie-house movies every Saturday afternoon and cheering when his smiling visage burst onto the screen to introduce a cartoon—felt Mickey was one of us, a bridge to the adult world of which Donald Duck was, for all of his childish sailor suit, an irascible, tyrannical member. Mickey didn't seek trouble, and he didn't complain; he rolled with the punches, and surprised himself as much as us when, as in *The Little Tailor,* he showed warrior resourcefulness and won, once again, a blushing kiss from dear, all but identical Minnie. His minimal, decent nature meant that he would yield, in the Disney animated cartoons, the starring role to combative, sputtering Donald Duck and even to Goofy, with his "gawshes" and Gary Cooper*–like gawkiness. But for an occasional comeback like the "Sorcerer's Apprentice" episode of *Fantasia,* and last year's rather souped-up *The Prince and the Pauper,* Mickey was through as a star by 1940. But as with Marilyn Monroe when her career was over, his life as an icon gathered strength. The America that is not symbolized by that imperial Yankee Uncle Sam is symbolized by Mickey Mouse. He is America as it feels to itself— plucky, put-on, inventive, resilient, good-natured, game.

Like America, Mickey has a lot of black blood. This fact was   5 revealed to me in conversation by Saul Steinberg**, who, in attempting to depict the racially mixed reality of New York streets for the supersensitive and race-blind *New Yorker* of the sixties and seventies, hit upon scribbling numerous Mickeys as a way of representing what was jauntily and scruffily and unignorably there. From just the way Mickey swings along in his classic, trademark pose, one three-fingered gloved hand held on high, he is jiving. Along with round black ears and yellow shoes, Mickey has soul. Looking back to such early animations as the early Looney Tunes' Bosko and Honey series (1930–36) and the Arab figures in Disney's own *Mickey in Arabia* of 1932, we see that blacks were drawn much like cartoon animals, with round button noses and great white eyes creating the double arch of the curious peaked skullcaps. Cartoon characters' rubberiness, their jazziness, their cheerful buoyance and idleness, all chimed with popular images of African Americans, earlier embodied in minstrel shows and in Joel Chandler Harris's tales of Uncle Remus, which Disney was to make into an animated feature, *Song of the South,* in 1946.

Up to 1950, animated cartoons, like films in general, contained   6 caricatures of blacks that would be unacceptable now; in fact, *Song of the South* raised objections from the NAACP when it was released. . . . Not even the superb crows section of *Dumbo* would be made now. But there is a sense in which all animated cartoon characters are more or less black. Steven Spielberg's hectic tribute to animation, *Who Framed Roger Rabbit?,* has them all, from the singing trees of Silly Symphonies to Daffy Duck and Woody Woodpecker, living in a Los Angeles ghetto, Toonville. As blacks were second-class citizens with entertaining qualities, so the animated shorts were second-class movies, with unreal actors who mocked

---

*EDS. NOTE—American film actor (1901–1961) known for his roles as a shy, silent, but strong hero in Westerns.

**EDS. NOTE—an artist who has drawn many cover illustrations for the *New Yorker* magazine.

and illuminated from underneath the real world, the live-actor cinema. Of course, even in a ghetto there are class distinctions. Porky Pig and Bugs Bunny have homes that they tend and defend, whereas Mickey started out, like those other raffish stick figures and dancing blots from the twenties, as a free spirit, a wanderer. As Richard Schickel has pointed out, "The locales of his adventures throughout the 1930s ranged from the South Seas to the Alps to the deserts of Africa. He was, at various times, a gaucho, teamster, explorer, swimmer, cowboy, fireman, convict, pioneer, taxi driver, castaway, fisherman, cyclist, Arab, football player, inventor, jockey, storekeeper, camper, sailor, Gulliver*, boxer," and so forth. He was, in short, a rootless vaudevillian who would play any part that the bosses at Disney Studios assigned him. And though the comic strip, which still persists, has fitted him with all of a white man's household comforts and headaches, it is as an unencumbered drifter whistling along on the road of hard knocks, ready for whatever adventure waits at the next turning, that he lives in our minds.

Cartoon characters have soul as Carl Jung defined it in his *Archetypes and the Collective Unconscious:* "soul is a life-giving demon who plays his elfin game above and below human existence." Without the "leaping and twinkling of the soul," Jung says, "man would rot away in his greatest passion, idleness." The Mickey Mouse of the thirties shorts was a whirlwind of activity, with a host of unsuspected skills and a reluctant heroism that rose to every occasion. Like Chaplin and Douglas Fairbanks** and Fred Astaire, he acted out our fantasies of endless nimbleness, of perfect weightlessness. Yet withal, there was nothing aggressive or self-promoting about him, as there was about Popeye. Disney, interviewed in the thirties, said, "Sometimes I've tried to figure out why Mickey appealed to the whole world. Everybody's tried to figure it out. So far as I know, nobody has. He's a pretty nice fellow who never does anybody any harm, who gets into scrapes through no fault of his own, but always manages to come up grinning." This was perhaps Disney's image of himself: for twenty years he did Mickey's voice in the films, and would often say, "There's a lot of the Mouse in me." Mickey was a character created with his own pen, and nurtured on Disney's memories of his mouse-ridden Kansas City studio and of the Missouri farm where his struggling father tried for a time to make

7

*EDS. NOTE—main character in *Gulliver's Travels* (1726) by Jonathan Swift (1667–1745).

**EDS. NOTE—American film actor (1883–1939) who played brave, daredevil characters.

a living. Walt's humble, scrambling beginnings remained embodied in the mouse, whom the Nazis, in a fury against the Mickey-inspired Allied legions (the Allied code word on D-Day was "Mickey Mouse"), called "the most miserable ideal ever revealed . . . mice are dirty."

But was Disney, like Mickey, just "a pretty nice fellow"? He was until crossed in his driving perfectionism, his Napoleonic capacity to marshal men and take risks in the service of an artistic and entrepreneurial vision. He was one of those great Americans, like Edison and Henry Ford, who invented themselves in terms of a new technology. The technology—in Disney's case, film animation—would have been there anyway, but only a few driven men seized the full possibilities and made empires. In the dozen years between *Steamboat Willie* and *Fantasia,* the Disney studios took the art of animation to heights of ambition and accomplishment it would never have reached otherwise, and Disney's personal zeal was the animating force. He created an empire of the mind, and its emperor was Mickey Mouse.

The thirties were Mickey's conquering decade. His image circled the globe. In Africa, tribesmen painfully had tiny mosaic Mickey Mouses inset into their front teeth, and a South African tribe refused to buy soap unless the cakes were embossed with Mickey's image, and a revolt of some native bearers was quelled when the safari masters projected some Mickey Mouse cartoons for them. Nor were the high and mighty immune to Mickey's elemental appeal— King George V and Franklin Roosevelt insisted that all film showings they attended include a dose of Mickey Mouse. But other popular phantoms, like Felix the Cat, have faded, where Mickey has settled into the national collective consciousness. The television program revived him for my children's generation, and the theme parks make him live for my grandchildren's. Yet survival cannot be imposed through weight of publicity; Mickey's persistence springs from something unhyped, something timeless in the image that has allowed it to pass in status from a fad to an icon.

To take a bite out of our imaginations, an icon must be simple. The ears, the wiggly tail, the red shorts, give us a Mickey. Donald Duck and Goofy, Bugs Bunny and Woody Woodpecker are inextricably bound up with the draftsmanship of the artists who make them move and squawk, but Mickey floats free. It was Claes Oldenburg's pop art that first alerted me to the fact that Mickey Mouse had passed out of the realm of commercially generated image into that of artifact. A new Disney gadget, advertised on television, is a camera-like box that spouts bubbles when a key is turned; the key consists of three circles, two mounted on a larger one, and the image is unmistakably Mickey. Like yin and yang, like the Christian cross and the star of Israel, Mickey can be seen everywhere—a sign, a rune, a hieroglyphic trace of a secret power, an electricity we want to plug into. Like totem poles, like African masks, Mickey stands at that intersection of abstraction and representation where magic connects.

Usually cartoon figures do not age, and yet their audience does age, as generation succeeds generation, so that a weight of allusion and sentimental reference increases. To the movie audiences of the early thirties, Mickey Mouse was a piping-voiced live wire, the latest thing in entertainment; by the time of *Fantasia* he was already a sentimental figure, welcomed back. *The Mickey Mouse Club,* with its slightly melancholy pack leader, Jimmie Dodd, created a Mickey more removed and marginal than in his first incarnation. The generation that watched it grew up into the rebels of the sixties, to whom Mickey became camp, a symbol of U.S. cultural fast food, with a touch of the old rodent raffishness. Politically, Walt, stung by the studio strike of 1940, moved to the right, but Mickey remains one of the thirties proletariat, not uncomfortable in the cartoon-rickety, cheerfully verminous crash pads of the counterculture. At the Florida and California theme parks, Mickey manifests himself as a short real person wearing an awkward giant head, costumed as a ringmaster; he is in danger, in these nineties, of seeming not merely venerable kitsch but part of the great trash problem, one more piece of visual litter being moved back and forth by the bulldozers of consumerism.

But never fear, his basic goodness will shine through. Beyond recall, perhaps, is the simple love felt by us of the generation that grew up with him. He was five years my senior and felt like a playmate. I remember crying when the local newspaper, cutting down its comic pages to help us win World War II, eliminated the Mickey Mouse strip. I was old enough, nine or ten, to write an angry letter to the editor. In fact, the strips had been eliminated by the votes of a readership poll, and my indignation and sorrow stemmed from my incredulous realization that not everybody loved Mickey Mouse as I did. In an account of my boyhood written over thirty years ago, "The Dogwood Tree," I find these sentences concerning another boy, a rival: "When we both collected Big Little Books, he outbid me for my supreme find (in the attic of a third boy), the first Mickey Mouse. I can still see that book. I wanted it so badly, its paper tan with age and its drawings done in Disney's primitive style, when Mickey's black chest is naked like a child's and his eyes are two nicked oblongs." And I once tried to write a short story called "A

11

12

Sensation of Mickey Mouse," trying to superimpose on adult experience, as a shiver-inducing revenant, that indescribable childhood sensation—a rubbery taste, a licorice smell, a feeling of supernatural clarity and close-in excitement that Mickey Mouse gave me, and gives me, much dimmed by the years, still. He is a "genius" in the primary dictionary sense of "an attendant spirit," with his vulnerable bare black chest, his touchingly big yellow shoes, the mysterious place at the back of his shorts where his tail came out, the little cleft cushion of a tongue, red as a valentine and glossy as candy, always peeping through the catenary curves of his undiscourageable smile. Not to mention his ears.

COMPREHENSION

1. What does Updike mean in paragraph 1 when he says, referring to Mickey Mouse, "It's all in the ears"?

2. What changes has Mickey undergone since his inception? What does Updike see as the significance of these changes?

3. According to Updike, in what ways does Mickey suggest "the overlookable democratic man" (4)? How does Mickey symbolize the United States?

4. How did cartoons of the 1930s and 1940s depict blacks? In what ways, according to Updike, does Mickey reinforce these stereotypes?

5. What reasons does Updike give for the persistence of the image of Mickey Mouse?

PURPOSE AND AUDIENCE

1. In your own words, state the thesis of this essay.

2. Is Updike's general purpose in writing this essay to express feelings, to present information, or to argue a point? How can you tell?

3. What preconceptions do you think Updike believes his readers have about Mickey Mouse? In what way is his detailed description of Mickey meant to break down these preconceptions?

STYLE AND STRUCTURE

1. Is this essay an objective or a subjective description? What leads you to your conclusion?

2. What strategy does Updike use in his introduction? Can you think of another strategy that would introduce the essay more effectively?

3. Why do you think Updike begins his description of Mickey Mouse with the ears? What organizing scheme does he use? Is it the best scheme for the topic?

4. What words and phrases convey Updike's personal, subjective reactions to Mickey? In what ways do these words help Updike make his point?

5. In his conclusion Updike relates two personal anecdotes concerning Mickey Mouse. What is the point of these stories? How effectively do they end the essay?

VOCABULARY PROJECTS

1. Define each of the following words as it is used in this selection.

zoomorphic (1)	impudence (3)	hieroglyphic (10)
humanoids (1)	manifestation (3)	intersection (10)
enmeshed (1)	pipsqueak (3)	marginal (11)
machinations (1)	undercapitalized (4)	camp (11)
genesis (1)	archetypes (7)	proletariat (11)
pretentious (1)	elfin (7)	verminous (11)
concocted (1)	nimbleness (7)	counterculture (11)
prosthesis (1)	nurtured (7)	incredulous (12)
resilience (2)	embossed (9)	superimpose (12)
spherical (2)	persistence (9)	vulnerable (12)
optical (2)	artifact (10)	
iconic (3)	rune (10)	

2. Choose ten words from the list above and supply a synonym for each word. In what way does the synonym change the meaning of the original word?

JOURNAL ENTRY

What does Updike mean by the statement "Like America, Mickey has a lot of black blood"? How credible is the case he makes in paragraphs 5 and 6 for this assertion? Do you find this section of the essay offensive?

WRITING WORKSHOP

1. Find a picture of an animal in a magazine or a book. Write an objective description of the animal, and then write a subjective description.

2. Who or what do you think symbolizes the United States? Describe this person or thing, making sure your description supports your conclusion.

3. Write an essay in which you describe a popular contemporary cartoon figure (or several figures) with which you are familiar. Include a thesis that attempts to account for the popularity of the figure(s) you describe.

THEMATIC CONNECTIONS

- "Why Mr. Ed Still Talks Good Horse Sense" (p. 198)
- "Television: The Plug-In Drug" (p. 303)
- "Let's Tell the Story of All America's Cultures" (p. 586)

ON SEEING ENGLAND FOR THE FIRST TIME

Jamaica Kincaid

Jamaica Kincaid was born Elaine Potter Richardson in 1949 in St. John's, the capital of the Caribbean island of Antigua, then a British colony. She came to the United States alone in 1966 when she was seventeen. After many odd jobs and one year at Franconia College in New Hampshire, Kincaid began writing. She has been a contributor to The New Yorker *since 1974 and is now a staff writer for the magazine. Her books include three autobiographical works of fiction,* At the Bottom of the River *(1984),* Annie John *(1985), and* Lucy *(1990);* A Small Place *(1988), a nonfiction work about racism and corruption in Antigua; and* Autobiography of My Mother *(1994). In "On Seeing England for the First Time," which was published in the journal* Transition *in 1991, Kincaid describes her difficulty as a child in fitting together in her mind the English culture to which she was exposed at school and the realities of life in the West Indies.*

When I saw England for the first time, I was a child in school 1 sitting at a desk. The England I was looking at was laid out on a map gently, beautifully, delicately, a very special jewel; it lay on a bed of sky blue—the background of the map—its yellow form mysterious, because though it looked like a leg of mutton, it could not really look like anything so familiar as a leg of mutton because it was England—with shadings of pink and green, unlike any shadings of pink and green I had seen before, squiggly veins of red running in every direction. England was a special jewel all right, and only special people got to wear it. The people who got to wear England were English people. They wore it well and they wore it everywhere: in jungles, in deserts, on plains, on top of the highest mountains, on all the oceans, on all the seas, in places where they were not welcome, in places they should not have been. When my teacher had pinned this map up on the blackboard, she said, "This is England"— and she said it with authority, seriousness, and adoration, and we all sat up. It was as if she had said, "This is Jerusalem, the place you will go to when you die but only if you have been good." We understood then—we were meant to understand then—that England was to be our source of myth and the source from which we got our sense of reality, our sense of what was meaningful, our sense of what was meaningless—and much about our own lives and much about the very idea of us headed that last list.

At the time I was a child sitting at my desk seeing England for the first time, I was already very familiar with the greatness of it. Each morning before I left for school, I ate a breakfast of half a grapefruit, an egg, bread and butter and a slice of cheese, and a cup of cocoa; or half a grapefruit, a bowl of oat porridge, bread and butter and a slice of cheese, and a cup of cocoa. The can of cocoa was often left on the table in front of me. It had written on it the name of the company, the year the company was established, and the words "Made in England." Those words, "Made in England," were written on the box the oats came in too. They would also have been written on the box the shoes I was wearing came in; a bolt of gray linen cloth lying on the shelf of a store from which my mother had bought three yards to make the uniform that I was wearing had written along its edge those three words. The shoes I wore were made in England; so were my socks and cotton undergarments and the satin ribbons I wore tied at the end of two plaits of my hair. My father, who might have sat next to me at breakfast, was a carpenter and cabinet maker. The shoes he wore to work would have been made in England, as were his khaki shirt and trousers, his underpants and undershirt, his socks and brown felt hat. Felt was not the proper material from which a hat that was expected to provide shade from the hot sun should be made, but my father must have seen and admired a picture of an Englishman wearing such a hat in England, and this picture that he saw must have been so compelling that it caused him to wear the wrong hat for a hot climate most of his long life. And this hat—a brown felt hat—became so central to his character that it was the first thing he put on in the morning as he stepped out of bed and the last thing he took off before he stepped back into bed at night. As we sat at breakfast a car might go by. The car, a Hillman or a Zephyr, was made in England. The very idea of the meal itself, breakfast, and its substantial quality and quantity was an idea from England; we somehow knew that in England they began the day with this meal called breakfast and a proper breakfast was a big breakfast. No one I knew liked eating so much food so early in the day; it made us feel sleepy, tired. But this breakfast business was Made in England like almost everything else that surrounded us, the exceptions being the sea, the sky, and the air we breathed.

At the time I saw this map—seeing England for the first time—I did not say to myself, "Ah, so that's what it looks like," because there was no longing in me to put a shape to those three words that ran through every part of my life, no matter how small; for me to have had such a longing would have meant that I lived in a certain atmosphere, an atmosphere in which those three words were felt as a burden. But I did not live in such an atmosphere. My father's brown felt hat would develop a hole in its crown, the lining would separate from the hat itself, and six weeks before he thought that he could not be seen wearing it—he was a very vain man—he would order another hat from England. And my mother taught me to eat my food in the English way: the knife in the right hand, the fork in the left, my elbows held still close to my side, the food carefully balanced on my fork and then brought up to my mouth. When I had finally mastered it, I overheard her saying to a friend, "Did you see how nicely she can eat?" But I knew then that I enjoyed my food more when I ate it with my bare hands, and I continued to do so when she wasn't looking. And when my teacher showed us the map, she asked us to study it carefully, because no test we would ever take would be complete without this statement: "Draw a map of England."

I did not know then that the statement "Draw a map of England" 4 was something far worse than a declaration of war, for in fact a flat-out declaration of war would have put me on alert, and again in fact, there was no need for war—I had long ago been conquered. I did not know then that this statement was part of a process that would result in my erasure, not my physical erasure, but my erasure all the same. I did not know then that this statement was meant to make me feel in awe and small whenever I heard the word "England": awe at its existence, small because I was not from it. I did not know very much of anything then—certainly not what a blessing it was that I was unable to draw a map of England correctly.

After that there were many times of seeing England for the first 5 time. I saw England in history. I knew the names of all the kings of England. I knew the names of their children, their wives, their disappointments, their triumphs, the names of people who betrayed them, I knew the dates on which they were born and the dates they died. I knew their conquests and was made to feel glad if I figured in them; I knew their defeats. I knew the details of the year 1066 (the Battle of Hastings, the end of the reign of the Anglo-Saxon kings) before I know the details of the year 1832 (the year slavery was abolished). It wasn't as bad as I make it sound now; it was worse. I did like so much hearing again and again how Alfred the Great, traveling in disguise, had been left to watch cakes, and because he wasn't used to this the cakes got burned, and Alfred burned his hands pulling them out of the fire, and the woman who

had left him to watch the cakes screamed at him. I loved King
Alfred. My grandfather was named after him; his son, my uncle, was
named after King Alfred; my brother is named after King Alfred.
And so there are three people in my family named after a man they
have never met, a man who died over ten centuries ago. The first
view I got of England then was not unlike the first view received by
the person who named my grandfather.

This view, though—the naming of the kings, their deeds, their 6
disappointments—was the vivid view, the forceful view. There were
other views, subtler ones, softer, almost not there—but these were the
ones that made the most lasting impression on me, these were the
ones that made me really feel like nothing. "When morning touched
the sky" was one phrase, for no morning touched the sky where I
lived. The mornings where I lived came on abruptly, with a shock of
heat and loud noises. "Evening approaches" was another, but the
evenings where I lived did not approach; in fact, I had no evening—I
had night and I had day and they came and went in a mechanical
way: on, off; on, off. And then there were gentle mountains and low
blue skies and moors over which people took walks for nothing but
pleasure, when where I lived a walk was an act of labor, a burden,
something only death or the automobile could relieve. And there
were things that a small turn of a head could convey—entire worlds,
whole lives would depend on this thing, a certain turn of a head.
Everyday life could be quite tiring, more tiring than anything I was
told not to do. I was told not to gossip, but they did that all the time.
And they ate so much food, violating another of those rules they
taught me: do not indulge in gluttony. And the foods they ate
actually: if only sometime I could eat cold cuts after theater, cold
cuts of lamb and mint sauce, and Yorkshire pudding and scones, and
clotted cream, and sausages that came from up-country (imagine,
"up-country"). And having troubling thoughts at twilight, a good
time to have troubling thoughts, apparently; and servants who stole
and left in the middle of a crisis, who were born with a limp or some
other kind of deformity, not nourished properly in their mother's
womb (that last part I figured out for myself; the point was, oh to
have an untrustworthy servant); and wonderful cobbled streets onto
which solid front doors opened; and people whose eyes were blue and
who had fair skins and who smelled only of lavender, or sometimes
sweet pea or primrose. And those flowers with those names: del-
phiniums, foxgloves, tulips, daffodils, floribunda, peonies; in bloom,
a striking display, being cut and placed in large glass bowls, crystal,
decorating rooms so large twenty families the size of mine could fit
in comfortably but used only for passing through. And the weather

was so remarkable because the rain fell gently always, only occasionally in deep gusts, and it colored the air various shades of gray, each an appealing shade for a dress to be worn when a portrait was being painted; and when it rained at twilight, wonderful things happened: people bumped into each other unexpectedly and that would lead to all sorts of turns of events—a plot, the mere weather caused plots. I saw that people rushed: they rushed to catch trains, they rushed toward each other and away from each other; they rushed and rushed and rushed. That word: rushed! I did not know what it was to do that. It was too hot to do that, and so I came to envy people who would rush, even though it had no meaning to me to do such a thing. But there they are again. They loved their children; their children were sent to their own rooms as a punishment, rooms larger than my entire house. They were special, everything about them said so, even their clothes; their clothes rustled, swished, soothed. The world was theirs, not mine; everything told me so.

If now as I speak of all this I give the impression of someone on the outside looking in, nose pressed up against a glass window, that is wrong. My nose was pressed up against a glass window all right, but there was an iron vise at the back of my neck forcing my head to stay in place. To avert my gaze was to fall back into something from which I had been rescued, a hole filled with nothing, and that was the word for everything about me, nothing. The reality of my life was conquests, subjugation, humiliation, enforced amnesia. I was forced to forget. Just for instance, this: I lived in a part of St. John's, Antigua, called Ovals. Ovals was made up of five streets, each of them named after a famous English seaman—to be quite frank, an officially sanctioned criminal: Rodney Street (after George Rodney), Nelson Street (after Horatio Nelson), Drake Street (after Francis Drake), Hood Street, and Hawkins Street (after John Hawkins). But John Hawkins was knighted after a trip he made to Africa, opening up a new trade, the slave trade. He was then entitled to wear as his crest a Negro bound with a cord. Every single person living on Hawkins Street was descended from a slave. John Hawkins's ship, the one in which he transported the people he had bought and kidnapped, was called *The Jesus*. He later became the treasurer of the Royal Navy and rear admiral.

Again, the reality of my life, the life I led at the time I was being shown these views of England for the first time, for the second time, for the one-hundred-millionth time, was this: the sun shone with what sometimes seemed to be a deliberate cruelty; we must have done something to deserve that. My dresses did not rustle in the evening air as I strolled to the theater (I had no evening, I had no theater; my dresses were made of a cheap cotton, the weave of which would give way after not too many washings). I got up in the morning, I did my chores (fetched water from the public pipe for my mother, swept the yard), I washed myself, I went to a woman to have my hair combed freshly every day (because before we were allowed into our classroom our teachers would inspect us, and children who had not bathed that day, or had dirt under their fingernails, or whose hair had not been combed anew that day, might not be allowed to attend class). I ate that breakfast. I walked to school. At school we gathered in an auditorium and sang a hymn, "All Things Bright and Beautiful," and looking down on us as we sang were portraits of the Queen of England and her husband; they wore jewels and medals and they smiled. I was a Brownie. At each meeting we would form a little group around a flagpole, and after raising the Union Jack, we would say, "I promise to do my best, to do my duty to God and the Queen, to help other people every day and obey the scouts' law."

Who were these people and why had I never seen them, I mean really seen them, in the place where they lived? I had never been to England. No one I knew had ever been to England, or I should say, no one I knew had ever been and returned to tell me about it. All the people I knew who had gone to England had stayed there. Sometimes they left behind them their small children, never to see them again. England! I had seen England's representatives. I had seen the governor general at the public grounds at a ceremony celebrating the Queen's birthday. I had seen an old princess and I had seen a young princess. They had both been extremely not beautiful, but who of us would have told them that? I had never seen England, really seen it, I had only met a representative, seen a picture, read books, memorized its history. I had never set foot, my own foot, in it. . . . 9

COMPREHENSION

1. Where does Kincaid see England for the first time?

2. Why is England so important to Kincaid and to the people she mentions?

3. What does Kincaid mean when she says, "I did not know then that the statement 'Draw a map of England' was something far worse than a declaration of war . . ." (4)?

4. What were the subtler views that Kincaid mentions in paragraph 6? Why were the impressions these views made the most lasting?

5. In what ways was Kincaid's everyday life different from the English life she read about? Why does she say that to avert her gaze from England was "to fall back into something from which I had been rescued . . ." (7)?

PURPOSE AND AUDIENCE

1. Where does Kincaid state her thesis? What would she have gained or lost had she used an implied thesis?

2. Does Kincaid expect her readers to be sympathetic or unsympathetic with her situation? On what do you base your conclusion?

3. What dominant impression of England do you think Kincaid is trying to create? How successful is she?

STYLE AND STRUCTURE

1. What is the effect of the repetition of the phrase "Made in England" in paragraph 2? How does this repetition reinforce the idea Kincaid is conveying in this paragraph?

2. Identify examples of figurative language in the essay. How do these examples help Kincaid make her point?

3. Underline the topic sentence of each paragraph in the essay. In what way do transitional words and phrases in these topic sentences connect ideas throughout the essay?

4. Why does the introduction begin with the statement, "When I saw England for the first time" and the conclusion contain the statement "I had never been to England"? What has changed?

VOCABULARY PROJECTS

1. Define each of the following words as it is used in this selection.
   mutton (1)   gluttony (6)   Union Jack (8)
   porridge (2)   crest (7)

2. Look up the word *colonialism* in a dictionary. What words does Kincaid use to suggest her attitude toward English colonialism?

JOURNAL ENTRY

Why do you think Kincaid and the other children in Antigua were taught more about England than about their own country?

WRITING WORKSHOP

1. Write an essay in which you describe a place as you saw it for the first time. Be sure to decide in advance whether you are going to write an objective or a subjective description.

2. Did you, like Kincaid, ever feel like someone "on the outside looking in" (7)? Write an essay describing your surroundings and yourself so that you convey the contrast to your readers.

3. Write an essay in which you describe your impressions of a place you always wanted to visit. In your description convey how the place was like and unlike your preconception of it.

THEMATIC CONNECTIONS

- "Just Walk On By" (p. 209)
- "The Civil Rights Movement: What Good Was It?" (p. 315)
- "Aria: A Memoir of a Bilingual Childhood" (p. 401)

THE WAY TO RAINY MOUNTAIN

N. Scott Momaday

N. Scott Momaday was born in 1934 in Lawton, Oklahoma, of Kiowa ancestry. He graduated from the University of New Mexico in 1958 and was awarded a doctorate from Stanford University in 1963. He has taught English at the University of California campuses at Santa Barbara and Berkeley as well as at Stanford, and he currently teaches at the University of Arizona. In 1969 Momaday won a Pulitzer Prize for his first novel, House Made of Dawn *(1968). His second book,* The Way to Rainy Mountain *(1969), is a collection of Kiowa legends and folk tales.* The Names: A Memoir *(1976) describes a personal quest for a Native American identity. Momaday's poetry is collected in* Angle of Geese and Other Poems *(1974) and* The Gourd Dancer *(1976). His most recent books are* The Ancient Child *(1989), a novel in which he shapes an ancient Kiowa myth into a contemporary search for identity, and* In the Presence of the Sun: Stories and Poems, 1961–1991 *(1992). In addition to writing poetry and prose, Momaday is an accomplished artist. He began drawing and painting in 1974 while teaching at the University of Moscow; he has received awards for his art, which has been exhibited in galleries and museums. The following essay is excerpted from the introduction to* The Way to Rainy Mountain, *in which Momaday traces the migration of the Kiowas to Oklahoma.*

A single knoll rises out of the plain in Oklahoma, north and west   1
of the Wichita Range. For my people, the Kiowas, it is an old
landmark, and they gave it the name Rainy Mountain. The hardest
weather in the world is there. Winter brings blizzards, hot tornadic
winds arise in the spring, and in summer the prairie is an anvil's
edge. The grass turns brittle and brown, and it cracks beneath your
feet. There are green belts along the rivers and creeks, linear groves
of hickory and pecan, willow and witch hazel. At a distance in July
or August the steaming foliage seems almost to writhe in fire. Great
green-and-yellow grasshoppers are everywhere in the tall grass,
popping up like corn to sting the flesh, and tortoises crawl about on
the red earth, going nowhere in the plenty of time. Loneliness is an
aspect of the land. All things in the plain are isolate; there is no
confusion of objects in the eye, but *one* hill or *one* tree or *one* man. To

look upon that landscape in the early morning, with the sun at your back, is to lose the sense of proportion. Your imagination comes to life, and this, you think, is where Creation was begun.

I returned to Rainy Mountain in July. My grandmother had died 2 in the spring, and I wanted to be at her grave. She had lived to be very old and at last infirm. Her only living daughter was with her when she died, and I was told that in death her face was that of a child.

I like to think of her as a child. When she was born, the Kiowas 3 were living that last great moment of their history. For more than a hundred years they had controlled the open range from the Smoky Hill River to the Red, from the headwaters of the Canadian to the fork of the Arkansas and Cimarron. In alliance with the Comanches, they had ruled the whole of the southern Plains. War was their sacred business, and they were among the finest horsemen the world has ever known. But warfare for the Kiowas was preeminently a matter of disposition rather than of survival, and they never understood the grim, unrelenting advance of the U.S. Cavalry. When at last, divided and ill-provisioned, they were driven onto the Staked Plains in the cold rains of autumn, they fell into panic. In Palo Duro Canyon they abandoned their crucial stores to pillage and had nothing then but their lives. In order to save themselves, they surrendered to the soldiers at Fort Sill and were imprisoned in the old stone corral that now stands as a military museum. My grandmother was spared the humiliation of those high gray walls by eight or ten years, but she must have known from birth the affliction of defeat, the dark brooding of old warriors.

Her name was Aho, and she belonged to the last culture to evolve 4 in North America. Her forebears came down from the high country in western Montana nearly three centuries ago. They were a mountain people, a mysterious tribe of hunters whose language has never been positively classified in any major group. In the late seventeenth century they began a long migration to the south and east. It was a long journey toward the dawn, and it led to a golden age. Along the way the Kiowas were befriended by the Crows, who gave them the culture and religion of the Plains. They acquired horses, and their ancient nomadic spirit was suddenly free of the ground. They acquired Tai-me, the sacred Sun Dance doll, from that moment the object and symbol of their worship, and so shared in the divinity of the sun. Not least, they acquired the sense of destiny, therefore courage and pride. When they entered upon the southern Plains, they had been transformed. No longer were they slaves to the simple necessity of survival; they were a lordly and dangerous society of fighters and thieves, hunters and priests of the sun. According to their origin myth, they entered the world through a hollow log. From one point of view, their migration was the fruit of an old prophecy, for indeed they emerged from a sunless world.

Although my grandmother lived out her long life in the shadow of 5 Rainy Mountain, the immense landscape of the continental interior lay like memory in her blood. She could tell of the Crows, whom she had never seen, and of the Black Hills, where she had never been. I wanted to see in reality what she had seen more perfectly in the mind's eye, and traveled fifteen hundred miles to begin my pilgrimage.

Yellowstone, it seemed to me, was the top of the world, a region of 6 deep lakes and dark timber, canyons and waterfalls. But, beautiful as it is, one might have the sense of confinement there. The skyline in all directions is close at hand, the high wall of the woods and deep cleavages of shade. There is a perfect freedom in the mountains, but it belongs to the eagle and the elk, the badger and the bear. The Kiowas reckoned their stature by the distance they could see, and they were bent and blind in the wilderness.

Descending eastward, the highland meadows are a stairway to the 7 plain. In July the inland slope of the Rockies is luxuriant with flax and buckwheat, stonecrop and larkspur. The earth unfolds and the limit of the land recedes. Clusters of trees and animals grazing far in the distance cause the vision to reach away and wonder to build upon the mind. The sun follows a longer course in the day, and the sky is immense beyond all comparison. The great billowing clouds that sail upon it are shadows that move upon the grain like water, dividing light. Farther down, in the land of the Crows and Blackfeet, the plain is yellow. Sweet clover takes hold of the hills and bends upon itself to cover and seal the soil. There the Kiowas paused on their way; they had come to the place where they must change their lives. The sun is at home in the plains. Precisely there does it have the certain character of a god. When the Kiowas came to the land of the Crows, they could see the dark lees of the hills at dawn across the Bighorn River, the profusion of light on the grain shelves, the oldest deity ranging after the solstices. Not yet would they veer southward to the caldron of the land that lay below; they must wean their blood from the northern winter and hold the mountains a while longer in their view. They bore Tai-me in procession to the east.

A dark mist lay over the Black Hills, and the land was like iron. 8 At the top of a ridge I caught sight of Devil's Tower upthrust against the gray sky as if in the birth of time the core of the earth had broken through its crust and the motion of the world was begun. There are things in nature that engender an awful quiet in the heart of man; Devil's Tower is one of them. Two centuries ago, because they could not do otherwise, the Kiowas made a legend at the base of the rock. My grandmother said:

> "Eight children were there at play, seven sisters and their brother. Suddenly the boy was struck dumb; he trembled and began to run upon his hands and feet. His fingers became claws, and his body was covered with fur. Directly there was a bear where the boy had been. The sisters were terrified; they ran, and the bear after them. They came to the stump of a great tree, and the tree spoke to them. It bade them climb upon it, and as they did so, it began to rise into the air. The bear came to kill them, but they were just beyond its reach. It reared against the tree and scored the bark all around with its claws. The seven sisters were borne into the sky, and they became the stars of the Big Dipper."

From that moment, and so long as the legend lives, the Kiowas have kinsmen in the night sky. Whatever they were in the mountains, they could be no more. However tenuous their well-being, however much they had suffered and would suffer again, they had found a way out of the wilderness.

My grandmother had a reverence for the sun, a holy regard that 9 now is all but gone out of mankind. There was a wariness in her, and an ancient awe. She was a Christian in her later years, but she had come a long way about, and she never forgot her birthright. As a child she had been to the Sun Dances; she had taken part in those annual rites, and by them she had learned the restoration of her people in the presence of Tai-me. She was about seven when the last Kiowa Sun Dance was held in 1887 on the Washita River above Rainy Mountain Creek. The buffalo were gone. In order to consummate the ancient sacrifice—to impale the head of a buffalo bull upon the medicine tree—a delegation of old men journeyed into Texas, there to beg and barter for an animal from the Goodnight herd. She was ten when the Kiowas came together for the last time as a living Sun Dance culture. They could find no buffalo; they had to hang an old hide from the sacred tree. Before the dance could begin, a company of soldiers rode out from Fort Sill under orders to disperse the tribe. Forbidden without cause the essential act of their faith, having seen the wild herds slaughtered and left to rot upon the ground, the Kiowas backed away forever from the medicine tree. That was July 20, 1890, at the great bend of the Washita. My grandmother was there. Without bitterness, and for as long as she lived, she bore a vision of deicide.

Now that I can have her only in memory, I see my grandmother in 10 the several postures that were peculiar to her: standing at the wood stove on a winter morning and turning meat in a great iron skillet; sitting at the south window, bent above her beadwork, and afterwards, when her vision had failed, looking down for a long time into the fold of her hands; going out upon a cane, very slowly as she did when the weight of age came upon her; praying. I remember her most often at prayer. She made long, rambling prayers out of suffering and hope, having seen many things. I was never sure that I had the right to hear, so exclusive were they of all mere custom and company. The last time I saw her she prayed standing by the side of her bed at night, naked to the waist, the light of a kerosene lamp moving upon her dark skin. Her long, black hair, always drawn and braided in the day, lay upon her shoulders and against her breasts like a shawl. I do not speak Kiowa, and I never understood her prayers, but there was something inherently sad in the sound, some merest hesitation upon the syllables of sorrow. She began in a high and descending pitch, exhausting her breath to silence; then again and again—and always the same intensity of effort, of something that is, and is not, like urgency in the human voice. Transported so in the dancing light among the shadows of her room, she seemed beyond the reach of time. But that was illusion; I think I knew then that I should not see her again.

COMPREHENSION

1. What is the significance of the essay's title?

2. What does Momaday mean when he says that his grandmother was born when the Kiowas were living the "last great moment of their history" (3)?

3. How did meeting the Crows change the Kiowas (3)?

4. What effect did the soldiers have on the religion of the Kiowas?

PURPOSE AND AUDIENCE

1. Is Momaday writing simply to express emotions, or does he have other purposes as well? Explain.

2. What assumptions does Momaday make about his audience? What elements of the essay lead you to your conclusion?

3. Why does Momaday include the legend of Devil's Tower in his essay?

STYLE AND STRUCTURE

1. Why does Momaday begin his essay with a description of Rainy Mountain?

2. What determines the order in which Momaday arranges details in his description of his grandmother?

3. Bracket the narrative passages that Momaday uses in his essay, and explain how they help him describe his grandmother.

4. Why does Momaday end his essay with a description of his grandmother praying?

VOCABULARY PROJECTS

1. Define each of the following words as it is used in this selection.

   infirm (2)   billowing (7)   consummate (9)
   preeminently (3)   profusion (7)   impale (9)
   nomadic (4)   engender (8)   deicide (9)
   luxuriant (7)   tenuous (8)   inherently (10)

2. Find three examples of figurative language in the essay. How do these examples help Momaday convey his impressions to his readers?

JOURNAL ENTRY

Which people in your family connect you to your ethnic or cultural heritage? How do they do so?

WRITING WORKSHOP

1. Write an essay describing a grandparent or any older person who has had a great influence on you. Make sure that you include background information as well as a detailed physical description.

2. Describe a place that has played an important part in your life. Include a narrative passage that conveys its significance to your readers.

3. Describe a ritual—such as a wedding or a confirmation—that you have witnessed or one in which you have participated.

THEMATIC CONNECTIONS

- "Only Daughter" (p. 73)
- "My Mother Never Worked" (p. 85)
- "Aria: A Memoir of a Bilingual Childhood" (p. 401)

ONCE MORE TO THE LAKE

E. B. White

Elwyn Brooks White (1899–1985) was born in Mount Vernon, New York, and graduated from Cornell University in 1921. He joined the newly founded New Yorker *in 1925 and was associated with the magazine until his death. White wrote many editorials, features, and essays for the* New Yorker, *including many of the anonymous "Notes and Comments" that appeared in the "Talk of the Town" section. In 1937 White moved to a farm in North Brooklin, Maine, and began a monthly column for* Harper's Magazine *entitled "One Man's Meat," which revealed a more serious side to his writing than had been evident in the earlier* New Yorker *pieces. His published books include the children's classics* Stuart Little *(1945) and* Charlotte's Web *(1952). His numerous writings are collected in several volumes, including* Every Day Is Saturday *(1934),* Quo Vadimus? *(1939),* One Man's Meat *(1944),* The Second Tree from the Corner *(1954),* The Points of My Compass *(1962),* Letters *(1976),* Essays of E. B. White *(1977), and* Poems and Sketches of E. B. White *(1981). White also revised a grammar handbook by William Strunk, a professor of English at Cornell, that he had used as a student; this handbook,* The Elements of Style *(1959), became a national bestseller. "Once More to the Lake" (1941), reprinted from* One Man's Meat, *is a classic essay of personal reminiscence. Using precise detail and vivid language, White masterfully recreates the lakeside camp he visited with his son.*

One summer, along about 1904, my father rented a camp on a lake 1 in Maine and took us all there for the month of August. We all got ringworm from some kittens and had to rub Pond's Extract on our arms and legs night and morning, and my father rolled over in a canoe with all his clothes on; but outside of that the vacation was a success and from then on none of us ever thought there was any place in the world like that lake in Maine. We returned summer after summer—always on August 1st for one month. I have since become a salt-water man, but sometimes in summer there are days when the restlessness of the tides and the fearful cold of the sea water and the incessant wind which blows across the afternoon and into the evening make me wish for the placidity of a lake in the woods. A few weeks ago this feeling got so strong I bought myself a couple of bass hooks and a spinner and returned to the lake where we used to go, for a week's fishing and to revisit old haunts.

I took along my son, who had never had any fresh water up his   2
nose and who had seen lily pads only from train windows. On the
journey over to the lake I began to wonder what it would be like. I
wondered how time would have marred this unique, this holy spot—
the coves and streams, the hills that the sun set behind, the camps
and the paths behind the camps. I was sure that the tarred road
would have found it out and I wondered in what other ways it would
be desolated. It is strange how much you can remember about places
like that once you allow your mind to return into the grooves which
lead back. You remember one thing, and that suddenly reminds you
of another thing. I guess I remembered clearest of all the early
mornings, when the lake was cool and motionless, remembered how
the bedroom smelled of the lumber it was made of and of the wet
woods whose scent entered through the screen. The partitions in the
camp were thin and did not extend clear to the top of the rooms, and
as I was always the first up I would dress softly so as not to wake the
others, and sneak out into the sweet outdoors and start out in the
canoe, keeping close along the shore in the long shadows of the pines.
I remembered being very careful never to rub my paddle against the
gunwale for fear of disturbing the stillness of the cathedral.

The lake had never been what you would call a wild lake. There   3
were cottages sprinkled around the shores, and it was in farming
country although the shores of the lake were quite heavily wooded.
Some of the cottages were owned by nearby farmers, and you would
live at the shore and eat your meals at the farmhouse. That's what
our family did. But although it wasn't wild, it was a fairly large and
undisturbed lake and there were places in it which, to a child at
least, seemed infinitely remote and primeval.

I was right about the tar: it led to within half a mile of the shore.   4
But when I got back there, with my boy, and we settled into a camp
near a farmhouse and into the kind of summertime I had known, I
could tell that it was going to be pretty much the same as it had been
before—I knew it, lying in bed the first morning, smelling the
bedroom, and hearing the boy sneak quietly out and go off along the
shore in a boat. I began to sustain the illusion that he was I, and
therefore, by simple transposition, that I was my father. This
sensation persisted, kept cropping up all the time we were there. It
was not an entirely new feeling, but in this setting it grew much
stronger. I seemed to be living a dual existence. I would be in the
middle of some simple act, I would be picking up a bait box or laying
down a table fork, or I would be saying something, and suddenly it
would be not I but my father who was saying the words or making
the gesture. It gave me a creepy sensation.

We went fishing the first morning. I felt the same damp moss   5
covering the worms in the bait can, and saw the dragonfly alight on
the tip of my rod as it hovered a few inches from the surface of the
water. It was the arrival of this fly that convinced me beyond any
doubt that everything was as it always had been, that the years
were a mirage and there had been no years. The small waves were
the same, chucking the rowboat under the chin as we fished at
anchor, and the boat was the same boat, the same color green and
the ribs broken in the same places, and under the floor-boards the
same freshwater leavings and débris—the dead helgramite,* the
wisps of moss, the rusty discarded fishhook, the dried blood from
yesterday's catch. We stared silently at the tips of our rods, at the
dragonflies that came and went. I lowered the tip of mine into the
water, tentatively, pensively dislodging the fly, which darted two feet
away, poised, darted two feet back, and came to rest again a little
farther up the rod. There had been no years between the ducking of
this dragonfly and the other one—the one that was part of memory.
I looked at the boy, who was silently watching his fly, and it was my
hands that held his rod, my eyes watching. I felt dizzy and didn't
know which rod I was at the end of.

We caught two bass, hauling them in briskly as though they were   6
mackerel, pulling them over the side of the boat in a businesslike
manner without any landing net, and stunning them with a blow on
the back of the head. When we got back for a swim before lunch, the
lake was exactly where we had left it, the same number of inches
from the dock, and there was only the merest suggestion of a breeze.
This seemed an utterly enchanted sea, this lake you could leave to
its own devices for a few hours and come back to, and find that it had
not stirred, this constant and trustworthy body of water. In the
shallows, the dark, water-soaked sticks and twigs, smooth and old,
were undulating in clusters on the bottom against the clean ribbed
sand, and the track of the mussel was plain. A school of minnows
swam by, each minnow with its small individual shadow, doubling
the attendance, so clear and sharp in the sunlight. Some of the other
campers were in swimming, along the shore, one of them with a cake
of soap, and the water felt thin and clear and unsubstantial. Over
the years there had been this person with the cake of soap, this
cultist, and here he was. There had been no years.

Up to the farmhouse to dinner through the teeming, dusty field,   7
the road under our sneakers was only a two-track road. The middle
track was missing, the one with the marks of the hooves and the

*Eds. note—an insect larva often used as bait.

splotches of dried, flaky manure. There had always been three tracks to choose from in choosing which track to walk in; now the choice was narrowed down to two. For a moment I missed terribly the middle alternative. But the way led past the tennis court, and something about the way it lay there in the sun reassured me; the tape had loosened along the backline, the alleys were green with plantains and other weeds, and the net (installed in June and removed in September) sagged in the dry noon, and the whole place steamed with midday heat and hunger and emptiness. There was a choice of pie for dessert, and one was blueberry and one was apple, and the waitresses were the same country girls, there having been no passage of time, only the illusion of it as in a dropped curtain— the waitresses were still fifteen; their hair had been washed, that was the only difference—they had been to the movies and seen the pretty girls with the clean hair.

Summertime, oh summertime, pattern of life indelible, the fade- 8 proof lake, the woods unshatterable, the pasture with the sweetfern and the juniper forever and ever, summer without end; this was the background, and the life along the shore was the design, the cottages with their innocent and tranquil design, their tiny docks with the flagpole and the American flag floating against the white clouds in the blue sky, the little paths over the roots of the trees leading from camp to camp and the paths leading back to the outhouses and the can of lime for sprinkling, and at the souvenir counters at the store the miniature birch-bark canoes and the post cards that showed things looking a little better than they looked. This was the American family at play, escaping the city heat, wondering whether the newcomers in the camp at the head of the cove were "common" or "nice," wondering whether it was true that the people who drove up for Sunday dinner at the farmhouse were turned away because there wasn't enough chicken.

It seemed to me, as I kept remembering all this, that those times 9 and those summers had been infinitely precious and worth saving. There had been jollity and peace and goodness. The arriving (at the beginning of August) had been so big a business in itself, at the railway station the farm wagon drawn up, the first smell of the pineladen air, the first glimpse of the smiling farmer, and the great importance of the trunks and your father's enormous authority in such matters, and the feel of the wagon under you for the long ten-mile haul, and at the top of the last long hill catching the first view of the lake after eleven months of not seeing this cherished body of water. The shouts and cries of the other campers when they saw you, and the trunks to be unpacked, to give up their rich burden.

(Arriving was less exciting nowadays, when you sneaked up in your car and parked it under a tree near the camp and took out the bags and in five minutes it was all over, no fuss, no loud wonderful fuss about trunks.)

Peace and goodness and jollity. The only thing that was wrong now, really, was the sound of the place, an unfamiliar nervous sound of the outboard motors. This was the note that jarred, the one thing that would sometimes break the illusion and set the years moving. In those other summertimes all motors were inboard; and when they were at a little distance, the noise they made was a sedative, an ingredient of summer sleep. They were one-cylinder and two-cylinder engines, and some were make-and-break and some were jump-spark, but they all made a sleepy sound across the lake. The one-lungers throbbed and fluttered, and the twin-cylinder ones purred and purred, and that was a quiet sound too. But now the campers all had outboards. In the daytime, in the hot mornings, these motors made a petulant, irritable sound; at night, in the still evening when the afterglow lit the water, they whined about one's ears like mosquitoes. My boy loved our rented outboard, and his great desire was to achieve singlehanded mastery over it, and authority, and he soon learned the trick of choking it a little (but not too much), and the adjustment of the needle valve. Watching him I would remember the things you could do with the old one-cylinder engine with the heavy flywheel, how you could have it eating out of your hand if you got really close to it spiritually. Motor boats in those days didn't have clutches, and you would make a landing by shutting off the motor at the proper time and coasting in with a dead rudder. But there was a way of reversing them, if you learned the trick, by cutting the switch and putting it on again exactly on the final dying revolution of the flywheel, so that it would kick back against compression and begin reversing. Approaching a dock in a strong following breeze, it was difficult to slow up sufficiently by the ordinary coasting method, and if a boy felt he had complete mastery over his motor, he was tempted to keep it running beyond its time and then reverse it a few feet from the dock. It took a cool nerve, because if you threw the switch a twentieth of a second too soon you could catch the flywheel when it still had speed enough to go up past center, and the boat would leap ahead, charging bull-fashion at the dock.

We had a good week at the camp. The bass were biting well and the sun shone endlessly, day after day. We would be tired at night and lie down in the accumulated heat of the little bedrooms after the long hot day and the breeze would stir almost imperceptibly outside and the smell of the swamp drift in through the rusty screens. Sleep would come easily and in the morning the red squirrel would be on the roof, tapping out his gay routine. I kept remembering everything, lying in bed in the mornings—the small steamboat that had a long rounded stern like the lip of a Ubangi,* and how quietly she ran on the moonlight sails, when the older boys played their mandolins and the girls sang and we ate doughnuts dipped in sugar, and how sweet the music was on the water in the shining night, and what it had felt like to think about girls then. After breakfast we would go up to the store and the things were in the same place—the minnows in a bottle, the plugs and spinners disarranged and pawed over by the youngsters from the boys' camp, the fig newtons and the Beeman's gum. Outside, the road was tarred and cars stood in front of the store. Inside, all was just as it had always been, except there was more Coca-Cola and not so much Moxie and root beer and birch beer and sarsaparilla. We would walk out with a bottle of pop apiece and sometimes the pop would backfire up our noses and hurt. We explored the streams, quietly, where the turtles slid off the sunny logs and dug their way into the soft bottom; and we lay on the town wharf and fed worms to the tame bass. Everywhere we went I had trouble making out which was I, the one walking at my side, the one walking in my pants.

One afternoon while we were there at that lake a thunderstorm 12 came up. It was like the revival of an old melodrama that I had seen long ago with childish awe. The second-act climax of the drama of the electrical disturbance over a lake in America had not changed in any important respect. This was the big scene, still the big scene. The whole thing was so familiar, the first feeling of oppression and heat and a general air around camp of not wanting to go very far away. In midafternoon (it was all the same) a curious darkening of the sky, and a lull in everything that had made life tick; and then the way the boats suddenly swung the other way at their moorings with the coming of a breeze out of the new quarter, and the premonitory rumble. Then the kettle drum, then the snare, then the bass drum and cymbals, then crackling light against the dark, and the gods grinning and licking their chops in the hills. Afterward the calm, the rain steadily rustling in the calm lake, the return of light and hope and spirits, and the campers running out in joy and relief to go swimming in the rain, their bright cries perpetuating the deathless joke about how they were getting simply drenched, and the children screaming with delight at the new sensation of bathing in the rain,

*EDS. NOTE—an African tribe whose members wear mouth ornaments that stretch their lips into a saucerlike shape.

and the joke about getting drenched linking the generations in a strong indestructible chain. And the comedian who waded in carrying an unbrella.

When the others went swimming my son said he was going in too. 13 He pulled his dripping trunks from the line where they had hung all through the shower, and wrung them out. Languidly, and with no thought of going in, I watched him, his hard little body, skinny and bare, saw him wince slightly as he pulled up around his vitals the small, soggy, icy garment. As he buckled the swollen belt suddenly my groin felt the chill of death.

COMPREHENSION

1. In what ways are the author and his son alike? In what ways are they different? What does White mean when he says, "I seem to be living a dual existence" (4)?

2. In paragraph 5 White says there seemed to be "no years" between past and present; elsewhere, he senses that things are different. How do you account for these conflicting feelings?

3. Why does White feel disconcerted when he discovers that the road to the farmhouse has two tracks, not three? What do you make of his comment that "now the choice was narrowed down to two"?

4. To what is White referring in the last sentence?

PURPOSE AND AUDIENCE

1. What is the thesis of this essay? Is it stated or implied?

2. Does White expect the ending of his essay to be a surprise to his audience? Explain.

3. To what age group do you think this essay would appeal most? Why?

STYLE AND STRUCTURE

1. Why does White begin his essay with a short narrative about his trip to the lake in 1904? How does this opening provide a context for the entire essay?

2. What ideas and images does White repeat throughout his essay? What is the purpose of this repetition?

3. White goes to great lengths to describe how things look feel, smell, taste, and sound. How does this help him achieve his purpose in this essay?

4. In what way does White's conclusion refer back to the first paragraph of the essay?

VOCABULARY PROJECTS

1. Define each of the following words as it is used in this selection.

placidity (1)	pensively (5)	melodrama (12)
gunwale (2)	jollity (9)	premonitory (12)
primeval (3)	petulant (10)	perpetuating (12)
transposition (4)	imperceptibly (11)	languidly (13)

2. Underline ten words in the essay that refer to one of the five senses. Make a list of synonyms you could use for these words. How close do you come to capturing White's meaning?

JOURNAL ENTRY

Do you identify with the father or the son in this essay? Explain why you feel the way you do.

WRITING WORKSHOP

1. Write a description of a scene you remember from your childhood. In your essay discuss how your current view of the scene differs from the view you had when you were a child.

2. Assume that you are a travel agent. Write a description calculated to bring tourists to the lake. Be specific, and stress the benefits that White mentions in his essay.

THEMATIC CONNECTIONS

- "Only Daughter" (p. 73)
- "On Seeing England for the First Time" (p. 146)
- "The Company Man" (p. 507)

THE GRAVE

Katherine Anne Porter

Katherine Anne Porter (1890–1980) was born in Indian Creek, Texas, where she was raised by her paternal grandmother after her mother's death in 1892 and educated in convent schools. Porter worked on newspapers in Texas, Denver, and Chicago before and during World War I and lived for extended periods in Mexico and Europe; later, she did some screenwriting for MGM. She also lectured widely, gave public readings of her work, and succeeded William Faulkner as writer in residence at the University of Virginia in 1958. Her short story collections are Flowering Judas and Other Stories *(1930),* Pale Horse, Pale Rider *(1939), and* The Leaning Tower and Other Stories *(1944). Porter also published a selection of her reviews, essays, and translations in* The Days Before *(1952), and she wrote one novel,* Ship of Fools *(1962). Her* Collected Stories *were published in 1965. In* "The Grave," *published in* The Leaning Tower, *Porter describes a childish afternoon of rabbit-hunting that brings death close enough to be seen and understood.*

The grandfather, dead for more than thirty years, had been twice disturbed in his long repose by the constancy and possessiveness of his widow. She removed his bones first to Louisiana and then to Texas as if she had set out to find her own burial place, knowing well she would never return to the places she had left. In Texas she set up a small cemetery in a corner of her first farm, and as the family connection grew, and oddments of relations came over from Kentucky to settle, it contained at last about twenty graves. After the grandmother's death, part of her land was to be sold for the benefit of certain of her children, and the cemetery happened to lie in the part set aside for sale. It was necessary to take up the bodies and bury them again in the family plot in the big new public cemetery, where the grandmother had been buried. At last her husband was to lie beside her for eternity, as she had planned.

The family cemetery had been a pleasant small neglected garden of tangled rose bushes and ragged cedar trees and cypress, the simple flat stones rising out of uncropped sweet-smelling wild grass. The graves were lying open and empty one burning day when Miranda and her brother Paul, who often went together to hunt rabbits and doves, propped their twenty-two Winchester rifles carefully

168

against the rail fence, climbed over and explored among the graves. She was nine years old and he was twelve.

They peered into the pits all shaped alike with such purposeful accuracy, and looking at each other with pleased adventurous eyes, they said in solemn tones: "These were graves!" trying by words to shape a special, suitable emotion in their minds, but they felt nothing except an agreeable thrill of wonder: they were seeing a new sight, doing something they had not done before. In them both there was also a small disappointment at the entire commonplaceness of the actual spectacle. Even if it had once contained a coffin for years upon years, when the coffin was gone a grave was just a hole in the ground. Miranda leaped into the pit that had held her grandfather's bones. Scratching around aimlessly and pleasurably as any young animal, she scooped up a lump of earth and weighed it in her palm. It had a pleasantly sweet, corrupt smell, being mixed with cedar needles and small leaves, and as the crumbs fell apart, she saw a silver dove no larger than a hazel nut, with spread wings and a neat fan-shaped tail. The breast had a deep round hollow in it. Turning it up to the fierce sunlight, she saw that the inside of the hollow was cut in little whorls. She scrambled out, over the pile of loose earth that had fallen back into one end of the grave, calling to Paul that she had found something, he must guess what . . . His head appeared smiling over the rim of another grave. He waved a closed hand at her. "I've got something too!" They ran to compare treasures, making a game of it, so many guesses each, all wrong, and a final showdown with opened palms. Paul had found a thin wide gold ring carved with intricate flowers and leaves. Miranda was smitten at sight of the ring and wished to have it. Paul seemed more impressed by the dove. They made a trade, with some little bickering. After he had got the dove in his hand, Paul said, "Don't you know what this is? This is a screw head for a *coffin!* . . . I'll bet nobody else in the world has one like this!"

Miranda glanced at it without covetousness. She had the gold ring on her thumb; it fitted perfectly. "Maybe we ought to go now," she said, "maybe one of the niggers'll see us and tell somebody." They knew the land had been sold, the cemetery was no longer theirs, and they felt like trespassers. They climbed back over the fence, slung their rifles loosely under their arms—they had been shooting at targets with various kinds of firearms since they were seven years old—and set out to look for the rabbits and doves or whatever small game might happen along. On these expeditions Miranda always followed at Paul's heels along the path, obeying instructions about handling her gun when going through fences; learning how to stand it up properly so it would not slip and fire unexpectedly; how to wait her time for a shot and not just bang away in the air without looking, spoiling shots for Paul, who really could hit things if given a chance. Now and then, in her excitement at seeing birds whizz up suddenly before her face, or a rabbit leap across her very toes, she lost her head, and almost without sighting she flung her rifle up and pulled the trigger. She hardly ever hit any sort of mark. She had no proper sense of hunting at all. Her brother would be often completely disgusted with her. "You don't care whether you get your bird or not," he said. "That's no way to hunt." Miranda could not understand his indignation. She had seen him smash his hat and yell with fury when he had missed his aim. "What I like about shooting," said Miranda, with exasperating inconsequence, "is pulling the trigger and hearing the noise."

"Then, by golly," said Paul, "whyn't you go back to the range and shoot at bulls-eyes?" 5

"I'd just as soon," said Miranda, "only like this, we walk around more." 6

"Well, you just stay behind and stop spoiling my shots," said Paul, 7 who, when he made a kill, wanted to be certain he had made it. Miranda, who alone brought down a bird once in twenty rounds, always claimed as her own any game they got when they fired at the same moment. It was tiresome and unfair and her brother was sick of it.

"Now, the first dove we see, or the first rabbit, is mine," he told her. 8 "And the next will be yours. Remember that and don't get smarty."

"What about snakes?" asked Miranda idly. "Can I have the first 9 snake?"

Waving her thumb gently and watching her gold ring glitter, 10 Miranda lost interest in shooting. She was wearing her summer roughing outfit: dark blue overalls, a light blue shirt, a hired-man's straw hat, and thick brown sandals. Her brother had the same outfit except his was a sober hickory-nut color. Ordinarily Miranda preferred her overalls to any other dress, though it was making rather a scandal in the countryside, for the year was 1903, and in the back country the law of female decorum had teeth in it. Her father had been criticized for letting his girls dress like boys and go careering around astride barebacked horses. Big sister Maria, the really independent and fearless one, in spite of her rather affected ways, rode at a dead run with only a rope knotted around her horse's nose. It was said the motherless family was running down, with the Grandmother no longer there to hold it together. It was known that she had discriminated against her son Harry in her will, and that he was in straits about money. Some of his old neighbors reflected with vicious satisfaction that now he would probably not be so stiff-necked, nor have any more high-stepping horses either. Miranda knew this, though she could not say how. She had met along the road old women of the kind who smoked corn-cob pipes, who had treated her grandmother with most sincere respect. They slanted their gummy old eyes side-ways at the granddaughter and said, "Ain't you ashamed of yoself, Missy? It's aginst the Scriptures to dress like that. Whut yo Pappy thinkin about?" Miranda, with her powerful social sense, which was like a fine set of antennae radiating from every pore of her skin, would feel ashamed because she knew well it was rude and ill-bred to shock anybody, even bad-tempered old crones, though she had faith in her father's judgment and was perfectly comfortable in the clothes. Her father had said, "They're just what you need, and they'll save your dresses for school . . ." This sounded quite simple and natural to her. She had been brought up in rigorous economy. Wastefulness was vulgar. It was also a sin. These were truths; she had heard them repeated many times and never once disputed.

Now the ring, shining with the serene purity of fine gold on her rather grubby thumb, turned her feelings against her overalls and sockless feet, toes sticking through the thick brown leather straps. She wanted to go back to the farmhouse, take a good cold bath, dust herself with plenty of Maria's violet talcum powder—provided Maria was not present to object, of course—put on the thinnest, most becoming dress she owned, with a big sash, and sit in a wicker chair under the trees . . . These things were not all she wanted, of course; she had vague stirrings of desire for luxury and a grand way of living which could not take precise form in her imagination but were founded on family legend of past wealth and leisure. These immediate comforts were what she could have, and she wanted them at once. She lagged rather far behind Paul, and once she thought of just turning back without a word and going home. She stopped, thinking that Paul would never do that to her, and so she would have to tell him. When a rabbit leaped, she let Paul have it without dispute. He killed it with one shot.   11

When she came up with him, he was already kneeling, examining the wound, the rabbit trailing from his hands. "Right through the head," he said complacently, as if he had aimed for it. He took out his sharp, competent bowie knife and started to skin the body. He did it very cleanly and quickly. Uncle Jimbilly knew how to prepare the skins so that Miranda always had fur coats for her dolls, for though she never cared much for her dolls she liked seeing them in fur coats.   12

The children knelt facing each other over the dead animal. Miranda watched admiringly while her brother stripped the skin away as if he were taking off a glove. The flayed flesh emerged dark scarlet, sleek, firm; Miranda with thumb and finger felt the long fine muscles with the silvery flat strips binding them to the joints. Brother lifted the oddly bloated belly. "Look," he said, in a low amazed voice. "It was going to have young ones."

Very carefully he slit the thin flesh from the center ribs to the flanks, and a scarlet bag appeared. He slit again and pulled the bag open, and there lay a bundle of tiny rabbits, each wrapped in a thin scarlet veil. The brother pulled these off and there they were, dark gray, their wet down lying in minute even ripples, like a baby's head just washed, their unbelievably small delicate ears folded close, their little blind faces almost featureless.   13

Miranda said, "Oh, I want to *see,*" under her breath. She looked and looked—excited but not frightened, for she was accustomed to the sight of animals killed in hunting—filled with pity and astonishment and a kind of shocked delight in the wonderful little creatures for their own sakes, they were so pretty. She touched one of them ever so carefully, "Ah, there's blood running over them," she said and began to tremble without knowing why. Yet she wanted most deeply to see and to know. Having seen, she felt at once as if she had known all along. The very memory of her former ignorance faded, she had always known just this. No one had ever told her anything outright, she had been rather unobservant of the animal life around her because she was so accustomed to animals. They seemed simply disorderly and unaccountably rude in their habits, but altogether natural and not very interesting. Her brother had spoken as if he had known about everything all along. He may have seen all this before. He had never said a word to her, but she knew now a part at least of what he knew. She understood a little of the secret, formless intuitions in her own mind and body, which had been clearing up, taking form, so gradually and so steadily she had not realized that she was learning what she had to know. Paul said cautiously, as if he were talking about something forbidden: "They were just about ready to be born." His voice dropped on the last word. "I know," said Miranda, "like kittens. I know, like babies." She was quietly and terribly agitated, standing again with her rifle under her arm, looking down at the bloody heap. "I don't want the skin," she said, "I won't have it." Paul buried the young rabbits again in their mother's body, wrapped the skin around her, carried her to a clump of sage bushes, and hid her away. He came out again at once   14 and said to Miranda, with an eager friendliness, a confidential tone quite unusual in him, as if he were taking her into an important secret on equal terms: "Listen now. Now you listen to me, and don't ever forget. Don't you ever tell a living soul that you saw this. Don't tell a soul. Don't tell Dad because I'll get into trouble. He'll say I'm leading you into things you ought not to do. He's always saying that. So now don't you go and forget and blab out sometime the way you're always doing . . . Now, that's a secret. Don't you tell."

Miranda never told, she did not even wish to tell anybody. She thought about the whole worrisome affair with confused unhappiness for a few days. Then it sank quietly into her mind and was heaped over by accumulated thousands of impressions, for nearly twenty years. One day she was picking her path among the puddles and crushed refuse of a market street in a strange city of a strange country, when without warning, plain and clear in its true colors as if she looked through a frame upon a scene that had not stirred nor changed since the moment it happened, the episode of that far-off day leaped from its burial place before her mind's eye. She was so reasonlessly horrified she halted suddenly staring, the scene before her eyes dimmed by the vision back of them. An Indian vendor had held up before her a tray of dyed sugar sweets, in the shapes of all kinds of small creatures: birds, baby chicks, baby rabbits, lambs, baby pigs. They were in gay colors and smelled of vanilla, maybe. . . . It was a very hot day and the smell in the market, with its piles of raw flesh and wilting flowers, was like the mingled sweetness and corruption she had smelled that other day in the empty cemetery at home: the day she had remembered always until now vaguely as the time she and her brother had found treasure in the opened graves. Instantly upon this thought the dreadful vision faded, and she saw clearly her brother, whose childhood face she had forgotten, standing again in the blazing sunshine, again twelve years old, a pleased sober smile in his eyes, turning the silver dove over and over in his hands.

THINKING ABOUT LITERATURE

1. What is the significance of the dove? The ring? The rabbit?

2. What is so meaningful about the event described in the story that Miranda remembers it twenty years later?

3. In what way do specific, concrete details contribute to the effect of the story?

JOURNAL ENTRY

In "The Grave" Porter describes how a memory "leaped from its burial place" years later. Write an entry about a childhood incident you remembered and understood only after having forgotten about it for several years.

THEMATIC CONNECTIONS

- "Shooting an Elephant" (p. 96)
- "Once More to the Lake" (p. 160)
- "Samuel" (p. 226)

WRITING ASSIGNMENTS FOR DESCRIPTION

1. Choose a character from a work of fiction or film who you think is truly interesting. Write a descriptive essay in which you demonstrate what makes this character so special.

2. Describe your reaction to a movie, concert, or sports event you have attended. Be certain to include the reactions of the other spectators as well.

3. Locate some photographs of your relatives. Describe three of these pictures, including details that provide insight into the lives of the people you discuss.

4. Visit a local art museum and select a painting that interests you. Study it carefully, and write an essay-length description of it. Make certain that you decide on a scheme of organization in advance.

5. Select an object that you are familiar with, and write an objective description of it. Include a diagram if you wish.

6. Assume that you are writing a letter to someone in another country who knows little about life in the United States. Describe to this person something that is typically American—a video arcade, a baseball stadium, or a shopping mall, for example.

7. Visit your college library, and write an objective description of the reference section. Be specific, and be sure to select an organizing principle before you begin your essay. Your goal is to acquaint students with the reference materials they will use.

8. Describe your neighborhood to a visitor who knows nothing about it. Include as much specific detail as you can.

9. After reconsidering both "Salvador" and "The Grave," write a description of a sight or scene that shocked you. Be sure your description explains why you were so stunned by what you saw.

10. Write an essay in which you describe an especially frightening horror film. What specific sights and sounds made this film so horrifying? Include a thesis that assesses the film's success as a horror film. Be careful to do more than merely recount the plot of the film.

COLLABORATIVE ACTIVITY FOR DESCRIPTION

Working in groups of six students, select a famous person—one you can reasonably expect your classmates to recognize. Then work as a group to write a description of that individual, being careful to include as much physical detail as possible. Give your description a general title—

politician, movie or television star, or person in the news, for example. Finally, have one person read the description aloud to the class, and see whether they can guess the person's identity.

4

Exemplification

WHAT IS EXEMPLIFICATION?

Exemplification uses one or more particular cases, or **examples,** to make a general point specific or an abstract concept concrete. In the following paragraph from *Sexism and Language,* Alleen Pace Nilsen uses a number of well-chosen examples to illustrate and explain her assertion that the armed forces use words that have positive male connotations to encourage recruitment.

<table>
<tr><td>Topic sentence</td><td>The armed forces, particularly the Marines, use the positive masculine connotation as part of their recruitment psychology. They promote the idea that to join the Marines (or the Army, Navy, or Air Force) guarantees that you will become a man. But this brings up a problem, because much of the work that is necessary to keep a large organization running is what is traditionally thought of as woman's work. Now, how can the Marines ask someone who has signed up for a man-sized job to do woman's work? Since they can't, they euphemize and give the jobs titles that are more prestigious or, at least, don't make people</td></tr>
<tr><td>Series of related examples</td><td>think of females. Waitresses are called orderlies, secretaries are called clerk-typists, nurses are called medics, assistants are called adjutants, and cleaning up an area is called policing the area. The same kind of word glorification is used in civilian life to bolster a man's ego when he is doing such tasks as cooking and sewing. For example, a chef has higher prestige than a cook and a tailor has higher prestige than a seamstress.</td></tr>
</table>

You have probably noticed, when watching television talk shows or listening to classroom discussions, that the most interesting and persuasive exchanges take place when those involved illustrate their points with specific examples. It is one thing to say, "The mayor is corrupt and should not be reelected," and another to exemplify his corruption by saying, "The mayor should not be reelected because he has fired two city workers who refused to contribute to his campaign fund, put his family and friends on the city payroll, and used public employees to make improvements on his home." The same principle applies to writing: Many of the most effective and convincing essays use examples extensively. Exemplification is used in every kind of writing situation, either as a basic essay pattern or in combination with other patterns of development, to explain and clarify, to add interest, and to persuade.

Using Examples to Explain and Clarify

On a midterm exam in a film course, you might write, "Even though horror movies seem modern, they really are not." You may think your statement is perfectly clear, but if this is all you say about this idea, you should not be surprised if your exam comes back with a question mark in the margin next to this sentence. After all, you have gone no further than making a general statement or claim about horror movies. It is not specific, nor does it anticipate a reader's questions about the ways in which horror movies are not modern. Furthermore, it includes no examples, your best means of ensuring clarity and avoiding ambiguity. To make sure your audience knows exactly what you mean, you should state your point precisely: "Despite the fact that horror movies seem modern, the two most memorable ones are adaptations of nineteenth-century Gothic novels." Then, you could illustrate your point by discussing these two films, *Frankenstein,* directed by James Whale, and *Dracula,* directed by Todd Browning, and by linking them with the novels on which they are based. With the benefit of these specific examples, a reader would know you meant that the literary roots of such movies are in the past, not that their cinematic techniques or their production methods are dated. Moreover, a reader would know to which literary sources you were referring. With these illustrations, then, your point would be clear.

Using Examples to Add Interest

Well-chosen examples add life to relatively bland or straightforward statements. Laurence J. Peter and Raymond Hull skillfully use this technique in their essay "The Peter Principle," which appears later in this chapter. In itself, their assertion that each employee in a system rises to a level of authority at which he or she is incompetent is not particularly intriguing. It becomes interesting, however, when supported by specific examples, such as the cases of the affable foreman who becomes the indecisive supervisor, the exacting mechanic who becomes the disorganized foreman, and the charismatic battlefield general who becomes the impotent and self-destructive field marshal.

When you use exemplification to support your assertions, look for examples that are interesting as well as pertinent. Test the effectiveness of your examples by putting yourself in your readers' place. If you would not find your own essay lively and absorbing, chances are that neither will your readers. If this is the case, rewrite it, adding more engaging, spirited examples. After all, your goal is to communicate your ideas to your readers, and energetic, imaginative examples can make the difference between an engrossing essay and one that is a chore to read.

Using Examples to Persuade

Although you may use examples simply to explain an idea or to interest or entertain your readers, examples are also an effective way of convincing others that what you are saying is reasonable and worth considering. A few well-chosen examples can eliminate pages of general, and many times unconvincing, explanations. For instance, a statement in response to a question on an economics quiz that adequate health insurance is now out of reach for many Americans needs support to be convincing. Including appropriate examples—such as that in a typical working-class neighborhood one out of every six primary wage earners is now jobless and that most of these unemployed workers can no longer afford health insurance—can help persuade readers that the statement is valid. Similarly, a statement in a biology paper that despite recent moves to revise its status, DDT should continue to be banned, is unconvincing without persuasive examples such as these to support it:

- Although DDT has been banned since December 31, 1972, traces are still being found in the eggs of various fish and waterfowl.
- Certain lakes and streams still cannot be used for sport and recreation because DDT levels are dangerously high, presumably because of farmland runoff.

- DDT has been found in the milk of nursing mothers.
- DDT residues, apparently carried by global air currents, have even been found in meltwater samples from Antarctica.
- Because of its stability as a compound, DDT does not degrade quickly; therefore, existent residues will threaten the environment well into the twenty-first century.

Because examples are so often necessary to convince, you should consider both the quality and the quantity of your examples when deciding which ones to include in an essay. Keep in mind that for examples to work, they should be concrete illustrations of your thesis; otherwise, they are beside the point and thus cannot serve as support.

Using Examples to Test Your Point

Examples can help you test your ideas as well as the ideas of others. For instance, suppose you plan to write a paper for a composition class about the decline in verbal skills of students nationwide. Your tentative thesis is that writing well is an inborn talent and that teachers can do little to help people write better. But is this really true? Has it been true in your own case? To test your point, you go back over your academic career and brainstorm about the various teachers who tried to help you improve your writing.

As you assemble your list, you remember Mrs. Colson, a teacher you had when you were a junior in high school. She was strict, required lots of writing, and seemed to accept nothing less than perfection. At the time neither you nor your classmates liked her; in fact, her nickname was Warden Colson. But looking back, you recall her one-on-one conferences, her organized lessons, and her pointed comments. You also remember her careful review of essay tests and realize that after your year with her, you felt much more comfortable taking such tests. After examining some papers that you saved, you are surprised to see how much your writing actually improved that year. These examples lead you to reevaluate your ideas and revise your tentative thesis. Now, you conclude that even though some people naturally are better writers than others, a good teacher can still make a difference in a person's writing.

Providing Enough Examples

Unfortunately, no general rule exists to tell you how many examples to use to support your ideas. The number you should use depends on your thesis. If, for instance, your thesis is that an educational institution, like a business, needs careful financial management, a detailed examination of your own college or university could work well. This single example could provide all the detail necessary to make your point. In this case, you would not need to include examples from a number of schools. In fact, too many examples could be tedious and undercut your points.

On the other hand, if your thesis were that conflict between sons and fathers is a major theme in the writing of Franz Kafka, several examples would be necessary. A single example would show only that the theme is present in *one* of Kafka's works. In this case, the more examples you include, the more effectively you prove your point. Of course, for some theses even several examples would not be enough. You could not, for instance, demonstrate convincingly through examples alone that children from small families have more successful careers than children from large families. This thesis would have to be supported with a statistical study—that is, by collecting and interpreting numerical data representing a great many examples.

Selecting a sufficient *range* of examples is just as important as choosing an appropriate number. If you wanted to convince a reader that Douglas MacArthur was an able general, you would choose examples from more than just the early part of his career. Likewise, if you wanted to argue that outdoor advertising was ruining the scenic view from local highways, you would discuss an area larger than your immediate neighborhood. Your object in each case is to select a cross section of examples appropriate for the boundaries of your topic.

Lawrence J. Peter and Raymond Hull use a variety of long and short examples to support their points in "The Peter Principle." The use of an assortment of brief examples allows them to present a wide range of examples in a small space. The use of a few examples that are more fully developed allows them to explore certain ideas in depth.

Choosing Representative Examples

Just as professional pollsters take great pains to ensure that their samples actually do reflect the makeup of the group whose opinions they want to determine, you should make sure that your examples fairly represent the group you are discussing. If you want to propose a ban on smoking in all public buildings, you should not choose only the supporting points that illustrate the benefits of such a ban for restaurants. To be convincing, you would have to widen your scope to include other public places, such as government office buildings, hospital lobbies, and movie theaters. For the same reason, one person's experience or one school's problems do not constitute sufficient evidence to support a conclusion about many others unless you can establish that the experience or problems are typical.

If you decide that you cannot cite enough representative examples to support your thesis, reexamine it. Rather than switching to a new topic, you may be able to make your thesis narrower. After all, the only way your paper will be convincing is if your readers believe that your examples and your claim about your topic correspond—that is, that your thesis is supported by your examples and that your examples fairly represent the breadth of your topic.

Of course, to be convincing you must not simply choose examples effectively but *use* them effectively to support your essay's main idea. One way to reinforce the connection between your examples and your thesis is by carefully using transitional words and phrases ("Another example of successful programs for the homeless . . ."). In addition, you should be sure you keep your thesis in mind as you write, taking care that you do not get so involved with one example that you wander off into a digression that is not relevant to your thesis. No matter how carefully developed, no matter how specific, lively, and appropriate they are, your examples accomplish nothing if they do not address your essay's main idea.

STRUCTURING AN EXEMPLIFICATION ESSAY

Exemplification essays usually begin with an *introduction* that includes the thesis statement, which is supported by examples in the body of the essay. Each *body* paragraph may develop a separate example, present a point illustrated by several brief examples, or explore one aspect of a single extended example that is developed throughout the essay. The *conclusion* restates the thesis and reinforces the main idea of the essay. At times, however, variations of this basic pattern are advisable, even necessary. For instance, beginning your paper with a striking example might stimulate your reader's interest and curiosity; ending with one might vividly reinforce your thesis.

Exemplification presents one special organizational problem. In an essay of this type, a large number of examples is not unusual. If these examples are not handled properly, your paper can become a thesis followed by a list or by ten or fifteen very brief, choppy paragraphs. One way to avoid this problem is to select your best examples for full development in separate paragraphs and to discard the others. Another way is to group related examples in paragraphs. Within each paragraph, examples can then be arranged in order of increasing importance or persuasiveness, to allow your audience's interest to build. The following informal outline for a paper evaluating the nursing care at a hospital illustrates one way to arrange examples. Notice how the author groups his examples under four general categories: *private rooms, semiprivate rooms, emergency wards,* and *outpatient clinics.*

Introduction: Thesis statement—The excellent quality of nursing care at Montgomery Hospital can serve as a model for nursing staff at other medical facilities.

Private rooms
   Example 1:   Responsiveness
   Example 2:   Effective rapport
   Example 3:   Good bedside care

Semiprivate rooms
   Example 4:   Efficient use of time
   Example 5:   Small ratio of nurses to patients
   Example 6:   Patient-centered care

Emergency wards
   Example 7:   Adequate staffing
   Example 8:   Nurses circulating among patients in the waiting room
   Example 9:   Satisfactory working relationship between doctors and nurses

Outpatient clinics
   Example 10:   Nurses preparing patients
   Example 11:   Nurses assisting during treatment
   Example 12:   Nurses instructing patients after treatment

Conclusion: Restatement of thesis

STUDENT WRITERS: EXEMPLIFICATION

Exemplification is frequently used in nonacademic writing situations, such as fiscal reports, memos, progress reports, and proposals. One of the more important uses you may make of exemplification is in applying for a job. Elizabeth Bensley's letter of application to a prospective employer follows this pattern of development.

295 Main Street
Mount Kisco, NY 10549
October 3, 1994

Mr. Steven Seltzer
The Wall Street Journal
420 Lexington Avenue
New York, NY 10017

Dear Mr. Seltzer:

Opening   Please consider my application for the position of   1
management trainee that you advertised in the October 1,
1994 edition of the Wall Street Journal. My advisor, Dr.
David Sutton, an editorial consultant to the Journal, has
inspired much of my enthusiasm about my field and about
this opportunity to work in your business office. I am
Thesis   confident that my education and my experience qualify me
statement   to fulfill the responsibilities of this job.

Series of brief   I am currently a senior in the College of Business at Drexel   2
examples   University and will graduate with a degree in management
in June. I have completed courses in accounting, data
processing, economics, management, and communications.
In addition, I have taken a number of computer courses and
have a working knowledge of systems programming.
Throughout my college career, I have maintained a 3.3
average and have been secretary of the Management Society.

Major   Drexel's five-year curriculum includes four work-study   3
example   periods, during which students gain practical experience in
the business world. During my latest work-study period, I
worked in the business office of the Philadelphia Inquirer. I

was responsible for accounts payable and worked closely with a number of people in the accounting department. During my six months in this position, I gained a working knowledge of the IBM Series 370 computer, which recorded charges and payments. Eventually my supervisor, Ms. Nancy Viamonte, put me in charge of training and supervising two other work-study students. While at the <u>Inquirer</u>, I developed a computer program that verified charges and ensured the prompt disposition and payment of accounts.

Closing   I believe that my education and my work experience make   4 me a good candidate for your position. I have enclosed a résumé for your convenience and will be available for an interview any time after October 15. I look forward to meeting with you to discuss my qualifications.

Sincerely,

Elizabeth Bensley

Elizabeth Bensley

Points for Special Attention

Organization.   Exemplification is ideally suited for letters of application. The only way Elizabeth Bensley can persuasively support her claims about her qualifications for the job for which she is applying is to set forth her experience and knowledge. The body of her letter is divided into two categories: educational record and work-study experience. Each of the body paragraphs has a clear purpose and function. Paragraph 2 contains a series of brief examples pertaining to Elizabeth's educational record. Paragraph 3 contains a more fully developed example that deals with her work-study experience. All of these examples are included to tell the prospective employer what qualifies Elizabeth for the job. In her body paragraphs, she uses order of importance to arrange not only her claims but also her examples. Although her academic record is important, in this case it is not as significant to a potential employer as her experience. Because her practical knowledge directly relates to the position she wants, Elizabeth considers this her strongest point and wisely chooses to present it last.

Elizabeth ends her letter with a request for an interview. Here, she not only asserts her willingness to be interviewed but also gives the date after which she will be available. Because people remember best what they read last, a strong conclusion is as essential here as it is in other writing situations.

Persuasive Examples.   To support a thesis convincingly, examples should convey specific information, not just judgments. Saying "I am a good student who works hard at her studies" means very little. It is better to say, as Elizabeth Bensley does, "Throughout my college career, I have maintained a 3.3 average." A letter of application should show a prospective employer how your strengths and background correspond to the employer's needs, and specific examples can help such a reader reach the proper conclusions.

Focus on Revision.   Elizabeth's letter is quite effective, but even so, it could be improved. Although she outlines her experience, Elizabeth could explain how her work at the *Philadelphia Inquirer* makes her useful to the *Wall Street Journal*. She could point out, for example, that her experience in the accounting department at the *Inquirer* would enable her to work either in the accounting department or in collections. In addition, Elizabeth could explain why her training and supervising two work-study students is important. If her purpose is to show that she is able to assume responsibility, she should say so. If it is to illustrate that she has managerial ability, she should make this clear. When she revises her letter, Elizabeth should make certain that the connection between her past experience and the job for which she is applying is clear.

The following essay by Grace Ku illustrates a more academic use of the exemplification pattern. Written for a composition class, it responds to the assignment "Write an essay about the worst job you (or someone you know) ever had."

MIDNIGHT

| Introduction | It was eight o'clock, and like millions of other | 1 |
| | Americans, I was staring at the television set wondering | |

what kind of a lesson Mr. Huxtable was going to teach his children next on The Bill Cosby Show. I was glued to the set like an average eleven-year-old couch potato while leisurely eating a can of cold Chef Boyardee spaghetti in my empty living room. As I watched the show, I gradually fell asleep on the floor fully clothed in a pair of blue jeans and a T-shirt, wondering when my parents would come home. Around midnight I suddenly woke up to a rustling noise when my parents finally arrived from a long day at work. I **Thesis statement** could see in their tired faces the grief and the hardship of working at a dry cleaner.

Transitional paragraph: Provides background They worked in modern times, but in conditions similar to those of eighteenth-century factory workers. Because they were immigrants with little formal education and spoke broken English, only hard, physically demanding jobs were available to them. Therefore, they worked at a dry cleaner that was as big as a factory, a place where smaller cleaners sent their clothes to be cleaned. 2

Series of brief examples: Physical demands My parents had to fulfill certain quotas: Several hundred garments--shirts, pants, and other clothing--had to be cleaned and pressed per day. By themselves, every day, they did an amount of work that should have taken four laborers to complete. The muscles of my mother's shoulders and arms became as firm as iron from working with the press, which is considered a difficult job even for a man. In addition to pressing, my father washed the clothes in the machines, which is the reason a strong odor of oil was permanently embedded in his working clothes. 3

Example: Long hours Not only were my parents' jobs physically demanding, but they also had to work long hours. They went to work at five o'clock in the morning and came home anytime between nine o'clock at night and midnight. They worked over twelve hours daily at the dry cleaner, where the eight- 4 hour work day did not exist. Their only rest was two ten- to twenty-minute breaks--one for lunch and one for dinner. **Example: Frequent burns** They did not stop even when they were burned by the hot press or by the steam rising from it. It was obvious that they worked at a dry cleaner because of the scars on their arms. Their burned skin would blister and later peel off, showing their raw flesh. In time they would heal, but other burns would soon follow.

Example: Low pay Along with having to work overtime without 5 compensation and suffering injuries without treatment, my parents were paid below the minimum wage. These two people who did the work of four laborers together received a paycheck equivalent to that of a single worker. This money was then spent to feed and house a household of five people.

As my parents silently entered our home around 6 **Conclusion** midnight, they did not have to complain about their jobs. I could see their anguish in the wrinkles on their foreheads and their fatigue in the languid movements of their bodies. **Restatement of thesis** Their eyes looked toward me saying, "We hate our jobs, but we have to work in order to survive."

Points for Special Attention

Organization. Grace Ku begins her introduction by describing herself as an eleven-year-old sitting on the floor watching television. At first, her behavior seems typical of many American children, but two things suggest problems: First, she is eating her cold dinner out of a can, and second, even though it is quite late, she is waiting for her parents to return from work. These remarks set the stage for her thesis that her parents' jobs produce only grief and hardship.

In the body of her essay, Grace presents the examples that support her thesis. In the second paragraph she sets the stage for the discussion to follow, explaining that her parents' working conditions are similar to those of eighteenth-century factory workers, and in paragraph 3 she presents a series of related examples that illustrate how physically demanding their jobs are. In the remaining body paragraphs, she gives three other examples to show how unpleasant the jobs are: how long her parents work, how often they are injured, and how little they are paid. Grace concludes her essay by returning to the scene she depicts in her introduction, concluding with a quotation calculated to stay with her readers after they have finished the essay.

Enough Examples. Certainly no single example, no matter how graphic, could adequately support the thesis of this essay. To establish the pain and difficulty her parents' jobs produce, Grace uses several well-chosen examples. Although more examples could have added depth to the essay, the ones she uses are vivid and compelling enough to reinforce her thesis that her parents have to endure great hardship to make a living.

Representative Examples. Grace selects examples that illustrate the full range of her subject. She draws from the daily experience of her parents and does not include examples that seem atypical or that do not fairly represent her parents' situation. She also includes enough detail so that her readers, who she assumes do not know much about working in a dry cleaner, will understand her points. She does not, however, use so much detail that her readers will lose interest or become confused.

Effective Examples. All of Grace's examples support her thesis. While developing these examples, she never loses sight of her main idea; consequently, she does not wander from her topic or get bogged down in irrelevant digressions. She also avoids the temptation to preach to her readers about the injustice of her parents' situation. By allowing her examples to speak for themselves, Grace presents a powerful portrait of her parents and their hardships.

Focus on Revision. In a revised version of this essay, Grace could go into more detail about her parents' situation. She could explain her examples in more depth—perhaps writing about the quotas her parents had to fulfill or the additional physical dangers of their jobs. In addition, she could expand the discussion in paragraph 5 about the low wages her parents receive, perhaps anticipating questions some of her readers might have about working conditions. For example, is it legal for her parents' employer to require them to work overtime without compensation or to pay them less than the minimum wage? If not, how is the employer able to get away with such practices? Grace might also consider moving the information about her parents' work-related injuries from paragraph 4 to paragraph 3, where she discusses the physical demands of their jobs. Finally, she might include comments by her parents to make their experiences more immediate to readers.

The selections that appear in this chapter all depend on exemplification to explain and clarify, to add interest, or to persuade.

THE PETER PRINCIPLE

Laurence J. Peter and Raymond Hull

Laurence J. Peter (1919–1990) was an educator and academic, and Raymond Hull (1919–1985) was a writer and dramatist. Together they wrote The Peter Principle: Why Things Always Go Wrong *(1969), a book that so pointedly analyzes American organizations and the way their social structures foster and reward ineptitude that the term "Peter Principle" has been absorbed into our language. This term refers to Peter's contention that in a hierarchy every employee tends to be promoted to a level at which he or she is incompetent to perform the duties of the position. Peter wrote two sequels,* Why Things Go Wrong: Or the Peter Principle Revisited *(1984), containing anecdotes, historical footnotes, and autobiographical illustrations of the principle; and* The Peter Pyramid: Or, Will We Ever Get the Point? *(1986), using the image of the inverted pyramid to illustrate how most systems start small and grow until they are no longer stable. The following selection, the first chapter of* The Peter Principle, *presents the book's thesis along with several supporting examples.*

When I was a boy I was taught that the men upstairs knew what 1
they were doing. I was told, "Peter, the more you know, the further you go." So I stayed in school until I graduated from college and then went forth into the world clutching firmly these ideas and my new teaching certificate. During the first year of teaching I was upset to find that a number of teachers, school principals, supervisors and superintendents appeared to be unaware of their professional responsibilities and incompetent in executing their duties. For example my principal's main concerns were that all window shades be at the same level, that classrooms should be quiet and that no one step on or near the rose beds. The superintendent's main concerns were that no minority group, no matter how fanatical, should ever be offended and that all official forms be submitted on time. The children's education appeared farthest from the administrator's mind.

At first I thought this was a special weakness of the school system 2
in which I taught so I applied for certification in another province. I filled out the special forms, enclosed the required documents and complied willingly with all the red tape. Several weeks later, back came my application and all the documents!

No, there was nothing wrong with my credentials; the forms were ₃
correctly filled out; an official departmental stamp showed that they
had been received in good order. But an accompanying letter said,
"The new regulations require that such forms cannot be accepted by
the Department of Education unless they have been registered at
the Post Office to ensure safe delivery. Will you please remail the
forms to the Department, making sure to register them this time?"

I began to suspect that the local school system did not have a ₄
monopoly on incompetence.

As I looked further afield, I saw that every organization contained ₅
a number of persons who could not do their jobs.

A UNIVERSAL PHENOMENON

Occupational incompetence is everywhere. Have you noticed it? ₆
Probably we have all noticed it.

We see indecisive politicians posing as resolute statesmen and the ₇
"authoritative source" who blames his misinformation on "situational
imponderables." Limitless are the public servants who are indolent
and insolent; military commanders whose behavioral timidity belies
their dreadnought rhetoric, and governors whose innate servility
prevents their actually governing. In our sophistication, we virtually
shrug aside the immoral cleric, corrupt judge, incoherent attorney,
author who cannot write and English teacher who cannot spell. At
universities we see proclamations authored by administrators whose
own office communications are hopelessly muddled, and droning lectures from inaudible or incomprehensible instructors.

Seeing incompetence at all levels of every hierarchy—political, ₈
legal, educational and industrial—I hypothesized that the cause
was some inherent feature of the rules governing the placement of
employees. Thus began my serious study of the ways in which employees move upward through a hierarchy, and of what happens to
them after promotion.

For my scientific data hundreds of case histories were collected. ₉
Here are three typical examples.

Municipal Government File, Case No. 17. J. S. Minion[1] was ₁₀
a maintenance foreman in the public works department of Excelsior
City. He was a favorite of the senior officials at City Hall. They all
praised his unfailing affability.

"I like Minion," said the superintendent of works. "He has good ₁₁
judgment and is always pleasant and agreeable."

[1] Some names have been changed, in order to protect the guilty.

This behavior was appropriate for Minion's position: he was not   12
supposed to make policy, so he had no need to disagree with his
superiors.

The superintendent of works retired and Minion succeeded him.   13
Minion continued to agree with everyone. He passed to his foreman
every suggestion that came from above. The resulting conflicts in
policy, and the continual changing of plans, soon demoralized the
department. Complaints poured in from the Mayor and other
officials, from taxpayers and from the maintenance-workers' union.

Minion still says "Yes" to everyone, and carries messages briskly   14
back and forth between his superiors and his subordinates. Nomi-
nally a superintendent, he actually does the work of a messenger.
The maintenance department regularly exceeds its budget, yet fails
to fulfill its program of work. In short, Minion, a competent foreman,
became an incompetent superintendent.

Service Industries File, Case No. 3.   E. Tinker was excep-   15
tionally zealous and intelligent as an apprentice at G. Reece Auto
Repair Inc., and soon rose to journeyman mechanic. In this job he
showed outstanding ability in diagnosing obscure faults, and endless patience in correcting them. He was promoted to foreman of the
repair shop.

But here his love of things mechanical and his perfectionism be-   16
came liabilities. He will undertake any job that he thinks looks
interesting, no matter how busy the shop may be. "We'll work it in
somehow," he says.

He will not let a job go until he is fully satisfied with it.   17

He meddles constantly. He is seldom to be found at his desk. He is   18
usually up to his elbows in a dismantled motor and while the man
who should be doing the work stands watching, other workmen sit
around waiting to be assigned new tasks. As a result the shop is
always overcrowded with work, always in a muddle, and delivery
times are often missed.

Tinker cannot understand that the average customer cares little   19
about perfection—he wants his car back on time! He cannot understand that most of his men are less interested in motors than in
their pay checks. So Tinker cannot get on with his customers or with
his subordinates. He was a competent mechanic, but is now an
incompetent foreman.

Military File, Case No. 8.   Consider the case of the late re-   20
nowned General A. Goodwin. His hearty, informal manner, his racy
style of speech, his scorn for petty regulations and his undoubted

personal bravery made him the idol of his men. He led them to many well-deserved victories.

When Goodwin was promoted to field marshal he had to deal, not   21
with ordinary soldiers, but with politicians and allied generalissimos.

He would not conform to the necessary protocol. He could not turn   22
his tongue to the conventional courtesies and flatteries. He quar-
reled with all the dignitaries and took to lying for days at a time,
drunk and sulking, in his trailer. The conduct of the war slipped out
of his hands into those of his subordinates. He had been promoted to
a position that he was incompetent to fill.

AN IMPORTANT CLUE!

In time I saw that all such cases had a common feature. The em-   23
ployee had been promoted from a position of competence to a position
of incompetence. I saw that, sooner or later, this could happen to
every employee in every hierarchy.

Hypothetical Case File, Case No. 1. Suppose you own a pill-   24
rolling factory, Perfect Pill Incorporated. Your foreman pill roller dies
of a perforated ulcer. You need a replacement. You naturally look
among your rank-and-file pill rollers.

Miss Oval, Mrs. Cylinder, Mr. Ellipse and Mr. Cube all show   25
various degrees of incompetence. They will naturally be ineligible
for promotion. You will choose—other things being equal—your
most competent pill roller, Mr. Sphere, and promote him to foreman.

Now suppose Mr. Sphere proves competent as foreman. Later,   26
when your general foreman, Legree, moves up to Works Manager,
Sphere will be eligible to take his place.

If, on the other hand, Sphere is an incompetent foreman, he will   27
get no more promotion. He has reached what I call his "level of
incompetence." He will stay there till the end of his career.

Some employees, like Ellipse and Cube, reach a level of incom-   28
petence in the lowest grade and are never promoted. Some, like
Sphere (assuming he is not a satisfactory foreman), reach it after
one promotion.

E. Tinker, the automobile repair-shop foreman, reached his level of   29
incompetence on the third stage of the hierarchy. General Goodwin
reached his level of incompetence at the very top of the hierarchy.

So my analysis of hundreds of cases of occupational incompetence   30
led me on to formulate *The Peter Principle:*

*In a Hierarchy Every Employee Tends
to Rise to His Level of Incompetence*

A NEW SCIENCE!

Having formulated the Principle, I discovered that I had inadvert- 31
ently founded a new science, hierarchiology, the study of hierarchies.

The term "hierarchy" was originally used to describe the system of 32
church government by priests graded into ranks. The contemporary
meaning includes any organization whose members or employees
are arranged in order of rank, grade or class.

Hierarchiology, although a relatively recent discipline, appears 33
to have great applicability to the fields of public and private
administration.

THIS MEANS YOU!

My Principle is the key to an understanding of all hierarchal 34
systems, and therefore to an understanding of the whole structure of
civilization. A few eccentrics try to avoid getting involved with
hierarchies, but everyone in business, industry, trade-unionism,
politics, government, the armed forces, religion and education is so
involved. All of them are controlled by the Peter Principle.

Many of them, to be sure, may win a promotion or two, moving 35
from one level of competence to a higher level of competence. But
competence in that new position qualifies them for still another
promotion. For each individual, for *you,* for *me,* the final promotion
is from a level of competence to a level of incompetence.[2]

So, given enough time—and assuming the existence of enough 36
ranks in the hierarchy—each employee rises to, and remains at, his
level of incompetence. Peter's Corollary states:

> *In time, every post tends to be occupied by an employee who is incom-* 37
> *petent to carry out its duties.*

WHO TURNS THE WHEELS?

You will rarely find, of course, a system in which *every* employee 38
has reached his level of incompetence. In most instances, something
is being done to further the ostensible purposes for which the hierarchy exists.

> *Work is accomplished by those employees who have not yet reached* 39
> *their level of incompetence.*

[2]The phenomena of "percussive sublimation" (commonly referred to as "being
kicked upstairs") and of "the lateral arabesque" are not, as the casual observer might
think, exceptions to the Principle. They are only pseudo-promotions. . . .

COMPREHENSION

1. What things disillusioned Peter during his first year of teaching? What did he find out about organizations?

2. What is the Peter Principle? What happens when an employee reaches his "level of incompetence?"

3. What do Peter and Hull mean by *hierarchiology?* How did hierarchiology lead Peter to the Peter Principle?

4. If the Peter Principle operates in hierarchies, who does the work?

PURPOSE AND AUDIENCE

1. Is this essay aimed at a general or an expert audience? What led you to your conclusion?

2. What is the essay's thesis? Why do the authors wait so long to state it?

3. How serious are the authors? What words or phrases indicate whether their purpose is humorous or serious—or both?

STYLE AND STRUCTURE

1. Why do the authors begin the essay with an example? Why do they present a series of brief examples before introducing the "typical case histories"?

2. Why do Peter and Hull say they collected hundreds of case histories for data? Why are the three case histories analyzed here typical?

3. Does the reliance on hypothetical examples strengthen or weaken the authors' case? Explain.

4. Do the authors use a sufficient range of examples? Explain.

VOCABULARY PROJECTS

1. Define each of the following words as it is used in this selection.

imponderables (7)	incomprehensible (7)	protocol (22)
indolent (7)	hypothesized (8)	subordinates (22)
insolent (7)	hierarchy (8)	eccentrics (34)
dreadnought (7)	minion (10)	ostensible (38)
inaudible (7)	dismantled (18)	

2. Do the authors use figures of speech in their discussion? Why do you think they do or do not?

JOURNAL ENTRY

What examples of the Peter Principle have you encountered in your life?

WRITING WORKSHOP

1. Do Peter and Hull overstate their case? Write a letter to them in the form of an exemplification essay pointing out the weaknesses of their position.

2. Study a school, business, or organization with which you are familiar. Write an exemplification essay showing how the Peter Principle applies.

3. Do you know someone who has progressed to the highest level of his or her incompetence? Write an exemplification essay showing how the Peter Principle applies.

THEMATIC CONNECTIONS

- "Shooting an Elephant" (p. 96)
- "The Company Man" (p. 507)
- "The Catbird Seat" (p. 522)

WHY MR. ED STILL TALKS GOOD HORSE SENSE

Michael Dorris

*Michael Dorris was born in Dayton, Washington, in 1945, gradu-
ated from Georgetown University in 1967, and received his master's
degree from Yale University in 1970. In 1972 Dorris, a member of
the Modoc tribe through his father, began teaching anthropology
and Native American studies at Dartmouth College, where he is
currently an adjunct professor. He has also taught at the University
of New Hampshire and the University of Auckland in New Zealand.
Dorris is the author of several books on Native Americans, including*
The Broken Cord *(1989), an examination of fetal alcohol syndrome
which is based on the life of Dorris's adopted Native American son
and was named the best nonfiction book of 1989 by the National
Book Critics Circle. Dorris's most recent works are* The Crown of
Columbus *(1991), a novel written with his wife, the poet and
novelist Louise Erdrich;* Morning Girl *(1992), a children's novel;*
Rooms in the House of Stone *(1993), a collection of essays; and*
Working Men *(1993), a collection of short stories. "Why Mister Ed
Still Talks Good Horse Sense," published in* TV Guide *in 1988, suggests that cultural values are passed on to new generations through
cartoons and television characters in much the same way as they are
through myths, fables, and fairy tales.*

The sun is descending. The pale, enlarged shadow of the moon 1
hangs low in the violet sky. Work for the day is done, and soon the
family will consume the evening meal. It is an hour when children
gather hushed before the storyteller to hear the very words their
parents heard before them, at the same age, at the same time of day
and in the same place. The light flickers, casting images that catch
and lodge in the memory, and the ageless tales unfold—tales that
entertain, tales that resonate with particular significance according
to the listener's age and level of accomplishment, tales in which good
ultimately triumphs over evil, tales that in subtle but important
ways underlie and support the society's values of cooperation,
competition and fair play.

"M-I-C," the opening chant intones, "K-E-Y M-O-U-S-E." 2

We Americans are tempted to distinguish ourselves from other 3
current and former inhabitants of this planet by assuming that we

198

are ruled by "progress." Last year's passion, in clothing style, music, literature or food, instantly fades before the latest trend. National magazines inform us that yuppies will soon be consigned to the same scrapbook as hippies and flappers, and we seek to dispose of rather than recycle everything from diapers to slang. Newness is interesting, exciting, full of promise. Old is, well, used.

When we think of non-Western societies, we often imagine that they are different, bound to boring repetitions of tradition, with each generation replicating the lives of its parents. As they are depicted in popular media, tribal societies appear static, frozen in the past, remote and forbidding.

Anthropologists report that some nonliterate peoples go so far as to preserve an archaic version of their language exclusively for the education of their young, guarding against the slightest syllabic alteration lest something precious in the ancient wisdom be lost forever. Since there are no libraries, no videocassette archives in which to store excess knowledge, information must be compressed, packaged in an easily transmitted dramatic format and passed on. Only the most streamlined, most universally understandable stories survive—"the girl who brought light to the world," "the boy who found fire"—and they, in time, become myth.

Yet are we really so different? This thought occurred to me recently as I sat on the couch reading the newspaper while my two youngest daughters, Persia, 4, and Pallas, 3, waited for their favorite program to appear on the Disney cable-television channel. Promptly at 4 o'clock the familiar fanfare of *The Mickey Mouse Club* anthem began, and I found myself humming along. Thirty years had passed for me, but as if out of a time warp danced Jimmie and Bobby and Doreen and Annette and especially (sigh) Darlene. They were wholesome, enthusiastic, brimming with the excitement of being child stars, the envy of hundreds of thousands of other baby boomers, before we acquired the name. "As we continue through the years/We won't forget the Mouseketeers," they promised, and they were right. They introduced Spin and Marty, still embroiled in the adventures of their dude-ranch camp; they talked earnestly about their hobbies, their ambitions for the future; and then, their voices reverential and serious, they adjourned with song "the club that's made for you and me."

Of course time does count for something. I *know* what happened to Annette's career, for instance—a few hit records, a few beach movies, then peanut butter commercials; yet that didn't detract from my nostalgia for the youthful exuberance she and the others projected. For me the show was a bridge, a visit to an uncomplicated era when

I was not forced to worry about income taxes and Government deficit spending, before I knew enough to realize that there should have been minority mousketeers, before terrorists and AIDS and anxiety over the danger of nuclear war.

But for Persia and Pallas, Cubby and Karen and the gang were 8 absolute contemporaries, children whom they could, as I used to do, measure themselves against, imitate and critique. So familiar was my daughters' conversation, so similar to one I probably had with my cousin Frank after watching the identical program, also at 4 o'clock, in the 1950s, that it was almost as if I remembered rather than overheard their remarks.

And we weren't over yet. Before dinner, with the magic of a sat- 9 ellite dish and a limitless variety of stations from which to choose, we aimed at the point in space where at 4:30 Lassie still barks instructions at obtuse human beings.

"Just wait," I advised my girls, like some wizened prophet or witch 10 doctor. "One of these days Jeff is going to disappear and Lassie will belong to a new little boy named Timmy." They looked skeptical, so I didn't tell them about the eventual forest ranger. Let them be surprised.

Mister Ed still talks good horse sense. Samantha can still clean a 11 messy kitchen with the twitch of her nose (and Darrin still, maddeningly, irrationally, doesn't want her to). Mighty Mouse still saves the day.

One definition of cultural continuity might be that each generation 12 participates during its childhood in a comparable learning process and then retains and reinterprets those lessons throughout a lifetime. As our perspective matures we peel away layers of meaning, enjoying the same tales at a greater moral depth and intellectual complexity. The specifics may change—a calculator may replace the abacus and the map of the world may display more or less color as the boundaries of nations are altered—but within the context of a healthy society some concepts must remain core. The necessity of loyalty between friends, the responsibility that the strong owe the infirm, the illusion of ill-gotten gain, the rewards of hard work, honesty and trust—these are enduring truths glimpsed and judged first through the imagination, first through art.

And whether these values are initially transmitted by a tribal 13 elder reciting fables around the fire, by parents reading their favorite fairy tales to their offspring before bedtime, or by Persia, Pallas and me donning mouseka-ears together for half an hour, the result is what matters: each method creates a shared set of formative impressions, a common cultural shorthand that collapses the barriers of time and experience, a bond that permits old and young to harmoniously inhabit, however temporarily, the same world.

COMPREHENSION

1. What function does Dorris say tales and myths serve in a society?

2. According to Dorris, how do Americans attempt to distinguish themselves from non-Western societies?

3. Dorris and his children experience *The Mickey Mouse Club* in different ways. Explain.

4. In what sense, according to Dorris, does television serve the same function in our society as the storyteller does in a non-Western society?

PURPOSE AND AUDIENCE

1. What is the thesis of this essay?

2. Does Dorris assume his readers will be familiar with the shows he discusses? With non-Western myths? How can you tell?

3. What preconceptions does Dorris expect his readers to have about television reruns? Does he attempt to reinforce or undercut these preconceptions?

STYLE AND STRUCTURE

1. In what way does Dorris attempt to create interest in his introduction? Is he successful?

2. Does Dorris use enough examples to support his thesis? Would additional examples have added to or detracted from the essay?

3. Do you think Dorris should have developed the examples he mentioned in paragraphs 9–11 in more depth? Explain.

4. Dorris has one style—concrete and informal—when he talks about television programs and another—abstract and academic—when he talks about anthropology. Is this inconsistency a problem? Explain.

5. What points does Dorris reinforce in his conclusion? Do you think he should have mentioned any other points?

VOCABULARY PROJECTS

1. Define each of the following words as it is used in this selection.

intones (2)	reverential (6)	irrationally (11)
replicating (4)	detract (7)	continuity (12)
anthropologists (5)	exuberance (7)	enduring (12)
syllabic (5)	critique (8)	formative (13)
baby boomers (6)	skeptical (10)	

2. What exactly does Dorris mean by the phrase *horse sense?*

JOURNAL ENTRY

What other examples of classic television shows could Dorris use to support his thesis? Why is each suitable?

WRITING WORKSHOP

1. Write an essay in which you discuss the importance of reruns. Which are your favorites, and why?

2. Write an exemplification essay in which you draw from your own experience to dispute the author's assertion that reruns, like old tribal tales, teach enduring values.

3. Use a single extended example—a single episode of your favorite contemporary television show—to support the thesis that television programs teach important values.

THEMATIC CONNECTIONS

- "The Mystery of Mickey Mouse" (p. 136)
- "The Way to Rainy Mountain" (p. 154)
- "Television: The Plug-In Drug" (p. 303)

THE SAME DIFFERENCE

Amy Wang

Amy Wang was born in 1969 in Pittsburgh to parents who had come to the United States from Taiwan two years earlier. She graduated from Cornell University in 1990 and received her master's degree from Columbia University's journalism school in 1993. Wang is currently a copy editor at the Philadelphia Inquirer. *In this personal essay, published in the* Inquirer's Sunday *magazine in 1993, she looks at the difference race makes in the way she is treated and the way she treats others.*

It was on my way home that the moment of truth swept by—again.

There we were, a friend and I, heading north on the Pennsylvania Turnpike to central New York to visit my parents. Somehow our conversation had parted the curtains before my childhood memories, and before I knew it, I was telling him about an incident I have never quite forgotten.

As I spoke, it was almost as if my adult self were back in Pittsburgh, watching; strange how in my memory the sun is always glinting through a bright haze on that day. The trees are bare, or nearly so, with dark branches that reach out to splinter the sun's rays. I am walking alone, down a white concrete sidewalk littered with leaves, twigs, buckeyes. School is out for the day, and everyone is going home.

From behind come shouts, and I turn to see a group of children from school. A moment passes, and I realize they are shouting at me. I listen for several seconds before the words whip into clarity:

Chink! Hey, chink! Chinky chinky chink!

They are running. I am frozen, my heart the only part of me moving, and it is pounding. Then one of them stoops, picks up a twig and hurls it at me. It lands short, a foot away on the sidewalk. Then I turn, still blocks from home, and run. The twigs keep coming, clattering close behind as the others shout and follow. As I run, I think of the steep steps to the front door and despair.

But when I reach the steps and turn around, only silence follows. And when my mother answers the doorbell's ring, she sees only her daughter, cheeks a little flushed, waiting to be let in. Almost instinctively, I know I must not tell her. It would only hurt her, and there is nothing she can do. Besides, it is nothing I want to discuss.

"Wow," he said. "And you were in sixth grade when this happened?" 8

"Six," I said. "I was 6 when this happened. I was in first grade." 9

He was clearly appalled, his eyes in far focus as he tried to 10
understand how such a thing could happen to a small child. I was concentrating on the road, but even a sidelong glance showed he did not, could not, quite understand. And it was then that I felt the familiar stab of disappointment: the realization that no matter how long we traveled together, we would always be on parallel roads, moving on either side of a great divide. I would never know his assurance as he made his way through a world where his skin color was an assumption, and he would never know my anxiety as I made my way through a world where my skin color was an anguish.

We were silent, and after a while he fell asleep. "Wake me up when 11
we get to Allentown," he had said as he drifted off, and we both smiled, remembering a classmate who had once padded an expense account for profit by driving from New York to Allentown and back twice in two days.

The thought of the old mill town triggered memories of another 12
old mill town, where I had gotten my first job out of college. It was at the local newspaper, working nights on the copy desk. Our shifts ended at 1 A.M., and I often drove home through deserted streets, the hush broken only by the whir of an occasional street-cleaning machine or the clanking of a distant garbage truck. The other drivers on the streets at that hour seemed just as weary, just as intent on getting to bed.

In such an atmosphere I often dream, and so to this day a 13
shadowy, slowed-down quality suffuses the memory of turning my head and looking out the side window one night just in time to see an old red Dodge draw up in the next lane at a traffic light. Inside, four young white crewcut men dressed in denim and flannel strain toward me, their faces distorted with hate, their mouths twisted with invective. Our windows are closed, so I am spared their actual words, but their frenzied pantomime leaves little to be imagined.

When the light turns green I pull away hastily, but they cruise 14
alongside for the next few blocks. By the time they tire of me and swing into a left turn, I am seething with fear and rage. I wait until they are committed to the turn, then raise my middle finger. One of them looks back for a final insult, sees my gesture, and gapes—but only for a moment. He turns, and I know he is screaming at the driver to turn back. I gun it.

They never come after me, and I make it home alive. Numb, I   15
crawl into bed. It is only after I lie down that I realize how they
might have hurt me, the four of them with their huge Dodge against
my tiny Nissan, and I begin to shake. As my mind tumbles, the
phone rings. For a moment I think it is them, and then logic returns.
I answer, and it is my boyfriend, calling from Boston. I tell him what
happened, melting into tears. He is sympathetic, but then he asks:
"How do you know they weren't yelling at you because you were a
woman?"

I don't, of course, but that is not the point. His whiteness rushes   16
through the line with the very question. "It doesn't matter," I tell
him, and suddenly I can't stand to hear his voice. I tell him I don't
want to discuss it anymore, and hang up.

Somewhere along Route 79 in New York he said, "This is beauti-   17
ful." I smiled, remembering the years I spent in Finger Lakes
country: middle school, high school, college. Here were trees I had
climbed, hills I had sledded down, malls I knew by heart; here were
roads that led to memories and people who knew my history.

And it was because I had to come back here that another He was   18
able to betray me. It was during the first summer I spent away from
home, working at a magazine in New York. Picture now a pavilion on
the grounds of a quiet country club where the staff is enjoying the
annual company picnic, and there I am by the jukebox, hovering
over the glassed-in 45s as a light mist dampens the grass. As The
Contours wail "Do You Love Me," I sway to the beat, attracting a
stranger's eyes. In a moment he is introducing himself; in an hour he
is sitting by me in the bus taking us back to the city; in a week he is
asking me out to dinner.

I am no longer thinking clearly. On my last day at the magazine,   19
he watches as I clean out my desk, then asks me, in a low but urgent
tone, not to forget him. He tells me he wants my address, and a
sudden foreboding chill nearly stuns me with its iciness, sending
shivers through my hand as I write out the address and phone
number. Then I ask for his address and phone number. I do not think
to ask him not to forget me.

Weeks go by without a word, and then one night, I know. The chill   20
comes back: For days I hate white men, all of them, they all bear the
blame for his misdeed. But I have known too many good ones for my
fury to last, and finally I am forced to admit that I have been a fool,
and that this time, at least, it had nothing to do with race.

"It could have happened to anyone," a (white male) friend tells me.   21
"It happens to everyone."

I am not immediately consoled. But time goes on, and finally, so 22
do I.

By the time we pulled into my parents' driveway, it was nearly 23
dinnertime. I sprang out, glad to stretch, and bounded into the
house, but he was slow to follow, and I had discarded my shoulder
bag and greeted everyone by the time he finally appeared in the
doorway. I went to introduce him, wondering why he was hanging
back. Then he raised his eyes to mine as he came up the stairs, and
I realized he was nervous: He was in my world now, and he was
finally getting an inkling of what I went through every day.

Payback time. At last. 24

Then my mother was there, smiling and shaking his hand, and my 25
father was right behind her, also smiling.

"Welcome," he said. 26

For a moment, I could see the horizon, where parallel lines 27
sometimes seem to meet.

COMPREHENSION

1. What is "the moment of truth" to which Wang refers in paragraph 1?

2. Why does Wang not tell her mother about the racial harassment she
   experienced as she walked home from school?

3. What does Wang mean when she says of her male friend that "no
   matter how long we traveled together, we would always be on parallel
   roads . . ." (10)?

4. Why does Wang consider her visit to her parents' house "payback
   time" (24) for her boyfriend?

PURPOSE AND AUDIENCE

1. What is Wang's thesis? Do you think she should have used an
   explicitly stated thesis instead of an implied thesis?

2. What function does the boyfriend's voice have in the essay? Whose
   point of view do you think he is supposed to reflect? Is Wang's
   portrayal of him critical? Flattering? Explain.

3. Does Wang expect her readers to be sympathetic, neutral, or hostile?
   On what do you base your conclusion?

STYLE AND STRUCTURE

1. Wang uses a single sentence to introduce her essay. Should she have expanded this sentence into a full introductory paragraph, or is it effective as it stands? Explain.

2. The body of Wang's essay consists of three examples. What would she have gained or lost by using a single extended example?

3. Does Wang present enough examples to support her thesis? Does she offer readers a sufficient range of examples? Do any of the examples seem irrelevant? Explain.

4. How are the three examples Wang presents similar? In what ways are they different?

5. Wang concludes her essay with a single sentence. What point does she choose to reinforce? Is this ending effective, or would another ending have been stronger?

VOCABULARY PROJECTS

1. Define each of the following words as it is used in this selection.

   appalled (10)   foreboding (19)   inkling (23)
   suffuses (13)   consoled (22)

2. *Chink* is a word that many Chinese find highly offensive. Why does Wang use it in her essay? Would a less distasteful term have been equally effective?

JOURNAL ENTRY

Is Wang overreacting—as her boyfriend suggests—to the incidents she describes? According to her, "It doesn't really matter" (16). Do you agree?

WRITING WORKSHOP

1. Write a letter to Wang's boyfriend explaining to him why she reacts the way she does to the incidents she describes. Make sure your letter has a thesis and that your examples directly support your thesis.

2. Using a single extended example, write an essay about a time when you, like Amy Wang, experienced prejudice.

3. Write an essay in which you challenge the stereotypes associated with a group of people. Use a variety of examples from your own experience to support your conclusions.

THEMATIC CONNECTIONS

- "Finishing School" (p. 78)
- "Just Walk On By" (p. 209)
- "Let's Tell the Story of All America's Cultures" (p. 586)

JUST WALK ON BY: A BLACK MAN PONDERS HIS POWER TO ALTER PUBLIC SPACE

Brent Staples

Born in Chester, Pennsylvania, in 1951, Brent Staples received his bachelor's degree from Widener University in 1973 and his doctorate in psychology from the University of Chicago in 1982. After deciding on a career in journalism, he wrote for the Chicago Sun-Times, *the* Chicago Reader, Chicago *magazine, and* Down Beat *magazine. Staples joined the* New York Times *in 1985, writing on culture and politics, and he became a member of its editorial board in 1990. He contributes articles to many other publications, including* New York Woman, Ms., *and* Harper's, *in which the following article was published in 1986. Staples has also written a memoir,* Parallel Time: Growing Up in Black and White *(1994), about his escape from the violence and poverty of his childhood. In "Just Walk On By," Staples recounts the many instances in which people have reacted to him as a potentially dangerous person solely because of the color of his skin.*

My first victim was a woman—white, well dressed, probably in her early twenties. I came upon her late one evening on a deserted street in Hyde Park, a relatively affluent neighborhood in an otherwise mean, impoverished section of Chicago. As I swung onto the avenue behind her, there seemed to be a discreet, uninflammatory distance between us. Not so. She cast back a worried glance. To her, the youngish black man—a broad six feet two inches with a beard and billowing hair, both hands shoved into the pockets of a bulky military jacket—seemed menacingly close. After a few more quick glimpses, she picked up her pace and was soon running in earnest. Within seconds she disappeared into a cross street.

That was more than a decade ago. I was 22 years old, a graduate student newly arrived at the University of Chicago. It was in the echo of that terrified woman's footfalls that I first began to know the unwieldy inheritance I'd come into—the ability to alter public space in ugly ways. It was clear that she thought herself the quarry of a mugger, a rapist, or worse. Suffering a bout of insomnia, however, I was stalking sleep, not defenseless wayfarers. As a softy who is scarcely able to take a knife to a raw chicken—let alone hold it to a person's throat—I was surprised, embarrassed, and dismayed all at once. Her flight made me feel like an accomplice in tyranny. It also made it clear that I was indistinguishable from the muggers who occasionally seeped into the area from the surrounding ghetto. That first encounter, and those that followed, signified that a vast, unnerving gulf lay between nighttime pedestrians—particularly women—and me. And I soon gathered that being perceived as dangerous is a hazard in itself. I only needed to turn a corner into a dicey situation, or crowd some frightened, armed person in a foyer somewhere, or make an errant move after being pulled over by a policeman. Where fear and weapons meet—and they often do in urban America—there is always the possibility of death.

In that first year, my first away from my hometown, I was to be- 3 come thoroughly familiar with the language of fear. At dark, shadowy intersections in Chicago, I could cross in front of a car stopped at a traffic light and elicit the *thunk, thunk, thunk, thunk* of the driver—black, white, male, or female—hammering down the door locks. On less traveled streets after dark, I grew accustomed to but never comfortable with people who crossed to the other side of the street rather than pass me. Then there were the standard unpleasantries with police, doormen, bouncers, cab drivers, and others whose business it is to screen out troublesome individuals *before* there is any nastiness.

I moved to New York nearly two years ago and I have remained an 4 avid night walker. In central Manhattan, the near-constant crowd cover minimizes tense one-on-one street encounters. Elsewhere— visiting friends in SoHo, where sidewalks are narrow and tightly spaced buildings shut out the sky—things can get very taut indeed.

Black men have a firm place in New York mugging literature. 5 Norman Podhoretz in his famed (or infamous) 1963 essay, "My Negro Problem—And Ours," recalls growing up in terror of black males; they "were tougher than we were, more ruthless," he writes— and as an adult on the Upper West Side of Manhattan, he continues, he cannot constrain his nervousness when he meets black men on certain streets. Similarly, a decade later, the essayist and novelist Edward Hoagland extols a New York where once "Negro bitterness bore down mainly on other Negroes." Where some see mere panhandlers, Hoagland sees "a mugger who is clearly screwing up his nerve to do more than just *ask* for money." But Hoagland has "the New Yorker's quick-hunch posture for broken-field maneuvering," and the bad guy swerves away.

I often witness that "hunch posture," from women after dark on 6
the warrenlike streets of Brooklyn where I live. They seem to set
their faces on neutral and, with their purse straps strung across
their chests bandolier style, they forge ahead as though bracing
themselves against being tackled. I understand, of course, that the
danger they perceive is not a hallucination. Women are particularly
vulnerable to street violence, and young black males are drastically
overrepresented among the perpetrators of that violence. Yet these
truths are no solace against the kind of alienation that comes of
being ever the suspect, against being set apart, a fearsome entity
with whom pedestrians avoid making eye contact.

It is not altogether clear to me how I reached the ripe old age of 22 7
without being conscious of the lethality nighttime pedestrians
attributed to me. Perhaps it was because in Chester, Pennsylvania,
the small, angry industrial town where I came of age in the 1960s,
I was scarcely noticeable against a backdrop of gang warfare, street
knifings, and murders. I grew up one of the good boys, had perhaps
a half-dozen fist fights. In retrospect, my shyness of combat has
clear sources.

Many things go into the making of a young thug. One of those 8
things is the consummation of the male romance with the power to
intimidate. An infant discovers that random flailings send the baby
bottle flying out of the crib and crashing to the floor. Delighted, the
joyful babe repeats those motions again and again, seeking to
duplicate the feat. Just so, I recall the points at which some of my
boyhood friends were finally seduced by the perception of themselves as tough guys. When a mark cowered and surrendered his
money without resistance, myth and reality merged—and paid off. It
is, after all, only manly to embrace the power to frighten and
intimidate. We, as men, are not supposed to give an inch of our lane
on the highway; we are to seize the fighter's edge in work and in play
and even in love; we are to be valiant in the face of hostile forces.

Unfortunately, poor and powerless young men seem to take all this 9
nonsense literally. As a boy, I saw countless tough guys locked away;
I have since buried several, too. They were babies, really—a teenage
cousin, a brother of 22, a childhood friend in his mid-twenties—all
gone down in episodes of bravado played out in the streets. I came to
doubt the virtues of intimidation early on. I chose, perhaps even
unconsciously, to remain a shadow—timid, but a survivor.

The fearsomeness mistakenly attributed to me in public places 10
often has a perilous flavor. The most frightening of these confusions
occurred in the late 1970s and early 1980s when I worked as a
journalist in Chicago. One day, rushing into the office of a magazine

I was writing for with a deadline story in hand, I was mistaken for a burglar. The office manager called security and, with an ad hoc posse, pursued me through the labyrinthine halls, nearly to my editor's door. I had no way of proving who I was. I could only move briskly toward the company of someone who knew me.

Another time I was on assignment for a local paper and killing 11 time before an interview. I entered a jewelry store on the city's affluent Near North Side. The proprietor excused herself and returned with an enormous red Doberman pinscher straining at the end of a leash. She stood, the dog extended toward me, silent to my questions, her eyes bulging nearly out of her head. I took a cursory look around, nodded, and bade her good night. Relatively speaking, however, I never fared as badly as another black male journalist. He went to nearby Waukegan, Illinois, a couple of summers ago to work on a story about a murderer who was born there. Mistaking the reporter for the killer, police hauled him from his car at gunpoint and but for his press credentials would probably have tried to book him. Such episodes are not uncommon. Black men trade tales like this all the time.

In "My Negro Problem—And Ours," Podhoretz writes that the 12 hatred he feels for blacks makes itself known to him through a variety of avenues—one being his discomfort with that "special brand of paranoid touchiness" to which he says blacks are prone. No doubt he is speaking here of black men. In time, I learned to smother the rage I felt at so often being taken for a criminal. Not to do so would surely have led to madness—via that special "paranoid touchiness" that so annoyed Podhoretz at the time he wrote the essay.

I began to take precautions to make myself less threatening. I 13 move about with care, particularly late in the evening. I give a wide berth to nervous people on subway platforms during the wee hours, particularly when I have exchanged business clothes for jeans. If I happen to be entering a building behind some people who appear skittish, I may walk by, letting them clear the lobby before I return, so as not to seem to be following them. I have been calm and extremely congenial on those rare occasions when I've been pulled over by the police.

And on late-evening constitutionals along streets less traveled by, 14 I employ what has proved to be an excellent tension-reducing measure: I whistle melodies from Beethoven and Vivaldi and the more popular classical composers. Even steely New Yorkers hunching toward nighttime destinations seem to relax, and occasionally they even join in the tune. Virtually everybody seems to sense that a mugger wouldn't be warbling bright, sunny selections from Vivaldi's *Four Seasons*. It is my equivalent of the cowbell that hikers wear when they know they are in bear country.

COMPREHENSION

1. Why does Staples characterize the woman he encounters in paragraph 1 as a "victim"?

2. What does Staples mean when he says he has the power to "alter public space" (2)?

3. Why does Staples walk the streets at night?

4. What things does Staples say go into the making of a young thug? Why are young, poor, and powerless men especially likely to become what he calls "thugs"?

5. In what ways does Staples attempt to make himself less threatening?

PURPOSE AND AUDIENCE

1. What is Staples's thesis? Does he state it or imply it?

2. Does Staples use logic, emotion, or a combination of the two to appeal to his readers? How appropriate is his strategy?

3. What preconceptions does Staples assume his audience has? In what ways does he challenge these preconceptions?

STYLE AND STRUCTURE

1. Why does Staples mention Norman Podhoretz? Could he have made the same points without referring to Podhoretz's essay?

2. Staples begins his essay with an anecdote. How effective is this strategy? Would another opening strategy have been more effective? Explain.

3. Does Staples present enough examples to support his thesis? Are they representative? Would other types of examples have been more convincing? Explain.

4. Why do you think Staples introduces the discussion of the young thug? Is this an effective strategy? Does it support or undercut Staples's point?

VOCABULARY PROJECTS

1. Define each of the following words as it is used in this selection.

discreet (1)	quarry (2)	constrain (5)
uninflammatory (1)	wayfarers (2)	bravado (9)
billowing (1)	insomnia (2)	constitutionals (14)

2. Throughout his essay, Staples uses various adjectives to describe the way people perceive him. Paragraph 1 of the essay is especially vivid. Rewrite this paragraph from the point of view of the young woman. Use as many descriptive adjectives as you can to convey her view of Staples. Then write the paragraph from the point of view of someone who knows Staples, portraying him in a much more positive light.

JOURNAL ENTRY

Have you ever reacted in the way Staples describes? What caused your reaction? After reading Staples's essay, do you still think your reaction was justified?

WRITING WORKSHOP

1. Use the journal entry above to help you write an essay in which you use an extended example to support the statement "When walking alone at night, you can (or cannot) be too careful."

2. Relying on examples from your own experience, write an essay in which you discuss what part you think race played in people's reactions to Staples. Do you think that his perceptions were accurate or that he was being overly sensitive?

3. How accurate is Staples's observation concerning the "male romance with the power to intimidate"? What does he mean by this statement? Can you give examples from your experience to illustrate that this is a characteristic of male upbringing in our society?

THEMATIC CONNECTIONS

- "The Civil Rights Movement: What Good Was It?" (p. 315)
- "The Arab World" (p. 382)
- "How the Pot Got to Call the Kettle Black" (p. 614)

THE HUMAN COST OF AN ILLITERATE SOCIETY

Jonathan Kozol

Jonathan Kozol was born in Boston in 1936 and graduated from Harvard University in 1958. After studying as a Rhodes Scholar at Oxford University, he began teaching in public schools in Boston and its suburbs. He has also taught at numerous colleges, including Yale University, Trinity College in Connecticut, and the University of Massachusetts at Amherst. Kozol has written for The Los Angeles Times, USA Today, *the* New York Times Book Review, *and* The New Yorker. *His numerous books on education and literacy and their social impact include the critically acclaimed* Death at an Early Age *(1967) and, more recently,* Illiterate America *(1985),* Rachel and Her Children: Homeless Families in America *(1988), and* Savage Inequalities: Children in America's Schools *(1991). In* Illiterate America, *Kozol examines the human and financial costs of illiteracy in America, pointing out that more than 35 million people read below the level needed to function in this society and that, in certain cities, almost forty percent of the adult population is functionally illiterate. The following essay, taken from that book, uses examples to convey to readers what it means to be illiterate.*

PRECAUTIONS. READ BEFORE USING.
Poison: Contains sodium hydroxide (caustic soda-lye).
Corrosive: Causes severe eye and skin damage, may cause blindness.
Harmful or fatal if swallowed.
If swallowed, give large quantities of milk or water.
Do not induce vomiting.
Important: Keep water out of can at all times to prevent contents from violently erupting . . .

—warning on a can of Drano

Questions of literacy, in Socrates' belief, must at length be judged as matters of morality. Socrates could not have had in mind the moral compromise peculiar to a nation like our own. Some of our Founding Fathers did, however, have this question in their minds. One of the wisest of those Founding Fathers (one who may not have been most compassionate but surely was more prescient than some of his peers) recognized the special dangers that illiteracy would pose to basic equity in the political construction that he helped to shape.

"A people who mean to be their own governors," James Madison   2
wrote, "must arm themselves with the power knowledge gives. A
popular government without popular information or the means of
acquiring it, is but a prologue to a farce or a tragedy, or perhaps
both."

Tragedy looms larger than farce in the United States today.   3
Illiterate citizens seldom vote. Those who do are forced to cast a vote
of questionable worth. They cannot make informed decisions based
on serious print information. Sometimes they can be alerted to their
interests by aggressive voter education. More frequently, they vote
for a face, a smile, or a style, not for a mind or character or body of
beliefs.

The number of illiterate adults exceeds by 16 million the entire   4
vote cast for the winner in the 1980 presidential contest. If even one
third of all illiterates could vote, and read enough and do sufficient
math to vote in their self-interest, Ronald Reagan would not likely
have been chosen president. There is, of course, no way to know for
sure. We do know this: Democracy is a mendacious term when used
by those who are prepared to countenance the forced exclusion of
one third of our electorate. So long as 60 million people are denied
significant participation, the government is neither of, nor for, nor
by, the people. It is a government, at best, of those two thirds whose
wealth, skin color, or parental privilege allows them opportunity to
profit from the provocation and instruction of the written word.

The undermining of democracy in the United States is one   5
"expense" that sensitive Americans can easily deplore because it
represents a contradiction that endangers citizens of all political
positions. The human price is not so obvious at first.

Since I first immersed myself within this work I have often had   6
the following dream: I find that I am in a railroad station or a large
department store within a city that is utterly unknown to me and
where I cannot understand the printed words. None of the signs or
symbols is familiar. Everything looks strange: like mirror writing of
some kind. Gradually I understand that I am in the Soviet Union.
All the letters on the walls around me are Cyrillic. I look for my
pocket dictionary but I find that it has been mislaid. Where have I
left it? Then I recall that I forgot to bring it with me when I packed
my bags in Boston. I struggle to remember the name of my hotel. I
try to ask somebody for directions. One person stops and looks at me
in a peculiar way. I lose the nerve to ask. At last I reach into my
wallet for an ID card. The card is missing. Have I lost it? Then I
remember that my card was confiscated for some reason, many
years before. Around this point, I wake up in a panic.

This panic is not so different from the misery that millions of adult   7
illiterates experience each day within the course of their routine
existence in the U.S.A.

Illiterates cannot read the menu in a restaurant.   8

They cannot read the cost of items on the menu in the *window* of   9
the restaurant before they enter.

Illiterates cannot read the letters that their children bring home   10
from their teachers. They cannot study school department circulars
that tell them of the courses that their children must be taking if they
hope to pass the SAT exams. They cannot help with homework. They
cannot write a letter to the teacher. They are afraid to visit in the
classroom. They do not want to humiliate their child or themselves.

Illiterates cannot read instructions on a bottle of prescription   11
medicine. They cannot find out when a medicine is past the year of
safe consumption; nor can they read of allergenic risks, warnings to
diabetics, or the potential sedative effect of certain kinds of nonpre-
scription pills. They cannot observe preventive health care admoni-
tions. They cannot read about "the seven warning signs of cancer" or
the indications of blood-sugar fluctuations or the risks of eating
certain foods that aggravate the likelihood of cardiac arrest.

Illiterates live, in more than literal ways, an uninsured existence.   12
They cannot understand the written details on a health insurance
form. They cannot read the waivers that they sign preceding
surgical procedures. Several women I have known in Boston have
entered a slum hospital with the intention of obtaining a tubal
ligation and have emerged a few days later after having been
subjected to a hysterectomy. Unaware of their rights, incognizant of
jargon, intimidated by the unfamiliar air of fear and atmosphere of
ether that so many of us find oppressive in the confines even of the
most attractive and expensive medical facilities, they have signed
their names to documents they could not read and which nobody, in
the hectic situation that prevails so often in those overcrowded hospitals that serve the urban poor, had even bothered to explain.

Childbirth might seem to be the last inalienable right of any   13
female citizen within a civilized society. Illiterate mothers, as we
shall see, already have been cheated of the power to protect their
progeny against the likelihood of demolition in deficient public
schools and, as a result, against the verbal servitude within which
they themselves exist. Surgical denial of the right to bear that child
in the first place represents an ultimate denial, an unspeakable
metaphor, a final darkness that denies even the twilight gleamings
of our own humanity. What greater violation of our biological, our
biblical, our spiritual humanity could possibly exist than that which

takes place nightly, perhaps hourly these days, within such over-burdened and benighted institutions as the Boston City Hospital? Illiteracy has many costs; few are so irreversible as this.

Even the roof above one's head, the gas or other fuel for heating   14
that protects the residents of northern city slums against the threat of illness in the winter months become uncertain guarantees. Illiterates cannot read the lease that they must sign to live in an apartment which, too often, they cannot afford. They cannot manage check accounts and therefore seldom pay for anything by mail. Hours and entire days of difficult travel (and the cost of bus or other public transit) must be added to the real cost of whatever they consume. Loss of interest on the check accounts they do not have, and could not manage if they did, must be regarded as another of the excess costs paid by the citizen who is excluded from the common instruments of commerce in a numerate society.

"I couldn't understand the bills," a woman in Washington, D.C.,   15
reports, "and then I couldn't write the checks to pay them. We signed things we didn't know what they were."

Illiterates cannot read the notices that they receive from welfare   16
offices or from the IRS. They must depend on word-of-mouth instruction from the welfare worker—or from other persons whom they have good reason to mistrust. They do not know what rights they have, what deadlines and requirements they face, what options they might choose to exercise. They are half-citizens. Their rights exist in print but not in fact.

Illiterates cannot look up numbers in a telephone directory. Even   17
if they can find the names of friends, few possess the sorting skills to make use of the yellow pages; categories are bewildering and trade names are beyond decoding capabilities for millions of non-readers. Even the emergency numbers listed on the first page of the phone book—"Ambulance," "Police," and "Fire"—are too frequently beyond the recognition of nonreaders.

Many illiterates cannot read the admonition on a pack of ciga-   18
rettes. Neither the Surgeon General's warning nor its reproduction on the package can alert them to the risks. Although most people learn by word of mouth that smoking is related to a number of grave physical disorders, they do not get the chance to read the detailed stories which can document this danger with the vividness that turns concern into determination to resist. They can see the handsome cowboy or the slim Virginia lady lighting up a filter cigarette; they cannot heed the words that tell them that this product is (not "may be") dangerous to their health. Sixty million men and women are condemned to be the unalerted, high-risk candidates for cancer.

Illiterates do not buy "no-name" products in the supermarkets. 19
They must depend on photographs or the familiar logos that are
printed on the packages of brand-name groceries. The poorest people, therefore, are denied the benefits of the least costly products.

Illiterates depend almost entirely upon label recognition. Many 20
labels, however, are not easy to distinguish. Dozens of different
kinds of Campbell's soup appear identical to the nonreader. The
purchaser who cannot read and does not dare to ask for help, out of
the fear of being stigmatized (a fear which is unfortunately realistic), frequently comes home with something which she never wanted
and her family never tasted.

Illiterates cannot read instructions on a pack of frozen food. Pack- 21
ages sometimes provide an illustration to explain the cooking preparations; but illustrations are of little help to someone who must
"boil water, drop the food—*within* its plastic wrapper—in the boiling
water, wait for it to simmer, instantly remove."

Even when labels are seemingly clear, they may be easily mis- 22
taken. A woman in Detroit brought home a gallon of Crisco for her
children's dinner. She thought that she had bought the chicken that
was pictured on the label. She had enough Crisco now to last a
year—but no more money to go back and buy the food for dinner.

Recipes provided on the packages of certain staples sometimes 23
tempt a semiliterate person to prepare a meal her children have not
tasted. The longing to vary the uniform and often starchy content
of low-budget meals provided to the family that relies on food stamps
commonly leads to ruinous results. Scarce funds have been wasted
and the food must be thrown out. The same applies to distribution
of food-surplus produce in emergency conditions. Government in-
ducements to poor people to "explore the ways" by which to make
a tasty meal from tasteless noodles, surplus cheese, and powdered
milk are useless to nonreaders. Intended as benevolent advice,
such recommendations mock reality and foster deeper feelings of resentment and of inability to cope. (Those, on the other hand, who
cautiously refrain from "innovative" recipes in preparation of their
children's meals must suffer the opprobrium of "laziness," "lack of
imagination. . . .")

Illiterates cannot travel freely. When they attempt to do so, they 24
encounter risks that few of us can dream of. They cannot read traffic
signs and, while they often learn to recognize and to decipher symbols, they cannot manage street names which they haven't seen before. The same is true for bus and subway stops. While ingenuity can
sometimes help a man or woman to discern directions from familiar landmarks, buildings, cemeteries, churches, and the like, most

illiterates are virtually immobilized. They seldom wander past the streets and neighborhoods they know. Geographical paralysis becomes a bitter metaphor for their entire existence. They are immobilized in almost every sense we can imagine. They can't move up. They can't move out. They cannot see beyond. Illiterates may take an oral test for drivers' permits in most sections of America. It is a questionable concession. Where will they go? How will they get there? How will they get home? Could it be that some of us might like it better if they stayed where they belong?

Travel is only one of many instances of circumscribed existence. 25 Choice, in almost all its facets, is diminished in the life of an illiterate adult. Even the printed TV schedule, which provides most people with the luxury of preselection, does not belong within the arsenal of options in illiterate existence. One consequence is that the viewer watches only what appears at moments when he happens to have time to turn the switch. Another consequence, a lot more common, is that the TV set remains in operation night and day. Whatever the program offered at the hour when he walks into the room will be the nutriment that he accepts and swallows. Thus, to passivity, is added frequency—indeed, almost uninterrupted continuity. Freedom to select is no more possible here than in the choice of home or surgery or food.

"You don't choose," said one illiterate woman. "You take your 26 wishes from somebody else." Whether in perusal of a menu, selection of highways, purchase of groceries, or determination of affordable enjoyment, illiterate Americans must trust somebody else: a friend, a relative, a stranger on the street, a grocery clerk, a TV copywriter.

"All of our mail we get, it's hard for her to read. Settin' down and 27 writing a letter, she can't do it. Like if we get a bill . . . we take it over to my sister-in-law . . . My sister-in-law reads it."

Billing agencies harass poor people for the payment of the bills for 28 purchases that might have taken place six months before. Utility companies offer an agreement for a staggered payment schedule on a bill past due. "You have to trust them," one man said. Precisely for this reason, you end up by trusting no one and suspecting everyone of possible deceit. A submerged sense of distrust becomes the corollary to a constant need to trust. "They are cheating me . . . I have been tricked . . . I do not know . . ."

Not knowing: This is a familiar theme. Not knowing the right 29 word for the right thing at the right time is one form of subjugation. Not knowing the world that lies concealed behind those words is a more terrifying feeling. The longitude and latitude of one's existence are beyond all easy apprehension. Even the hard, cold stars within the firmament above one's head begin to mock the possibilities for self-location. Where am I? Where did I come from? Where will I go?

"I've lost a lot of jobs," one man explains. "Today, even if you're a   30
janitor, there's still reading and writing . . . They leave a note saying, 'Go to room so-and-so . . .' You can't do it. You can't read it. You don't know."

"The hardest thing about it is that I've been places where I didn't   31
know where I was. You don't know where you are . . . You're lost."

"Like I said: I have two kids. What do I do if one of my kids starts   32
choking? I go running to the phone . . . I can't look up the hospital phone number. That's if we're at home. Out on the street, I can't read the sign. I get to a pay phone. 'Okay, tell us where you are. We'll send an ambulance.' I look at the street sign. Right there, I can't tell you what it says. I'd have to spell it out, letter for letter. By that time, one of my kids would be dead . . . These are the kinds of fears you go with, every single day . . ."

"Reading directions, I suffer with. I work with chemicals . . .   33
That's scary to begin with . . ."

"You sit down. They throw the menu in front of you. Where do you   34
go from there? Nine times out of ten you say, 'Go ahead. Pick out something for the both of us.' I've eaten some weird things, let me tell you!"

Menus. Chemicals. A child choking while his mother searches for   35
a word she does not know to find assistance that will come too late. Another mother speaks about the inability to help her kids to read: "I can't read to them. Of course that's leaving them out of something they should have. Oh, it matters. You *believe* it matters! I ordered all these books. The kids belong to a book club. Donny wanted me to read a book to him. I told Donny: 'I can't read,' He said: 'Mommy, you sit down. I'll read it to you.' I tried it one day, reading from the pictures. Donny looked at me. He said, 'Mommy, that's not right.' He's only five. He knew I couldn't read . . .'"

A landlord tells a woman that her lease allows him to evict her if   36
her baby cries and causes inconvenience to her neighbors. The consequence of challenging his words conveys a danger which appears, unlikely as it seems, even more alarming than the danger of eviction. Once she admits that she can't read, in the desire to maneuver for the time in which to call a friend, she will have defined herself in terms of an explicit impotence that she cannot endure. Capitulation in this case is preferable to self-humiliation. Resisting the definition of oneself in terms of what one cannot do, what others take for granted, represents a need so great that other imperatives (even one so urgent as the need to keep one's home in winter's cold)

evaporate and fall away in face of fear. Even the loss of home and shelter, in this case, is not so terrifying as the loss of self.

"I come out of school. I was sixteen. They had their meetings. The directors meet. They said that I was wasting their school paper. I was wasting pencils . . ." 37

Another illiterate, looking back, believes she was not worthy of her teacher's time. She believes that it was wrong of her to take up space within her school. She believes that it was right to leave in order that somebody more deserving could receive her place. 38

Children choke. Their mother chokes another way: on more than chicken bones. 39

People eat what others order, know what others tell them, struggle not to see themselves as they believe the world perceives them. A man in California speaks about his own loss of identity, of self-location, definition: 40

"I stood at the bottom of the ramp. My car had broke down on the freeway. There was a phone. I asked for the police. They was nice. They said to tell them where I was. I looked up at the signs. There was one that I had seen before. I read it to them: ONE WAY STREET. They thought it was a joke. I told them I couldn't read. There was other signs above the ramp. They told me to try. I looked around for somebody to help. All the cars was going by real fast. I couldn't make them understand that I was lost. The cop was nice. He told me: 'Try once more.' I did my best. I couldn't read. I only knew the sign above my head. The cop was trying to be nice. He knew that I was trapped. 'I can't send out a car to you if you can't tell me where you are.' I felt afraid. I nearly cried. I'm forty-eight years old. I only said: 'I'm on a one-way street . . .'" 41

The legal problems and the courtroom complications that confront illiterate adults have been discussed above. The anguish that may underlie such matters was brought home to me this year while I was working on this book. I have spoken, in the introduction, of a sudden phone call from one of my former students, now in prison for a criminal offense. Stephen is not a boy today. He is twenty-eight years old. He called to ask me to assist him in his trial, which comes up next fall. He will be on trial for murder. He has just knifed and killed a man who first enticed him to his home, then cheated him, and then insulted him—as "an illiterate subhuman." 42

Stephen now faces twenty years to life. Stephen's mother was illiterate. His grandparents were illiterate as well. What parental curse did not destroy was killed off finally by the schools. Silent violence is repaid with interest. It will cost us $25,000 yearly to maintain this 43 broken soul in prison. But what is the price that has been paid by Stephen's victim? What is the price that will be paid by Stephen?

Perhaps we might slow down a moment here and look at the reali-   44
ties described above. This is the nation that we live in. This is a society that most of us did not create but which our President and other leaders have been willing to sustain by virtue of malign neglect. Do we possess the character and courage to address a problem which so many nations, poorer than our own, have found it natural to correct?

The answers to these questions represent a reasonable test of our   45
belief in the democracy to which we have been asked in public school to swear allegiance.

COMPREHENSION

1. Why is illiteracy a danger to a democratic society?

2. What does Kozol mean when he says that our reactions to the problem of illiteracy in America test our belief in democracy?

3. What does Kozol mean when he says that an illiterate person leads a "circumscribed existence" (25)? How does being illiterate limit a person's choices?

4. What are the legal problems and courtroom complications that confront illiterate adults?

PURPOSE AND AUDIENCE

1. What is Kozol's thesis? Where does he state it?

2. Kozol aims his essay at a wide general audience. How does he address the needs of this audience? In what ways would his discussion differ if it were intended for an audience of reading specialists? Of politicians?

3. Is Kozol's purpose to inform, persuade, express emotions, or some combination of these three? Does he have additional, more specific purposes as well? Explain.

STYLE AND STRUCTURE

1. Why does Kozol introduce his essay with references to Socrates and James Madison? How does this strategy help him establish his thesis?

2. In paragraph 6 Kozol recounts a dream that he has often had. Why does he include this anecdote? How does it help him move from his introduction to the body of his essay?

3. How effective is Kozol's use of statistics? Do the statistics complement or undercut his illustrations of the personal cost of illiteracy?

4. Why did Kozol choose to end his essay with the example of Stephen, one of his former students, who is in jail awaiting trial for murder? How does this anecdote help Kozol set up his concluding remarks in paragraphs 44 and 45?

VOCABULARY PROJECTS

1. Define each of the following words as it is used in this selection.

prescient (1)	sedative (11)	concession (24)
farce (2)	admonitions (11)	firmament (29)
mendacious (4)	incognizant (12)	capitulation (36)
countenance (4)	jargon (12)	
Cyrillic (6)	oppobrium (23)	

2. Reread paragraphs 23 and 24 and determine which words convey Kozol's feelings toward his subject. Rewrite these paragraphs, eliminating as much subjective language as you can. Do your changes make the paragraphs more appealing or less so to a general audience? To a group of sociologists? To a group of reading teachers?

JOURNAL ENTRY

Keep a journal for a day, noting the difficulty you would have carrying out each activity in your daily routine if you were illiterate.

WRITING WORKSHOP

1. Using your journal entry as a starting point, write an essay in which you describe the tasks you would have difficulty accomplishing if you could not read. Do not forget to include an explicit thesis and to use examples to illustrate your points.

2. People have not always had to read to function in society. Several hundred years ago, in fact, the majority of people could not read. Write an essay giving examples of the kinds of jobs you could hold today if you could not read.

3. Using Kozol's essay as source material, write an essay in which your thesis is Madison's statement, "A people who mean to be their own

governors must arm themselves with the power knowledge gives." Do not forget to document information that you borrow from Kozol.

THEMATIC CONNECTIONS

- "Midnight" (p. 186)
- "Aria: A Memoir of a Bilingual Childhood" (p. 401)
- "How the Pot Got to Call the Kettle Black" (p. 614)

SAMUEL

Grace Paley

Grace Paley was born in 1922 and grew up in New York City. She attended Hunter College and taught at Columbia University, Syracuse University, City College of New York, and Sarah Lawrence College, from which she retired in 1988. Paley's short stories have appeared in The New Yorker, Ms., Mother Jones, *and many other magazines, and they have been published in the collections* The Little Disturbances of Man *(1959);* Enormous Changes at the Last Minute *(1974), in which "Samuel" is published;* Later the Same Day *(1985); and* The Collected Stories of Grace Paley *(1994). Paley has also published two collections of poems,* Leaning Forward *(1985), and* New and Collected Poems *(1992), and two books of stories and poems on peace,* 365 Reasons Not to Have Another War *(1989) and* Long Walks and Intimate Talks *(1991). In "Samuel," Paley uses a simple narrative to raise complex emotions and questions.*

Some boys are very tough. They're afraid of nothing. They are the ones who climb a wall and take a bow at the top. Not only are they brave on the roof, but they make a lot of noise in the darkest part of the cellar where even the super hates to go. They also jiggle and hop on the platform between the locked doors of the subway cars.

Four boys are jiggling on the swaying platform. Their names are Alfred, Calvin, Samuel, and Tom. The men and the women in the cars on either side watch them. They don't like them to jiggle or jump but don't want to interfere. Of course some of the men in the cars were once brave boys like these. One of them had ridden the tail of a speeding truck from New York to Rockaway Beach without getting off, without his sore fingers losing hold. Nothing happened to him then or later. He had made a compact with other boys who preferred to watch: starting at Eighth Avenue and Fifteenth Street, he would get to some specified place, maybe Twenty-third and the river, by hopping the tops of the moving trucks. This was hard to do when one truck turned a corner in the wrong direction and the nearest truck was a couple of feet too high. He made three or four starts before succeeding. He had gotten this idea from a film at school called *The Romance of Logging*. He had finished high school, married a good friend, was in a responsible job and going to night school.

These two men and others looked at the four boys jumping and   3
jiggling on the platform and thought, It must be fun to ride that way,
especially now the weather is nice and we're out of the tunnel and
way high over the Bronx. Then they thought, These kids do seem to
be acting sort of stupid. They *are* little. Then they thought of some of
the brave things they had done when they were boys and jiggling
didn't seem so risky.

The ladies in the car became very angry when they looked at the   4
four boys. Most of them brought their brows together and hoped the
boys could see their extreme disapproval. One of the ladies wanted
to get up and say, be careful you dumb kids, get off that platform or
I'll call a cop. But three of the boys were Negroes and the fourth was
something else she couldn't tell for sure. She was afraid they'd be
fresh and laugh at her and embarrass her. She wasn't afraid they'd
hit her, but she was afraid of embarrassment. Another lady thought,
their mothers never know where they are. It wasn't true in this
particular case. Their mothers all knew that they had gone to see the
missile exhibit on Fourteenth Street.

Out on the platform, whenever the train accelerated, the boys   5
would raise their hands and point them up to the sky to act like
rockets going off, then they rat-tat-tatted the shatterproof glass
pane like machine guns, although no machine guns had been
exhibited.

For some reason known only to the motorman, the train began a   6
sudden slowdown. The lady who was afraid of embarrassment saw
the boys jerk forward and backward and grab the swinging guard
chains. She had her own boy at home. She stood up with determination and went to the door. She slid it open and said, "You boys will
be hurt. You'll be killed. I'm going to call the conductor if you don't
just go into the next car and sit down and be quiet."

Two of the boys said, "Yes'm," and acted as though they were   7
about to go. Two of them blinked their eyes a couple of times and
pressed their lips together. The train resumed its speed. The door
slid shut, parting the lady and the boys. She leaned against the side
door because she had to get off at the next stop.

The boys opened their eyes wide at each other and laughed. The   8
lady blushed. The boys looked at her and laughed harder. They
began to pound each other's back. Samuel laughed the hardest and
pounded Alfred's back until Alfred coughed and the tears came.
Alfred held tight to the chain hook. Samuel pounded him even
harder when he saw the tears. He said, "Why you bawling? You a
baby, huh?" and laughed. One of the men whose boyhood had been
more watchful than brave became angry. He stood up straight and

looked at the boys for a couple of seconds. Then he walked in a citizenly way to the end of the car, where he pulled the emergency cord. Almost at once, with a terrible hiss, the pressure of air abandoned the brakes and the wheels were caught and held.

People standing in the most secure places fell forward, then back-   9
ward. Samuel had let go of his hold on the chain so he could pound Tom as well as Alfred. All the passengers in the cars whipped back and forth, but he pitched only forward and fell head first to be crushed and killed between the cars.

The train had stopped hard, halfway into the station, and the   10
conductor called at once for the trainmen who knew about this kind of death and how to take the body from the wheels and brakes. There was silence except for passengers from other cars who asked, What happened! What happened! The ladies waited around wondering if he might be an only child. The men recalled other afternoons with very bad endings. The little boys stayed close to each other, leaning and touching shoulders and arms and legs.

When the policeman knocked at the door and told her about it,   11
Samuel's mother began to scream. She screamed all day and moaned all night, though the doctors tried to quiet her with pills.

Oh, oh, she hopelessly cried. She did not know how she could ever   12
find another boy like that one. However, she was a young woman and she became pregnant. Then for a few months she was hopeful. The child born to her was a boy. They brought him to be seen and nursed. She smiled. But immediately she saw that this baby wasn't Samuel. She and her husband together have had other children, but never again will a boy exactly like Samuel be known.

THINKING ABOUT LITERATURE

1. The story supports its main point with a single example. What is the example?

2. The story begins with the observation, "Some boys are very tough." Is Samuel really tough? What do you think Paley wants her readers to realize about Samuel?

3. What point do you think the story makes about bravery? Which of the characters would you consider brave?

4. What effect does the incident have on the other characters? What do their reactions indicate about them? What, if anything, do these characterizations reveal about Grace Paley's values?

JOURNAL ENTRY

Do you consider Samuel a hero? Is it true, as the narrator asserts, that "never again will a boy exactly like Samuel be known" (12)?

THEMATIC CONNECTIONS

- "38 Who Saw Murder Didn't Call the Police" (p. 91)
- "It's Just Too Late" (p. 325)

WRITING ASSIGNMENTS FOR EXEMPLIFICATION

1. Interview several business people in your community. Explain the Peter Principle to them if they are unfamiliar with it, ask them their feelings about this concept, and take notes on their responses. Then write an essay about your findings that includes quotations from your notes.

2. Write a humorous essay about a ritual you have experienced and the types of people who participate in it. Make a point about the ritual, and use the people as examples to support your point.

3. Write an essay in which you establish that you are an optimistic or a pessimistic person. Use two or three extended examples to support your case.

4. If you could change three things at your college or university, what would they be? Use examples from your own experience to support your claims, and be sure to tie the three examples together with a single thesis.

5. Write an essay in which you discuss two or three of the greatest challenges facing the United States.

6. Using your family and friends as examples, write an essay in which you suggest some of the positive or negative characteristics of Americans.

7. Write an essay in which you present your formula for achieving success in college. You may, if you wish, talk about things like scheduling time, maintaining a high energy level, and learning how to relax. Use examples from your own experience to make your point.

8. Write an exemplification essay in which you discuss how cooperation has helped you achieve some important goal. Support your thesis with a single extended example.

9. Choose an event that you believe illustrates a less-than-admirable moment in your life. Write an essay explaining your feelings.

10. Several of the selections in this chapter address personal problems. Write an essay in which you identify and discuss what you believe is the most pressing personal problem you have faced and overcome.

COLLABORATIVE ACTIVITY FOR EXEMPLIFICATION

The following passage appeared in a handbook given to parents of entering students at a Midwestern university:

The freshman experience is like no other—at once challenging, exhilarating, and fun. Students face academic challenges as they are exposed to many new ideas. They also face personal challenges as they meet many new people from diverse backgrounds. It is a time to mature and grow. It is an opportunity to explore new subjects and familiar ones. There may be no more challenging and exciting time of personal growth than the first year of university study.

Working in groups of four, brainstorm for examples that support or refute the idea that "[t]here may be no more challenging and exciting time of personal growth" than the first year of college. One person from each group should tell the class what position the group took and explain the list of examples you collected. Finally, work together to write an essay that presents your group's position. Have one student write the first draft, two others revise this draft, and the last edit and proofread the revised draft.

5

Process

WHAT IS PROCESS?

A **process** essay presents a sequence of steps and shows how those steps lead toward a particular result. In the following paragraph from *Language in Thought and Action,* the semanticist S. I. Hayakawa uses process to explain how an editor of a dictionary decides on a word's definition.

<table>
<tr>
<td>Process presents series of steps in chronological order</td>
<td>To define a word, then, the dictionary-editor places before him the stack of cards illustrating that word; each of the cards represents an actual use of the word by a writer of some literary or historical importance. He reads the cards carefully, discards some, rereads the rest, and divides up the stack according to what he thinks are the several senses of the word. Finally, he writes his definitions, following the hard-and-fast rule that each definition must be based on what the quotations in front of him reveal about the meaning of the word. The editor cannot be</td>
</tr>
<tr>
<td>Topic sentence</td>
<td>influenced by what he thinks a given word ought to mean. <u>He must work according to the cards or not at all.</u></td>
</tr>
</table>

Process, like narrative, presents events in chronological order. Unlike a narrative, however, a process essay details a particular series of events that produces the same outcome whenever it is duplicated. Because these events form a sequence that often has a fixed order, clarity is extremely important. Whether your reader is actually to perform the process or simply to understand how it occurs, your paper must make clear the exact order of the individual steps as well as their relationships to one another and to the process as a whole. Not only must you provide clear, logical transitions between the steps in a process, but you must also present the steps in *strict* chronological order—that is, in the order in which they occur or are to be performed.

Instructions and Process Explanations

Depending on its purpose, a process essay can use either of two formats. The purpose of a set of *instructions* is to enable readers to perform the process. Instructions have many practical uses. A recipe, a handout about using your library's catalog, or an operating manual for your car or your stereo are all written as sets of instructions. So are directions for locating an office building in Washington, D.C., or for driving from Houston to Pensacola, Florida. Instructions use the present tense and, like commands, the imperative mood, speaking directly to the readers who are to perform the tasks described: "Disconnect the system, and check the electrical source."

The purpose of a *process explanation* is not to enable readers to perform the process but rather to help them understand how it is carried out. Explanation essays may therefore examine anything from how silkworms spin their cocoons to how Michelangelo and Leonardo da Vinci painted their masterpieces on plaster walls and ceilings. A process explanation may employ the first person *(I, we)* or the third *(he, she, it, they)*, the past tense or the present. (Because its readers need to understand, not perform, the process, the explanation does not use the second person or the imperative mood used for instructions.) The style of a process explanation will vary depending on whether a writer is explaining a process that takes place regularly or one that occurred in the past, and on whether the writer or someone else carried out the steps. The chart below suggests some of the options available to writers of process explanations.

	First Person	*Third Person*
Present	"After I pin the pattern to the fabric, I cut it out with a sharp pair of scissors." (habitual process performed by the writer)	"After the photographer places the chemicals in the tray. . . ." (habitual process performed by someone other than the writer)
Past	"After I pinned the pattern to the fabric. . . ." (process performed in the past by the writer)	"When the mixture was cool, he added. . . ." (process performed in the past by someone other than the writer)

Uses of Process Essays

College writing frequently calls for instructions or process explanations, with the process pattern shaping a section of a paper or an entire piece of writing. For example, in a biology term paper on genetic engineering, you might devote a paragraph to an explanation of the process of amniocentesis; in an editorial on the negative side of fraternity life, you might decide to include a brief summary of the process of pledging. Or, you can organize an entire paper around a process pattern: In a literature essay, you might trace the developmental steps through which a fictional character reached new insight; on a finance midterm, you might be asked to explain the procedure for approving a commercial loan.

You can use process writing to persuade or simply to present information. If its purpose is persuasive, a process paper may take a strong stand like "Applying for public assistance is a needlessly complex process that discourages many potential recipients" or "The process of slaughtering baby seals is inhumane and sadistic." Many process essays, however, aim to communicate nothing more debatable than the idea that learning the procedure for blood typing can introduce students to some basic laboratory techniques. Even in such a case, a process essay should have a clear thesis that identifies the process and perhaps why it is performed: "Typing your own blood can familiarize you with some fundamental laboratory procedures."

STRUCTURING A PROCESS ESSAY

Like other essays, a full-length process essay generally consists of three main sections. The *introduction* names the process and indicates why and under what circumstances it is performed. This section may also include information about materials or preliminary preparations, or it may present an overview of the process, perhaps even listing its major stages. The paper's thesis is also usually stated in the introduction.

Each paragraph in the *body* of the essay typically treats one major stage of the procedure. Each stage may group several steps, depending on the nature and complexity of the process. These steps are presented in chronological order, interrupted only for essential definitions, explanations, or cautions. Every step must be included and must appear in its proper place. Throughout the body of a process essay, transitional words and phrases ensure that each step, each stage, and each paragraph lead logically to the next. Transitions like *first, second, meanwhile, after this, next, then, when you have finished,* and *finally* establish sequential and chronological relationships that help readers follow the process.

A short process essay may not need a formal *conclusion.* If an essay does include a conclusion, however, it will often briefly review the procedure's major stages. Such an ending is especially useful if the paper has outlined a very long and complex or particularly technical procedure that may seem complicated to general readers. The conclusion may also reinforce the thesis by summarizing the results of the process or explaining its significance.

Before you can arrange your ideas into a coherent process essay, you must have a clear understanding of your essay's purpose. As you write, you should keep your readers' needs in mind. When necessary, you should explain the reasons for performing the steps, describe unfamiliar materials or equipment, define unfamiliar terms, and warn readers about possible snags during the process. Sometimes you may even need to include illustrations. Besides complete information, your readers need a clear and consistent discussion without ambiguities or surprises. For this reason, you should avoid unnecessary shifts in tense, person, voice, and mood. You should also include appropriate articles *(a, an,* and *the)* so that your discussion moves smoothly, like an essay—not abruptly, like a cookbook.

Always be careful to depict a process accurately. For instance, you should distinguish between what usually or always happens and what occasionally or rarely happens, between necessary steps and optional ones. You should also mentally test all the steps in sequence to be sure that the process will really work as you explain it. Check carefully for omitted steps or incorrect information. If you are writing from firsthand observation, try to test your explanation after writing it by observing the process again. This precaution can help you avoid omissions or errors.

Suppose you are taking a midterm examination in a course in childhood and adolescent behavior. One essay question calls for a process explanation: "Trace the stages that children go through in acquiring language." After thinking about the question, you develop the following thesis: "Although individual cases may differ, most children acquire language in a predictable series of stages." You then plan your essay, an extended account of the process by which children learn language, and develop an outline. An informal outline for your essay might look like this:

Introduction: Thesis statement—Although individual cases may differ, most children acquire language in a predictable series of stages.

First stage (two to twelve months):	Prelinguistic behavior, including "babbling" and appropriate responses to nonverbal cues
Second stage (end of first year):	Single words as commands or requests; infant catalogs his or her environment
Third stage (beginning of second year):	Expressive jargon, a flow of sounds that imitates adult speech; real words along with jargon
Fourth (and final) stage (middle of second year to beginning of third year):	Child begins combining real words into two-word phrases and then longer strings; missing parts of speech appear, and foundations of language are established
Conclusion:	Restatement of thesis; summary of key points

This essay, when completed, will show not only what the stages of the process are but how they relate to one another. It also will develop its thesis that children learn language through a well-defined process.

STUDENT WRITERS: PROCESS

The following student essays, Joseph Miksitz's set of instructions and Melany Hunt's explanation of how a process was conducted, were both written in response to the same assignment: "Write an essay in which you give instructions for a process that can change a person's appearance—or explain a process that changed your own appearance in some way."

PUMPING IRON

Introduction   Students of high school and college age are often   1
dissatisfied with their appearance. They see actors and
models on television and in magazines, and they want to be
thinner, stronger, or better looking. Sometimes this quest
for perfection gets young adults into trouble, leading them
to eating disorders or drug use. A healthier way to improve
Thesis   your appearance is through a weight-training program,
statement   which can increase not only your strength but also your
self-esteem.

Overview of the process: Getting started

If you want to avoid injury, you should begin gradually. In the first week, you might lift only two days, concentrating on thigh and calf muscles in the lower body and triceps, biceps, chest, back, and shoulders in the upper body. For the next three or four weeks, lift three days a week, adding more exercises each week. By the fourth week, you will probably start to feel stronger. At this point, you can begin a four-day lifting program, which many experts believe is the most productive and shows the best results.

Steps in process of upper-body workout

On Monday and Thursday, concentrate on your upper body. Begin with the bench press (to work chest muscles) and then move on to the military press (for the shoulders). After that, work your back muscles with the lat pull-down exercise on the Universal machine and some heavy and light weight dead lifts. Finally, concentrate on your arms, doing bicep curls, tricep extensions, and wrist curls (for the forearms). To cool down, do a few sets of sit-ups.

Steps in process of lower-body workout

On Tuesday and Friday, focus on your lower body with a leg workout. Start with the weight-gaining bulk exercise, the leg press. (Always begin your workout with your most strenuous exercise, which is usually the exercise that works the largest muscles.) Next, do some leg extensions to build the thigh muscles in the front of your leg, and then move on to leg curls to strengthen your hamstring muscle. After that, do calf raises to work your calf muscles. When you are finished, be sure to stretch all the major muscles to prevent tightness and injuries.

Warnings and reminders

Of course, a balanced weight-training program involves more than just lifting weights. During your weight training, you should eat four high-protein/high-carbohydrate meals a day, limiting fat and eating four or five servings of fruit and vegetables daily. You should also monitor your progress

carefully, paying attention to your body's aches and pains
and consulting a professional trainer when necessary--
especially if you think you may have injured yourself.

Conclusion Above all, don't let your weight-training regimen take 6
over your life. If you integrate it into the rest of your life,
balancing exercise with school, work, and social activities, a
weight-training program can make you look and feel
terrific.

Points for Special Attention

Introduction. The first paragraph of Joseph Miksitz's essay
includes a thesis statement that presents the advantages of embark-
ing on a weight-training program. Joseph begins with an overview of
the image problems faced by young adults and then narrows his
focus to present weight training as a possible solution to those
problems.

Structure. After the paper's introduction, Joseph includes a
paragraph that presents guidelines for getting started. The third
and fourth paragraphs enumerate the steps in each of the two processes he describes: upper- and lower-body workouts. In his fifth paragraph, Joseph includes reminders and cautions calculated to help
his readers get the most out of their exercise program while avoiding
overexertion or injury. (The parenthetical sentence in paragraph 4
offers another helpful tip.) In his conclusion Joseph advises readers
to keep their exercise program in perspective and (echoing his thesis
statements) reminds them of its benefits.

Purpose and Style. Because Joseph's essay is designed to enable readers to duplicate the process, he has written it as a set of
instructions rather than as an explanation of how a process is or was
performed. Therefore, he uses the second person (*"you* will probably
start to feel stronger") and present-tense verbs in the form of
commands (*"Begin* with the bench press. . . .").

Transitions. To make his essay clear and easy to follow, Joseph
has included transitions that indicate the order in which each step
is to be performed ("After that," "Next," "Finally," etc.), as well as
specific time markers ("On Monday and Thursday," "On Tuesday

and Friday") to distinguish the two related processes on which his essay focuses.

Focus on Revision. Joseph is careful to name various parts of the body and to identify different exercises as well as the general objective of each. Many other key details, however, have been omitted. For example, how much time should be spent on each exercise? What exactly is a bench press? A bicep curl? How are "light" and "heavy" weights defined? How many is "some" leg extensions or "a few sets" of sit-ups? How many repetitions of each exercise should be done? What specific danger signs should alert readers to possible overexertion or injury? Is the routine Joseph describes appropriate for females as well as males? When revising his essay, Joseph needs to remember that his audience may not be familiar with the processes he describes and will therefore need much more detailed explanations.

Finally, Joseph's essay, while clear and straightforward, is not very lively or interesting. Keep in mind, though, that his purpose is not to entertain readers but to present information. Given this purpose, an overly cute or clever essay would be inappropriate.

In contrast to "Pumping Iron," Melany Hunt's essay is a process explanation.

MEDIUM ASH BROWN

Introduction

The beautiful chestnut-haired woman pictured on the box seemed to beckon to me. I reached for the box of Medium Ash Brown hair dye just as my friend Veronica grabbed the box labeled Sparkling Sherry. I can't remember our reasons for wanting to change our hair color, but they seemed to make sense at the time. Maybe we were just bored. I do remember that the idea of transforming our appearance came up unexpectedly. Impulsively, we decided to change our hair color--and, we hoped, ourselves--that **Thesis statement** very evening. Now I know that some impulses should definitely be resisted.

Materials assembled

We decided to use my bathroom to dye our hair. Inside each box of hair color, we found two little bottles and a

1

2

small tube wrapped in a page of instructions. Attached to the instruction page itself were two very large, one-size-fits-all plastic gloves, which looked and felt like plastic sandwich bags. The directions recommended having some old towels around to soak up any spills or drips that might occur. Under the sink we found some old, frayed towels that I figured my mom had forgotten about, and we spread them around the bathtub. After we put our gloves on, we began the actual dyeing process. First we poured the first bottle into the second, which was half-full of some odd-smelling liquid. The smell was not much better after we poured the two bottles together. The directions advised us to cut off a small section of hair to use as a sample. For some reason, we decided to skip this step.

First stage of process: Preparing the dye

At this point, Veronica and I took turns leaning over the tub to wet our hair for the dye. The directions said to leave the dye on the hair for fifteen to twenty minutes. We found a little timer and set it for fifteen minutes. Next, we applied the dye to our hair. Again, we took turns squeezing the bottle in order to cover all our hair. We then wrapped one of the old towels around our sour-smelling hair and went outside to get some fresh air.

Second stage of process: Applying the dye

3

After the fifteen minutes were up, we rinsed our hair. According to the directions, we were to add a little water and scrub as if we were shampooing our hair. The dye lathered up, and we rinsed our hair until the water ran clear. So far, so good.

Third stage of process: Rinsing

4

The last part of the process involved applying the small tube of conditioner to our hair (because dyed hair becomes brittle and easily damaged). We used the conditioner as directed, and then we dried our hair so that we could see the actual color. Even before I looked in the mirror, I heard Veronica's gasp.

Last stage of process: Applying conditioner

5

Outcome of
process
"Nice try," I said, assuming she was just trying to make   6
me nervous, "But you're not funny."

"Mel," she said, "look in the mirror." Slowly, I turned   7
around. My stomach turned into a lead ball when I saw my
reflection. My hair was the putrid greenish-brown color of a
winter lawn, dying in patches yet still a nice green in the
shade.

The next day in school, I wore my hair tied back under   8
a baseball cap. I told only my close friends what I had done.
After they were finished laughing, they offered their
deepest, most heartfelt condolences. They also offered
many suggestions--none very helpful--on what to do to get
my old hair color back.

Conclusion
It is now three months later, and I still have no idea   9
what prompted me to dye my hair. My only consolation is
that I resisted my first impulse--to dye my hair a wild color,
like blue or fuchsia. Still, as I wait for my hair to grow out
and assemble a larger and larger collection of baseball caps,
it is small consolation indeed.

Points for Special Attention

Structure.   In her opening paragraph, Melany includes a thesis
statement that makes it very clear that the experience she describes
is not one she would recommend to others. The temptation she
describes in her introduction's first few sentences lures readers into
her essay just as the picture on the box lured her. Her second paragraph enumerates the contents of the box of hair dye and explains
how she and her friend assembled the other necessary materials.
Then the first stage in the process, preparing the dye, is explained.
Paragraphs 3–5 describe the other stages in the process in chronological order, and paragraphs 6–8 record Melany's and Veronica's
reactions to their experiment. In paragraph 9 Melany sums up the
impact of her experience and once again conveys her annoyance
with herself for her impulsive act.

Purpose and Style. Melany's purpose is *not* to enable others to duplicate the process she explains; on the contrary, she is trying to discourage readers from doing what she did. Consequently, she presents her process not as a set of instructions but as a process explanation, using first person and past tense to explain the actions of herself and her friend. She also largely eliminates cautions and reminders that her readers, not likely to undertake the process, will therefore not need to know.

Detail. Melany's essay is full of the kind of vivid descriptive detail necessary to convey to readers a clear sense of the unpleasantness of the process she explains—and of its outcome. Throughout, her emphasis is on the negative aspects of the process—the "odd-smelling liquid" and the "putrid greenish-brown color" of her hair, for instance—and this emphasis is consistent with her essay's purpose.

Transitions. To move readers smoothly through the process, Melany includes clear transitions ("First," "At this point," "Next," "then," and so on) and clearly identifies the beginning of the process ("After we put our gloves on, we began the actual dyeing process") and the end ("The last part of the process . . .").

Focus on Revision. Melany's essay is clearly written and structured, and its ironic, self-mocking tone is well suited to her audience and purpose. Some minor revisions, however, could make her essay even more effective. Paragraph 2, for example, needs a bit of work. For one thing, this paragraph begins quite abruptly: Paragraph 1 records the purchase of the hair dye, and paragraph 2 opens with the sentence "We decided to use my bathroom to dye our hair," leaving readers wondering how much time has passed between purchase and application. Given the fact that the thesis rests on the idea of the foolishness of an impulsive gesture, it is important that readers know that the girls presumably went immediately from the store to Melany's house. Under the circumstances, then, a clearer opening for paragraph 2 might be "As soon as we paid for the dye, we returned to my house, where, eager to begin our transformation, we locked ourselves in my bathroom. Inside each box. . . ." It might also make sense to divide paragraph 2 into two paragraphs, one describing the materials and another beginning with "After we put our gloves on . . . ," which introduces the first step in the process.

Another possible revision might be the further development of the character of Veronica. Although both girls purchase and apply hair color, readers never learn what happens to Veronica. Following paragraph 7, Melany could easily add a brief paragraph describing Veronica's "Sparkling Sherry" hair in humorous terms.

The following selections illustrate how varied the purposes of process writing can be. All, however, provide orderly and clear explanations so that readers can follow the process easily.

MY FIRST CONK

Malcolm X

The term "conk" needs to be explained before reading

#b explained BETTER Here!

Malcolm X was born Malcolm Little in Omaha, Nebraska, in 1925 and was assassinated in New York City in 1965. The son of a Baptist minister, he converted to Islam while serving a prison term for burglary and became a Muslim minister and advocate of black separatism upon his release in 1952. Malcolm X was a vocal member of the Black Muslims (known as the Nation of Islam) and a disciple of their leader, Elijah Muḥammad. In 1963, however, he left the Black Muslim movement, and following a 1964 trip to Mecca he converted to orthodox Islam and founded the black nationalist Organization for Afro-American Unity. It is believed that his assassination was motivated by the tension between the two movements after Malcolm X left the Black Muslims. The Autobiography of Malcolm X *(1964), from which the following excerpt is taken, relates his rise from poverty to national prominence as a lecturer and religious leader. The autobiography was dictated to Alex Haley, who later wrote* Roots. *"My First Conk" explains a ritual procedure that was part of Malcolm X's young manhood and also reflects his adult view of the process.*

Shorty soon decided that my hair was finally long enough to be conked. He had promised to school me in how to beat the barber shops' three- and four-dollar price by making up congolene, and then conking ourselves.

I took the little list of ingredients he had printed out for me, and went to a grocery store, where I got a can of Red Devil lye, two eggs, and two medium-sized white potatoes. Then at a drugstore near the poolroom, I asked for a large jar of vaseline, a large bar of soap, a large-toothed comb and a fine-toothed comb, one of those rubber hoses with a metal spray-head, a rubber apron and a pair of gloves.

"Going to lay on that first conk?" the drugstore man asked me. I proudly told him, grinning, "Right!"

Shorty paid six dollars a week for a room in his cousin's shabby apartment. His cousin wasn't at home. "It's like the pad's mine, he spends so much time with his woman," Shorty said. "Now, you watch me—"

He peeled the potatoes and thin-sliced them into a quart-sized Mason fruit jar, then started stirring them with a wooden spoon as

245

he gradually poured in a little over half the can of lye. "Never use a metal spoon; the lye will turn it black," he told me.

A jelly-like, starchy-looking glop resulted from the lye and pota- 6 toes, and Shorty broke in the two eggs, stirring real fast—his own conk and dark face bent down close. The congolene turned pale-yellowish. "Feel the jar," Shorty said. I cupped my hand against the outside, and snatched it away. "Damn right, it's hot, that's the lye," he said. "So you know it's going to burn when I comb it in—it burns bad. But the longer you can stand it, the straighter the hair."

He made me sit down, and he tied the string of the new rubber 7 apron tightly around my neck, and combed up my bush of hair. Then, from the big vaseline jar, he took a handful and massaged it hard all through my hair and into the scalp. He also thickly vaselined my neck, ears and forehead. "When I get to washing out your head, be sure to tell me anywhere you feel any little stinging," Shorty warned me, washing his hands, then pulling on the rubber gloves, and tying on his own rubber apron. "You always got to remember that any congolene left in burns a sore into your head."

The congolene just felt warm when Shorty started combing it in. 8 But then my head caught fire.

I gritted my teeth and tried to pull the sides of the kitchen table 9 together. The comb felt as if it was raking my skin off.

My eyes watered, my nose was running. I couldn't stand it any 10 longer; I bolted to the washbasin. I was cursing Shorty with every name I could think of when he got the spray going and started soap lathering my head.

He lathered and spray-rinsed, lathered and spray-rinsed, maybe 11 ten or twelve times, each time gradually closing the hot-water faucet, until the rinse was cold, and that helped some.

"You feel any stinging spots?" 12

"No," I managed to say. My knees were trembling. 13

"Sit back down, then. I think we got it all out okay." 14

The flame came back as Shorty, with a thick towel, started drying 15 my head, rubbing hard. "*Easy, man, easy!*" I kept shouting.

"The first time's always worst. You get used to it better before 16 long. You took it real good, homeboy. You got a good conk."

When Shorty let me stand up and see in the mirror, my hair hung 17 down in limp, damp strings. My scalp still flamed, but not as badly; I could bear it. He draped the towel around my shoulders, over my rubber apron, and began again vaselining my hair.

I could feel him combing, straight back, first the big comb, then 18 the fine-tooth one.

Then, he was using a razor, very delicately, on the back of my neck.   19
Then, finally, shaping the sideburns.

My first view in the mirror blotted out the hurting. I'd seen some   20
pretty conks, but when it's the first time, on your *own* head, the
transformation, after the lifetime of kinks, is staggering.

The mirror reflected Shorty behind me. We both were grinning   21
and sweating. And on top of my head was this thick, smooth sheen
of shining red hair—real red—as straight as any white man's.

How ridiculous I was! Stupid enough to stand there simply lost in   22
admiration of my hair now looking "white," reflected in the mirror in
Shorty's room. I vowed that I'd never again be without a conk, and
I never was for many years.

This was my first really big step toward self-degradation: when I   23
endured all of that pain, literally burning my flesh to have it look
like a white man's hair. I had joined that multitude of Negro men
and women in America who are brainwashed into believing that the
black people are "inferior"—and white people "superior"—that they
will even violate and mutilate their God-created bodies to try to look
"pretty" by white standards.

Look around today, in every small town and big city, from two-bit   24
catfish and soda-pop joints into the "integrated" lobby of the
Waldorf-Astoria, and you'll see conks on black men. And you'll see
black women wearing these green and pink and purple and red and
platinum-blonde wigs. They're all more ridiculous than a slapstick
comedy. It makes you wonder if the Negro has completely lost his
sense of identity, lost touch with himself.

You'll see the conk worn by many, many so-called "upper class"   25
Negroes, and, as much as I hate to say it about them, on all too many
Negro entertainers. One of the reasons that I've especially admired
some of them, like Lionel Hampton and Sidney Poitier, among
others, is that they have kept their natural hair and fought to the
top. I admire any Negro man who has never had himself conked, or
who has had the sense to get rid of it—as I finally did.

I don't know which kind of self-defacing conk is the greater   26
shame—the one you'll see on the heads of the black so-called "middle class" and "upper class," who ought to know better, or the one
you'll see on the heads of the poorest, most downtrodden, ignorant
black men. I mean the legal-minimum-wage ghetto-dwelling kind of
Negro, as I was when I got my first one. It's generally among these
poor fools that you'll see a black kerchief over the man's head, like
Aunt Jemima; he's trying to make his conk last longer, between
trips to the barbershop. Only for special occasions is this kerchief-

Emblem of Shame. he is black.

protected conk exposed—to show off how "sharp" and "hip" its owner is. The ironic thing is that I have never heard any woman, white or black, express any admiration for a conk. Of course, any white woman with a black man isn't thinking about his hair. But I don't see how on earth a black woman with any race pride could walk down the street with any black man wearing a conk—the emblem of his shame that he is black.

To my own shame, when I say all of this I'm talking first of all about myself—because you can't show me any Negro who ever conked more faithfully than I did. I'm speaking from personal experience when I say of any black man who conks today, or any white-wigged black woman, that if they gave the brains in their heads just half as much attention as they do their hair, they would be a thousand times better off.

COMPREHENSION

· *African Americans*

1. What exactly is a conk? *Hair straightening* Why did Malcolm X want to get his hair conked? What did the conk symbolize to him at the time he got it? What did it symbolize at the time he wrote about it? *Wearing a conk the emblem of shame he is black.*

Right of passage from boy to young man.

2. List the materials Shorty asked Malcolm X to buy. Is the purpose of each explained? If so, where? *Red Devil Lye, 2 eggs, 2 med potatoes soap etc. Then directs when each ingredient added*

3. Outline the major stages in the procedure Malcolm X describes. Are they in chronological order? Which, if any, of the major stages are out of place? *Yes.*

to make the conk and equipment used during the process.

PURPOSE AND AUDIENCE

1. Why does Malcolm X write this selection as a process explanation instead of as a set of instructions?

2. This process explanation has an explicit thesis that makes its purpose clear. What is this thesis?

3. *The Autobiography of Malcolm X* was published in 1964, when many African Americans got their hair straightened regularly. Is the thesis of the selection still relevant today?

4. Why does Malcolm X include so many references to the pain and discomfort he endured as part of the process?

5. What is the relationship between Malcolm X's personal narrative and the universal statement he makes about conking in this selection?

STYLE AND STRUCTURE

1. Identify some of the transitional words Malcolm X uses to move from step to step.

2. Only about half of this selection is devoted to the process explanation. Where does the process begin? Where does it end?

3. In paragraphs 22–26, Malcolm X encloses several words in quotation marks, occasionally prefacing them with the phrase *so-called*. What is the effect of these quotation marks?

VOCABULARY PROJECTS

1. Define each of the following words as it is used in this selection.

   vowed (22)   mutilate (23)   downtrodden (26)
   self-degradation (23)   slapstick (24)   emblem (26)
   multitude (23)   self-defacing (26)

2. Because this is an informal narrative, Malcolm X uses conversational slang terms. Substitute a more formal word for each of the following.

   beat (1)   glop (6)   "sharp" (26)
   pad (4)   real (6)   "hip" (26)

Evaluate the possible impact of your substitutions. Do they improve the essay or weaken it?

JOURNAL ENTRY

Did you ever engage in behavior that you came to view as unacceptable as your beliefs changed or your social consciousness developed? What made you change your attitude toward this behavior?

WRITING WORKSHOP

1. Write a process explanation of an unpleasant experience you or someone you know has often gone through in order to conform to others' standards of physical beauty (for instance, dieting or strenuous exercise). Include a thesis that conveys your disapproval of the process.

2. Rewrite Malcolm X's process explanation as he might have written it when he still thought of conking as a desirable process, worth all the trouble. Include all his steps, but change his thesis and slant your writing to make conking sound painless and worthwhile.

THEMATIC CONNECTIONS

THE SPIDER AND THE WASP

Alexander Petrunkevitch

Alexander Petrunkevitch (1875–1964) was born in Pliski, Russia, and educated at the University of Moscow and the University of Freiburg in Germany, where he received his doctorate in 1901. Petrunkevitch taught zoology at several universities in the United States, including Yale University from 1910 to 1944. He wrote several scholarly books, including An Inquiry into the Natural Classification of Spiders *(1933) and* Principles of Classification *(1952). In addition to these scientific works, Petrunkevitch also translated the poetry of Lord Byron into Russian and that of the Russian writer Alexander Pushkin into English, and he wrote an essay, "The Role of the Intellectuals in the Liberating Movement in Russia," that was published in 1918 in a collection entitled* The Russian Revolution. *"The Spider and the Wasp," first published in* Scientific American *in 1952, examines how a wasp is able to attack and kill a tarantula without any resistance from the spider until the last moment.*

In the feeding and safeguarding of their progeny insects and [1] spiders exhibit some interesting analogies to reasoning and some crass examples of blind instinct. The case I propose to describe here is that of the tarantula spiders and their archenemy, the digger wasps of the genus *Pepsis*. It is a classic example of what looks like intelligence pitted against instinct—a strange situation in which the victim, though fully able to defend itself, submits unwittingly to its destruction.

Most tarantulas live in the tropics, but several species occur in the [2] temperate zone and a few are common in the southern U.S. Some varieties are large and have powerful fangs with which they can inflict a deep wound. These formidable-looking spiders do not, however, attack man; you can hold one in your hand, if you are gentle, without being bitten. Their bite is dangerous only to insects and small mammals such as mice; for man it is no worse than a hornet's sting.

Tarantulas customarily live in deep cylindrical burrows, from [3] which they emerge at dusk and into which they retire at dawn. Mature males wander about after dark in search of females and occasionally stray into houses. After mating, the male dies in a few weeks, but a female lives much longer and can mate several years in succession. In a Paris museum is a tropical specimen which is said to have been living in captivity for 25 years.

A fertilized female tarantula lays from 200 to 400 eggs at a time; thus it is possible for a single tarantula to produce several thousand young. She takes no care of them beyond weaving a cocoon of silk to enclose the eggs. After they hatch, the young walk away, find convenient places in which to dig their burrows and spend the rest of their lives in solitude. The eyesight of tarantulas is poor, being limited to a sensing of change in the intensity of light and to the perception of moving objects. They apparently have little or no sense of hearing, for a hungry tarantula will pay no attention to a loudly chirping cricket placed in its cage unless the insect happens to touch one of its legs. 4

But all spiders, and especially hairy ones, have an extremely delicate sense of touch. Laboratory experiments prove that tarantulas can distinguish three types of touch: pressure against the body wall, stroking of the body hair, and riffling of certain very fine hairs on the legs called trichobothria. Pressure against the body, by the finger or the end of a pencil, causes the tarantula to move off slowly for a short distance. The touch excites no defensive response unless the approach is from above where the spider can see the motion, in which case it rises on its hind legs, lifts its front legs, opens its fangs and holds this threatening posture as long as the object continues to move. 5

The entire body of a tarantula, especially its legs, is thickly clothed with hair. Some of it is short and wooly, some long and stiff. Touching this body hair produces one of two distinct reactions. When the spider is hungry, it responds with an immediate and swift attack. At the touch of a cricket's antennae the tarantula seizes the insect so swiftly that a motion picture taken at the rate of 64 frames per second shows only the result and not the process of capture. But when the spider is not hungry, the stimulation of its hairs merely causes it to shake the touched limb. An insect can walk under its hairy belly unharmed. 6

The trichobothria, very fine hairs growing from disklike membranes on the legs, are sensitive only to air movement. A light breeze makes them vibrate slowly, without disturbing the common hair. When one blows gently on the trichobothria, the tarantula reacts with a quick jerk of its four front legs. If the front and hind legs are stimulated at the same time, the spider makes a sudden jump. This reaction is quite independent of the state of its appetite. 7

These three tactile responses—to pressure on the body wall, to moving of the common hair, and to flexing of the trichobothria—are so different from one another that there is no possibility of confusing 8 them. They serve the tarantula adequately for most of its needs and enable it to avoid most annoyances and dangers. But they fail the spider completely when it meets its deadly enemy, the digger wasp *Pepsis.*

These solitary wasps are beautiful and formidable creatures. Most 9 species are either a deep shiny blue all over, or deep blue with rusty wings. The largest have a wing span of about 4 inches. They live on nectar. When excited, they give off a pungent odor—a warning that they are ready to attack. The sting is much worse than that of a bee or common wasp, and the pain and swelling last longer. In the adult stage the wasp lives only a few months. The female produces but a few eggs, one at a time at intervals of two or three days. For each egg the mother must provide one adult tarantula, alive but paralyzed. The mother wasp attaches the egg to the paralyzed spider's abdomen. Upon hatching from the egg, the larva is many hundreds of times smaller than its living but helpless victim. It eats no other food and drinks no water. By the time it has finished its single Gargantuan meal and become ready for wasphood, nothing remains of the tarantula but its indigestible chitinous skeleton.

The mother wasp goes tarantula-hunting when the egg in her 10 ovary is almost ready to be laid. Flying low over the ground late on a sunny afternoon, the wasp looks for its victim or for the mouth of a tarantula burrow, a round hole edged by a bit of silk. The sex of the spider makes no difference, but the mother is highly discriminating as to species. Each species of *Pepsis* requires a certain species of tarantula, and the wasp will not attack the wrong species. In a cage with a tarantula which is not its normal prey, the wasp avoids the spider and is usually killed by it in the night.

Yet when a wasp finds the correct species, it is the other way 11 about. To identify the species the wasp apparently must explore the spider with her antennae. The tarantula shows an amazing tolerance to this exploration. The wasp crawls under it and walks over it without evoking any hostile response. The molestation is so great and so persistent that the tarantula often rises on all eight legs, as if it were on stilts. It may stand this way for several minutes. Meanwhile the wasp, having satisfied itself that the victim is of the right species, moves off a few inches to dig the spider's grave. Working vigorously with legs and jaws, it excavates a hole 8 to 10 inches deep with a diameter slightly larger than the spider's girth. Now and again the wasp pops out of the hole to make sure that the spider is still there.

When the grave is finished, the wasp returns to the tarantula to 12 complete her ghastly enterprise. First she feels it all over once more with her antennae. Then her behavior becomes more aggressive. She bends her abdomen, protruding her sting, and searches for the soft membrane at the point where the spider's legs join its body—the only spot where she can penetrate the horny skeleton. From time to time, as the exasperated spider slowly shifts ground, the wasp turns on her back and slides along with the aid of her wings, trying to get under the tarantula for a shot at the vital spot. During all this maneuvering, which can last for several minutes, the tarantula makes no move to save itself. Finally the wasp corners it against some obstruction and grasps one of its legs in her powerful jaws. Now at last the harassed spider tries a desperate but vain defense. The two contestants roll over and over on the ground. It is a terrifying sight and the outcome is always the same. The wasp finally manages to thrust her sting into the soft spot and holds it there for a few seconds while she pumps in the poison. Almost immediately the tarantula falls paralyzed on its back. Its legs stop twitching; its heart stops beating. Yet it is not dead, as is shown by the fact that if taken from the wasp it can be restored to some sensitivity by being kept in a moist chamber for several months.

After paralyzing the tarantula, the wasp cleans herself by drag- 13
ging her body along the ground and rubbing her feet, sucks a drop of blood oozing from the wound in the spider's abdomen, then grabs a leg of the flabby, helpless animal in her jaws and drags it down to the bottom of the grave. She stays there for many minutes, sometimes for several hours, and what she does all that time in the dark we do not know. Eventually she lays her egg and attaches it to the side of the spider's abdomen with a sticky secretion. Then she emerges, fills the grave with soil carried bit by bit in her jaws, and finally tramples the ground all around to hide any trace of the grave from prowlers. Then she flies away, leaving her descendant safely started in life.

In all this the behavior of the wasp evidently is qualitatively dif- 14
ferent from that of the spider. The wasp acts like an intelligent animal. This is not to say that instinct plays no part or that she reasons as man does. But her actions are to the point; they are not automatic and can be modified to fit the situation. We do not know for certain how she identifies the tarantula—probably it is by some olfactory or chemo-tactile sense—but she does it purposefully and does not blindly tackle a wrong species.

On the other hand, the tarantula's behavior shows only confusion. 15
Evidently the wasp's pawing gives it no pleasure, for it tries to move away. That the wasp is not simulating sexual stimulation is certain because male and female tarantulas react in the same way to its

advances. That the spider is not anesthetized by some odorless secretion is easily shown by blowing slightly at the tarantula and making it jump suddenly. What, then, makes the tarantula behave as stupidly as it does?

No clear, simple answer is available. Possibly the stimulation by   16
the wasp's antennae is masked by a heavier pressure on the spider's body, so that it reacts as when prodded by a pencil. But the explanation may be much more complex. Initiative in attack is not in the nature of tarantulas; most species fight only when cornered so that escape is impossible. Their inherited patterns of behavior apparently prompt them to avoid problems rather than attack them. For example, spiders always weave their webs in three dimensions, and when a spider finds that there is insufficient space to attach certain threads in the third dimension, it leaves the place and seeks another, instead of finishing the web in a single plane. This urge to escape seems to arise under all circumstances, in all phases of life, and to take the place of reasoning. For a spider to change the pattern of its web is as impossible as for an inexperienced man to build a bridge across a chasm obstructing his way.

In a way the instinctive urge to escape is not only easier but often   17
more efficient than reasoning. The tarantula does exactly what is most efficient in all cases except in an encounter with a ruthless and determined attacker dependent for the existence of her own species on killing as many tarantulas as she can lay eggs. Perhaps in this case the spider follows its usual pattern of trying to escape, instead of seizing and killing the wasp, because it is not aware of its danger. In any case, the survival of the tarantula species as a whole is protected by the fact that the spider is much more fertile than the wasp.

COMPREHENSION

1. List some of the tarantula's most striking physical features. List some of the wasp's most striking physical features.

2. Why *must* the wasp paralyze the tarantula?

3. What does Petrunkevitch see as the single most obvious contrast between the behavior of the wasp and that of the spider?

4. Why, according to Petrunkevitch, does the spider behave with such apparent stupidity in its encounter with the wasp?

5. Why is the fact that the tarantula is more fertile than the wasp so important?

PURPOSE AND AUDIENCE

1. Does "The Spider and the Wasp" include an explicitly stated thesis? If so, what is it? If not, why not?

2. *Scientific American,* in which "The Spider and the Wasp" first appeared, is a periodical aimed not at scientists but at a well-educated audience with an interest in science. What techniques are used by Petrunkevitch, a zoologist, to attract and hold the interest of this audience?

3. What do you think is Petrunkevitch's purpose in spending so much more time describing the spider than the wasp? Does he accomplish this end? Explain.

STYLE AND STRUCTURE

1. Where does Petrunkevitch actually begin his discussion of the process by which a wasp kills a tarantula?

2. In the essay's opening paragraphs, Petrunkevitch describes first the spider and then the wasp. How does he indicate his movement from one subject to the other?

3. Why does Petrunkevitch supply detailed descriptions of both the spider and the wasp before he begins to describe the process?

4. In the section of the essay devoted to the process explanation, what transitional words and phrases help readers to follow the steps of the process?

5. What verb tense does Petrunkevitch use in his explanation of the process? Why does he select this tense?

6. In paragraph 11 Petrunkevitch uses an analogy to help readers visualize the tarantula's reaction to the wasp. What is this analogy? Where else does Petrunkevitch use analogies to clarify his explanations?

7. Petrunkevitch makes frequent use of *parallelism* in his essay. One example of this technique is "They serve the tarantula adequately. ... But they fail the spider completely...." Give some additional examples of parallel constructions. How does parallelism strengthen the essay?

VOCABULARY PROJECTS

1. Define each of the following words as it is used in this selection.

progeny (1)   tactile (8)   olfactory (14)
crass (1)   Gargantuan (9)
unwittingly (1) chitinous (9)

2. Although Petrunkevitch knows his audience is not composed of zoologists, his topic requires that he use an occasional technical term. Still, he is careful to accommodate his audience by defining such terms or by placing them in a context that suggests their meaning. Give examples of two or three such technical terms, and explain the concessions Petrunkevitch makes to his audience in each case.

3. At times Petrunkevitch uses distinctly unscientific language—for example, "the wasp pops out of the hole" (11); "her ghastly enterprise" (12). Give other examples of such language, and explain why you think Petrunkevitch uses it.

JOURNAL ENTRY

Choose one paragraph of "The Spider and the Wasp," and rewrite it so that it is appropriate for an elementary school science textbook. When you have finished your revision, make a list of the kinds of changes you have made and explain why each was necessary. (Note: You will need to use a dictionary for this exercise.)

WRITING WORKSHOP

1. In paragraph 1 Petrunkevitch calls the spider-wasp confrontation "a classic example of what looks like intelligence pitted against instinct—a strange situation in which the victim, though fully able to defend itself, submits unwittingly to its destruction." Write a process essay in which you explain a similar "strange situation" from your own reading or experience—for example, deciding not to respond to a dangerous physical challenge or not to pursue an argument even though you believed you were right.

2. Retell the "story" of the encounter between the spider and the wasp as an animal fable like Aesop's "The Fox and the Grapes." Keep the process structure of the original essay, but try to portray the spider and the wasp as more fully realized characters. Include dialogue if you like, and be sure to include a moral at the end of your story.

3. Describe the process Petrunkevitch outlines from the point of view of either the spider or the wasp. Use first person and present tense.

THEMATIC CONNECTIONS

- "The Lottery" (p. 272)
- "It's Just Too Late" (p. 325)
- "The Catbird Seat" (p. 522)

ANATOMY OF A JOKE

Garry Trudeau

Garry Trudeau was born in 1948 in New York City and attended Yale University and Yale's School of Art and Architecture, from which he received a master's degree in fine arts in 1970. He is the creator of the comic strip "Doonesbury," which is syndicated nationwide. The strips have been compiled in numerous books. Trudeau won a Pulitzer Prize for editorial cartooning in 1975 and was nominated for an Academy Award in 1977 for the animated film A Doonesbury Special. *He is also an occasional contributor to the Op-Ed page of the* New York Times, *where "Anatomy of a Joke" appeared in 1993. In this piece, Trudeau outlines the detailed procedure by which a single joke for* The Tonight Show *is developed from the initial idea to the comic's delivery.*

In the wake of last week's press "availabilities" of funnymen Dave Letterman, Jay Leno, Chevy Chase et al., there was much rim-shot critiquing, all of it missing the point.

The real jokes, the ones that count, occur not at press events but during those extraordinary little set pieces called monologues. Despite the popular conception of the monologue as edgy and unpredictable, it is actually as formal and structured as anything found in traditional kabuki. The stakes are too high for it to be otherwise. Even the ad-libs, rejoinders and recoveries are carefully scripted. While it may suit Leno's image to portray the "Tonight" show monologue as something that's banged out over late-night pizza with a few cronies, in fact each joke requires the concerted effort of a crack team of six highly disciplined comedy professionals. To illustrate how it works, let's follow an actual topical joke, told the night of Monday, July 26, as it makes its way through the pipeline.

The inspiration for a topical joke is literally torn from the headlines by a professional comedy news "clipper." Comedy news reading is sometimes contracted out to consultants, but the big-budget "Tonight" show has 12 of its own in-house clippers who peruse some 300 newspapers every day. Clippers know that the idea for the joke must be contained in the headline or, at worst, the subhead. If the idea is in the body text, then the general public has probably missed it and won't grasp the reference the joke is built around. In this case, the clipper has spied an item about flood relief.

A20 Friday, July 23, 1993

House Delays Final Flood Aid Vote

$3 Billion Package Stalls in Dispute Over Budget Limits

The Washington Post

The news clip is then passed on to a comedy "engineer," whose job 4
is to decide what shape the joke should take. After analyzing the
headline, the engineer decides how many parts the joke should have,
the velocity of its build, whether it contains any red herrings (rare
on the "Tonight" show), and the dynamics of the payoff and underlaughing. With Monday's joke, the engineer chose a simple inter-
rogatory setup, which telegraphs to the often sleepy audience that
the next line contains a payoff. The finished sequencing is then sent
on to the "stylist."

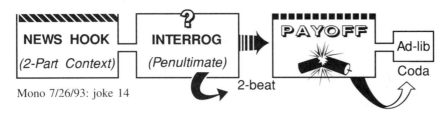

NEWS HOOK   INTERROG   PAYOFF   Ad-lib

(2-Part Context)   (Penultimate)   Coda

Mono 7/26/93: joke 14   2-beat

The comedy stylist is the writer who actually fashions the raw 5
joke. The stylist is the prima donna of the team, the best paid, the
worst dressed—and never in the office. The stylist, who is typically
a per diem session player, is faxed the original headline, the structural scheme and a gross time count, and from those elements
creates the rough draft for the joke. It's up to him to find the joke's
"spring," that tiny component of universal truth that acts as the
joke's fulcrum. In this case, the joke hinges on the public's resentment of Congress, a hoary but proven truism. The stylist then faxes
his finished rough to the "polish man."

```
1./It looks like the House of Representatives is
having trouble voting flood relief because they're
worried about where to appropriate the money from./
2. /Here's my question./
3./ How come when the House votes itself a pay raise,
they never worry about that appropriation?
```

    ⊘ *too long*   (*Senate*)

It looks like the ~~House of Representatives~~ is

          passing, ⊘ *where?* *for the midwest*)

having troub~~le voting~~ flood relief because ~~they're~~

(*some Senators are*)   (*is going to come*)

worried about where ~~to appropriate~~ the money from.

(*Now,*)

Here's my question: How come when the ~~House~~ (*Senate*) votes

     big   (*wonder where*)

itself a pay raise, they never ~~worry about~~ that

money's coming from?

~~appropriation?~~   *ad-libs: Ever notice that?*

It just seems to fall from the sky.

The polish man, usually a woman, is the joke's editor, charged 6
with burnishing the joke until it gleams. Obscure references, awkward phrasing and puns are all removed, and any potentially offensive material is run by an outside anti-defamation consultant. Unlike the stylist, who usually works at his beach house, the polish man is always on the premises, available in the event of emergency rewrites. For Monday's joke, the polish man adds a "fall from the sky" coda that will allow Leno some physical business. The decision to use it, however, ultimately rests with the "timing coach."

The timing coach is responsible for timing out the phrasing and 7
pauses, and bringing the 21-joke routine in under its seven-minute limit. Running over is a major no-no. During the Carson era, a timing coach, who asked not to be identified, signed off on a monologue that ran 13.5 seconds long, a deficit that came out of Barbra Streisand's guest segment. The coach was summarily sacked. Such errors are rare today, however, as the monologues are now digitalized on disk. A timer can modulate the phrasing pattern to within 0.01 of a second, well beyond the performance sensitivity of any comic but Robin Williams.

(6.3 sec. to pause) IT LOOKS LIKE...FLOOD RELIEF...WORRIED...
MONEY IS GOING TO COME FROM. (.95 sec. beat) NOW, HERE'S
MY QUESTION; (.6 second beat; 3.45 sec. to ad-lib) HOW COME...
BIG PAY RAISE...WHERE <u>THAT</u> MONEY'S COMING FROM? (ad-lib
under laugh; see menu).

The final joke is then E-mailed to the "talent," in this case Jay   8
Leno. Leno dry-runs the joke in his office, adding spin and body
movement, and locks in his ad-libs, including recovery lines in case
the joke bombs. (Carson had such good recovery material that he
used to commission intentionally bad jokes, but Leno has not yet
reached that pinnacle of impeccability.) Once Leno approves the
joke, it is transferred to a hard disk and laser-printed on cue cards
with a special font to make it look hand-lettered. Finally, at exactly
5:30 P.M., California taping time, Leno walks out on stage and reads
it to 15 million people.

COMPREHENSION

1. Identify each of the six people involved in writing a typical joke, and
   explain what each contributes to the process.

2. What is the inspiration for most of the jokes that are told in late-night
   talk-show monologues? Why do you suppose this is so?

PURPOSE AND AUDIENCE

1. Trudeau, the creator of the *Doonesbury* comic strip, is known primarily as a cartoonist, yet this essay originally appeared as a column in
   the *New York Times*. What, if anything, do these details and Trudeau's
   comments in paragraphs 1 and 2 suggest about his purpose for
   explaining how a joke is created?

2. Does Trudeau seem to assume his audience is familiar with late-night
   comedy programs? If so, do you believe this assumption is justified?
   Explain.

3. Where does Trudeau state his essay's thesis? Restate it in your own
   words. Do you think such a restatement of the thesis should appear in
   the essay's conclusion? Explain.

STYLE AND STRUCTURE

1. List the individual stages in the process Trudeau describes.

2. What transitional expressions does Trudeau use to move his readers
   through each stage of the process? How does he connect one stage to
   the next? Are any additional transitions necessary for clarity?

3. Do you think Trudeau is being serious when he refers to the joke
   writers as a "crack team of six highly disciplined comedy professionals" (2)? Explain your reasoning.

4. What elements typically included in a process explanation are absent here? Why?

5. Could Trudeau have used another pattern to support his thesis? If so, which one? If not, why not?

6. Do you think the illustrations are necessary? Do they add to or detract from the essay's effectiveness? Explain.

VOCABULARY PROJECTS

1. Define each of the following words as it is used in this selection.

anatomy (title)	fulcrum (5)	summarily (7)
kabuki (2)	hoary (5)	spin (8)
rejoinders (2)	truism (5)	pinnacle (8)
velocity (4)	burnishing (6)	impeccability (8)
red herrings (4)	coda (6)	
per diem (5)	business (6)	

2. Trudeau's essay includes many examples of *colloquialisms,* such as paragraph 2's "cronies" and "banged out." Choose one paragraph and identify additional examples of colloquialisms. What other features can you identify that mark this essay's style as informal?

3. The essay also includes a good deal of *jargon,* such as paragraph 4's "underlaughing" and "sequencing." Do you think Trudeau should define these terms? Why?

JOURNAL ENTRY

Does Trudeau's essay change the way you view your favorite late-night television talk-show host? If so, how?

WRITING WORKSHOP

1. Write an essay (serious or humorous) in which you explain your process of writing and revision. Include a thesis statement that assesses the effectiveness of your writing process.

2. Write a set of instructions in which your goal is to convince a younger student of the importance of revision. If you like, you may include an illustration like the one that follows paragraph 6 in Trudeau's essay.

3. Record the process of writing your own topical joke. Begin with an idea "literally torn from the headlines," and include a thesis that comments on how difficult the process is.

THEMATIC CONNECTIONS

- "The Open Window" (p. 106)
- "Television: The Plug-In Drug" (p. 303)
- "The Catbird Seat" (p. 522)

THE EMBALMING
OF MR. JONES

Jessica Mitford

Jessica Mitford was born in 1917 in Batsford Mansion, England, to a wealthy, aristocratic family. She rebelled against her sheltered upbringing, becoming involved in left-wing politics and eventually emigrating to the United States. Mitford has written two volumes of autobiography, Daughters and Rebels *(1960), about her eccentric family, and* A Fine Old Conflict *(1976), about her and her husband's involvement with the Communist Party. After leaving the party in the 1950s, she began a career in investigative journalism, which has produced the books* The American Way of Death *(1963), on the mortuary business;* Kind and Unusual Punishment: The Prison Business *(1973), on the prison system;* Poison Penmanship: The Gentle Art of Muckraking *(1979), a collection of articles; and most recently* The American Way of Birth *(1992), about the crisis in American obstetrical care and the role of midwives. "The Embalming of Mr. Jones" is excerpted from* The American Way of Death. *This book criticized the funeral industry and sharpened public scrutiny of the way funerals are handled; it also prompted angry responses from morticians. Here Mitford painstakingly and ironically describes the dual process of embalming and restoring a cadaver.*

Embalming is indeed a most extraordinary procedure, and one must wonder at the docility of Americans who each year pay hundreds of millions of dollars for its perpetuation, blissfully ignorant of what it is all about, what is done, how it is done. Not one in ten thousand has any idea of what actually takes place. Books on the subject are extremely hard to come by. They are not to be found in most libraries or bookshops.

In an era when huge television audiences watch surgical operations in the comfort of their living rooms, when, thanks to the animated cartoon, the geography of the digestive system has become familiar territory even to the nursery school set, in a land where the satisfaction of curiosity about almost all matters is a national pastime, the secrecy surrounding embalming can, surely, hardly be attributed to the inherent gruesomeness of the subject. Custom in this regard has within this century suffered a complete reversal. In the early days of American embalming, when it was performed in the home of the deceased, it was almost mandatory for some relative to stay by the embalmer's side and witness the procedure. Today, family members who might wish to be in attendance would certainly be dissuaded by the funeral director. All others, except apprentices, are excluded by law from the preparation room.

A close look at what does actually take place may explain in large measure the undertaker's intractable reticence concerning a procedure that has become his major *raison d'être*. Is it possible he fears that public information about embalming might lead patrons to wonder if they really want this service? If the funeral men are loath to discuss the subject outside the trade, the reader may, understandably, be equally loath to go on reading at this point. For those who have the stomach for it, let us part the formaldehyde curtain. . . .

The body is first laid out in the undertaker's morgue—or rather, Mr. Jones is reposing in the preparation room—to be readied to bid the world farewell.

The preparation room in any of the better funeral establishments has the tiled and sterile look of a surgery, and indeed the embalmer-restorative artist who does his chores there is beginning to adopt the term "dermasurgeon" (appropriately corrupted by some mortician-writers as "demisurgeon") to describe his calling. His equipment, consisting of scalpels, scissors, augers, forceps, clamps, needles, pumps, tubes, bowls and basins, is crudely imitative of the surgeon's as is his technique, acquired in a nine- or twelve-month post-high-school course in an embalming school. He is supplied by an advanced chemical industry with a bewildering array of fluids, sprays, pastes, oils, powders, creams, to fix or soften tissue, shrink or distend it as needed, dry it here, restore the moisture there. There are cosmetics, waxes and paints to fill and cover features, even plaster of Paris to replace entire limbs. There are ingenious aids to prop and stabilize the cadaver: a Vari-Pose Head Rest, the Edwards Arm and Hand Positioner, the Repose Block (to support the shoulders during the embalming), and the Throop Foot Positioner, which resembles an old-fashioned stocks.

Mr. John H. Eckels, president of the Eckels College of Mortuary Science, thus describes the first part of the embalming procedure: "In the hands of a skilled practitioner, this work may be done in a comparatively short time and without mutilating the body other than by slight incision—so slight that it scarcely would cause serious inconvenience if made upon a living person. It is necessary to remove all the blood, and doing this not only helps in the disinfecting, but removes the principal cause of disfigurements due to discoloration."

Another textbook discusses the all-important time element: "The earlier this is done, the better, for every hour that elapses between death and embalming will add to the problems and complications encountered. . . ." Just how soon should one get going on the embalming? The author tells us, "On the basis of such scanty information made available to this profession through its rudimentary and haphazard system of technical research, we must conclude that the best results are to be obtained if the subject is embalmed before life is completely extinct—that is, before cellular death has occurred. In the average case, this would mean within an hour after somatic death." For those who feel that there is something a little rudimentary, not to say haphazard, about this advice, a comforting thought is offered by another writer. Speaking of fears entertained in early days of premature burial, he points out, "One of the effects of embalming by chemical injection, however, has been to dispel fears of live burial." How true; once the blood is removed, chances of live burial are indeed remote.

To return to Mr. Jones, the blood is drained out through the veins and replaced by embalming fluid pumped in through the arteries. As noted in *The Principles and Practices of Embalming,* "every operator has a favorite injection and drainage point—a fact which becomes a handicap only if he fails or refuses to forsake his favorites when conditions demand it." Typical favorites are the carotid artery, femoral artery, jugular vein, subclavian vein. There are various choices of embalming fluid. If Flextone is used, it will produce a "mild, flexible rigidity. The skin retains a velvety softness, the tissues are rubbery and pliable. Ideal for women and children." It may be blended with B. and G. Products Company's Lyf-Lyk tint, which is guaranteed to reproduce "nature's own skin texture . . . the velvety appearance of living tissue." Suntone comes in three separate tints: Suntan; Special Cosmetic Tint, a pink shade "especially indicated for young female subjects"; and Regular Cosmetic Tint, moderately pink.

About three to six gallons of a dyed and perfumed solution of formaldehyde, glycerin, borax, phenol, alcohol and water is soon circulating through Mr. Jones, whose mouth has been sewn together with a "needle directed upward between the upper lip and gum and brought out through the left nostril," with the corners raised slightly "for a more pleasant expression." If he should be buck-toothed, his teeth are cleaned with Bon Ami and coated with colorless nail polish. His eyes, meanwhile, are closed with flesh-tinted eye caps and eye cement.

The next step is to have at Mr. Jones with a thing called a trocar. This is a long, hollow needle attached to a tube. It is jabbed into the abdomen, poked around the entrails and chest cavity, the contents of which are pumped out and replaced with "cavity fluid." This is done, and the hole in the abdomen sewed up, Mr. Jones's face is heavily creamed (to protect the skin from burns which may be caused by leakage of the chemicals), and he is covered with a sheet and left unmolested for a while. But not for long—there is more, much more, in store for him. He has been embalmed, but not yet restored, and the best time to start restorative work is eight to ten hours after embalming, when the tissues have become firm and dry.

The object of all this attention to the corpse, it must be remem- 11
bered, is to make it presentable for viewing in an attitude of healthy repose. "Our customs require the presentation of our dead in the semblance of normality . . . unmarred by the ravages of illness, disease or mutilation," says Mr. J. Sheridan Mayer in his *Restorative Art.* This is rather a large order since few people die in the full bloom of health, unravaged by illness and unmarked by some disfigurement. The funeral industry is equal to the challenge: "In some cases the gruesome appearance of a mutilated or disease-ridden subject may be quite discouraging. The task of restoration may seem impossible and shake the confidence of the embalmer. This is the time for intestinal fortitude and determination. Once the formative work is begun and affected tissues are cleaned or removed, all doubts of success vanish. It is surprising and gratifying to discover the results which may be obtained."

The embalmer, having allowed an appropriate interval to elapse, 12
returns to the attack, but now he brings into play the skill and equipment of sculptor and cosmetician. Is a hand missing? Casting one in plaster of Paris is a simple matter. "For replacement purposes, only a cast of the back of the hand is necessary; this is within the ability of the average operator and is quite adequate." If a lip or two, a nose or an ear should be missing, the embalmer has at hand a variety of restorative waxes with which to model replacements. Pores and skin texture are simulated by stippling with a little brush, and over this cosmetics are laid on. Head off? Decapitation cases are rather routinely handled. Ragged edges are trimmed, and head joined to torso with a series of splints, wires and sutures. It is a good idea to have a little something at the neck—a scarf or high collar—when time for viewing comes. Swollen mouth? Cut out tissue as needed from inside the lips. If too much is removed, the surface contour can easily be restored by padding with cotton. Swollen necks and cheeks are reduced by removing tissue through vertical incisions made down each side of the neck. "When the deceased is casketed, the pillow will hide the suture incisions . . . as an extra precaution against leakage, the suture may be painted with liquid sealer."

The opposite condition is more likely to be present itself—that 13
of emaciation. His hypodermnic syringe now loaded with massage
cream, the embalmer seeks out and fills the hollowed and sunken
areas by injection. In this procedure the backs of the hands and
fingers and the under-chin area should not be neglected.

Positioning the lips is a problem that recurrently challenges the 14
ingenuity of the embalmer. Closed too tightly, they tend to give
a stern, even disapproving expression. Ideally, embalmers feel, the
lips should give the impression of being ever so slightly parted, the
upper lip protruding slightly for a more youthful appearance. This
takes some engineering, however, as the lips tend to drift apart. Lip
drift can sometimes be remedied by pushing one or two straight pins
through the inner margin of the lower lip and then inserting them
between the two front upper teeth. If Mr. Jones happens to have no
teeth, the pins can just as easily be anchored in his Armstrong Face
Former and Denture Replacer. Another method to maintain lip closure is to dislocate the lower jaw, which is then held in its new position by a wire run through holes which have been drilled through
the upper jaws at the midline. As the French are fond of saying, *il
faut souffrir pour être belle.**

If Mr. Jones has died of jaundice, the embalming fluid will very 15
likely turn him green. Does this deter the embalmer? Not if he has
intestinal fortitude. Masking pastes and cosmetics are heavily laid
on, burial garments and casket interiors are color-correlated with
particular care, and Jones is displayed beneath rose-colored lights.
Friends will say, "How *well* he looks." Death by carbon monoxide,
on the other hand, can be rather a good thing from the embalmer's
viewpoint: "One advantage is the fact that this type of discoloration
is an exaggerated form of a natural pink coloration." This is nice
because the healthy glow is already present and needs but little
attention.

The patching and filling completed, Mr. Jones is now shaved, 16
washed and dressed. Cream-based cosmetic, available in pink, flesh,
suntan, brunette and blonde, is applied to his hands and face, his
hair is shampooed and combed (and, in the case of Mrs. Jones, set),
his hands manicured. For the horny-handed son of toil special care
must be taken; cream should be applied to remove ingrained grime,
and the nails cleaned. "If he were not in the habit of having them
manicured in life, trimming and shaping is advised for better
appearance—never questioned by kin."

*Eds. Note—It is necessary to suffer in order to be beautiful.

Jones is now ready for casketing (this is the present participle of   17
the verb "to casket"). In this operation his right shoulder should be
depressed slightly "to turn the body a bit to the right and soften the
appearance of lying flat on the back." Positioning the hands is a matter of importance, and special rubber positioning blocks may be used.
The hands should be cupped slightly for a more lifelike, relaxed appearance. Proper placement of the body requires a delicate sense of
balance. It should lie as high as possible in the casket, yet not so
high that the lid, when lowered, will hit the nose. On the other hand,
we are cautioned, placing the body too low "creates the impression
that the body is in a box."

Jones is next wheeled into the appointed slumber room where a   18
few last touches may be added—his favorite pipe placed in his hand
or, if he was a great reader, a book propped into position. (In the case
of little Master Jones a Teddy bear may be clutched.) Here he will
hold open house for a few days, visiting hours 10 A.M. to 9 P.M.

COMPREHENSION

1. How, according to Mitford, has the public's knowledge of embalming
   changed? How does she explain this change?

2. To what other professionals does Mitford liken the embalmer? Are
   these analogies flattering or critical? Explain.

3. What are the major stages in the process of embalming and restoration?

PURPOSE AND AUDIENCE

1. Mitford's purpose in this essay is to convince her audience of something. What is her thesis?

2. Does Mitford expect her audience to agree with her thesis? How can
   you tell?

3. In one of her books, Mitford refers to herself as a muckraker, one who
   informs the public of misconduct. Does she achieve this status here?
   Cite specific examples.

4. Mitford's tone in this essay is very subjective. What effect does her
   tone have on you? Does it encourage you to trust her? Should she have
   presented her facts in a more objective way? Explain.

STYLE AND STRUCTURE

1. Identify the stylistic features that distinguish this process explanation from a set of instructions.

2. In this selection, as in many process essays, a list of necessary materials precedes the procedure. What additional details does Mitford include in her list in paragraph 5? How do these additions affect you?

3. Go through the essay and locate the author's remarks about the language of embalming. How are these comments about euphemisms, newly coined words, and other aspects of language consistent with Mitford's thesis?

4. Throughout the essay, Mitford quotes a series of experts. How does she use their remarks to support her thesis?

5. What phrases signal Mitford's transitions between stages?

VOCABULARY PROJECTS

1. Define each of the following words as it is used in this selection.

   perpetuation (1)   rudimentary (7)   stippling (12)
   inherent (2)   haphazard (7)   emaciation (13)
   mandatory (2)   entertained (7)   recurrently (14)
   dissuaded (2)   pliable (8)   jaundice (15)
   intractable (3)   repose (11)   toil (16)
   reticence (3)   unravaged (11)
   loath (3)   fortitude (11)

2. Substitute another word for each of the following.

   territory (2)   ingenious (5)   presentable (11)
   gruesomeness (2)   jabbed (10)

   What effect does each of your changes have on Mitford's meaning?

3. Reread paragraphs 5–9 very carefully. Then, list all the words in this section of the essay that suggest surgical technique and all the words that suggest cosmetic artistry. What do your lists tell you about Mitford's intent in these paragraphs?

JOURNAL ENTRY

What are your thoughts about the way your religious or ethnic group deals with death and dying? What practices, if any, make you uncomfortable? Why?

WRITING WORKSHOP

1. Rewrite this process explanation as a set of instructions for undertakers, condensing it so that your essay is about five hundred words long. Unlike Mitford, keep your essay objective.

2. In the role of a funeral director, write a letter to Mitford in which you take issue with her essay. Explain the practice of embalming as necessary and practical. Design your process explanation, unlike Mitford's, to defend the practice.

3. Write an explanation of a process which you personally find disgusting—or delightful. Make your attitude clear in your thesis statement and your choice of words.

THEMATIC CONNECTIONS

- "My First Conk" (p. 245)
- "The Ways We Lie" (p. 455)

THE LOTTERY

Shirley Jackson

Shirley Jackson (1919–1965) was born in California and graduated from Syracuse University in 1940. Jackson is best known for her horror stories exploring human motivation and social behavior and for her suspense novels, macabre tales of loneliness and isolation, which include The Haunting of Hill House *(1959) and* We Have Always Lived in the Castle *(1962). Jackson also wrote accounts of her life as a wife and the mother of four children in* Life Among the Savages *(1953) and* Raising Demons *(1957). Two posthumous volumes,* The Magic of Shirley Jackson *(1966) and* Come Along with Me *(1968), collect Jackson's stories, novels, and lectures. "The Lottery," Jackson's best-known story, first appeared in 1948 in* The New Yorker, *where this haunting tale of an annual ritual inspired a flood of letters of protest and outrage as well as praise.*

The morning of June 27th was clear and sunny, with the fresh warmth of a full-summer day; the flowers were blossoming profusely and the grass was richly green. The people of the village began to gather in the square, between the post office and the bank, around ten o'clock; in some towns there were so many people that the lottery took two days and had to be started on June 26th, but in this village, where there were only about three hundred people, the whole lottery took less than two hours, so it could begin at ten o'clock in the morning and still be through in time to allow the villagers to get home for noon dinner.

The children assembled first, of course. School was recently over for the summer, and the feeling of liberty sat uneasily on most of them; they tended to gather together quietly for a while before they broke into boisterous play, and their talk was still of the classroom and the teacher, of books and reprimands. Bobby Martin had already stuffed his pockets full of stones, and the other boys soon followed his example, selecting the smoothest and roundest stones; Bobby and Harry Jones and Dickie Delacroix—the villagers pronounced his name "Dellacroy"—eventually made a great pile of stones in one corner of the square and guarded it against the raids of the other boys. The girls stood aside, talking among themselves, looking over their shoulders at the boys, and the very small children rolled in the dust or clung to the hands of their older brothers or sisters.

Soon the men began to gather, surveying their own children, speaking of planting and rain, tractors and taxes. They stood together, away from the pile of stones in the corner, and their jokes were quiet and they smiled rather than laughed. The women, wearing faded house dresses and sweaters, came shortly after their menfolk. They greeted one another and exchanged bits of gossip as they went to join their husbands. Soon the women, standing by their husbands, began to call to their children, and the children came reluctantly, having to be called four or five times. Bobby Martin ducked under his mother's grasping hand and ran, laughing, back to the pile of stones. His father spoke up sharply, and Bobby came quickly and took his place between his father and his oldest brother. 3

The lottery was conducted—as were the square dances, the teenage club, the Halloween program—by Mr. Summers, who had time and energy to devote to civic activities. He was a round-faced, jovial man and he ran the coal business, and people were sorry for him, because he had no children and his wife was a scold. When he arrived in the square, carrying the black wooden box, there was a murmur of conversation among the villagers, and he waved and called, "Little late today, folks." The postmaster, Mr. Graves, followed him, carrying a three-legged stool, and the stool was put in the center of the square and Mr. Summers set the black box down on it. The villagers kept their distance, leaving a space between themselves and the stool, and when Mr. Summers said, "Some of you fellows want to give me a hand?" there was a hesitation before two men, Mr. Martin and his oldest son, Baxter, came forward to hold the box steady on the stool while Mr. Summers stirred up the papers inside it. 4

The original paraphernalia for the lottery had been lost long ago, and the black box now resting on the stool had been put into use even before Old Man Warner, the oldest man in town, was born. Mr. Summers spoke frequently to the villagers about making a new box, but no one liked to upset even as much tradition as was represented by the black box. There was a story that the present box had been made with some pieces of the box that had preceded it, the one that had been constructed when the first people settled down to make a village here. Every year, after the lottery, Mr. Summers began talking again about a new box, but every year the subject was allowed to fade off without anything's being done. The black box grew shabbier each year; by now it was no longer completely black but splintered badly along one side to show the original wood color, and in some places faded or stained. 5

Mr. Martin and his oldest son, Baxter, held the black box securely on the stool until Mr. Summers had stirred the papers thoroughly 6 with his hand. Because so much of the ritual had been forgotten or discarded, Mr. Summers had been successful in having slips of paper substituted for the chips of wood that had been used for generations. Chips of wood, Mr. Summers had argued, had been all very well when the village was tiny, but now that the population was more than three hundred and likely to keep on growing, it was necessary to use something that would fit more easily into the black box. The night before the lottery, Mr. Summers and Mr. Graves made up the slips of paper and put them in the box, and it was then taken to the safe of Mr. Summers' coal company and locked up until Mr. Summers was ready to take it to the square next morning. The rest of the year, the box was put away, sometimes one place, sometimes another; it had spent one year in Mr. Graves' barn and another year underfoot in the post office, and sometimes it was set on a shelf in the Martin grocery and left there.

There was a great deal of fussing to be done before Mr. Summers   7 declared the lottery open. There were the lists to make up—of heads of families, heads of households in each family, members of each household in each family. There was the proper swearing-in of Mr. Summers by the postmaster, as the official of the lottery; at one time, some people remembered, there had been a recital of some sort, performed by the official of the lottery, a perfunctory, tuneless chant that had been rattled off duly each year; some people believed that the official of the lottery used to stand just so when he said or sang it, others believed that he was supposed to walk among the people, but years and years ago this part of the ritual had been allowed to lapse. There had been, also, a ritual salute, which the official of the lottery had had to use in addressing each person who came up to draw from the box, but this also had changed with time, until now it was felt necessary only for the official to speak to each person approaching. Mr. Summers was very good at all this; in his clean white shirt and blue jeans, with one hand resting carelessly on the black box, he seemed very proper and important as he talked interminably to Mr. Graves and the Martins.

Just as Mr. Summers finally left off talking and turned to the   8 assembled villagers, Mrs. Hutchinson came hurriedly along the path to the square, her sweater thrown over her shoulders, and slid into place in the back of the crowd. "Clean forgot what day it was," she said to Mrs. Delacroix, who stood next to her, and they both laughed softly. "Thought my old man was out back stacking wood," Mrs. Hutchinson went on, "and then I looked out the window and the kids were gone, and then I remembered it was the twenty-seventh and came a-running." She dried her hands on her apron, and Mrs. Delacroix said, "You're in time, though. They're still talk-ing away up there."

Mrs. Hutchinson craned her neck to see through the crowd and found her husband and children standing near the front. She tapped Mrs. Delacroix on the arm as a farewell and began to make her way through the crowd. The people separated good-humoredly to let her through; two or three people said, in voices just loud enough to be heard across the crowd, "Here comes your Missus, Hutchinson," and "Bill, she made it after all." Mrs. Hutchinson reached her husband, and Mr. Summers, who had been waiting, said cheerfully, "Thought we were going to have to get on without you, Tessie." Mrs. Hutch-inson said, grinning, "Wouldn't have me leave m'dishes in the sink, now, would you, Joe?," and soft laughter ran through the crowd as the people stirred back into position after Mrs. Hutchinson's arrival. 9

"Well, now," Mr. Summers said soberly, "guess we better get started, get this over with, so's we can go back to work. Anybody ain't here?" 10

"Dunbar," several people said. "Dunbar, Dunbar." 11

Mr. Summers consulted his list. "Clyde Dunbar," he said. "That's right. He's broke his leg, hasn't he? Who's drawing for him?" 12

"Me, I guess," a woman said, and Mr. Summers turned to look at her. "Wife draws for her husband," Mr. Summers said. "Don't you have a grown boy to do it for you, Janey?" Although Mr. Summers and everyone else in the village knew the answer perfectly well, it was the business of the official of the lottery to ask such questions formally. Mr. Summers waited with an expression of polite interest while Mrs. Dunbar answered. 13

"Horace's not but sixteen yet," Mrs. Dunbar said regretfully. "Guess I gotta fill in for the old man this year." 14

"Right," Mr. Summers said. He made a note on the list he was holding. Then he asked, "Watson boy drawing this year?" 15

A tall boy in the crowd raised his hand. "Here," he said. "I'm drawing for m'mother and me." He blinked his eyes nervously and ducked his head as several voices in the crowd said things like "Good fellow, Jack," and "Glad to see your mother's got a man to do it." 16

"Well," Mr. Summers said, "guess that's everyone. Old Man Warner make it?" 17

"Here," a voice said, and Mr. Summers nodded. 18

A sudden hush fell on the crowd as Mr. Summers cleared his throat and looked at the list. "All ready?" he called. "Now, I'll read the names—heads of families first—and the men come up and take a paper out of the box. Keep the paper folded in your hand without looking at it until everyone has had a turn. Everything clear?" 19

The people had done it so many times that they only half listened 20 to the directions; most of them were quiet, wetting their lips, not looking around. Then Mr. Summers raised one hand high and said, "Adams." A man disengaged himself from the crowd and came forward. "Hi, Steve," Mr. Summers said, and Mr. Adams said, "Hi, Joe." They grinned at one another humorlessly and nervously. Then Mr. Adams reached into the black box and took out a folded paper. He held it firmly by one corner as he turned and went hastily back to his place in the crowd, where he stood a little apart from his family, not looking down at his hand.

"Allen." Mr. Summers said. "Anderson. . . . Bentham." 21

"Seems like there's no time at all between lotteries any more," 22 Mrs. Delacroix said to Mrs. Graves in the back row. "Seems like we got through with the last one only last week."

"Time sure goes fast," Mrs. Graves said. 23

"Clark. . . . Delacroix." 24

"There goes my old man," Mrs. Delacroix said. She held her breath 25 while her husband went forward.

"Dunbar," Mr. Summers said, and Mrs. Dunbar went steadily to 26 the box while one of the women said, "Go on, Janey," and another said, "There she goes."

"We're next," Mrs. Graves said. She watched while Mr. Graves 27 came around from the side of the box, greeted Mr. Summers gravely, and selected a slip of paper from the box. By now, all through the crowd there were men holding the small folded papers in their large hands, turning them over and over nervously. Mrs. Dunbar and her two sons stood together, Mrs. Dunbar holding the slip of paper.

"Harburt. . . . Hutchinson." 28

"Get up there, Bill," Mrs. Hutchinson said, and the people near 29 her laughed.

"Jones." 30

"They do say," Mr. Adams said to Old Man Warner, who stood next 31 to him, "that over in the north village they're talking of giving up the lottery."

Old Man Warner snorted. "Pack of crazy fools," he said. "Listening 32 to the young folks, nothing's good enough for *them*. Next thing you know, they'll be wanting to go back to living in caves, nobody work any more, live *that* way for a while. Used to be a saying about 'Lottery in June, corn be heavy soon.' First thing you know, we'd all be eating stewed chickweed and acorns. There's *always* been a lottery," he added petulantly. "Bad enough to see young Joe Summers up there joking with everybody."

"Some places have already quit lotteries," Mrs. Adams said.   33

"Nothing but trouble in *that,*" Old Man Warner said stoutly. "Pack   34
of young fools."

"Martin." And Bobby Martin watched his father go forward.   35
"Overdyke. . . . Percy."

"I wish they'd hurry," Mrs. Dunbar said to her older son. "I wish   36
they'd hurry."

"They're almost through," her son said.   37

"You get ready to run tell Dad," Mrs. Dunbar said.   38

Mr. Summers called his own name and then stepped forward   39
precisely and selected a slip from the box. Then he called, "Warner."

"Seventy-seventh year I been in the lottery," Old Man Warner said   40
as he went through the crowd. "Seventy-seventh time."

"Watson." The tall boy came awkwardly through the crowd. Some-   41
one said, "Don't be nervous, Jack," and Mr. Summers said, "Take
your time, son."

"Zanini."   42

After that, there was a long pause, a breathless pause, until Mr.   43
Summers, holding his slip of paper in the air, said, "All right fellows." For a minute, no one moved, and then all the slips of paper
were opened. Suddenly, all the women began to speak at once, saying, "Who is it," "Who's got it?," "Is it the Dunbars?," "Is it the Wat-
sons?" Then the voices began to say, "It's Hutchinson. It's Bill," "Bill
Hutchinson's got it."

"Go tell your father," Mrs. Dunbar said to her older son.   44

People began to look around to see the Hutchinsons. Bill Hutch-   45
inson was standing quiet, staring down at the paper in his hand.
Suddenly, Tessie Hutchinson shouted to Mr. Summers, "You didn't
give him time enough to take any paper he wanted. I saw you. It
wasn't fair!"

"Be a good sport, Tessie," Mrs. Delacroix called, and Mrs. Graves   46
said, "All of us took the same chance."

"Shut up, Tessie," Bill Hutchinson said.   47

"Well, everyone," Mr. Summers said, "that was done pretty fast,   48
and now we've got to be hurrying a little more to get it done in time."
He consulted his next list. "Bill," he said, "you draw for the Hutchinson family. You got any other households in the Hutchinsons?"

"There's Don and Eva," Mrs. Hutchinson yelled. "Make *them* take   49
their chance!"

"Daughters draw with their husbands' families, Tessie," Mr. Sum-   50
mers said gently. "You know that as well as anyone else."

"It wasn't *fair,*" Tessie said. 51

"I guess not, Joe," Bill Hutchinson said regretfully. "My daughter 52
draws with her husband's family, that's only fair. And I've got no
other family except the kids."

"Then, as far as drawing for families is concerned, it's you," Mr. 53
Summers said in explanation, "and as far as drawing for households
is concerned, that's you, too. Right?"

"Right," Bill Hutchinson said." 54

"How many kids, Bill?" Mr. Summers asked formally. 55

"Three," Bill Hutchinson said. "There's Bill, Jr., and Nancy, and 56
little Dave. And Tessie and me."

"All right, then," Mr. Summers said. "Harry, you got their tickets 57
back?"

Mr. Graves nodded and held up the slips of paper. "Put them in the 58
box, then," Mr. Summers directed. "Take Bill's and put it in."

"I think we ought to start over," Mrs. Hutchinson said, as quietly 59
as she could. "I tell you it wasn't *fair.* You didn't give him time
enough to choose. *Every*body saw that."

Mr. Graves had selected the five slips and put them in the box, 60
and he dropped all the paper but those onto the ground, where the
breeze caught them and lifted them off.

"Listen, everybody," Mrs. Hutchinson was saying to the people 61
around her.

"Ready, Bill?" Mr. Summers asked, and Bill Hutchinson, with one 62
quick glance around at his wife and children, nodded.

"Remember," Mr. Summers said, "take the slips and keep them 63
folded until each person has taken one. Harry, you help little Dave."
Mr. Graves took the hand of the little boy, who came willingly with
him up to the box. "Take a paper out of the box, Davy," Mr. Summers
said. Davy put his hand into the box and laughed. "Take just *one*
paper," Mr. Summer said. "Harry, you hold it for him." Mr. Graves
took the child's hand and removed the folded paper from the tight
fist and held it while little Dave stood next to him and looked up at
him wonderingly.

"Nancy next," Mr. Summers said. Nancy was twelve, and her 64
school friends breathed heavily as she went forward, switching her
skirt, and took a slip daintily from the box. "Bill, Jr.," Mr. Summers
said, and Billy, his face red and his feet over-large, nearly knocked
the box over as he got a paper out. "Tessie," Mr. Summers said. She
hesitated for a minute, looking around defiantly, and then set her
lips and went up to the box. She snatched a paper out and held it
behind her.

"Bill," Mr. Summers said, and Bill Hutchinson reached into the 65 box and felt around, bringing his hand out at last with the slip of paper in it.

The crowd was quiet. A girl whispered, "I hope it's not Nancy," and the sound of the whisper reached the edges of the crowd. 66

"It's not the way it used to be," Old Man Warner said clearly. "People ain't the way they used to be." 67

"All right," Mr. Summers said. "Open the papers. Harry, you open little Dave's." 68

Mr. Graves opened the slip of paper and there was a general sigh through the crowd as he held it up and everyone could see that it was blank. Nancy and Bill, Jr., opened theirs at the same time, and both beamed and laughed, turning around to the crowd and holding their slips of paper above their heads. 69

"Tessie," Mr. Summers said. There was a pause, and then Mr. Summers looked at Bill Hutchinson, and Bill unfolded his paper and showed it. It was blank. 70

"It's Tessie," Mr. Summers said, and his voice was hushed. "Show us her paper, Bill." 71

Bill Hutchinson went over to his wife and forced the slip of paper out of her hand. It had a black spot on it, the black spot Mr. Summers had made the night before with the heavy pencil in the coal-company office. Bill Hutchinson held it up, and there was a stir in the crowd. 72

"All right, folks," Mr. Summers said. "Let's finish quickly." 73

Although the villagers had forgotten the ritual and lost the original black box, they still remembered to use stones. The pile of stones the boys had made earlier was ready; there were stones on the ground with the blowing scraps of paper that had come out of the box. Mrs. Delacroix selected a stone so large she had to pick it up with both hands and turned to Mrs. Dunbar. "Come on," she said. "Hurry up." 74

Mrs. Dunbar had small stones in both hands, and she said, gasping for breath, "I can't run at all. You'll have to go ahead and I'll catch up with you." 75

The children had stones already, and someone gave little Davy Hutchinson a few pebbles. 76

Tessie Hutchinson was in the center of a cleared space by now, and she held her hands out desperately as the villagers moved in on her. "It isn't fair," she said. A stone hit her on the side of the head. 77

Old Man Warner was saying, "Come on, come on, everyone." Steve Adams was in the front of the crowd of villagers, with Mrs. Graves beside him. 78

"It isn't fair, it isn't right," Mrs. Hutchinson screamed, and then they were upon her. 79

THINKING ABOUT LITERATURE

1. List the stages in the process of the lottery. Then, identify passages that explain the reasons behind each step. How logical are these explanations?

2. What is the significance of the fact that the process has continued essentially unchanged for so many years? What does this fact suggest about the people in the town?

3. Do you see this story as an explanation of a brutal process carried out in one particular town, or do you see it as a universal statement about dangerous tendencies in modern society—or in human nature? Explain your reasoning.

JOURNAL ENTRY

What do you think it would take to stop a process like the lottery? What could be done—and who would have to do it?

THEMATIC CONNECTIONS

- "38 Who Saw Murder Didn't Call the Police" (p. 91)
- "Shooting an Elephant" (p. 96)
- "Samuel" (p. 226)

WRITING ASSIGNMENTS FOR PROCESS

1. Write a short explanation of the process you follow when you compose on a computer.

2. Write a set of instructions explaining in very objective terms how the lottery Shirley Jackson describes should be conducted. Imagine you are setting these steps down in writing for generations of your fellow townspeople to follow.

3. Write a consumer-oriented article for your school newspaper in which you explain how to apply for financial aid, a work-study job, or a student internship.

4. List the steps in the process you follow when you study for a major exam. Then, interview a friend about how he or she studies, and take notes about his or her customary procedure. Finally, combine the most helpful strategies into a set of instructions aimed at students entering your school.

5. Write a set of instructions explaining how to use one of these reference works: a thesaurus, the *Readers' Guide to Periodical Literature,* or the *Encyclopaedia Britannica.* If you like, you may substitute another reference work with which you are more familiar.

6. Think of a series of steps in a bureaucratic process, a process you had to go through to accomplish something: registering to vote, getting a driver's license, or applying to college, for instance. Write an essay in which you explain that process, and include a thesis that evaluates the efficiency of the process.

7. Imagine you have encountered a visitor from another country (or another planet) who is not familiar with a social ritual you take for granted. Try to outline the steps involved in one such ritual—for instance, choosing sides for a game or pledging a fraternity or sorority.

8. Write a process essay explaining how you went about putting together a collection, a scrapbook, or an album of some kind. Be sure your essay makes clear why you collected or compiled your materials.

9. Explain how a certain ritual or ceremony is conducted in your religion. Make sure someone of another faith will be able to understand the process.

10. Think of a process you believe should be modified or discontinued. Formulate a persuasive thesis that presents your negative feelings, and then explain the process so that you make your objections to it clear to your readers.

COLLABORATIVE ACTIVITY FOR PROCESS

Working with three other students, create an illustrated instructional pamphlet to help new students survive four of your college's first "ordeals"—registering for classes, purchasing textbooks, eating in the cafeteria, moving into a dorm, and so on. Before beginning, decide as a group which processes to write about, whether you want your pamphlet to be practical and serious or humorous and irreverent, and what kind of illustrations it should include. Then decide which of you will write about which process—each student should do one of them—and who will be responsible for the illustrations. When all of you are ready, assemble your individual efforts into a single piece of writing.

6

Cause and Effect

WHAT IS CAUSE AND EFFECT?

Process describes *how* something happens; **cause and effect** analyzes *why* something happens. Cause-and-effect essays examine causes, describe effects, or do both. In the following passage from a *New York Times* column entitled "The Pump on the Well," Tom Wicker considers the effects of a technological advance on a village in India.

<table>
<tr><td>Cause</td><td rowspan="6">When a solar-powered water pump was provided for a well in India, the village headman took it over and sold the water, until stopped. The new liquid abundance attracted hordes of unwanted nomads. Village boys who had drawn water in buckets had nothing to do, and some became criminals. The gap between rich and poor widened, since the poor had no land to benefit from irrigation. Finally, village women broke the pump, so they could gather again around the well that had been the center of their social lives. <u>Moral: technological advances have social, cultural and economic consequences, often unanticipated.</u></td></tr>
<tr><td></td></tr>
<tr><td></td></tr>
<tr><td></td></tr>
<tr><td>Effects</td></tr>
<tr><td>Topic sentence</td></tr>
</table>

Cause and effect, like narration, links situations and events together in time, with causes preceding effects. But causality involves more than sequence: Cause-and-effect analysis explains why something happened—or is happening—and it predicts what probably will happen.

Sometimes many different causes can be responsible for one effect. For example, many elements may contribute to an individual's decision to leave his or her native country and come to the United States.

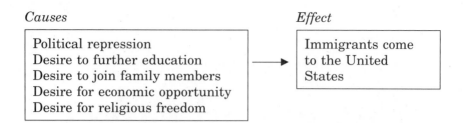

Causes

Political repression
Desire to further education
Desire to join family members
Desire for economic opportunity
Desire for religious freedom

Effect

Immigrants come
to the United
States

Similarly, many different effects can be produced by a single cause. Immigration, for instance, has had a variety of effects on the United States.

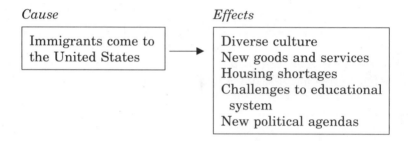

Cause

Immigrants come to
the United States

Effects

Diverse culture
New goods and services
Housing shortages
Challenges to educational
system
New political agendas

Of course, causal relationships are rarely as neat as these boxes suggest. Such relationships are often subtle and complex. As you examine situations that seem suited to cause-and-effect analysis, you will discover that most complex situations involve numerous causes and many different effects. Consider this example.

For over twenty years, from the 1960s to the 1980s, the college board scores of high school seniors steadily declined. This decline began soon after television became popular, and therefore many people concluded that the two events were connected. The idea is plausible because children did seem to be reading less in order to watch television more and because reading comprehension is one of the chief skills the tests evaluate.

But many other elements might have contributed to the lowering of test scores. During the same period, for example, many schools reduced the number of required courses and deemphasized traditional subjects and skills, such as reading. Adults were reading less than they used to, and perhaps they were not encouraging their children to read. Furthermore, during the 1960s and 1970s, many colleges changed their policies and admitted students who previously would not have qualified. These new admission standards encouraged students who would not have taken college boards in earlier years to take the tests. Therefore, the scores may have been lower because they now measured the top third of high school seniors rather than the top fifth. In any case, the reason for the lower scores is not clear. Perhaps television was the cause after all, but now—with SAT verbal scores apparently starting to creep upward again, but with the percentage of students scoring below 400 still climbing steadily while television watching remains fairly constant—nobody knows for sure. In such a case, it is easy—too easy—to claim a cause-and-effect relationship without the evidence to support it.

Just as the lower scores may have had many causes, television watching may have had many effects. For instance, it may have made those same students better observers and listeners, even if they did less well on standardized written tests. It may have given them a national or even international outlook instead of a narrow interest in local affairs. In other words, even if watching television may have limited people in some ways, it may have broadened them in others.

To give your readers a balanced analysis, you should try to consider all causes and effects, not just the most obvious ones or the first ones you think of. For example, suppose a professional basketball team, recently stocked with the best players money can buy, has had a mediocre season. Because the individual players are talented and because they were successful under other coaches, fans blame the current coach for the team's losing streak and want him fired. But can the coach alone be responsible? Maybe the inability of the players to mesh well as a team is responsible for their poor performance. Perhaps some of the players are suffering from injuries, personal problems, or drug dependency. Or maybe the drop in attendance at games has affected the team's morale. Clearly, other elements besides the new coach could have caused the losing streak. Indeed, the suspected cause of the team's decline—the coach—may actually have saved the team from total collapse by keeping the players from quarreling with one another. In writing about such a situation, you must carefully identify these complex causes and effects.

Main and Contributory Causes

Even when you have identified several causes of an effect, one—the **main cause**—is always more important than the others—the **contributory causes.** Understanding the distinction between the main or most important cause and the contributory or less important causes is vital for planning a cause-and-effect paper: When you can identify the main cause, you can emphasize it in your paper and downplay the less important causes. How can you tell which is the main, or most important, cause? Sometimes the main cause is obvious, but often it is not, as the following example shows.

During one winter a number of years ago, an abnormally large amount of snow accumulated on the roof of the Civic Center Auditorium in Hartford, Connecticut, and the roof fell in. Newspapers reported that the weight of the snow had caused the collapse, and they were partly right. Other buildings, however, had not been flattened by the snow, so the main cause seemed to lie elsewhere. Insurance investigators eventually decided that the design of the roof, not the weight of the snow, was the main cause of the disaster.

This diagram outlines the cause-and-effect relationships in the situation summarized above.

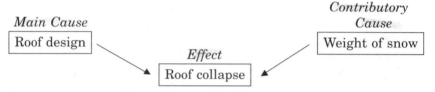

Because the main cause is not always obvious, it is important that you consider the significance of each cause very carefully as you plan your essay—and that you continue to evaluate the relative importance of your main cause and to consider possible alternatives to it as you write and revise.

Immediate and Remote Causes

Another important distinction is the difference between an *immediate cause* and a *remote cause*. An **immediate cause** closely precedes an effect and therefore is relatively easy to recognize. A **remote cause** is less obvious, perhaps because it takes place further in the past or farther away. Assuming that the most obvious cause is always the most important can be dangerous as well as shortsighted.

For example, look again at the Hartford roof collapse. Most people agreed that the snow was the immediate, or most obvious, cause of the roof collapse. But further study by insurance investigators uncovered remote causes that were not so apparent. The design of the roof was the most important remote cause of the collapse. In addition, perhaps the materials used in the roof's construction were partly to blame. Maybe maintenance crews had not done their jobs properly, or necessary repairs had not been made. If you were the insurance investigator analyzing the causes of this event, you would want to assess all possible contributing factors rather than just the most obvious. If you did not consider the remote as well as the immediate causes, you would reach an oversimplified and illogical conclusion.

This diagram outlines the cause-and-effect relationships in the situation summarized above.

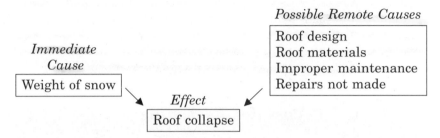

Possible Remote Causes

Roof design
Roof materials
Improper maintenance
Repairs not made

Immediate Cause

Weight of snow

Effect

Roof collapse

In this situation, the remote causes are extremely important; in fact, as we have seen, it is a remote cause—the roof design—that was the main cause of the accident.

The Causal Chain

Sometimes an effect can also be a cause. This is true in a **causal chain,** where A causes B, B causes C, C causes D, and so on.

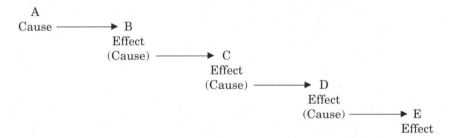

A
Cause ⟶ B
Effect
(Cause) ⟶ C
Effect
(Cause) ⟶ D
Effect
(Cause) ⟶ E
Effect

If your analysis of a situation reveals a causal chain, this discovery can be useful in your writing. The very operation of a causal chain suggests an organizational pattern for a paper, and following the chain keeps you from discussing links out of their logical order. Be careful, however, to keep your emphasis on the causal connections and not to lapse into narration.

A simple example of a causal chain starts with the conclusion of World War II in 1945. Beginning in 1946, as thousands of American soldiers returned home, the United States birth rate began to rise dramatically. As the numbers of births increased, the creation of goods and services designed to meet the needs of this growing new population also increased. As advertisers competed to attract this group's attention to these products, the so-called "baby boom generation" became more and more visible. Consequently, baby boomers were perceived as more and more powerful—as voters as well as consumers. As a result, this group's emergence has been a major factor in shaping American political, social, cultural, and economic life.

In a causal chain like this one, the result of one action is the cause of another. Leaving out any link in the chain, or putting any link in improper order, destroys the logic and continuity of the chain.

Post Hoc *Reasoning*

When developing a cause-and-effect paper, you should not assume that simply because event A *precedes* event B, event A has *caused* event B. This illogical assumption, called **post hoc reasoning,** equates a chronological sequence with causality. When you fall into this trap—assuming, for instance, that you failed an exam because a black cat crossed your path the day before—you are mistaking coincidence for causality.

Consider another situation that illustrates *post hoc* reasoning. Until the late nineteenth century, many scientists accepted the notion of spontaneous generation—that is, they believed living things could arise directly from nonliving matter. To support their beliefs, they pointed to specific situations. For example, they observed that maggots, the larvae of the housefly, seemed to arise directly from the decaying flesh of dead animals.

What these scientists were doing was confusing sequence with causality, assuming that just because the presence of decaying meat preceded the appearance of maggots, the two were connected in a causal relationship. In fact, because the dead animals were exposed to the air, flies were free to lay eggs in the animals' bodies. These eggs hatched into maggots. Therefore, the living maggots were not a direct result of the presence of nonliving matter. Although these scientists were applying the best technology and scientific theory of their time, hindsight reveals that their conclusions were not valid.

In your writing as well as in your observations, it is neither logical nor fair for you to assume that a causal relationship exists in the absence of clear, strong evidence to support the connection. When you revise a cause-and-effect paper, make sure you have not confused words like *because, therefore,* and *consequently*—words that show a causal relationship—with words like *subsequently, later,* and *afterward*—words that show a chronological relationship. When you use a word like *because*, you are signaling your readers that you are telling *why* something happened; when you use a word like *later* you are only showing what did happen and when.

Being able to identify and analyze cause-and-effect relationships; to distinguish causes from effects and recognize causal chains; and to distinguish immediate from remote, main from contributory, and logical from illogical causes are all skills that will help you write. Understanding the nature of the cause-and-effect relationship will help you to decide when to use this pattern to structure a paper.

STRUCTURING A CAUSE-AND-EFFECT ESSAY

After you have sorted out the cause-and-effect relationships you will write about, you are ready to plan your paper. You have three basic options: to discuss causes, to discuss effects, or to discuss both causes and effects. Often your topic will suggest which of these options to use. Here are a few likely topics for cause-and-effect treatment:

Focus on finding causes
{
Discuss the causes of the Spanish-American War. (history exam)

Discuss the factors that have contributed to the declining population of state mental hospitals. (social work paper)
}

Focus on describing or predicting effects
{
Evaluate the probable effects of moving elementary school children from a highly structured classroom to a relatively open classroom. (education paper)

Discuss the impact of World War I on two of Ernest Hemingway's characters. (literature exam)
}

Focus on both causes and effects
{
The 1840s were very volatile years in Europe. Choose one social, political, or economic event that occurred during those years, analyze its causes, and briefly note how the event influenced later developments in European history. (history exam)
}

Of course, a cause-and-effect essay usually does more than just enumerate causes or effects. For example, an economics paper treating the major effects of the Vietnam War on the U.S. economy could be a straightforward presentation of factual information—an attempt to inform readers of the war's economic impact. More likely, however, the paper will indicate the significance of the war's effects, not just list them. In fact, cause-and-effect analysis often requires you to judge various factors so that you can assess the relative significance of causes or effects.

When you formulate a thesis statement, you will want to be sure that it clarifies the relationships among the specific causes or effects you will discuss. This thesis statement should tell your readers three things: the points you plan to consider, the position you will take, and whether your emphasis is on causes, effects, or both. Your thesis statement may also indicate explicitly or implicitly the cause or effect you consider most important and the order in which you will treat your points.

You have several options when deciding on the sequence in which you will present causes or effects. One strategy, of course, is chronology—you can present causes or effects in the order in which they occurred. Another option is to introduce the main cause first and then the contributory causes—or to do just the opposite. If you want to stress positive consequences, begin by briefly discussing the negative ones; if you prefer to emphasize negative results, summarize the less important positive effects first. Still another possibility is to begin by dismissing any events that were *not* causes and then to go on to explain what the real causes were. This method is especially effective if you think your readers are likely to jump to *post hoc* conclusions. Finally, you can begin with the most obvious causes or effects and move on to more subtle factors and then to your analysis and conclusion.

Finding Causes

Suppose you are planning the social work paper mentioned earlier: "Discuss the factors that have contributed to the declining population of state mental hospitals." Your assignment specifies an effect—the declining population of state hospitals—and asks you to discuss possible causes. Causes might include the following:

- An increasing acceptance of mental illness in our society
- Prohibitive costs of in-patient care

Drop-Off Package Receipt: 1 of 1

THIS IS NOT A SHIPPING LABEL. PLEASE SAVE FOR YOUR RECORDS.

DROP-OFF LOCATION:
The UPS Store #6067
1016 THOMAS DR
PANAMA CITY BEACH FL 32408-74

DROP-OFF DATE/TIME:
Sat 5 Mar 2016 3:03 PM

ESTIMATED PICKUP DATE:
UPS   Mon 7 Mar 2016   1pkg

CUSTOMER:
FORESGREN
ID Type: Not Provided   TOTAL PACKAGES: 1pkg

TRACKING NUMBER	CARRIER & SERVICE	WEIGHT
1Z8Y5R529071264619	UPS Ground	7.30 lbs

This receipt lists each package received by The UPS Store #6067 and
indicates that the information for each package has been transmitted to each
carrier's data system. This receipt is not confirmation that the carrier has
picked up the packages. To verify when and if a package has been picked up,
enter one of the following web addresses in your browser and enter the
tracking numbers listed above.   http://theupsstore.com (select Tracking,
then enter Tracking #)   You acknowledge that the shipment services
provided by The UPS Store #6067 for the listed packages are subject to and
governed by each Carrier Agreement, if applicable, the Rates and Service
Guide for each carrier, and the tariff in effect at the time of shipment.

Everyone needs a helping hand now and then.
Join our FREE email program
For great offers and resources visit www.theupsstore.com/email

Powered by iShip(r)
03/05/2016 01:04 PM Pacific Time

TO REORDER YOUR UPS DIRECT THERMAL LABELS:

1. Access our supply ordering web site at **UPS.COM**®
   or Contact UPS at 800-877-8652.
2. Please refer to Label # 01774006 when ordering.

01774006   IR

- Increasing numbers of mental-health professionals, facilitating treatment outside the hospital

Many health professionals, however, believe that the most important cause is the development and use of psychotropic drugs, such as chlorpromazine (Thorazine), which can alter behavior. To emphasize this cause in your paper, you could construct the following thesis statement:

Less important causes	Although society's increasing acceptance of the mentally ill, the high cost of in-patient care, and the rise in the number of health professionals have all been influential in reducing the population of state mental hospitals, the most important cause of this reduction is the development and use of psychotropic drugs.
Effect	
Most important cause	

This thesis statement fully prepares your readers for your essay. It identifies the points you will consider, and it also reveals your position—your assessment of the relative significance of the causes you identify. It states the less important causes first and indicates their secondary importance with *although*. In the body of your essay the less important causes would be considered first so that the essay could gradually build up to the most convincing material, the information that is likely to have the greatest impact on the reader. An informal outline for your paper might look like this:

Introduction:	Thesis statement—Although society's increasing acceptance of the mentally ill, the high cost of in-patient care, and the rise in the number of health professionals have all been influential in reducing the population of state mental hospitals, the most important cause of this reduction is the development and use of psychotropic drugs.
First cause:	Increased acceptance of the mentally ill
Second cause:	High cost of in-patient care
Third cause:	Rise in the number of health professionals
Fourth (and most important) cause:	Development and use of psychotropic drugs
Conclusion:	Restatement of thesis; summary of key points

Describing or Predicting Effects

Suppose you were planning the education paper mentioned earlier: "Evaluate the probable effects of moving elementary school children from a highly structured classroom to a relatively open classroom." You would use a procedure similar to the one above to consider effects rather than find causes. After brainstorming and deciding which specific points to discuss, you might formulate this thesis statement:

> **Cause**   Moving children from a highly structured classroom to a relatively open one is desirable because it is likely to en-
> **Effects**   courage more independent play, more flexibility in forming friendship groups, and ultimately more creativity.

This thesis statement clearly tells readers the stand you will take and the main points your essay will consider in support of that stand; the thesis also clearly specifies that these points are effects of the open classroom. After introducing the cause, your essay would treat these three effects in the order in which they are presented in the thesis statement, building up to the most important point. An informal outline of your paper might look like this:

Introduction:	Thesis statement—Moving children from a highly structured classroom to a relatively open one is desirable because it is likely to encourage more independent play, more flexibility in forming friendship groups, and, ultimately, more creativity.
First effect:	More independent play
Second effect:	More flexible friendship groups
Third (and most important) effect:	More creativity
Conclusion:	Restatement of thesis; summary of key points

A STUDENT WRITER: CAUSE AND EFFECT

The following midterm examination, written for a history class, analyzes both causes and effects of the Irish potato famine that occurred during the 1840s. Notice how the writer, Evelyn Pellicane, concentrates on causes but also discusses briefly the effects of this tragedy, just as the exam question directs.

> *Question*: The 1840s were very volatile years in Europe. Choose one social, political, or economic event that occurred during those years, analyze its causes, and briefly note how the event influenced later developments in European history.

THE IRISH FAMINE, 1845-1849

**Thesis
statement**
  The Irish famine, which brought hardship and tragedy 1
to Ireland during the 1840s, was caused and prolonged by
four basic factors: the failure of the potato crop, the
landlord-tenant system, errors in government policy, and the
long-standing prejudice of the British toward Ireland.

First cause
  The immediate cause of the famine was the failure of 2
the potato crop. In 1845, potato disease struck the crop, and
potatoes rotted in the ground. The 1846 crop also failed, and
before long people were eating weeds. The 1847 crop was
healthy, but there were not enough potatoes to go around,
and in 1848 the blight struck again, leading to more and
more evictions of tenants by landlords.

Second cause
  The tenants' position on the land had never been very 3
secure. Most had no leases and could be turned out by their
landlords at any time. If a tenant owed rent, he was evicted--
or, worse, put in prison, leaving his family to starve. The
threat of prison caused many tenants to leave their land;
those who could leave Ireland did so, sometimes with
money provided by their landlords. Some landlords did try
to take care of their tenants, but most did not. Many were
absentee landlords who spent their rent money abroad.

Third cause
  Government policy errors, while not an immediate 4
cause of the famine, played an important role in creating an
unstable economy and perpetuating starvation. In 1846, the
government decided not to continue selling corn, as it had
during the first year of the famine, claiming that low-cost
purchases of corn by Ireland had paralyzed British trade by
interfering with free enterprise. Therefore, 1846 saw a
starving population, angry demonstrations, and panic; even
those with money were unable to buy food. Still the

government insisted that, if it sent food to Ireland, prices would rise in the rest of the United Kingdom and that this would be unfair to hardworking English and Scots. As a result, no food was sent. Throughout the years of the famine, the British government aggravated an already grave situation: They did nothing to improve agricultural operations, to help people adjust to another crop, to distribute seeds, or to reorder the landlord-tenant system which made the tenants' position so insecure.

Fourth cause   At the root of this poor government policy was the   5
long-standing British prejudice against the Irish. Hostility between the two countries went back some six hundred years, and the British were simply not about to inconvenience themselves to save the Irish. When the Irish so desperately needed grain to replace the damaged potatoes, it was clear that grain had to be imported from England. This meant, however, that the Corn Laws, which had been enacted to keep the price of British corn high by taxing imported grain, had to be repealed. The British were unwilling to repeal the Corn Laws. Even when they did supply corn meal, they made no attempt to explain to the Irish how to cook this unfamiliar food. Moreover, the British government was determined to make Ireland pay for its own poor, and so it forced the collection of taxes. Since many landlords just did not have the tax money, they were forced to evict their tenants. The British government's callous and indifferent treatment of the Irish has been called genocide.

Effects   As a result of this devastating famine, the population of   6
Ireland was reduced from about nine million to about six and one-half million. During the famine years, men roamed the streets looking for work, begging when they found none. Epidemics of "famine fever" and dysentery reduced the

population drastically. The most important historical result of the famine, however, was the massive emigration to the United States, Canada, and Great Britain of poor, unskilled people who had to struggle to fit into a skilled economy and who brought with them a deep-seated hatred of the British. (This same hatred remained strong in Ireland itself--so strong that at the time of World War II, Ireland, then independent, remained neutral rather than coming to England's aid.) Irish immigrants faced slums, fever epidemics, joblessness, and hostility--even anti-Catholic and anti-Irish riots--in Boston, New York, London, Glasgow, and Quebec. In Ireland itself, poverty and discontent continued, and by 1848 those emigrating from Ireland included a more highly skilled class of farmer, the ones Ireland needed to recover and to survive.

Conclusion (includes restatement of thesis)   The Irish famine, one of the great tragedies of the   7
nineteenth century, was a natural disaster compounded by the insensitivity of the British government and the archaic agricultural system of Ireland. While the deaths that resulted depleted Ireland's resources even more, the men and women who emigrated to other countries permanently enriched those nations.

Points for Special Attention

Structure. This is a relatively long essay; if it were not so clearly organized, it would be difficult to follow. Because the essay is to focus primarily on causes, Evelyn first introduces the effect—the famine itself—and then considers its causes. After she has examined the causes, she moves on to the results of the famine, treating the most important result last. In this essay, then, the famine is first treated as an effect and then, toward the end, as a cause. In fact, it is the central link in a causal chain. Evelyn devotes one paragraph to her introduction and one to each cause; she sums up the effects or results in a separate paragraph and devotes the final paragraph to her conclusion. (Depending on a given paper's length and complexity, of course, more—or less—than one paragraph may be devoted to each cause or effect.) An informal outline for her paper might have looked like this:

- Introduction—including thesis statement
- First cause: Failure of the potato crop
- Second cause: The landlord–tenant system
- Third cause: Errors in government policy
- Fourth cause: British prejudice
- Results of the famine
- Conclusion

Because Evelyn believes that all the causes are very important and that they are interrelated, she does not attempt to present them in order of increasing importance. Instead, she begins with the immediate cause of the famine—the failure of the potato crop—and then digs more deeply until she arrives at the most remote cause, British prejudice. The immediate cause is also the main (most important) cause, for the other situations had existed all along.

Transitions. The cause-and-effect relationships in this essay are both subtle and complex; Evelyn considers a series of interconnected relationships and an intricate causal chain. Throughout the essay, many words suggest cause-and-effect connections: *so, therefore, because, as a result, since, led to, brought about, caused,* and the like. These are the most effective transitions for such an essay.

Answering an Examination Question. Before planning and writing her answer, Evelyn carefully studied the exam question. She noted that it asked for both causes and effects but that its wording directed her to spend more time on causes ("analyze") than on effects ("briefly note"). Consequently, she organizes her discussion to conform to these directions and is careful to indicate *explicitly* which are the causes ("government policy . . . played an important role") and which are the effects ("The most important historical result . . .").

Evelyn's purpose is to convey factual information and, in doing so, to demonstrate her understanding of the course material. Rather than waste her limited time choosing a clever opening strategy or making elaborate attempts to engage her audience, Evelyn begins her essay with a direct statement of her thesis.

Evelyn has obviously been influenced by outside sources; the ideas in the essay are not completely her own. Because this is an exam, however, and because the instructor expects that students will base their essays on class notes and assigned readings, Evelyn does not have to acknowledge and document her sources.

Focus on Revision.   Because this essay was an exam answer, Evelyn had no time—and no need—to revise it further. If she had been preparing this assignment outside of class, however, she might have done more. For example, she could have added a more arresting opening, such as a brief eyewitness account of the famine's effects. Her conclusion—appropriately brief and straightforward for an exam answer—could also have been strengthened, perhaps with the addition of information about the nation's eventual recovery. Finally, the addition of statistics, quotations by historians, or a brief summary of Irish history before the famine could also have enriched the essay.

All the selections that follow focus on cause-and-effect relationships. Some readings focus on causes, others on effects. As these essays illustrate, the cause-and-effect pattern is so versatile that it may be used to examine topics as dissimilar as boxing, television, the civil rights movement, a young girl's life, and the environment.

WHO KILLED BENNY PARET?

Norman Cousins

*Norman Cousins (1915–1990) was born in Union City, New Jersey,
and graduated from Columbia University's Teachers College in
1933. He began his career in journalism writing for* The New York
Evening Post *and* Current History *magazine. In 1940 Cousins
joined the* Saturday Review, *where he served as editor from 1942 to
1978. Cousins lectured widely on world affairs, was a social critic
and a strong advocate of nuclear controls, and arranged for victims
of the atomic bombing of Hiroshima to come to the United States for
medical treatment. From 1978 until his death, he was an adjunct
professor in the department of psychiatry and biobehavioral science
at U.C.L.A. Medical School. Cousins published numerous books, including many urging a positive outlook to combat illness:* Anatomy
of an Illness *(1979), about his own struggle with a life-threatening
form of arthritis;* Human Options: An Autobiographical Notebook
(1981); Healing and Belief *(1982);* The Healing Heart: Antidotes to
Panic and Helplessness *(1983);* The Pathology of Power *(1987); and
his last book, about the effect of the emotions on the body's resistance
to disease,* Head First: The Biology of Hope *(1989). In his 1962 essay
"Who Killed Benny Paret?" Cousins investigates the causes of a
boxer's death. In answering the question posed by his essay's title,
Cousins takes a strong stand against violence in sports.*

Sometime about 1935 or 1936 I had an interview with Mike 1
Jacobs, the prize-fight promoter. I was a fledgling reporter at that
time; my beat was education but during the vacation season I found
myself on varied assignments, all the way from ship news to sports
reporting. In this way I found myself sitting opposite the most
powerful figure in the boxing world.

There was nothing spectacular in Mr. Jacobs' manner or appear- 2
ance; but when he spoke about prize fights, he was no longer a bland
little man but a colossus who sounded the way Napoleon must have
sounded when he reviewed a battle. You knew you were listening to
Number One. His saying something made it true.

We discussed what to him was the only important element in 3
successful promoting—how to please the crowd. So far as he was
concerned, there was no mystery to it. You put killers in the ring and
the people filled your arena. You hire boxing artists—men who are

adroit at feinting, parrying, weaving, jabbing, and dancing, but who don't pack dynamite in their fists—and you wind up counting your empty seats. So you searched for the killers and sluggers and maulers—fellows who could hit with the force of a baseball bat.

I asked Mr. Jacobs if he was speaking literally when he said people 4 came out to see the killer.

"They don't come out to see a tea party," he said evenly. "They 5 come out to see the knockout. They come out to see a man hurt. If they think anything else, they're kidding themselves."

Recently, a young man by the name of Benny Paret was killed in 6 the ring. The killing was seen by millions; it was on television. In the twelfth round, he was hit hard in the head several times, went down, was counted out, and never came out of the coma.

The Paret fight produced a flurry of investigations. Governor 7 Rockefeller was shocked by what happened and appointed a committee to assess the responsibility. The New York State Boxing Commission decided to find out what was wrong. The District Attorney's office expressed its concern. One question that was solemnly studied in all three probes concerned the action of the referee. Did he act in time to stop the fight? Another question had to do with the role of the examining doctors who certified the physical fitness of the fighters before the bout. Still another question involved Mr. Paret's manager; did he rush his boy into the fight without adequate time to recuperate from the previous one?

In short, the investigators looked into every possible cause except 8 the real one. Benny Paret was killed because the human fist delivers enough impact, when directed against the head, to produce a massive hemorrhage in the brain. The human brain is the most delicate and complex mechanism in all creation. It has a lacework of millions of highly fragile nerve connections. Nature attempts to protect this exquisitely intricate machinery by encasing it in a hard shell. Fortunately, the shell is thick enough to withstand a great deal of pounding. Nature, however, can protect man against everything except man himself. Not every blow to the head will kill a man—but there is always the risk of concussion and damage to the brain. A prize fighter may be able to survive even repeated brain concussions and go on fighting, but the damage to his brain may be permanent.

In any event, it is futile to investigate the referee's role and seek 9 to determine whether he should have intervened to stop the fight earlier. That is not where the primary responsibility lies. The primary responsibility lies with the people who pay to see a man hurt. The referee who stops a fight too soon from the crowd's viewpoint can expect to be booed. The crowd wants the knockout; it wants to see a man stretched out on the canvas. This is the supreme moment in boxing. It is nonsense to talk about prize fighting as a test of boxing skills. No crowd was ever brought to its feet screaming and cheering at the sight of two men beautifully dodging and weaving out of each other's jabs. The time the crowd comes alive is when a man is hit hard over the heart or the head, when his mouthpiece flies out, when the blood squirts out of his nose or eyes, when he wobbles under the attack and his pursuer continues to smash at him with pole-axe impact.

Don't blame it on the referee. Don't even blame it on the fight managers. Put the blame where it belongs—on the prevailing mores that regard prize fighting as a perfectly proper enterprise and vehicle of entertainment. No one doubts that many people enjoy prize fighting and will miss it if it should be thrown out. And that is precisely the point. 10

COMPREHENSION

1. Why, according to Mike Jacobs, do people come to see a prizefight? Does Cousins agree with him?

2. What was the immediate cause of Paret's death? What remote causes did the investigators consider? What, according to Cousins, is the main cause? (That is, where does the "primary responsibility" lie?)

3. Why does Cousins believe that "it is futile to investigate the referee's role" (9)?

4. Cousins ends his essay with "And that is precisely the point." What is the "point" to which he refers?

PURPOSE AND AUDIENCE

1. This persuasive essay has a strong thesis. What is it?

2. This essay appeared on May 5, 1962, a month after Paret died. What do you suppose its impact was on its audience? Is the impact the same today, or has it changed?

3. At whom is this essay aimed—boxing enthusiasts, sportswriters, or a general audience? What led you to your conclusion?

4. Does Cousins expect his audience to agree with his thesis? How does he try to win their sympathy for his position?

Persuasive
Essay -
Cause & effect
org.

STYLE AND STRUCTURE

1. The essay begins with a brief narrative describing a meeting between Cousins and Mike Jacobs. Where does this narrative introduction end? What is its function in the essay?

2. Once Paret's death is mentioned and the persuasive portion of the essay begins, the introductory narrative never resumes. Why not? Do you think this weakens the essay? Explain.

3. Does Cousins include enough detail to convince readers? Explain. Where, if anywhere, might more detail be helpful?

4. Sort out the complex cause-and-effect relationships discussed in paragraph 9.

5. What strategy does Cousins use in his conclusion? Is it effective? Explain.

VOCABULARY PROJECTS

1. Define each of the following words as it is used in this selection.

   promoter (1)   feinting (3)   lacework (8)
   fledgling (1)   parrying (3)   encasing (8)
   colossus (2)   maulers (3)   intervened (9)

2. The specialized vocabulary of boxing is prominent in this essay, but the facts Cousins presents would apply equally well to any sport in which violence is a potential problem.
   a. Assuming that you are writing a similar essay about football, hockey, rugby, or another sport, substitute appropriate equivalent words for the following:

      promoter (1)   feinting, parrying, weaving,   knockout (5)
      prize fights (2)   jabbing, and dancing (3)   referee (7)
      in the ring (3)   killers and sluggers   fighters/fight (7)
      boxing artists (3)   and maulers(3)

   b. Rewrite this sentence so that it suits the sport you have chosen: "The crowd wants the knockout; it wants to see a man stretched out on the canvas. . . . It is nonsense to talk about prize fighting as a test of boxing skills. No crowd was ever brought to its feet screaming and cheering at the sight of two men beautifully dodging and weaving out of each other's jabs."

JOURNAL ENTRY

Do Cousins's graphic descriptions convince you that boxing should be outlawed? Explain.

WRITING WORKSHOP

1. Write a cause-and-effect essay examining how the demands of the public affect a professional sport. (You might examine violence in hockey or football, for example, or the ways in which an individual player cultivates an image for the fans.)

2. Write a cause-and-effect essay about a time when you did something you felt was dishonest or unwise in response to peer pressure. Be sure to identify the causes for your actions.

3. Why do you think a young man might turn to a career in boxing? Write a cause-and-effect essay in which you examine his possible motives.

THEMATIC CONNECTIONS

- "38 Who Saw Murder Didn't Call the Police" (p. 91)
- "Shooting an Elephant" (p. 96)
- "The Spider and the Wasp" (p. 251)
- "Ex-Basketball Player" (p. 409)

TELEVISION:
THE PLUG-IN DRUG

Marie Winn

Marie Winn was born in 1936 in Prague, Czechoslovakia, and came to the United States in 1939. She was educated at Radcliffe College and Columbia University. As a freelance writer, Winn has contributed articles to the New York Times Magazine, *the* New York Times Book Review, Parade, *and the* Village Voice. *She has written books for children, including* The Sick Book *and* The Baby Reader, *and edited* The Fireside Book of Children's Songs *(1966) and* The Fireside Book of Fun and Game Songs *(1975). Winn also writes books for parents and teachers, including* The Plug-In Drug: Television, Children, and the Family *(1977), where the following selection first appeared;* Children Without Childhood *(1983); and* Unplugging the Plug-In Drug *(1987). In "Television: The Plug-In Drug" (originally titled "Family Life"), Winn considers the effects of television on the American family.*

A quarter of a century after the introduction of television into 1 American society, a period that has seen the medium become so deeply ingrained in American life that in at least one state the television set has attained the rank of a legal necessity, safe from repossession in case of debt along with clothes, cooking utensils, and the like, television viewing has become an inevitable and ordinary part of daily life. Only in the early years of television did writers and commentators have sufficient perspective to separate the activity of watching television from the actual content it offers the viewer. In those early days writers frequently discussed the effects of television on family life. However, a curious myopia afflicted those early observers: almost without exception they regarded television as a favorable, beneficial, indeed, wondrous influence upon the family.

"Television is going to be a real asset in every home where there 2 are children," predicts a writer in 1949.

"Television will take over your way of living and change your 3 children's habits, but this change can be a wonderful improvement," claims another commentator.

"No survey's needed, of course, to establish that television has 4 brought the family together in one room," writes *The New York Times* television critic in 1949.

303

Each of the early articles about television is invariably accompa- 5
nied by a photograph or illustration showing a family cozily sitting
together before the television set, Sis on Mom's lap, Buddy perched
on the arm of Dad's chair, Dad with his arm around Mom's shoulder.
Who could have guessed that twenty or so years later Mom would be
watching a drama in the kitchen, the kids would be looking at cartoons in their room, while Dad would be taking in the ball game in
the living room?

Of course television sets were enormously expensive in those early 6
days. The idea that by 1975 more than 60 percent of American families would own two or more sets was preposterous. The splintering
of the multiple-set family was something the early writers could not
foresee. Nor did anyone imagine the numbers of hours children
would eventually devote to television, the common use of television
by parents as a child pacifier, the changes television would effect
upon child-rearing methods, the increasing domination of family
schedules by children's viewing requirements—in short, the *power*
of the new medium to dominate family life.

After the first years, as children's consumption of the new medium 7
increased, together with parental concern about the possible effects
of so much television viewing, a steady refrain helped to soothe and
reassure anxious parents. "Television always enters a pattern of influences that already exist: the home, the peer group, the school, the
church and culture generally," write the authors of an early and
influential study of television's effects on children. In other words, if
the child's home life is all right, parents need not worry about the
effects of all that television watching.

But television does not merely influence the child; it deeply in- 8
fluences that "pattern of influences" that is meant to ameliorate its
effects. Home and family life has changed in important ways since
the advent of television. The peer group has become television-
oriented, and much of the time children spend together is occupied
by television viewing. Culture generally has been transformed by
television. Therefore it is improper to assign to television the sub-
sidiary role its many apologists (too often members of the television
industry) insist it plays. Television is not merely one of a number of
important influences upon today's child. Through the changes it has
made in family life, television emerges as *the* important influence in
children's lives today.

Television's contribution to family life has been an equivocal one. 9
For while it has, indeed, kept the members of the family from dis-
persing, it has not served to bring them *together*. By its domination
of the time families spend together, it destroys the special quality
that distinguishes one family from another, a quality that depends

to a great extent on what a family *does,* what special rituals, games, recurrent jokes, familiar songs, and shared activities it accumulates.

"Like the sorcerer of old," writes Urie Bronfenbrenner, "the television set casts its magic spell, freezing speech and action, turning the living into silent statues so long as the enchantment lasts. The primary danger of the television screen lies not so much in the behavior it produces—although there is danger there—as in the behavior it prevents: the talks, the games, the family festivities and arguments through which much of the child's learning takes place and through which his character is formed. Turning on the television set can turn off the process that transforms children into people."

Yet parents have accepted a television-dominated family life so completely that they cannot see how the medium is involved in whatever problems they might be having. A first-grade teacher reports:

"I have one child in the group who's an only child. I wanted to find out more about her family life because this little girl was quite isolated from the group, didn't make friends, so I talked to her mother. Well, they don't have time to do anything in the evening, the mother said. The parents come home after picking up the child at the babysitter's. Then the mother fixes dinner while the child watches TV. Then they have dinner and the child goes to bed. I said to this mother. 'Well, couldn't she help you fix dinner? That would be a nice time for the two of you to talk,' and the mother said, 'Oh, but I'd hate to have her miss "Zoom." It's such a good program!'"

Even when families make efforts to control television, too often its very presence counterbalances the positive features of family life. A writer and mother of two boys aged 3 and 7 described her family's television schedule in an article in *The New York Times:*

> We were in the midst of a full-scale War. Every day was a new battle and every program was a major skirmish. We agreed it was a bad scene all around and were ready to enter diplomatic negotiations. . . . In principle we have agreed on 2 1/2 hours of TV a day, "Sesame Street," "Electric Company" (with dinner gobbled up in between) and two half-hour shows between 7 and 8:30 which enables the grown-ups to eat in peace and prevents the two boys from destroying one another. Their pre-bedtime choice is dreadful, because, as Josh recently admitted, "There's nothing much on I really like." So . . . it's "What's My Line" or "To Tell the Truth" . . . Clearly there is a need for first-rate children's shows at this time. . . .

Consider the "family life" described here: Presumably the father comes home from work during the "Sesame Street"—"Electric Company" stint. The children are either watching television, gobbling their dinner, or both. While the parents eat their dinner in peaceful privacy, the children watch another hour of television. Then there is only a half-hour left before bedtime, just enough time for baths, getting pajamas on, brushing teeth, and so on. The children's evening is regimented with an almost military precision. They watch their favorite programs, and when there is "nothing much on I really like," they watch whatever else is on—because *watching* is the important thing. Their mother does not see anything amiss with watching programs just for the sake of watching; she only wishes there were some first-rate children's shows on at those times.

Without conjuring up memories of the Victorian era with family games and long, leisurely meals, and large families, the question arises: isn't there a better family life available than this dismal, mechanized arrangement of children watching television for however long is allowed them, evening after evening? 15

Of course, families today still do *special* things together at times: go camping in the summer, go to the zoo on a nice Saturday, take various trips and expeditions. But their *ordinary* daily life together is diminished—that sitting around at the dinner table, that spontaneous taking up of an activity, those little games invented by children on the spur of the moment when there is nothing else to do, the scribbling, the chatting, and even the quarreling, all the things that form the fabric of a family, that define a childhood. Instead, the children have their regular schedule of television programs and bedtime, and the parents have their peaceful dinner together. 16

The author of the article in the *Times* notes that "keeping a family sane means mediating between the needs of both children and adults." But surely the needs of adults are being better met than the needs of the children, who are effectively shunted away and rendered untroublesome, while their parents enjoy a life as undemanding as that of any childless couple. In reality, it is those very demands that young children make upon a family that lead to growth, and it is the way parents accede to those demands that builds the relationships upon which the future of the family depends. If the family does not accumulate its backlog of shared experiences, shared *everyday* experiences that occur and recur and change and develop, then it is not likely to survive as anything other than a caretaking institution. 17

FAMILY RITUALS

Ritual is defined by sociologists as "that part of family life that the family likes about itself, is proud of and wants formally to continue." 18

Another text notes that "the development of a ritual by a family is an index of the common interest of its members in the family as a group."

What has happened to family rituals, those regular, dependable, recurrent happenings that gave members of a family a feeling of *belonging* to a home rather than living in it merely for the sake of convenience, those experiences that act as the adhesive of family unity far more than any material advantages? [19]

Mealtime rituals, going-to-bed rituals, illness rituals, holiday rituals, how many of these have survived the inroads of the television set? [20]

A young woman who grew up near Chicago reminisces about her childhood and gives an idea of the effects of television upon family rituals: [21]

"As a child I had millions of relatives around—my parents both come from relatively large families. My father had nine brothers and sisters. And so every holiday there was this great swoop-down of aunts, uncles, and millions of cousins. I just remember how wonderful it used to be. These thousands of cousins would come and everyone would play and ultimately, after dinner, all the women would be in the front of the house, drinking coffee and talking, all the men would be in the back of the house, drinking and smoking, and all the kids would be all over the place, playing hide and seek. Christmas time was particularly nice because everyone always brought all their toys and games. Our house had a couple of rooms with go-through closets, so there was always kids running in a great circle route. I remember it was just wonderful. [22]

"And then all of a sudden one year I remember becoming suddenly aware of how different everything had become. The kids were no longer playing Monopoly or Clue or the other games we used to play together. It was because we had a television set which had been turned on for a football game. All of that socializing that had gone on previously had ended. Now everyone was sitting in front of the television set, on a holiday, at a family party! I remember being stunned by how awful that was. Somehow the television had become more attractive." [23]

As families have come to spend more and more of their time together engaged in the single activity of television watching, those rituals and pastimes that once gave family life its special quality have become more and more uncommon. Not since prehistoric times when cave families hunted, gathered, ate, and slept, with little time remaining to accumulate a culture of any significance, have families been reduced to such a sameness. [24]

REAL PEOPLE

It is not only the activities that a family might engage in together 25
that are diminished by the powerful presence of television in the
home. The relationships of the family members to each other are
also affected, in both obvious and subtle ways. The hours that the
young child spends in a one-way relationship with television people,
an involvement that allows for no communication or interaction,
surely affect his relationships with real-life people.

Studies show the importance of eye-to-eye contact, for instance, in 26
real-life relationships, and indicate that the nature of a person's
eye-contact patterns, whether he looks another squarely in the eye
or looks to the side or shifts his gaze from side to side, may play a
significant role in his success or failure in human relationships. But
no eye contact is possible in the child-television relationship, although in certain children's programs people purport to speak directly to the child and the camera fosters this illusion by focusing
directly upon the person being filmed. (Mr. Rogers is an example,
telling the child "I like you, you're special," etc.) How might such a
distortion of real-life relationships affect a child's development of
trust, of openness, of an ability to relate well to other *real* people?

Bruno Bettelheim writes: 27

> Children who have been taught, or conditioned, to listen passively
> most of the day to the warm verbal communications coming from the
> TV screen, to the deep emotional appeal of the so-called TV person-
> ality, are often unable to respond to real persons because they arouse
> so much less feeling than the skilled actor. Worse, they lose the ability
> to learn from reality because life experiences are much more compli-
> cated than the ones they see on the screen. . . .

A teacher makes a similar observation about her personal viewing 28
experiences:

"I have trouble mobilizing myself and dealing with real people 29
after watching a few hours of television. It's just hard to make that
transition from watching television to a real relationship. I suppose
it's because there was no effort necessary while I was watching, and
dealing with real people always requires a bit of effort. Imagine,
then, how much harder it might be to do the same thing for a small
child, particularly one who watches a lot of television every day."

But more obviously damaging to family relationships is the elimi- 30
nation of opportunities to talk, and perhaps more important, to argue,
to air grievances, between parents and children and brothers and
sisters. Families frequently use television to avoid confronting their

problems, problems that will not go away if they are ignored but will only fester and become less easily resolvable as time goes on.

A mother reports:

"I find myself, with three children, wanting to turn on the TV set when they're fighting. I really have to struggle not to do it because I feel that's telling them this is the solution to the quarrel—but it's so tempting that I often do it."

A family therapist discusses the use of television as an avoidance mechanism:

"In a family I know the father comes home from work and turns on the television set. The children come and watch him and the wife serves them their meal in front of the set. He then goes and takes a shower, or works on the car or something. She then goes and has her own dinner in front of the television set. It's a symptom of a deeper-rooted problem, sure. But it would help them all to get rid of the set. It would be far easier to work on what the symptom really means without the television. The television simply encourages a double avoidance of each other. They'd find out more quickly what was going on if they weren't able to hide behind the TV. Things wouldn't necessarily be better, of course, but they wouldn't be anesthetized."

The decreased opportunities for simple conversation between parents and children in the television-centered home may help explain an observation made by an emergency room nurse at a Boston hospital. She reports that parents just seem to sit there these days when they come in with a sick or seriously injured child, although talking to the child would distract and comfort him. "They don't seem to know *how* to talk to their own children at any length," the nurse observes. Similarly, a television critic writes in *The New York Times*: "I had just a day ago taken my son to the emergency ward of a hospital for stitches above his left eye, and the occasion seemed no more real to me than Maalot or 54th Street, south-central Los Angeles. There was distance and numbness and an inability to turn off the total institution. I didn't behave at all; I just watched. . . ."

A number of research studies substantiate the assumption that television interferes with family activities and the formation of family relationships. One survey shows that 78 percent of the respondents indicated no conversation taking place during viewing except at specified times such as commercials. The study notes: "The television atmosphere in most households is one of quiet absorption on the part of family members who are present. The nature of the family social life during a program could be described as 'parallel' rather than interactive, and the set does seem to dominate family life when it is on." Thirty-six percent of the respondents in another study indicated that television viewing was the only family activity participated in during the week.

In a summary of research findings on television's effect on family 37 interactions James Gabardino states: "The early findings suggest that television had a disruptive effect upon interaction and thus presumably human development. . . . It is not unreasonable to ask: 'Is the fact that the average American family during the 1950s came to include two parents, two children and a television set somehow related to the psychosocial characteristics of the young adults of the 1970s?'"

UNDERMINING THE FAMILY

In its effect on family relationships, in its facilitation of parental 38 withdrawal from an active role in the socialization of their children, and in its replacement of family rituals and special events, television has played an important role in the disintegration of the American family. But of course it has not been the only contributing factor, perhaps not even the most important one. The steadily rising divorce rate, the increase in the number of working mothers, the decline of the extended family, the breakdown of neighborhoods and communities, the growing isolation of the nuclear family—all have seriously affected the family.

As Urie Bronfenbrenner suggests, the sources of family break- 39 down do not come from the family itself, but from the circumstances in which the family finds itself and the way of life imposed upon it by those circumstances. "When those circumstances and the way of life they generate undermine relationships of trust and emotional security between family members, when they make it difficult for parents to care for, educate and enjoy their children, when there is no support or recognition from the outside world for one's role as a parent and when time spent with one's family means frustration of career, personal fulfillment and peace of mind, then the development of the child is adversely affected," he writes.

But while the roots of alienation go deep into the fabric of Amer- 40 ican social history, television's presence in the home fertilizes them, encourages their wild and unchecked growth. Perhaps it is true that America's commitment to the television experience masks a spiritual vacuum, an empty and barren way of life, a desert of materialism. But it is television's dominant role in the family that anesthetizes the family into accepting its unhappy state and prevents it from struggling to better its condition, to improve its relationships, and to regain some of the richness it once possessed.

Others have noted the role of mass media in perpetuating an un-   41
satisfactory *status quo*. Leisure-time activity, writes Irving Howe,
"must provide relief from work monotony without making the return
to work too unbearable; it must provide amusement without insight
and pleasure without disturbance—as distinct from art which gives
pleasure through disturbance. Mass culture is thus oriented towards a central aspect of industrial society: the depersonalization of
the individual." Similarly, Jacques Ellul rejects the idea that television is a legitimate means of educating the citizen: "Education . . .
takes place only incidentally. The clouding of his consciousness is
paramount. . . ."

And so the American family muddles on, dimly aware that some-   42
thing is amiss but distracted from an understanding of its plight by
an endless stream of television images. As family ties grow weaker
and vaguer, as children's lives become more separate from their parents', as parents' educational role in their children's lives is taken
over by television and schools, family life becomes increasingly more
unsatisfying for both parents and children. All that seems to be left
is Love, an abstraction that family members *know* is necessary but
find great difficulty giving each other because the traditional opportunities for expressing love within the family have been reduced or
destroyed.

For contemporary parents, love toward each other has increas-   43
ingly come to mean successful sexual relations, as witnessed by the
proliferation of sex manuals and sex therapists. The opportunities
for manifesting other forms of love through mutual support, understanding, nurturing, even, to use an unpopular word, *serving* each
other, are less and less available as mothers and fathers seek their
independent destinies outside the family.

As for love of children, this love is increasingly expressed through   44
supplying material comforts, amusements, and educational opportunities. Parents show their love for their children by sending them
to good schools and camps, by providing them with good food and
good doctors, by buying them toys, books, games, and a television set
of their very own. Parents will even go further and express their love
by attending PTA meetings to improve their children's schools, or by
joining groups that are acting to improve the quality of their children's television programs.

But this is love at a remove, and is rarely understood by children.   45
The more direct forms of parental love require time and patience,
steady, dependable, ungrudgingly given time actually spent *with* a
child, reading to him, comforting him, playing, joking, and working
with him. But even if a parent were eager and willing to demon-

strate that sort of direct love to his children today, the opportunities are diminished. What with school and Little League and piano lessons and, of course, the inevitable television programs, a day seems to offer just enough time for a good-night kiss.

COMPREHENSION

1. How did early observers view television? How, in general, does Winn's own view differ from theirs?

2. How has the nature of family television viewing changed since its inception? How does Winn account for this change?

3. How does television keep families apart? In what sense does Winn see television as a threat to the very nature of the family?

4. How does Winn define "family rituals"? How does she believe television has affected these rituals?

5. What other factors besides the presence of television does Winn see as having a negative effect on the family?

6. Why does Winn believe today's families have such difficulty expressing love?

PURPOSE AND AUDIENCE

1. Winn states her thesis in paragraph 8. What is it?

2. In paragraphs 10 and 27, Winn quotes two noted psychologists. What effect do you think she expects their words to have on her audience?

3. What effect do you believe the young woman's testimony in paragraphs 22–23 is calculated to have on Winn's readers?

4. In paragraph 24, Winn makes an analogy between modern families and cave families. What is her purpose in doing this?

STYLE AND STRUCTURE

1. Winn does not state her thesis until paragraph 8. What does she achieve in the paragraphs that precede this?

2. The length of Winn's paragraphs varies considerably. What effect do you think short paragraphs such as paragraphs 2, 3, 4, and 20 are likely to have?

3. From what different kinds of sources does Winn draw the many quotations she uses in this essay? How does the varied nature of these quotations help support her thesis?

4. This essay includes three headings: "Family Rituals," "Real People," and "Undermining the Family." What functions do these headings serve?

5. Winn's focus in this essay is on the effects of television on the American family. In the last four paragraphs, however, her focus widens, and she touches on television only incidentally. Does this concluding strategy strengthen or weaken her essay? Explain.

VOCABULARY PROJECTS

1. Define each of the following words as it is used in this selection.

myopia (1)	counterbalances (13)	facilitation (38)
ameliorate (8)	regimented (14)	perpetuating (41)
advent (8)	mediating (17)	depersonalization (41)
subsidiary (8)	adhesive (19)	amiss (42)
apologists (8)	fosters (26)	abstraction (42)
equivocal (9)	substantiate (36)	remove (45)

2. One important effect of television has been seen in our vocabulary: Television has spawned new words (for example, *sitcom*) and suggested new uses for old words (for instance, *tube*). List as many television-inspired words as you can, and define each.

JOURNAL ENTRY

What effects—positive or negative—do you think television has had on your life? What would your life be like without it?

WRITING WORKSHOP

1. Write an essay in which you consider the effects (including any possible future effects) of one of these inventions on the American family: The telephone, the personal computer, the microwave oven, the hand-held calculator, the VCR, the Walkman, Nintendo.

2. Write a cause-and-effect essay in which you discuss the *positive* effects of television on American society.

3. Consider what other causes might have produced some of the same effects Winn identifies, and explore those causes in an essay. For

instance, what economic, political, or social events might have contributed to changing the nature of family life? Consider, for example, why the details of family life presented in paragraphs 13–16 and elsewhere do not really characterize many of today's families.

THEMATIC CONNECTIONS

- "Once More to the Lake" (p. 160)
- "Why Mr. Ed Still Talks Good Horse Sense" (p. 198)
- "The Human Cost of an Illiterate Society" (p. 215)

THE CIVIL RIGHTS MOVEMENT: WHAT GOOD WAS IT?

Alice Walker

Born in 1944 in Eatonton, Georgia, to a sharecropping family, Alice Walker attended Spelman College and graduated from Sarah Lawrence College in 1965. After college Walker taught at Jackson State College in Mississippi, where she was active in the civil rights movement. Walker's writing focuses on the problems of African-American families, particularly women. She became a leading spokesperson for black feminism, coining the term "womanist" to describe the focus of her writing. Her novels include The Color Purple *(1982), which won both the Pulitzer Prize and the American Book Award for fiction in 1983 and was made into an award-winning film in 1985,* The Temple of My Familiar *(1989), and* Possessing the Secret of Joy *(1992). Walker has also published a biography of Langston Hughes and collections of short stories and of poetry, including most recently* Her Blue Body Everything We Know: Earthling Poems, 1965–1990 *(1991). Her essays and articles are collected in* In Search of Our Mothers' Gardens: Womanist Prose *(1983) and* Living By the Word: Selected Writings *(1988). "The Civil Rights Movement: What Good Was It?", Walker's first published essay, won first prize in* The American Scholar *essay contest when she was twenty-three. At a time when many observers were asking whether the civil rights movement of the early 1960s was losing its momentum without having accomplished significant changes, Walker provides a passionate tribute to its effects on her life and the lives of all African Americans.*

Someone said recently to an old black lady from Mississippi, whose legs had been badly mangled by local police who arrested her for "disturbing the peace," that the Civil Rights Movement was dead, and asked, since it was dead, what she thought about it. The old lady replied, hobbling out of his presence on her cane, that the Civil Rights Movement was like herself, "if it's dead, it shore ain't ready to lay down!"

This old lady is a legendary freedom fighter in her small town in the Delta. She has been severely mistreated for insisting on her rights as an American citizen. She has been beaten for singing Movement songs, placed in solitary confinement in prisons for talking about freedom, and placed on bread and water for praying aloud to God for her jailers' deliverance. For such a woman the Civil Rights Movement will never be over as long as her skin is black. It also will never be over for twenty million others with the same "affliction," for whom the Movement can never "lay down," no matter how it is killed by the press and made dead and buried by the white American public. As long as one black American survives, the struggle for equality with other Americans must also survive. This is a debt we owe to those blameless hostages we leave to the future, our children.

Still, white liberals and deserting Civil Rights sponsors are quick   3
to justify their disaffection from the Movement by claiming that it is all over. "And since it is over," they will ask, "would someone kindly tell me what has been gained by it?" They then list statistics supposedly showing how much more advanced segregation is now than ten years ago—in schools, housing, jobs. They point to a gain in conservative politicians during the last few years. They speak of ghetto riots and of the survey that shows that most policemen are admittedly too anti-Negro to do their jobs in ghetto areas fairly and effectively. They speak of every area that has been touched by the Civil Rights Movement as somehow or other going to pieces.

They rarely talk, however, about human attitudes among Negroes   4
that have undergone terrific changes just during the past seven to ten years (not to mention all those years when there was a Movement and only the Negroes knew about it). They seldom speak of changes in personal lives because of the influence of people in the Movement. They see general failure and few, if any, individual gains.

They do not understand what it is that keeps the Movement from   5
"laying down" and Negroes from reverting to their former *silent* second-class status. They have apparently never stopped to wonder why it is always the white man—on his radio and in his newspaper and on his television—who says that the Movement is dead. If a Negro were audacious enough to make such a claim, his fellows might hanker to see him shot. The Movement is dead to the white man because it no longer interests him. And it no longer interests him because he can afford to be uninterested: he does not have to live by it, with it, or for it, as Negroes must. He can take a rest from the news of beatings, killings, and arrests that reach him from North and South—if his skin is white. Negroes cannot now and will never be able to take a rest from the injustices that plague them, for they—not the white man—are the target.

Perhaps it is naive to be thankful that the Movement "saved" a   6
large number of individuals and gave them something to live for,

even if it did not provide them with everything they wanted. (Materially, it provided them with precious little that they wanted.) When a movement awakens people to the possibilities of life, it seems unfair to frustrate them by then denying what they had thought was offered. But what was offered? What was promised? What was it all about? What good did it do? Would it have been better, as some have suggested, to leave the Negro people as they were, unawakened, unallied with one another, unhopeful about what to expect for their children in some future world?

I do not think so. If knowledge of my condition is all the freedom 7 I get from a "freedom movement," it is better than unawareness, forgottenness, and hopelessness, the existence that is like the existence of a beast. Man only truly lives by knowing; otherwise he simply performs, copying the daily habits of others, but conceiving nothing of his creative possibilities as a man, and accepting someone else's superiority and his own misery.

When we are children, growing up in our parents' care, we await 8 the spark from the outside world. Sometimes our parents provide it—if we are lucky—sometimes it comes from another source far from home. We sit, paralyzed, surrounded by our anxiety and dread, hoping we will not have to grow up into the narrow world and ways we see about us. We are hungry for a life that turns us on; we yearn for a knowledge of living that will save us from our innocuous lives that resemble death. We look for signs in every strange event; we search for heroes in every unknown face.

It was just six years ago that I began to be alive. I had, of course, 9 been living before—for I am now twenty-three—but I did not really know it. And I did not know it because nobody told me that I—a pensive, yearning, typical high-school senior, but Negro—existed in the minds of others as I existed in my own. Until that time my mind was locked apart from the outer contours and complexion of my body as if it and the body were strangers. The mind possessed both thought and spirit—I wanted to be an author or a scientist—which the color of the body denied. I had never seen myself and existed as a statistic exists, or as a phantom. In the white world I walked, less real to them than a shadow; and being young and well hidden among the slums, among people who also did not exist—either in books or in films or in the government of their own lives—I waited to be called to life. And, by a miracle, I was called.

There was a commotion in our house that night in 1960. We had 10 managed to buy our first television set. It was battered and overpriced, but my mother had gotten used to watching the afternoon soap operas at the house where she worked as maid, and nothing could satisfy her on days when she did not work but a continuation of her "stories." So she pinched pennies and bought a set.

I remained listless throughout her "stories," tales of pregnancy, abortion, hypocrisy, infidelity, and alcoholism. All these men and women were white and lived in houses with servants, long stair-cases that they floated down, patios where liquor was served four times a day to "relax" them. But my mother, with her swollen feet eased out of her shoes, her heavy body relaxed in our only comfort-able chair, watched each movement of the smartly coiffed women, heard each word, pounced upon each innuendo and inflection, and for the duration of these "stories" she saw herself as one of them. She placed herself in every scene she saw, with her braided hair turned blond, her two hundred pounds compressed into a sleek size-seven dress, her rough dark skin smooth and *white*. Her husband became "dark and handsome," talented, witty, urbane, charming. And when she turned to look at my father sitting near her in his sweat shirt with his smelly feet raised on the bed to "air," there was always a tragic look of surprise on her face. Then she would sigh and go out to the kitchen looking lost and unsure of herself. My mother, a truly great woman who raised eight children of her own and half a dozen of the neighbors' without a single complaint, was convinced that she did not exist compared to "them." She subordinated her soul to theirs and became a faithful and timid supporter of the "Beau-tiful White People." Once she asked me, in a moment of vicarious pride and despair, if I didn't think that "they" were "jest naturally smarter, prettier, better." My mother asked this: a woman who never got rid of any of her children, never cheated on my father, was never a hypocrite if she could help it, and never even tasted liquor. She could not even bring herself to blame "them" for making her believe what they wanted her to believe: that if she did not look like them, think like them, be sophisticated and corrupt-for-comfort's-sake like them, she was a nobody. Black was not a color on my mother; it was a shield that made her invisible.

Of course, the people who wrote the soap-opera scripts always made the Negro maids in them steadfast, trusty, and wise in a home-remedial sort of way; but my mother, a maid for nearly forty years, never once identified herself with the scarcely glimpsed black servant's face beneath the ruffled cap. Like everyone else, in her daydreams at least, she thought she was free.

Six years ago, after half-heartedly watching my mother's soap operas and wondering whether there wasn't something more to be asked of life, the Civil Rights Movement came into my life. Like a good omen for the future, the face of Dr. Martin Luther King, Jr., was the first black face I saw on our new television screen. And, as in a fairy tale, my soul was stirred by the meaning for me of his mission—at the time he was being rather ignominiously dumped into a police van for having led a protest march in Alabama—and I fell in love with the sober and determined face of the Movement. The singing of "We Shall Overcome"—that song betrayed by nonbelievers in it—rang for the first time in my ears. The influence that my mother's soap operas might have had on me became impossible. The life of Dr. King, seeming bigger and more miraculous than the man himself, because of all he had done and suffered, offered a pattern of strength and sincerity I felt I could trust. He had suffered much because of his simple belief in nonviolence, love, and brotherhood. Perhaps the majority of men could not be reached through these beliefs, but because Dr. King kept trying to reach them in spite of danger to himself and his family, I saw in him the hero for whom I had waited so long.

What Dr. King promised was not a ranch-style house and an acre 14
of manicured lawn for every black man, but jail and finally freedom. He did not promise two cars for every family, but the courage one day for all families everywhere to walk without shame and unafraid on their own feet. He did not say that one day it will be us chasing prospective buyers out of our prosperous well-kept neighborhoods, or in other ways exhibiting our snobbery and ignorance as all other ethnic groups before us have done; what he said was that we had a right to live anywhere in this country we chose, and a right to a meaningful well-paying job to provide us with the upkeep of our homes. He did not say we had to become carbon copies of the white American middle class; but he did say we had the right to become whatever we wanted to become.

Because of the Movement, because of an awakened faith in the 15
newness and imagination of the human spirit, because of "black and white together"—for the first time in our history in some human relationship on and off TV—because of the beatings, the arrests, the hell of battle during the past years, I have fought harder for my life and for a chance to be myself, to be something more than a shadow or a number, than I had ever done before in my life. Before, there had seemed to be no real reason for struggling beyond the effort for daily bread. Now there was a chance at that other that Jesus meant when He said we could not live by bread alone.

I have fought and kicked and fasted and prayed and cursed and 16
cried myself to the point of existing. It has been like being born again, literally. Just "knowing" has meant everything to me. Knowing has pushed me out into the world, into college, into places, into people.

Part of what existence means to me is knowing the difference ¹⁷
between what I am now and what I was then. It is being capable of
looking after myself intellectually as well as financially. It is being
able to tell when I am being wronged and by whom. It means being
awake to protect myself and the ones I love. It means being a part of
the world community, and being *alert* to which part it is that I have
joined, and knowing how to change to another part if that part does
not suit me. To know is to exist: to exist is to be involved, to move
about, to see the world with my own eyes. This, at least, the Movement has given me.

The hippies and other nihilists would have me believe that it is all ¹⁸
the same whether the people in Mississippi have a movement behind them or not. Once they have their rights, they say, they will run
all over themselves trying to be just like everybody else. They will be
well fed, complacent about things of the spirit, emotionless, and
without the marvelous humanity and "soul" that the Movement has
seen them practice time and time again. "What has the Movement
done," they ask, "with the few people it has supposedly helped?" "Got
them white-collar jobs, moved them into standardized ranch houses
in white neighborhoods, given them nondescript gray flannel suits?"
"What are these people now?" they ask. And then they answer themselves, "Nothings!"

I would find this reasoning—which I have heard many, many ¹⁹
times from hippies and nonhippies alike—amusing if I did not also
consider it serious. For I think it is a delusion, a cop-out, an excuse
to disassociate themselves from a world in which they feel too little
has been changed or gained. The real question, however, it appears
to me, is not whether poor people will adopt the middle-class mentality once they are well fed; rather, it is whether they will ever be
well fed enough to be able to choose whatever mentality they think
will suit them. The lack of a movement did not keep my mother from
wishing herself bourgeois in her daydreams.

There is widespread starvation in Mississippi. In my own state of ²⁰
Georgia there are more hungry families than Lester Maddox* would
like to admit—or even see fed. I went to school with children who ate
red dirt. The Movement has prodded and pushed some liberal senators into pressuring the government for food so that the hungry
may eat. Food stamps that were two dollars and out of the reach of
many families not long ago have been reduced to fifty cents. The
price is still out of the reach of some families, and the government,

---

*Eds. Note—Governor of Georgia between 1967 and 1971, Maddox was widely
known for his segregationist views.

it seems to a lot of people, could spare enough free food to feed its own people. It angers people in the Movement that it does not; they point to the billions in wheat we send free each year to countries abroad. Their government's slowness while people are hungry, its unwillingness to believe that there are Americans starving, its stingy cutting of the price of food stamps, make many Civil Rights workers throw up their hands in disgust. But they do not give up. They do not withdraw into the world of psychedelia. They apply what pressure they can to make the government give away food to hungry people. They do not plan so far ahead in their disillusionment with society that they can see these starving families buying identical ranch-style houses and sending their snobbish children to Bryn Mawr and Yale. They take first things first and try to get them fed.

They do not consider it their business, in any case, to say what kind of life the people they help must lead. How one lives is, after all, one of the rights left to the individual—when and if he has opportunity to choose. It is not the prerogative of the middle class to determine what is worthy of aspiration. There is also every possibility that the middle-class people of tomorrow will turn out ever so much better than those of today. I even know some middle-class people of today who are not *all* bad.

I think there are so few Negro hippies because middle-class Negroes, although well fed, are not careless. They are required by the treacherous world they live in to be clearly aware of whoever or whatever might be trying to do them in. They are middle class in money and position, but they cannot afford to be middle class in complacency. They distrust the hippie movement because they know that it can do nothing for Negroes as a group but "love" them, which is what all paternalists claim to do. And since the only way Negroes can survive (which they cannot do, unfortunately, on love alone) is with the support of the group, they are wisely wary and stay away.

A white writer tried recently to explain that the reason for the relatively few Negro hippies is that Negroes have built up a "supercool" that cracks under LSD and makes them have a "bad trip." What this writer doesn't guess at is that Negroes are needing drugs less than ever these days for any kind of trip. While the hippies are "tripping," Negroes are going after power, which is so much more important to their survival and their children's survival than LSD and pot.

Everyone would be surprised if the Israelis ignored the Arabs and took up "tripping" and pot smoking. In this country we are the Israelis. Everybody who can do so would like to forget this, of course. But for us to forget it for a minute would be fatal. "We Shall Overcome" is just a song to most Americans, *but we must do it*. Or die.

What good was the Civil Rights Movement? If it had just given this country Dr. King, a leader of conscience, for once in our lifetime, it would have been enough. If it had just taken black eyes off white television stories, it would have been enough. If it had fed one starving child, it would have been enough. 25

If the Civil Rights Movement is "dead," and if it gave us nothing else, it gave us each other forever. It gave some of us bread, some of us shelter, some of us knowledge and pride, all of us comfort. It gave us our children, our husbands, our brothers, our fathers, as men reborn and with a purpose for living. It broke the pattern of black servitude in this country. It shattered the phony "promise" of white soap operas that sucked away so many pitiful lives. It gave us history and men far greater than Presidents. It gave us heroes, selfless men of courage and strength, for our little boys and girls to follow. It gave us hope for tomorrow. It called us to life. 26

Because we live, it can never die. 27

COMPREHENSION

1. Is this essay's focus on finding causes, describing effects, or both?

2. According to Walker, how do white liberals view the civil rights movement?

3. According to Walker, what good *was* the civil rights movement?

4. What was it that called Walker to life at the age of seventeen? Why was she affected so strongly?

5. With whom did Walker's mother identify as she watched soap operas? Why?

6. What, specifically, were the effects of the civil rights movement on Walker herself?

7. What does Walker think the "hippies and other nihilists" would have her believe? What is her reaction to their opinion of the "Movement"?

8. When her essay was written, what did Walker believe still remained to be accomplished?

PURPOSE AND AUDIENCE

1. What do you think Walker hoped to accomplish in writing this essay in the late 1960s? Do you think she had different expectations for it when she decided to include it in her 1983 book? Explain.

2. Is Walker writing for an audience that is primarily African American, or does she expect to reach a larger interracial audience? How can you tell?

3. What is the essay's thesis?

4. What purpose does Walker's digression about her mother's soap operas serve?

5. What does Walker hope to accomplish with her analogy between African Americans and Israelis? Is it as effective an analogy today as it might have been twenty-five years ago? Explain.

STYLE AND STRUCTURE

1. What advantage does Walker gain by beginning with the anecdote about the elderly woman? What is the connection between this opening and the essay's conclusion?

2. Walker frequently uses *we* in her essay. Whom does she mean by *we*? Why do you think she uses this word?

3. Walker frequently uses stylistic techniques that Martin Luther King used—for example, *parallelism* (as in "She has been *beaten* . . . *placed* in solitary confinement . . . and *placed* on bread and water" [paragraph 2]) and *antithesis,* a rhetorical technique in which opposing ideas are expressed within a balanced grammatical structure (for instance, "He did not say we had to become carbon copies of the white American middle class, but he did say we had the right to become whatever we wanted to become" [paragraph 14]). Find another example of each technique. What do these stylistic techniques contribute to the essay?

4. Where in this essay does Walker use narration? Why does she use this pattern of development?

VOCABULARY PROJECTS

1. Define each of the following words as it is used in this selection.

mangled (1)	pensive (9)	nihilists (18)
deliverance (2)	listless (11)	complacent (18)
affliction (2)	hypocrisy (11)	bourgeois (19)
disaffection (3)	coiffed (11)	psychedelia (20)
reverting (5)	innuendo (11)	prerogative (21)
audacious (5)	urbane (11)	paternalists (22)
hanker (5)	vicarious (11)	
innocuous (8)	ignominiously (13)	

2. What words and expressions used in this essay are not often used today? Are there any expressions you have never heard? How can you explain this?

JOURNAL ENTRY

Do you think there is still a need for a civil rights movement? Or, do you think policies like affirmative action and legislation like the Voting Rights Act and the Equal Employment Opportunities Act have made such a movement unnecessary?

WRITING WORKSHOP

1. What good, in your opinion, was the civil rights movement? Expanding Walker's focus to include more recent advances—and, if you wish, to include its effects on whites as well as on blacks—write a cause-and-effect essay on this topic.

2. Write a cause-and-effect essay on the topic "The Women's Movement: What Good Was (or Is) It?" Or, consider the animal rights movement, the environmental movement, or the gay rights movement. You may focus on positive or negative effects (or both).

3. Reread paragraphs 11–12 of Walker's essay. Then, write an essay in which you consider how the characters and values portrayed in soap operas have affected the way you view your own life.

THEMATIC CONNECTIONS

- "The Same Difference" (p. 203)
- "An Argument against the Anna Todd Jennings Scholarship" (p. 550)
- "Letter from Birmingham Jail" (p. 562)
- "Let's Tell the Story of All America's Cultures" (p. 586)
- "How the Pot Got to Call the Kettle Black" (p. 614)

IT'S JUST TOO LATE

Calvin Trillin

Calvin Trillin was born in 1935 in Kansas City, Missouri, and graduated from Yale University in 1957. He has written investigative journalism, humor columns, short stories, a novel, and social and political commentary for several magazines. Trillin was a staff writer for The New Yorker *for almost twenty years, and some of his pieces from that magazine are collected in* U.S. Journals *(1971), about disputes and conflicts of ordinary people in small towns across the country;* Killings *(1984), on the ways Americans get killed; and most recently* American Stories *(1991). Trillin's writings on American food, prompted by his extensive travels as a journalist, are collected in* American Fried *(1974),* Alice, Let's Eat *(1978), and* Third Helpings *(1983). His humor columns, written originally for* The Nation *and since 1986 for newspaper syndication, have also been published in several collections, including* Enough's Enough (And Other Rules of Life) *(1990). Trillin's most recently published book is* Remembering Denny *(1993), a memoir that tries to understand the suicide of a college friend in 1991 by reflecting on the constricting social environment of the 1950s in which the two men grew up. "It's Just Too Late," which comes from* Killings, *examines the events leading up to a fatal car accident.*

Knoxville, Tennessee
March 1979

Until she was sixteen, FaNee Cooper was what her parents some- 1
times called an ideal child. "You'd never have to correct her," FaNee's
mother has said. In sixth grade, FaNee won a spelling contest. She
played the piano and the flute. She seemed to believe what she
heard every Sunday at the Beaver Dam Baptist Church about good
and evil and the hereafter. FaNee was not an outgoing child. Even as
a baby, she was uncomfortable when she was held and cuddled. She
found it easy to tell her parents she loved them but difficult to
confide in them. Particularly compared to her sister, Kristy, a cheerful, open little girl two and a half years younger, she was reserved
and introspective. The thoughts she kept to herself, though, were apparently happy thoughts. Her eighth-grade essay on Christmas—
written in a remarkably neat hand—talked of the joys of helping put
together toys for her little brother, Leo, Jr., and the importance of
her parents reminder that Christmas is the birthday of Jesus. Her

parents were the sort of people who might have been expected to have an ideal child. As a boy, Leo Cooper had been called "one of the greatest high-school basketball players ever developed in Knox County." He went on to play basketball at East Tennessee State, and he married the homecoming queen, JoAnn Henson. After college, Cooper became a high-school basketball coach and teacher and, eventually, an administrator. By the time FaNee turned thirteen, in 1973, he was in his third year as the principal of Gresham Junior High School, in Fountain City—a small Knox County town that had been swallowed up by Knoxville when the suburbs began to move north. A tall man with curly black hair going on gray, Leo Cooper has an elaborate way of talking ("Unless I'm very badly mistaken, he has never related to me totally the content of his conversation") and a manner that may come from years of trying to leave errant junior-high-school students with the impression that a responsible adult is magnanimous, even humble, about invariably being in the right. His wife, a high-school art teacher, paints and does batik, and created the name FaNee because she liked the way it looked and sounded— it sounds like "Fawn*ee*" when the Coopers say it—but the impression she gives is not of artiness but of soft-spoken small-town gentility. When she found, in the course of cleaning up FaNee's room, that her ideal thirteen-year-old had been smoking cigarettes, she was, in her words, crushed. "FaNee was such a perfect child before that," JoAnn Cooper said some time later. "She was angry that we found out. She knew we knew that she had done something we didn't approve of, and then the rebellion started. I was hurt. I was very hurt. I guess it came through as disappointment."

Several months later, FaNee's grandmother died. FaNee had been devoted to her grandmother. She wrote a poem in her memory—an almost joyous poem, filled with Christian faith in the afterlife ("Please don't grieve over my happiness/Rejoice with me in the presence of the Angels of Heaven"). She also took some keepsakes from her grandmother's house, and was apparently mortified when her parents found them and explained that they would have to be returned. By then, the Coopers were aware that FaNee was going to have a difficult time as a teenager. They thought she might be self-conscious about the double affliction of glasses and braces. They thought she might be uncomfortable in the role of the principal's daughter at Gresham. In ninth grade, she entered Halls High School, where JoAnn Cooper was teaching art. FaNee was a loner at first. Then she fell in with what could only be considered a bad crowd.

Halls, a few miles to the north of Fountain City, used to be known as Halls Crossroads. It is what Knoxville people call "over the ridge"—on the side of Black Oak Ridge that has always been thought of as rural. When FaNee entered Halls High, the Coopers were already in the process of building a house on several acres of land they had bought in Halls, in a sparsely settled area along Brown Gap road. Like two or three other houses along the road, it was to be constructed basically of huge logs taken from old buildings—a house that Leo Cooper describes as being, like the name FaNee, "just a little bit different." Ten years ago, Halls Crossroads was literally a crossroads. Then some of the Knoxville expansion that had swollen Fountain City spilled over the ridge, planting subdivisions here and there on roads that still went for long stretches with nothing but an occasional house with a cow or two next to it. The increase in population did not create a town. Halls has no center. Its commercial area is a series of two or three shopping centers strung together on the Maynardville Highway, the four-lane that leads north into Union County—a place almost synonymous in east Tennessee with mountain poverty. Its restaurant is the Halls Freezo Drive-In. The gathering place for the group FaNee Cooper eventually found herself in was the Maynardville Highway Exxon station.

At Halls High School, the social poles were represented by the 4
Jocks and the Freaks. FaNee found her friends among the Freaks. "I am truly enlighted upon irregular trains of thought aimed at strange depots of mental wards," she wrote when she was fifteen. "Yes! Crazed farms for the mental off—Oh! I walked through the halls screams & loud laughter fill my ears—Orderlys try to reason with me—but I am unreasonable! The joys of being a FREAK in a circus of imagination." The little crowd of eight or ten young people that FaNee joined has been referred to by her mother as "the Union County group." A couple of the girls were from backgrounds similar to FaNee's, but all the boys had the characteristics, if not the precise addresses, that Knoxville people associate with the poor whites of Union County. They were the sort of boys who didn't bother to finish high school, or finished it in a special program for slow learners, or get ejected from it for taking a swing at the principal.

"I guess you can say they more or less dragged us down to their 5
level with the drugs," a girl who was in the group—a girl who can be called Marcia—said recently. "And somehow we settled for it. It seems like we had to get ourselves in the pit before we could look out." People in the group used marijuana and Valium and LSD. They sneered at the Jocks and the "prim and proper little ladies" who went with Jocks. "We set ourselves aside," Marcia now says. "We put ourselves above everyone. How we did that I don't know." In a Knox County high school, teenagers who want to get themselves in the pit

need not mainline heroin. The Jocks they mean to be compared to do not merely show up regularly for classes and practice football and wear clean clothes; they watch their language and preach temperance and go to prayer meetings on Wednesday nights and talk about having a real good Christian witness. Around Knoxville, people who speak of well-behaved high-school kids often seem to use words like "perfect," or even "angels." For FaNee's group, the opposite was not difficult to figure out. "We were into wicked things, strange things," Marcia says. "It was like we were on some kind of devil trip." FaNee wrote about demons and vultures and rats. "Slithering serpents eat my sanity and bite my ass," she wrote in an essay called "The Lovely Road of Life," just after she turned sixteen, "while tornadoes derail and ever so swiftly destroy every car in my train of thought." She wrote a lot about death.

FaNee's girl friends spoke of her as "super-intelligent." Her English teacher found some of her writing profound—and disturbing. She was thought to be not just super-intelligent but super-mysterious, and even, at times, super-weird—an introverted girl who stared straight ahead with deep-brown, nearly black eyes and seemed to have thoughts she couldn't share. Nobody really knew why she had chosen to run with the Freaks—whether it was loneliness or rebellion or simple boredom. Marcia thought it might have had something to do with a feeling that her parent had settled on Kristy as their perfect child. "I guess she figured she couldn't be the best," Marcia said recently. "So she decided she might as well be the worst." 6

Toward the spring of FaNee's junior year at Halls, her problems seemed to deepen. Despite her intelligence, her grades were sliding. She was what her mother called "a mental dropout." Leo Cooper had to visit Halls twice because of minor suspensions. Once, FaNee had been caught smoking. Once, having ducked out of a required assembly, she was spotted by a favorite teacher, who turned her in. At home, she exchanged little more than short, strained formalities with Kristy, who shared their parents' opinion of FaNee's choice of friends. The Coopers had finished their house—a large house, its size accentuated by the huge old logs and a great stone fireplace and outsize "Paul Bunyan"-style furniture—but FaNee spent most of her time there in her own room, sleeping or listening to rock music through earphones. One night, there was a terrible scene when FaNee returned from a concert in a condition that Leo Cooper knew had to be the result of marijuana. JoAnn Cooper, who ordinarily strikes people as too gentle to raise her voice, found herself losing her temper regularly. Finally, Leo Cooper asked a counsellor he 7 knew, Jim Griffin, to stop in at Halls High School and have a talk with FaNee—unofficially.

Griffin—a young man with a warm, informal manner—worked for 8
the Juvenile Court of Knox County. He had a reputation for being able to reach teenagers who wouldn't talk to their parents or to school administrators. One Friday in March of 1977, he spent an hour and a half talking to FaNee Cooper. As Griffin recalls the interview, FaNee didn't seem alarmed by his presence. She seemed to him calm and controlled—Griffin thought it was something like talking to another adult—and, unlike most of the teenagers he dealt with, she looked him in the eye the entire time. Griffin, like some of FaNee's friends, found her eyes unsettling—"the coldest, most distant, but, at the same time, the most knowing eyes I'd ever seen." She expressed affection for her parents, but she didn't seem interested in exploring ways of getting along better with them. The impression she gave Griffin was that they were who they were, and she was who she was, and there didn't happen to be any connection. Several times, she made the same response to Griffin's suggestions: "It's too late."

That weekend, neither FaNee nor her parents brought up the 9
subject of Griffin's visit. Leo Cooper has spoken of the weekend as being particularly happy; a friend of FaNee's who stayed over remembers it as particularly strained. FaNee stayed home from school on Monday because of a bad headache—she often had bad headaches—but felt well enough on Monday evening to drive to the library. She was to be home at nine. When she wasn't, Mrs. Cooper began to phone her friends. Finally, around ten, Leo Cooper got into his other car and took a swing around Halls—past the teenage hangouts like the Exxon station and the Pizza Hut and the Smoky Mountain Market. Then he took a second swing. At eleven, FaNee was still not home.

She hadn't gone to the library. She had picked up two girl friends 10
and driven to the home of a third, where everyone took five Valium tablets. Then the four girls drove over to the Exxon station, where they met four boys from their crowd. After a while, the group bought some beer and some marijuana and reassembled at Charlie Stevens's trailer. Charlie Stevens was five or six years older than everyone else in the group—a skinny, slow-thinking young man with long black hair and a sparse beard. He was married and had a child, but he and his wife had separated; she was back in Union County with the baby. Stevens had remained in their trailer—parked in the yard near his mother's house, in a back-road area of Knox County dom-

inated by decrepit, unpainted sheds and run-down trailers and rusted-out automobiles. Stevens had picked up FaNee at home once or twice—apparently, more as a driver for the group than as a date—and the Coopers, having learned that his unsuitability extended to being married, had asked her not to see him.

In Charlie's trailer, which had no heat or electricity, the group drank beer and passed around joints, keeping warm with blankets. By eleven or so, FaNee was what one of her friends has called "super-messed-up." Her speech was slurred. She was having trouble keeping her balance. She had decided not to go home. She had apparently persuaded herself that her parents intended to send her away to some sort of home for incorrigibles. "It's too late," she said to one of her friends. "It's just too late." It was decided that one of the boys, David Munsey, who was more or less the leader of the group, would drive the Coopers' car to FaNee's house, where FaNee and Charlie Stevens would pick him up in Stevens's car—a worn Pinto with four bald tires, one light, and a dragging muffler. FaNee wrote a note to her parents, and then, perhaps because her handwriting was suffering the effects of beer and marijuana and Valium, asked Stevens to rewrite it on a large piece of paper, which would be left on the seat of the Coopers' car. The Stevens version was just about the same as FaNee's, except that Stevens left out a couple of sentences about trying to work things out ("I'm willing to try") and, not having won any spelling championship himself, he misspelled a few words, like "tomorrow." The note said, "Dear Mom and Dad. Sorry I'm late. Very late. I left your car because I thought you might need it tomorrow. I love you all, but this is something I just had to do. The man talked to me privately for one and a half hours and I was really scared, so this is something I just had to do, but don't worry. I'm with a very good friend. Love you all. FaNee. P.S. Please try to understand I love you all very much, really I do. Love me if you have a chance."

At eleven-thirty or so, Leo Cooper was sitting in his living room, looking out the window at his driveway—a long gravel road that runs almost four hundred feet from the house to Brown Gap Road. He saw the car that FaNee had been driving pull into the driveway. "She's home," he called to his wife, who had just left the room. Cooper walked out on the deck over the garage. The car had stopped at the end of the driveway, and the lights had gone out. He got into his other car and drove to the end of the driveway. David Munsey had already joined Charlie Stevens and FaNee, and the Pinto was just leaving, travelling at a normal rate of speed. Leo Cooper pulled out on the road behind them.

Stevens turned left on Crippen Road, a road that has a field on one   13
side and two or three small houses on the other, and there Cooper
pulled his car in front of the Pinto and stopped, blocking the way.
He got out and walked toward the Pinto. Suddenly, Stevens put the
car in reverse, backed into a driveway a hundred yards behind him,
and sped off. Cooper jumped in his car and gave chase. Stevens raced
back to Brown Gap Road, ran a stop sign there, ran another stop
sign at Maynardville Highway, turned north, veered off onto the old
Andersonville Pike, a nearly abandoned road that runs parallel to
the highway, and then crossed back over the highway to the narrow,
dark country roads on the other side. Stevens sometimes drove with
his lights out. He took some of the corners by suddenly applying his
hand brake to make the car swerve around in a ninety-degree turn.
He was in familiar territory—he actually passed his trailer—and
Cooper had difficulty keeping up. Past the trailer, Stevens swept
down a hill into a sharp left turn that took him onto Foust Hollow
Road, a winding, hilly road not much wider than one car.

At a fork, Cooper thought he had lost the Pinto. He started to   14
go right and then saw what seemed to be a spark from Stevens's
dragging muffler off to the left, in the darkness. Cooper took the left
fork, down Salem Church Road. He went down a hill and then up a
long, curving hill to a crest, where he saw the Stevens car ahead.
"I saw the car airborne. Up in the air," he later testified. "It was
up in the air. And then it completely rolled over one more time. It
started to make another flip forward, and just as it started to flip to
the other side it flipped back this way, and my daughter's body came
out."

Cooper slammed on his brakes and skidded to a stop up against   15
the Pinto. "Book!" Stevens shouted—the group's equivalent of
"Scram!" Stevens and Munsey disappeared into the darkness. "It
was dark, no one around, and so I started yelling for FaNee," Cooper
had testified. "I thought it was an eternity before I could find her
body, wedged under the back end of that car. . . . I tried everything I
could, and saw that I couldn't get her loose. So I ran to a trailer back
up to the top of the hill back up there to try to get that lady to call
to get me some help, and then apparently she didn't think that I was
serious. . . . I took the jack out of my car and got under, and it was
dark, still couldn't see too much what was going on . . . and started
prying and got her loose, and I don't know how. And then I dragged
her over to the side, and, of course, at the time I felt reasonably
assured that she was gone, because her head was completely—on
one side just as if you had taken a sledgehammer and just hit it and

bashed it in. And I did have the pleasure of one thing. I had the pleasure of listening to her breathe about the last three times she ever breathed in her life."

David Munsey did not return to the wreck that night, but Charlie Stevens did. Leo Cooper was kneeling next to his daughter's body. Cooper insisted that Stevens come close enough to see FaNee. "He was kneeling down next to her," Stevens later testified. "And he said, 'Do you know what you've done? Do you really know what you've done?' Like that. And I just looked at her, and I said. 'Yes,' and just stood there. Because I couldn't say nothing." There was, of course, a legal decision to be made about who was responsible for FaNee Cooper's death. In a deposition, Stevens said he had been fleeing for his life. He testified that when Leo Cooper blocked Crippen Road, FaNee had said that her father had a gun and intended to hurt them. Stevens was bound over and eventually indicted for involuntary manslaughter. Leo Cooper testified that when he approached the Pinto on Crippen Road, FaNee had a strange expression that he had never seen before. "It wasn't like FaNee, and I knew something was wrong," he said. "My concern was to get FaNee out of the car." The district attorney's office asked that Cooper be bound over for reckless driving, but the judge declined to do so. "Any father would have done what he did," the judge said. "I can see no criminal act on the part of Mr. Cooper." 16

Almost two years passed before Charlie Stevens was brought to trial. Part of the problem was assuring the presence of David Munsey, who had joined the Navy but seemed inclined to assign his own leaves. In the meantime, the Coopers went to court with a civil suit—they had "uninsured-motorist coverage," which requires their insurance company to cover any defendant who has no insurance of his own—and they won a judgment. There were ways of assigning responsibility, of course, which had nothing to do with the law, civil or criminal. A lot of people in Knoxville thought that Leo Cooper had, in the words of his lawyer, "done what any daddy worth his salt would have done." There were others who believed that FaNee Cooper had lost her life because Leo Cooper had lost his temper. Leo Cooper was not among those who expressed any doubts about his actions. Unlike his wife, whose eyes filled with tears at almost any mention of FaNee, Cooper seemed able, even eager to go over the details of the accident again and again. With the help of a school-board security man, he conducted his own investigation. He drove over the route dozens of times. "I've thought about it every day, and I guess I will the rest of my life," he said as he and his lawyer and 17

the prosecuting attorney went over the route again the day before
Charlie Stevens's trial finally began. "But I can't tell any alternative
for a father. I simply wanted her out of that car. I'd have done the
same thing again, even at the risk of losing her."

Tennessee law permits the family of a victim to hire a special   18
prosecutor to assist the district attorney. The lawyer who acted for
the Coopers in the civil case helped prosecute Charlie Stevens. Both
he and the district attorney assured the jurors that the presence of
a special prosecutor was not to be construed to mean that the
Coopers were vindictive. Outside the courtroom, Leo Cooper said
that the verdict was of no importance to him—that he felt sorry, in
a way, for Charlie Stevens. But there were people in Knoxville who
thought Cooper had a lot riding on the prosecution of Charlie
Stevens. If Stevens was not guilty of FaNee Cooper's death—found
so by twelve of his peers—who was?

At the trial, Cooper testified emotionally and remarkably graph-   19
ically about pulling FaNee out from under the car and watching
her die in his arms. Charlie Stevens had shaved his beard and cut
his hair, but the effort did not transform him into an impressive
witness. His lawyer—trying to argue that it would have been impossible for Stevens to concoct the story about FaNee's having mentioned a gun, as the prosecution strongly implied—said, "His mind
is such that if you ask him a question you can hear his mind go
around, like an old mill creaking." Stevens did not deny the reck-
lessness of his driving or the sorry condition of his car. It happened
to be the only car he had available to flee in, he said, and he had fled
in fear for his life.

The prosecution said that Stevens could have let FaNee out of the   20
car when her father stopped them, or could have gone to the commercial strip on the Maynardville Highway for protection. The prosecution said that Leo Cooper had done what he might have been
expected to do under the circumstances—alone, late at night, his
daughter in danger. The defense said precisely the same about
Stevens: he had done what he might have been expected to do when
being pursued by a man he had reason to be afraid of. "I don't fault
Mr. Cooper for what he did, but I'm sorry he did it," the defense
attorney said. "I'm sorry the girl said what she said." The jury
deliberated for eighteen minutes. Charlie Stevens was found guilty.
The jury recommended a sentence of from two to five years in the
state penitentiary. At the announcement, Leo Cooper broke down
and cried, JoAnn Cooper's eyes filled with tears; she blinked them
back and continued to stare straight ahead.

In a way, the Coopers might still strike a casual visitor as an ideal   21
family—handsome parents, a bright and bubbly teenage daughter, a
little boy learning the hook shot from his father, a warm house with
some land around it. FaNee's presence is there, of course. A picture
of her, with a small bouquet of flowers over it, hangs in the living
room. One of her poems is displayed in a frame on a table. Even if
Leo Cooper continues to think about that night for the rest of his life,
there are questions he can never answer. Was there a way that Leo
and JoAnn Cooper could have prevented FaNee from choosing the
path she chose? Would she still be alive if Leo Cooper had not jumped
into his car and driven to the end of the driveway to investigate? Did
she in fact tell Charlie Stevens that her father would hurt them—or
even that her father had a gun? Did she want to get away from her
family even at the risk of tearing around dark country roads in
Charlie Stevens's dismal Pinto? Or did she welcome the risk? The
poem of FaNee's that the Coopers have displayed is one she wrote a
week before her death:

> I think I'm going to die
> And I really don't know why.
> But look in my eye
> When I tell you good-bye.
> I think I'm going to die.

COMPREHENSION

1. What early signs suggested that FaNee was not really an "ideal
   child"?

2. During her high school years, what specific kinds of behavior caused
   FaNee's parents to worry about her?

3. In what ways might FaNee's parents have contributed to her problems? Consider their backgrounds, their personalities, and their position in the town. What other factors might have caused her problems?

4. In what ways did the social structure of the town of Halls—and, in
   particular, of Halls High School—lead FaNee to become a "Freak"?

5. Identify the immediate cause of FaNee's death. What other, more
   remote, causes do you see as significant?

6. In what sense might FaNee's decline be described as a causal chain?

7. What do you think Trillin means when he says, in paragraph 17,
   "There were ways of assigning responsibility . . . which had nothing to
   do with the law, civil or criminal"?

8. What do you think FaNee meant by the statement "It's just too late"? What do you think Trillin means to suggest by using this statement as his essay's title?

PURPOSE AND AUDIENCE

1. Do you believe Trillin's primary purpose in this essay is to report information about FaNee and her family in a case study, or to suggest that her story has wider social or even moral implications for readers? Explain.

2. In paragraph 5 Trillin says, "In a Knox County high school, teenagers who want to get themselves in the pit need not mainline heroin. The Jocks they mean to be compared to do not merely show up regularly for classes and practice football and wear clean clothes; they watch their language and preach temperance and go to prayer meetings on Wednesday nights and talk about having a real good Christian witness." Why do you think Trillin finds it necessary to include this explanation? What does it suggest about his view of his audience?

3. "It's Just Too Late" does not have an explicitly stated thesis. What do you think the essay's main idea is? State it in a single sentence. Why do you think Trillin chose not to include such a statement?

STYLE AND STRUCTURE

1. Trillin's essay might be divided into three parts: background (paragraphs 1–8); the events of the night FaNee died (9–15); and the aftermath of that night, including the trial (16–21). How does Trillin signal movement from one part of the "story" to the next? Do you think he needs to make these signals more explicit? Could internal headings be useful? Explain.

2. What do you think Trillin hopes to accomplish by quoting FaNee's writing in paragraphs 2, 4, 5, 11, and 21? Is he successful?

3. What do the quotations from FaNee's parents, her friend Marcia, Jim Griffin, and others add to the essay? What other voices would you like to hear?

4. Trillin is a reporter, and his writing is both detailed and objective. Why is this level of detail and objectivity so important here? Where, if anywhere, does he reveal his own opinions?

5. In the last paragraph of his essay, Trillin asks (but does not answer) a series of questions. What do you think he hopes these unanswered questions will suggest to readers?

VOCABULARY PROJECTS

1. Define each of the following words as it is used in this selection.

   introspective (1)   affliction (2)   graphically (19)
   errant (1)   temperance (5)
   magnanimous (1)   bald (11)

2. "At Halls High School," Trillin explains, "the social poles were represented by the Jocks and the Freaks." Write one-sentence definitions of *jock* and *freak*. Then, suggest a few alternate names for each group, being careful to choose words that convey the same meanings as the original terms.

JOURNAL ENTRY

Who, if anyone, do you think could have "saved" FaNee? Or do you believe it really was "just too late"?

WRITING WORKSHOP

1. Write an essay in which you consider the possible effects of FaNee's death on those who knew her—her parents, her teachers, her friends.

2. Who or what do you see as responsible for FaNee's death? Write an essay in which you consider both the main cause of her death and the contributory causes.

3. Taking the point of view of a school counselor, write a report in which you make specific recommendations for addressing FaNee's needs and problems. In your report, be sure to explain the beneficial results of the plan you propose.

THEMATIC CONNECTIONS

- "Television: The Plug-In Drug" (p. 303)
- "Suicide Note" (p. 347)
- "The Perfect Family" (p. 511)

SHIPS IN THE DESERT

Al Gore

Albert Gore, Jr., was born in Washington, D.C., in 1948 and grew up there, where his father served as a representative and later a senator from Tennessee. Gore graduated from Harvard University in 1969 with a degree in government and then served as an army reporter in Vietnam for two years. Returning to Tennessee, where he had spent his childhood summers on his parents' farm, he worked as an investigative reporter and editorial writer for the Nashville Tennessean, *as a home builder and land developer, and as a livestock and tobacco farmer. He also studied philosophy for a year and law for two years at Vanderbilt University. In 1976 Gore was elected a Democratic U.S. representative from Tennessee, and he served four terms before being elected to the Senate in 1984. He ran an unsuccessful campaign for the 1988 Democratic presidential nomination, but was elected vice president in 1992 as Bill Clinton's running mate. As a senator, Gore focused his attention on health-related issues, environmental dangers, and nuclear arms and disarmament. He is the author of* Biotechnology: Implications for Public Policy *(1985);* Earth in the Balance: Ecology and the Human Spirit *(1992);* Putting People First: How We Can All Change America *(1992), written with Clinton and outlining the policies of their campaign; and* From Red Tape to Results: Creating a Government That Works Better and Costs Less *(1993), Gore's report on reinventing the way government functions. "Ships in the Desert," from* Earth in the Balance, *examines the complex interrelationship of human civilization and the global environment.*

I was standing in the sun on the hot steel deck of a fishing ship   1
capable of processing a fifty-ton catch on a good day. But it wasn't a
good day. We were anchored in what used to be the most productive
fishing site in all of central Asia, but as I looked out over the bow, the
prospects of a good catch looked bleak. Where there should have
been gentle blue-green waves lapping against the side of the ship,
there was nothing but hot dry sand—as far as I could see in all
directions. The other ships of the fleet were also at rest in the sand,
scattered in the dunes that stretched all the way to the horizon.

Oddly enough, it made me think of a fried egg I had seen back in   2
the United States on television the week before. It was sizzling and
popping the way a fried egg should in a pan, but it was in the middle

of a sidewalk in downtown Phoenix. I guess it sprang to mind because, like the ship on which I was standing, there was nothing wrong with the egg itself. Instead, the world beneath it had changed in an unexpected way that made the egg seem—through no fault of its own—out of place. It was illustrating the newsworthy point that at the time Arizona wasn't having an especially good day, either, because for the second day in a row temperatures had reached a record 122 degrees.

As a camel walked by on the dead bottom of the Aral Sea, my   3
thoughts returned to the unlikely ship of the desert* on which I stood, which also seemed to be illustrating the point that its world had changed out from underneath it with sudden cruelty. Ten years ago the Aral was the fourth-largest inland sea in the world, comparable to the largest of North America's Great Lakes. Now it is disappearing because the water that used to feed it has been diverted in an ill-considered irrigation scheme to grow cotton in the desert. The new shoreline was almost forty kilometers across the sand from where the fishing fleet was now permanently docked. Meanwhile, in the nearby town of Muynak the people were still canning fish— brought not from the Aral Sea but shipped by rail through Siberia from the Pacific Ocean, more than a thousand miles away.

I had come to the Aral Sea in August 1990 to witness at first hand   4
the destruction taking place there on an almost biblical scale. But during the trip I encountered other images that also alarmed me. For example, the day I returned to Moscow from Muynak, my friend Alexei Yablokov, possibly the leading environmentalist in the Soviet Union, was returning from an emergency expedition to the White Sea, where he had investigated the mysterious and unprecedented death of several *million* starfish, washed up into a knee-deep mass covering many miles of beach. That night, in his apartment, he talked of what it was like for the residents to wade through the starfish in hip boots, trying to explain their death.

Later investigations identified radioactive military waste as the   5
likely culprit in the White Sea deaths. But what about all of the other mysterious mass deaths washing up on beaches around the world? French scientists recently concluded that the explanation for the growing number of dead dolphins washing up along the Riviera was accumulated environmental stress, which, over time, rendered the animals too weak to fight off a virus. This same phenomenon may also explain the sudden increase in dolphin deaths along the Gulf Coast in Texas as well as the mysterious deaths of 12,000 seals

---

*Eds. Note—The camel is often called "the ship of the desert."

whose corpses washed up on the shores of the North Sea in the summer of 1988. Of course, the oil-covered otters and seabirds of Prince William Sound* a year later presented less of a mystery to science, if no less an indictment of our civilization.

As soon as one of these troubling images fades, another takes its place, provoking new questions. What does it mean, for example, that children playing in the morning surf must now dodge not only the occasional jellyfish but the occasional hypodermic needle washing in with the waves? Needles, dead dolphins, and oil-soaked birds—are all these signs that the shores of our familiar world are fast eroding, that we are now standing on some new beach, facing dangers beyond the edge of what we are capable of imagining? 6

With our backs turned to the place in nature from which we came, we sense an unfamiliar tide rising and swirling around our ankles, pulling at the sand beneath our feet. Each time this strange new tide goes out, it leaves behind the flotsam and jetsam of some giant shipwreck far out at sea, startling images washed up on the sands of our time, each a fresh warning of hidden dangers that lie ahead if we continue on our present course. 7

My search for the underlying causes of the environmental crisis has led me to travel around the world to examine and study many of these images of destruction. At the very bottom of the earth, high in the Trans-Antarctic Mountains, with the sun glaring at midnight through a hole in the sky, I stood in the unbelievable coldness and talked with a scientist in the late fall of 1988 about the tunnel he was digging through time. Slipping his parka back to reveal a badly burned face that was cracked and peeling, he pointed to the annual layers of ice in a core sample dug from the glacier on which we were standing. He moved his finger back in time to the ice of two decades ago. "Here's where the U.S. Congress passed the Clean Air Act," he said. At the bottom of the world, two continents away from Washington, D.C., even a small reduction in one country's emissions had changed the amount of pollution found in the remotest and least accessible place on earth. 8

But the most significant change thus far in the earth's atmosphere is the one that began with the industrial revolution early in the last century and has picked up speed ever since. Industry meant coal, and later oil, and we began to burn lots of it—bringing rising levels of carbon dioxide (CO_2), with its ability to trap more heat in the atmosphere and slowly warm the earth. Fewer than a hundred 9

*Eds. Note—site in Alaska of the 1989 *Exxon Valdez* oil spill.

yards from the South Pole, upwind from the ice runway where the ski plane lands and keeps its engines running to prevent the metal parts from freeze-locking together, scientists monitor the air several times every day to chart the course of that inexorable change. During my visit, I watched one scientist draw the results of that day's measurements, pushing the end of a steep line still higher on the graph. He told me how easy it is—there at the end of the earth—to see that this enormous change in the global atmosphere is still picking up speed.

Two and a half years later I slept under the midnight sun at the   10
other end of our planet, in a small tent pitched on a twelve-foot-thick slab of ice floating in the frigid Arctic Ocean. After a hearty breakfast, my companions and I traveled by snowmobiles a few miles farther north to a rendezvous point where the ice was thinner—only three and a half feet thick—and a nuclear submarine hovered in the water below. After it crashed through the ice, took on its new passengers, and resubmerged, I talked with scientists who were trying to measure more accurately the thickness of the polar ice cap, which many believe is thinning as a result of global warming. I had just negotiated an agreement between ice scientists and the U.S. Navy to secure the release of previously top secret data from submarine sonar tracks, data that could help them learn what is happening to the north polar cap. Now, I wanted to see the pole itself, and some eight hours after we met the submarine, we were crashing through that ice, surfacing, and then I was standing in an eerily beautiful snowscape, windswept and sparkling white, with the horizon defined by little hummocks, or "pressure ridges" of ice that are pushed up like tiny mountain ranges when separate sheets collide. But here too, CO_2 levels are rising just as rapidly, and ultimately temperatures will rise with them—indeed, global warming is expected to push temperatures up much more rapidly in the polar regions than in the rest of the world. As the polar air warms, the ice here will thin; and since the polar cap plays such a crucial role in the world's weather system, the consequences of a thinning cap could be disastrous.

Considering such scenarios is not a purely speculative exercise.   11
Six months after I returned from the North Pole, a team of scientists reported dramatic changes in the pattern of ice distribution in the Arctic, and a second team reported a still controversial claim (which a variety of data now suggest) that, overall, the north polar cap has thinned by 2 percent in just the last decade. Moreover, scientists established several years ago that in many land areas north of the Arctic Circle, the spring snowmelt now comes earlier every year, and

deep in the tundra below, the temperature of the earth is steadily rising.

As it happens, some of the most disturbing images of environmental destruction can be found exactly halfway between the North and South poles—precisely at the equator in Brazil—where billowing clouds of smoke regularly blacken the sky above the immense but now threatened Amazon rain forest. Acre by acre, the rain forest is being burned to create fast pasture for fast-food beef; as I learned when I went there in early 1989, the fires are set earlier and earlier in the dry season now, with more than one Tennessee's worth of rain forest being slashed and burned each year. According to our guide, the biologist Tom Lovejoy, there are more different species of birds in each square mile of the Amazon than exist in all of North America— which means we are silencing thousands of songs we have never even heard. 12

But for most of us the Amazon is a distant place, and we scarcely notice the disappearance of these and other vulnerable species. We ignore these losses at our peril, however. They're like the proverbial miners' canaries*, silent alarms whose message in this case is that living species of animals and plants are now vanishing around the world *one thousand times faster* than at any time in the past 65 million years. 13

To be sure, the deaths of some of the larger and more spectacular animal species now under siege do occasionally capture our attention. I have also visited another place along the equator, East Africa, where I encountered the grotesquely horrible image of a dead elephant, its head mutilated by poachers who had dug out its valuable tusks with chain saws. Clearly, we need to change our purely aesthetic consideration of ivory, since its source is now so threatened. To me, its translucent whiteness seems different now, like evidence of the ghostly presence of a troubled spirit, a beautiful but chill apparition, inspiring both wonder and dread. 14

A similar apparition lies just beneath the ocean. While scuba diving in the Caribbean, I have seen and touched the white bones of a dead coral reef. All over the earth, coral reefs have suddenly started to "bleach" as warmer ocean temperatures put unaccustomed stress on the tiny organisms that normally live in the skin of the coral and give the reef its natural coloration. As these organisms—nicknamed 15

---

*Eds. Note—Because a canary will die from lack of air well before a human being will, miners traditionally carried canaries down into the mines with them to serve as a warning of a shortage of oxygen.

"zooks"—leave the membrane of the coral, the coral itself becomes transparent, allowing its white limestone skeleton to shine through—hence its bleached appearance. In the past, bleaching was almost always an occasional and temporary phenomenon, but repeated episodes can exhaust the coral. In the last few years, scientists have been shocked at the sudden occurrence of extensive worldwide bleaching episodes from which increasing numbers of coral reefs have failed to recover. Though dead, they shine more brightly than before, haunted perhaps by the same ghost that gives spectral light to an elephant's tusk.

But one doesn't have to travel around the world to witness humankind's assault on the earth. Images that signal the distress of our global environment are now commonly seen almost anywhere. A few miles from the Capitol, for example, I encountered another startling image of nature out of place. Driving in the Arlington, Virginia, neighborhood where my family and I live when the Senate is in session, I stepped on the brake to avoid hitting a large pheasant walking across the street. It darted between the parked cars, across the sidewalk, and into a neighbor's backyard. Then it was gone. But this apparition of wildness persisted in my memory as a puzzle: Why would a pheasant, let alone such a large and beautiful mature specimen, be out for a walk in my neighborhood? Was it a much wilder place than I had noticed? Were pheasants, like the trendy Vietnamese potbellied pigs, becoming the latest fashion in unusual pets? I didn't solve the mystery until weeks later, when I remembered that about three miles away, along the edge of the river, developers were bulldozing the last hundred acres of untouched forest in the entire area. As the woods fell to make way for more concrete, more buildings, parking lots, and streets, the wild things that lived there were forced to flee. Most of the deer were hit by cars; other creatures—like the pheasant that darted into my neighbor's backyard—made it a little farther. 16

Ironically, before I understood the mystery, I felt vaguely comforted to imagine that perhaps this urban environment, so similar to the one in which many Americans live, was not so hostile to wild things after all. I briefly supposed that, like the resourceful raccoons and possums and squirrels and pigeons, all of whom have adapted to life in the suburbs, creatures as wild as pheasants might have a fighting chance. Now I remember that pheasant when I take my children to the zoo and see an elephant or a rhinoceros. They too inspire wonder and sadness. They too remind me that we are creating a world that is hostile to wildness, that seems to prefer concrete to natural landscapes. We are encountering these creatures on a 17 path we have paved—one that ultimately leads to their extinction.

On some nights, in high northern latitudes, the sky itself offers another ghostly image that signals the lose of ecological balance now in progress. If the sky is clear after sunset—and if you are watching from a place where pollution hasn't blotted out the night sky altogether—you can sometimes see a strange kind of cloud high in the sky. This "noctilucent cloud" occasionally appears when the earth is first cloaked in the evening darkness; shimmering above us with a translucent whiteness, these clouds seem quite unnatural. And they should: noctilucent clouds have begun to appear more often because of a huge buildup of methane gas in the atmosphere. (Also called natural gas, methane is released from landfills, from coal mines and rice paddies, from billions of termites that swarm through the freshly cut forestland, from the burning of biomass and from a variety of other human activities.) Even though noctilucent clouds were sometimes seen in the past, all this extra methane carries more water vapor into the upper atmosphere, where it condenses at much higher altitudes to form more clouds that the sun's rays still strike long after sunset has brought the beginning of night to the surface far beneath them.

What should we feel toward these ghosts in the sky? Simple wonder or the mix of emotions we feel at the zoo? Perhaps we should feel awe for our own power: just as men tear tusks from elephants' heads in such quantity as to threaten the beast with extinction, we are ripping matter from its place in the earth in such volume as to upset the balance between daylight and darkness. In the process, we are once again adding to the threat of global warming, because methane has been one of the fastest-growing greenhouse gases, and is third only to carbon dioxide and water vapor in total volume, changing the chemistry of the upper atmosphere. But, without even considering that threat, shouldn't it startle us that we have now put these clouds in the evening sky which glisten with a spectral light? Or have our eyes adjusted so completely to the bright lights of civilization that we can't see these clouds for what they are—a physical manifestation of the violent collision between human civilization and the earth?

COMPREHENSION

1. Why do the ships in the desert remind Gore of a fried egg on the sidewalk?

2. What do you think Gore means in paragraph 4 when he says the destruction he witnesses is "on an almost biblical scale"?

3. According to Gore, what effect has the industrial revolution of the nineteenth century had on the environment? What effect has the increase of carbon dioxide levels had on the polar ice cap?

4. Why is the Amazon rain forest being destroyed? What effect will this destruction ultimately have?

5. How does Gore account for the appearance of noctilucent clouds? How do these clouds contribute to global warming?

6. Where does Gore ultimately place the blame for the environmental destruction he witnesses?

PURPOSE AND AUDIENCE

1. In paragraph 7 Gore expresses the main idea of his essay. State this main idea in the form of a one-sentence thesis. Do you think Gore should have included such a statement earlier in his essay? Explain.

2. In paragraph 5 Gore refers to one environmental disaster as "an indictment of our civilization." Do you think he is intentionally exaggerating the problem? If so, what might be his motive for doing so? Do you think this statement suggests his primary purpose in this essay is to assign blame for the destruction he witnesses? Or do you believe he has another, more important purpose?

3. Gore wrote this essay when he was a U.S. senator. Despite his high office, he presents his position not in the form of a technical exploration of abstract scientific issues but rather as a personal journey, what he calls "My search for the underlying causes of the environmental crisis" (8). Why do you think he chose this perspective? How do you suppose he expected it to affect his audience?

4. Throughout his essay Gore makes an effort to appeal to his readers' emotions. How does he do this? Would a less emotional, more objective presentation have been more or less effective? Explain.

5. What does Gore assume his audience knows about the situation he identifies? Does he expect them to be sympathetic to his position? How can you tell?

STYLE AND STRUCTURE

1. Gore opens his essay with the unexpected image, echoed in the title, of ships "scattered in the dunes." Evaluate the effectiveness of this opening strategy.

2. In paragraph 2 Gore draws an **analogy** between the ship he is on and a fried egg on the sidewalk. Is this analogy effective, or are the ship and the egg too dissimilar to be comparable? Explain.

3. Gore gives many specific examples of the kind of "troubling images" that suggest environmental disaster. List as many of these examples as you can. Do they convince you of the seriousness of the problem, or does he need more (or different) examples? Which particular examples do you find most compelling? Why?

4. Is this essay's focus on causes, effects, or both? Explain.

5. Paragraphs 9 through 11 can be summarized as a causal chain. What are the elements of this chain? Can you identify any other causal chains in the essay?

6. Gore's style is informal and down to earth, and his tone is personal. Identify specific words and expressions that characterize his writing as informal and personal.

7. Although his essay is written for a lay audience rather than for scientists, Gore does cite the views of a number of experts. Why does he do so? Should he have included more expert opinion? More technical terms? Statistics? Explain.

8. Gore takes a very subjective, even emotional, view of the environmental crisis. Do you think this attitude is appropriate for his subject matter? For someone in his position?

VOCABULARY PROJECTS

1. Define each of the following words as it is used in this selection.

dunes (1)	flotsam and jetsam (7)	tundra (11)
culprit (5)	emissions (8)	proverbial (13)
rendered (5)	rendezvous (10)	translucent (14)
indictment (5)	hummocks (10)	apparition (14)
eroding (6)	scenarios (11)	spectral (15)

2. What technical terms does Gore use in his discussion of this scientific subject? Does he define the terms he uses? Does he need to? Explain.

JOURNAL ENTRY

Do you react as passionately as Gore does to the images of the dry Aral Sea, dead dolphins, oil-covered otters, burned-out rain forests, extinct birds, and mutilated elephants? Or do you have a hard time seeing these disasters as relevant to your own life?

WRITING WORKSHOP

1. Although, as Gore says, "for most of us the Amazon is a distant place" (13), many of us, like Gore, have witnessed environmental destruction closer to home. Write a cause and effect essay in which you explain the causes and/or effects of "humankind's assault on the earth" (16) in your own community.

2. Write a letter to Gore arguing that serious as the environmental crisis is, another problem—violence, drugs, world hunger, AIDS, illiteracy, or racism—needs more immediate attention. Outline the effects the problem you identify has had on you and your world, and predict the effects it will have in the future if action is not taken.

THEMATIC CONNECTIONS

- "The Valley of Windmills" (p. 124)
- "Once More to the Lake" (p. 160)
- "The Human Cost of an Illiterate Society" (p. 215)
- "On Dumpster Diving" (p. 664)

SUICIDE NOTE

Janice Mirikitani

*Janice Mirikitani, born in 1942, is a Japanese-American poet,
editor, and community activist in San Francisco. Her book* Shedding Silence *(1987) is a collection of poetry and prose addressing
racism in the United States—how it affects Asians and Asian-
Americans, and particularly how it affected the thousands of
Japanese-Americans held in internment camps during World War
II. She is also the author of* Awake in the River *(1978), another
collection of poetry and prose; the editor of* Time to Greez! Incanta-
tions from the Third World *(1975) and* Ayumi: A Japanese American Anthology *(1980); and the co-editor of* I Have Something to Say
about This Big Trouble: Children of the Tenderloin Speak Out
*(1989), a collection of drawings, poems, and prose by children of the
underclass in San Francisco's Tenderloin neighborhood. In "Suicide
Note," which appears in* Shedding Silence, *a note of apology from a
young Asian-American college student to her parents reveals the
extreme pressure to excel placed upon her by her parents and her
culture.*

How many notes written . . .
ink smeared like birdprints in snow.

    not good enough   not pretty enough   not smart enough
dear mother and father.
5 I apologize
for disappointing you.
I've worked very hard,
                not good enough
harder, perhaps to please you.
10 If only I were a son, shoulders broad
as the sunset threading through pine,
I would see the light in my mother's
eyes, or the golden pride reflected
in my father's dream
15 of my wide, male hands worthy of work
and comfort.
I would swagger through life
muscled and bold and assured,
drawing praises to me
20 like currents in the bed of wind, virile
with confidence.

347

      not good enough   not strong enough   not good enough
I apologize.
Tasks do not come easily.

25   Each failure, a glacier.
Each disapproval, a bootprint.
Each disappointment,
ice above my river.
So I have worked hard.

30   not good enough
My sacrifice I will drop
bone by bone, perched
on the ledge of my womanhood,
fragile as wings.

35   not strong enough
It is snowing steadily
surely not good weather
for flying—this sparrow
sillied and dizzied by the wind

40   on the edge.
                   not smart enough
I make this ledge my altar
to offer penance.
This air will not hold me,

45   the snow burdens my crippled wings,
my tears drop like bitter cloth
softly into the gutter below.
      not good enough   not strong enough   not smart enough

                   Choices thin as shaved
50   ice. Notes shredded
                   drift like snow

on my broken body,
covers me like whispers
of sorries
55   sorries.
Perhaps when they find me
they will bury
my bird bones beneath
a sturdy pine
60   and scatter my feathers like
unspoken song
over this white and cold and silent
breast of earth.

THINKING ABOUT LITERATURE

1. A note accompanying this poem explained the main cause of the student's death:

   "An Asian American college student was reported to have jumped to her death from her dormitory window. Her body was found two days later under a deep cover of snow. Her suicide note contained an apology to her parents for having received less than a perfect four point grade average. . . ."

   What other causes might have contributed to her suicide?

2. Why does the speaker believe her life would have been happier if she had been male? Do you think she is correct?

3. What words, phrases, and images are repeated in this poem? What effect do these repetitions have on you?

JOURNAL ENTRY

Who (or what) do you blame for teenage suicides such as the one the poem describes? How might the causes be eliminated?

THEMATIC CONNECTIONS

- "Only Daughter" (p. 73)
- "College Pressures" (p. 425)
- "The Company Man" (p. 507)

WRITING ASSIGNMENTS FOR CAUSE AND EFFECT

1. "On Dumpster Diving," "Who Killed Benny Paret?," "Ships in the Desert," and "38 Who Saw Murder Didn't Call the Police" all (directly or undirectly) encourage readers to take action rather than remain uninvolved bystanders. Using information gleaned from all four of these essays as examples, write an essay in which you explore the possible consequences of apathy.

2. Both "Letter from Birmingham Jail" and "The Civil Rights Movement: What Good Was It?" consider some of the factors that made the United States ripe for the civil rights movement. Citing these two essays when necessary, write a cause-and-effect essay in which you explore those factors.

3. Various technological and social developments have contributed to the decline of letter writing. One of these is the telephone. Consider some other possible causes, and write an essay explaining why letter writing has become less popular. You may also consider the *effects* of this decline.

4. How do you account for the popularity of one of the following phenomena: shopping malls, MTV, romance novels, fast food, E-mail, heavy metal, rap music, soap operas, sensationalist tabloids like the *National Enquirer*? Write an essay in which you consider remote as well as immediate causes for the success of the phenomenon you choose.

5. Between 1946 and 1964, the birth rate increased considerably. Some of the effects attributed to this "baby boom" include the 1960s antiwar movement, the increase in the crime rate, and the development of feminism. Write an essay in which you explore some possible effects of the baby boom generation's growing older. What trends would you expect to find as the bulk of the baby boomers reach middle age? When they reach retirement?

6. Write an essay in which you trace a series of events from your life that constitutes a causal chain. Be sure to indicate clearly both the sequence of events and the causal connections among them.

7. Consider the effects, or possible effects, of one of these scientific developments on your life and/or on the lives of your contemporaries: genetic engineering, space exploration, artificial intelligence, in vitro fertilization. Consider negative as well as positive effects.

8. Currently almost half of American marriages end in divorce. To what do you attribute this high divorce rate? Be as specific as possible, citing "case studies" of families with which you are familiar.

9. What do you see as the major cause of any *one* of these problems: acquaintance rape, alcohol or drug abuse among college students, or academic cheating? Based on your identification of its causes, formulate some specific solutions for the problem you select.

10. Write an essay in which you consider the likely effects of a severe, protracted shortage of one of the following commodities: food, rental housing, medical care, computer hardware, reading matter. You may consider a community-, city-, or statewide shortage or a nation- or worldwide crisis.

COLLABORATIVE ACTIVITY FOR CAUSE AND EFFECT

Working in groups of four, discuss your feelings about the increasing homeless population, and then list four *effects* the presence of these homeless people is having on you, your community, and our nation. Assign each member of your group to write a paragraph explaining one of the effects the group identifies, and then arrange the paragraphs in order of increasing importance, moving from the least to the most significant consequence. Finally, work together to write an introduction, a conclusion, and transitions between paragraphs for the essay your paragraphs create, including a thesis statement in paragraph 1.

7

Comparison
and Contrast

WHAT IS COMPARISON AND CONTRAST?

In the narrowest sense, *comparison* shows how two or more things are similar, and *contrast* shows how they are different. In most writing situations, however, you use the two related processes of **comparison and contrast** to consider both similarities and differences. In the following paragraph from *Disturbing the Universe*, Freeman Dyson compares and contrasts two different styles of human endeavor, which he calls "the gray and the green."

<table>
<tr>
<td>

Topic sentence (outlines elements of comparison)

Point-by-point comparison

</td>
<td>

In everything we undertake, either on earth or in the sky, we have a choice of two styles, which I call the gray and the green. The distinction between the gray and green is not sharp. Only at the extremes of the spectrum can we say without qualification, this is green and that is gray. The difference between green and gray is better explained by examples than by definitions. Factories are gray, gardens are green. Physics is gray, biology is green. Plutonium is gray, horse manure is green. Bureaucracy is gray, pioneer communities are green. Self-reproducing machines are gray, trees and children are green. Human technology is gray, God's technology is green. Clones are gray, clades* are green. Army field manuals are gray, poems are green.

</td>
</tr>
</table>

A special form of comparison, called **analogy,** looks for similarities between two essentially dissimilar things. With analogy you

*Eds. Note—a group of organisms that evolved from a common ancestor.

explain one thing by comparing it to a second thing that is more familiar than the first. In the following paragraph from *The Shopping Mall High School,* Arthur G. Powell, Eleanor Farrar, and David K. Cohen use analogy to shed light on the nature of American high schools.

> If Americans want to understand their high schools at work, they should imagine them as shopping malls. Secondary education is another consumption experience in an abundant society. Shopping malls attract a broad range of customers with different tastes and purposes. Some shop at Sears, others at Woolworth's or Bloomingdale's. In high schools a broad range of students also shop. They too can select from an astonishing variety of products and services conveniently assembled in one place with ample parking. Furthermore, in malls and schools many different kinds of transactions are possible. Both institutions bring hopeful purveyors and potential purchasers together. The former hope to maximize sales but can take nothing for granted. Shoppers have a wide discretion not only about what to buy but also about whether to buy.

Throughout our lives we are bombarded with countless bits of information from newspapers, television, radio, and personal experience: The police strike in Memphis; city workers walk out in Philadelphia; the Senate debates government spending; taxes are lowered in New Jersey. Somehow we must make sense of the jumbled facts and figures that surround us. One way we have of understanding information like this is to put it side by side with other data and then to compare and contrast. Do the police in Memphis have the same complaints as the city workers in Philadelphia? What are the differences between the two situations? Is the national debate on spending analogous to the New Jersey debate on taxes? How do they differ? We make similar distinctions every day about matters that directly affect us. When we make personal decisions, we consider alternatives, asking ourselves whether one option seems better than another. Should I buy a car with manual or automatic transmission? Should I major in history or business? What job opportunities will each major offer me? Should I register as a Democrat or a Republican, or should I join a smaller political party? What are the positions of each on government spending, welfare, and taxes?

Because this way of thinking is central to our understanding of the world, comparison and contrast is often called for in papers and on essay examinations:

Compare and contrast the attitudes toward science and technology expressed in Fritz Lang's *Metropolis* and George Lucas's *Star Wars*. (film)

What are the similarities and differences between mitosis and meiosis? (biology)

Discuss the relative merits of establishing a partnership and a corporation. (business law)

Discuss the advantages and disadvantages of heterogeneous grouping of pupils. (education)

Using Comparison and Contrast

You are not likely to sit down and say to yourself, "I think I'll write a comparison-and-contrast essay today. Now what can I write about?" Instead, you will use comparison and contrast because your assignment suggests that you do so or because you decide it suits your purpose. In the examples above, for instance, the instructors have phrased their questions to tell students how to treat the material. When you read the questions, certain key words and phrases— *compare and contrast, similarities and differences, relative merits, advantages and disadvantages*—indicate that you should use a comparison-and-contrast pattern to organize your essay. Sometimes you may not even need such key phrases. Consider the question, "Which of the two Adamses, John or Samuel, had the greater influence on the timing and course of the American Revolution?" The word *greater* is enough to suggest a contrast.

Even when you are not given an assignment that is worded to suggest comparison and contrast, your purpose may point to this organization strategy. For instance, when you evaluate, you frequently employ comparison and contrast. If, as a student in a course in hospital management, you were asked to evaluate two health-care systems, you could begin by researching the standards used by experts in their evaluations. You could then compare each system's performance with those standards, and then contrast the systems with each other, concluding perhaps that both systems met minimum standards but that one was more cost-efficient than the other. Or if you were evaluating two of this year's new cars for a consumer newsletter, you might establish some criteria—fuel economy, handling, comfort, sturdiness, style—and compare and contrast the cars with respect to each criterion. If each of the cars was better in different categories, your readers would have to decide which features mattered most.

Establishing a Basis of Comparison

Before you can compare or contrast two things, you must determine what elements they have in common. For example, although cats and dogs are very different pets, both can learn from their owners. Cats and dogs may be taught different behaviors in different ways, but these differences can be analyzed because both animals share a common element: Both are trainable. Without a common element, there would be no basis for analysis—that is, no **basis of comparison.**

A comparison should lead you, and thus your readers, beyond the obvious. For instance, at first the idea of a comparison-and-contrast essay based on an analogy between bees and people might seem absurd. After all, these two creatures differ in species, physical structure, and intelligence. Their differences are so obvious that an essay based on them would seem to be pointless. But, after further analysis, you might decide there are quite a few similarities between the two. Both are social animals that live in complex social structures, and both have tasks to perform and roles to fulfill in their respective societies. Therefore, you *could* write about them, but you would focus your essay on the common elements that seem most provocative—social structures and roles—rather than those elements that lead nowhere—species, physical structure, and intelligence. If you tried to draw an analogy between bees and Jeeps or humans and golf tees, however, you would run into trouble. Although some points of comparison could be found, they would be trivial. Why bother to point out that both bees and Jeeps travel great distances or that both people and tees are needed to play golf? Neither statement establishes a significant basis of comparison.

When two subjects are very similar, it is the contrast that may be worth writing about. And when two subjects are not very much alike, you may find enlightening similarities.

Selecting Points for Discussion

When you know what subjects you will compare and contrast, you then need to select the points you want to discuss. You do this by determining your emphasis—on similarities, differences, or both—and the major focus of your paper. If your purpose for comparing two types of house plants is to explain that one is easier to grow than the other, you would contrast points having to do with plant care, not those having to do with plant biology.

When you compare and contrast, make sure that you treat the same, or at least similar, elements for each subject you discuss. For instance, if you were going to compare and contrast two novels, you might consider the following elements in both works:

Novel A	*Novel B*
Major characters	Major characters
Minor characters	Minor characters
Themes	Themes

You should avoid the common error of discussing entirely different elements for each subject. Such an approach obscures any basis of comparison that might exist. The two novels, for example, could not be meaningfully compared or contrasted if you discussed elements such as these:

Novel A	*Novel B*
Major characters	Plot
Minor characters	Author's life
Themes	Symbolism

Formulating a Thesis Statement

After you decide on the points you want to discuss, you are ready to formulate your thesis statement. This thesis establishes the significance of the comparison or contrast and perhaps the relative merits of the items discussed.

As in other kinds of essays, your thesis statement should tell your readers what to expect in your essay. It should mention not only the subjects to be compared and contrasted but also the point you will make about them. Your thesis should also indicate whether you will concentrate on similarities or differences or whether you will balance the two. In addition, it may list the points of comparison and contrast in the order in which they are discussed in the essay.

The structure of your thesis sentence can help to show the focus of your essay. As the following sentences illustrate, a thesis statement can emphasize the central concern of the essay by stating it in the main, rather than the subordinate, clause of the sentence. The structure of the first sentence emphasizes similarities, and the structure of the second highlights differences:

Despite the fact that doctors and nurses perform distinctly different tasks at a hospital, their functions overlap when they interact with patients.

Although Melville's *Moby-Dick* and London's *The Sea Wolf* are both about the sea, the major characters, minor characters, and themes of *Moby-Dick* establish its greater complexity.

STRUCTURING A COMPARISON-AND-CONTRAST ESSAY

Like every other type of essay examined in this book, a comparison-and-contrast essay has an introduction, several body paragraphs, and a conclusion. Within the body of your paper, there are two basic comparison-and-contrast patterns you can follow: You can discuss each subject separately, devoting one or more paragraphs to subject A and then the same number to subject B; or you can discuss one element common to the two subjects in each section of the paper, making your points about subject A and subject B in turn. As you might expect, both organizational patterns have advantages and disadvantages that you should consider before you use them.

Using Subject-by-Subject Comparison

When composing a subject-by-subject comparison, you essentially write a separate essay about each subject, but you discuss the same points for both subjects. In discussing each subject, you use the *same basis of comparison* to guide your selection of supporting points, and you arrange these points in some logical order, usually in order of their increasing significance. The following informal outline illustrates a subject-by-subject comparison:

Introduction: Thesis statement—Despite the fact that doctors and nurses
                perform distinctly different tasks at a hospital, their func-
                tions overlap when they interact with patients.
Doctors' functions
   Point 1:   Teaching patients
   Point 2:   Assessing patients
   Point 3:   Dispensing medication
Nurses' functions
   Point 1:   Teaching patients
   Point 2:   Assessing patients
   Point 3:   Dispensing medication
Conclusion: Restatement of thesis

Subject-by-subject comparisons are most appropriate for short, uncomplicated papers. In longer papers, where many points are made about each subject, this organizational pattern puts too many demands on your readers, requiring them to keep track of all your points throughout your paper. In addition, because of the length of each section, your paper may seem less like a unified, coherent whole than like two separate essays weakly connected by a transitional phrase. For longer or more complex papers, then, it is best to use a point-by-point comparison.

Using Point-by-Point Comparison

When you write a point-by-point comparison, you first make a point about one subject and then follow it with a comparable point about the other. This alternating pattern continues throughout the body of your essay until all your comparisons or contrasts have been made. The following informal outline illustrates a point-by-point comparison:

Introduction: Thesis statement—Melville's *Moby-Dick* has more fully developed characters and more complex themes than does London's *The Sea Wolf.*
Minor characters
    Book 1: *The Sea Wolf*
    Book 2: *Moby-Dick*
Major characters
    Book 1: *The Sea Wolf*
    Book 2: *Moby-Dick*
Themes
    Book 1: *The Sea Wolf*
    Book 2: *Moby-Dick*
Conclusion: Restatement of thesis

Point-by-point comparisons are especially useful for longer, more complicated essays where you discuss a number of different points. (If you treat only one or two points of comparison, then you should consider a subject-by-subject organization.) In the point-by-point pattern, readers can easily follow comparisons or contrasts and do not have to wait several paragraphs to find out the differences between *Moby-Dick* and *The Sea Wolf* or to remember on page six what was said on page three. Nevertheless, it is easy to fall into a monotonous, back-and-forth movement between points when you write a point-by-point comparison. To avoid this problem, use clear transitions, and vary sentence structure as you move from point to point.

STUDENT WRITERS: COMPARISON AND CONTRAST

Both of the following essays illustrate comparison and contrast. The first, written by Bettina Sacklowski for a film and literature class, is an example of a subject-by-subject comparison. The second, written by Margaret Depner for her composition class, illustrates a point-by-point comparison.

Bettina's essay was written in response to the following assignment: "Write a comparison of Arthur Miller's *Death of a Salesman* and Frank Capra's *It's a Wonderful Life,* focusing on the characters' reactions to their economic and social environments."

A COMPARISON OF DEATH OF A SALESMAN AND IT'S A WONDERFUL LIFE

Introduction   The United States's entrance into World War II in the   1
winter of 1941 radically changed American society. Within
five years, the nation moved from a state of economic
stagnation and depression to one of economic prosperity,
and in the process, major corporations increased their
control over all aspects of American life. World War II also
marked America's emergence as a superpower. These
events had a major impact on the generation of Americans
who experienced both the collapse and the rebirth of the
American economy. On the one hand, the majority of
Americans experienced a new faith in progress and modern
capitalism. On the other hand, many--especially those who
did not benefit from the new prosperity--felt a need to return
to the comforting values of the past. Both the 1949 play
Death of a Salesman, by Arthur Miller, and the 1946 movie
It's a Wonderful Life, directed by Frank Capra, reflect the
problems many Americans had coping with the changes

Thesis   taking place in post-World War II America. Although these
statement
(emphasizing   works examine similar issues, they present two very
differences)   different solutions to the problems Americans faced.

First subject:
Death of a
Salesman

Death of a Salesman is described by Miller as a modern 2
tragedy. The main character, Willy Loman, is a tragic--and
somewhat pathetic--figure who struggles against the
economic forces that were changing postwar American

Faith in
modern
capitalism

society. Even so, Willy has faith in the future and in his
ability to make one last big sale. Ironically, it is Willy's faith
in the American dream that makes it hard for him to
succeed: He turns down the opportunity to "make it big in
Alaska" in order to pursue his fantasy of starting small and
working his way to the top of his company. Although Willy
is a firm believer in the American dream of success and
upward mobility, he is cast off by it when he outlives his
usefulness. Not only does he raise his children with the
same unrealistic beliefs, he also cheats on his wife when he
feels frustrated by his apparent lack of success. Like many

Need for
traditional
values

Americans after 1945, Willy yearns for the simpler times of
the past even while putting his faith in progress and
technology. He constantly tells his son Biff about the "good
old days" when a salesman could make a comfortable living
and a deal could be sealed with a handshake. Willy also lives
vicariously through Biff, recalling the time when his son was
a star of his high school football game. By the end of the play,
however, Willy comes to the realization that people like him
are only "a dime a dozen" and concludes that he can save
his family from disaster only by committing suicide.

Second
subject: ***It's a***
Wonderful Life

Unlike Miller's modern tragedy, It's a Wonderful Life 3
is a modern-day fairy tale. Although the main character,

Faith in
modern
capitalism

George Bailey, has embraced capitalism, he is a decent,
unselfish man. He is, therefore, in danger of being displaced
by larger, less compassionate forces. Like Willy Loman,
George sees suicide as a way to save his family and free
himself from an economically oppressive society. In fact,
had Capra written the movie as a realistic drama--with

George committing suicide--it too would have been a modern tragedy. However, because It's a Wonderful Life is a fantasy, it resolves the tensions between George and the economic system that tries to destroy him in an unrealistic way. Like Miller, Capra stresses the importance of

Need for traditional values

traditional values, implying that friends and community solidarity can overcome the pressures of capitalism and the breakdown of community. According to Capra, the audience is left with the message that "each man's life touches so many others" and that "no man is a failure." Thus, Capra's message is far different from--and far more optimistic than-- Miller's. George Bailey survives while Willy Loman is sucked dry by the postwar economic forces that were changing the country.

Conclusion

Both Death of a Salesman and It's a Wonderful Life   4
react to the economic and social forces that seemed to be pulling American society away from its comforting and

Restatement of the thesis

traditional past. Where Miller's play presents a realistic and tragic view of a family that is destroyed by these forces, Capra's movie sidesteps the implications of these changes and forces a happy ending. Even so, both works suggest that an entire generation of American people were apprehensive about accepting an uncertain future if it meant losing the reassuring values of the past.

Points for Special Attention

Basis of Comparison. At first, Bettina was puzzled because she did not think that *Death of a Salesman* and *It's a Wonderful Life* had much in common. After brainstorming about them, however, she decided that even though they appear to be dissimilar, they actually address many of the same issues. Both are family dramas, both focus on American society after World War II, and both reflect many of the social and economic tensions that were present at that time. She decided that the major difference between the two works was the way in which the major characters resolve the problems they face.

Structure.   Bettina makes two points about the works she compares: Both reflect the then-present faith in progress and capitalism, and both reflect the desire to return to the values of the past. Because readers can easily keep these two ideas in mind, a subject-by-subject discussion is a good strategy. Of course Bettina could have chosen to do a point-by-point discussion and written an equally convincing paper. (Indeed, in paragraph 3 of her essay she includes a short section of point-by-point comparison to underscore the similarities between Willy Loman and George Bailey.) Often the choice is a matter of preference—a different writer might simply have liked a different strategy better.

Transitions.   Any essay needs transitions to make it coherent. This is especially true for comparison-and-contrast essays. Without adequate transitions, a point-by-point comparison can produce a series of choppy paragraphs, and a subject-by-subject comparison can read like two separate essays. In addition to connecting the sections of an essay, transitional words and phrases like the following can clearly identify similarities and differences for your readers:

on the one hand . . . on the other hand	both
even though	like
on the contrary	likewise
in spite of	similarly
although	despite
unlike	

Notice, for example, how the addition of the transitional phrases *on the one hand . . . on the other hand* makes the contrast between the following sentences from paragraph 1 clear:

Without transitions	The majority of Americans experienced a new faith in progress and modern capitalism. Many—especially those who did not benefit from the new prosperity—felt a need to return to the comforting values of the past.
With transitions	On the one hand, the majority of Americans experienced a new faith in progress and modern capitalism. On the other hand, many—especially those

who did not benefit from the new prosperity—felt a
need to return to the comforting values of the past.

Topic Sentences. A topic sentence presents the main idea of a
paragraph; often it is the paragraph's first sentence. Like transitional phrases, topic sentences help to guide readers through your
essay. When reading a comparison-and-contrast essay, readers can
easily miss the transition from one subject to another, especially if
the paper is long or complex. Direct, clearly stated topic sentences
act as guideposts, alerting readers to the comparisons and contrasts
you are making. For example, Bettina's straightforward topic sentence at the beginning of paragraph 3 clearly moves readers from
one work (*Death of a Salesman*) to the other (*It's a Wonderful Life*).
In addition, as in any effective comparison-and-contrast essay, a
point discussed about one subject is also discussed about the other,
and Bettina's topic sentences reinforce this balance.

Death of a Salesman is defined by Miller as a modern tragedy (paragraph
2).

Unlike Miller's modern tragedy, *It's a Wonderful Life* is a modern-day
fairy tale (paragraph 3).

Focus on Revision. Bettina is vague in describing how economic and political change after World War II affected American
society in general and Willy Loman and George Bailey in particular.
She might have explained more specifically the social and economic
situation of these characters and the reasons they were depicted
as economic failures at a time of growing prosperity. She could also
divide paragraphs 2 and 3 into two paragraphs each, presenting
separate discussions of each character's faith in progress and capitalism and each one's desire to return to the values of the past. She
would still have to emphasize the major points of her discussion
with topic sentences and to discuss the same points in the same
order for both works.

Unlike the essay above, Margaret Depner's paper uses point-by-
point comparision.

THE BIG MOVE

Introduction   The adjustment began when I was a sophomore in high   1

school. I was fifteen--a typical American teenager. I lived

to talk on the telephone, hang out at the mall, watch lots of television, and go to the movies. Everything about my life seemed satisfying. I loved my neighborhood, my school, and my friends. But suddenly everything changed. One night my parents told me that my father had been transferred and that we were going to move to England. I felt as if everything I had grown to love was being torn away from me. I was going to have to start over, and I did not want to go. My parents ignored my pleas and told me in no uncertain terms that I had no choice in the matter. My fate was sealed. When we finally arrived in England I was so

Thesis statement (Emphasizing differences) frightened that I felt sick. Not only would I have to get used to a new neighborhood and a new school, but I would also have to get used to a new way of life.

First point: Adjusting to a new neighborhood The first thing I had to adjust to was living in a new 2
neighborhood. The Boston suburb we had left was a known quantity, and perhaps for this reason, I liked it. At home we lived in a new development that was just starting to get built up. There were single houses everywhere with a few small trees scattered in between. Our house had a large lawn that my brother and I tried to avoid cutting whenever we could.

Neighborhood in U.S. Moms carting children around in mini vans was a common sight. My dad belonged to a neighborhood watch program and coached a girls' soccer team. My mom had a part-time job and rushed around on weekends catching up on all the things she could not do during the week. Every fall kids came to the door selling Girl Scout cookies or raising money to fight heart disease. Every spring and summer lawnmowers hummed away on Saturday mornings, and everyone went to church on Sunday. Everything was familiar . . . almost predictable.

Neighborhood in England Our neighborhood outside of London, however, was far 3
different from what I was used to. The house we lived in

was cozy but much smaller than the house we had left in the United States. It had a cute little lawn in front--which my brother and I still argued about cutting--and was exactly like the house next door. Near our house was a forest in which outlaws were said to have lived several hundred years ago. Most of the women in this area worked full time to supplement their husbands' income, and my mother was no exception. She got a job with my father's company and was very busy most of the time. There was no need for a neighborhood watch program because there was almost no crime. (The only crimes I ever heard about were a parked car that was sideswiped and a cat that had allegedly been stolen.) Although there was a soccer team, girls were not allowed on it. (In England soccer is considered a boy's game, like tackle football.) Some things were the same, however. Just as they did at home, people cut their lawns on Saturday--with a push, not a power, mower--and went to church every Sunday.

Second point: Adjusting to a new school

The next thing I had to adjust to was a new school. In 4 the United States I had attended a large suburban public high school. It had been built in the 1970s and held almost two thousand students. Sweatshirts and jeans were the most common articles of clothing for the students, and informality was a way of life. Several of my teachers even encouraged students to call them by their first names and to talk whenever they had something to say. I was able to choose from a long list of classes and take almost any

School in U.S.

course I wanted to. Classes had a relaxed atmosphere, to say the least. Some students had private conversations during class and paid little attention to the teacher. The only time they focused on the class was when the teacher called on them or when they made a funny comment or a sarcastic remark. We frequently had no homework, and we didn't study much, except for a test. Although most of us wanted to go on to college, none of us seemed to take learning seriously. If anyone did, he or she was usually teased by the rest of us.

School in England

The school I attended in England was quite different   5
from the one I attended in the United States. It was small even by English standards--only four hundred students-- and the building was over three hundred years old. All the students wore uniforms--a black blazer, a freshly-ironed white shirt, and a pleated skirt if you were female or black pants if you were male. The teachers were the epitome of formality. You called them "Sir" or "Ma'am" and always showed respect. I never dreamed of using their first names. The atmosphere in the classroom was also quite formal. Students worked quietly and spoke to the teachers only when they were called on. When we were called on, our teachers expected us to respond intelligently. No one joked or made sarcastic remarks. All of us were serious about our work. I spent hours studying each night and wrote a thousand-word essay each week. I always had papers to hand in or a tutorial to prepare for. Eventually, I got used to the workload and was able to budget my time so I could go out on the weekends.

Third point: Adjusting to a new way of life

My greatest challenge, however, was to adjust to a new   6
way of life. In the United States my social life was predictable, if not very interesting. Most of my friends lived in my neighborhood within walking distance of my house. I spent hours talking on the phone each night. Every Friday

Life in U.S.

my friends and I would hang out at the local mall or go to the movies. On Saturday we would get together at someone's house and watch TV or rent a movie. Sometimes we would go to a party or take a train into the city and go to Quincy Market. During the summer my friends and I would go to the beach or just lie around the house complaining that we had nothing to do. Although occasionally I would volunteer to help a teacher, my friends and I did not consider it acceptable to be too involved with school. Once, when I tried out for a school play, they teased me for weeks.

Life in England   In England my social life was quite different. Most of   7
my friends lived almost an hour away. There were no malls to hang out in, we never went to the movies, and I spent little time on the phone. At first, my whole life seemed upside down, but gradually I grew to like it. I found new things to do. I got interested in sports and other school activities. I became involved in community service, joined the debating team, and was elected to student council. Instead of hanging out at the mall, my friends and I went to plays and concerts in London. During the summer, I went on trips to Spain and to the Isle of Wight. Perhaps the most interesting thing I did was meet people from all over the world and find out about their customs. And I don't ever remember sitting around the house wondering what to do.

Conclusion   In my one year in England, I accomplished more than I   8
had dreamed I would before I left the United States. It was hard to give up everything that was familiar to me, but for the first time I understood what my mother had meant when she said, "Sometimes, you need to lose something to gain something." By the end of the year, when we had returned home, I knew that year had changed me and that I would never be the same person I had been before.

Points for Special Attention

Structure. In this point-by-point comparison, Margaret introduces three points of contrast between her two subjects, and she is careful to present these three points in the same order for both subjects. With this method of organization she can be sure her readers will easily follow her comparison between her life in the United States and her life in England. Had Margaret used a subject-by-subject comparison, her readers would have had to keep all three of her major points in mind as they read her discussion of each subject.

Topic Sentences. Without clear transitions, Margaret's readers would have a difficult time determining where each discussion of life in the United States ended and one about life in England began. Margaret makes sure that her readers can follow her discussion by distinguishing the two subjects of her comparison with topic sentences that make the contrast between them clear:

> The Boston suburb we had left was a known quantity, and perhaps for this reason, I liked it.
> Our neighborhood outside of London, however, was far different from what I was used to.

> In the United States I had attended a large suburban public high school. The school I attended in England was quite different from the one I attended in the United States.

> In the United States, my social life was predictable, if not very interesting. In England my social life was quite different.

Transitions. In addition to the clear and straightforward topic sentences that identify the differences between life in the United States and life in England, Margaret also includes transitional sentences that help readers move through the essay. Notice that by establishing a parallel structure, these sentences form a pattern that reinforces the essay's thesis:

> The first thing I had to adjust to was living in England.
> The next thing I had to adjust to was a new school.
> My greatest challenge, however, was to adjust to a new way of life.

Focus on Revision. The biggest strength of Margaret's essay is its use of detail, which makes the contrast between the United States and England clear. Even more detail could improve the essay. For example, in paragraph 3 Margaret could describe her London suburb more precisely than she does. In paragraph 7 she could provide insight into how her English friends were different from her friends back in the United States. Margaret could also improve her conclusion. As it is, it is little more than a loose collection of ideas, which, although adequate, adds little to the discussion. An anecdote that sums up her feelings about leaving England would be an improvement. So would a summary of how her experience changed her life once she returned to the United States.

The selections that follow illustrate both point-by-point and subject-by-subject comparisons. Each uses transitional elements and topic sentences to enhance clarity and to reinforce the comparison. Although the reading selections vary in their organization, length, and complexity, each is primarily concerned with the similarities and differences between its subjects.

GRANT AND LEE:
A STUDY IN CONTRASTS

Bruce Catton

Bruce Catton (1899–1978) was born in Petoskey, Michigan, and attended Oberlin College. His studies were interrupted by his service in World War I, after which he worked as a journalist and then as a public official for various government agencies. Catton edited American Heritage *magazine from 1954 until his death. His first book,* The War Lords of Washington *(1948), grew out of his service with the War Production Board during World War II. Catton was an authority on the Civil War, and among his many books on the subject are* Mr. Lincoln's Army *(1951);* Glory Road *(1952);* A Stillness at Appomattox *(1953), which won both a Pulitzer Prize and a National Book Award;* This Hallowed Ground *(1956);* Terrible Swift Sword *(1963); and* Gettysburg: The Final Fury *(1974). He also wrote a memoir,* Waiting for the Morning Train *(1972), in which he recalls listening as a young boy to the memories of Union Army veterans. A book based on tape recordings that Catton had made for educational purposes,* Reflections on the Civil War *(1981, edited by John Leekley), was published posthumously. "Grant and Lee: A Study in Contrasts" first appeared in a collection of historical essays entitled* The American Story. *This essay identifies not only differences but also important similarities between the two generals who headed the opposing armies of the Civil War.*

When Ulysses S. Grant and Robert E. Lee met in the parlor of a 1
modest house at Appomattox Court House, Virginia, on April 9,
1865, to work out the terms for the surrender of Lee's Army of
Northern Virginia, a great chapter in American life came to a close,
and a great new chapter began.

These men were bringing the Civil War to its virtual finish. To be 2
sure, other armies had yet to surrender, and for a few days the
fugitive Confederate government would struggle desperately and
vainly, trying to find some way to go on living now that its chief
support was gone. But in effect it was all over when Grant and Lee
signed the papers. And the little room where they wrote out the
terms was the scene of one of the poignant, dramatic contrasts in
American history.

They were two strong men, these oddly different generals, and ₃ they represented the strengths of two conflicting currents that, through them, had come into final collision.

Back of Robert E. Lee was the notion that the old aristocratic con- ₄ cept might somehow survive and be dominant in American life.

Lee was tidewater Virginia, and in his background were family, ₅ culture, and tradition . . . the age of chivalry transplanted to a New World which was making its own legends and its own myths. He embodied a way of life that had come down through the age of knighthood and the English country squire. America was a land that was beginning all over again, dedicated to nothing much more complicated than the rather hazy belief that all men had equal rights and should have an equal chance in the world. In such a land Lee stood for the feeling that it was somehow of advantage to human society to have a pronounced inequality in the social structure. There should be a leisure class, backed by ownership of land; in turn, society itself should be keyed to the land as the chief source of wealth and influence. It would bring forth (according to this ideal) a class of men with a strong sense of obligation to the community; men who lived not to gain advantage for themselves, but to meet the solemn obligations which had been laid on them by the very fact that they were privileged. From them the country would get its leadership; to them it could look for the higher values—of thought, of conduct, of personal deportment—to give it strength and virtue.

Lee embodied the noblest elements of this aristocratic ideal. ₆ Through him, the landed nobility justified itself. For four years, the Southern states had fought a desperate war to uphold the ideals for which Lee stood. In the end, it almost seemed as if the Confederacy fought for Lee; as if he himself was the Confederacy . . . the best thing that the way of life for which the Confederacy stood could ever have to offer. He had passed into legend before Appomattox. Thousands of tired, underfed, poorly clothed Confederate soldiers, long since past the simple enthusiasm of the early days of the struggle, somehow considered Lee the symbol of everything for which they had been willing to die. But they could not quite put this feeling into words. If the Lost Cause, sanctified by so much heroism and so many deaths, had a living justification, its justification was General Lee.

Grant, the son of a tanner on the Western frontier, was everything ₇ Lee was not. He had come up the hard way and embodied nothing in particular except the eternal toughness and sinewy fiber of the men who grew up beyond the mountains. He was one of a body of men who owed reverence and obeisance to no one, who were self-reliant to a fault, who cared hardly anything for the past but who had a sharp eye for the future.

These frontier men were the precise opposites of the tidewater aristocrats. Back of them, in the great surge that had taken people over the Alleghenies and into the opening Western country, there was a deep, implicit dissatisfaction with a past that had settled into grooves. They stood for democracy, not from any reasoned conclusion about the proper ordering of human society, but simply because they had grown up in the middle of democracy and knew how it worked. Their society might have privileges, but they would be privileges each man had won for himself. Forms and patterns meant nothing. No man was born to anything, except perhaps to a chance to show how far he could rise. Life was competition. 8

Yet along with this feeling had come a deep sense of belonging to a national community. The Westerner who developed a farm, opened a shop, or set up in business as a trader, could hope to prosper only as his own community prospered—and his community ran from the Atlantic to the Pacific and from Canada down to Mexico. If the land was settled, with towns and highways and accessible markets, he could better himself. He saw his fate in terms of the nation's own destiny. As its horizons expanded, so did his. He had, in other words, an acute dollars-and-cents stake in the continued growth and development of his country. 9

And that, perhaps, is where the contrast between Grant and Lee becomes most striking. The Virginia aristocrat, inevitably, saw himself in relation to his own region. He lived in a static society which could endure almost anything except change. Instinctively, his first loyalty would go to the locality in which that society existed. He would fight to the limit of endurance to defend it, because in defending it he was defending everything that gave his own life its deepest meaning. 10

The Westerner, on the other hand, would fight with an equal tenacity for the broader concept of society. He fought so because everything he lived by was tied to growth, expansion, and a constantly widening horizon. What he lived by would survive or fall with the nation itself. He could not possibly stand by unmoved in the face of an attempt to destroy the Union. He would combat it with everything he had, because he could only see it as an effort to cut the ground out from under his feet. 11

So Grant and Lee were in complete contrast, representing two diametrically opposed elements in American life. Grant was the modern man emerging; beyond him, ready to come on the stage, was 12 the great age of steel and machinery, of crowded cities and a restless burgeoning vitality. Lee might have ridden down from the old age of chivalry, lance in hand, silken banner fluttering over his head. Each man was the perfect champion of his cause, drawing both his strengths and his weaknesses from the people he led.

Yet it was not all contrast, after all. Different as they were—in background, in personality, in underlying aspiration—these two great soldiers had much in common. Under everything else, they were marvelous fighters. Furthermore, their fighting qualities were really very much alike. 13

Each man had, to begin with, the great virtue of utter tenacity and fidelity. Grant fought his way down the Mississippi Valley in spite of acute personal discouragement and profound military handicaps. Lee hung on in the trenches at Petersburg after hope itself had died. In each man there was an indomitable quality . . . the born fighter's refusal to give up as long as he can still remain on his feet and lift his two fists. 14

Daring and resourcefulness they had, too; the ability to think faster and move faster than the enemy. These were the qualities which gave Lee the dazzling campaigns of Second Manassas and Chancellorsville and won Vicksburg for Grant. 15

Lastly, and perhaps greatest of all, there was the ability, at the end, to turn quickly from war to peace once the fighting was over. Out of the way these two men behaved at Appomattox came the possibility of a peace of reconciliation. It was a possibility not wholly realized, in the years to come, but which did, in the end, help the two sections to become one nation again . . . after a war whose bitterness might have seemed to make such a reunion wholly impossible. No part of either man's life became him more than the part he played in this brief meeting in the McLean house at Appomattox. Their behavior there put all succeeding generations of Americans in their debt. Two great Americans, Grant and Lee—very different, yet under everything very much alike. Their encounter at Appomattox was one of the great moments of American history. 16

COMPREHENSION

1. What took place at Appomattox Court House on April 9, 1865? Why did the meeting at Appomattox signal the closing of "a great chapter in American life"?

2. How does Robert E. Lee represent aristocracy? How does Ulysses S. Grant represent Lee's opposite?

3. According to Catton, where is it that "the contrast between Grant and Lee becomes most striking"?

4. What similarities does Catton see between the two men?

PURPOSE AND AUDIENCE

1. Catton's purpose in contrasting Grant and Lee is to make a general statement about the differences between two currents in American history. Summarize these differences. Do you think the differences still exist today?

2. Is Catton's purpose in comparing Grant and Lee the same as his purpose in contrasting them? That is, do their similarities also make a statement about United States history? Explain.

3. State the essay's thesis in your own words.

STYLE AND STRUCTURE

1. Does Catton use subject-by-subject or point-by-point comparison? Why do you think he chose the structure he did?

2. In this essay, topic sentences are extremely helpful to the reader. Explain the functions of the following sentences: "Grant . . . was everything Lee was not" (paragraph 7); "So Grant and Lee were in complete contrast . . ." (12); "Yet it was not all contrast, after all" (13); "Lastly, and perhaps greatest of all . . ." (16).

3. Catton uses transitions skillfully in his essay. Identify the transitional words or expressions that link each paragraph to the preceding one.

4. Why do you suppose Catton provides the background for the meeting at Appomattox but presents no information about the dramatic meeting itself?

VOCABULARY PROJECTS

1. Define each of the following words as it is used in this selection.

poignant (2)	obeisance (7)	tenacity (14)
chivalry (5)	implicit (8)	fidelity (14)
deportment (5)	inevitably (10)	indomitable (14)
sanctified (6)	diametrically (12)	reconciliation (16)
embodied (7)	burgeoning (12)	
sinewy (7)	aspiration (13)	

2. Look up synonyms for the following words and determine which would and would not have been as effective as the original word. Explain your choices.

deportment (5)   obeisance (7)   indomitable (14)
sanctified (6)   diametrically (12)

JOURNAL ENTRY

Compare your attitudes about the United States with either Grant's or Lee's.

WRITING WORKSHOP

1. Write a similar "study in contrasts" about two people you know well—two teachers, your parents, two relatives, two friends—or about two fictional characters with whom you are very familiar. Be sure you include a thesis statement.

2. Write a dialogue between two people you know that reveals their contrasting attitudes toward school, work, or any other subject.

3. Write an essay about two individuals from periods of American history other than the Civil War to make the same points Catton makes. Do some research if necessary.

THEMATIC CONNECTIONS

- "Aria: A Memoir of a Bilingual Childhood" (p. 401)
- "Letter from Birmingham Jail" (p. 562)
- "A Negative Vote on Affirmative Action" (p. 625)

OFF THE LADDER

Michael Scofield

Michael Scofield lives in New Jersey, where he works as a health-data analyst. In "Off the Ladder," published in the "About Men" column of the New York Times Magazine *in 1993, Scofield examines how affirmative action has affected career opportunities for women and men climbing the corporate ladder.*

Back in the mid-1980's, when I was in my mid-30's, I braved a career change. I went from being an administrator at a small hospital to working in the human-resources department of a giant corporation. It turned out that my new place of employment was in the midst of its own changes. Women were moving into senior management positions just as the layers of management were being reduced. As a result, the number of new male bosses was also reduced.

This was the first time I had experienced affirmative action. I had come from the private, not-for-profit world where women were well represented at all levels of the hierarchy. There was no "glass ceiling."

But in my new company even the most chauvinistic executives had come to realize that it made good business sense to involve women in management. After all, they reasoned, women were beginning to make up an increasing proportion of the work force.

So what does a company do if it wants to spread more women throughout the management ranks, especially when those ranks are thinning? It tries to promote women whenever possible. My company even offers management development courses like "Becoming a Promotable Woman," "Corporate Issues for Women" and "Women, Leadership and Power."

At first, I paid little attention to the promotions of my female colleagues. My attention was focused on the men. I had noticed that many of them with important titles seemed no smarter or harder-working than I. It wouldn't be long, I thought, before I, too, would ascend the corporate ladder. No one in the company thought to tell me that, while drive and enthusiasm were welcomed, they wouldn't necessarily be rewarded with more responsibility, status or money.

After several smashing performance appraisals but no promotions, it dawned on me that men also faced a glass ceiling, but theirs was generally set lower than that for women. Nowhere was this more apparent than in the human-resources department, where women were especially well represented in management. I heard two theories explaining women's advantages there:

Theory A: Human-resource work can be done well by anyone who is bright, hard-working and has a modicum of business sense. Therefore, it's a good place to put promotable women who lack the specific skills of a particular business function like marketing or finance.

Theory B: Human resources is a good department for women because there they can't get in the way of running the business.

Are these the rationalizations of an average performer in a company where only a few hard-working stars make it to the top? Possibly. But over my first few years with the company I was led to believe the ladder was there for me to climb. For example, I was placed in the "Leadership Continuity Program" for "high performing, high potential" managers. Nothing happened. Perhaps the company changed its mind about continuing to have leadership. I was informed I was on the "immediately promotable list." That was long ago. Maybe they lost the list. A department head once told me I was his choice for a new position in his group. He was overridden by his boss, a woman, who gave the job to someone else, also a woman. She was qualified. So was I. She has since had another promotion. I'm still waiting.

I had always fancied myself a socially responsible and progressive thinker. So it was hard to rationalize my revised version of a longstanding belief: Qualified people from underrepresented groups should be given every opportunity for success—*except when it affects me.* And as I saw women getting jobs I wanted, I sure did feel affected!

I wrestled with feelings of failure and frustration for a long time, mulling over my options. Daily resentment? Too painful. Lackadaisical performance? Too boring. A job change? Too risky. Another career change? To what? For quite a while I hung on to the fantasy that something *big* would suddenly happen to my career.

But slowly a different view of reality began to emerge. I considered the facts. I really loved my job. It was stimulating and meaningful, and I was always learning something new. I worked for, and with, a nice bunch of people who respected me and appreciated my contributions. I had as much job security as I could expect in uncertain times.

Why, I started asking myself, did I want a promotion so badly? The managers above me spent most of their time in meetings and on conference calls. I found most meetings boring and the disembodied communication of conference calls tedious. What I really wanted was more money and status for doing the work I enjoyed.

At about this time, my wife, Barbara, was offered the chance to return to teaching. Barbara and I decided our children were old enough for her to go back to work, so our income jumped instantly by more than any promotion of mine would have meant. 14

So much for more money. That left status. I didn't have legions of admiring subordinates. My gray desk and beige bookcases were made of metal, not wood, which comes with real importance. My office didn't have a window. My goodness, was it tough to bear! 15

I've struggled over not having "made it." But time, contemplation and the shared insights of some wonderful people have helped me realize a new freedom, a different perspective. For example, I'm freed from the nagging question that used to hang over every decision: How will this affect my career? The answer is—it won't! 16

On the job, I'm freer to speak my mind. I can choose not to play office politics, though sometimes I play just for sport. I don't volunteer for lousy assignments because I'm not looking for any more "developmental experiences." I do volunteer to coach Little League and to stay home when the kids are sick. I can wear short-sleeved shirts and Hush Puppies to the office! 17

Some would say I've lowered my goals to meet reality. I say I've exchanged career goals for a vision of life. I have never felt happier or more content. There's much more to my life today than just making a living. 18

Of course, if I ever had any chance for upward corporate mobility it's gone now. I couldn't take the grind. Whether real or imagined, that glass ceiling has become an invisible shield. It has protected me from aspiring to a life filled with meetings, conference calls, long hours, long sleeves and red suspenders. 19

Once again, being a man has had its advantages. 20

COMPREHENSION

1. How did the situation at Scofield's company change in the mid-1980s?

2. How, according to Scofield, is the glass ceiling different for women and for men? What leads him to this conclusion?

3. What idea challenges Scofield's view of himself as a "socially responsible and progressive thinker" (10)? How exactly does he change?

4. In what way does Scofield respond to his failure to be promoted? What conclusion does he draw about this situation?

5. How has Scofield's new perspective affected his prospects at his job? How does he feel about the professional position in which he now finds himself?

PURPOSE AND AUDIENCE

1. What is Scofield's thesis? Why does he place it near the end of his essay?

2. What preconceptions about success does Scofield have? Do you think he expects his readers to share these preconceptions? What makes you think so? In what way does he address the reservations they might have about his actions?

3. What do you think Scofield's reason is for writing this essay? Is he trying to change people's opinion or just explain (or defend) why he did what he did?

STYLE AND STRUCTURE

1. What two subjects is Scofield comparing? Does he use a subject-by-subject or a point-by-point comparison? What are the advantages of this method of organization?

2. Scofield uses a good bit of narrative in his essay. Where does he use it? Do you think these passages are useful? Distracting? Could he have developed his comparison in another way? Explain.

3. How would you describe Scofield's tone in his essay? Choose several words in the essay that convey Scofield's attitude toward his subject. Do you think these words reinforce or undercut his purpose?

4. Why does Scofield include Theory A and Theory B in his discussion? What use does he make of these theories in his discussion?

5. Scofield's essay has a one-sentence conclusion. How effective is this strategy?

VOCABULARY PROJECTS

1. Define each of the following words as it is used in this selection.

   modicum (7)   mulling (11)   disembodied (13)
   continuity (9)   lackadaisical (11)

2. In your own words, describe what Scofield means when he talks about "making it."

3. Explain what Scofield means by each of the following business terms: *glass ceiling* (2), *management ranks* (4), *promotable woman* (4), *corporate ladder* (5), *performance appraisal* (6). What other business terms does he use? Could he have used other expressions in their place?

JOURNAL ENTRY

Are you one of the people who believes that Scofield has "lowered [his] goals to meet reality"? Or do you agree that he has "exchanged career goals for a vision of life" (18)? Is there a difference?

WRITING WORKSHOP

1. Write an essay in which you compare your career expectations with those of a friend. What are the similarities? What are the differences? How do you explain them?

2. Write a letter to Scofield from the woman who he says got the promotion he should have gotten. Compare her interpretation of what happened with his. Be creative, but use the facts presented in the essay.

3. If you are a woman, how have your own work experiences been different from those of your male coworkers? In your essay, you may consider topics like the glass ceiling, sexual harassment, duties assigned, pay, bosses' expectations, and so on.

THEMATIC CONNECTIONS

- "My Mother Never Worked" (p. 85)
- "The Company Man" (p. 507)
- "How the Pot Got to Call the Kettle Black" (p. 614)

THE ARAB WORLD

Edward T. Hall

Edward T. Hall was born in 1914 in Webster Groves, Missouri. He graduated from the University of Denver in 1936, received a master's degree from the University of Arizona in 1938, and earned a doctorate from Columbia University in 1942. He has taught anthropology at numerous universities and done fieldwork with Native Americans in the Southwest and with Micronesians in the Pacific. His books include The Silent Language *(1959), on nonverbal communication;* The Hidden Dimension *(1966), on human perceptions of space;* Beyond Culture *(1976), on the unconscious attitudes that mold behavior;* The Dance of Life: The Other Dimension of Time *(1983), on the cultural influence of time; and* An Anthropology of Everyday Life: An Autobiography *(1992). Currently a consultant to business and government agencies, Hall continues to do research in intercultural communication. He has written several books on this subject with his wife, Mildred Reed Hall, including* Hidden Differences: Doing Business with the Japanese *(1987) and* Understanding Cultural Differences: Keys to Success in West Germany, France, and the United States *(1990). "The Arab World," excerpted from* The Hidden Dimension, *examines how Arabs' perceptual world differs from the one occupied by Americans. By studying proxemic patterns—spatial relations among people and their interactions with their environment—Hall reveals the hidden cultural frames that influence perception.*

In spite of over two thousand years of contact, Westerners and Arabs still do not understand each other. Proxemic research reveals some insights into this difficulty. Americans in the Middle East are immediately struck by two conflicting sensations. In public they are compressed and overwhelmed by smells, crowding, and high noise levels; in Arab homes Americans are apt to rattle around, feeling exposed and often somewhat inadequate because of too much space! (The Arab houses and apartments of the middle and upper classes which Americans stationed abroad commonly occupy are much larger than the dwellings such Americans usually inhabit.) Both the high sensory stimulation which is experienced in public places and the basic insecurity which comes from being in a dwelling that is too large provide Americans with an introduction to the sensory world of the Arab.

BEHAVIOR IN PUBLIC

Pushing and shoving in public places is characteristic of Middle   2
Eastern culture. Yet it is not entirely what Americans think it is
(being pushy and rude) but stems from a different set of assumptions concerning not only the relations between people but how one
experiences the body as well. Paradoxically, Arabs consider northern
Europeans and Americans pushy, too. This was very puzzling to
me when I started investigating these two views. How could Americans who stand aside and avoid touching be considered pushy? I
used to ask Arabs to explain this paradox. None of my subjects
was able to tell me specifically what particulars of American behavior were responsible, yet they all agreed that the impression was
widespread among Arabs. After repeated unsuccessful attempts to
gain insight into the cognitive world of the Arab on this particular
point, I filed it away as a question that only time would answer.
When the answer came, it was because of a seemingly inconsequen-
tial annoyance.

While waiting for a friend in a Washington, D.C., hotel lobby and   3
wanting to be both visible and alone, I had seated myself in a solitary chair outside the normal stream of traffic. In such a setting
most Americans follow a rule, which is all the more binding because
we seldom think about it, that can be stated as follows: as soon as a
person stops or is seated in a public place, there balloons around him
a small sphere of privacy which is considered inviolate. The size of
the sphere varies with the degree of crowding, the age, sex, and the
importance of the person, as well as the general surroundings. Anyone who enters this zone and stays there is intruding. In fact, a
stranger who intrudes, even for a specific purpose, acknowledges the
fact that he has intruded by beginning his request with "Pardon me,
but can you tell me . . . ?"

To continue, as I waited in the deserted lobby, a stranger walked   4
up to where I was sitting and stood close enough so that not only
could I easily touch him but I could even hear him breathing. In
addition, the dark mass of his body filled the peripheral field of
vision on my left side. If the lobby had been crowded with people, I
would have understood his behavior, but in an empty lobby his presence made me exceedingly uncomfortable. Feeling annoyed by this
intrusion, I moved my body in such a way as to communicate annoyance. Strangely enough, instead of moving away, my actions
seemed only to encourage him, because he moved even closer. In
spite of the temptation to escape the annoyance, I put aside thoughts
of abandoning my post, thinking, "To hell with it. Why should I

move? I was here first and I'm not going to let this fellow drive me out even if he is a boor." Fortunately, a group of people soon arrived whom my tormentor immediately joined. Their mannerisms explained his behavior, for I knew from both speech and gestures that they were Arabs. I had not been able to make this crucial identification by looking at my subject when he was alone because he wasn't talking and he was wearing American clothes.

In describing the scene later to an Arab colleague, two contrasting   5
patterns emerged. My concept and my feelings about my own circle of privacy in a "public" place immediately struck my Arab friend as strange and puzzling. He said, "After all, it's a public place, isn't it?" Pursuing this line of inquiry, I found that in Arab thought I had no rights whatsoever by virtue of occupying a given spot; neither my place nor by body was inviolate! For the Arab, there is no such thing as an intrusion in public. Public means public. With this insight, a great range of Arab behavior that had been puzzling, annoying, and sometimes even frightening began to make sense. I learned, for example, that if A is standing on a street corner and B wants his spot, B is within his rights if he does what he can to make A uncomfortable enough to move. In Beirut only the hardy sit in the last row in a movie theater, because there are usually standees who want seats and who push and shove and make such a nuisance that most people give up and leave. Seen in this light, the Arab who "intruded" on my space in the hotel lobby had apparently selected it for the very reason I had: it was a good place to watch two doors and the elevator. My show of annoyance, instead of driving him away, had only encouraged him. He thought he was about to get me to move.

Another silent source of friction between Americans and Arabs is   6
in an area that Americans treat very informally—the manners and rights of the road. In general, in the United States we tend to defer to the vehicle that is bigger, more powerful, faster, and heavily laden. While a pedestrian walking along a road may feel annoyed he will not think it unusual to step aside for a fast-moving automobile. He knows that because he is moving he does not have the right to the space around him that he has when he is standing still (as I was in the hotel lobby). It appears that the reverse is true with the Arabs who apparently *take on rights to space as they move*. For someone else to move into a space an Arab is also moving into is a violation of his rights. It is infuriating to an Arab to have someone else cut in front of him on the highway. It is the American's cavalier treatment of moving space that makes the Arab call him aggressive and pushy.

CONCEPTS OF PRIVACY

The experience described above and many others suggested to me 7
that Arabs might actually have a wholly contrasting set of assumptions concerning the body and the rights associated with it. Certainly the Arab tendency to shove and push each other in public and to feel and pinch women in public conveyances would not be tolerated by Westerners. It appeared to me that they must not have any concept of a private zone outside the body. This proved to be precisely the case.

In the Western world, the person is synonymous with an individual inside a skin. And in northern Europe generally, the skin and 8
even the clothes may be inviolate. You need permission to touch either if you are a stranger. This rule applies in some parts of France, where the mere touching of another person during an argument used to be legally defined as assault. For the Arab the location of the person in relation to the body is quite different. The person exists somewhere down inside the body. The ego is not completely hidden, however, because it can be reached very easily with an insult. It is protected from touch but not from words. The dissociation of the body and the ego may explain why the public amputation of a thief's hand is tolerated as standard punishment in Saudi Arabia. It also sheds light on why an Arab employer living in a modern apartment can provide his servant with a room that is a boxlike cubicle approximately 5 by 10 by 4 feet in size that is not only hung from the ceiling to conserve floor space but has an opening so that the servant can be spied on.

As one might suspect, deep orientations toward the self such as 9
the one just described are also reflected in the language. This was brought to my attention one afternoon when an Arab colleague who is the author of an Arab-English dictionary arrived in my office and threw himself into a chair in a state of obvious exhaustion. When I asked him what had been going on, he said: "I have spent the entire afternoon trying to find the Arab equivalent of the English word 'rape'. There is no such word in Arabic. All my sources, both written and spoken, can come up with no more than an approximation, such as 'He took her against her will.' There is nothing in Arabic approaching your meaning as it is expressed in that one word."

Differing concepts of the placement of the ego in relation to the 10
body are not easily gasped. Once an idea like this is accepted, however, it is possible to understand many other facets of Arab life that would otherwise be difficult to explain. One of these is the high

population density of Arab cities like Cairo, Beirut, and Damascus. According to the animal studies described in the earlier chapters, the Arabs should be living in a perpetual behavioral sink. While it is probable that Arabs are suffering from population pressures, it is also just as possible that continued pressure from the desert has resulted in a cultural adaptation to high density which takes the form described above. Tucking the ego down inside the body shell not only would permit higher population densities but would explain why it is that Arab communications are stepped up as much as they are when compared to northern European communication patterns. Not only is the sheer noise level much higher, but the piercing look of the eyes, the touch of the hands, and the mutual bathing in the warm moist breath during conversation represent stepped-up sensory inputs to a level which many Europeans find unbearably intense.

The Arab dream is for lots of space in the home, which unfortunately many Arabs cannot afford. Yet when he has space, it is very different from what one finds in most American homes. Arab spaces inside their upper middle-class homes are tremendous by our standards. They avoid partitions because Arabs *do not like to be alone.* The form of the home is such as to hold the family together inside a single protective shell, because Arabs are deeply involved with each other. Their personalities are intermingled and take nourishment from each other like the roots and soil. If one is not with people and actively involved in some way, one is deprived of life. An old Arab saying reflects this value: "Paradise without people should not be entered because it is Hell." Therefore, Arabs in the United States often feel socially and sensorially deprived and long to be back where there is human warmth and contact. 11

Since there is no physical privacy as we know it in the Arab family, not even a word for privacy, one could expect that the Arabs might use some other means to be alone. Their way to be alone is to stop talking. Like the English, an Arab who shuts himself off in this way is not indicating that anything is wrong or that he is withdrawing, only that he wants to be alone with his own thoughts or does not want to be intruded upon. One subject said that her father would come and go for days at a time without saying a word, and no one in the family thought anything of it. Yet for this very reason, an Arab exchange student visiting a Kansas farm failed to pick up the cue that his American hosts were mad at him when they gave him the "silent treatment." He only discovered something was wrong when they took him to town and tried forcibly to put him on a bus to Washington, D.C., the headquarters of the exchange program responsible for his presence in the U.S. 12

ARAB PERSONAL DISTANCES

Like everyone else in the world, Arabs are unable to formulate   13
specific rules for their informal behavior patterns. In fact, they often
deny that there are any rules, and they are made anxious by suggestions that such is the case. Therefore, in order to determine how
the Arab sets distances, I investigated the use of each sense separately. Gradually, definite and distinctive behavioral patterns began
to emerge.

Olfaction occupies a prominent place in the Arab life. Not only is   14
it one of the distance-setting mechanisms, but it is a vital part of a
complex system of behavior. Arabs consistently breathe on people
when they talk. However, this habit is more than a matter of different manners. To the Arab good smells are pleasing and a way of
being involved with each other. To smell one's friend is not only nice
but desirable, for to deny him your breath is to act ashamed. Americans, on the other hand, trained as they are not to breathe in people's faces, automatically communicate shame in trying to be polite.
Who would expect that when our highest diplomats are putting on
their best manners they are also communicating shame? Yet this is
what occurs constantly, because diplomacy is not only "eyeball to
eyeball" but breath to breath.

By stressing olfaction, Arabs do not try to eliminate all the body's   15
odors, only to enhance them and use them in building human relationships. Nor are they self-conscious about telling others when they
don't like the way they smell. A man leaving his house in the morning may be told by his uncle, "Habib, your stomach is sour and your
breath doesn't smell too good. Better not talk too close to people today." Smell is even considered in the choice of a mate. When couples
are being matched for marriage, the man's go-between will sometimes
ask to smell the girl, who may be turned down if she doesn't "smell
nice." Arabs recognize that smell and disposition may be linked.

In a word, the olfactory boundary performs two roles in Arab life.   16
It enfolds those who want to relate and separates those who don't.
The Arab finds it essential to stay inside the olfactory zone as a
means of keeping tab on changes in emotion. What is more, he may
feel crowded as soon as he smells something unpleasant. While not
much is known about "olfactory crowding," this may prove to be as
significant as any other variable in the crowding complex because it
is tied directly to the body chemistry and hence to the state of health
and emotions. . . . It is not surprising, therefore, that the olfactory
boundary constitutes for the Arabs an informal distance-setting
mechanism in contrast to the visual mechanisms of the Westerner.

FACING AND NOT FACING

One of my earliest discoveries in the field of intercultural com-   17
munication was that the position of the bodies of people in conversation varies with the culture. Even so, it used to puzzle me that a
special Arab friend seemed unable to walk and talk at the same
time. After years in the United States, he could not bring himself to
stroll along, facing forward while talking. Our progress would be
arrested while he edged ahead, cutting slightly in front of me and
turning sideways so we could see each other. Once in this position,
he would stop. His behavior was explained when I learned that for
Arabs to view the other person peripherally is regarded as impolite,
and to sit or stand back-to-back is considered very rude. You must be
involved when interacting with Arabs who are friends.

One mistaken American notion is that Arabs conduct all conver-   18
sations at close distances. This is not the case at all. On social occasions, they may sit on opposite sides of the room and talk across the
room to each other. They are, however, apt to take offense when Americans use what are to them ambiguous distances, such as the four- to
seven-foot social-consultative distance. They frequently complain
that Americans are cold or aloof or "don't care." This was what an
elderly Arab diplomat in an American hospital thought when the
American nurses used "professional" distance. He had the feeling
that he was being ignored, that they might not take good care of
him. Another Arab subject remarked, referring to American behavior, "What's the matter? Do I smell bad? Or are they afraid of me?"

Arabs who interact with Americans report experiencing a certain   19
flatness traceable in part to a very different use of the eyes in private and in public as well as between friends and strangers. Even
though it is rude for a guest to walk around the Arab home eying
things, Arabs look at each other in ways which seem hostile or challenging to the American. One Arab informant said that he was in
constant hot water with Americans because of the way he looked at
them without the slightest intention of offending. In fact, he had on
several occasions barely avoided fights with American men who
apparently thought their masculinity was being challenged because
of the way he was looking at them. As noted earlier, Arabs look each
other in the eye when talking with an intensity that makes most
Americans highly uncomfortable.

INVOLVEMENT

As the reader must gather by now, Arabs are involved with each   20
other on many different levels simultaneously. Privacy in a public

place is foreign to them. Business transactions in the bazaar, for example, are not just between buyer and seller, but are participated in by everyone. Anyone who is standing around may join in. If a grownup sees a boy breaking a window, he must stop him even if he doesn't know him. Involvement and participation are expressed in other ways as well. If two men are fighting, the crowd must intervene. On the political level, *to fail to intervene* when trouble is brewing is to take sides, which is what our State Department always seems to be doing. Given the fact that few people in the world today are even remotely aware of the cultural mold that forms their thoughts, it is normal for Arabs to view *our* behavior as though it stemmed from *their* own hidden set of assumptions.

FEELINGS ABOUT ENCLOSED SPACES

In the course of my interviews with Arabs the term "tomb" kept 21 cropping up in conjunction with enclosed space. In a word, Arabs don't mind being crowded by people but hate to be hemmed in by walls. They show a much greater overt sensitivity to architectural crowding than we do. Enclosed space must meet as least three requirements that I know of if it is to satisfy the Arabs: there must be plenty of unobstructed space in which to move around (possibly as much as a thousand square feet); very high ceilings—so high in fact that they do not normally impinge on the visual field; and, in addition, there must be an unobstructed view. It was spaces such as these in which the Americans referred to earlier felt so uncomfortable. One sees the Arab's need for a view expressed in many ways, even negatively, for to cut off a neighbor's view is one of the most effective ways of spiting him. In Beirut one can see what is known locally as the "spite house." It is nothing more than a thick, four-story wall, built at the end of a long fight between neighbors, on a narrow strip of land for the express purpose of denying a view of the Mediterranean to any house built on the land behind. According to one of my informants, there is also a house on a small plot of land between Beirut and Damascus which is completely surrounded by a neighbor's wall built high enough to cut off the view from all windows.

BOUNDARIES

Proxemic patterns tell us other things about Arab culture. For 22 example, the whole concept of the boundary as an abstraction is almost impossible to pin down. In one sense, there are no boundaries. "Edges" of town, yes, but permanent boundaries out in the country (hidden lines), no. In the course of my work with Arab subjects I had a difficult time translating our concept of a boundary into terms which could be equated with theirs. In order to clarify the distinctions between the two very different definitions, I thought it might be helpful to pinpoint acts which constituted trespass. To date, I have been unable to discover anything even remotely resembling our own legal concept of trespass.

Arab behavior in regard to their own real estate is apparently an extension of, and therefore consistent with, their approach to the body. My subjects simply failed to respond whenever trespass was mentioned. They didn't seem to understand what I meant by this term. This may be explained by the fact that they organize relationships with each other according to closed systems rather than spatially. For thousands of years Moslems, Marinites, Druses, and Jews have lived in their own villages, each with strong kin affliations. Their hierarchy of loyalties is: first to one's self, then to kinsman, townsman, or tribesman, co-religionist and/or countryman. Anyone not in these categories is a stranger. Strangers and enemies are very closely linked, if not synonymous, in Arab thought. Trespass in this context is a matter of who you are, rather than a piece of land or a space with a boundary that can be denied to anyone and everyone, friend and foe alike. 23

In summary, proxemic patterns differ. By examining them it is possible to reveal cultural frames that determine the structure of a given people's perceptual world. Perceiving the world differently leads to differential definitions of what constitutes crowded living, different interpersonal relations, and a different approach to both local and international politics. . . . 24

COMPREHENSION

1. How does Hall explain the pushing and shoving in public that he says is characteristic of Middle Eastern culture? In what way does the Arab sense of "public" extend to the rights of the road? How can the American's sense of "moving space" cause friction?

2. How does Hall say that the Arab sense of privacy differs from the Western sense of privacy?

3. According to Hall, what part does olfaction play in Arab life? What effect do American concepts of personal distance have on Arabs?

4. What do patterns of proximity reveal about the Arab's perceptual world?

PURPOSE AND AUDIENCE

1. What is Hall's purpose in describing the ways in which Arabs interact when they are close to one another?

2. What is the thesis of this essay? At what point does Hall state it? Why does he state it where he does?

3. What assumptions does Hall make about his audience's knowledge of Arab culture? How does Hall characterize his readers? Explain.

4. How would you expect an Arab audience to react to this essay? Do you think they might accuse Hall of stereotyping Arabs?

STYLE AND STRUCTURE

1. How does the introduction of this essay prepare readers for the discussion to follow?

2. Does Hall use a subject-by-subject or a point-by-point method of comparison, or a combination of the two? What is the advantage of the strategy that he uses?

3. What ideas does Hall emphasize with headings? Should he have used headings to emphasize any other ideas?

4. Does Hall discuss too many points? Should he have just concentrated on the points that he could develop in depth? Do the short discussions at the end of the essay add to the readers' understanding?

5. Throughout his essay Hall includes small bits of dialogue. What is the function of this dialogue?

VOCABULARY PROJECTS

1. Define each of the following words as it is used in this selection.

   proxemic (1)   olfaction (14)   Marinites (23)
   paradoxically (2)   peripherally (17)   Druses (23)
   inviolate (3)   bazaar (20)

2. For what English words does Hall say Arabs have no equivalents? Write a paragraph in which you discuss the significance of this fact.

JOURNAL ENTRY

Have you ever misunderstood a person from another culture? In what ways did your cultural preconceptions lead to this misunderstanding?

WRITING WORKSHOP

1. Write an essay in which you compare the value that you place on privacy with the value that Hall says Arabs place on privacy.

2. Write an essay in which you compare your "hierarchy of loyalities" with the one that Hall presents in paragraph 23.

3. Compare the hidden "cultural frames" (24) that exist for your peer group, family, or ethnic group with the ones that Hall identifies for Arabs.

THEMATIC CONNECTIONS

- "Shooting an Elephant" (p. 96)
- "On Seeing England for the First Time" (p. 146)
- "The Big Move" (p. 364)
- "Tortillas" (p. 499)

SEX, LIES, AND
CONVERSATION

Deborah Tannen

Deborah Tannen was born in Brooklyn, New York, in 1945. She graduated from the State University of New York at Binghamton, was awarded a doctorate from the University of California at Berkeley, and currently teaches at Georgetown University. Tannen has written and edited several scholarly books on the problems of communication across cultural, class, ethnic, and sexual divides. She has also presented her research to the general public in newspapers and magazines, including the New York Times Magazine *and* Newsweek; *in her best-selling books* That's Not What I Meant! How Conversational Style Makes or Breaks Relationships *(1986) and* You Just Don't Understand: Women and Men in Conversation *(1990); and through appearances on television news and talk shows. In 1992, Tannen conducted a seminar on gender dynamics for members of the Senate in the wake of the hearings into Anita Hill's charges of sexual harassment against Supreme Court nominee Clarence Thomas. "Sex, Lies, and Conversation," which appeared in* The Washington Post *in 1990, presents Tannen's views on conversational differences between women and men.*

I was addressing a small gathering in a suburban Virginia living room—a women's group that had invited men to join them. Throughout the evening, one man had been particularly talkative, frequently offering ideas and anecdotes, while his wife sat silently beside him on the couch. Toward the end of the evening, I commented that women frequently complain that their husbands don't talk to them. This man quickly concurred. He gestured toward his wife and said, "She's the talker in our family." The room burst into laughter; the man looked puzzled and hurt. "It's true," he explained. "When I come home from work I have nothing to say. If she didn't keep the conversation going, we'd spend the whole evening in silence."

This episode crystallizes the irony that although American men tend to talk more than women in public situations, they often talk less at home. And this pattern is wreaking havoc with marriage.

The pattern was observed by political scientist Andrew Hacker in the late '70s. Sociologist Catherine Kohler Riessman reports in her new book *Divorce Talk* that most of the women she interviewed—but only a few of the men—gave lack of communication as the reason for their divorces. Given the current divorce rate of nearly 50 percent, that amounts to millions of cases in the United States every year—a virtual epidemic of failed conversation.

In my own research, complaints from women about their hus- 4
bands most often focused not on tangible inequities such as having given up the chance for a career to accompany a husband to his, or doing far more than their share of daily life-support work like cleaning, cooking, social arrangements and errands. Instead, they focused on communication: "He doesn't listen to me," "He doesn't talk to me." I found, as Hacker observed years before, that most wives want their husbands to be, first and foremost, conversational partners, but few husbands share this expectation of their wives.

In short, the image that best represents the current crisis is the 5
stereotypical cartoon scene of a man sitting at the breakfast table with a newspaper held up in front of his face, while a woman glares at the back of it, wanting to talk.

LINGUISTIC BATTLE OF THE SEXES

How can women and men have such different impressions of com- 6
munication in marriage? Why the widespread imbalance in their interests and expectations?

In the April issue of *American Psychologist,* Stanford University's 7
Eleanor Maccoby reports the results of her own and others' research showing that children's development is most influenced by the social structure of peer interactions. Boys and girls tend to play with children of their own gender, and their sex-separate groups have different organizational structures and interactive norms.

I believe these systematic differences in childhood socialization 8
make talk between women and men like cross-cultural communication, heir to all the attraction and pitfalls of that enticing but difficult enterprise. My research on men's and women's conversations uncovered patterns similar to those described for children's groups.

For women, as for girls, intimacy is the fabric of relationships, and 9
talk is the thread from which it is woven. Little girls create and maintain friendships by exchanging secrets; similarly, women regard conversation as the cornerstone of friendship. So a woman expects her husband to be a new and improved version of a best friend. What is important is not the individual subjects that are discussed

but the sense of closeness, of a life shared, that emerges when people tell their thoughts, feelings, and impressions.

Bonds between boys can be as intense as girls', but they are based less on talking, more on doing things together. Since they don't assume talk is the cement that binds a relationship, men don't know what kind of talk women want, and they don't miss it when it isn't there. 10

Boys' groups are larger, more inclusive, and more hierarchical, so boys must struggle to avoid the subordinate position in the group. This may play a role in women's complaints that men don't listen to them. Some men really don't like to listen, because being the listener makes them feel one-down, like a child listening to adults or an employee to a boss. 11

But often when women tell men, "You aren't listening," and the men protest, "I am," the men are right. The impression of not listening results from misalignments in the mechanics of conversation. The misalignment begins as soon as a man and a woman take physical positions. This became clear when I studied videotapes made by psychologist Bruce Dorval of children and adults talking to their same-sex best friends. I found that at every age, the girls and women faced each other directly, their eyes anchored on each other's faces. At every age, the boys and men sat at angles to each other and looked elsewhere in the room, periodically glancing at each other. They were obviously attuned to each other, often mirroring each other's movements. But the tendency of men to face away can give women the impression they aren't listening even when they are. A young woman in college was frustrated: Whenever she told her boyfriend she wanted to talk to him, he would lie down on the floor, close his eyes, and put his arm over his face. This signaled to her, "He's taking a nap." But he insisted he was listening extra hard. Normally, he looks around the room, so he is easily distracted. Lying down and covering his eyes helped him concentrate on what she was saying. 12

Analogous to the physical alignment that women and men take in conversation is their topical alignment. The girls in my study tended to talk at length about one topic, but the boys tended to jump from topic to topic. The second-grade girls exchanged stories about people they knew. The second-grade boys teased, told jokes, noticed things in the room and talked about finding games to play. The sixth-grade girls talked about problems with a mutual friend. The sixth-grade boys talked about 55 different topics, none of which extended over more than a few turns. 13

LISTENING TO BODY LANGUAGE

Switching topics is another habit that gives women the impression men aren't listening, especially if they switch to a topic about themselves. But the evidence of the 10th-grade boys in my study indicates otherwise. The 10th-grade boys sprawled across their chairs with bodies parallel and eyes straight ahead, rarely looking at each other. They looked as if they were riding in a car, staring out the windshield. But they were talking about their feelings. One boy was upset because a girl had told him he had a drinking problem, and the other was feeling alienated from all his friends. 14

Now, when a girl told a friend about a problem, the friend responded by asking probing questions and expressing agreement and understanding. But the boys dismissed each other's problems. Todd assured Richard that his drinking was "no big problem" because "sometimes you're funny when you're off your butt." And when Todd said he felt left out, Richard responded, "Why should you? You know more people than me." 15

Women perceive such responses as belittling and unsupportive. But the boys seemed satisfied with them. Whereas women reassure each other by implying, "You shouldn't feel bad because I've had similar experiences," men do so by implying, "You shouldn't feel bad because your problems aren't so bad." 16

There are even simpler reasons for women's impression that men don't listen. Linguist Lynette Hirschman found that women make more listener-noise, such as "mhm," "uhuh," and "yeah," to show "I'm with you." Men, she found, more often give silent attention. Women who expect a stream of listener-noise interpret silent attention as no attention at all. 17

Women's conversational habits are as frustrating to men as men's are to women. Men who expect silent attention interpret a stream of listener-noise as overreaction or impatience. Also, when women talk to each other in a close, comfortable setting, they often overlap, finish each other's sentences and anticipate what the other is about to say. This practice, which I call "participatory listenership," is often perceived by men as interruption, intrusion and lack of attention. 18

A parallel difference caused a man to complain about his wife, "She just wants to talk about her own point of view. If I show her another view, she gets mad at me." When most women talk to each other, they assume a conversationalist's job is to express agreement and support. But many men see their conversational duty as pointing out the other side of an argument. This is heard as disloyalty by women, and refusal to offer the requisite support. It is not that 19 women don't want to see other points of view, but that they prefer them phrased as suggestions and inquiries rather than as direct challenges.

In his book *Fighting for Life,* Walter Ong points out that men use 20 "agonistic" or warlike, oppositional formats to do almost anything; thus discussion becomes debate, and conversation a competitive sport. In contrast, women see conversation as a ritual means of establishing rapport. If Jane tells a problem and June says she has a similar one, they walk away feeling closer to each other. But this attempt at establishing rapport can backfire when used with men. Men take too literally women's ritual "troubles talk," just as women mistake men's ritual challenges for real attack.

THE SOUNDS OF SILENCE

These differences begin to clarify why women and men have such 21 different expectations about communication in marriage. For women, talk creates intimacy. Marriage is an orgy of closeness: you can tell your feelings and thoughts, and still be loved. Their greatest fear is being pushed away. But men live in a hierarchical world, where talk maintains independence and status. They are on guard to protect themselves from being put down and pushed around.

This explains the paradox of the talkative man who said of his 22 silent wife, "She's the talker." In the public setting of a guest lecture, he felt challenged to show his intelligence and display his understanding of the lecture. But at home, where he has nothing to prove and no one to defend against, he is free to remain silent. For his wife, being home means she is free from the worry that something she says might offend someone, or spark disagreement, or appear to be showing off; at home she is free to talk.

The communication problems that endanger marriage can't be 23 fixed by mechanical engineering. They require a new conceptual framework about the role of talk in human relationships. Many of the psychological explanations that have become second nature may not be helpful, because they tend to blame either women (for not being assertive enough) or men (for not being in touch with their feelings). A sociolinguistic approach by which male-female conversation is seen as cross-cultural communication allows us to understand the problem and forge solutions without blaming either party.

Once the problem is understood, improvement comes naturally, as 24 it did to the young woman and her boyfriend who seemed to go to sleep when she wanted to talk. Previously, she had accused him of not listening, and he had refused to change his behavior, since that would be admitting fault. But then she learned about and explained to him the differences in women's and men's habitual ways of aligning themselves in conversation. The next time she told him she wanted to talk, he began, as usual, by lying down and covering his eyes. When the familiar negative reaction bubbled up, she reassured herself that he really was listening. But then he sat up and looked at her. Thrilled, she asked why. He said, "You like me to look at you when we talk, so I'll try to do it." Once he saw their differences as cross-cultural rather than right and wrong, he independently altered his behavior.

Women who feel abandoned and deprived when their husbands   25
won't listen to or report daily news may be happy to discover their husbands trying to adapt once they understand the place of small talk in women's relationships. But if their husbands don't adapt, the women may still be comforted that for men, this is not a failure of intimacy. Accepting the difference, the wives may look to their friends or family for that kind of talk. And husbands who can't provide it shouldn't feel their wives have made unreasonable demands. Some couples will still decide to divorce, but at least their decisions will be based on realistic expectations.

In these times of resurgent ethnic conflicts, the world desperately   26
needs cross-cultural understanding. Like charity, successful cross-cultural communication should begin at home.

COMPREHENSION

1. What pattern of communication does Tannen identify at the beginning of her essay?

2. According to Tannen, what do women complain about most in their marriages?

3. What gives women the impression that men do not listen?

4. What characteristics of women's speech do men find frustrating?

5. According to Tannen, what can men and women do to remedy the communication problems that exist in most marriages?

PURPOSE AND AUDIENCE

1. What is Tannen's thesis?

2. What is Tannen's purpose in writing this essay? Does she want to inform or to persuade? On what do you base your conclusion?

3. Is Tannen writing to an expert audience or an audience of general readers? Explain.

STYLE AND STRUCTURE

1. Why does Tannen begin her essay with an anecdote? How does this story set the stage for the rest of the essay?

2. What does Tannen gain by stating her thesis in paragraph 2 of the essay? Would there be any advantage in postponing the thesis until the end? Explain.

3. Is this essay a subject-by-subject or a point-by-point comparison? What does Tannen gain by organizing her essay the way she does?

4. Throughout her essay, Tannen refers to scholarly studies and quotes statistics. How effectively does this information support her points? Could she have made a strong case without this material?

5. Would you say Tannen's tone is hopeful, despairing, sarcastic, angry, or something else?

6. Tannen concludes her essay with a far-reaching statement. What do you think she hopes to accomplish with this conclusion? Is she successful?

VOCABULARY PROJECTS

1. Define each of the following words as it is used in this selection.

concurred (1)	pitfall (8)	rapport (20)
crystallizes (2)	subordinate (11)	ritual (20)
inequities (4)	misalignment (12)	orgy (21)
imbalance (6)	analogous (13)	sociolinguistic (23)
peer (7)	alienated (14)	forge (23)
organizational (7)	intrusion (18)	

2. Where does Tannen use professional jargon in this essay? Would the essay be more or less effective without these words? Explain.

JOURNAL ENTRY

Based on your own observations of male-female communication, how accurate is Tannen's analysis? Can you relate an anecdote from your own life that illustrates her thesis?

WRITING WORKSHOP

1. In another essay, Tannen contrasts the communication patterns of male and female students in classroom settings. After observing a few of your own classes, write an essay in which you too draw a comparison between the linguistic behavior of your male and female classmates.

2. Write an essay in which you compare the way men or women speak in films or on television and the way you actually communicate. Use examples from your own experience to support your point.

THEMATIC CONNECTIONS

- "The Grave" (p. 168)
- "Aria: A Memoir of a Bilingual Childhood" (p. 401)
- "Sexism in English: A 1990s Update" (p. 441)
- "It's a Jungle Out There" (p. 635)

ARIA: A MEMOIR
OF A BILINGUAL CHILDHOOD

Richard Rodriguez

*Born in San Francisco in 1944 to Mexican immigrants, Richard
Rodriguez learned to speak English as an elementary school student
in Sacramento, California. He graduated from Stanford University
in 1967, received a master's degree from Columbia University, and
later earned a doctorate in English Renaissance literature from the
University of California at Berkeley, where he taught for a time
before devoting himself solely to writing. He is now an editor for the
Pacific News Service and an essayist for* The MacNeil-Lehrer News
Hour *on public television. Rodriguez's essays and articles have appeared in* The American Scholar, College English, Change, *and*
Harper's. *In a series of autobiographical essays collected in the book*
Hunger of Memory: The Education of Richard Rodriguez *(1982), he
explores his ambivalent feelings about what he gained—and lost—
by leaving his immigrant culture and entering American society.
Another collection of essays,* Days of Obligation: An Argument With
My Mexican Father *(1992), focuses on the conflicts Rodriguez sees,
within himself and elsewhere, between Mexican fatalism and American optimism. In "Aria: A Memoir of a Bilingual Childhood," originally published in* The American Scholar *in 1981 and later collected
in* Hunger of Memory, *Rodriguez compares the conflicting pulls of
home and school, family and outsiders, Spanish and English.*

I remember to start with that day in Sacramento—a California 1
now nearly thirty years past—when I first entered a classroom, able
to understand some fifty stray English words.

The third of four children, I had been preceded to a neighborhood 2
Roman Catholic school by an older brother and sister. But neither of
them had revealed very much about their classroom experiences.
Each afternoon they returned, as they left in the morning, always
together, speaking in Spanish as they climbed the five steps of the
porch. And their mysterious books, wrapped in shopping-bag paper,
remained on the table next to the door, closed firmly behind them.

An accident of geography sent me to a school where all my class- 3
mates were white, many the children of doctors and lawyers and
business executives. All my classmates certainly must have been uneasy on that first day of school—as most children are uneasy—to

find themselves apart from their families in the first institution of their lives. But I was astonished.

The nun said, in a friendly but oddly impersonal voice, "Boys and girls, this is Richard Rodriguez." (I heard her sound out: *Richard Road-ree-guess*.) It was the first time I had heard anyone name me in English. "Richard," the nun repeated more slowly, writing my name down in her black leather book. Quickly I turned to see my mother's face dissolve in a watery blur behind the pebbled glass door.

Many years later there is something called bilingual education—a scheme proposed in the late 1960s by Hispanic-American social activists, later endorsed by a congressional vote. It is a program that seeks to permit non-English-speaking children, many from lower-class homes, to use their family language as the language of school. (Such is the goal its supporters announce.) I hear them and am forced to say no: It is not possible for a child—any child—ever to use his family's language in school. Not to understand this is to misunderstand the public uses of schooling and to trivialize the nature of intimate life—a family's "language."

Memory teaches me what I know of these matters; the boy reminds the adult. I was a bilingual child, a certain kind—socially disadvantaged—the son of working-class parents, both Mexican immigrants.

In the early years of my boyhood, my parents coped very well in America. My father had steady work. My mother managed at home. They were nobody's victims. Optimism and ambition led them to a house (our home) many blocks from the Mexican south side of town. We lived among *gringos* and only a block from the biggest, whitest houses. It never occurred to my parents that they couldn't live wherever they chose. Nor was the Sacramento of the fifties bent on teaching them a contrary lesson. My mother and father were more annoyed than intimidated by those two or three neighbors who tried initially to make us unwelcome. ("Keep your brats away from my sidewalk!") But despite all they achieved, perhaps because they had so much to achieve, any deep feeling of ease, the confidence of "belonging" in public was withheld from them both. They regarded the people at work, the faces in crowds, as very distant from us. They were the others, *los gringos*. That term was interchangeable in their speech with another, even more telling, *los americanos*.

I grew up in a house where the only regular guests were my relations. For one day, enormous families of relatives would visit and there would be so many people that the noise and the bodies would spill out to the backyard and front porch. Then, for weeks, no one came by. (It was usually a salesman who rang the doorbell.) Our house stood apart. A gaudy yellow in a row of white bungalows. We were the people with the noisy dog. The people who raised pigeons and chickens. We were the foreigners on the block. A few neighbors smiled and waved. We waved back. But no one in the family knew the names of the old couple who lived next door; until I was seven years old, I did not know the names of the kids who lived across the street.

In public, my father and mother spoke a hesitant, accented, not always grammatical English. And they would have to strain—their bodies tense—to catch the sense of what was rapidly said by *los gringos*. At home they spoke Spanish. The language of their Mexican past sounded in counterpoint to the English of public society. The words would come quickly, with ease. Conveyed through those sounds was the pleasing, soothing, consoling reminder of being at home.

During those years when I was first conscious of hearing, my mother and father addressed me only in Spanish; in Spanish I learned to reply. By contrast, English (*inglés*), rarely heard in the house, was the language I came to associate with *gringos*. I learned my first words of English overhearing my parents speak to strangers. At five years of age, I knew just enough English for my mother to trust me on errands to stores one block away. No more.

I was a listening child, careful to hear the very different sounds of Spanish and English. Wide-eyed with hearing, I'd listen to sounds more than words. First, there were English (*gringo*) sounds. So many words were still unknown that when the butcher or the lady at the drugstore said something to me, exotic polysyllabic sounds would bloom in the midst of their sentences. Often the speech of people in public seemed to me very loud, booming with confidence. The man behind the counter would literally ask, "What can I do for you?" But by being so firm and so clear, the sound of his voice said that he was a *gringo*; he belonged in public society.

I would also hear then the high nasal notes of middle-class American speech. The air stirred with sound. Sometimes, even now, when I have been traveling abroad for several weeks, I will hear what I heard as a boy. In hotel lobbies or airports, in Turkey or Brazil, some Americans will pass, and suddenly I will hear it again—the high sound of American voices. For a few seconds I will hear it with pleasure, for it is now the sound of *my* society—a reminder of home. But inevitably—already on the flight headed for home—the sound fades with repetition. I will be unable to hear it anymore.

When I was a boy, things were different. That accent of *los gringos* was never pleasing nor was it hard to hear. Crowds at Safeway or at bus stops would be noisy with sound. And I would be forced to edge away from the chirping chatter above me.

I was unable to hear my own sounds, but I knew very well that I 14
spoke English poorly. My words could not stretch far enough to form complete thoughts. And the words I did speak I didn't know well enough to make into distinct sounds. (Listeners would usually lower their heads, better to hear what I was trying to say.) But it was one thing for *me* to speak English with difficulty. It was more troubling for me to hear my parents speak in public: their high-whining vowels and guttural consonants; their sentences that got stuck with "eh" and "ah" sounds; the confused syntax; the hesitant rhythm of sounds so different from the way *gringos* spoke. I'd notice, moreover, that my parents' voices were softer than those of *gringos* we'd meet.

I am tempted now to say that none of this mattered. In adulthood 15
I am embarrassed by childhood fears. And, in a way, it didn't matter very much that my parents could not speak English with ease. Their linguistic difficulties had no serious consequences. My mother and father made themselves understood at the county hospital clinic and at government offices. And yet, in another way, it mattered very much—it was unsettling to hear my parents struggle with English. Hearing them, I'd grow nervous, my clutching trust in their protection and power weakened.

There were many times like the night at a brightly lit gasoline 16
station (a blaring white memory) when I stood uneasily, hearing my father. He was talking to a teenaged attendant. I do not recall what they were saying, but I cannot forget the sounds my father made as he spoke. At one point his words slid together to form one word—sounds as confused as the threads of blue and green oil in the puddle next to my shoes. His voice rushed through what he had left to say. And, toward the end, reached falsetto notes, appealing to his listener's understanding. I looked away to the lights of passing automobiles. I tried not to hear anymore. But I heard only too well the calm, easy tones in the attendant's reply. Shortly afterward, walking toward home with my father, I shivered when he put his hand on my shoulder. The very first chance that I got, I evaded his grasp and ran on ahead into the dark, skipping with feigned boyish exuberance.

But then there was Spanish. *Español*: my family's language. *Es-* 17
pañol: the language that seemed to me a private language. I'd hear strangers on the radio and in the Mexican Catholic church across town speaking in Spanish, but I couldn't really believe that Spanish was a public language, like English. Spanish speakers, rather, seemed related to me, for I sensed that we shared—through our language—the experience of feeling apart from *los gringos*. It was thus a ghetto

Spanish that I heard and I spoke. Like those whose lives are bound by a barrio, I was reminded by Spanish of my separateness from *los otros, los gringos* in power. But more intensely than for most barrio children—because I did not live in a barrio—Spanish seemed to me the language of home. (Most days it was only at home that I'd hear it.) It became the language of joyful return.

A family member would say something to me and I would feel   18
myself specially recognized. My parents would say something to me and I would feel embraced by the sounds of their words. Those sound said: *I am speaking with ease in Spanish. I am addressing you in words I never use with* los gringos. *I recognize you as someone special, close, like no one outside. You belong with us. In the family.*

(Ricardo.)   19

At the age of five, six, well past the time when most other children   20
no longer easily notice the difference between sounds uttered at home and words spoken in public, I had a different experience. I lived in a world magically compounded of sounds. I remained a child longer than most; I lingered too long, poised at the edge of language—often frightened by the sounds of *los gringos,* delighted by the sounds of Spanish at home. I shared with my family a language that was startlingly different from that used in the great city around us.

For me there were none of the gradations between public and pri-   21
vate society so normal to a maturing child. Outside the house was public society; inside the house was private. Just opening or closing the screen door behind me was an important experience. I'd rarely leave home all alone or without reluctance. Walking down the sidewalk, under the canopy of tall trees, I'd warily notice the—suddenly—silent neighborhood kids who stood warily watching me. Nervously, I'd arrive at the grocery store to hear there the sounds of the *gringo*—foreign to me—reminding me that in this world so big, I was a foreigner. But then I'd return. Walking back toward our house, climbing the steps from the sidewalk, when the front door was open in summer, I'd hear voices beyond the screen door talking in Spanish. For a second or two, I'd stay, linger there, listening. Smiling, I'd hear my mother call out, saying in Spanish (words): "Is that you, Richard?" All the while her sounds would assure me: *You are home now; come closer; inside. With us.*

"Si," I'd reply.   22

Once more inside the house I would resume (assume) my place in   23
the family. The sounds would dim, grow harder to hear. Once more at home, I would grow less aware of that fact. It required, however, no more than the blurt of the doorbell to alert me to listen to sounds all over again. The house would turn instantly still while my mother

went to the door. I'd hear her hard English sounds. I'd wait to hear her voice return to soft-sounding Spanish, which assured me, as surely as did the clicking tongue of the lock on the door, that the stranger was gone.

Plainly, it is not healthy to hear such sounds so often. It is not healthy to distinguish public words from private sounds so easily. I remained cloistered by sounds, timid and shy in public, too dependent on voices at home. And yet it needs to be emphasized: I was an extremely happy child at home. I remember many nights when my father would come back from work, and I'd hear him call out to my mother in Spanish, sounding relieved. In Spanish, he'd sound light and free notes he never could manage in English. Some nights I'd jump up just at hearing his voice. With *mis hermanos* I would come running into the room where he was with my mother. Our laughing (so deep was the pleasure!) became screaming. Like others who know the pain of public alienation, we transformed the knowledge of our public separateness and made it consoling—the reminder of intimacy. Excited, we joined our voices in a celebration of sounds. *We are speaking now the way we never speak out in public. We are alone— together,* voices sounded, surrounded to tell me. Some nights, no one seemed willing to loosen the hold sounds had on us. At dinner, we invented new words. (Ours sounded Spanish, but made sense only to us.) We pieced together new words by taking, say, an English verb and giving it Spanish endings. My mother's instructions at bedtime would be lacquered with mock-urgent tones. Or a word like *si* would become, in several notes, able to convey added measures of feeling. Tongues explored the edges of words, especially the fat vowels. And we happily sounded that military drum roll, the twirling roar of the Spanish *r.* Family language: my family's sounds. The voices of my parents and sisters and brother. Their voices insisting: *You belong here. We are family members. Related. Special to one another. Listen!* Voices singing and sighing, rising, straining, then surging, teeming with pleasure that burst syllables into fragments of laughter. At times it seemed there was steady quiet only when, from another room, the rustling whispers of my parents faded and I moved closer to sleep.

24

COMPREHENSION

1. What things made Rodriguez ill at ease on his first day of school? In what ways was he different from the other children?

2. To the young Rodriguez, how did the sounds of English differ from the sounds of Spanish? Why did Spanish seem to be a private language?

3. What does Rodriguez mean in paragraph 24 when he says, "It is not healthy to distinguish public words from private sounds so easily"?

4. In addition to the differences between public and private language, what other oppositions does Rodriguez encounter?

5. Does Rodriguez consider his experiences to be similar to or different from those faced by other Mexican–American children? What statements in the essay lead you to your conclusion?

PURPOSE AND AUDIENCE

1. What is Rodriguez's thesis? Where does he state it?

2. Is Rodriguez writing this essay to enlighten, persuade, debunk, educate, or entertain? Explain.

3. This essay is addressed to a well-educated audience largely made up of *los gringos*. What concessions does Rodriguez make to this audience?

4. Does Rodriguez consider his audience to be hostile or friendly? Well informed or misinformed? Explain your answer.

STYLE AND STRUCTURE

1. Why are some passages italicized?

2. Rodriguez's essay does not move in a straight line from one time period or episode to the next; different periods blend together. How is this indefinite sense of time consistent with the aims of the essay? What would have been gained or lost if Rodriguez had presented events in chronological order?

3. What transitional words and phrases does Rodriguez use to indicate comparisons?

4. In the first four paragraphs, Rodriguez uses a flashback to highlight an episode that occurred when he was a child. How does this technique set the stage for the thesis?

5. Does Rodriguez present his ideas objectively or subjectively? Could he be accused of sentimentalizing the nature of family life and its reliance on a "private language"? Explain.

VOCABULARY PROJECTS

1. Define each of the following words as it is used in this selection.

   bilingual (5)   polysyllabic (11)   guttural (14)   barrio (17)

2. What Spanish words does Rodriguez use in this essay? Does he make sure that his English-speaking readers understand their meaning? What effect does he achieve by including them? Write a paragraph in which you explain your reaction to their use.

JOURNAL ENTRY

Do you agree with Rodriguez's comments about bilingual education? Do you think it is desirable for children who speak no English to be taught in their native language?

WRITING WORKSHOP

1. Think of a time when you felt like an outsider. Write an essay in which you compare your ideas with those held by the members of the group from which you felt estranged.

2. Has anyone you know come from a family whose private language, unique culture, or special customs set them apart from you and your family? Write an essay in which you compare your family and the person that you know and explain how these differences manifested themselves.

3. Write an essay in which you respond to Rodriguez's thesis that it is not possible for a child to use his or her private language in school. Compare your ideas about the public uses of language with the ideas that Rodriguez expresses in paragraph 5.

THEMATIC CONNECTIONS

- "Finishing School" (p. 78)
- "The Same Difference" (p. 203)
- "Let's Tell the Story of All America's Cultures" (p. 586)

EX-BASKETBALL PLAYER

John Updike

"Ex-Basketball Player," published in The Carpentered Hen and Other Tame Creatures *(1958), looks back at the talents and accomplishments of a young athlete through a description of what his life has become. (For biographical information on John Updike, see page 136.)*

Pearl Avenue runs past the high-school lot,
Bends with the trolley tracks, and stops, cut off
Before it has a chance to go two blocks,
At Colonel McComsky Plaza. Berth's Garage
5 Is on the corner facing west, and there,
Most days, you'll find Flick Webb, who helps Berth out.

Flick stands tall among the idiot pumps—
Five on a side, the old bubble-head style,
Their rubber elbows hanging loose and low.
10 One's nostrils are two S's, and his eyes
An E and O. And one is squat, without
A head at all—more of a football type.

Once Flick played for the high-school team, the Wizards.
He was good: in fact, the best. In '46
15 He bucketed three hundred ninety points,
A county record still. The ball loved Flick.
I saw him rack up thirty-eight or forty
In one home game. His hands were like wild birds.

He never learned a trade, he just sells gas,
20 Checks oil, and changes flats. Once in a while,
As a gag, he dribbles an inner tube,
But most of us remember anyway.
His hands are fine and nervous on the lug wrench.
It makes no difference to the lug wrench, though.

25 Off work, he hangs around Mae's luncheonette.
Grease-gray and kind of coiled, he plays pinball,
Smokes those thin cigars, nurses lemon phosphates.
Flick seldom says a word to Mae, just nods
Beyond her face toward bright applauding tiers
30 Of Necco Wafers, Nibs, and Juju Beads.

THINKING ABOUT LITERATURE

1. What two things are being compared in the poem? What strategies does the speaker use to let readers know when he is shifting from one subject to another?

2. Do you know any people like Flick? How accurate do you think the speaker's characterization is? Do you think the speaker is stereotyping Flick? Explain.

3. What comment is the poem making about the role of sports in our society? About the relationship between education and sports?

JOURNAL ENTRY

What do you think went wrong with Flick's sports career? Why is Flick not a success today?

THEMATIC CONNECTIONS

- "The Human Cost of an Illiterate Society" (p. 215)
- "Who Killed Benny Paret?" (p. 298)
- "College Pressures" (p. 425)

WRITING ASSIGNMENTS FOR COMPARISON AND CONTRAST

1. Find a description of the same event in two different magazines or newspapers. Write a comparison-and-contrast essay in which you discuss the similarities and differences between these two stories.

2. Go to the library and locate two children's books on the same subject, one written in the 1950s and one written today. Write an essay discussing which elements are the same and which are different. Include a thesis that makes a point about the significance of the differences between the two books.

3. Write a comparison-and-contrast essay in which you show how your knowledge of an academic subject has either increased or decreased your enthusiasm for it.

4. Write an essay about a relative or friend you knew when you were a child. Consider in what respects your opinion of this person has changed and in what sense it has remained the same.

5. Are the academic standards for athletes different from the standards applied to other students at your school? Compare the academic requirements and other expectations for athletes and nonathletes, including a thesis that states your opinion about any discrepancies you identify.

6. Since you started college, how have you changed and how have you stayed the same?

7. Watch a local television news program and then a national news broadcast. Write an essay in which you compare the two television programs, paying particular attention to the news content and to the broadcasting styles of the journalists.

8. Write an essay in which you compare your own early memories of school with those of Richard Rodriguez.

9. Do students who work to finance their own education have different attitudes toward that education than students who do not? If so, why? Your thesis should explain why you believe a difference does (or does not) exist.

10. Write an essay in which you compare any two groups that have divergent values: vegetarians vs. meat-eaters and smokers vs. non-smokers, for example.

COLLABORATIVE ACTIVITY FOR COMPARISON AND CONTRAST

Form groups of six students. Assume you are consultants who have been asked by your college to suggest solutions for several problems that students have been complaining about. Select the three areas—food, dorm space, and recreational activities, for example—that you think are most in need of improvement. Then, as a group, write a short report to your college in which you describe the present conditions in these areas and compare them with the improvements you envision. (Be sure to organize your report as a comparison-and-contrast essay.) Finally, have one person from each group read the group's report to the class, and then decide as a class which of the groups has the best suggestions.

8

Classification and Division

WHAT IS CLASSIFICATION AND DIVISION?

Division is the process of breaking a whole into parts; *classification* is the act of sorting individual items into categories. In the following paragraph from "Fans," Paul Gallico divides sports fans into categories based on the different sports they watch.

Parts: Kinds of sports fans   The fight crowd is a beast that lurks in the darkness behind the fringe of white light shed over the first six rows by the incandescents atop the ring, and is not to be trusted with pop bottles or other hardware. The tennis crowd is the pansy of all the great sports mobs and is always preening and shushing itself. The golf crowd is the most unwieldy and most sympathetic, and is the only horde given to mass production of that absurd noise written generally as "tsk tsk tsk tsk," and made between tongue and teeth with head-waggings to denote extreme commiseration. The baseball crowd is the most hysterical, the football crowd the best-natured and the polo crowd the most aristocratic. Racing crowds are the most restless, wrestling crowds the most tolerant, and soccer crowds the most easily incitable to riot and disorder. **Topic sentence identifies whole (sports fans)** Every sports crowd takes on the characteristics of the individuals who compose it. Each has its particular note of hysteria, its own little cruelties, mannerisms, and bad mannerisms, its own code of sportsmanship and its own method of expressing its emotions.

Through **classification and division,** we can make sense of seemingly random ideas by putting scattered bits of information into useful, coherent order. By breaking a large group into smaller categories and bringing separate items together into particular categories, we are able to identify relationships between the whole and its parts and to recognize similarities and differences among the parts themselves. (Remember, though, that simply enumerating representative examples does not constitute classification; when you classify, you always sort individual examples into categories according to some grouping principle.)

In countless practical situations classification and division brings order to chaos. Items in a Sunday newspaper are *classified* in clearly defined sections—international news, sports, travel, entertainment, comics, and so on—so that hockey scores, for example, are not mixed up with real estate listings. Similarly, department stores are *divided* into different departments so that managers can assign merchandise to particular areas and shoppers can know where to look for a particular item. Without such organization, an item might be anywhere in a store. Thus, order is brought to newspapers and department stores—and to supermarkets, biological hierarchies, and libraries—when a whole is divided into categories or sections and individual items are assigned to one or another of these subgroups.

 The interrelated processes of classification and division invariably occur together; nevertheless, they are two separate operations. When you *classify,* you begin with individual items and sort them into categories. Most things have several different attributes, and so they can be classified in any of several different ways. Take as an example the students who attend your school. The most obvious way to classify these individuals might be according to their year in college—freshman, sophomore, junior, or senior. But you could also classify students according to their major, racial or ethnic background, home state, grade point average, political affiliation, or any number of other principles. The principle of classification you choose would depend on how you wished to approach the members of this large and diverse group.

Division is the opposite of classification. When you *divide,* you start with a whole (an entire class) that you break into its individual parts—smaller, more specific classes, called subclasses. For example, you might start with the large general class *television shows* and divide it into smaller subclasses: *comedy, drama, action/adventure,* and so forth. You could divide each of these subclasses still further— *action/adventure programs,* for example, might include *westerns, police shows,* and so on—and each of these subclasses could be further divided as well. Eventually you would need to determine a particular principle to help you assign specific programs to one category or another—that is, to classify them.

Guidelines for Classification and Division

Three guidelines can help ensure proper division and classification:

1. All the categories should result from the same principle. If you
    decide to divide *television shows* into *soap operas, police shows,*
    and the like, it is not logical to include the subclass *children's
    programs,* for this subclass results from one principle—target
    audience—while the others result from another principle—
    genre. Similarly, if you are classifying undergraduates at your
    school according to their year, you cannot include the subclass
    students receiving financial aid.
2. All of the subclasses should be on the same level. In the series
    comedy, drama, action/adventure, and *westerns,* the last of
    these items, *westerns,* does not belong because it is on a lower
    level—that is, it is a subclass of *action/adventure.* Likewise,
    sophomores (a subclass of *undergraduates*) does not belong
    in the series *undergraduates, graduate students, extension
    students.*
3. You should treat all subclasses that are significant and rel-
    evant to your discussion and include enough subclasses to
    make your point, with no important omissions and no overlap-
    ping categories. In a review of a network's fall television lineup,
    the series *sitcoms, soap operas, police shows,* and *detective
    shows* is incomplete because it omits important subclasses like
    news programs, game shows, talk shows, and *documentaries;*
    moreover, *detective shows* may overlap with *police shows.* In
    the same way, the series *freshmen, sophomores, juniors,* and
    transfers is also illogical: The important group *seniors* has been
    omitted, while *transfers* may include *freshmen, sophomores,*
    and *juniors.*

Uses of Classification and Division

Whenever you write an essay, you use classification and division to bring order to the invention stage of the writing process. For
example, when you brainstorm, as Chapter 1 explains, you begin
with your paper's topic, listing all the related points you can think of.
Next, you *divide* your topic into logical categories and *classify* the
items in your brainstorming notes into one category or another,
perhaps narrowing, expanding, or eliminating some categories—or
some points—as you go along. This picking and choosing, sorting

and grouping, reduces your material until it is manageable and eventually suggests your thesis and the main points of your essay.

In addition, because of the way they are worded, certain topics and questions immediately suggest you use a classification-and-division pattern to structure your essay. Suppose, for example, you are asked, "What kinds of policies can be used to direct and control the national economy?" Here the word *kinds* suggests classification and division. Other words, such as *types, varieties,* and *categories,* can also serve as clues.

STRUCTURING A CLASSIFICATION-AND-DIVISION ESSAY

Once you decide to use classification and division as your pattern of development, you need to plan your essay. Before you begin, you must decide what *principle of classification* you are going to use—what quality you regard your items as having in common. Your system must be logical and consistent. Just as a clear basis of comparison determines the points in a comparison-and-contrast essay, so a clear principle of classification determines the system you use to categorize items. Every group of people, things, or ideas can be categorized in many ways. When you are at the bookstore with only twenty dollars, the cost of different books may be the only principle by which you select them. As you decide which books to carry across campus, however, weight may matter more. Finally, as you study and read, the quality of the books should determine which ones you concentrate on. Similarly, when you organize an essay, your principle of classification and division is determined by your writing situation—your assignment, your purpose, your audience, and your special knowledge and interests.

Once you define your principle and apply it to your topic, you must select your categories by dividing a whole class into parts and grouping a number of different items together within each part. Next, you should decide how you will treat the categories in your essay. Just as a comparison-and-contrast essay makes comparable points about its subjects, so your classification-and-division essay should treat all categories similarly. When you discuss comparable points for each, you ensure that your readers see your distinctions among categories and understand your definition of each category.

Finally, you should arrange your categories in some logical order, preferably so that one leads to the next and the least important to the most important. Such an order ensures that your readers see how the categories are related and how significant each is. Whatever this order, it should be consistent with your purpose and support your thesis.

Like other essays, a classification-and-division essay must have a thesis. This thesis should identify your subject, enumerate the categories you will discuss, and perhaps show readers the relationships of your categories to one another and to the subject as a whole. In addition, your thesis should convince your readers why your categories are significant or establish their relative value. Listing different kinds of investments would be pointless if you did not evaluate the strengths and weaknesses of each and then make recommendations based on your assessment. Similarly, a term paper about a writer's major works would accomplish little if it merely categorized his or her writings. Instead, your thesis should communicate your evaluation of these works to your readers, perhaps demonstrating that some deserve higher public regard than others.

Once you have formulated your essay's main idea and established your subclasses, you should plan your classification-and-division essay around the same three major sections that other essays have: introduction, body, and conclusion. Your *introduction* should orient your readers by mentioning your topic, the principle by which your material is divided and classified, and the individual subclasses you plan to discuss. Your paper's thesis should also usually be stated in the introduction. Once your readers have this information, they can easily follow your paper as it develops. In the subsequent *body* paragraphs, you should treat the categories one by one in the order in which your introduction presents them. Finally, your *conclusion* should restate your thesis, summing up the points you have made, and then perhaps move on to consider their implications.

Suppose that you are preparing a term paper on Mark Twain's nonfiction works for an American literature course. You have read *Roughing It, Life on the Mississippi,* and *The Innocents Abroad.* Besides these travel narratives, you have read Twain's autobiography as well as some of his correspondence and essays. When you realize that the works you have studied can easily be classified as four different types of Twain's nonfiction—travel narratives, essays, letters, and autobiography—you decide to use classification and division to structure your essay. Therefore, you first divide the large class *Twain's nonfiction prose* into major subclasses—his travel narratives, essays, autobiography, and letters. Then you go on to classify the individual works—that is, to assign the works you plan to discuss to these subclasses, which you plan to discuss one at a time. Your categories make sense to you as a way to organize your paper, but you know that you also need a strong thesis statement so that your paper does more than just list various works. You decide that your purpose is to persuade readers to reconsider the reputations of some of these works, and you formulate your thesis accordingly. You might then prepare a formal outline like this one for the body of your paper:

Thesis statement: Most readers know Mark Twain as a writer of novels such as *Huckleberry Finn,* but his nonfiction works—his travel narratives, his essays, his letters, and especially his autobiography—deserve more attention.

Division

I. Travel narratives

A. *Roughing It*

Class

B. *The Innocents Abroad*

C. *Life on the Mississippi*

II. Essays

A. "Fenimore Cooper's Literary Offenses"

B. "How To Tell A Story"

C. "The Awful German Language"

III. Letters

A. To W. D. Howells

B. To his family

IV. Autobiography

Because this will be a long term paper, each of the outline's divisions will have several subdivisions, and each subdivision might require several paragraphs.

This outline illustrates each of the characteristics of an effective classification-and-division essay. To begin with, Twain's nonfiction works are classified according to a single principle of classification—literary genre. Depending on your purpose, of course, another principle—for example, theme, subject matter, stage in Twain's career, or contemporary critical reception—could have worked just as well. If you had written your term paper for a political science course, for example, you might have decided to examine Twain as a social critic by classifying his works according to the amount or kind of political commentary in each. Literary genre, however, is an appropriate principle of classification for the writing situation at hand. (If you had arranged Twain's works into novels, essays, short stories, letters, and political works, you would have mixed two principles of classification—genre and content. As a result, a highly political novel like *The Gilded Age* would have fit more than one category.) In addition to being derived from a single principle of classification, all the paper's subclasses are on the same level (you could not, for example, treat Twain's essays, letters, autobiography, and *Roughing It* as your four major divisions). And all relevant subclasses are included. Had you left out the subclass *essays,* for example, you would have been unable to classify several significant works of nonfiction.

Note too that this outline arranges the four subclasses so they will support your thesis most effectively. Because you believe Twain's travel narratives, though familiar to many readers, are somewhat overrated, you plan to discuss them early in your paper. Similarly, because you think the autobiography would make your best case for the merit of the nonfiction works as a whole, you decide it would be most effective placed last. Of course, you could have arranged your categories in several other orders, such as shorter to longer works or least to most popular, depending on the details of your argument.

Finally, this outline helps guide you to treat all of your categories comparably in your paper. In fact, you should go on to verify this consistency by identifying each main point in your rough draft and cross-checking the order of points from category to category. Your case would be weakened if, for example, you inadvertently skipped style in your discussion of Twain's letters while including it for every other category. This omission might lead your readers to suspect either that you could not discuss this point because you had not done enough research on the letters or that you had ignored the point because the style of Twain's letters did not measure up somehow to the style of his other works.

A STUDENT WRITER: CLASSIFICATION AND DIVISION

The following classification-and-division essay was written by Roger Bauer for a course in American literature. The essay *divides* a whole entity—fiction of the American West—into four parts, or elements, using a principle of division common in literary analysis. In addition, it *classifies* material—details about fiction of the American West—into categories.

THE WESTERN:

MORE THAN JUST "POPULAR" LITERATURE

Introduction   A work of popular fiction--a detective story, a gothic   1

novel, or a Western, for example--is usually not regarded

very highly by literary critics. This evaluation is justified in most cases. All too often in popular fiction characters are familiar stereotypes, plot devices are predictable (and sometimes improbable), settings are overly familiar or only vaguely described, and themes are simplistic or undeveloped. To some extent, these characteristics apply to fiction of the American West--not only to contemporary Westerns, but also to those novels and stories that have

Thesis (identifies four elements to be discussed) achieved status as classics. Still, although clichéd characters and trite plots dominate even classic Westerns, a strong sense of place and timeless themes give the Western the power to transcend the "popular fiction" category.

First element: Characters Readers encounter familiar characters in novels and short stories with Western settings. The cast of characters is likely to include at least a few of the following: the cowboy, the dance hall girl, the sheriff, the deputy, the madam, the miner, the schoolmarm, the Easterner, the gambler, the rancher, the hired hand, the store owner, the preacher, the traveling salesman, and assorted cavalry soldiers, cattle rustlers, Indians, and Mexicans. These people are seldom fully developed; rather, they are stock characters who play exactly the roles readers expect them to play. Some classic stories, such as "The Outcasts of Poker Flat" and "Stage to Lordsburg," gather an assortment of these characters together in an isolated setting, playing them off against one another in a way that emphasizes their status as types rather

Second element: Plot than individuals. The plot elements are just as predictable. Often a gang terrorizes innocent settlers or ranchers or townspeople, as in Shane; just as often a desperado is on the loose, as in "The Bride Comes to Yellow Sky." Other common elements are a showdown on a dusty street, as in "The Tin Star," or an ambush, as in "Stage to Lordsburg." Scenes of chase and capture are staples from James Fenimore Cooper to Louis L'Amour, and standard boy-

2

meets-girl plots can be traced from <u>The Virginian</u> to current popular novels.

Third element: Setting

But the Western has the potential to transcend the limits   3
of these familiar materials. A particular strength is its geographical setting, which includes an unusually varied landscape and some magnificent scenery. The setting in Western fiction is special for a variety of reasons. First, the West is beautiful and exotic. Second, the West is huge: Towns are widely separated, and characters travel great distances. As a result, a sense of loneliness and isolation pervades the Western. Third, the West is frightening and unpredictable, characterized by untamed landscapes, wild animals, and terrifying extremes of weather. The harshness and unpredictability of the climate are especially frightening to newcomers to the West (and to readers). Still, the very extreme conditions (tornadoes, blizzards, desert sun) and unfamiliar topography (mesas, plains, canyons) that are so disturbing are also fascinating. Ultimately, the setting can be friend or enemy: Zane Grey's <u>Riders of the Purple Sage</u> ends with its lovers isolated in a canyon by a rock slide; in Max Brand's "Wine on the Desert," a man dies of thirst in the hostile sun. In these and other Western stories, the setting is a powerful presence that is always strongly felt.

Fourth element: Theme

Perhaps even more powerful than the setting are the   4
themes of the Western--themes found in all great literature. Each of these themes adds interest to the Western, giving it substance and stature. One such theme is the classic conflict between East and West, civilization and the wilderness, illustrated in novels as diverse as Cooper's <u>The Prairie</u> and Wister's <u>The Virginian</u>. (In <u>The Virginian</u>, as in Crane's "The Bride Comes to Yellow Sky," it is the woman who is the symbol of civilization.) Typically, the East is portrayed

as rigid, sterile, and limiting, while the West is natural and spontaneous, untamed and beautiful. Another classic theme frequently seen in Western literature is the initiation theme. Here a young man or a boy (or, occasionally, a girl) is initiated into the mysteries of adulthood through participation in a physical test of his courage--for example, a fistfight, a gun battle, or a feat of strength. This theme is developed in "The Tin Star" as well as in High Noon, the 1952 Gary Cooper film. A third theme frequently explored in Western fiction is the journey or search. The vast spaces and dangerous climate and topography of the West make it an ideal setting for this theme. In works as diverse as Charles Portis's True Grit, Louis L'Amour's Down the Long Hills, and the classic John Ford film The Searchers, the journey figures prominently. Whether the quest is for a long-lost relative, for land or gold or silver, or for knowledge or experience, the search theme dominates many works of Western literature, particularly longer works.

Conclusion (restates thesis)   Balancing the familiar plot elements and stereotypical   5
characters of Western fiction are two other elements, setting and theme, that set it apart from other kinds of popular fiction. In addition to its vivid settings and universal themes, the Western also boasts a strong sense of history and an identity as a uniquely American genre. These two qualities should give it a lasting importance consistent with its continuing popularity.

Points for Special Attention

Thesis and Support.   Roger Bauer's purpose in writing this essay was not just to describe the fiction of the American West but also to evaluate it. Consequently, his thesis presents his assessment of the genre's literary value, and his body paragraphs support his position with analysis and examples.

Organization.   Roger planned his essay carefully, and his organization scheme keeps the four elements he discusses distinct; in addition, both the space he allots to each element and the order in which he presents them convey his emphasis to his readers. Thus, paragraph 2 combines a discussion of the two elements Roger does not consider to be particularly noteworthy; in paragraphs 3 and 4 he goes on to give fuller treatment to the two elements of major importance to his thesis, setting and theme. Because he considers some elements to be more important than others, his treatment of the four categories is necessarily unequal. Still, Roger is careful to provide specific examples from various works of Western literature in all four cases.

Transition between Categories.   Roger uses clear transitional sentences to introduce each individual element of literature he discusses: "Readers encounter familiar characters in novels and short stories with Western settings"; "The plot elements are just as predictable"; "A particular strength is its geographical setting, which provides it with an unusually varied landscape and some magnificent scenery"; and "Perhaps even more powerful than the setting are the themes of the Western—themes found in all great literature." To indicate his shift from what he considers less important elements to more significant ones, Roger uses another strong transition: "But the Western has the potential to transcend the limits of these familiar materials." Each of these transitional sentences not only distinguishes the four elements from one another but also conveys Roger's direction and emphasis to his readers.

Writing about Literature.   Because he is writing for a course in American literature, Roger pays special attention to certain conventions that apply to writing about literature. He uses present tense when referring to literary works, and he places titles of short stories within quotation marks and underlines titles of novels and films. Also, he presents his interpretations and evaluations straightforwardly, without using unnecessary phrases like *In my opinion* and *I think.*

Focus on Revision.   In order to make a stronger case for the value of the fiction of the American West without writing a much longer essay, Roger could condense paragraph 2, which deals with the formulaic aspects of such fiction. He could then expand the paragraphs about setting and theme, which he considers to be more important. If he were writing a longer essay, Roger could provide brief plot summaries of the works he mentions in order to accommodate readers who might not be familiar with them. In any case, additional examples—particularly from modern Westerns, which apply the conventions of the genre somewhat differently—would strengthen the essay.

Each of the following reading selections is developed by means of classification and division. In some cases, the pattern is used to explain ideas; in others, it is used to persuade the reader.

COLLEGE PRESSURES

William Zinsser

Born in 1922 in New York City, William Zinsser graduated from Princeton University in 1944. He worked at the New York Herald Tribune *as a feature and editorial writer, a drama editor, and a film critic, and he was a columnist for* Life *magazine and the* New York Times. *Zinsser has also taught English at Yale University and served as general editor for the Book-of-the-Month Club. He is the author of several books on writing, including* On Writing Well: An Informal Guide to Writing Nonfiction *(1976) and* Writing to Learn *(1988). He has also written works on American culture, including* Spring Training *(1989), about the culture of baseball as Zinsser observed it at the Pittsburgh Pirates' training camp, and most recently* American Places: A Writer's Pilgrimage to 15 of This Country's Most Visited and Cherished Sites *(1992). In "College Pressures," written for* Country Journal *magazine in 1979, Zinsser analyzes the different forces contributing to the anxiety of students at Yale.*

Dear Carlos: I desperately need a dean's excuse for my chem midterm which will begin in about 1 hour. All I can say is that I totally blew it this week. I've fallen incredibly, inconceivably behind. 1

Carlos: Help! I'm anxious to hear from you. I'll be in my room and won't leave it until I hear from you. Tomorrow is the last day for. . . . 2

Carlos: I left town because I started bugging out again. I stayed up all night to finish a take home make-up exam & am typing it to hand in on the 10th. It was due on the 5th. P.S. I'm going to the dentist. Pain is pretty bad. 3

Carlos: Probably by Friday I'll be able to get back to my studies. Right now I'm going to take a long walk. This whole thing has taken a lot out of me. 4

Carlos: I'm really up the proverbial creek. The problem is I really *bombed* the history final. Since I need that course for my major. . . . 5

Carlos: Here follows a tale of woe. I went home this weekend, had to help my Mom, & caught a fever so didn't have much time to study. My professor. . . . 6

Carlos: Aargh! Nothing original but everything's piling up at once. To be brief, my job interview. . . . 7

Hey Carlos, good news! I've got mononucleosis. 8

Who are these wretched supplicants, scribbling notes so laden 9
with anxiety, seeking such miracles of postponement and balm?
They are men and women who belong to Bradford College, one of the
twelve residential colleges at Yale University, and the messages
are just a few of the hundreds that they left for their dean, Carlos
Hortas—often slipped under his door at 4 A.M.—last year.

But students like the ones who wrote those notes can also be 10
found on campuses from coast to coast—especially in New England
and at many other private colleges across the country that have high
academic standards and highly motivated students. Nobody could
doubt that the notes are real. In their urgency and their gallows
humor they are authentic voices of a generation that is panicky to
succeed.

My own connection with the message writers is that I am master 11
of Bradford College. I live in its Gothic quadrangle and know the
students well. (We have 485 of them.) I am privy to their hopes and
fears—and also to their stereo music and their piercing cries in the
dead of night ("Does anybody *ca-a-are?*"). If they went to Carlos to
ask how to get through tomorrow, they come to me to ask how to get
through the rest of their lives.

Mainly I try to remind them that the road ahead is a long one and 12
that it will have more unexpected turns than they think. There will
be plenty of time to change jobs, change careers, change whole
attitudes and approaches. They don't want to hear such liberating
news. They want a map—right now—that they can follow unswerv-
ingly to career security, financial security, Social Security and,
presumably, a prepaid grave.

What I wish for all students is some release from the clammy grip 13
of the future. I wish them a chance to savor each segment of their
education as an experience in itself and not as a grim preparation
for the next step. I wish them the right to experiment, to trip and
fall, to learn that defeat is as instructive as victory and is not the end
of the world.

My wish, of course, is naive. One of the few rights that America 14
does not proclaim is the right to fail. Achievement is the national
god, venerated in our media—the million-dollar athlete, the wealthy
executive—and glorified in our praise of possessions. In the presence of such a potent state religion, the young are growing up old.

I see four kinds of pressure working on college students today; eco- 15
nomic pressure, parental pressure, peer pressure, and self-induced
pressure. It is easy to look around for villains—to blame the colleges
for charging too much money, the professors for assigning too much
work, the parents for pushing their children too far, the students for
driving themselves too hard. But there are no villains, only victims.

"In the late 1960s," one dean told me, "the typical question that I 16
got from students was 'Why is there so much suffering in the world?'
or 'How can I make a contribution?' Today it's 'Do you think it would
look better for getting into law school if I did a double major in
history and political science, or just majored in one of them?'" Many
other deans confirmed this pattern. One said: "They're trying to find
an edge—the intangible something that will look better on paper if
two students are about equal."

Note the emphasis on looking better. The transcript has become 17
a sacred document, the passport to security. How one appears on
paper is more important than how one appears in person. *A* is for
Admirable and *B* is for Borderline, even though, in Yale's official system of grading, *A* means "excellent" and *B* means "very good." Today,
looking very good is no longer good enough, especially for students
who hope to go on to law school or medical school. They know that
entrance into the better schools will be an entrance into the better
law firms and better medical practices where they will make a lot of
money. They also know that the odds are harsh. Yale Law School for
instance, matriculates 170 students from an applicant pool of 3,700;
Harvard enrolls 550 from a pool of 7,000.

It's all very well for those of us who write letters of recommenda- 18
tion for our students to stress the qualities of humanity that will
make them good lawyers or doctors. And it's nice to think that admission officers are really reading our letters and looking for the
extra dimension of commitment or concern. Still, it would be hard
for a student not to visualize these officers shuffling so many transcripts studded with *A*s that they regard a *B* as positively shameful.

The pressure is almost as heavy on students who just want to 19
graduate and get a job. Long gone are the days of the "gentleman's
C," when students journeyed through college with a certain relax-
ation, sampling a wide variety of courses—music, art, philosophy,
classics, anthropology, poetry, religion—that would send them out as
liberally educated men and women. If I were an employer I would
rather employ graduates who have this range and curiosity than
those who narrowly pursued safe subjects and high grades. I know
countless students whose inquiring minds exhilarate me. I like to
hear the play of their ideas. I don't know if they are getting *A*s or *C*s,

and I don't care. I also like them as people. The country needs them, and they will find satisfying jobs. I tell them to relax. They can't.

Nor can I blame them. They live in a brutal economy. Tuition, 20 room, and board at most private colleges now comes to at least $7,000, not counting books and fees. This might seem to suggest that the colleges are getting rich. But they are equally battered by inflation. Tuition covers only 60 percent of what it costs to educate a student, and ordinarily the remainder comes from what colleges receive in endowments, grants, and gifts. Now the remainder keeps being swallowed by the cruel costs—higher every year—of just opening the doors. Heating oil is up. Insurance is up. Postage is up. Health-premium costs are up. Everything is up. Deficits are up. We are witnessing in America the creation of a brotherhood of paupers—colleges, parents, and students, joined by the common bond of debt.

Today it is not unusual for a student, even if he works part time 21 at college and full time during the summer, to accrue $5,000 in loans after four years—loans that he must start to repay within one year after graduation. Exhorted at commencement to go forth into the world, he is already behind as he goes forth. How could he not feel under pressure throughout college to prepare for this day of reckoning? I have used "he," incidentally, only for brevity. Women at Yale are under no less pressure to justify their expensive education to themselves, their parents, and society. In fact, they are probably under more pressure. For although they leave college superbly equipped to bring fresh leadership to traditionally male jobs, society hasn't yet caught up with this fact.

Along with economic pressure goes parental pressure. Inevitably, 22 the two are deeply intertwined.

I see many students taking pre-medical courses with joyless 23 tenacity. They go off to their labs as if they were going to the dentist. It saddens me because I know them in other corners of their life as cheerful people.

"Do you want to go to medical school?" I ask them. 24

"I guess so," they say, without conviction, or "Not really." 25

"Then why are you going?" 26

"Well, my parents want me to be a doctor. They're paying all this 27 money and . . ."

Poor students, poor parents. They are caught in one of the oldest 28 webs of love and duty and guilt. The parents mean well; they are trying to steer their sons and daughters toward a secure future. But the sons and daughters want to major in history or classics or philosophy—subjects with no "practical" value. Where's the payoff on the humanities? It's not easy to persuade such loving parents that the humanities do indeed pay off. The intellectual faculties developed by studying subjects like history and classics—an ability to synthesize and relate, to weigh cause and effect, to see events in perspective—are just the faculties that make creative leaders in business or almost any general field. Still, many fathers would rather put their money on courses that point toward a specific profession—courses that are pre-law, pre-medical, pre-business, or, as I sometimes heard it put, "pre-rich."

But the pressure on students is severe. They are truly torn. One 29 part of them feels obligated to fulfill their parents' expectations, after all, their parents are older and presumably wiser. Another part tells them that the expectations that are right for their parents are not right for them.

I know a student who wants to be an artist. She is very obviously 30 an artist and will be a good one—she has already had several modest exhibits. Meanwhile she is growing as a well-rounded person and taking humanistic subjects that will enrich the inner resources out of which her art will grow. But her father is strongly opposed. He thinks that an artist is a "dumb" thing to be. The student vacillates and tries to please everybody. She keeps up with her art somewhat furtively and takes some of the "dumb" courses her father wants her to take—at least they are dumb courses for her. She is a free spirit on a campus of tense students—no small achievement in itself—and she deserves to follow her muse.

Peer pressure and self-induced pressure are also intertwined, and 31 they begin almost at the beginning of freshman year.

"I had a freshman student I'll call Linda," one dean told me, "who 32 came in and said she was under terrible pressure because her roommate, Barbara, was much brighter and studied all the time. I couldn't tell her that Barbara had come in two hours earlier to say the same thing about Linda."

The story is almost funny—except that it's not. It's symptomatic of 33 all the pressures put together. When every student thinks every other student is working harder and doing better, the only solution is to study harder still. I see students going off to the library every night after dinner and coming back when it closes at midnight. I wish they could sometimes forget about their peers and go to a movie. I hear the clacking of typewriters in the hours before dawn. I see the tension in their eyes when exams are approaching and papers are due: *"Will I get everything done?"*

Probably they won't. They will get sick. They will get "blocked." 34 They will sleep. They will oversleep. They will bug out. *Hey Carlos, help!*

Part of the problem is that they do more than they are expected to do. A professor will assign five-page papers. Several students will start writing ten-page papers to impress him. Then more students will write ten-page papers, and a few will raise the ante to fifteen. Pity the poor student who is still just doing the assignment. 35

"Once you have twenty or thirty percent of the student population deliberately overexerting," one dean points out, "it's bad for everybody. When a teacher gets more and more effort from his class, the student who is doing normal work can be perceived as not doing well. The tactic works, psychologically." 36

Why can't the professor just cut back and not accept longer papers? He can, and he probably will. But by then the term will be half over and the damage done. Grade fever is highly contagious and not easily reversed. Besides, the professor's main concern is with his course. He knows his students only in relation to the course and doesn't know that they are also overexerting in their other courses. Nor is it really his business. He didn't sign up for dealing with the student as a whole person and with all the emotional baggage the student brought along from home. That's what deans, masters, chaplains, and psychiatrists are for. 37

To some extent this is nothing new: a certain number of professors have always been self-contained islands of scholarship and shyness, more comfortable with books than with people. But the new pauperism has widened the gap still further, for professors who actually like to spend time with students don't have as much time to spend. They also are overexerting. If they are young, they are busy trying to publish in order not to perish, hanging by their finger nails onto a shrinking profession. If they are old and tenured, they are buried under the duties of administering departments—as departmental chairmen or members of committees—that have been thinned out by the budgetary axe. 38

Ultimately it will be the students' own business to break the circles in which they are trapped. They are too young to be prisoners of their parents' dreams and their classmates' fears. They must be jolted into believing in themselves as unique men and women who have the power to shape their own future. 39

"Violence is being done to the undergraduate experience," says Carlos Hortas. "College should be open-ended: at the end it should open many, many roads. Instead, students are choosing their goal in advance, and their choices narrow at they go along. It's almost as if they think that the country has been codified in the type of jobs that exist—that they've got to fit into certain slots. Therefore, fit into the best-paying slot. 40

"They ought to take chances. Not taking chances will lead to a life 41
of colorless mediocrity. They'll be comfortable. But something in the
spirit will be missing."

I have painted too drab a portrait of today's students, making 42
them seem a solemn lot. That is only half of their story; if they were
so dreary I wouldn't so thoroughly enjoy their company. The other
half is that they are easy to like. They are quick to laugh and to offer
friendship. They are not introverts. They are usually kind and are
more considerate of one another than any student generation I have
known.

Nor are they so obsessed with their studies that they avoid sports 43
and extracurricular activities. On the contrary, they juggle their
crowded hours to play on a variety of teams, perform with musical
and dramatic groups, and write for campus publications. But this in
turn is one more cause of anxiety. There are too many choices. Aca-
demically, they have 1,300 courses to select from; outside class they
have to decide how much spare time they can spare and how to
spend it.

This means that they engage in fewer extracurricular pursuits 44
than their predecessors did. If they want to row on the crew and play
in the symphony they will eliminate one; in the '60s they would have
done both. They also tend to choose activities that are self-limiting.
Drama, for instance, is flourishing in all twelve of Yale's residential
colleges as it never has before. Students hurl themselves into these
productions—as actors, directors, carpenters, and technicians—with
a dedication to create the best possible play, knowing that the day
will come when the run will end and they can get back to their
studies.

They also can't afford to be the willing slave of organizations like 45
the *Yale Daily News.* Last spring at the one-hundredth anniversary
banquet of that paper—whose past chairmen include such once and
future kings as Potter Stewart, Kingman Brewster, and William F.
Buckley, Jr.*—much was made of the fact that the editorial staff
used to be small and totally committed and that "newsies" routinely
worked fifty hours a week. In effect they belonged to a club; Newsies
is how they defined themselves at Yale. Today's student will write
one or two articles a week, when he can, and he defines himself as
a student. I've never heard the word Newsie except at the banquet.

If I have described the modern undergraduate primarily as a 46
driven creature who is largely ignoring the blithe spirit inside who

---

*Eds. note—Stewart is a former U.S. Supreme Court Justice; Brewster is a former
president of Yale; and Buckley is a conservative editor and columnist.

keeps trying to come out and play, it's because that's where the crunch is, not only at Yale but throughout American education. It's why I think we should all be worried about the values that are nurturing a generation so fearful of risk and so goal-obsessed at such an early age.

I tell students that there is no one "right" way to get ahead—that each of them is a different person, starting from a different point and bound for a different destination. I tell them that change is a tonic and that all the slots are not codified nor the frontiers closed. One of my ways of telling them is to invite men and women who have achieved success outside the academic world to come and talk informally with my students during the year. They are heads of companies or ad agencies, editors of magazines, politicians, public officials, television magnates, labor leaders, business executives, Broadway producers, artists, writers, economists, photographers, scientists, historians—a mixed bag of achievers. 47

I ask them to say a few words about how they got started. The students assume that they started in their present profession and knew all along that it was what they wanted to do. Luckily for me, most of them got into their field by a circuitous route, to their surprise, after many detours. The students are startled. They can hardly conceive of a career that was not pre-planned. They can hardly imagine allowing the hand of God or chance to nudge them down some unforeseen trail. 48

COMPREHENSION

1. What advice does Zinsser give to students when they bring their problems to him?

2. What does Zinsser wish for his students? Why does he believe his wish is naive?

3. What are the four kinds of pressures Zinsser identifies?

4. Whom does Zinsser blame for the existence of the pressures? Explain.

5. How, according to Zinsser, is his evaluation of students different from their own and from their potential employers' assessments?

6. Why does Zinsser believe that women are probably under even more pressure than men?

7. How does what Zinsser calls the "new pauperism" affect professors?

8. Who, according to Zinsser, is ultimately responsible for eliminating college pressures? Explain.

9. In what sense are sports and other extracurricular activities another source of anxiety for students? How do they adapt to this pressure?

PURPOSE AND AUDIENCE

1. In your own words, state Zinsser's thesis. Is his intent in this essay simply to expose a difficult situation or to effect change? Explain.

2. On what kind of audience do you think this essay would have the most significant impact: students, teachers, parents, potential employers, graduate school admissions committees, or college administrators? Explain.

3. What do you think Zinsser hopes to accomplish in paragraphs 42–46? How might the essay be different without this section?

4. What assumptions does Zinsser make about his audience? Are they valid? Explain.

STYLE AND STRUCTURE

1. Evaluate the essay's introductory strategy. What impact do you think Zinsser hopes the notes to Carlos will have on his readers? Do they have the desired impact? Explain.

2. Identify the boundaries of the actual classification. How does Zinsser introduce the first category? How does he indicate that his treatment of the final category is complete?

3. What function do paragraphs 22 and 31 serve in the essay?

4. Zinsser is careful to explain that when he refers to students as *he,* he includes female students as well. However, he also refers to professors as *he* (for example, in paragraphs 35–37). Assuming that not all professors at Yale are male, what other stylistic options does Zinsser have in this situation?

5. At various points in this essay Zinsser quotes deans and students at Yale. What is the effect of these quotations?

6. Zinsser notes that his categories are "intertwined." In what ways do the categories overlap? Does this overlap weaken the essay? Explain.

7. What, if anything, seems to determine the order in which Zinsser introduces his categories? Is this order effective?

VOCABULARY PROJECTS

1. Define each of the following words as it is used in this selection.

   proverbial (5)   intangible (16)   blithe (46)
   supplicants (9)   accrue (21)   tonic (47)
   balm (9)   exhorted (21)   codified (47)
   privy (11)   tenacity (23)
   venerated (14)   faculties (28)

2. At times Zinsser uses religious language—*national god, sacred document*—to describe the students' quest for success. Identify other examples of such language, and explain why it is used.

JOURNAL ENTRY

Which of the pressures Zinsser identifies has the greatest effect on you? Why?

WRITING WORKSHOP

1. Are the pressures you experience as a college student similar to or different from the ones Zinsser describes at Yale in the late 1970s? Classify your own college pressures, and write an essay with a thesis that takes a strong stand against the forces responsible for the pressures.

2. Write a classification essay in which you support a thesis about college students' drive for success by categorizing students you know on the basis of either the degree of their need to succeed or the different ways in which they wish to succeed.

3. Zinsser takes a negative view of the college pressures he identifies. Using his four categories, write an essay that argues that in the long run, these pressures are not only necessary but valuable.

THEMATIC CONNECTIONS

- "Suicide Note" (p. 347)
- "Off the Ladder" (p. 377)
- "The Company Man" (p. 507)

THE MEN WE CARRY
IN OUR MINDS

Scott Russell Sanders

Scott Russell Sanders, born in 1945, is a professor of English at Indiana University and has written science fiction, folktales, children's stories, essays, and novels. His books include Stone Country *(1985), a documentary narrative about Indiana's limestone region;* The Paradise of Bombs *(1987), a collection of essays;* The Invisible Company *(1989), a novel; and, most recently, the essay collections* Secrets of the Universe: Scenes from the Journey Home *(1991) and* Staying Put: Making a Home in a Restless World *(1993). In "The Men We Carry in Our Minds," from* The Paradise of Bombs, *Sanders explains why as a man from a poor rural background he sees the men from his childhood community as very far from the positions of power that some women from more privileged circumstances think of and envy as typically male.*

The first men, besides my father, I remember seeing were black   1
convicts and white guards, in the cottonfield across the road from our farm on the outskirts of Memphis. I must have been three or four. The prisoners wore dingy gray-and-black zebra suits, heavy as canvas, sodden with sweat. Hatless, stooped, they chopped weeds in the fierce heat, row after row, breathing the acrid dust of boll-weevil poison. The overseers wore dazzling white shirts and broad shadowy hats. The oiled barrels of their shotguns flashed in the sunlight. Their faces in memory are utterly blank. Of course those men, white and black, have become for me an emblem of racial hatred. But they have also come to stand for the twin poles of my early vision of manhood—the brute toiling animal and the boss.

When I was a boy, the men I knew labored with their bodies. They   2
were marginal farmers, just scraping by, or welders, steel workers, carpenters; they swept floors, dug ditches, mined coal, or drove trucks, their forearms ropy with muscle; they trained horses, stoked furnaces, built tires, stood on assembly lines wrestling parts onto cars and refrigerators. They got up before light, worked all day long whatever the weather, and when they came home at night they looked as though somebody had been whipping them. In the evenings and on weekends they worked on their own places, tilling

435

gardens that were lumpy with clay, fixing broken-down cars, hammering on houses that were always too drafty, too leaky, too small.

The bodies of the men I knew were twisted and maimed in ways   3
visible and invisible. The nails of their hands were black and split, the hands tattooed with scars. Some had lost fingers. Heavy lifting had given many of them finicky backs and guts weak from hernias. Racing against conveyor belts had given them ulcers. Their ankles and knees ached from years of standing on concrete. Anyone who had worked for long around machines was hard of hearing. They squinted, and the skin of their faces was creased like the leather of old work gloves. There were times, studying them, when I dreaded growing up. Most of them coughed, from dust or cigarettes, and most of them drank cheap wine or whiskey, so their eyes looked bloodshot and bruised. The fathers of my friends always seemed older than the mothers. Men wore out sooner. Only women lived into old age.

As a boy I also knew another sort of men, who did not sweat and   4
break down like mules. They were soldiers, and so far as I could tell they scarcely worked at all. During my early school years we lived on a military base, an arsenal in Ohio, and every day I saw GIs in the guardshacks, on the stoops of barracks, at the wheels of olive drab Chevrolets. The chief fact of their lives was boredom. Long after I left the Arsenal I came to recognize the sour smell the soldiers gave off as that of souls in limbo. They were all waiting—for wars, for transfers, for leaves, for promotions, for the end of their hitch—like so many braves waiting for the hunt to begin. Unlike the warriors of older tribes, however, they would have no say about when the battle would start or how it would be waged. Their waiting was broken only when they practiced for war. They fired guns at targets, drove tanks across the churned-up fields of the military reservation, set off bombs in the wrecks of old fighter planes. I knew this was all play. But I also felt certain that when the hour for killing arrived, they would kill. When the real shooting started, many of them would die. This was what soldiers were *for*, just as a hammer was for driving nails.

Warriors and toilers: those seemed, in my boyhood vision, to be the   5
chief destinies for men. They weren't the only destinies, as I learned from having a few male teachers, from reading books, and from watching television. But the men on television—the politicians, the astronauts, the generals, the savvy lawyers, the philosophical doctors, the bosses who gave orders to both soldiers and laborers— seemed as remote and unreal to me as the figures in tapestries. I could no more imagine growing up to become one of these cool, potent creatures than I could imagine becoming a prince.

A nearer and more hopeful example was that of my father, who   6
had escaped from a red-dirt farm to a tire factory, and from the as-

sembly line to the front office. Eventually he dressed in a white shirt and tie. He carried himself as if he had been born to work with his mind. But his body, remembering the earlier years of slogging work, began to give out on him in his fifties, and it quit on him entirely before he turned sixty-five. Even such a partial escape from man's fate as he had accomplished did not seem possible for most of the boys I knew. They joined the Army, stood in line for jobs in the smoky plants, helped build highways. They were bound to work as their fathers had worked, killing themselves or preparing to kill others.

A scholarship enabled me not only to attend college, a rare enough feat in my circle, but even to study in a university meant for the children of the rich. Here I met for the first time young men who had assumed from birth that they would lead lives of comfort and power. And for the first time I met women who told me that men were guilty of having kept all the joys and privileges of the earth for themselves. I was baffled. What privileges? What joys? I thought about the maimed, dismal lives of most of the men back home. What had they stolen from their wives and daughters? The right to go five days a week, twelve months a year, for thirty or forty years to a steel mill or a coal mine? The right to drop bombs and die in war? The right to feel every leak in the roof, every gap in the fence, every cough in the engine, as a wound they must mend? The right to feel, when the lay-off comes or the plant shuts down, not only afraid but ashamed?

I was slow to understand the deep grievances of women. This was because, as a boy, I had envied them. Before college, the only people I had ever known who were interested in art or music or literature, the only ones who read books, the only ones who ever seemed to enjoy a sense of ease and grace were the mothers and daughters. Like the menfolk, they fretted about money, they scrimped and made-do. But, when the pay stopped coming in, they were not the ones who had failed. Nor did they have to go to war, and that seemed to me a blessed fact. By comparison with the narrow, ironclad days of fathers, there was an expansiveness, I thought, in the days of mothers. They went to see neighbors, to shop in town, to run errands at school, at the library, at church. No doubt, had I looked harder at their lives, I would have envied them less. It was not my fate to become a woman, so it was easier for me to see the graces. Few of them held jobs outside the home, and those who did filled thankless roles as clerks and waitresses. I didn't see, then, what a prison a house could be, since houses seemed to me brighter, handsomer places than any factory. I did not realize—because such things were never spoken of—how often women suffered from men's bullying. I did learn about the wretchedness of abandoned wives, single mothers, widows; but I also learned about the wretchedness of lone men. Even then I could see how exhausting it was for a mother to cater all day to the needs of young children. But if I had been asked, as a boy, to choose between tending a baby and tending a machine, I think I would have chosen the baby. (Having now tended both, I know I would choose the baby.)

So I was baffled when the women at college accused me and my sex of having cornered the world's pleasures. I think something like my bafflement has been felt by other boys (and by girls as well) who grew up in dirt-poor farm country, in mining country, in black ghettos, in Hispanic barrios, in the shadows of factories, in Third World nations—any place where the fate of men is as grim and bleak as the fate of women. Toilers and warriors. I realize now how ancient these identities are, how deep the tug they exert on men, the undertow of a thousand generations. The miseries I saw, as a boy, in the lives of nearly all men I continue to see in the lives of many—the body-breaking toil, the tedium, the call to be tough, the humiliating powerlessness, the battle for a living and for territory.

When the women I met at college thought about the joys and privileges of men, they did not carry in their minds the sort of men I had known in my childhood. They thought of their fathers, who were bankers, physicians, architects, stockbrokers, the big wheels of the big cities. These fathers rode the train to work or drove cars that cost more than any of my childhood houses. They were attended from morning to night by female helpers, wives and nurses and secretaries. They were never laid off, never short of cash at month's end, never lined up for welfare. These fathers made decisions that mattered. They ran the world.

The daughters of such men wanted to share in this power, this glory. So did I. They yearned for a say over their future, for jobs worthy of their abilities, for the right to live at peace, unmolested, whole. Yes, I thought, yes yes. The difference between me and these daughters was that they saw me, because of my sex, as destined from birth to become like their fathers, and therefore as an enemy to their desires. But I knew better. I wasn't an enemy, in fact or in feeling. I was an ally. If I had known, then, how to tell them so, would they have believed me? Would they now?

COMPREHENSION

1. What does Sanders mean in paragraph 1 when he characterizes the black convicts and white guards as "an emblem of racial hatred"? In what sense do they represent "the twin poles of [his] early vision of manhood"?

2. When he was a child, what did Sanders expect to become when he grew up? Why? How did he escape this destiny?

3. What advantages did Sanders attribute to women? Why? What challenged his assumptions?

4. What kind of men do the women Sanders meets in college carry in their minds? Why do they see him as "an enemy to their desires"? How does he defend himself against their charges?

PURPOSE AND AUDIENCE

1. What purpose do you think Sanders had in mind when he wrote this essay? Is his essay intended as a personal memoir, or does he have another agenda? Explain.

2. What is the essay's thesis?

3. Is this essay directed primarily at workers like the ones Sanders grew up watching or at the "children of the rich"? At men or at women? On whom would you expect it to have the greatest impact? Explain.

STYLE AND STRUCTURE

1. What is Sanders categorizing in this essay? What categories does he name? What other, unnamed categories does he identify?

2. What principle of classification determines the categories Sanders discusses?

3. What, if anything, determines the order in which Sanders discusses his categories?

4. Is the treatment of the various categories in this essay balanced, or does Sanders give more attention to some than to others? If some are given more attention, does this weaken the essay? Explain.

VOCABULARY PROJECTS

1. Define each of the following words as it is used in this selection.

acrid (1)	finicky (3)	expansiveness (8)
boll weevil (1)	slogging (6)	undertow (9)
overseers (1)	fretted (8)	unmolested (11)
maimed (3)	ironclad (8)	

2. Create descriptive titles for the categories Sanders does not name. Be sure to include categories that cover women's roles as well as men's, and be sure your categories do not overlap.

JOURNAL ENTRY

Do you think it is true, as Sanders suggests, that men have harder lives than women do?

WRITING WORKSHOP

1. Imagine the possible kinds of work available to you in the field you expect to study. Write a division-and-classification essay in which you discuss several categories of possible future employment, arranging them from least to most desirable.

2. Consider the adult workers you know best—your relatives, your friends' parents, your employers, your teachers—and others with whom you come in contact on a regular basis (merchants, for example). Write a classification-and-division essay in which you devise categories that distinguish different types of workers. Then, discuss these categories of workers in terms of how fortunate they are. Consider income level, job security, working conditions, prestige, and job satisfaction in your discussion of each category. In your essay's introduction and conclusion, consider how the employment categories you have devised are like or unlike Sanders's.

3. What kinds of jobs do you see as "dream jobs"? Why? List as many of these ideal jobs as you can, and then group them into logical categories according to a single principle of classification.

THEMATIC CONNECTIONS

- "Midnight" (p. 186)
- "Off the Ladder" (p. 377)
- "Ex-Basketball Player" (p. 409)

SEXISM IN ENGLISH:
A 1990s UPDATE

Alleen Pace Nilsen

Alleen Pace Nilsen was born in 1936 in Phoenix, Arizona, and grad-
uated from Brigham Young University in 1958. She received her
doctorate from the University of Iowa in 1973, writing her disser-
tation on the effect of sexist language in children's literature. In 1975
Nilsen began teaching at Arizona State University, where she be-
came professor of education and assistant dean of the graduate col-
lege and is currently professor of English. Nilsen writes articles on
young adult literature for several scholarly journals. She has also
written, coauthored, or edited several books, including Sexism and
Language *(1977), a collection of scholarly essays;* Presenting M. E.
Kerr *(1986), a study of Kerr's young adult fiction; and the fourth*
edition of Literature for Today's Young Adults *(1993). The original*
version of the following essay was titled "Sexism in English: A Fem-
inist View" and appeared in a collection published in 1972. In this
version, written in 1990, Nilsen brings up to date her examination
of how language, in particular the terms used for women and men,
reveals much about social attitudes and assumptions.

Twenty years ago I embarked on a study of the sexism inherent in   1
American English. I had just returned to Ann Arbor, Michigan, after
living for two years (1967–69) in Kabul, Afghanistan, where I had
begun to look critically at the role society assigned to women. The
Afghan version of the *chaderi** prescribed for Moslem women was
particularly confining. Afghan jokes and folklore were blatantly sexist, such as this proverb: "If you see an old man, sit down and take
a lesson; if you see an old woman, throw a stone."

But it wasn't only the native culture that made me question   2
women's roles, it was also the American community.

Most of the American women were like myself—wives and moth-   3
ers whose husbands were either career diplomats, employees of
USAID, or college professors who had been recruited to work on
various contract teams. We were suddenly bereft of our traditional
roles: some of us became alcoholics, others got very good at bridge,

**Eds. Note—full-length outer garment traditionally worn by Muslim women in
public.*

441

while still others searched desperately for ways to contribute either to our families or to the Afghans. The local economy provided few jobs for women and certainly none for foreigners; we were isolated from former friends and the social goals we had grown up with.

When I returned in the fall of 1969 to the University of Michigan in Ann Arbor, I was surprised to find that many other women were also questioning the expectations they had grown up with. In the spring of 1970, a women's conference was announced. I hired a baby-sitter and attended, but I returned home more troubled than ever. The militancy of these women frightened me. Since I wasn't ready for a revolution, I decided I would have my own feminist movement. I would study the English language and see what it could tell me about sexism. I started reading a desk dictionary and making note-cards on every entry that seemed to tell something about male and female. I soon had a dog-eared dictionary, along with a collection of notecards filling two shoe boxes. 4

Ironically, I started reading the dictionary because I wanted to avoid getting involved in social issues, but what happened was that my notecards brought me right back to looking at society. Language and society are as intertwined as a chicken and an egg. The language a culture uses is telltale evidence of the values and beliefs of that culture. And because there is a lag in how fast a language changes—new words can easily be introduced, but it takes a long time for old words and usages to disappear—a careful look at English will reveal the attitudes that our ancestors held and that we as a culture are therefore predisposed to hold. My notecards revealed three main points. Friends have offered the opinion that I didn't need to read the dictionary to learn such obvious facts. Nevertheless, it was interesting to have linguistic evidence of sociological observations. 5

WOMEN ARE SEXY; MEN ARE SUCCESSFUL

First, in American culture a woman is valued for the attractiveness and sexiness of her body, while a man is valued for his physical strength and accomplishments. A woman is sexy. A man is successful. 6

A persuasive piece of evidence supporting this view are the eponyms—words that have come from someone's name—found in English. I had a two-and-a-half-inch stack of cards taken from men's names but less than a half-inch stack from women's names, and most of those came from Greek mythology. In the words that came into American English since we separated from Britain, there are 7 many eponyms based on the names of famous American men: *Bartlett pear, boysenberry, diesel engine, Franklin stove, Ferris wheel, Gatling gun, mason jar, sideburns, sousaphone, Schick test,* and *Winchester rifle.* The only common eponyms taken from American women's names are *Alice blue* (after Alice Roosevelt Longworth), *bloomers* (after Amelia Jenks Bloomer), and *Mae West jacket* (after the buxom actress). Two out of the three feminine eponyms relate closely to a woman's physical anatomy, while the masculine eponyms (except for *sideburns* after General Burnsides) have nothing to do with the namesake's body but, instead, honor the man for an accomplishment of some kind.

Although in Greek mythology women played a bigger role than   8
they did in the biblical stories of the Judeo-Christian cultures and so the names of goddesses are accepted parts of the language in such place names as *Pomona* from the goddess of fruit and *Athens* from Athena and in such common words as *cereal* from Ceres, *psychology* from Psyche, and *arachnoid* from Arachne, the same tendency to think of women in relation to sexuality is seen in the eponyms *aphrodisiac* from Aphrodite, the Greek name for the goddess of love and beauty, and *venereal disease* from Venus, the Roman name for Aphrodite.

Another interesting word from Greek mythology is *Amazon.*   9
According to Greek folk etymology, the *a* means "without" as in *atypical* or *amoral,* while *mazon* comes from *mazos* meaning "breast" as still seen in *mastectomy.* In the Greek legend, Amazon women cut off their right breasts so that they could better shoot their bows. Apparently, the storytellers had a feeling that for women to play the active, "masculine" role the Amazons adopted for themselves, they had to trade in part of their femininity.

This preoccupation with women's breasts is not limited to ancient   10
stories. As a volunteer for the University of Wisconsin's *Dictionary of American Regional English (DARE),* I read a western trapper's diary from the 1930s. I was to make notes of any unusual usages or language patterns. My most interesting finding was that the trapper referred to a range of mountains as *The Teats,* a metaphor based on the similarity between the shapes of mountains and women's breasts. Because today we use the French wording, *The Grand Tetons,* the metaphor isn't as obvious, but I wrote to mapmakers and found the following listings: *Nippletop* and *Little Nipple Top* near Mount Marcy in the Adirondacks; *Nipple Mountain* in Archuleta County, Colorado; *Nipple Peak* in Coke County, Texas; *Nipple Butte* in Pennington, South Dakota; *Squaw Peak* in Placer County, California (and many other locations); *Maiden's Peak* and *Squaw Tit*

(they're the same mountain) in the Cascade Range in Oregon; *Mary's Nipple* near Salt Lake City, Utah; and *Jane Russell Peaks* near Stark, New Hampshire.

Except for the movie star Jane Russell, the women being referred to are anonymous—it's only a sexual part of their body that is mentioned. When topographical features are named after men, it's probably not going to be to draw attention to a sexual part of their bodies but instead to honor individuals for an accomplishment. For example, no one thinks of a part of the male body when hearing a reference to Pike's Peak, Colorado, or Jackson Hole, Wyoming. 11

Going back to what I learned from my dictionary cards, I was surprised to realize how many pairs of words we have in which the feminine word has acquired sexual connotations while the masculine word retains a serious businesslike aura. For example, a *callboy* is the person who calls actors when it is time for them to go on stage, but a *callgirl* is a prostitute. Compare *sir* and *madam*. *Sir* is a term of respect, while *madam* has acquired the specialized meaning of a brothel manager. Something similar has happened to *master* and *mistress*. Would you rather have a painting by an *old master* or an *old mistress*? 12

It's because the word *woman* had sexual connotations, as in "She's his woman," that people began avoiding its use, hence such terminology as *ladies' room, lady of the house,* and *girls' school* or *school for young ladies*. Feminists, who ask that people use the term *woman* rather than *girl* or *lady*, are rejecting the idea that *woman* is primarily a sexual term. They have been at least partially successful in that today *woman* is commonly used to communicate gender without intending implications about sexuality. 13

I found two hundred pairs of words with masculine and feminine forms, e.g., *heir-heiress, hero-heroine, steward-stewardess, usher-usherette*. In nearly all such pairs, the masculine word is considered the base, with some kind of a feminine suffix being added. The masculine form is the one from which compounds are made, e.g., from *king-queen* comes *kingdom* but not *queendom,* from *sportsman-sportslady* comes *sportsmanship* but not *sportsladyship*. There is one—and only one—semantic area in which the masculine word is not the base or more powerful word. This is in the area dealing with sex and marriage. When someone refers to a *virgin,* a listener will probably think of a female, unless the speaker specifies *male* or uses a masculine pronoun. The same is true for *prostitute*. 14

In relation to marriage, there is much linguistic evidence showing that weddings are more important to women than to men. A woman cherishes the wedding and is considered a bride for a whole year, but 15 a man is referred to as a groom only on the day of the wedding. The word *bride* appears in *bridal attendant, bridal gown, bridesmaid, bridal shower,* and even *bridegroom. Groom* comes from the Middle English *grom,* meaning "man," and in the sense is seldom used outside of the wedding. With most pairs of male/female words, people habitually put the masculine word first, *Mr. and Mrs., his and hers, boys and girls, men and women, kings and queens, brothers and sisters, guys and dolls,* and *host and hostess,* but it is the *bride and groom* who are talked about, not the *groom and bride.*

The importance of marriage to a woman is also shown by the fact   16
that when a marriage ends in death, the woman gets the title of *widow.* A man gets the derived title of *widower.* This term is not used in other phrases or contexts, but *widow* is seen in *widowhood, widow's peak,* and *widow's walk.* A *widow* in a card game is an extra hand of cards, while in typesetting it is an extra line of type.

How changing cultural ideas bring changes to language is clearly   17
visible in this semantic area. The feminist movement has caused the differences between the sexes to be downplayed, and since I did my dictionary study two decades ago, the word *singles* has largely replaced such sex specific and value-laden terms as *bachelor, old maid, spinster, divorcee, widow,* and *widower.* And in 1970 I wrote that when a man is called *a professional* he is thought to be a doctor or a lawyer, but when people hear a woman referred to as *a professional* they are likely to think of a prostitute. That's not as true today because so many women have become doctors and lawyers that it's no longer incongruous to think of women in those professional roles.

Another change that has taken place is in wedding announce-   18
ments. They used to be sent out from the bride's parents and did not even give the name of the groom's parents. Today, most couples choose to list either all or none of the parents' names. Also it is now much more likely that both the bride and groom's picture will be in the newspaper, while a decade ago only the bride's picture was published on the "Women's" or the "Society" page. Even the traditional wording of the wedding ceremony is being changed. Many officials now pronounce the couple "husband and wife" instead of the old "man and wife," and they ask the bride if she promises "to love, honor, and cherish," instead of "to love, honor, and obey."

WOMEN ARE PASSIVE; MEN ARE ACTIVE

The wording of the wedding ceremony also relates to the second   19
point that my cards showed, which is that women are expected to play a passive or weak role while men play an active or strong role.

In the traditional ceremony, the official asks, "Who gives the bride away?" and the father answers, "I do." Some fathers answer, "Her mother and I do," but that doesn't solve the problem inherent in the question. The idea that a bride is something to be handed over from one man to another bothers people because it goes back to the days when a man's servants, his children, and his wife were all considered to be his property. They were known by his name because they belonged to him, and he was responsible for their actions and their debts.

The grammar used in talking or writing about weddings as well as other sexual relationships shows the expectation of men playing the active role. Men *wed* women while women *become* brides of men. A man *possesses* a woman; he *deflowers* her; he *performs;* he *scores;* he *takes away* her virginity. Although a woman can *seduce* a man, she cannot offer him her virginity. When talking about virginity, the only way to make the woman the actor in the sentence is to say that "She lost her virginity," but people lose things by accident rather than by purposeful actions, and so she's only the grammatical, not the real-life, actor.   20

The reason that women tried to bring the term *Ms.* into the language to replace *Miss* and *Mrs.* relates to this point. Married women resent being identified only under their husband's names. For example, when Susan Glascoe did something newsworthy, she would be identified in the newspaper only as Mrs. John Glascoe. The dictionary cards showed what appeared to be an attitude on the part of the editors that it was almost indecent to let a respectable woman's name march unaccompanied across the pages of a dictionary. Women were listed with male names whether or not the male contributed to the woman's reason for being in the dictionary or in his own right was as famous as the woman. For example, Charlotte Brontë was identified as Mrs. Arthur B. Nicholls, Amelia Earhart as Mrs. George Palmer Putnam, Helen Hayes as Mrs. Charles MacArthur, Jenny Lind as Mme. Otto Goldschmit, Cornelia Otis Skinner as the daughter of Otis, Harriet Beecher Stowe as the sister of Henry Ward Beecher, and Edith Sitwell as the sister of Osbert and Sacheverell.* A very small number of women got into the dictionary without the benefit of a masculine escort. They were rebels and   21

*Eds. Note—Charlotte Brontë (1816–55), author of *Jane Eyre;* Amelia Earhart (1898–1937), first woman to fly over the Atlantic; Helen Hayes (1900–   ), actress; Jenny Lind (1820–87), Swedish soprano known as the "Swedish nightingale"; Cornelia Otis Skinner (1901–79), actress and writer; Harriet Beecher Stowe (1811–96), author of *Uncle Tom's Cabin;* and Edith Sitwell (1877–1964), English poet and critic.

crusaders: temperance leaders Frances Elizabeth Caroline Willard and Carry Nation, women's rights leaders Carrie Chapman Catt and Elizabeth Cady Stanton, birth control educator Margaret Sanger, religious leader Mary Baker Eddy, and slaves Harriet Tubman and Phillis Wheatley.

Etiquette books used to teach that if a woman had *Mrs.* in front of her name, then the husband's name should follow because *Mrs.* is an abbreviated form of *Mistress* and a woman couldn't be a mistress of herself. As with many arguments about "correct" language usage, this isn't very logical because *Miss* is also an abbreviation of *Mistress.* Feminists hoped to simplify matters by introducing *Ms.* as an alternative to both *Mrs.* and *Miss,* but what happened is that *Ms.* largely replaced *Miss,* to become a catch-all business title for women. Many married women still prefer the title *Mrs.,* and some resent being addressed with the term *Ms.* As one frustrated newspaper reporter complained, "Before I can write about a woman, I have to know not only her marital status but also her political philosophy." The result of such complications may contribute to the demise of titles, which are already being ignored by many computer programmers who find it more efficient to simply use names, for example in a business letter: "Dear Joan Garcia," instead of "Dear Mrs. Joan Garcia," "Dear Ms. Garcia," or "Dear Mrs. Louis Garcia."

The titles given to royalty provide an example of how males can be disadvantaged by the assumption that they are always to play the more powerful role. In British royalty, when a male holds a title, his wife is automatically given the feminine equivalent. But the reverse is not true. For example, a *count* is a high political officer with a *countess* being his wife. The same is true for a *duke* and a *duchess* and a *king* and a *queen.* But when a female holds the royal title, the man she marries does not automatically acquire the matching title. For example, Queen Elizabeth's husband has the title of *prince* rather than *king,* but if Prince Charles should become king while he is still married to Lady or Princess Diana, she will be known as the queen. The reasoning appears to be that since masculine words are stronger, they are reserved for true heirs and withheld from males coming into the royal family by marriage. If Prince Phillip were called *King Phillip,* it would be much easier for British subjects to forget where the true power lies.

The names that people give their children show the hopes and dreams they have for them, and when we look at the differences between male and female names in a culture, we can see the cumulative expectations of that culture. In our culture girls often have names taken from small, aesthetically pleasing items, e.g., *Ruby,*

Jewel, and *Pearl. Esther* and *Stella* mean "star," *Ada* means "ornament," and *Vanessa* means "butterfly." Boys are more likely to be given names with meanings of power and strength, e.g., *Neil* means "champion," *Martin* is from Mars, the God of War, *Raymond* means "wise protection," *Harold* means "chief of the army," *Ira* means "vigilant," *Rex* means "king," and *Richard* means "strong king."

We see similar differences in food metaphors. Food is a passive   25
substance just sitting there waiting to be eaten. Many people have recognized this and so no longer feel comfortable describing women as "delectable morsels." However, when I was a teenager, it was considered a compliment to refer to a girl (we didn't call anyone a *woman* until she was middle-aged) as a *cute tomato, a peach,* a *dish,* a *cookie, honey, sugar,* or *sweetie-pie.* When being affectionate, women will occasionally call a man *honey* or *sweetie,* but in general, food metaphors are used much less often with men than with women. If a man is called *a fruit,* his masculinity is being questioned. But it's perfectly acceptable to use a food metaphor if the food is heavier and more substantive than that used for women. For example pin-up pictures of women have long been known as *cheesecake,* but when Burt Reynolds posed for a nude centerfold the picture was immediately dubbed *beefcake,* c.f., *a hunk of meat.* That such sexual references to men have come into the language is another reflection of how society is beginning to lessen the differences between their attitudes toward men and women.

Something similar to the *fruit* metaphor happens with references   26
to plants. We insult a man by calling him a *pansy,* but it wasn't considered particularly insulting to talk about a girl being a *wallflower,* a *clinging vine,* or a *shrinking violet,* or to give girls such names as *Ivy, Rose, Lily, Iris, Daisy, Camellia, Heather,* and *Flora.* A plant metaphor can be used with a man if the plant is big and strong, for example, Andrew Jackson's nickname of *Old Hickory.* Also, the phrases *blooming idiots* and *budding geniuses* can be used with either sex, but notice how they are based on the most active thing a plant can do, which is to bloom or bud.

Animal metaphors also illustrate the different expectations for   27
males and females. Men are referred to as *studs, bucks,* and *wolves* while women are referred to with such metaphors as *kitten, bunny, beaver, bird, chick,* and *lamb.* In the 1950s we said that boys went *tomcatting,* but today it's just *catting around* and both boys and girls do it. When the term *foxy,* meaning that someone was sexy, first became popular it was used only for girls, but now someone of either sex can be described as *a fox.* Some animal metaphors that are used predominantly with men have negative connotations based on the size and/or strength of the animals, e.g., *beast, bullheaded, jackass,*

rat, loanshark, and *vulture.* Negative metaphors used with women are based on smaller animals, e.g., *social butterfly, mousy, catty,* and *vixen.* The feminine terms connote action, but not the same kind of large scale action as with the masculine terms.

WOMEN ARE CONNECTED WITH NEGATIVE CONNOTATIONS; MEN WITH POSITIVE CONNOTATIONS

The final point that my notecards illustrated was how many posi-   28
tive connotations are associated with the concept of masculine, while there are either trivial or negative connotations connected with the corresponding feminine concept. An example from the animal metaphors makes a good illustration. The word *shrew* taken from the name of a small but especially vicious animal was defined in my dictionary as "an ill-tempered scolding woman," but the word *shrewd* taken from the same root was defined as "marked by clever, discerning awareness" and was illustrated with the phrase "a shrewd businessman."

Early in life, children are conditioned to the superiority of the mas-   29
culine role. As child psychologists point out, little girls have much more freedom to experiment with sex roles than do little boys. If a little girl acts like a *tomboy,* most parents have mixed feelings, being at least partially proud. But if their little boy acts like a *sissy* (derived from *sister*), they call a psychologist. It's perfectly acceptable for a little girl to sleep in the crib that was purchased for her brother, to wear his hand-me-down jeans and shirts, and to ride the bicycle that he has outgrown. But few parents would put a boy baby in a white and gold crib decorated with frills and lace, and virtually no parents would have their little boys wear his sister's hand-me-down dresses, nor would they have their son ride a girl's pink bicycle with a flower-bedecked basket. The proper names given to girls and boys show this same attitude. Girls can have "boy" names—*Cris, Craig, Jo, Kelly, Shawn, Teri, Toni,* and *Sam*—but it doesn't work the other way around. A couple of generations ago, *Beverley, Francis, Hazel, Marion,* and *Shirley* were common boys' names. As parents gave these names to more and more girls, they fell into disuse for males, and some older men who have these names prefer to go by their initials or by such abbreviated forms as *Haze* or *Shirl.*

When a little girl is told to *be a lady,* she is being told to sit with   30
her knees together and to be quiet and dainty. But when a little boy is told to *be a man* he is being told to be noble, strong, and virtuous—to have all the qualities that the speaker looks on as desirable. The concept of manliness has such positive connotations that it used to be a compliment to call someone a *he-man,* to say that he was

doubly a man. Today many people are more ambivalent about this term and respond to it much as they do to the word *macho.* But calling someone a *manly man* or a *virile man* is nearly always meant as a compliment. *Virile* comes from the Indo-European *vir* meaning "man," which is also the basis for *virtuous.* Contrast the positive connotations of both *virile* and *virtuous* with the negative connotations of *hysterical.* The Greeks took this latter word from their name for *uterus* (as still seen in *hysterectomy*). They thought that women were the only ones who experienced uncontrolled emotional outbursts, and so the condition must have something to do with a part of the body that only women have.

Differences in the connotations between positive male and negative female can be seen in several pairs of words that differ denotatively only in the matter of sex. *Bachelor* as compared to *spinster* or *old maid* has such positive connotations that women try to adopt them by using the term *bachelor-girl* or *bachelorette.* *Old maid* is so negative that it's the basis for metaphors: pretentious and fussy old men are called *old maids,* as are the leftover kernels of unpopped popcorn, and the last card in a popular children's game. 31

Patron and *matron* (Middle English for *father* and *mother*) have such different levels of prestige that women try to borrow the more positive masculine connotations with the word *patroness,* literally "female father." Such a peculiar term came about because of the high prestige attached to *patron* in such phrases as *a patron of the arts* or *a patron saint. Matron* is more apt to be used in talking about a woman in charge of a jail or a public restroom. 32

When men are doing jobs that women often do, we apparently try to pay the men extra by giving them fancy titles; for example, a male cook is more likely to be called a *chef* while a male seamstress will get the title of *tailor.* The armed forces have a special problem in that they recruit under such slogans as "The Marine Corps builds men!" and "Join the Army! Become a Man." Once the recruits are enlisted, they find themselves doing much of the work that has been traditionally thought of as "women's work." The solution to getting the work done and not insulting anyone's masculinity was to change the titles as shown below: 33

waitress	orderly
nurse	medic or corpsman
secretary	clerk-typist
assistant	adjutant
dishwasher or	KP (kitchen police)
kitchen helper	

Compare *brave* and *squaw.* Early settlers in America truly admired   34
Indian men and hence named them with a word that carried connotations of youth, vigor, and courage. But they used the Algonquin's
name for "woman" and over the years it developed almost opposite
connotations to those of *brave. Wizard* and *witch* contrast almost as
much. The masculine *wizard* implies skill and wisdom combined with
magic, while the feminine *witch* implies evil intentions combined
with magic. Part of the unattractiveness of both *witch* and *squaw* is
that they have been used so often to refer to old women, something
with which our culture is particularly uncomfortable, just as the
Afghans were. Imagine my surprise when I ran across the phrases
grandfatherly advice and *old wives' tales* and realized that the
underlying implication is the same as the Afghan proverb about old
men being worth listening to while old women talk only foolishness.

Other terms that show how negatively we view old women as   35
compared to young women are *old nag* as compared to *filly, old crow*
or *old bat* as compared to *bird,* and being *catty* as compared to being *kittenish.* There is no matching set of metaphors for men. The
chicken metaphor tells the whole story of a woman's life. In her
youth she is a *chick.* Then she marries and begins *feathering her
nest.* Soon she begins feeling *cooped up,* so she goes to *hen parties*
where she *cackles* with her friends. Then she has her *brood,* begins
to *henpeck* her husband, and finally turns into an *old biddy.*

I embarked on my study of the dictionary not with the intention of   36
prescribing language change but simply to see what the language
would tell me about sexism. Nevertheless I have been both surprised
and pleased as I've watched the changes that have occurred over the
past two decades. I'm one of those linguists who believes that new
language customs will cause a new generation of speakers to grow
up with different expectations. This is why I'm happy about people's
efforts to use inclusive language, to say *he or she* or *they* when speaking about individuals whose names they do not know. I'm glad that
leading publishers have developed guidelines to help writers use
language that is fair to both sexes, and I'm glad that most newspapers and magazines list women by their own names instead of only
by their husbands' names and that educated and thoughtful people
no longer begin their business letters with "Dear Sir" or "Gentlemen," but instead use a memo form or begin with such salutations as
"Dear Colleagues," "Dear Reader," or "Dear Committee Members."
I'm also glad that such words as *poetess, authoress, conductress,* and
aviatrix now sound quaint and old-fashioned and that *chairman* is
giving way to *chair* or *head, mailman* to *mail carrier, clergyman* to
clergy, and *stewardess* to *flight attendant.* I was also pleased when

the National Oceanic and Atmospheric Administration bowed to feminist complaints and in the late 1970s began to alternate men's and women's names for hurricanes. However, I wasn't so pleased to discover that the change did not immediately erase sexist thoughts from everyone's mind, as shown by a headline about Hurricane David in a 1979 New York tabloid, "David Rapes Virgin Islands." More recently a similar metaphor appeared in a headline in the *Arizona Republic* about Hurricane Charlie, "Charlie Quits Carolinas, Flirts with Virginia."

What these incidents show is that sexism is not something existing independently in American English or in the particular dictionary that I happened to read. Rather, it exists in people's minds. Language is like an X-ray in providing visible evidence of invisible thoughts. The best thing about people being interested in and discussing sexist language is that as they make conscious decisions about what pronouns they will use, what jokes they will tell or laugh at, how they will write their names, or how they will begin their letters, they are forced to think about the underlying issue of sexism. This is good because as a problem that begins in people's assumptions and expectations, it's a problem that will be solved only when a great many people have given it a great deal of thought.

37

COMPREHENSION

1. Why did Nilsen first decide to study the English language? Why does she now see irony in her motive?

2. What are some of the examples Nilsen uses to support the idea that language portrays women as sexy and men as successful?

3. How, according to Nilsen, does language suggest "weddings are more important to women than to men" (15)?

4. According to Nilsen, how have marriage customs changed since she wrote her original essay?

5. What are some of the examples Nilsen uses to support the idea that language casts women as weak and passive?

6. Why was the term *Ms.* introduced? Does Nilsen believe it has solved the problems feminists hoped it would? Explain.

7. What are some of the examples Nilsen uses to support the idea that men are associated with positive connotations while women are associated with negative connotations?

8. Does Nilsen still see the English language as sexist, or does she believe that changes in language customs have largely eliminated such bias?

PURPOSE AND AUDIENCE

1. Is the primary purpose of this essay to inform or to persuade? Explain your conclusion. What is Nilsen's thesis? Do you think the thesis should take a more argumentative stance—for example, suggesting the dangers of sexist language? Explain.

2. This essay updates one Nilsen published twenty years earlier. Would you expect audience reaction in the 1970s to be different from audience reaction in the 1990s? If so, how? If not, why not?

STYLE AND STRUCTURE

1. Into what three categories does Nilsen divide sexist language?

2. Where, if anywhere, do Nilsen's categories overlap? Is this overlap to be expected, or does it reveal a flaw in Nilsen's classification system? Explain.

3. Nilsen uses headings to identify her categories. Are these headings helpful? Necessary? Misleading? Distracting? Does she need additional headings? Subheadings? Explain.

4. What function does the essay's introduction (paragraphs 1–5) serve? Do you think it could be condensed? How much of it do you consider essential to your understanding and appreciation of the essay that follows?

5. Which paragraph or paragraphs constitute Nilsen's conclusion? Should it be expanded? If so, what could be added?

6. Does Nilsen include enough examples to convince readers that sexism exists in English?

7. Nilsen uses contractions and first-person pronouns in her essay, giving it an informal, even conversational, style. Is this style appropriate for her subject matter? Explain.

8. Do paragraphs 15–18 represent a digression, or do they illustrate the statement "Women are sexy; men are successful"? Do any other paragraphs strike you as digressions? Explain.

VOCABULARY PROJECTS

1. Define each of the following words as it is used in this selection.

   inherent (1)   buxom (7)   ambivalent (30)
   blatantly (1)   semantic (14)
   bereft (3)   connote (27)

2. List as many additional examples as you can of words that illustrate each of the three points Nilsen discusses.

3. Nilsen has updated her essay for the 1990s. Nevertheless, you may find that some of the usages she describes are no longer current. Identify any words that you believe are no longer used as Nilsen says they are.

JOURNAL ENTRY

In recent years, some feminists have begun spelling the word *women* as *womyn* or *wimmin* so it will not include the word *men*. What is your reaction to this practice?

WRITING WORKSHOP

1. What special kinds of language are used in sports—for example, by players, fans, and sportswriters? How do various sports differ in their idioms? Answer these questions in a classification-and-division essay about the language of sports. (How you organize your essay will depend on whether you write about one particular sport or several different ones.)

2. How does today's advertising portray women? Using Nilsen's general categories (and her headings if you like), collect examples to support the thesis that advertising, like language, has a sexist bias.

3. Many people believe that the English language reflects not only the sexism in people's minds but also the racism. Write an essay called "Racism in English." Begin by listing individual words and usage patterns you consider racist, and then divide your list into categories determined by a single principle of classification—for example, kinds of racist language, kinds of language applied to different racial groups, or different motives for using racist language. Your thesis can simply sum up current practices or take a stand against them. Reading (or rereading) some of the essays on this topic that appear in other chapters of this book, such as "'What's in a Name?'" "The Same Difference," and "Finishing School," might help you as you plan your paper.

THEMATIC CONNECTIONS

- "My Field of Dreams" (p. 68)
- "Only Daughter" (p. 73)
- "Sex, Lies, and Conversation" (p. 393)
- "The Catbird Seat" (p. 522)

THE WAYS WE LIE

Stephanie Ericsson

Stephanie Ericsson is a screenwriter and advertising copywriter. She has published three books on the subject of mourning: Shame Faced: The Road to Recovery *(1986),* Recovering Together, *and* Companion Through Darkness: Inner Dialogues on Grief *(1993). Ericsson is currently working on a new book from which the following is taken. "The Ways We Lie," published in the* Utne Reader *in 1992, looks at the many ways we deceive ourselves and others.*

The bank called today and I told them my deposit was in the mail, even though I hadn't written a check yet. It'd been a rough day. The baby I'm pregnant with decided to do aerobics on my lungs for two hours, our three-year-old daughter painted the living-room couch with lipstick, the IRS put me on hold for an hour, and I was late to a business meeting because I was tired.

I told my client the traffic had been bad. When my partner came home, his haggard face told me his day hadn't gone any better than mine, so when he asked, "How was your day?" I said, "Oh, fine," knowing that one more straw might break his back. A friend called and wanted to take me to lunch. I said I was busy. Four lies in the course of a day, none of which I felt the least bit guilty about.

We lie. We all do. We exaggerate, we minimize, we avoid confrontation, we spare people's feelings, we conveniently forget, we keep secrets, we justify lying to the big-guy institutions. Like most people, I indulge in small falsehoods and still think of myself as an honest person. Sure I lie, but it doesn't hurt anything. Or does it?

I once tried going a whole week without telling a lie, and it was paralyzing. I discovered that telling the truth all the time is nearly impossible. It means living with some serious consequences: The bank charges me $60 in overdraft fees, my partner keels over when I tell him about my travails, my client fires me for telling her I didn't feel like being on time, and my friend takes it personally when I say I'm not hungry. There must be some merit to lying.

But if I justify lying, what makes me any different from slick politicians or the corporate robbers who raided the S&L industry? Saying it's okay to lie one way and not another is hedging. I cannot seem to escape the voice deep inside me that tells me: When someone lies, someone loses.

What far-reaching consequences will I, or others, pay as a result of my lie? Will someone's trust be destroyed? Will someone else pay *my* penance because I ducked out? We must consider the *meaning of our actions*. Deception, lies, capital crimes, and misdemeanors all carry meanings. *Webster's* definition of *lie* is specific: 6

> 1: a false statement or action especially made with the intent to deceive; 2: anything that gives or is meant to give a false impression.

A definition like this implies that there are many, many ways to tell a lie. Here are just a few. 7

THE WHITE LIE

> A man who won't lie to a woman has very little consideration for her feelings.
> —Bergen Evans

The white lie assumes that the truth will cause more damage than a simple, harmless untruth. Telling a friend he looks great when he looks like hell can be based on a decision that the friend needs a compliment more than a frank opinion. But, in effect, it is the liar deciding what is best for the lied to. Ultimately, it is a vote of no confidence. It is an act of subtle arrogance for anyone to decide what is best for someone else. 8

Yet not all circumstances are quite so cut-and-dried. Take, for instance, the sergeant in Vietnam who knew one of his men was killed in action but listed him as missing so that the man's family would receive indefinite compensation instead of the lump-sum pittance the military gives widows and children. His intent was honorable. Yet for twenty years this family kept their hopes alive, unable to move on to a new life. 9

FACADES

> Et tu, Brute? —Caesar*

We all put up facades to one degree or another. When I put on a suit to go to see a client, I feel as though I am putting on another 10

*EDS. NOTE—"And you, Brutus?" In Shakespeare's play *Julius Caesar,* Caesar asks this question when he sees Brutus, whom he has believed to be his friend, among the conspirators who are stabbing him.

face, obeying the expectation that serious businesspeople wear suits rather than sweatpants. But I'm a writer. Normally, I get up, get the kid off to school, and sit at my computer in my pajamas until four in the afternoon. When I answer the phone, the caller thinks I'm wearing a suit (though the UPS man knows better).

But facades can be destructive because they are used to seduce   11 others into an illusion. For instance, I recently realized that a former friend was a liar. He presented himself with all the right looks and the right words and offered lots of new consciousness theories, fabulous books to read, and fascinating insights. Then I did some business with him, and the time came for him to pay me. He turned out to be all talk and no walk. I heard a plethora of reasonable excuses, including in-depth descriptions of the big break around the corner. In six months of work, I saw less than a hundred bucks. When I confronted him, he raised both eyebrows and tried to convince me that I'd heard him wrong, that he'd made no commitment to me. A simple investigation into his past revealed a crowded graveyard of disenchanted former friends.

IGNORING THE PLAIN FACTS

Well, you must understand that Father Porter is only human . . .
—A Massachusetts priest

In the '60s, the Catholic Church in Massachusetts began hearing   12 complaints that Father James Porter was sexually molesting children. Rather than relieving him of his duties, the ecclesiastical authorities simply moved him from one parish to another between 1960 and 1967, actually providing him with a fresh supply of unsuspecting families and innocent children to abuse. After treatment in 1967 for pedophilia, he went back to work, this time in Minnesota. The new diocese was aware of Father Porter's obsession with children, but they needed priests and recklessly believed treatment had cured him. More children were abused until he was relieved of his duties a year later. By his own admission, Porter may have abused as many as a hundred children.

Ignoring the facts may not in and of itself be a form of lying, but   13 consider the context of this situation. If a lie is *a false action done with the intent to deceive,* then the Catholic Church's conscious covering for Porter created irreparable consequences. The church became a co-perpetrator with Porter.

DEFLECTING

When you have no basis for an argument, abuse the plaintiff.

—Cicero

I've discovered that I can keep anyone from seeing the true me by 14 being selectively blatant. I set a precedent of being up-front about intimate issues, but I never bring up the things I truly want to hide; I just let people assume I'm revealing everything. It's an effective way of hiding.

Any good liar knows that the way to perpetuate an untruth is to 15 deflect attention from it. When Clarence Thomas exploded with accusations that the Senate hearings were a "high-tech lynching," he simply switched the focus from a highly charged subject to a radioactive subject. Rather than defending himself, he took the offensive and accused the country of racism. It was a brilliant maneuver. Racism is now politically incorrect in official circles—unlike sexual harassment, which still rewards those who can get away with it.

Some of the most skillful deflectors are passive-aggressive people 16 who, when accused of inappropriate behavior, refuse to respond to the accusations. This you-don't-exist stance infuriates the accuser, who, understandably, screams something obscene out of frustration. The trap is sprung and the act of deflection successful, because now the passive-aggressive person can indignantly say, "Who can talk to someone as unreasonable as you?" The real issue is forgotten and the sins of the original victim become the focus. Feeling guilty of name-calling, the victim is fully tamed and crawls into a hole, ashamed. I have watched this fighting technique work thousands of times in disputes between men and women, and what I've learned is that the real culprit is not necessarily the one who swears the loudest.

OMISSION

The cruelest lies are often told in silence.

—R.L. Stevenson

Omission involves telling most of the truth minus one or two key 17 facts whose absence changes the story completely. You break a pair of glasses that are guaranteed under normal use and get a new pair, without mentioning that the first pair broke during a rowdy game of basketball. Who hasn't tried something like that? But what about omission of information that could make a difference in how a person lives his or her life?

For instance, one day I found out that rabbinical legends tell of   18
another woman in the Garden of Eden before Eve. I was stunned.
The omission of the Sumerian goddess Lilith from Genesis—as well
as her demonization by ancient misogynists as an embodiment of
female evil—felt like spiritual robbery. I felt like I'd just found out
my mother was really my stepmother. To take seriously the tradition
that Adam was created out of the same mud as his equal counterpart, Lilith, redefines all of Judeo-Christian history.

Some renegade Catholic feminists introduced me to a view of   19
Lilith that had been suppressed during the many centuries when
this strong goddess was seen only as a spirit of evil. Lilith was a
proud goddess who defied Adam's need to control her, attempted
negotiations, and when this failed, said adios and left the Garden
of Eden.

This omission of Lilith from the Bible was a patriarchal strategy   20
to keep women weak. Omitting the strong-woman archetype of
Lilith from Western religions and starting the story with Eve the Rib
has helped keep Christian and Jewish women believing they were
the lesser sex for thousands of years.

STEREOTYPES AND CLICHÉS

Where opinion does not exist, the status quo becomes stereotyped and
all originality is discouraged.
                                                        —Bertrand Russell

Stereotype and cliché serve a purpose as a form of shorthand. Our   21
need for vast amounts of information in nanoseconds has made the stereotype vital to modern communication. Unfortunately, it often shuts
down original thinking, giving those hungry for the truth a candy bar
of misinformation instead of a balanced meal. The stereotype explains
a situation with just enough truth to seem unquestionable.

All the 'isms'—racism, sexism, ageism, et al.—are founded on and   22
fueled by the stereotype and the cliché, which are lies of exaggeration, omission, and ignorance. They are always dangerous. They
take a single tree and make it a landscape. They destroy curiosity.
They close minds and separate people. The single mother on welfare
is assumed to be cheating. Any black male could tell you how much
of his identity is obliterated daily by stereotypes. Fat people, ugly
people, beautiful people, old people, large-breasted women, short
men, the mentally ill, and the homeless all could tell you how much
more they are like us than we want to think. I once admitted to a
group of people that I had a mouth like a truck driver. Much to my

surprise, a man stood up and said, "I'm a truck driver, and I never cuss." Needless to say, I was humbled.

GROUPTHINK

Who is more foolish, the child afraid of the dark, or the man afraid of the light?

—Maurice Freehill

Irving Janis, in *Victims of GroupThink,* defines this sort of lie 23 as a psychological phenomenon within decision-making groups in which loyalty to the group has become more important than any other value, with the result that dissent and the appraisal of alternatives are suppressed. If you've ever worked on a committee or in a corporation, you've encountered groupthink. It requires a combination of other forms of lying—ignoring facts, selective memory, omission, and denial, to name a few.

The textbook example of groupthink came on December 7, 1941. 24 From as early as the fall of 1941, the warnings came in, one after another, that Japan was preparing for a massive military operation. The Navy command in Hawaii assumed Pearl Harbor was invulnerable—the Japanese weren't stupid enough to attack the United States' most important base. On the other hand, racist stereotypes said the Japanese weren't smart enough to invent a torpedo effective in less than 60 feet of water (the fleet was docked in 30 feet); after all, U.S. technology hadn't been able to do it.

On Friday, December 5, normal weekend leave was granted to all 25 the commanders at Pearl Harbor, even though the Japanese consulate in Hawaii was busy burning papers. Within the tight, good-ole-boy cohesiveness of the U.S. command in Hawaii, the myth of invulnerability stayed well entrenched. No one in the group considered the alternatives. The rest is history.

OUT-AND-OUT LIES

The only form of lying that is beyond reproach is lying for its own sake.

—Oscar Wilde

Of all the ways to lie, I like this one the best, probably because I 26 get tired of trying to figure out the real meanings behind things. At least I can trust the bald-faced lie. I once asked my five-year-old nephew, "Who broke the fence?" (I had seen him do it.) He answered, "The murderers." Who could argue?

At least when this sort of lie is told it can be easily confronted. As the person who is lied to, I know where I stand. The bald-faced lie doesn't toy with my perceptions—it argues with them. It doesn't try to refashion reality, it tries to refute it. *Read my lips* . . . No sleight of hand. No guessing. If this were the only form of lying, there would be no such thing as floating anxiety or the adult-children of alcoholics movement.

DISMISSAL

Pay no attention to that man behind the curtain! I am the Great Oz!
—The Wizard of Oz

Dismissal is perhaps the slipperiest of all lies. Dismissing feelings, perceptions, or even the raw facts of a situation ranks as a kind of lie that can do as much damage to a person as any other kind of lie.

The roots of many mental disorders can be traced back to the dismissal of reality. Imagine that a person is told from the time she is a tot that her perceptions are inaccurate. *"Mommy, I'm scared."* "No you're not, darling." *"I don't like that man next door, he makes me feel icky."* "Johnny, that's a terrible thing to say, of course you like him. You go over there right now and be nice to him."

I've often mused over the idea that madness is actually a sane reaction to an insane world. Psychologist R.D. Laing supports this hypothesis in *Sanity, Madness & The Family,* an account of his investigations into the families of schizophrenics. The common thread that ran through all of the families he studied was a deliberate, staunch dismissal of the patient's perceptions from a very early age. Each of the patients started out with an accurate grasp of reality, which, through meticulous and methodical dismissal, was demolished until the only reality the patient could trust was catatonia.

Dismissal runs the gamut. Mild dismissal can be quite handy for forgiving the foibles of others in our day-to-day lives. Toddlers who have just learned to manipulate their parents' attention sometimes are dismissed out of necessity. Absolute attention from the parents would require so much energy that no one would get to eat dinner. But we must be careful and attentive about how far we take our "necessary" dismissals. Dismissal is a dangerous tool, because it's nothing less than a lie.

DELUSION

We lie loudest when we lie to ourselves.

—Eric Hoffer

I could write the book on this one. Delusion, a cousin of dismissal, 32 is the tendency to see excuses as facts. It's a powerful lying tool because it filters out information that contradicts what we want to believe. Alcoholics who believe that the problems in their lives are legitimate reasons for drinking rather than results of the drinking offer the classic example of deluded thinking. Delusion uses the mind's ability to see things in myriad ways to support what it wants to be the truth.

But delusion is also a survival mechanism we all use. If we were 33 to fully contemplate the consequences of our stockpiles of nuclear weapons or global warming, we could hardly function on a day-to-day level. We don't want to incorporate that much reality into our lives because to do so would be paralyzing.

Delusion acts as an adhesive to keep the status quo intact. It 34 shamelessly employs dismissal, omission, and amnesia, among other sorts of lies. Its most cunning defense is that it cannot see itself.

The liar's punishment . . . is that he cannot believe anyone else.

—George Bernard Shaw

These are only a few of the ways we lie. Or are lied to. As I said 35 earlier, it's not easy to entirely eliminate lies from our lives. No matter how pious we may try to be, we will still embellish, hedge, and omit to lubricate the daily machinery of living. But there is a world of difference between telling functional lies and living a lie. Martin Buber* once said, "The lie is the spirit committing treason against itself." Our acceptance of lies becomes a cultural cancer that eventually shrouds and reorders reality until moral garbage becomes as invisible to us as water is to a fish.

How much do we tolerate before we become sick and tired of being 36 sick and tired? When will we stand up and declare our *right* to trust? When do we stop accepting that the real truth is in the fine print? Whose lips do we read this year when we vote for president? When will we stop being so reticent about making judgments? When do we stop turning over our personal power and responsibility to liars?

Maybe if I don't tell the bank the check's in the mail I'll be less 37 tolerant of the lies told me every day. A country song I once heard

*EDS. NOTE—Jewish philosopher (1878–1965).

said it all for me: "You've got to stand for something or you'll fall for anything."

COMPREHENSION

1. List and define each of the ten kinds of lies Ericsson identifies.

2. Why, in Ericsson's view, is each kind of lie necessary?

3. According to Ericsson, what is the danger of each kind of lie?

4. Why does Ericsson like "out-and-out lies" (26–27) best?

5. Why is dismissal the "slipperiest of all lies" (28)?

PURPOSE AND AUDIENCE

1. Is Ericsson's thesis simply that "there are many, many ways to tell a lie" (7)? Or is she defending—or attacking—the process of lying? Try to state her thesis in a single sentence.

2. Do you think Ericsson's choice of examples reveals a political bias? If so, what do you think this bias reveals about the attitudes she expects her intended audience to have?

STYLE AND STRUCTURE

1. Despite the seriousness of her subject matter, Ericsson's essay is informal; her opening paragraphs are especially personal and breezy. Why do you think she uses this kind of opening? Do you think her decision makes sense?

2. A dictionary definition is quite a familiar—even tired—strategy for an essay's introduction. Would you have advised Ericsson to delete the definition in paragraph 6 for this reason, or do you believe it is necessary? Explain.

3. Ericsson introduces each category of lie with a quotation. What function do these quotations serve? Would the essay be more or less effective without them?

4. In addition to a heading and a quotation, what other elements does Ericsson include in her discussion of each category of lie? Are all the discussions parallel—that is, does each include *all* the standard elements, and *only* those elements? If not, do you think this lack of balance is a problem? Explain.

5. What, if anything, determines the order in which Ericsson arranges her categories? Should any category be relocated? Explain.

6. Throughout her essay, Ericsson uses *rhetorical questions,* questions to which no answer is expected (or given). Why do you suppose she uses this stylistic device?

7. Ericsson occasionally cites the views of experts. Why does she do so? If she wished to cite additional experts, what professional backgrounds or fields of study should they represent? Why?

8. In paragraph 29 Ericsson says, "Imagine that a person is told from the time she is a tot. . . ." Does she use *she* in similar contexts elsewhere in the essay? Do you find the feminine form of the personal pronoun distracting? Explain.

9. Paragraphs 35–37 constitute Ericsson's conclusion. How is this conclusion related to the essay's introduction in terms of style, structure, and content?

VOCABULARY PROJECTS

1. Define each of the following words as it is used in this selection.

travails (4)	deflectors (16)	staunch (30)
hedging (5)	passive-aggressive (16)	catatonia (30)
pittance (9)	misogynists (18)	gamut (31)
facades (10)	counterpart (18)	foibles (31)
plethora (11)	archetype (20)	reticent (36)
pedophilia (12)	nanoseconds (21)	
blatant (14)	obliterated (22)	

2. Ericsson uses many *colloquialisms* in this essay—for example, "I could write the book on this one" (32). Identify as many such expressions as you can. Why do you think she uses these colloquialisms instead of more formal expressions? Do they have a positive or negative effect on your reaction to her ideas? Explain.

JOURNAL ENTRY

In paragraph 3 Ericsson says, "We lie. We all do." Later in the paragraph she comments, "Sure I lie, but it doesn't hurt anything. Or does it?" Answer her question.

WRITING WORKSHOP

1. Choose three or four of Ericsson's categories and write a classification-and-division essay called "The Ways I Lie." Base your essay on per-

sonal experience, and include an explicit thesis that defends these lies—or that is sharply critical of their use.

2. In paragraph 22 Ericsson includes a statement that condemns stereotypes. Write a classification-and-division essay with the thesis "Stereotypes are sometimes inaccurate, often negative, and always dangerous." Consider the stereotypes applied to the following groups: the disabled, the overweight, the elderly, and teenagers.

3. Using the same thesis suggested in question 2, write a classification-and-division essay that considers the stereotypes applied to police officers, librarians, used-car dealers, flight attendants, and lawyers.

THEMATIC CONNECTIONS

- "38 Who Saw Murder Didn't Call the Police" (p. 91)
- "The Lottery" (p. 272)
- "Civility and Its Discontents" (p. 593)

REVELATION

Flannery O'Connor

*Flannery O'Connor (1925–1964) was born in Savannah and lived
with her mother in Milledgeville, Georgia, for most of her life. She
graduated from Georgia State College for Women in 1945 and
received an M.F.A. from the University of Iowa in 1947. In spite of
suffering from the debilitating effects of lupus, O'Connor was able to
write, travel, and lecture until she died at the age of thirty-nine. She
wrote two novels,* Wise Blood *(1952) and* The Violent Bear It Away
(1960), and many short stories, which are collected in A Good Man
Is Hard to Find *(1955) and* Everything That Rises Must Converge
(1965). Her other writings are collected in Mystery and Manners:
Occasional Prose *(1969),* The Habit of Being: Letters of Flannery
O'Connor *(1979), and* The Presence of Grace and Other Book
Reviews *(1983). Her* Complete Stories *was published in 1971 and
her* Collected Works *in 1988. In "Revelation," O'Connor describes
the unraveling of a woman's rigidly organized view of the world.*

The doctor's waiting room, which was very small, was almost full 1
when the Turpins entered and Mrs. Turpin, who was very large,
made it look even smaller by her presence. She stood looming at the
head of the magazine table set in the center of it, a living demon-
stration that the room was inadequate and ridiculous. Her little
bright black eyes took in all the patients as she sized up the seating
situation. There was one vacant chair and a place on the sofa occupied by a blond child in a dirty blue romper who should have been
told to move over and make room for the lady. He was five or six, but
Mrs. Turpin saw at once that no one was going to tell him to move
over. He was slumped down in the seat, his arms idle at his sides and
his eyes idle in his head; his nose ran unchecked.

Mrs. Turpin put a firm hand on Claud's shoulder and said in a 2
voice that included everyone that wanted to listen, "Claud, you sit in
that chair there," and gave him a push down into the vacant one.
Claud was florid and bald and sturdy, somewhat shorter than Mrs.
Turpin, but he sat down as if he were accustomed to doing what she
told him to.

Mrs. Turpin remained standing. The only man in the room besides 3
Claud was a lean stringy old fellow with a rusty hand spread out on
each knee, whose eyes were closed as if he were asleep or dead or

pretending to be so as not to get up and offer her his seat. Her gaze settled agreeably on a well-dressed grey-haired lady whose eyes met hers and whose expression said: if that child belonged to me, he would have some manners and move over—there's plenty of room there for you and him too.

Claud looked up with a sigh and made as if to rise.   4

"Sit down," Mrs. Turpin said. "You know you're not supposed to   5
stand on that leg. He has an ulcer on his leg," she explained.

Claud lifted his foot onto the magazine table and rolled his trouser   6
leg up to reveal a purple swelling on a plump marble-white calf.

"My!" the pleasant lady said. "How did you do that?"   7

"A cow kicked him," Mrs. Turpin said.   8

"Goodness!" said the lady.   9

Claud rolled his trouser leg down.   10

"Maybe the little boy would move over," the lady suggested, but   11
the child did not stir.

"Somebody will be leaving in a minute," Mrs. Turpin said. She   12
could not understand why a doctor—with as much money as they made charging five dollars a day just to stick their head in the hospital door and look at you—couldn't afford a decent-sized waiting room. This one was hardly bigger than a garage. The table was cluttered with limp-looking magazines and at one end of it there was a big green glass ash tray full of cigaret butts and cotton wads with little blood spots on them. If she had had anything to do with the running of the place, that would have been emptied every so often. There were no chairs against the wall at the head of the room. It had a rectangular-shaped panel in it that permitted a view of the office where the nurse came and went and the secretary listened to the radio. A plastic fern in a gold pot sat in the opening and trailed its fronds down almost to the floor. The radio was softly playing gospel music.

Just then the inner door opened and a nurse with the highest   13
stack of yellow hair Mrs. Turpin had ever seen put her face in the crack and called for the next patient. The woman sitting beside Claud grasped the two arms of her chair and hoisted herself up; she pulled her dress free from her legs and lumbered through the door where the nurse had disappeared.

Mrs. Turpin eased into the vacant chair, which held her tight as a   14
corset. "I wish I could reduce," she said, and rolled her eyes and gave a comic sigh.

"Oh, *you* aren't fat," the stylish lady said.   15

"Ooooo I am too," Mrs. Turpin said. "Claud he eats all he wants to   16
and never weighs over one hundred and seventy-five pounds, but me I just look at something good to eat and I gain some weight," and her

stomach and shoulders shook with laughter. "You can eat all you want to, can't you, Claud?" she asked turning to him.

Claud only grinned. 17

"Well, as long as you have such a good disposition," the stylish 18 lady said, "I don't think it makes a bit of difference what size you are. You just can't beat a good disposition."

Next to her was a fat girl of eighteen or nineteen, scowling into a 19 thick blue book which Mrs. Turpin saw was entitled *Human Development*. The girl raised her head and directed her scowl at Mrs. Turpin as if she did not like her looks. She appeared annoyed that anyone should speak while she tried to read. The poor girl's face was blue with acne and Mrs. Turpin thought how pitiful it was to have a face like that at that age. She gave the girl a friendly smile but the girl only scowled the harder. Mrs. Turpin herself was fat but she had always had good skin, and, though she was forty-seven years old, there was not a wrinkle in her face except around her eyes from laughing too much.

Next to the ugly girl was the child, still in exactly the same posi- 20 tion, and next to him was a thin leathery old woman in a cotton print dress. She and Claud had three sacks of chicken feed in their pump house that was in the same print. She had seen from the first that the child belonged with the old woman. She could tell by the way they sat—kind of vacant and white-trashy, as if they would sit there until Doomsday if nobody called and told them to get up. And at right angles but next to the well-dressed pleasant lady was a lank-faced woman who was certainly the child's mother. She had on a yellow sweat shirt and wine-colored slacks, both gritty-looking, and the rims of her lips were stained with snuff. Her dirty yellow hair was tied behind with a piece of red paper ribbon. Worse than niggers any day, Mrs. Turpin thought.

The gospel hymn playing was, "When I looked up and He looked 21 down," and Mrs. Turpin, who knew it, supplied the last line mentally, "And wona these days I know I'll we-eara crown."

Without appearing to, Mrs. Turpin always noticed people's feet. 22 The well-dressed lady had on red and grey suede shoes to match her dress. Mrs. Turpin had on her good black patent leather pumps. The ugly girl had on Girl Scout shoes and heavy socks. The old woman had on tennis shoes and the white-trashy mother had on what appeared to be bedroom slippers, black straw with gold braid threaded through them—exactly what you would have expected her to have on.

Sometimes at night when she couldn't go to sleep, Mrs. Turpin 23 would occupy herself with the question of who she would have chosen to be if she couldn't have been herself. If Jesus had said to her before he made her, "There's only two places available for you. You can either be a nigger or white-trash," what would she have said? "Please, Jesus, please," she would have said, "just let me wait until there's another place available," and he would have said, "No, you have to go right now and I have only those two places so make up your mind." She would have wiggled and squirmed and begged and pleaded but it would have been no use and finally she would have said, "All right, make me a nigger then—but that don't mean a trashy one." And he would have made her a neat clean respectable Negro woman, herself but black.

Next to the child's mother was a red-headed youngish woman, 24 reading one of the magazines and working a piece of chewing gum, hell for leather, as Claud would say. Mrs. Turpin could not see the woman's feet. She was not white-trash, just common. Sometimes Mrs. Turpin occupied herself at night naming the classes of people. On the bottom of the heap were most colored people, not the kind she would have been if she had been one, but most of them; then next to them—not above, just away from—were the white-trash; then above them were the home-owners, and above them the home-and-land owners, to which she and Claud belonged. Above she and Claud were people with a lot of money and much bigger houses and much more land. But here the complexity of it would begin to bear in on her, for some of the people with a lot of money were common and ought to be below she and Claud and some of the people who had good blood had lost their money and had to rent and then there were colored people who owned their homes and land as well. There was a colored dentist in town who had two red Lincolns and a swimming pool and a farm with registered white-face cattle on it. Usually by the time she had fallen asleep all the classes of people were moiling and roiling around in her head, and she would dream they were all crammed in together in a box car, being ridden off to be put in a gas oven.

"That's a beautiful clock," she said and nodded to her right. It was 25 a big wall clock, the face encased in a brass sunburst.

"Yes, it's very pretty," the stylish lady said agreeably. "And right on 26 the dot too," she added, glancing at her watch.

The ugly girl beside her cast an eye upward at the clock, smirked, 27 then looked directly at Mrs. Turpin and smirked again. Then she returned her eyes to her book. She was obviously the lady's daughter because, although they didn't look anything alike as to disposition, they both had the same shape of face and same blue eyes. On the lady they sparkled pleasantly but in the girl's seared face they appeared alternately to smolder and to blaze.

What if Jesus had said, "All right, you can be white-trash or a   28
nigger or ugly!"

Mrs. Turpin felt an awful pity for the girl, though she thought it   29
was one thing to be ugly and another to act ugly.

The woman with the snuff-stained lips turned around in her chair   30
and looked up at the clock. Then she turned back and appeared to
look a little to the side of Mrs. Turpin. There was a cast in one of her
eyes. "You want to know wher you can get one of themther clocks?"
she asked in a loud voice.

"No, I already have a nice clock," Mrs. Turpin said. Once somebody   31
like her got a leg in the conversation, she would be all over it.

"You can get you one with green stamps," the woman said. "That's   32
most likely wher he got hisn. Save you up enough, you can get you
most anythang. I got me some joo'ry."

Ought to have got you a wash rag and some soap, Mrs. Turpin   33
thought.

"I get contour sheets with mine," the pleasant lady said.   34

The daughter slammed her book shut. She looked straight in front   35
of her, directly through Mrs. Turpin and on through the yellow curtain and the plate glass window which made the wall behind her.
The girl's eyes seemed lit all of a sudden with a peculiar light, an unnatural light like night road signs give. Mrs. Turpin turned her head
to see if there was anything going on outside that she should see, but
she could not see anything. Figures passing cast only a pale shadow
through the curtain. There was no reason the girl should single her
out for her ugly looks.

"Miss Finley," the nurse said, cracking the door. The gum-chewing   36
woman got up and passed in front of her and Claud and went into
the office. She had on red high-heeled shoes.

Directly across the table, the ugly girl's eyes were fixed on Mrs.   37
Turpin as if she had some very special reason for disliking her.

"This is wonderful weather, isn't it?" the girl's mother said.   38

"It's good weather for cotton if you can get the niggers to pick it,"   39
Mrs. Turpin said, "but niggers don't want to pick cotton any more.
You can't get the white folks to pick it and now you can't get the
niggers—because they got to be right up there with the white folks."

"They gonna *try* anyways," the white-trash woman said, leaning   40
forward.

"Do you have one of those cotton-picking machines?" the pleasant   41
lady asked.

"No," Mrs. Turpin said, "they leave half the cotton in the field. We   42
don't have much cotton anyway. If you want to make it farming now,
you have to have a little of everything. We got a couple of acres of

cotton and a few hogs and chickens and just enough white-face that Claud can look after them himself."

"One thang I don't want," the white-trash woman said, wiping her mouth with the back of her hand. "Hogs. Nasty stinking things, a-gruntin and a-rootin all over the place." 43

Mrs. Turpin gave her the merest edge of her attention. "Our hogs are not dirty and they don't stink," she said. "They're cleaner than some children I've seen. Their feet never touch the ground. We have a pig-parlor—that's where you raise them on concrete," she explained to the pleasant lady, "and Claud scoots them down with the hose every afternoon and washes off the floor." Cleaner by far than that child right there, she thought. Poor nasty little thing. He had not moved except to put the thumb of his dirty hand into his mouth. 44

The woman turned her face away from Mrs. Turpin. "I know I wouldn't scoot down no hog with no hose," she said to the wall. 45

You wouldn't have no hog to scoot down, Mrs. Turpin said to herself. 46

"A-gruntin and a-rootin and a-groanin," the woman muttered. 47

"We got a little of everything," Mrs. Turpin said to the pleasant lady. "It's no use in having more than you can handle yourself with help like it is. We found enough niggers to pick our cotton this year but Claud he has to go after them and take them home again in the evening. They can't walk that half a mile. No they can't. I tell you," she said and laughed merrily, "I sure am tired of buttering up niggers, but you got to love em if you want em to work for you. When they come in the morning, I run out and I say, 'Hi yawl this morning?' and when Claud drives them off to the field I just wave to beat the band and they just wave back." And she waved her hand rapidly to illustrate. 48

"Like you read out of the same book," the lady said, showing she understood perfectly. 49

"Child, yes," Mrs. Turpin said. "And when they come in from the field, I run out with a bucket of icewater. That's the way it's going to be from now on," she said. "You may as well face it." 50

"One thang I know," the white-trash woman said. "Two thangs I ain't going to do: love no niggers or scoot down no hog with no hose." And she let out a bark of contempt. 51

The look that Mrs. Turpin and the pleasant lady exchanged indicated they both understood that you had to *have* certain things before you could *know* certain things. But every time Mrs. Turpin exchanged a look with the lady, she was aware that the ugly girl's peculiar eyes were still on her, and she had trouble bringing her attention back to the conversation. 52

"When you got something," she said, "you got to look after it." And 53
when you ain't got a thing but breath and britches, she added to
herself, you can afford to come to town every morning and just sit on
the Court House coping and spit.

A grotesque revolving shadow passed across the curtain behind 54
her and was thrown palely on the opposite wall. Then a bicycle clat-
tered down against the outside of the building. The door opened and
a colored boy glided in with a tray from the drug store. It had two
large red and white paper cups on it with tops on them. He was a
tall, very black boy in discolored white pants and a green nylon
shirt. He was chewing gum slowly, as if to music. He set the tray
down in the office opening next to the fern and stuck his head
through to look for the secretary. She was not in there. He rested his
arms on the ledge and waited, his narrow bottom stuck out, swaying
slowly to the left and right. He raised a hand over his head and
scratched the base of his skull.

"You see that button there, boy?" Mrs. Turpin said. "You can 55
punch that and she'll come. She's probably in the back somewhere."

"Is thas right?" the boy said agreeably, as if he had never seen the 56
button before. He leaned to the right and put his finger on it. "She
sometime out," he said and twisted around to face his audience, his
elbows behind him on the counter. The nurse appeared and he
twisted back again. She handed him a dollar and he rooted in his
pocket and made the change and counted it out to her. She gave him
fifteen cents for a tip and he went out with the empty tray. The
heavy door swung to slowly and closed at length with the sound of
suction. For a moment no one spoke.

"They ought to send all them niggers back to Africa," the white- 57
trash woman said. "That's wher they come from in the first place."

"Oh, I couldn't do without my good colored friends," the pleasant 58
lady said.

"There's a heap of things worse than a nigger," Mrs. Turpin 59
agreed. "It's all kinds of them just like it's all kinds of us."

"Yes, and it takes all kinds to make the world go round," the lady 60
said in her musical voice.

As she said it, the raw-complexioned girl snapped her teeth to- 61
gether. Her lower lip turned downwards and inside out, revealing
the pale pink inside her mouth. After a second it rolled back up. It
was the ugliest face Mrs. Turpin had ever seen anyone make and for
a moment she was certain that the girl had made it at her. She was
looking at her as if she had known and disliked her all her life—all
of Mrs. Turpin's life, it seemed too, not just all the girl's life. Why,
girl, I don't even know you, Mrs. Turpin said silently.

She forced her attention back to the discussion. "It wouldn't be practical to send them back to Africa," she said. "They wouldn't want to go. They got it too good here."

"Wouldn't be what they wanted—if I had anythang to do with it," the woman said.

"It wouldn't be a way in the world you could get all the niggers back over there," Mrs. Turpin said. "They'd be hiding out and lying down and turning sick on you and wailing and hollering and raring and pitching. It wouldn't be a way in the world to get them over there."

"They got over here," the trashy woman said. "Get back like they got over."

"It wasn't so many of them then," Mrs. Turpin explained.

The woman looked at Mrs. Turpin as if here was an idiot indeed but Mrs. Turpin was not bothered by the look, considering where it came from.

"Nooo," she said, "they're going to stay here where they can go to New York and marry white folks and improve their color. That's what they all want to do, every one of them, improve their color."

"You know what comes of that, don't you?" Claud asked.

"No, Claud, what?" Mrs. Turpin said.

Claud's eyes twinkled. "White-faced niggers," he said with never a smile.

Everybody in the office laughed except the white-trash and the ugly girl. The girl gripped the book in her lap with white fingers. The trashy woman looked around her from face to face as if she thought they were all idiots. The old woman in the feed sack dress continued to gaze expressionless across the floor at the high-top shoes of the man opposite her, the one who had been pretending to be asleep when the Turpins came in. He was laughing heartily, his hands still spread out on his knees. The child had fallen to the side and was lying now almost face down in the old woman's lap.

While they recovered from their laughter, the nasal chorus on the radio kept the room from silence.

> *You go to blank blank*
> *And I'll go to mine*
> *But we'll all blank along*
> *To-geth-ther,*
> *And all along the blank*
> *We'll hep eachother out*
> *Smile-ling in any kind of*
> *Weath-ther!*

Mrs. Turpin didn't catch every word but she caught enough to agree with the spirit of the song and it turned her thoughts sober. To help anybody out that needed it was her philosophy of life. She never spared herself when she found somebody in need, whether they were white or black, trash or decent. And of all she had to be thankful for, she was most thankful that this was so. If Jesus had said, "You can be high society and have all the money you want and be thin and svelte-like, but you can't be a good woman with it," she would have had to say, "Well don't make me that then. Make me a good woman and it don't matter what else, how fat or how ugly or how poor!" Her heart rose. He had not made her a nigger or white-trash or ugly! He had made her herself and given her a little of everything. Jesus, thank you! she said. Thank you thank you thank you! Whenever she counted her blessings she felt as buoyant as if she weighed one hundred and twenty-five pounds instead of one hundred and eighty.

"What's wrong with your little boy?" the pleasant lady asked the white-trashy woman. 74

"He has an ulcer," the woman said proudly. "He ain't give me a minute's peace since he was born. Him and her are just alike," she said, nodding at the old woman, who was running her leathery fingers through the child's pale hair. "Look like I can't get nothing down them two but Co' Cola and candy." 75

That's all you try to get down em, Mrs. Turpin said to herself. Too lazy to light the fire. There was nothing you could tell her about people like them that she didn't know already. And it was not just that they didn't have anything. Because if you gave them everything, in two weeks it would all be broken or filthy or they would have chopped it up for lightwood. She knew all this from her own experience. Help them you must, but help them you couldn't. 76

All at once the ugly girl turned her lips inside out again. Her eyes were fixed like two drills on Mrs. Turpin. This time there was no mistaking that there was something urgent behind them. 77

Girl, Mrs. Turpin exclaimed silently, I haven't done a thing to you! The girl might be confusing her with somebody else. There was no need to sit by and let herself be intimidated. "You must be in college," she said boldly, looking directly at the girl. "I see you reading a book there." 78

The girl continued to stare and pointedly did not answer. 79

Her mother blushed at this rudeness. "The lady asked you a question, Mary Grace," she said under her breath. 80

"I have ears," Mary Grace said. 81

The poor mother blushed again. "Mary Grace goes to Wellesley College," she explained. She twisted one of the buttons on her dress. 82

"In Massachusetts," she added with a grimace. "And in the summer she just keeps right on studying. Just reads all the time, a real book worm. She's done real well at Wellesley; she's taking English and Math and History and Psychology and Social Studies," she rattled on, "and I think it's too much. I think she ought to get out and have fun."

The girl looked as if she would like to hurl them all through the plate glass window.   83

"Way up north," Mrs. Turpin murmured and thought, well, it hasn't done much for her manners.   84

"I'd almost rather to have him sick," the white-trash woman said, wrenching the attention back to herself. "He's so mean when he ain't. Look like some children just take natural to meanness. It's some gets bad when they get sick but he was the opposite. Took sick and turned good. He don't give me no trouble now. It's me waitin to see the doctor," she said.   85

If I was going to send anybody back to Africa, Mrs. Turpin thought, it would be your kind, woman. "Yes, indeed," she said aloud, but looking up at the ceiling, "it's a heap of things worse than a nigger." And dirtier than a hog, she added to herself.   86

"I think people with bad dispositions are more to be pitied than anyone on earth," the pleasant lady said in a voice that was decidedly thin.   87

"I thank the Lord he has blessed me with a good one," Mrs. Turpin said. "The day has never dawned that I couldn't find something to laugh at."   88

"Not since she married me anyways," Claud said with a comical straight face.   89

Everybody laughed except the girl and the white-trash.   90

Mrs. Turpin's stomach shook. "He's such a caution," she said, "that I can't help but laugh at him."   91

The girl made a loud ugly noise through her teeth.   92

Her mother's mouth grew thin and tight. "I think the worst thing in the world," she said, "is an ungrateful person. To have everything and not appreciate it. I know a girl," she said, "who has parents who would give her anything, a little brother who loves her dearly, who is getting a good education, who wears the best clothes, but who can never say a kind word to anyone, who never smiles, who just criticizes and complains all day long."   93

"Is she too old to paddle?" Claud asked.   94

The girl's face was almost purple.   95

"Yes," the lady said, "I'm afraid there's nothing to do but leave her to her folly. Some day she'll wake up and it'll be too late."   96

"It never hurt anyone to smile," Mrs. Turpin said. "It just makes you feel better all over." 97

"Of course," the lady said sadly, "but there are just some people you can't tell anything to. They can't take criticism." 98

"If it's one thing I am," Mrs. Turpin said with feeling, "it's grateful. When I think who all I could have been besides myself and what all I got, a little of everything, and a good disposition besides, I just feel like shouting, 'Thank you, Jesus, for making everything the way it is!' It could have been different!" For one thing, somebody else could have got Claud. At the thought of this, she was flooded with gratitude and a terrible pang of joy ran through her. "Oh thank you, Jesus, Jesus, thank you!" she cried aloud. 99

The book struck her directly over her left eye. It struck almost at the same instant that she realized the girl was about to hurl it. Before she could utter a sound, the raw face came crashing across the table toward her, howling. The girl's fingers sank like clamps into the soft flesh of her neck. She heard the mother cry out and Claud shout, "Whoa!" There was an instant when she was certain that she was about to be in an earthquake. 100

All at once her vision narrowed and she saw everything as if it were happening in a small room far away, or as if she were looking at it through the wrong end of a telescope. Claud's face crumpled and fell out of sight. The nurse ran in, then out, then in again. Then the gangling figure of the doctor rushed out of the inner door. Magazines flew this way and that as the table turned over. The girl fell with a thud and Mrs. Turpin's vision suddenly reversed itself and she saw everything large instead of small. The eyes of the white-trashy woman were staring hugely at the floor. There the girl, held down on one side by the nurse and on the other by her mother, was wrenching and turning in their grasp. The doctor was kneeling astride her, trying to hold her arm down. He managed after a second to sink a long needle into it. 101

Mrs. Turpin felt entirely hollow except for her heart which swung from side to side as if it were agitated in a great empty drum of flesh. 102

"Somebody that's not busy call for the ambulance," the doctor said in the off-hand voice young doctors adopt for terrible occasions. 103

Mrs. Turpin could not have moved a finger. The old man who had been sitting next to her skipped nimbly into the office and made the call, for the secretary still seemed to be gone. 104

"Claud!" Mrs. Turpin called. 105

He was not in his chair. She knew she must jump up and find him but she felt like some one trying to catch a train in a dream, when everything moves in slow motion and the faster you try to run the slower you go. 106

"Here I am," a suffocated voice, very unlike Claud's, said. 107

He was doubled up in the corner on the floor, pale as paper, 108
holding his leg. She wanted to get up and go to him but she could not
move. Instead, her gaze was drawn slowly downward to the churn-
ing face on the floor, which she could see over the doctor's shoulder.

The girl's eyes stopped rolling and focused on her. They seemed a 109
much lighter blue than before, as if a door that had been tightly
closed behind them was now open to admit light and air.

Mrs. Turpin's head cleared and her power of motion returned. She 110
leaned forward until she was looking directly into the fierce brilliant
eyes. There was no doubt in her mind that the girl did know her,
knew her in some intense and personal way, beyond time and place
and condition. "What you got to say to me?" she asked hoarsely and
held her breath, waiting, as for a revelation.

The girl raised her head. Her gaze locked with Mrs. Turpin's. "Go 111
back to hell where you came from, you old wart hog," she whispered.
Her voice was low but clear. Her eyes burned for a moment as if she
saw with pleasure that her message had struck its target.

Mrs. Turpin sank back in her chair. 112

After a moment the girl's eyes closed and she turned her head 113
wearily to the side.

The doctor rose and handed the nurse the empty syringe. He 114
leaned over and put both hands for a moment on the mother's
shoulders, which were shaking. She was sitting on the floor, her lips
pressed together, holding Mary Grace's hand in her lap. The girl's
fingers were gripped like a baby's around her thumb. "Go on to the
hospital," he said. "I'll call and make the arrangements."

"Now let's see that neck," he said in a jovial voice to Mrs. Turpin. 115
He began to inspect her neck with his two fingers. Two little moon-
shaped lines like pink fish bones were indented over her windpipe.
There was the beginning of an angry red swelling above her eye. His
fingers passed over this also.

"Let me be," she said thickly and shook him off. "See about Claud. 116
She kicked him."

"I'll see about him in a minute," he said and felt her pulse. He was 117
a thin grey-haired man, given to pleasantries. "Go home and have
yourself a vacation the rest of the day," he said and patted her on the
shoulder.

Quit your pattin me, Mrs. Turpin growled to herself. 118

"And put an ice pack over that eye," he said. Then he went and 119
squatted down beside Claud and looked at his leg. After a moment
he pulled him up and Claud limped after him into the office.

Until the ambulance came, the only sounds in the room were the 120
tremulous moans of the girl's mother, who continued to sit on the

floor. The white-trash woman did not take her eyes off the girl. Mrs. Turpin looked straight ahead at nothing. Presently the ambulance drew up, a long dark shadow, behind the curtain. The attendants came in and set the stretcher down beside the girl and lifted her expertly onto it and carried her out. The nurse helped the mother gather up her things. The shadow of the ambulance moved silently away and the nurse came back in the office.

"That ther girl is going to be a lunatic, ain't she?" the white-trash 121
woman asked the nurse, but the nurse kept on to the back and never answered her.

"Yes, she's going to be a lunatic," the white-trash woman said to 122
the rest of them.

"Po' critter," the old woman murmured. The child's face was still in 123
her lap. His eyes looked idly out over her knees. He had not moved during the disturbance except to draw one leg up under him.

"I thank Gawd," the white-trash woman said fervently, "I ain't a 124
lunatic."

Claud came limping out and the Turpins went home. 125

As their pick-up truck turned into their own dirt road and made 126
the crest of the hill, Mrs. Turpin gripped the window ledge and looked out suspiciously. The land sloped gracefully down through a field dotted with lavender weeds and at the start of the rise their small yellow frame house, with its little flower beds spread out around it like a fancy apron, sat primly in its accustomed place between two giant hickory trees. She would not have been startled to see a burnt wound between two blackened chimneys.

Neither of them felt like eating so they put on their house clothes 127
and lowered the shade in the bedroom and lay down, Claud with his leg on a pillow and herself with a damp washcloth over her eye. The instant she was flat on her back, the image of a razor-backed hog with warts on its face and horns coming out behind its ears snorted into her head. She moaned, a low quiet moan.

"I am not," she said tearfully, "a wart hog. From hell." But the 128
denial had no force. The girl's eyes and her words, even the tone of her voice, low but clear, directed only to her, brooked no repudiation. She had been singled out for the message, though there was trash in the room to whom it might justly have been applied. The full force of this fact struck her only now. There was a woman there who was neglecting her own child but she had been overlooked. The message had been given to Ruby Turpin, a respectable, hard-working, churchgoing woman. The tears dried. Her eyes began to burn instead with wrath.

She rose on her elbow and the washcloth fell into her hand. Claud 129 was lying on his back, snoring. She wanted to tell him what the girl had said. At the same time, she did not wish to put the image of herself as a wart hog from hell into his mind.

"Hey, Claud," she muttered and pushed his shoulder. 130

Claud opened one pale baby blue eye. 131

She looked into it warily. He did not think about anything. He just went his way. 132

"Wha, whasit?" he said and closed the eye again. 133

"Nothing," she said. "Does your leg pain you?" 134

"Hurts like hell," Claud said. 135

"It'll quit terreckly," she said and lay back down. In a moment Claud was snoring again. For the rest of the afternoon they lay there. Claud slept. She scowled at the ceiling. Occasionally she raised her fist and made a small stabbing motion over her chest as if she was defending her innocence to invisible guests who were like the comforters of Job, reasonable-seeming but wrong. 136

About five-thirty Claud stirred. "Got to go after those niggers," he sighed, not moving. 137

She was looking straight up as if there were unintelligible handwriting on the ceiling. The protuberance over her eye had turned a greenish-blue. "Listen here," she said. 138

"What?" 139

"Kiss me." 140

Claud leaned over and kissed her loudly on the mouth. He pinched her side and their hands interlocked. Her expression of ferocious concentration did not change. Claud got up, groaning and growling, and limped off. She continued to study the ceiling. 141

She did not get up until she heard the pick-up truck coming back with the Negroes. Then she rose and thrust her feet in her brown oxfords, which she did not bother to lace, and stumped out onto the back porch and got her red plastic bucket. She emptied a tray of ice cubes into it and filled it half full of water and went out into the back yard. Every afternoon after Claud brought the hands in, one of the boys helped him put out hay and the rest waited in the back of the truck until he was ready to take them home. The truck was parked in the shade under one of the hickory trees. 142

"Hi yawl this evening?" Mrs. Turpin asked grimly, appearing with the bucket and the dipper. There were three women and a boy in the truck. 143

"Us doin nicely," the oldest woman said. "Hi you doin?" and her gaze struck immediately on the dark lump on Mrs. Turpin's forehead. "You done fell down, ain't you?" she asked in a solicitous voice. The old woman was dark and almost toothless. She had on an old 144 felt hat of Claud's set back on her head. The other two women were younger and lighter and they both had new bright green sun hats. One of them had hers on her head; the other had taken hers off and the boy was grinning beneath it.

Mrs. Turpin set the bucket down on the floor of the truck. "Yawl hep yourselves," she said. She looked around to make sure Claud had gone. "No. I didn't fall down," she said, folding her arms. "It was something worse than that." 145

"Ain't nothing bad happen to you!" the old woman said. She said it as if they all knew that Mrs. Turpin was protected in some special way by Divine Providence. "You just had you a little fall." 146

"We were in town at the doctor's office for where the cow kicked Mr. Turpin," Mrs. Turpin said in a flat tone that indicated they could leave off their foolishness. "And there was this girl there. A big fat girl with her face all broke out. I could look at that girl and tell she was peculiar but I couldn't tell how. And me and her mama were just talking and going along and all of a sudden WHAM! She throws this big book she was reading at me and . . ." 147

"Naw!" the old woman cried out. 148

"And then she jumps over the table and commences to choke me." 149

"Naw!" they all exclaimed, "naw!" 150

"Hi come she do that?" the old woman asked. "What ail her?" 151

Mrs. Turpin only glared in front of her. 152

"Somethin ail her," the old woman said. 153

"They carried her off in an ambulance," Mrs. Turpin continued, "but before she went she was rolling on the floor and they were trying to hold her down to give her a shot and she said something to me." She paused. "You know what she said to me?" 154

"What she say?" they asked. 155

"She said," Mrs. Turpin began, and stopped, her face very dark and heavy. The sun was getting whiter and whiter, blanching the sky overhead so that the leaves of the hickory tree were black in the face of it. She could not bring forth the words. "Something real ugly," she muttered. 156

"She sho shouldn't said nothin ugly to you," the old woman said. "You so sweet. You the sweetest lady I know." 157

"She pretty too," the one with the hat on said. 158

"And stout," the other one said. "I never knowed no sweeter white lady." 159

"That's the truth befo' Jesus," the old woman said. "Amen! You jes as sweet and pretty as you can be." 160

Mrs. Turpin knew just exactly how much Negro flattery was worth and it added to her rage. "She said," she began again and finished 161 this time with a fierce rush of breath, "that I was an old wart hog from hell."

There was an astounded silence. 162

"Where she at?" the youngest woman cried in a piercing voice. 163

"Lemme see her. I'll kill her!" 164

"I'll kill her with you!" the other one cried. 165

"She b'long in the sylum," the old woman said emphatically. "You the sweetest white lady I know." 166

"She pretty too," the other two said. "Stout as she can be and sweet. Jesus satisfied with her!" 167

"Deed he is," the old woman declared. 168

Idiots! Mrs. Turpin growled to herself. You could never say anything intelligent to a nigger. You could talk at them but not with them. "Yawl ain't drunk your water," she said shortly. "Leave the bucket in the truck when you're finished with it. I got more to do than just stand around and pass the time of day," and she moved off and into the house. 169

She stood for a moment in the middle of the kitchen. The dark protuberance over her eye looked like a miniature tornado cloud which might any moment sweep across the horizon of her brow. Her lower lip protruded dangerously. She squared her massive shoulders. Then she marched into the front of the house and out the side door and started down the road to the pig parlor. She had the look of a woman going single-handed, weaponless, into battle. 170

The sun was a deep yellow now like a harvest moon and was rising westward very fast over the far tree line as if it meant to reach the hogs before she did. The road was rutted and she kicked several good-sized stones out of her path as she strode along. The pig parlor was on a little knoll at the end of a lane that ran off from the side of the barn. It was a square of concrete as large as a small room, with a board fence about four feet high around it. The concrete floor sloped slightly so that the hog wash could drain off into a trench where it was carried to the field for fertilizer. Claud was standing on the outside, on the edge of the concrete, hanging onto the top board, hosing down the floor inside. The hose was connected to the faucet of a water trough nearby. 171

Mrs. Turpin climbed up beside him and glowered down at the hogs inside. There were seven long-snouted bristly shoats in it—tan with liver-colored spots—and an old sow a few weeks off from farrowing. She was lying on her side grunting. The shoats were running about shaking themselves like idiot children, their little slit pig eyes searching the floor for anything left. She had read that pigs were the most intelligent animal. She doubted it. They were supposed to be 172 smarter than dogs. There had even been a pig astronaut. He had performed his assignment perfectly but died of a heart attack afterwards because they left him in his electric suit, sitting upright throughout his examination when naturally a hog should be on all fours.

A-gruntin and a-rootin and a-groanin. 173

"Gimme that hose," she said, yanking it away from Claud. "Go on 174 and carry them niggers home and then get off that leg."

"You look like you might have swallowed a mad dog," Claud 175 observed, but he got down and limped off. He paid no attention to her humors.

Until he was out of earshot, Mrs. Turpin stood on the side of the 176 pen, holding the hose and pointing the stream of water at the hind quarters of any shoat that looked as if it might try to lie down. When he had had time to get over the hill, she turned her head slightly and her wrathful eyes scanned the path. He was nowhere in sight. She turned back again and seemed to gather herself up. Her shoulders rose and she drew in her breath.

"What do you send me a message like that for?" she said in a low 177 fierce voice, barely above a whisper but with the force of a shout in its concentrated fury. "How am I a hog and me both? How am I saved and from hell too?" Her free fist was knotted and with the other she gripped the hose, blindly pointing the stream of water in and out of the eye of the old sow whose outraged squeal she did not hear.

The pig parlor commanded a view of the back pasture where their 178 twenty beef cows were gathered around the hay-bales Claud and the boy had put out. The freshly cut pasture sloped down to the highway. Across it was their cotton field and beyond that a dark green dusty wood which they owned as well. The sun was behind the wood, very red, looking over the paling of trees like a farmer inspecting his own hogs.

"Why me?" she rumbled. "It's no trash around here, black or 179 white, that I haven't given to. And break my back to the bone every day working. And do for the church."

She appeared to be the right size woman to command the arena 180 before her. "How am I a hog?" she demanded. "Exactly how am I like them?" and she jabbed the stream of water at the shoats. "There was plenty of trash there. It didn't have to be me."

"If you like trash better, go get yourself some trash then," she 181 railed. "You could have made me trash. Or a nigger. If trash is what you wanted why didn't you make me trash?" She shook her fist with the hose in it and a watery snake appeared momentarily in the air. "I could quit working and take it easy and be filthy," she growled.

"Lounge about the sidewalks all day drinking root beer. Dip snuff and spit in every puddle and have it all over my face. I could be nasty.

"Or you could have made me a nigger. It's too late for me to be a   182
nigger," she said with deep sarcasm, "but I could act like one. Lay down in the middle of the road and stop traffic. Roll on the ground."

In the deepening light everything was taking on a mysterious hue.   183
The pasture was growing a peculiar grassy green and the streak of highway had turned lavender. She braced herself for a final assault and this time her voice rolled out over the pasture. "Go on," she yelled, "call me a hog! Call me a hog again. From hell. Call me a wart hog from hell. Put that bottom rail on top. There'll still be a top and bottom!"

A garbled echo returned to her.   184

A final surge of fury shook her and she roared, "Who do you think   185
you are?"

The color of everything, field and crimson sky, burned for a mo-   186
ment with a transparent intensity. The question carried over the pasture and across the highway and the cotton field and returned to her clearly like an answer from beyond the wood.

She opened her mouth but no sound came out of it.   187

A tiny truck, Claud's, appeared on the highway, heading rapidly   188
out of sight. Its gears scraped thinly. It looked like a child's toy. At any moment a bigger truck might smash into it and scatter Claud's and the niggers' brains all over the road.

Mrs. Turpin stood there, her gaze fixed on the highway, all her   189
muscles rigid, until in five or six minutes the truck reappeared, re-turning. She waited until it had had time to turn into their own road. Then like a monumental statue coming to life, she bent her head slowly and gazed, as if through the very heart of mystery, down into the pig parlor at the hogs. They had settled all in one corner around the old sow who was grunting softly. A red glow suffused them. They appeared to pant with a secret life.

Until the sun slipped finally behind the tree line, Mrs. Turpin   190
remained there with her gaze bent to them as if she were absorbing some abysmal life-giving knowledge. At last she lifted her head. There was only a purple streak in the sky, cutting through a field of crimson and leading, like an extension of the highway, into the de-scending dusk. She raised her hands from the side of the pen in a gesture hieratic and profound. A visionary light settled in her eyes. She saw the streak as a vast swinging bridge extending upward from the earth through a field of living fire. Upon it a vast horde of souls were rumbling toward heaven. There were whole companies of white-trash, clean for the first time in their lives, and bands of black

niggers in white robes, and battalions of freaks and lunatics shouting and clapping and leaping like frogs. And bringing up the end of the procession was a tribe of people whom she recognized at once as those who, like herself and Claud, had always had a little of everything and the God-given wit to use it right. She leaned forward to observe them closer. They were marching behind the others with great dignity, accountable as they had always been for good order and common sense and respectable behavior. They alone were on key. Yet she could see by their shocked and altered faces that even their virtues were being burned away. She lowered her hands and gripped the rail of the hog pen, her eyes small but fixed unblinkingly on what lay ahead. In a moment the vision faded but she remained where she was, immobile.

At length she got down and turned off the faucet and made her slow way on the darkening path to the house. In the woods around her the invisible cricket choruses had struck up, but what she heard were the voices of the souls climbing upward into the starry field and shouting hallelujah.

191

THINKING ABOUT LITERATURE

1. What is Mrs. Turpin's revelation? What causes it? What, if anything, does it teach her about herself?

2. On what basis does Mrs. Turpin classify people? What categories does she identify? How do hogs fit into her system of classification?

3. How would you classify Mrs. Turpin, the "white-trash woman," and the "pleasant lady" in terms of their attitudes toward blacks? Whose attitudes do you find most—and least—offensive?

JOURNAL ENTRY

What dangers do you see in classification systems like Mrs. Turpin's? Who—or what—is most at risk?

THEMATIC CONNECTIONS

- "'What's in a Name?'" (p. 5)
- "The Same Difference" (p. 203)
- "Just Walk On By" (p. 209)

WRITING ASSIGNMENTS FOR CLASSIFICATION AND DIVISION

1. Choose a film you have seen recently and list all the different elements that you consider significant—plot, direction, acting, special effects, and so on. Then further subdivide each category (for instance, listing each of the special effects). Using this chart as an organizational guide, evaluate the film.

2. Write an essay in which you classify the teachers you have had into several distinct categories and make a judgment about the relative effectiveness of the teachers in each group. Give each category a name, and make certain your essay has a thesis statement.

3. What styles of dress do you observe on your college campus? Establish four or five distinct categories, and write an essay in which you classify students on the basis of how they dress. Give each group a descriptive title.

4. Do some research to help you identify the subclasses of a large class of animals or plants. Write an essay in which you enumerate and describe the subclasses in each class for an audience of elementary school students.

5. Violence in sports is considered by many to be a serious problem. Write an essay in which you express your views on this problem. Use a classification-and-division structure, categorizing information according to sources of violence (the players, the nature of the game, the fans, etc.).

6. Classify television shows according to type (action, drama, etc.), audience (preschoolers, school-age children, adults, etc.), or any other logical principle. Write an essay based on your system of classification, making sure to include a thesis statement. For instance, you might assert that the relative popularity of one kind of program over others reveals something about television watchers, or that one kind of program shows signs of becoming obsolete.

7. Write a lighthearted essay discussing kinds of snack foods, cartoons, pets, status symbols, toys, shoppers, parties, vacations, weight-loss diets, hair styles, or drivers.

8. Write an essay in which you assess the relative merits of several different politicians, news broadcasts, or academic majors.

9. What kinds of survival skills does a student need to get through college successfully? Write a classification-and-division essay in which you identify and discuss several kinds of skills, indicating why each category is important.

10. After attending a party, lecture, or concert, write an essay in which you divide the people you observe there into categories according to some logical principle and then classify several individuals into each category. Include a thesis statement that points out how diverse the group is.

COLLABORATIVE ACTIVITY FOR CLASSIFICATION AND DIVISION

Working in groups, devise a classification system that encompasses all the different kinds of popular music favored by the members of your group. You may begin with general categories like country, pop, and rhythm and blues, but you should also be sure to fit more specific categories, such as heavy metal and rap, into your classification system. When you have decided on categories and subcategories that represent the tastes of all members of your group, fill in examples for each category. Then discuss how, if you were going to write an essay about popular music, you would decide in what order to arrange your categories.

9

Definition

WHAT IS DEFINITION?

A **definition** tells what a term means and how it is different from other terms in its class. In the following paragraph from *The Medical Detectives,* Berton Roueché defines *mass hysteria.*

The word "hysteria" derives from the Greek *hystera,* meaning "uterus." This curious name reflects Hippocrates' notion of the point of origin of the disturbance. "For hysterical maidens," he wrote, "I prescribe marriage, for they are cured by pregnancy." His view prevailed in medicine until well into the nineteenth century, and is perhaps still prevalent in the lingering lay association of women and hysteria. The term "mass hysteria" is also a lay survival. **[Topic sentence]** The phenomenon is now preferably known to science as "collective obsessional behavior." Collective obsessions occur throughout the animal world (the cattle stampede, the flocking of starlings on the courthouse roof), and the human animal, despite—or maybe because of—its more finely tuned mentality, seems exquisitely susceptible to them. **[Extended definition defines term by means of its origin and by exemplification, comparison and contrast, and negation.]** Manifestations among the human race take many forms. These range in social seriousness from the transient tyranny of the fad (skate-boards, Farrah Fawcett-Majors, jogging, Perrier with a twist) and the eager lock-step of fashion (blue jeans, hoopskirts, stomping boots, white kid gloves, the beard, the wig) to the delirium of the My Lai massacre and the frenzy of the race riot and the witch hunt. Epidemic obsessional behavior differs from its companion compulsions in one prominent respect. It is not, as Alan C. Kerckhoff and Kurt W. Back, both of Duke University, have noted in "The June Bug: A Study of Hysterical Contagion" (1968), "an active response to some element in the situation; it is a passive experience. The

487

actors do not *do* something so much as something happens to them."

Any time you take an examination, you are likely to encounter questions that require definitions. You might, for example, be asked to define *behaviorism;* tell what a *cell* is; explain the meaning of the literary term *naturalism;* include a clear, comprehensive definition of *mitosis* in your answer; or define *authority*. Such exam questions cannot always be answered in one or two sentences. In fact, the definitions they call for often require several paragraphs.

Most people think of definition in terms of dictionaries, which give brief, succinct explanations of what words mean. But *definition* has much wider application. It also includes explaining what something, or even someone, *is*—that is, its essential nature. Sometimes a definition can be given in a sentence. At other times it requires a paragraph, an essay, or even a whole book. These longer, more complex definitions are called *extended definitions*.

Extended definitions are useful for many academic assignments besides exams. A thoughtful definition can clarify precise terms as well as more general concepts central to any academic discipline. Definitions can explain abstractions like *freedom* or controversial terms like *right to life* or slang terms whose meanings may vary from locale to locale or change as time passes. In a given writing situation, a definition can be essential because a term has more than one meaning, because you are using it in an uncommon way, or because you suspect the term is unfamiliar to your readers.

Many extended-definition essays include shorter definitions like those in the dictionary. Moreover, essays with other dominant patterns of development often incorporate brief definitions of terms to clarify points or establish basic information that equips the reader to understand the rest of the discussion. Whether it appears in another kind of essay or acts as a center for an extended definition, the brief formal (or dictionary) definition establishes the basic meaning of a term.

Formal (Dictionary) Definitions

Thumb through any dictionary, and you will see pages of words followed by definitions. These definitions all have a standard three-part structure: They present first the *term* to be defined, then the general *class* it is a part of, and finally the *qualities that differentiate it* from the other terms in the same class.

Term	*Class*	*Differentiation*
Behaviorism	is a theory	that regards the objective facts of a subject's actions as the only valid basis for psychological study.
A cell	is a unit of protoplasm	with a nucleus, cytoplasm, and an enclosing membrane.
Naturalism	is a literary movement	whose original adherents believed that writers should treat life with scientific objectivity.
Mitosis	is the process	of nuclear division of cells, consisting of prophase, metaphase, anaphase, and telophase.
Authority	is the power	to command and require obedience.

Supplying a dictionary definition of each term you use is seldom necessary or desirable. Readers generally will either know what a word means or be able to look it up easily. Sometimes, however, defining your terms is essential—for example, when a word has several meanings, each of which might fit your context, or when you want to use a word in a special way. Frequently a brief formal definition will be used in a longer definition essay to introduce the extended definition or even to help establish the essay's thesis. Remember, formal definitions include the term, its class, and its distinguishing qualities—the three components that pinpoint what something is and what it is not.

Extended (Essay-Length) Definitions

An extended definition includes the three basic parts of a formal definition—the term, its class, and its distinguishing characteristics. Beyond these essentials, an extended definition does not follow a set pattern. Instead, it uses whatever techniques best suit the term being defined and the writing situation. In fact, you can use any of the essay patterns illustrated in this book to structure a definition essay. As you plan your essay, jotting down your ideas about the term or subject, you will see which pattern emerges as most useful. The formal definitions of the five terms discussed above, for example, could be extended using five different patterns of development.

Exemplification. To explain what *behaviorism* is, you could give examples. Carefully chosen cases exemplifying behaviorist assumptions and methods could show how this theory of psychology applies in different situations. These examples could help your reader see exactly how behaviorism works and what it can and cannot account for. Often, examples can be the clearest way to explain something unusual, especially when it is unfamiliar to your readers. Defining dreams as "the symbolic representation of mental states" might convey little to readers who did not know much about psychology. But a few examples could help you make your point. Many students have dreams about taking exams—perhaps dreaming that they are late for the test, that they remember nothing about the course, or that they are writing their answers in disappearing ink. You might explain the nature of dreams by interpreting these particular dreams, which may reflect anxiety about a particular course or about school in general.

Description.   You can explain the nature of something by describing it. For example, the concept of a *cell* is difficult to grasp from just the formal definition alone, but your readers would understand the concept more clearly if you were to explain what the cell looks like, possibly with the aid of a diagram or two. Concentrating on the cell membrane, cytoplasm, and nucleus, you could detail each structure's appearance and function. These descriptions would enable readers to visualize the whole cell and understand its workings. Of course, there is more to description than the visual: A definition of Italian cooking might describe the taste and smell, as well as the appearance, of ravioli, and a definition of a disease might include a description of how its symptoms feel to a patient.

Comparison and Contrast.   An extended definition of *naturalism* could employ a comparison-and-contrast structure. Naturalism is one of several major movements in American literature, and its literary aims could be contrasted with those of other literary movements, such as romanticism or realism. Or you could compare and contrast the plots and characters of several naturalistic works with those of romantic or realistic works. When defining something unfamiliar, you can compare it to something familiar to your readers. For example, your readers may never have heard of the Chinese dish called sweet and sour cabbage, but you can help them understand it by saying that it tastes something like cole slaw. You may also define a thing by contrasting it with something very much unlike it, especially if the two have some qualities in common. One way to explain the British sport of rugby is by contrasting it with American football, which is not as violent.

Process.   An extended definition of *mitosis* should be organized as a process analysis because mitosis is a process. You could explain the stages of mitosis, making sure that you point out the transitions from one phase to another. By tracing the process from stage to stage for your readers, you could be certain that this type of cell division is clearly defined. Similarly, some objects must be defined in terms of what they do. A computer is a machine that carries out certain processes, and so an extended definition of a computer would probably include a process analysis.

Classification.   Finally, you could define *authority* using classification and division. Basing your extended definition on the model developed by the German sociologist Max Weber, you could divide the class *authority* into the subclasses traditional authority, charismatic authority, and legal-bureaucratic authority. Then, by explaining how each type of authority is made to seem legitimate or justifiable, you could clarify this very broad term for your reader. In both extended and formal definitions, classification can be very useful. By saying what class an object belongs to, you are explaining what kind of thing it is. For instance, *monetarism* is an economic theory; *The Adventures of Huckleberry Finn* is a novel; *emphysema* is a disease. And by dividing that class into subclasses, you can be more specific. Emphysema is not merely a disease, it is a disease of the lungs, which classifies it with tuberculosis but not with appendicitis.

Each of these patterns of development helps define by emphasizing one or more central, essential characteristics of the subject. Other options are also available. Cause and effect or narration can be used to structure definition papers, as can any combination of patterns. In addition, a few techniques are unique to definition:

- You can define a term by using *synonyms* (using words with similar meanings).
- You can define a term by using *negation* (telling what it is *not*).
- You can define a term by using *enumeration* (listing its characteristics).
- You can define a term by discussing its *origin and development* (examining the word's derivation, original meaning, and usages).

Although your definitions and definition essays may take many forms, you should be certain that they are clear and that they actually define. You should be sure you provide a true definition, not just a descriptive statement such as "Happiness is a four-day weekend." Likewise, repetition is not definition, so do not include the term you are defining in your definition. For instance, the statement "abstract art is a school of artists whose works are abstract" clarifies nothing for your readers. Finally, define as precisely as possible. Name the class of the term you are defining—state, for example, "mitosis is *a process in which* a cell divides" rather than "mitosis is *when* a cell divides"—and be sure to define this class as narrowly and as accurately as you can. Be specific when you differentiate your term from other members of its class. Careful attention to the language and structure of your definition will ensure that your meaning will be clear to your reader.

STRUCTURING A DEFINITION ESSAY

A definition essay should have an *introduction,* a *body,* and a *conclusion.* Although a dictionary definition strives for objectivity, an extended definition may not. Instead, it may define a term in a special light determined by your attitude toward the subject or your reason for defining it. For example, your extended-definition paper about literary naturalism could argue that the significance of this movement's major works has been underestimated by literary scholars, and your definition of *authority* could criticize its abuses. In such cases the thesis provides a center for a definition essay and makes it more than just a catalog of facts.

Suppose that you are assigned a short paper in your introductory psychology course. You decide to examine *behaviorism.* First, you have to recognize that your topic entails a definition. If the topic can be summed up in a form such as "The true nature of A is B" or "A means B," then it is a definition. Of course, you can define *behaviorism* as a *word* in one sentence, or possibly two. But to explain the *concept* of behaviorism and its position in the history and current knowledge of psychology, you must go beyond the dictionary.

Second, you have to decide what kinds of explanation are most suitable for your topic and for your intended audience. If you are trying to define *behaviorism* for readers who know very little about psychology, you might use comparisons that relate behaviorism to your readers' experiences, such as how they were brought up by their parents or how they trained their pets. You might use examples, but the examples would relate not to psychological experiments or clinical treatment but to experiences in everyday life. If, on the other hand, you direct your paper to your psychology instructor, who obviously already knows what behaviorism is, your purpose is to show that you know too. One way to show that you understand a theory is to compare it with other theories that attempt to explain human behavior. Another is to give examples of how it works in practice. You might also give some of the background and history of the theory. (In a term paper you might even use all of these strategies.) After considering your paper's scope and audience, you might decide that because behaviorism is still somewhat controversial, your best strategy is to supplement a formal definition with examples showing how behaviorist assumptions and methods are applied in specific situations. These examples, drawn from your class notes and your textbook, will support your thesis that behaviorism is a valid approach for treating certain psychological dysfunctions. In combination, your examples will define *behaviorism* as it is understood today.

An informal outline for your essay might look like this:

Introduction	Thesis statement—Contrary to its critics' assertions, behaviorism is a valid approach for treating a wide variety of psychological dysfunctions.
Background:	Definition of behaviorism, including its origins and evolution
First example:	The use of behaviorism to help psychotics function in an institutional setting
Second example:	The use of behaviorism to treat neurotic behavior, such as chronic anxiety, a phobia, or a pattern of destructive acts
Third example:	The use of behaviorism to treat normal but antisocial or undesirable behavior, such as heavy smoking or overeating
Conclusion:	Restatement of thesis; summary of key points

Notice how the three examples in this paper define behaviorism with the complexity, detail, and breadth that a formal definition could not duplicate. It is more like a textbook explanation—and, in fact, textbook explanations are often written as extended definitions.

A STUDENT WRITER: DEFINITION

The following student essay, written by Ajoy Mahtab for a composition course, defines the untouchables, a caste whose members are shunned in India. In his essay Ajoy, who grew up in Calcutta, presents a thesis that is sharply critical of the practice of ostracizing untouchables.

THE UNTOUCHABLE

Introduction:
Background

A word that is extremely common in India yet   1
uncommon to the point of incomprehension in the West is
the word <u>untouchable</u>. It is a word that has had extremely
sinister connotations throughout India's history. A
rigorously worked-out caste system existed in traditional
Indian society. At the top of the social ladder sat the
Brahmins, the clan of the priesthood. These people had
renounced the material world for a spiritual one. Below
them came the Kshatriyas, or the warrior caste. This caste
included the kings and all their nobles along with their
armies. Third on the social ladder were the Vaishyas, who
were the merchants of the land. Trade was their only form
of livelihood. Last came the Shudras--the menials. Shudras
were employed by the prosperous as sweepers and laborers.
Originally a person's caste was determined only by his
profession. Thus, if the son of a merchant joined the army,
he automatically converted from a Vaishya to a Kshatriya.
However, the system soon became hereditary and rigid.
Whatever one's occupation, one's caste was determined
from birth according to the caste of one's father.

Outside of this structure were a group of people, human   2
beings treated worse than dogs and shunned far more than
lepers, people who were not considered even human, people
who defiled with their very touch. These were the

Formal
definition

Achhoots: the untouchables. The word <u>untouchable</u> is
commonly defined as "that which cannot or should not be
touched." In India, however, it was taken to a far greater

History

extreme. The untouchables of a village lived in a separate
community downwind of the borders of the village. They
had a separate water supply, for they would make the village
water impure if they were to drink of it. When they walked

they were made to bang two sticks together continuously so that passersby could avoid an untouchable's shadow. Tied to their waists, trailing behind them, was a broom that would clean the ground they had walked on. The penalty for not following these or any other rules was death for the untouchable and, in many instances, for the entire untouchable community.

Present situation

One of the pioneers of the fight against untouchability 3 was Mahatma Gandhi. Thanks to his efforts and those of many others, untouchability no longer presents anything like the horrific picture painted above. In India today, in fact, recognition of untouchability is punishable by law. Theoretically, there is no such thing as untouchability anymore. But old traditions linger on, and such a deep-rooted fear passed down from generation to generation cannot disappear overnight. Even today, caste is an important factor in most marriages. Most Indian surnames reveal a person's caste immediately, and so it is a difficult thing to hide. The shunning of the untouchable is more prevalent in South India, where the general public is much more devout, than in the North. Some people would rather starve than share food and water with an untouchable. This concept is very difficult to accept in the West, but it is true all the same.

Example

I remember an incident from my childhood. I could not 4 have been more than eight or nine at the time. I was on a holiday staying at my family's house on the river Ganges. There was a festival going on and, as is customary, we were giving the servants small presents. I was handing them out when an old lady, bent with age, slowly hobbled into the room. She stood in the far corner of the room all alone, and no one so much as looked at her. When the entire line ended, she stepped hesitantly forward and stood in front of

me, looking down at the ground. She then held a cloth
stretched out in front of her. I was a little confused about
how I was supposed to hand her her present, since both her
hands were holding the cloth. Then, with the help of
prompting from someone behind me, I found out that I was
supposed to drop the gift into the cloth without touching the
cloth itself. It was only later that I found out that she was an
untouchable. This was the first time I had actually come
face to face with prejudice, and it felt like a slap in the face.
That incident was burned into my memory, and I do not
think I will ever forget it.

Conclusion begins   The word <u>untouchable</u> is not often used in the West,   5
and when it is, it is generally used as a complimentary term.
For example, an avid fan might say of an athlete, "He was
absolutely untouchable. Nobody could even begin to
compare with him." It seems rather ironic that in one
culture a word should be so favorable and in another so
derogatory. Why does a word that gives happiness in one
part of the world cause pain in another? Why does the same
word have different meanings to different people around the
globe? Why do certain words cause rifts and others forge
bonds? I do not think anyone can tell me the answer.

Conclusion continues   No actual parallel can be found in the world today that   6
can compare to the horrors of untouchability. For an
untouchable, life itself was a crime. The day was spent just
Thesis statement   trying to stay alive. From the misery of the untouchables,
the world should learn a lesson: Isolating and punishing any
group of people is dehumanizing and immoral.

Points for Special Attention

Thesis. Ajoy Mahtab's assignment was to write an extended
definition of a term he expected would be unfamiliar to his audience.

Because he had strong feelings about the unjust treatment of the untouchables, Ajoy wanted his essay to have a strong thesis that communicated his disapproval. Still, because he knew his American classmates would need a good deal of background information before they would be willing to accept such a thesis, he decided not to present it in his introduction but rather to lead up to it gradually and state it at the end of his essay.

Structure.   Ajoy's introduction establishes the direction of his essay by introducing the word he will define; he then places this word in context by explaining India's rigid caste system. In paragraph 2 he presents the formal definition of the word *untouchable* and goes on to sketch the term's historical framework. Paragraph 3 explains the status of the untouchables in present-day India, and paragraph 4 gives a vivid example of Ajoy's first encounter with an untouchable. As he begins his conclusion in paragraph 5, Ajoy brings his readers back to the word his essay defines. Here he uses two strategies to add interest: He contrasts one contemporary American usage of *untouchable* with its derogatory meaning in India, and he asks a series of **rhetorical questions.** In paragraph 6 Ajoy uses a summary of his position to lead in to his thesis statement.

Patterns of Development.   This essay uses a number of the strategies commonly encountered in extended definitions: It includes a formal definition, it explains the term's origin, and it explores some of the term's connotations. In addition, the essay uses several familiar patterns of development to develop an extended definition of the word *untouchable.* For instance, paragraph 1 uses *classification and division* to explain India's caste system; paragraphs 2 and 3 use brief *examples* to illustrate the plight of the untouchable; and paragraph 4 presents a *narrative.* Each of these patterns enriches the definition.

Focus on Revision.   To develop his definition further, Ajoy could use comparison and contrast, drawing *analogies* between the unfamiliar and the familiar. To help his readers understand the concept of untouchability, he could compare untouchables to other groups who are shunned—for example, people with AIDS. Although Ajoy states in his conclusion that no parallel exists, an attempt to find common ground between untouchables and other groups could make his essay more meaningful to his readers—and bring home to them an idea that is distinctly foreign. Such a connection could make an especially powerful conclusion.

The readings that follow employ exemplification, description, narration, and other methods of developing extended definitions. As you can see, no one pattern is more appropriate than another for a definition paper. In fact, combining several patterns may most effectively define the significant aspects of your term. Your choice of pattern or patterns should evolve naturally from your knowledge of your material, your purpose, and the needs of your audience.

TORTILLAS

José Antonio Burciaga

José Antonio Burciaga was born in 1940 in El Chuco, Texas, and served in the U.S. Air Force from 1960 to 1964. He graduated from the University of Texas at El Paso in 1968 and attended the Corcoran School of Art and the San Francisco Art Institute. Burciaga has been a resident fellow in the Chicano residences at Stanford University since 1985. He is the founder of Disseños Literarios, a publishing company in California, and he contributes fiction, poetry, and articles to many anthologies as well as to journals and newspapers, including Texas Monthly, Denver Quarterly, Christian Science Monitor, *and the* Los Angeles Times. *Burciaga has published several books of poems, drawings, and essays, including most recently the poetry collection* Undocumented Love *(1992) and the essay collection* Drink Cultura *(1993). He is currently working on another book of essays, titled* Spilling the Beans. *"Tortillas," originally titled "I Remember Masa," was first published in* Weedee Peepo *(1988), a bilingual collection of essays in Spanish and English. In this essay Burciaga discusses the numerous uses and transformations of the tortilla.*

My earliest memory of *tortillas* is my *Mamá* telling me not to play   1
with them. I had bitten eyeholes in one and was wearing it as a
mask at the dinner table.

As a child, I also used *tortillas* as hand warmers on cold days, and   2
my family claims that I owe my career as an artist to my early experiments with *tortillas.* According to them, my clowning around
helped me develop a strong artistic foundation. I'm not so sure,
though. Sometimes I wore a *tortilla* on my head, like a *yarmulke,*
and yet I never had any great urge to convert from Catholicism to
Judaism. But who knows? They may be right.

For Mexicans over the centuries, the *tortilla* has served as the   3
spoon and the fork, the plate and the napkin. *Tortillas* originated
before the Mayan civilizations, perhaps predating Europe's wheat
bread. According to Mayan mythology, the great god Quetzalcoatl,
realizing that the red ants knew the secret of using maize as food,
transformed himself into a black ant, infiltrated the colony of red
ants, and absconded with a grain of corn. (Is it any wonder that to
this day, black ants and red ants do not get along?) Quetzalcoatl
then put maize on the lips of the first man and woman, Oxomoco and

Cipactonal, so that they would become strong. Maize festivals are still celebrated by many Indian cultures of the Americas.

When I was growing up in El Paso, *tortillas* were part of my daily life. I used to visit a *tortilla* factory in an ancient adobe building near the open *mercado* in Ciudad Juárez. As I approached, I could hear the rhythmic slapping of the *masa* as the skilled vendors outside the factory formed it into balls and patted them into perfectly round corn cakes between the palms of their hands. The wonderful aroma and the speed with which the women counted so many dozens of *tortillas* out of warm wicker baskets still linger in my mind. Watching them at work convinced me that the most handsome and *deliciosas tortillas* are handmade. Although machines are faster, they can never adequately replace generation-to-generation experience. There's no place in the factory assembly line for the tender slaps that give each *tortilla* character. The best thing that can be said about mass-producing *tortillas* is that it makes it possible for many people to enjoy them.

In the *mercado* where my mother shopped, we frequently bought *taquitos de nopalitos,* small tacos filled with diced cactus, onions, tomatoes, and *jalapeños.* Our friend Don Toribio showed us how to make delicious, crunchy *taquitos* with dried, salted pumpkin seeds. When you had no money for the filling, a poor man's *taco* could be made by placing a warm *tortilla* on the left palm, applying a sprinkle of salt, then rolling the *tortilla* up quickly with the fingertips of the right hand. My own kids put peanut butter and jelly on *tortillas,* which I think is truly bicultural. And speaking of fast foods for kids, nothing beats a *quesadilla,* a *tortilla* grilled-cheese sandwich.

Depending on what you intend to use them for, *tortillas* may be made in various ways. Even a run-of-the-mill *tortilla* is more than a flat corn cake. A skillfully cooked homemade *tortilla* has a bottom and a top; the top skin forms a pocket in which you put the filling that folds your *tortilla* into a taco. Paper-thin *tortillas* are used specifically for *flautas,* a type of taco that is filled, rolled, and then fried until crisp. The name *flauta* means *flute,* which probably refers to the Mayan bamboo flute; however, the only sound that comes from an edible *flauta* is a delicious crunch that is music to the palate. In México *flautas* are sometimes made as long as two feet and then cut into manageable segments. The opposite of *flautas* is *gorditas,* meaning *little fat ones.* These are very thick small *tortillas.*

The versatility of *tortillas* and corn does not end here. Besides being tasty and nourishing, they have spiritual and artistic qualities as well. The Tarahumara Indians of Chihuahua, for example, concocted a corn-based beer called *tesgüino,* which their descendants still make today. And everyone has read about the woman in New Mexico who was cooking her husband a *tortilla* one morning when the image of Jesus Christ miraculously appeared on it. Before they knew what was happening, the man's breakfast had become a local shrine.

Then there is *tortilla* art. Various Chicano artists throughout the   8 Southwest have, when short of materials or just in a whimsical mood, used a dry *tortilla* as a small, round canvas. And a few years back, at the height of the Chicano movement, a priest in Arizona got into trouble with the Church after he was discovered celebrating mass using a *tortilla* as the host. All of which only goes to show that while the *tortilla* may be a lowly corn cake, when the necessity arises, it can reach unexpected distinction.

COMPREHENSION

1. What exactly is a tortilla?

2. List the functions—both practical and whimsical—tortillas serve.

3. In paragraph 7 Burciaga cites the "spiritual and artistic qualities" of tortillas. Do you think he is being serious? Explain.

4. Why are tortillas so important to Burciaga? Is it just their versatility he admires, or do they represent something more to him?

PURPOSE AND AUDIENCE

1. Burciaga states his thesis explicitly in his essay's final sentence. Paraphrase this thesis. Why do you think he does not state it sooner?

2. Do you think Burciaga expects most of his readers to be of Hispanic descent? To be familiar with tortillas? Explain.

3. Why does Burciaga use humor in this essay? Is it consistent with his essay's purpose? Could such humor have a negative effect on his audience? Explain.

STYLE AND STRUCTURE

1. Where does Burciaga provide a formal definition of *tortilla?* Why does he locate this formal definition so late in his essay?

2. Burciaga uses many Spanish words in this essay, but he defines only some of them—for example, *taquitos de nopalitos* and *quesadilla* in paragraph 5 and *flautas* and *gorditas* in paragraph 6. Why do you think he defines some terms but not others?

3. Burciaga uses several patterns of development in his extended definition. Where, for example, does he use description, narration, process, and exemplification? Does he use any other patterns?

4. Does Burciaga use synonyms or negation to define *tortilla?* Does he discuss the word's origin? If so, where? If not, do you think he should have used any of these strategies?

VOCABULARY PROJECTS

1. Define each of the following words as it is used in this selection.

   yarmulke (2)   absconded (3)   concocted (7)
   maize (3)   adobe (4)

2. Look up each of the following words in a Spanish-English dictionary and (if possible) supply its English equivalent.

   mercado (4)   *masa* (4)   *deliciosas* (4)   *jalapeños* (5)

JOURNAL ENTRY

Can you think of any additional uses—practical or frivolous—for tortillas that Burciaga does not discuss?

WRITING WORKSHOP

1. Write an essay in which you define a food that is important to your family, ethnic group, or circle of friends. Use a variety of patterns of development, as Burciaga does. Assume that your audience is not very familiar with the food you define.

2. Relying primarily on description and exemplification, define a food that is sure to be familiar to all your readers. Do not name the food until your essay's last sentence.

3. Write an essay defining a food—but include a thesis statement that paints a strongly favorable portrait of a much-maligned food (for example, brussels sprouts) or a very negative picture of a popular food (for example, ice cream).

THEMATIC CONNECTIONS

- "Once More to the Lake" (p. 160)
- "Aria: A Memoir of a Bilingual Childhood" (p. 401)
- "Let's Tell the Story of All America's Cultures" (p. 586)
- "The Park" (p. 660)

I WANT A WIFE

Judy Brady

*Judy Brady was born in San Francisco in 1937 and earned a B.F.A.
in painting from the University of Iowa in 1962. She has raised two
daughters, worked as a secretary, and published articles on many
social issues. Brady has been active in the women's movement since
1969, and this article appeared in the first issue of* Ms. *magazine in
1972. Most recently, Brady edited* Women and Cancer *(1990), an
anthology of writings by women, and* One in Three: Women with
Cancer Confront an Epidemic *(1991). In "I Want a Wife," Brady
adopts an ironic tone to present a definition of what she believes
society considers the ideal wife.*

I belong to that classification of people known as wives. I am A 1
Wife. And, not altogether incidentally, I am a mother.

Not too long ago a male friend of mine appeared on the scene fresh 2
from a recent divorce. He had one child, who is, of course, with his
ex-wife. He is looking for another wife. As I thought about him while
I was ironing one evening, it suddenly occurred to me that I, too,
would like to have a wife. Why do I want a wife?

I would like to go back to school so that I can become economically 3
independent, support myself, and if need be, support those dependent upon me. I want a wife who will work and send me to school.
And while I am going to school I want a wife to take care of my children. I want a wife to keep track of the children's doctor and dentist
appointments. And to keep track of mine, too. I want a wife to make
sure my children eat properly and are kept clean. I want a wife who
will wash the children's clothes and keep them mended. I want a
wife who is a good nurturant attendant to my children, who arranges for their schooling, makes sure that they have an adequate
social life with their peers, takes them to the park, the zoo, etc. I
want a wife who takes care of the children when they are sick, a wife
who arranges to be around when the children need special care, because, of course, I cannot miss classes at school. My wife must arrange to lose time at work and not lose the job. It may mean a small
cut in my wife's income from time to time, but I guess I can tolerate
that. Needless to say, my wife will arrange and pay for the care of the
children while my wife is working.

I want a wife who will take care of *my* physical needs. I want a 4
wife who will keep my house clean. A wife who will pick up after my

children, a wife who will pick up after me. I want a wife who will keep my clothes clean, ironed, mended, replaced when need be, and who will see to it that my personal things are kept in their proper place so that I can find what I need the minute I need it. I want a wife who cooks the meals, a wife who is a *good* cook. I want a wife who will plan the menus, do the necessary grocery shopping, prepare the meals, serve then pleasantly, and then do the cleaning up while I do my studying. I want a wife who will care for me when I am sick and sympathize with my pain and loss of time from school. I want a wife to go along when our family takes a vacation so that someone can continue to care for me and my children when I need a rest and change of scene.

I want a wife who will not bother me with rambling complaints 5 about a wife's duties. But I want a wife who will listen to me when I feel the need to explain a rather difficult point I have come across in my course of studies. And I want a wife who will type my papers for me when I have written them.

I want a wife who will take care of the details of my social life. 6 When my wife and I are invited out by my friends, I want a wife who will take care of the babysitting arrangements. When I meet people at school that I like and want to entertain, I want a wife who will have the house clean, will prepare a special meal, serve it to me and my friends, and not interrupt when I talk about things that interest me and my friends. I want a wife who will have arranged that the children are fed and ready for bed before my guests arrive so that the children do not bother us. I want a wife who takes care of the needs of my guests so that they feel comfortable, who makes sure that they have an ashtray, that they are passed the hors d'oeuvres, that they are offered a second helping of the food, that their wine glasses are replenished when necessary, that their coffee is served to them as they like it. And I want a wife who knows that sometimes I need a night out by myself.

I want a wife who is sensitive to my sexual needs, a wife who 7 makes love passionately and eagerly when I feel like it, a wife who makes sure that I am satisfied. And, of course, I want a wife who will not demand sexual attention when I am not in the mood for it. I want a wife who assumes the complete responsibility for birth control, because I do not want more children. I want a wife who will remain sexually faithful to me so that I do not have to clutter up my intellectual life with jealousies. And I want a wife who understands that *my* sexual needs may entail more than strict adherence to monogamy. I must, after all, be able to relate to people as fully as possible.

If, by chance, I find another person more suitable as a wife than 8 the wife I already have, I want the liberty to replace my present wife with another one. Naturally, I will expect a fresh, new life; my wife will take the children and be solely responsible for them so that I am left free.

When I am through with school and have a job, I want my wife to quit working and remain at home so that my wife can more fully and completely take care of a wife's duties.

My God, who *wouldn't* want a wife?

9

10

COMPREHENSION

1. In one sentence, define what Brady means by *wife*. Does this ideal wife actually exist? Explain.

2. List some of the specific duties of the wife Brady describes. Into what five general categories does Brady arrange these duties?

3. What complaints does Brady apparently have about the life she actually leads? To what does she seem to attribute her problems?

4. Under what circumstances does Brady say she would consider leaving her wife? What would happen to the children if she left?

PURPOSE AND AUDIENCE

1. This essay was first published in *Ms.* magazine. In what sense is it appropriate for the audience of this feminist publication?

2. Does this essay have an explicitly stated thesis? If so, where is it? If the thesis is implied, paraphrase it.

3. Do you think Brady *really* wants the kind of wife she describes? Explain.

STYLE AND STRUCTURE

1. What patterns of development does Brady use in developing her definition? Where does she use each pattern?

2. Throughout the essay, Brady repeats the words "I want a wife." What is the effect of this repetition?

3. The first and last paragraphs of this essay are quite brief. Does this weaken the essay? Explain.

4. In enumerating the wife's duties, Brady frequently uses the verb *arrange*. What other verbs does she use repeatedly? How do these verbs help her make her point?

5. Brady never uses the personal pronouns *he* or *she* to refer to the wife she defines. Why not?

6. Comment on Brady's use of phrases like *of course* (paragraphs 2, 4, and 7), *needless to say* (paragraph 3), *after all* (paragraph 7), *by chance* (paragraph 8), and *naturally* (paragraph 8). What do these expressions contribute to the sentences in which they appear? To the essay as a whole?

VOCABULARY PROJECTS

1. Define each of the following words as it is used in this selection.

   nurturant (3)   replenished (6)   adherence (7)   monogamy (7)

2. Going beyond the dictionary definitions, decide what Brady means to suggest by the following words. Is she using any of those words sarcastically? Explain.

   proper (4)   necessary (6)   suitable (8)
   pleasantly (4)   demand (7)   free (8)
   bother (6)   clutter up (7)

JOURNAL ENTRY

Do you think Brady's 1970 characterization of a wife is accurate today?

WRITING WORKSHOP

1. Write an essay in which you define your ideal spouse.

2. Write an essay entitled "I Want a Husband." Taking an ironic stance, use society's notions of the ideal husband to help you shape your definition.

3. Read "The Company Man" (p. 507). Using ideas gleaned from that essay and "I Want a Wife," as well as your own ideas, write a definition essay called "The Ideal Couple." Your essay can be serious or humorous. Develop your definition with examples.

THEMATIC CONNECTIONS

- "My Mother Never Worked" (p. 85)
- "The Men We Carry in Our Minds" (p. 435)
- "Date Rape Hysteria" (p. 646)

THE COMPANY MAN

Ellen Goodman

Ellen Goodman was born in 1941 in Newton, Massachusetts, and graduated from Radcliffe College in 1963. After working for Newsweek *and* The Detroit Free Press, *she began working for* The Boston Globe *in 1967 and is now a columnist and associate editor at the newspaper. Her regular column, "At Large," has been syndicated since 1976, and she has published several volumes of her columns, including* Close to Home *(1975) and, most recently,* Value Judgments *(1993). Goodman, who is also a frequent commentator on television and radio, received a Pulitzer Prize for commentary in 1980. She is also the author of* Turning Points *(1979), an examination, based on interviews, of changes in men's and women's lives as a result of the feminist movement. "The Company Man," from* Close to Home, *defines what clinicians call a "workaholic." Goodman develops her definition with an extended example of a man who literally worked himself to death.*

He worked himself to death, finally and precisely, at 3:00 A.M. Sunday morning. 1

The obituary didn't say that, of course. It said that he died of a 2 coronary thrombosis—I think that was it—but everyone among his friends and acquaintances knew it instantly. He was a perfect Type A, a workaholic, a classic, they said to each other and shook their heads—and thought for five or ten minutes about the way they lived.

This man who worked himself to death finally and precisely at 3 3:00 A.M. Sunday morning—on his day off—was fifty-one years old and a vice-president. He was, however, one of six vice-presidents, and one of three who might conceivably—if the president died or retired soon enough—have moved to the top spot. Phil knew that.

He worked six days a week, five of them until eight or nine at 4 night, during a time when his own company had begun the four-day week for everyone but the executives. He worked like the Important People. He had no outside "extracurricular interests," unless, of course, you think about a monthly golf game that way. To Phil, it was work. He always ate egg salad sandwiches at his desk. He was, of course, overweight, by 20 or 25 pounds. He thought it was okay, though, because he didn't smoke.

On Saturdays, Phil wore a sports jacket to the office instead of a ₅
suit, because it was the weekend.

He had a lot of people working for him, maybe sixty, and most of ₆
them liked him most of the time. Three of them will be seriously
considered for his job. The obituary didn't mention that.

But it did list his "survivors" quite accurately. He is survived by ₇
his wife, Helen, forty-eight years old, a good woman of no particular
marketable skills, who worked in an office before marrying and
mothering. She had, according to her daughter, given up trying to
compete with his work years ago, when the children were small. A
company friend said, "I know how much you will miss him." And she
answered, "I already have."

"Missing him all these years," she must have given up part of ₈
herself which had cared too much for the man. She would be "well
taken care of."

His "dearly beloved" eldest of the "dearly beloved" children is a ₉
hard-working executive in a manufacturing firm down South. In the
day and a half before the funeral, he went around the neighborhood
researching his father, asking the neighbors what he was like. They
were embarrassed.

His second child is a girl, who is twenty-four and newly married. ₁₀
She lives near her mother and they are close, but whenever she was
alone with her father, in a car driving somewhere, they had nothing
to say to each other.

The youngest is twenty, a boy, a high-school graduate who has ₁₁
spent the last couple of years, like a lot of his friends, doing enough
odd jobs to stay in grass and food. He was the one who tried to grab
at his father, and tried to mean enough to him to keep the man at
home. He was his father's favorite. Over the last two years, Phil
stayed up nights worrying about the boy.

The boy once said, "My father and I only board here." ₁₂

At the funeral, the sixty-year-old company president told the ₁₃
forty-eight-year-old widow that the fifty-one-year-old deceased had
meant much to the company and would be missed and would be hard
to replace. The widow didn't look him in the eye. She was afraid he
would read her bitterness and, after all, she would need him to
straighten out the finances—the stock options and all that.

Phil was overweight and nervous and worked too hard. If he wasn't ₁₄
at the office, he was worried about it. Phil was a Type A, a heart-
attack natural. You could have picked him out in a minute from a
lineup.

So when he finally worked himself to death, at precisely 3:00 A.M. ₁₅
Sunday morning, no one was really surprised.

By 5:00 P.M. the afternoon of the funeral, the company president 16
had begun, discreetly of course, with care and taste, to make inquiries about his replacement. One of three men. He asked around:
"Who's been working the hardest?"

COMPREHENSION

1. In one sentence, define *the company man*. What does Goodman's
   extended definition convey that your one-sentence definition lacks?

2. When Phil's widow is told by a friend, "I know how much you will miss
   him," she answers, "I already have." What does she mean?

3. Why does Phil's oldest son go around the neighborhood researching
   his father?

4. Why doesn't Phil's widow look the company president in the eye?

5. What kind of man will the company president seek for Phil's replacement?

PURPOSE AND AUDIENCE

1. What point is Goodman trying to make in this essay?

2. What assumptions does Goodman make about her readers? Considering whom she expects to read her essay, what effect do you think she
   hopes it to have?

3. Why does Goodman imply her thesis and not state it?

STYLE AND STRUCTURE

1. Why does Goodman state the time of Phil's death both at the beginning and at the end of her essay?

2. Is there a reason why Goodman waits until the end of paragraph 3
   before she uses "the company man's" name? Explain.

3. What is the effect of the bits of dialogue Goodman includes?

4. Goodman tells Phil's story in a flat, impersonal way. How does this
   tone help her achieve her purpose?

5. Why does Goodman put quotation marks around the phrases *extracurricular interests, survivors, missing him all these years, well taken
   care of,* and *dearly beloved*?

6. What patterns of development does Goodman use to define her subject?

VOCABULARY PROJECTS

1. Define each of the following words as it is used in this selection.

   coronary thrombosis (2)   classic (2)   stock options (13)
   workaholic (2)   conceivably (3)

2. This essay's style and vocabulary are quite informal. Substitute a more formal word or expression for each of the following:

   top spot (3)   odd jobs (11)   all that (13)
   okay (4)   grab at (11)   a heart-attack natural (14)

   How do your substitutions change the sentences in which they appear?

JOURNAL ENTRY

Do you know anyone like Phil? What do you think really motivates people like him? Do such forces drive women as well as men?

WRITING WORKSHOP

1. Write an essay defining the workaholic student (or the procrastinating student). As Goodman does, use an extended example to support your thesis.

2. Write a definition essay in which you define the company man (or the company woman), but use comparison and contrast to organize your definition.

3. Write a brief obituary for Phil, one that might appear in his company's trade magazine. Using the title "A Valued Employee," develop the obituary as a definition essay. Your aim is to show readers what traits such an employee must have.

THEMATIC CONNECTIONS

- "The Peter Principle" (p. 191)
- "Off the Ladder" (p. 377)
- "The Men We Carry in Our Minds" (p. 435)
- "The Catbird Seat" (p. 522)

THE PERFECT FAMILY

Alice Hoffman

Alice Hoffman was born in 1952 in New York City and grew up on Long Island. She graduated from Adelphi University in 1973 and earned her master of fine arts degree from Stanford University in 1975. Hoffman is the author of short stories, book reviews, screenplays, and ten novels. Her most recent books are At Risk *(1988),* Seventh Heaven *(1990), and* Turtle Moon *(1992), which were all best-sellers, and* Second Nature *(1994). Hoffman's novels often combine the familiar and the magical in stories of ordinary lives within families and communities. She frequently writes about single mothers and relationships between parents and children. "The Perfect Family," published in 1992, examines the idea of the ideal family represented in television shows of the 1950s and its relation to the lives many people, including Hoffman's mother, actually led.*

When I was growing up in the 50's, there was only one sort of 1 family, the one we watched on television every day. Right in front of us, in black and white, was everything we needed to know about family values: the neat patch of lawn, the apple tree, the mother who never once raised her voice, the three lovely children: a Princess, a Kitten, a Bud* and, always, the father who knew best.

People stayed married forever back then, and roses grew by the 2 front door. We had glass bottles filled with lightning bugs and brand-new swing sets in the backyard, and softball games at dusk. We had summer nights that lasted forever and well-balanced meals, three times a day, in our identical houses, on our identical streets. There was only one small bargain we had to make to exist in this world: we were never to ask questions, never to think about people who didn't have as much or who were different in any way. We ignored desperate marriages and piercing loneliness. And we were never, ever, to wonder what might be hidden from view, behind the unlocked doors, in the privacy of our neighbors' bedrooms and knotty-pine-paneled dens.

This was a bargain my own mother could not make. Having once 3 believed that her life would sort itself out to be like the television shows we watched, only real and in color, she'd been left to care for

*Eds. Note—characters in *Father Knows Best,* a popular television show from 1954 to 1962.

her children on her own, at a time when divorce was so uncommon I did not meet another child of divorced parents until 10 years later, when I went off to college.

Back then, it almost made sense when one of my best friends was not allowed to come to my house; her parents did not approve of divorce or my mother's life style. My mother, after all, had a job and a boyfriend and, perhaps even more incriminating, she was the one who took the silver-colored trash cans out to the curb on Monday nights. She did so faithfully, on evenings when she had already balanced the checkbook and paid the bills and ministered to sore throats and made certain we'd had dinner; but all up and down the street everybody knew the truth: taking out the trash was clearly a job for fathers.

When I was 10, my mother began to work for the Department of Social Services, a world in which the simple rules of the suburbs did not apply. She counseled young unwed mothers, girls and women who were not allowed to make their own choices, most of whom had not been allowed to finish high school or stay in their own homes, none of whom had been allowed to decide not to continue their pregnancies. Later, my mother placed most of these babies in foster care, and still later, she moved to the protective-services department, investigating charges of abuse and neglect, often having to search a child's back and legs for bruises or welts.

She would have found some on my friend, left there by her righteous father, the one who wouldn't allow her to visit our home but blackened her eye when, a few years later, he discovered that she was dating a boy he didn't approve of. But none of his neighbors had dared to report him. They would never have imagined that someone like my friend's father, whose trash cans were always tidily placed at the curb, whose lawn was always well cared for, might need watching.

To my mother, abuse was a clear-cut issue, if reported and found, but neglect was more of a judgment call. It was, in effect, passing judgment on the nature of love. If my father had not sent the child-support checks on time, if my mother hadn't been white and college-educated, it could have easily been us in one of those apartments she visited, where the heat didn't work on the coldest days, and the dirt was so encrusted you could mop all day and still be called a poor housekeeper, and there was often nothing more for dinner than Frosted Flakes and milk, or, if it was toward the end of the month, the cereal might be served with tap water. Would that have meant my mother loved her children any less, that we were less of a family?

My mother never once judged who was a fit mother on the basis of a clean floor, or an unbalanced meal, or a boyfriend who sometimes spent the night. But back then, there were good citizens who were only too ready to set their standards for women and children, factoring out poverty or exhaustion or simply a different set of beliefs.

There are always those who are ready to deal out judgment with   9
the ready fist of the righteous. I know this because before the age of 10 I was one of the righteous, too. I believed that mothers were meant to stay home and fathers should carry out the trash on Monday nights. I believed that parents could create a domestic life that was the next best thing to heaven, if they just tried. That is what I'd been told, that in the best of all worlds we would live identical lives in identical houses.

It's a simple view of the world, too simple even for childhood.   10
Certainly, it's a vision that is much too limited for the lives we live now, when only one in 19 families are made up of a wage-earner father, a mother who doesn't work outside the home and two or more children. And even long ago, when I was growing up, we paid too high a price when we cut ourselves off from the rest of the world. We ourselves did not dare to be different. In the safety we created, we became trapped.

There are still places where softball games are played at dusk and   11
roses grow by the front door. There are families with sons named Bud, with kind and generous fathers, and mothers who put up strawberry preserves every June and always have time to sing lullabies. But do these families love their children any more than the single mother who works all day? Are their lullabies any sweeter? If I felt deprived as a child, it was only when our family was measured against some notion of what we were supposed to be. The truth of it was, we lacked for little.

And now that I have children of my own, and am exhausted at the   12
end of the day in which I've probably failed in a hundred different ways, I am amazed that women alone can manage. That they do, in spite of everything, is a simple fact. They rise from sleep in the middle of the night when their children call out to them. They rush for the cough syrup and cold washcloths and keep watch till dawn. These are real family values, the same ones we knew when we were children. As far as we were concerned our mother could cure a fever with a kiss. This may be the only thing we ever need to know about love. The rest, no one can judge.

COMPREHENSION

1. What "one sort of family" was typical when Hoffman was growing up? How was her family different?

2. What bargain does Hoffman say her mother was unable to make? Why?

3. Why was the fact that Hoffman's mother was the one who took the trash cans to the curb so "incriminating" (4)?

4. Why, according to Hoffman, did it "almost make sense" (4) when a good friend was not allowed to visit her?

5. How are the "perfect" suburban families like the families Hoffman's mother works with? How are they different?

6. What does Hoffman mean when she says that her mother saw neglect as "in effect, passing judgment on the nature of love" (7)?

7. How do you interpret this statement: "In the safety we created, we became trapped" (10)?

PURPOSE AND AUDIENCE

1. Hoffman mentions the term *family values* in both her introduction and her conclusion. Why does she do so? What do you think the term means? How is this term related to her purpose in writing this essay?

2. Hoffman seems to expect her middle-class readers to have certain preconceived ideas about her subject. What ideas do you think they might have? How does paragraph 7 address these preconceptions?

3. This essay does not include an explicitly stated thesis. Write a one-sentence statement that sums up the main point Hoffman is making about what really constitutes the perfect family.

STYLE AND STRUCTURE

1. Throughout Hoffman's essay, certain images recur—images of roses, softball games, and neat lawns, for example. What point does she make with these images? What other images does she return to? Why?

2. What individuals and families does Hoffman compare in her essay? Why is this kind of comparison and contrast effective?

3. What patterns of development does Hoffman use in her extended definition? What additional patterns might she have used?

4. Does Hoffman define *the perfect family* by negation? Explain.

5. Early in her essay, Hoffman mentions that most people she knew—that is, most middle-class suburbanites—lived in "identical houses, on . . . identical streets" (2). In what sense is this characterization ironic?

VOCABULARY PROJECTS

1. Define each of the following words as it is used in this selection.

   incriminating (4)   welts (5)   fit (8)
   ministered (4)   righteous (6)   factoring (8)

2. Hoffman notes that her mother made a clear distinction between *abuse* and *neglect*. Look up each of these words in a dictionary, define each in a single sentence, and then write a short paragraph in which you illustrate the difference between them with specific examples.

JOURNAL ENTRY

What image of the family do today's television programs project? How is this image different from the one defined by 1950s television?

WRITING WORKSHOP

1. Expand your journal entry into a definition essay in which you define the typical family as it is portrayed in four or five contemporary television shows. Include a thesis that assesses the accuracy of this image.

2. What values are most important to your own family? Write an essay in which you develop your family's definition of *family values,* using exemplification, narration, and description as your primary patterns of development.

3. Hoffman mentions divorce as an anomaly in her childhood, but this is certainly not the case today; in fact, as she notes in paragraph 10, "only one in 19 families [is] made up of a wage-earner father, a mother who doesn't work outside the home and two or more children." Given the reality of today's families, write a definition called "The 90s Family," relying on exemplification and on classification and division to convey the variety of possible combinations of people that can constitute a family.

THEMATIC CONNECTIONS

- "Once More to the Lake" (p. 160)
- "Midnight" (p. 186)
- "Why Mr. Ed Still Talks Good Horse Sense" (p. 198)
- "Television: The Plug-In Drug" (p. 303)

DYSLEXIA

Eileen Simpson

Eileen Simpson is a psychotherapist and the author of short stories, a novel, and several nonfiction works. Her books include Poets in Their Youth *(1982), a memoir of the poet John Berryman, from whom Simpson was divorced in 1956, and* Orphans: Real and Imaginary *(1987), about growing up without parents, as Simpson herself did from the age of six. The following selection, from* Reversals: A Personal Account of Victory over Dyslexia *(1979), defines a developmental disorder that affects nearly 10 percent of Americans and has afflicted such noted figures as Hans Christian Andersen, W. B. Yeats, Thomas Edison, and Woodrow Wilson. Simpson had struggled all her life with dyslexia until she was finally able to overcome it by gaining an understanding of what it is. Here she presents a working definition for her readers, comparing the case studies she selects with her own experience as a child.*

Dyslexia (from the Greek, *dys,* faulty, + *lexis,* speech, cognate 1
with the Latin *legere,* to read), developmental or specific dyslexia as
it's technically called, the disorder I suffered from, is the inability of
otherwise normal children to read. Children whose intelligence is
below average, whose vision or hearing is defective, who have not
had proper schooling, or who are too emotionally disturbed or brain-
damaged to profit from it belong in other diagnostic categories. They,
too, may be unable to learn to read, but they cannot properly be
called dyslexics.

For more than seventy years the essential nature of the affliction 2
has been hotly disputed by psychologists, neurologists, and educators. It is generally agreed, however, that it is the result of a neuro-
physiological flaw in the brain's ability to process language. It is
probably inherited, although some experts are reluctant to say this
because they fear people will equate "inherited" with "untreatable."
Treatable it certainly is: not a disease to be cured, but a malfunction
that require retraining.

Reading is the most complex skill a child entering school is asked 3
to develop. What makes it complex, in part, is that letters are less
constant than objects. A car seen from a distance, close to, from
above, or below, or in a mirror still looks like a car even though the
optical image changes. The letters of the alphabet are more whim-

sical. Take the letter *b*. Turned upside down it becomes a *p*. Looked at in a mirror, it becomes a *d*. Capitalized, it becomes something quite different, a *B*. The *M* upside down is a *W*. The *E* flipped over becomes Ǝ. This reversed *E* is familiar to mothers of normal children who have just begun to go to school. The earliest examples of art work they bring home often have I LOVE YOU written on them.

Dyslexics differ from other children in that they read, spell, and write letters upside down and turned around far more frequently and for a much longer time. In what seems like a capricious manner, they also add letters, syllables, and words, or, just as capriciously, delete them. With palindromic words (was–saw, on–no), it is the order of the letters rather than the orientation they change. The new word makes sense, but not the sense intended. Then there are other words where the changed order—"sorty" for story—does not make sense at all.   4

The inability to recognize that g, *g*, and G are the same letter, the inability to maintain the orientation of the letters, to retain the order in which they appear, and to follow a line of text without jumping above or below it—all the results of the flaw—can make of an orderly page of words a dish of alphabet soup.   5

Also essential for reading is the ability to store words in memory and to retrieve them. This very particular kind of memory dyslexics lack. So, too, do they lack the ability to hear what the eye sees, and to see what they hear. If the eye sees "off," the ear must hear "off" and not "of," or "for." If the ear hears "saw," the eye must see that it looks like "saw" on the page and not "was." Lacking these skills, a sentence or paragraph becomes a coded message to which the dyslexic can't find the key.   6

It is only a slight exaggeration to say that those who learned to read without difficulty can best understand the labor reading is for a dyslexic by turning a page of text upside down and trying to decipher it.   7

While the literature is replete with illustrations of the way these children write and spell, there are surprisingly few examples of how they read. One, used for propaganda purposes to alert the public to the vulnerability of dyslexics in a literate society, is a sign warning that behind it are guard dogs trained to kill. The dyslexic reads: 8

Wurring
Guard God
Patoly

for

Warning
Guard Dog
Patrol

and, of course, remains ignorant of the danger.

Looking for a more commonplace example, and hoping to recap- 9
ture the way I must have read in fourth grade, I recently observed
dyslexic children at the Educational Therapy Clinic in Princeton,
through the courtesy of Elizabeth Travers, the director. The first
child I saw, eight-year-old Anna (whose red hair and brown eyes
reminded me of myself at that age), had just come to the Clinic and
was learning the alphabet. Given the story of "Little Red Riding
Hood," which is at the second grade level, she began confidently
enough, repeating the title from memory, then came to a dead stop.
With much coaxing throughout, she read as follows:

> Grandma you a top. Grandma [looks over at picture of Red Riding
> Hood]. Red Riding Hood [long pause, presses index finger into the
> paper. Looks at me for help. I urge: Go ahead] the a [puts head close
> to the page, nose almost touching] on Grandma

for

> Once upon a time there was a little girl who had a red coat with a red
> hood. Etc.

"Grandma" was obviously a memory from having heard the story 10
read aloud. Had I needed a reminder of how maddening my silences
must have been to Miss Henderson, and how much patience is required to teach these children, Anna, who took almost ten minutes
to read these few lines, furnished it. The main difference between
Anna and me at that age is that Anna clearly felt no need to invent.
She was perplexed, but not anxious, and seemed to have infinite tolerance for her long silences.

Toby, a nine-year old boy with superior intelligence, had a year of 11
tutoring behind him and could have managed "Little Red Riding
Hood" with ease. His text was taken from the *Reader's Digest's
Reading Skill Builder,* Grade IV. He read:

> A kangaroo likes as if he had but truck together warm. His saw neck
> and head do not . . . [Here Toby sighed with fatigue] seem to feel
> happy back. They and tried and so every a tiger Moses and shoots
> from lonesome day and shouts and long shore animals. And each farm
> play with five friends . . .

He broke off with the complaint, "This is too hard, Do I have to read any more?" 12

His text was: 13

> A kangaroo looks as if he had been put together wrong. His small neck and head do not seem to fit with his heavy back legs and thick tail. Soft eyes, a twinkly little nose and short front legs seem strange on such a large strong animal. And each front paw has five fingers, like a man's hand.

An English expert gives the following bizarre example of an adult dyslexic's performance: 14

> An the bee-what in the tel mother of the biothodoodoo to the majoram or that emidrate eni eni Krastrei, mestriet to Ketra lotombreidi to ra from treido as that.

His text, taken from a college catalogue the examiner happened to have close at hand, was: 15

> It shall be in the power of the college to examine or not every licenti-ate, previous to his admission to the fellowship, as they shall think fit.

That evening when I read aloud to Auntie for the first time, I probably began as Toby did, my memory of the classroom lesson keeping me close to the text. When memory ran out, and Auntie did not correct my errors, I began to invent. When she still didn't stop me, I may well have begun to improvise in the manner of this pa-tient—anything to keep going and keep up the myth that I was read-ing—until Auntie brought the "gibberish" to a halt. 16

COMPREHENSION

1. In one sentence, define *dyslexia*.

2. How are dyslexics different from normal children who are just learn-ing to read and write? What essential skills for reading do dyslexics lack?

3. How is Anna's behavior different from the behaivor of Simpson as a child? How can you account for this difference?

4. Why did Simpson, like other dyslexics, resort to "improvising" when she read aloud?

PURPOSE AND AUDIENCE

1. In paragraph 2, Simpson suggests her purpose in defining *dyslexia*. What is this purpose?

2. Does this essay include an explicitly stated thesis? If so, what is it? If not, state the thesis in one sentence.

3. Does Simpson expect her audience to be familiar with dyslexia? How can you tell?

STYLE AND STRUCTURE

1. In paragraph 1, Simpson uses formal definition and negation. Identify each of these strategies.

2. In the body of her essay, Simpson develops her definition with examples, description, and comparison and contrast. Find examples of each of these strategies.

3. Simpson concludes her essay with a personal note. Is this an effective conclusion? Why, or why not?

VOCABULARY PROJECTS

1. Define each of the following words as it is used in this selection.

cognate (1)	whimsical (3)	replete (8)
developmental (1)	capricious (4)	vulnerability (8)
neurologists (2)	palindromic (4)	literate (8)
neuro-physiological (2)	orientation (5)	commonplace (9)

2. Simpson uses a variety of terms to characterize dyslexia as a treatable condition, not a hopeless disease—for instance, *disorder* (paragraph 1), *affliction, flaw,* and *malfunction* (paragraph 2). Look up each of these four words in a dictionary and make sure you understand how they differ. Then, compile a list of near synonyms for each. Are there any contexts in the essay in which you believe one of these synonyms would be more appropriate than the word Simpson uses? Explain.

JOURNAL ENTRY

Do you think students with dyslexia or other learning disabilities should get preferential treatment in decisions regarding college admission? For example, students with certain visual or learning disabilities may be eligible to take untimed SATs. Do you think such an arrangement is fair?

WRITING WORKSHOP

1. Write an essay in which you define a disability you have or one you are familiar with through the experiences of a friend or family member. Use examples and any other appropriate techniques to develop your definition.

2. Use what you now know about dyslexia to write an essay in which you define a similar disability by comparing and contrasting it with dyslexia.

3. Even without a disability, you have probably found some task or skill very difficult to master, though others found it easy. Name and define the "condition" that hindered your learning, using whatever techniques are appropriate for your definition.

THEMATIC CONNECTIONS

- "The Human Cost of an Illiterate Society" (p. 215)
- "Aria: A Memoir of a Bilingual Childhood" (p. 401)
- "College Pressures" (p. 425)

THE CATBIRD SEAT

James Thurber

James Thurber (1894–1961) was born in Columbus, Ohio, and graduated from The Ohio State University in 1919. He joined the staff of The New Yorker in 1927, contributing his humorous and satirical stories, anecdotes, and sketches even after he resigned from the magazine in 1933. As his eyesight deteriorated, Thurber began to write more than he drew; he was almost totally blind for the last fifteen years of his life. His numerous books include Is Sex Necessary? (1929, with E.B. White); My Life and Hard Times (1933); My World and Welcome to It (1942), containing the well-known story "The Secret Life of Walter Mitty"; Men, Women, and Dogs (1943); The Thurber Carnival (1945); and The Thirteen Clocks (1950), a fable for children. Thurber also wrote a comedy with Elliott Nugent called The Male Animal (1940), which was produced on Broadway and later made into a film. His last book was The Years with Ross (1959), a biography of The New Yorker editor Harold Ross as well as a memoir of Thurber's years on the staff of the magazine. In "The Catbird Seat," the main character builds a case against an office rival and then plots her murder.

Mr. Martin bought the pack of Camels on Monday night in the most crowded cigar store on Broadway. It was theater time and seven or eight men were buying cigarettes. The clerk didn't even glance at Mr. Martin, who put the pack in his overcoat pocket and went out. If any of the staff at F & S had seen him buy the cigarettes, they would have been astonished, for it was generally known that Mr. Martin did not smoke, and never had. No one saw him. 1

It was just a week to the day since Mr. Martin had decided to rub out Mrs. Ulgine Barrows. The term "rub out" pleased him because it suggested nothing more than the correction of an error—in this case an error of Mr. Fitweiler. Mr. Martin had spent each night of the past week working out his plan and examining it. As he walked home now he went over it again. For the hundredth time he resented the element of imprecision, the margin of guesswork that entered into the business. The project as he had worked it out was casual and bold, the risks were considerable. Something might go wrong anywhere along the line. And therein lay the cunning of his scheme. No one would ever see in it the cautious, painstaking hand of Erwin Martin, head of the filing department at F & S, of whom Mr. Fit- 2 weiler had once said, "Man is fallible but Martin isn't." No one would see his hand, that is, unless it were caught in the act.

Sitting in his apartment, drinking a glass of milk, Mr. Martin reviewed his case against Mrs. Ulgine Barrows, as he had every night for seven nights. He began at the beginning. Her quacking voice and braying laugh had first profaned the halls of F & S on March 7, 1941 (Mr. Martin had a head for dates). Old Roberts, the personnel chief, had introduced her as the newly appointed special adviser to the president of the firm, Mr. Fitweiler. The woman had appalled Mr. Martin instantly, but he hadn't shown it. He had given her his dry hand, a look of studious concentration, and a faint smile. "Well," she had said, looking at the papers on his desk, "are you lifting the oxcart out of the ditch?" As Mr. Martin recalled that moment, over his milk, he squirmed slightly. He must keep his mind on her crimes as a special adviser, not on her peccadillos as a personality. This he found difficult to do, in spite of entering an objection and sustaining it. The faults of the woman as a woman kept chattering on in his mind like an unruly witness. She had, for almost two years now, baited him. In the halls, in the elevator, even in his own office, into which she romped now and then like a circus horse, she was constantly shouting out these silly questions at him. "Are you lifting the oxcart out of the ditch? Are you tearing up the pea patch? Are you hollering down the rain barrel? Are you scraping around the bottom of the pickle barrel? Are you sitting in the catbird seat?"

It was Joey Hart, one of Mr. Martin's two assistants, who had explained what the gibberish meant. "She must be a Dodger fan," he had said. "Red Barber announces the Dodger games over the radio and he uses those expressions—picked 'em up down South." Joey had gone on to explain one or two. "Tearing up the pea patch" meant going on a rampage; "sitting in the catbird seat" meant sitting pretty, like a batter with three balls and no strikes on him. Mr. Martin dismissed all this with an effort. It had been annoying, it had driven him near to distraction, but he was too solid a man to be moved to murder by anything so childish. It was fortunate, he reflected as he passed on to the important charges against Mrs. Barrows, that he had stood up under it so well. He had maintained always an outward appearance of polite tolerance. "Why, I even believe you like the woman," Miss Paird, his other assistant, had once said to him. He had simply smiled.

A gavel rapped in Mr. Martin's mind and the case proper was resumed. Mrs. Ulgine Barrows stood charged with willful, blatant, and persistent attempts to destroy the efficiency and system of F & S. It was competent, material, and relevant to review her advent and rise to power. Mr. Martin had got the story from Miss Paird, who seemed always able to find things out. According to her, Mrs. Barrows had met Mr. Fitweiler at a party, where she had rescued him from the embraces of a powerfully built drunken man who had mistaken the president of F & S for a famous retired Middle Western football coach. She had led him to a sofa and somehow worked upon him a monstrous magic. The aging gentleman had jumped to the conclusion there and then that this was a woman of singular attainments, equipped to bring out the best in him and in the firm. A week later he had introduced her into F & S as his special adviser. On that day confusion got its foot in the door. After Miss Tyson, Mr. Brundage, and Mr. Bartlett had been fired and Mr. Munson had taken his hat and stalked out, mailing in his resignation later, old Roberts had been emboldened to speak to Mr. Fitweiler. He mentioned that Mr. Munson's department had been "a little disrupted" and hadn't they perhaps better resume the old system there? Mr. Fitweiler had said certainly not. He had the greatest faith in Mrs. Barrows' ideas. "They require a little seasoning, a little seasoning, is all," he had added. Mr. Roberts had given it up. Mr. Martin reviewed in detail all the changes wrought by Mrs. Barrows. She had begun chipping at the cornices of the firm's edifice and now she was swinging at the foundation stones with a pickaxe.

Mr. Martin came now, in his summing up, to the afternoon of 6 Monday, November 2, 1942—just one week ago. On that day, at 3 P.M., Mrs. Barrows had bounced into his office. "Boo!" she had yelled. "Are you scraping around the bottom of the pickle barrel?" Mr. Martin had looked at her from under his green eyeshade, saying nothing. She had begun to wander about the office, taking it in with her great, popping eyes. "Do you really need *all* these filing cabinets?" she had demanded suddenly. Mr. Martin's heart had jumped. "Each of these files," he had said, keeping his voice even, "plays an indispensable part in the system of F & S." She had brayed at him, "Well, don't tear up the pea patch!" and gone to the door. From there she had bawled, "But you sure have got a lot of fine scrap in here!" Mr. Martin could no longer doubt that the finger was on his beloved department. Her pickaxe was on the upswing, poised for the first blow. It had not come yet; he had received no blue memo from the enchanted Mr. Fitweiler bearing nonsensical instructions deriving from the obscene woman. But there was no doubt in Mr. Martin's mind that one would be forthcoming. He must act quickly. Already a precious week had gone by. Mr. Martin stood up in his living room, still holding his milk glass. "Gentlemen of the jury," he said to himself, "I demand the death penalty for this horrible person."

The next day Mr. Martin followed his routine, as usual. He pol-   7
ished his glasses more often and once sharpened an already sharp
pencil, but not even Miss Paird noticed. Only once did he catch sight
of his victim; she swept past him in the hall with a patronizing "Hi!"
At five-thirty he walked home, as usual, and had a glass of milk, as
usual. He had never drunk anything stronger in his life—unless you
could count ginger ale. The late Sam Schlosser, the S of F & S, had
praised Mr. Martin at a staff meeting several years before for his
temperate habits. "Our most efficient worker neither drinks nor
smokes," he had said. "The results speak for themselves." Mr. Fitweiler had sat by, nodding approval.

Mr. Martin was still thinking about that red-letter day as he   8
walked over to the Schrafft's on Fifth Avenue near Forty-sixth
Street. He got there, as he always did, at eight o'clock. He finished
his dinner and the financial page of the *Sun* at a quarter to nine, as
he always did. It was his custom after dinner to take a walk. This
time he walked down Fifth Avenue at a casual pace. His gloved
hands felt moist and warm, his forehead cold. He transferred the
Camels from his overcoat to a jacket pocket. He wondered, as he did
so, if they did not represent an unnecessary note of strain. Mrs.
Barrows smoked only Luckies. It was his idea to puff a few puffs on
a Camel (after the rubbing-out), stub it out in the ashtray holding
her lipstick-stained Luckies, and thus drag a small red herring
across the trail. Perhaps it was not a good idea. It would take time.
He might even choke, too loudly.

Mr. Martin had never seen the house on West Twelfth Street   9
where Mrs. Barrows lived, but he had a clear enough picture of it.
Fortunately, she had bragged to everybody about her ducky first-
floor apartment in the perfectly darling three-story redbrick. There
would be no doorman or other attendants; just the tenants of the
second and third floors. As he walked along, Mr. Martin realized that
he would get there before nine-thirty. He had considered walking
north on Fifth Avenue from Schrafft's to a point from which it would
take him until ten o'clock to reach the house. At that hour people
were less likely to be coming in or going out. But the procedure
would have made an awkward loop in the straight thread of his
casualness, and he had abandoned it. It was impossible to figure
when people would be entering or leaving the house, anyway. There
was a great risk at any hour. If he ran into anybody, he would simply
have to place the rubbing-out of Ulgine Barrows in the inactive file
forever. The same thing would hold true if there were someone in her
apartment. In that case he would just say that he had been passing
by, recognized her charming house and thought to drop in.

It was eighteen minutes after nine when Mr. Martin turned into 10
Twelfth Street. A man passed him, and a man and a woman talking.
There was no one within fifty paces when he came to the house, halfway down the block. He was up the steps and in the small vestibule
in no time, pressing the bell under the card that said "Mrs. Ulgine
Barrows." When the clicking in the lock started, he jumped forward
against the door. He got inside fast, closing the door behind him. A
bulb in a lantern hung from the hall ceiling on a chain seemed to
give a monstrously bright light. There was nobody on the stair,
which went up ahead of him along the left wall. A door opened down
the hall in the wall on the right. He went toward it swiftly, on tiptoe.

"Well, for God's sake, look who's here!" bawled Mrs. Barrows, and 11
her braying laugh rang out like the report of a shotgun. He rushed
past her like a football tackle, bumping her. "Hey, quit shoving!" she
said, closing the door behind them. They were in her living room,
which seemed to Mr. Martin to be lighted by a hundred lamps.
"What's after you?" she said. "You're as jumpy as a goat." He found
he was unable to speak. His heart was wheezing in his throat. "I—
yes," he finally brought out. She was jabbering and laughing as
she started to help him off with his coat. "No, no," he said. "I'll put
it there." He took it off and put it on a chair near the door. "Your
hat and gloves, too," she said. "You're in a lady's house." He put his
hat on top of the coat. Mrs. Barrows seemed larger than he had
thought. He kept his gloves on. "I was passing by," he said. "I recognized—is there anyone here?" She laughed louder than ever. "No,"
she said, "we're all alone. You're as white as a sheet, you funny man.
Whatever *has* come over you? I'll mix you a toddy." She started
toward a door across the room. "Scotch-and-soda be all right? But
say, you don't drink, do you?" She turned and gave him her amused
look. Mr. Martin pulled himself together. "Scotch-and-soda will be
all right," he heard himself say. He could hear her laughing in the
kitchen.

Mr. Martin looked quickly around the living room for the weapon. 12
He had counted on finding one there. There were andirons and a
poker and something in a corner that looked like an Indian club.
None of them would do. It couldn't be that way. He began to pace
around. He came to a desk. On it lay a metal paper knife with an
ornate handle. Would it be sharp enough? He reached for it and
knocked over a small brass jar. Stamps spilled out of it and it fell to
the floor with a clatter. "Hey," Mrs. Barrows yelled from the kitchen,
"are you tearing up the pea patch?" Mr. Martin gave a strange laugh.
Picking up the knife, he tried its point against his left wrist. It was
blunt. It wouldn't do.

When Mrs. Barrows reappeared, carrying two highballs, Mr. Martin, standing there with his gloves on, became acutely conscious of the fantasy he had wrought. Cigarettes in his pocket, a drink prepared for him—it was all too grossly improbable. It was more than that; it was impossible. Somewhere in the back of his mind a vague idea stirred, sprouted. "For heaven's sake, take off those gloves," said Mrs. Barrows. "I always wear them in the house," said Mr. Martin. The idea began to bloom, strange and wonderful. She put the glasses on a coffee table in front of a sofa and sat on the sofa. "Come over here, you odd little man," she said. Mr. Martin went over and sat beside her. It was difficult getting a cigarette out of the pack of Camels, but he managed it. She held a match for him, laughing. "Well," she said, handing him his drink "this is perfectly marvelous. You with a drink and a cigarette." 13

Mr. Martin puffed, not too awkwardly, and took a gulp of the highball. "I drink and smoke all the time," he said. He clinked his glass against hers. "Here's nuts to that old windbag, Fitweiler," he said, and gulped again. The stuff tasted awful, but he made no grimace. "Really, Mr. Martin," she said, her voice and posture changing, "you are insulting our employer." Mrs. Barrows was now all special adviser to the president. "I am preparing a bomb," said Mr. Martin, "which will blow the old goat higher than hell." He had only had a little of the drink, which was not strong. It couldn't be that. "Do you take dope or something?" Mrs. Barrows asked coldly. "Heroin," said Mr. Martin. "I'll be coked to the gills when I bump that old buzzard off." "Mr. Martin!" she shouted, getting to her feet. "That will be all of that. You must go at once." Mr. Martin took another swallow of his drink. He tapped his cigarette out in the ashtray and put the pack of Camels on the coffee table. Then he got up. She stood glaring at him. He walked over and put on his hat and coat. "Not a word about this," he said, and laid an index finger against his lips. All Mrs. Barrows could bring out was "Really!" Mr. Martin put his hand on the doorknob. "I'm sitting in the catbird seat," he said. He stuck his tongue out at her and left. Nobody saw him go. 14

Mr. Martin got to his apartment, walking, well before eleven. No one saw him go in. He had two glasses of milk after brushing his teeth, and he felt elated. It wasn't tipsiness, because he hadn't been tipsy. Anyway, the walk had worn off all effects of the whisky. He got in bed and read a magazine for a while. He was asleep before midnight. 15

Mr. Martin got to the office at eight-thirty the next morning, as usual. At a quarter to nine, Ulgine Barrows, who had never before 16 arrived at work before ten, swept into his office. "I'm reporting to Mr. Fitweiler now!" she shouted. "If he turns you over to the police, it's no more than you deserve!" Mr. Martin gave her a look of shocked surprise. "I beg your pardon?" he said. Mrs. Barrows snorted and bounced out of the room, leaving Miss Paird and Joey Hart staring after her. "What's the matter with that old devil now?" asked Miss Paird. "I have no idea," said Mr. Martin, resuming his work. The other two looked at him and then at each other. Miss Paird got up and went out. She walked slowly past the closed door of Mr. Fitweiler's office. Mrs. Barrows was yelling inside, but she was not braying. Miss Paird could not hear what the woman was saying. She went back to her desk.

Forty-five minutes later, Mrs. Barrows left the president's office and went into her own, shutting the door. It wasn't until half an hour later that Mr. Fitweiler sent for Mr. Martin. The head of the filing department, neat, quiet, attentive, stood in front of the old man's desk. Mr. Fitweiler was pale and nervous. He took his glasses off and twiddled them. He made a small, bruffing sound in his throat. "Martin," he said, "you have been with us more than twenty years." "Twenty-two, sir," said Mr. Martin. "In that time," pursued the president, "your work and your—uh—manner have been exemplary." "I trust so, sir," said Mr. Martin. "I have understood, Martin," said Mr. Fitweiler, "that you have never taken a drink or smoked." "That is correct, sir," said Mr. Martin. "Ah, yes." Mr. Fitweiler polished his glasses. "You may describe what you did after leaving the office yesterday, Martin," he said. Mr. Martin allowed less than a second for his bewildered pause. "Certainly, sir," he said. "I walked home. Then I went to Schrafft's for dinner. Afterward I walked home again. I went to bed early, sir, and read a magazine for a while. I was asleep before eleven." "Ah, yes," said Mr. Fitweiler again. He was silent for a moment, searching for the proper words to say to the head of the filing department. "Mrs. Barrows," he said finally, "Mrs. Barrows has worked hard, Martin, very hard. It grieves me to report that she has suffered a severe breakdown. It has taken the form of a persecution complex accompanied by distressing hallucinations." "I am very sorry, sir," said Mr. Martin. "Mrs. Barrows is under the delusion," continued Mr. Fitweiler, "that you visited her last evening and behaved yourself in an—uh—unseemly manner." He raised his hand to silence Mr. Martin's little pained outcry. "It is the nature of these psychological diseases," Mr. Fitweiler said, "to fix upon the least likely and most innocent party as the—uh—source of persecution. These matters are not for the lay mind to grasp, Martin. I've just had my psychiatrist, Dr. Fitch, on the phone. He would not, of

17

course, commit himself, but he made enough generalizations to sub-stantiate my suspicions. I suggested to Mrs. Barrows when she had completed her—uh—story to me this morning, that she visit Dr. Fitch, for I suspected a condition at once. She flew, I regret to say, into a rage, and demanded—uh—requested that I call you on the carpet. You may not know, Martin, but Mrs. Barrows had planned a reorganization of your department—subject to my approval, of course, subject to my approval. This brought you, rather than anyone else, to her mind—but again that is a phenomenon for Dr. Fitch and not for us. So, Martin, I am afraid Mrs. Barrows' usefulness here is at an end." "I am dreadfully sorry, sir," said Mr. Martin.

It was at this point that the door to the office blew open with the suddenness of a gas-main explosion and Mrs. Barrows catapulted through it. "Is the little rat denying it?" she screamed. "He can't get away with that!" Mr. Martin got up and moved discreetly to a point beside Mr. Fitweiler's chair. "You drank and smoked at my apart-ment," she bawled at Mr. Martin, "and you know it! You called Mr. Fitweiler an old windbag and said you were going to blow him up when you got coked to the gills on your heroin!" She stopped yelling to catch her breath and a new glint came into her popping eyes. "If you weren't such a drab, ordinary little man," she said, "I'd think you'd planned it all. Sticking your tongue out, saying you were sit-ting in the catbird seat, because you thought no one would believe me when I told it! My God, it's really too perfect!" She brayed loudly and hysterically, and the fury was on her again. She glared at Mr. Fitweiler. "Can't you see how he has tricked us, you old fool? Can't you see his little game?" But Mr. Fitweiler had been surreptitiously pressing all the buttons under the top of his desk and employees of F & S began pouring into the room. "Stockton," said Mr. Fitweiler, "you and Fishbein will take Mrs. Barrows to her home. Mrs. Powell, you will go with them." Stockton, who had played a little football in high school, blocked Mrs. Barrows as she made for Mr. Martin. It took him and Fishbein together to force her out of the door into the hall, crowded with stenographers and office boys. She was still screaming imprecations at Mr. Martin, tangled and contradictory imprecations. The hubbub finally died out down the corridor.

"I regret that this has happened," said Mr. Fitweiler. "I shall ask you to dismiss it from your mind, Martin." "Yes, sir," said Mr. Mar-tin, anticipating his chief's "That will be all" by moving to the door. "I will dismiss it." He went out and shut the door, and his step was light and quick in the hall. When he entered his department he had slowed down to his customary gait, and he walked quietly across the room to the W20 file, wearing a look of studious concentration.

THINKING ABOUT LITERATURE

1. Define *catbird seat*. What is the term's origin?

2. What patterns of development are used to develop the definition of *catbird seat*?

3. If Mrs. Barrows had kept quiet about her encounter with Mr. Martin, *she* would have been in the catbird seat. Why, then, do you suppose she did not keep silent?

JOURNAL ENTRY

Could this story of office rivalry have been written about two men? About two women? Explain.

THEMATIC CONNECTIONS

- "The Peter Principle" (p. 191)
- "Off the Ladder" (p. 377)
- "The Company Man" (p. 507)

WRITING ASSIGNMENTS FOR DEFINITION

1. Choose a document or ritual that plays a significant part in your religious or cultural heritage. Define it, using any pattern or combination of patterns you choose but making sure to include a formal definition somewhere in your essay. Assume your readers are not familiar with the term you are defining.

2. Write an essay defining *catbird seat,* explaining a time when you were "sitting pretty."

3. The readings in this chapter define family and occupational roles, a disability, and a food. Write an essay in which you too define one of these topics—for instance, a stepmother (family role), the modern baseball player (occupational role), agoraphobia (disability), or spaghetti (food).

4. Do some research to learn the meaning of one of these medical terms: *angina, migraine, Hodgkin's disease, Down Syndrome, tubal ligation, osteoporosis, poliomyelitis, Alzheimer's disease.* Then, write an extended definition essay explaining the term to an audience of college students with no background in medicine.

5. Use an extended example to support a thesis in an essay that defines *racism, sexism,* or another type of bigoted behavior.

6. Choose a term that is central to one of your courses—for instance, *naturalism, behaviorism,* or *authority*—and write an essay in which you define the term. Assume that your audience is made up of students who have not yet taken the course. You may begin with an overview of the term's origin if you believe this is appropriate; then, develop your essay with examples and analogies that will facilitate your audience's understanding of the term.

7. Assuming your audience is a group from a culture not familiar with modern pastimes, write a definition essay in which you describe the form and function of a Frisbee, a Barbie doll, a G.I. Joe action figure, a Teenage Mutant Ninja Turtle, a jump rope, a boomerang, or baseball cards.

8. Review any one of the following narrative essays from Chapter 2, and use it to help you develop an extended definition of one of the following terms:

   "Only Daughter"—alienation
   "Finishing School"—prejudice
   "My Mother Never Worked"—work
   "38 Who Saw Murder Didn't Call the Police"—apathy
   "Shooting an Elephant"—power

9. What constitutes an education? Define the term *education* by iden-

tifying several different sources of knowledge, formal or informal, and explaining what each contributes.

10. What qualifies someone to be a hero? Developing your essay with a single extended example or a series of examples, define the word *hero.* Be sure your essay includes a formal definition.

COLLABORATIVE ACTIVITY FOR DEFINITION

Working as a group, choose one of the following words to define: *pride, hope, sacrifice, courage, justice.* Then, define the term with a series of extended examples drawn from films that members in your group have seen, with each of you developing an illustrative paragraph based on a different film. (Before beginning, your group may decide to focus on one particular genre of film.) When each paragraph has been read by everyone in the group, work together to formulate a thesis that asserts the vital importance of the quality your examples have defined. Then, write suitable opening and closing paragraphs for the essay and arrange the body paragraphs in a logical order, adding transitions where necessary.

10

Argumentation

WHAT IS ARGUMENTATION?

Argumentation is a reasoned, logical way of asserting the soundness of a position, belief, or conclusion. Argumentation takes a stand—supported by evidence—and urges people to share the writer's perspective and insights. In the following paragraph from "Test-Tube Babies: Solution or Problem?" Ruth Hubbard argues that before we endorse further development of the technology that allows for the creation of test-tube babies, we must consider the consequences.

Issue identified	In vitro fertilization of human eggs and the implantation of early embryos into women's wombs are new biotechnologies that may enable some women to bear children
Background presents both sides of issue	who have hitherto been unable to do so. In that sense, it may solve their particular infertility problems. On the other hand, this technology poses unpredictable hazards since it intervenes in the process of fertilization, in the first cell divisions of the fertilized egg, and in the implantation of the embryo into the uterus. At present we have no way to assess in what ways and to what extent these interventions may affect the women or the babies they acquire by this procedure. Since the use of the technology is only the beginning, the financial and technical invest-
Topic sentence (takes a stand)	ments it represents are still modest. <u>It is therefore important that we, as a society, seriously consider the wisdom of implementing and developing it further.</u>

Argumentation has several purposes: to convince other people to accept—or at least acknowledge the validity of—your position; to defend your position, even if others cannot be convinced to agree; and to question or refute a position you believe to be misguided, untrue, dangerous, or evil, perhaps without offering an alternative.

Argumentation and Persuasion

Although *persuasion* and *argumentation* are terms frequently used interchangeably, they are not equivalent. **Persuasion** is a general term that refers to the method by which a writer moves an audience to adopt a belief or follow a course of action. To persuade an audience, a writer relies on various appeals—to the *emotions*, to *reason*, or to *ethics*.

Argumentation is the appeal to reason. In an argument a writer connects a series of statements so that they lead logically to a conclusion. Argumentation is different from persuasion in that it does not try to move an audience to action; its primary purpose is to demonstrate to an audience that certain ideas are valid and that others are not. Unlike persuasion, argumentation has a formal structure: To support a conclusion, an argument makes points, supplies evidence, establishes a logical chain of reasoning, refutes opposing arguments, and accommodates the views of an audience.

As the readings in this chapter demonstrate, however, most effective arguments combine appeals: Even though their primary appeal is to logic, they also appeal to emotions. For example, you could use a combination of logical and emotional appeals to argue against lowering the drinking age in your state from twenty-one to eighteen years of age. You could appeal to *reason* by constructing an argument that leads to the conclusion that the state should not condone policies that have a high probability of injuring or killing citizens. You could support your conclusion by presenting statistics that show that alcohol-related traffic accidents kill more teenagers than disease does. You could also discuss studies that show that states with lower drinking ages have more fatal traffic accidents than states with higher drinking ages. In addition, you could include an appeal to the *emotions* by telling a particularly sad story about an eighteen-year-old alcoholic or by pointing out how an increased number of accidents involving drunk drivers would cost taxpayers more money and could even cost some their lives. These appeals to your audience's emotions could strengthen your argument by widening its appeal.

What appeals you choose and how you balance them depend in part on your purpose and your sense of your audience. But as you consider what appeals to use, remember that some extremely effective means of persuasion are simply unfair. Although most people would agree that lies, threats, and appeals to greed and prejudice are unacceptable ways of motivating an audience to action, such appeals are used in political campaigns, international diplomacy, and daily conversation. Still, in your college writing you should use only those appeals that most people would perceive as being fair.

Choosing a Topic

In an argumentative essay, as in all writing, choosing the right topic is important. Ideally, it should be one in which you have an intellectual or emotional stake. Nevertheless, you should be open-minded and willing to consider all sides of a question. If the evidence goes against your position, you should be willing to change your thesis. And you should be able, from the outset, to consider your topic from other people's viewpoints so that you understand what they believe and can use this knowledge to help you build a logical case. If you cannot, then you should abandon your topic and pick another one that you can deal with more objectively.

Other factors should also influence your selection of a topic. You should be well informed about your topic. In addition, you should select an issue narrow enough to be treated effectively in the space available to you, or confine your discussion to a single aspect of a broad issue. In selecting your topic you should also consider your purpose—what you expect your argument to accomplish and how you wish your audience to respond. If your topic is so far-reaching that you cannot identify what you want to convince readers to think, or your purpose so idealistic that your expectations of their response are impossible or unreasonable, your essay will suffer.

Taking a Stand

After you have chosen your topic, you are ready to take your stand—to state the position you will argue in the form of a thesis. Consider the following thesis statement:

Solar power is the best available solution to the impending energy crisis.

This thesis says that you believe there will be an energy crisis in the future, that there is more than one possible solution to the crisis, and that solar energy is a better solution than any other. In your argument you will have to support each of these three points logically and persuasively.

After stating your thesis, you should examine it to make sure that it is *debatable*. There is no point in arguing a statement of fact or a point that people accept as self-evident. A good argumentative thesis, therefore, would contain a proposition that has at least two sides. A good way to test the suitability of your thesis for an argumentation essay is to formulate an **antithesis,** a statement that asserts the opposite position. If you know that some people would argue in support of the antithesis, you can be certain that your thesis is indeed debatable.

Thesis: Because immigrants have contributed much to the development of the United States, immigration quotas should be relaxed.

Antithesis: Even though immigrants have contributed much to the development of the United States, immigration quotas should not be relaxed.

Analyzing Your Audience

Before writing any essay, you should analyze the characteristics, values, and interests of your audience. In argumentation it is especially important to assess what beliefs or opinions your readers are likely to hold and whether they are likely to be friendly, neutral, or hostile to your thesis. It is probably best to assume that some, if not most, of your readers are at least skeptically neutral. That assumption will keep you from making claims you cannot support. If your position is controversial, you should assume an informed and determined opposition is looking for holes in your argument.

The challenge that arguments must routinely meet is to appeal to readers who are neutral or even hostile to your position and to change their views so that they match your own more closely. For example, it would be relatively easy to convince college students that tuition should be lowered or instructors that faculty salaries should be raised. You could be reasonably sure, in advance, that each group would be friendly and would agree with your position. But argument requires more than telling people what they already believe. It would be much harder to convince college students that tuition should be raised to pay for an increase in instructors' salaries or to persuade instructors to forgo raises so that tuition can remain the same. Remember, your audience will not just take your word for things. You must provide evidence that will support your thesis and reasoning that will lead logically to your conclusion.

Gathering Evidence

All the points you make in your paper must be supported. If they are not, your audience will dismiss them as unfounded, irrelevant, or unclear. Sometimes you can support a statement with appeals to emotion, but most of the time you support the points of your argument by appealing to reason—by providing **evidence,** material presented in support of your position.

As you gather evidence and assess its effectiveness, keep in mind that evidence in an argumentative essay never proves anything conclusively. If it did, there would be no debate and hence no point in arguing. The best evidence can do is convince your audience that an assertion is reasonable and worth considering.

Kinds of Evidence. Evidence can be fact or opinion. *Facts* are statements that most people agree are true and that can be verified independently. Facts—including statistics—are the most commonly used type of evidence. It is a *fact,* for example, that fewer people per year were killed in automobile accidents in the 1990s than in the 1960s. Facts may be drawn from your own experience as well as from reading and observation. It may, for instance, be a fact that you yourself have had a serious automobile accident. Quite often, facts are more convincing when they are supplemented by *opinions,* interpretations of facts. To connect your facts about automobile accidents to the assertion that installation of airbags on all cars and trucks could reduce deaths still further, you could cite the opinions of experts—consumer advocate Ralph Nader, for example. His statements, along with the facts you have assembled and your own interpretations of those facts, could convince readers that your solution to the problem of highway deaths is reasonable.

Keep in mind that not all opinions are equally convincing. The opinions of experts are more convincing than are those of individuals who have less experience with or knowledge of an issue. Your personal opinions can be excellent evidence (provided you are knowledgeable about your subject) but they are usually less convincing to your audience than expert opinion or facts are. In the final analysis, what is important is not just the quality of the evidence, but also the credibility of the person offering the evidence.

As soon as you decide on a topic, you should begin to gather as much evidence as you can. Brainstorm to think of ideas and observations that support your claims. If your topic is technical or demands support beyond your own knowledge of the subject, go to the library and search reference books, print indexes, and computer databases to locate the facts and expert opinions you need.

Criteria for Evidence. As you select and review material, choose your evidence with three criteria in mind:

1. *Your evidence should be relevant.* It should support your thesis and should be pertinent to the argument you are making. As you present evidence, be careful not to concentrate so much on

a specific example that you lose sight of the point you are supporting. If you do, you may digress and your readers may become confused. In arguing for mandatory AIDS testing for all health-care workers, one student made the point that AIDS is at epidemic proportions. To illustrate this point he offered a discussion of the bubonic plague in fourteenth-century Europe. Although interesting, this example was not relevant because the writer did not link his discussion to his assertions about AIDS. To show its relevance he could, for instance, have compared the spread of the bubonic plague in the fourteenth century to the spread of AIDS today.

2. *Your evidence should be representative.* It should represent the *full range* of opinions about your subject, not just one side or the other. Examples and expert opinions should be typical, not aberrant. Suppose you are writing an argumentation essay in which you support the building of a trash-to-steam plant in your city. To support your thesis you present the example of Baltimore, which has a successful trash-to-steam program. As you consider your evidence, you should ask yourself if Baltimore's experience with trash-to-steam is typical. Did other cities have less success? Look especially hard at opinions that disagree with the position you plan to take. They will help you understand your opposition and enable you to refute it effectively when you write your paper.

3. *Your evidence should be sufficient.* You should include enough evidence to support your claims. The amount of evidence you need depends on the length of your paper, your audience, and your thesis. It stands to reason that you would use fewer examples in a two-page paper than in a ten-page research assignment. Similarly, an audience that is favorably disposed to your thesis might need only one or two examples to be convinced, while a skeptical audience would need many more. As you develop your thesis, consider the level of support you will need as you write your paper. You may decide that a narrower, more limited thesis might be easier to support than one that is more expansive.

What kind of evidence might change readers' minds? That depends on the readers, on the issue, and on the facts at hand. You need to put yourself in the place of your readers and ask what would make them agree with your thesis. Why should a student agree to pay higher tuition? You might concede that tuition is high but point out that it has not been raised for three years, while the college's costs have kept going up. Heating and maintaining the buildings costs more and professors' salaries have failed to keep pace with the cost of living, with the result that several excellent teachers have recently left the college for higher-paying jobs. Furthermore, cuts in federal and state funding have already caused a reduction in the number of courses offered. Similarly, how could you convince a professor to agree to accept no raise at all, especially in light of the fact that faculty salaries have not kept up with inflation? You could say that because cuts in government funding have already reduced course offerings and because the government has also reduced funds for loans for the many students from families whose incomes average $40,000 or less, any further rise in tuition to pay faculty salaries will cause some students to drop out—and that in turn would cost some instructors their jobs. As you can see, the evidence and reasoning you use in an argument depend to a great extent on whom you want to persuade and what you know about them.

Dealing with the Opposition

When gathering evidence, keep in mind that you cannot ignore arguments against your position. In fact, you should specifically address the most obvious—and sometimes the not-so-obvious—objections to your case. Try to anticipate the objections that a reasonable person would have to your thesis. By directly addressing these objections in your essay, you go a long way toward convincing readers that your arguments are sound. This part of an argument, called **refutation,** is essential to making the strongest case possible on behalf of your thesis.

You can refute opposing arguments by showing that they are unsound, unfair, or weak. Frequently, you present contrasting evidence to show the weakness of your opponent's case. Careful definition and cause-and-effect analysis may also prove effective. In the following passage from the classic essay "Politics and the English Language," George Orwell refutes an opponent's argument:

> I said earlier that the decadence of our language is probably curable. Those who deny this would argue, if they produced an argument at all, that language merely reflects existing social conditions, and that we cannot influence its development by any direct tinkering with words and constructions. So far as the general tone or spirit of a language goes, this may be true, but it is not true in detail. Silly words and expressions have often disappeared, though not through any evolutionary process but owing to the conscious actions of a minority.

Orwell begins by stating the point he wants to make. He goes on to define the argument against his position, and then he identifies its weakness. Later on in the essay Orwell bolsters his argument by presenting two examples that support his point.

When an opponent's argument is so compelling that it cannot be easily dismissed, you should concede its strength. By acknowledging that a point is well taken, you reinforce the impression that you are a fair-minded person. If possible, point out the limitations of the opposing position and then move your argument to more solid ground. Many times a strong point represents only *one* element in a multi-faceted problem.

When planning your argumentative essay, write down all possible arguments against your thesis that you can identify. Then, as you marshal your evidence, you can decide which points you will refute—keeping in mind that careful readers will expect you to refute intelligently the most compelling of your opponent's arguments. Take care, though, not to distort an opponent's argument or make it seem weaker than it actually is. This technique, called creating a *straw man,* can backfire and actually turn fair-minded readers against you.

Using Deductive and Inductive Argument

In an argument, you may move from evidence to conclusion in two basic ways. One, called **deductive reasoning,** proceeds from a general premise or assumption to a specific conclusion. Deduction is what most people mean when they speak of logic. Using strict logical form, deduction holds that if all the statements in the argument are true, the conclusion must also be true. The other method of moving from evidence to conclusion is called **inductive reasoning.** Induction proceeds from individual observations to a more general conclusion and uses no strict form. It requires only that all the relevant evidence be stated and that the conclusion fit the evidence better than any other conclusion would. Most written arguments use a combination of deductive and inductive reasoning, but it is simpler to discuss and illustrate them separately.

Deductive Arguments. The basic form of a deductive argument is a **syllogism.** A syllogism consists of a *major premise,* which is a general statement; a *minor premise,* which is a related but more specific statement; and a *conclusion,* which has to be drawn from those premises. Consider the following example:

Major premise: All Olympic runners are fast.
Minor premise: Florence Griffith Joyner is an Olympic runner.
  Conclusion: Therefore, Florence Griffith Joyner is fast.

As you can see, if you grant each of the premises, then you must also grant the conclusion—and it is the only conclusion that you can properly draw. You cannot conclude that Florence Griffith Joyner is slow, because that conclusion contradicts the premises. Nor can you conclude (even if it is true) that Florence Griffith Joyner is tall, because that conclusion goes beyond the premises.

Of course this argument seems obvious, and it is much simpler than an argumentative essay would be. But a deductive argument's premises can be fairly elaborate. The Declaration of Independence (p. 556) has at its core a deductive argument that might be summarized in this way:

Major premise: Tyrannical rulers deserve no loyalty.
Minor premise: King George III is a tyrannical ruler.
  Conclusion: Therefore, King George III deserves no loyalty.

The major premise is a truth the Declaration says is self-evident. Much of the Declaration consists of evidence to support the minor premise that King George is a tyrannical ruler. And the conclusion, because it is drawn from those premises, has the force of irrefutable logic: The king deserves no loyalty from his American subjects, who are therefore entitled to revolt against him.

When a conclusion follows logically from the major and minor premises, then the argument is said to be *valid*. But if the syllogism is not logical, the argument is not valid and the conclusion is not sound. For example, the following syllogism is not logical:

Major premise: All dogs are animals.
Minor premise: All cats are animals.
  Conclusion: Therefore, all dogs are cats.

Of course the conclusion is absurd. But how did we wind up with such a ridiculous conclusion when both premises are obviously true? The answer is that although both cats and dogs are animals, cats are not included in the major premise of the syllogism. Therefore, the form of the syllogism is defective, and the argument is invalid. Here is another example of an invalid argument:

Major premise: All dogs are animals.
Minor premise: Ralph is an animal.
  Conclusion: Therefore, Ralph is a dog.

Even without understanding formal logic, most of us can tell that there is a problem with this conclusion. This error in logic occurs when the minor premise refers to a term in the major premise that is *undistributed*—that is, it covers only some of the items in the class it denotes. In the major premise, *dogs* is the distributed term; it designates *all dogs*. The minor premise, however, refers not to *dogs* but to *animals,* which is undistributed because it refers only to animals that are dogs. Just because, as the minor premise establishes, Ralph is an animal, it does not follow that he is also a dog. He could be a cat, a horse, or even a human being.

But even if a syllogism is valid—that is, correct in its form—its conclusion will not necessarily be *true.* The following syllogism draws a false conclusion:

Major premise: All dogs are brown.
Minor premise: My poodle Toby is a dog.
   Conclusion: Therefore, Toby is brown.

As it happens, Toby is black. The conclusion is false because the major premise is false: Many dogs are not brown. If Toby had actually been brown, the conclusion would have been correct, but only by chance, not by logic. To be *sound,* the syllogism must be both logical and true.

The advantage of a deductive argument is that if you convince your audience to accept your major and minor premises, they should also accept your conclusion. The problem is to establish your basic assumptions. You try to select premises that you know your audience accepts or that are self-evident—that is, premises that most people would believe to be true. Do not assume, however, that "most people" refers only to your friends and acquaintances. Think, too, of those who may hold different views. If you think that your premises are too controversial or difficult to establish firmly, you should use inductive reasoning.

Inductive Arguments.   Inductive arguments move from specific examples or facts to a general conclusion. Unlike deduction, induction has no distinctive form, and its conclusions are less definitive than those of syllogisms whose forms are valid and whose premises are clearly true. Still, much inductive thinking and writing based on that thinking tends to follow a certain process. First, usually, you decide on a question to be answered—or, especially in scientific work, you identify a tentative answer to such a question, called a *hypothesis.* Then you gather all the evidence you can find that is relevant to the question and that may be important to finding the answer. Finally you draw a conclusion, called an *inference,* that answers the question and takes the evidence into account. Here is a very simple example:

Question: How did that living-room window get broken?
Evidence: There is a baseball on the living-room floor.
             The baseball was not there this morning.
             Some children were playing baseball this afternoon.
             They were playing in the vacant lot across from the window.
             They stopped playing a little while ago.
             They aren't in the vacant lot now.
Conclusion: One of the children hit or threw the ball through the
             window. Then they all ran away.

The conclusion, because it takes all of the evidence into account, seems obvious. But if it turned out that the children had been playing softball, not baseball, that one additional piece of evidence would make the conclusion very doubtful—and the true answer would be much harder to infer. And even if the conclusion is believable, you cannot necessarily assume it is true: After all, the window could have been broken in some other way. For example, perhaps a bird flew against it, and perhaps the baseball in the living room had been there unnoticed all day, so that the second piece of "evidence" is not true.

Because inductive arguments tend to be more complicated than the example above, you must consider how to move from the evidence you have collected to a sound conclusion. That crucial step can be a big one, and indeed it sometimes requires what is called an *inductive leap.* With induction, conclusions are never certain, only highly probable. Although the form of induction does not point to any particular type of conclusion the way deduction does, making sure that your evidence is *relevant, representative,* and *sufficient* (see pp. 537–38) can increase the probability of your conclusion's being sound. In addition, the more information you gather, the smaller the gap between your evidence and your conclusion.

Considering possible conclusions is a good way to avoid reaching an unjustified or false conclusion. In the example above, a hypothesis something like this might follow the question:

Hypothesis: One of those children playing baseball broke the living-
             room window.

Many people stop reasoning at this point, without considering the evidence. But when the gap between your evidence and your conclusion is too great, you can be accused of reaching a hasty conclusion or one that is not borne out by the facts. This well-named error is called *jumping to a conclusion* because it amounts to a premature inductive leap. In induction, the hypothesis is merely the starting point. The rest of the inductive process continues as if the question were still to be answered—as in fact it is until all the evidence has been taken into account.

Toulmin Logic.   Another method for structuring arguments has been advanced by the philosopher Stephen Toulmin. In an effort to describe argumentation as it actually occurs in everyday life, Toulmin put forth a model that divides arguments into three parts: *the claim, the grounds,* and *the warrant.* The **claim** is the main point of the essay. Usually the claim is stated directly as the thesis, but in some arguments it may be implied. The **grounds**—the material that a writer uses to support the claim—can be evidence (facts or expert opinion) or appeals to the emotions or values of the audience. The **warrant** is the inference that connects the claim to the grounds. It can be a belief that is taken for granted or an assumption that underlies the argument.

In the simplest terms, an argument following Toulmin logic would look like this:

Claim: Carol should be elected class president.
Grounds: Carol is an honor student.
Warrant: A person who is an honor student would make a good class president.

When you formulate an argument using Toulmin logic, you still use inductive and deductive reasoning. You derive your claim inductively from facts and examples, and you connect the grounds and warrant to your claim deductively. For example, the deductive argument in the Declaration of Independence that was summarized on page 541 can be represented this way:

Claim: King George III deserves no loyalty.
Grounds: King George III is a tyrannical ruler. (supported by facts and examples)
Warrant: Tyrannical rulers deserve no loyalty.

Recognizing Fallacies

Fallacies are statements that may sound reasonable or true but are not logically defensible and may actually be deceptive. When your readers detect them, such statements can backfire and turn even a sympathetic audience against your position. Here are some of the more common fallacies that you should try to avoid:

Begging the Question. Begging the question is a logical fallacy that assumes in the premise what the arguer is trying to prove in the conclusion. This tactic asks readers to agree that certain points are self-evident when they are not.

> The unfair and shortsighted legislation that limits free trade is clearly a threat to the American economy.

Restrictions against free trade may or may not be unfair and shortsighted, but emotionally loaded language does not constitute proof. The statement begs the question because it assumes what it should be proving—that restrictive legislation is dangerous.

Argument from Analogy. An **analogy** is a comparison of two unlike things. Although analogies can explain an abstract or unclear idea, they are not proof. An argument that is based on an analogy and ignores important dissimilarities between the two things being compared is a fallacy.

> The overcrowded conditions in some parts of our city have forced people together like rats in a cage. Like rats, they will eventually turn on one another, fighting and killing until a balance is restored. It is therefore necessary that we vote to appropriate funds to build low-cost housing.

No evidence is offered that people behave like rats under these or any other conditions. You should not assume that simply because two things have some characteristics in common, they are alike in other respects.

Personal Attack (Argument *Ad Hominem*). This fallacy tries to turn attention away from the facts of an issue by attacking the motives or character of one's opponents.

> The public should not take seriously Dr. Mason's plan for upgrading county health services. He is a recovering alcoholic whose second wife recently divorced him.

This attack on Dr. Mason's character says nothing about the quality of his plan. Sometimes a connection exists between a person's private and public lives—for example, a case of conflict of interest. But no evidence of such a connection is given here.

Hasty or Sweeping Generalization. A form of jumping to a conclusion, this fallacy occurs when a conclusion is reached on the basis of too little evidence.

Our son Marc really benefited socially from going to nursery school; I think every child should go.

Perhaps other children would benefit from nursery school, and perhaps not, but no conclusion about children in general can be reached on the basis of one child's experience.

False Dilemma (Either/Or Fallacy). This kind of argument assumes that there are only two alternatives when more exist.

We must choose between life and death, between intervention and genocide. There can be no neutral position on this issue.

An argument like this oversimplifies issues and forces people to choose between extremes instead of exploring more moderate positions.

Equivocation. This fallacy occurs when the meaning of a key term changes at some point in an argument. Equivocation makes it seem as if a conclusion follows from premises when it actually does not.

As a human endeavor computers are a praiseworthy and even remarkable accomplishment. But how human can we hope to be if we rely on computers to make our decisions?

The use of *human* in the first sentence refers to the entire human race. In the second sentence *human* means "merciful" or "civilized." By subtly shifting this term to refer to qualities characteristic of people as opposed to machines, the writer makes his argument seem more sound than it is.

Red Herring. This fallacy occurs when the focus of an argument is changed to divert the audience from the actual issue.

So far Mr. Bradley, our state representative, has spent months fighting the proposed tax bill. The governor has said that she needs the revenue that this bill offers, but Mr. Bradley refuses to support her. One can only wonder if Mr. Bradley has nothing better to do in his own district than to spend so much time opposing the governor.

The focus of this argument should be the merits of the tax bill. Instead, the writer shifts to the irrelevant issue of Mr. Bradley's spending too much time opposing the governor.

You Also (*Tu Quoque*). This fallacy asserts that an opponent's argument has no value because the opponent does not follow his or her own advice. In other words, an opponent is accused of acting in a way that is not in line with his or her stated position.

How can that judge favor stronger penalties for convicted drug dealers? During his confirmation hearings, he admitted having smoked marijuana when he was a student.

Appeal to Doubtful Authority. Often people will attempt to bolster an argument with references to experts or famous people. These appeals are valid when the person quoted or referred to is an expert in the area being discussed. They are fallacies, however, when the individuals cited have no expertise concerning the issue.

According to Ted Koppel, interest rates will remain low during the next fiscal year.

Although Ted Koppel is a respected journalist, he has no background in business or finance. In the final analysis, his pronouncements about interest rates are no more than a personal opinion or, at best, an educated guess.

Misleading Statistics. Although statistics are a powerful form of factual evidence, they can be misrepresented or distorted in an attempt to influence an audience.

Women will never be competent electricians; 50 percent of the women in the electrical technology section failed the exam.

Here the writer has neglected to mention that there were only two women in the course. Because this statistic is not based on a large enough sample, it cannot be used as evidence to support the argument.

***Post Hoc, Ergo Propter Hoc* (After This, Therefore Because of This).** This fallacy, known as ***post hoc* reasoning,** assumes that because two events occur close together in time, the first must cause the second.

Every time a Republican is elected president a recession follows. If we want to avoid another recession, we should elect a Democrat.

Even if it is true that recessions always occur during the tenure of Republican presidents, no causal connection has been established. (See pp. 288–89.)

***Non Sequitur* (It Does Not Follow).**   This fallacy occurs when a statement does not logically follow from a previous statement.

Disarmament weakened the United States after World War I. Disarmament also weakened the United States after the Vietnam War. For this reason, gun control will weaken the United States.

The historical effects of disarmament have nothing to do with current efforts to control the sale of guns. Therefore, the conclusion is a *non sequitur.*

STRUCTURING AN ARGUMENTATIVE ESSAY

An argumentative essay, like other kinds of essays, has an *introduction,* a *body,* and a *conclusion.* But an argumentative essay has its own special structure, one that ensures that ideas are presented logically and convincingly. The Declaration of Independence follows the classic design typical of many arguments:

Introduction: Introduces the issue.
               States the thesis.
     Body: Induction—offers evidence to support the thesis.
               Deduction—uses syllogisms to support the thesis.
               States the arguments against the thesis and refutes them.
Conclusion: Sums up the argument if it is long and complex.
               Restates the thesis.
               Makes a forceful closing statement.

Jefferson begins the Declaration by presenting the issue that the document addresses: the obligation of the people of the American colonies to tell the world why they must separate from Great Britain. Next Jefferson states his thesis that because of the tyranny of the British king, the colonies must replace his rule with another form of government. In the body of the Declaration, he offers as evidence twenty-eight examples of injustice endured by the colonies. Following the evidence, Jefferson refutes counterarguments by explaining how time and time again the colonists have appealed to the British for redress, but without result. In his concluding paragraph, he restates the thesis and reinforces it one final time. He ends with a flourish: Speaking for the representatives of the United States, he explicitly dissolves all political connections between England and America.

Not all arguments, however, follow this pattern. Your material, your thesis, your purpose, your audience, the type of argument you are writing, and the limitations of your assignment ultimately determine the strategies you use. If your thesis is especially novel or controversial, for example, the refutation of opposing arguments may come first. For the same reason, opposing positions may even be mentioned in the introduction—provided they are discussed more fully later in the argument.

Suppose your journalism instructor gives you the following assignment: "Select a controversial topic that interests you, and write a brief editorial. Direct your editorial to readers who do not share your views, and try to convince them that your position is reasonable. Be sure to acknowledge the view your audience holds and to refute possible criticisms of your argument." You are especially well informed about one local issue because you have just read a series of articles on it. A citizens group is lobbying for a local ordinance that would authorize government funding for parochial schools in your community. Because you have also recently studied the constitutional doctrine of separation of church and state in your American government class, you know you could argue fairly and strongly against the position taken by this group.

An informal outline of your essay might look like this:

Issue introduced:	Should public tax revenues be spent on aid to parochial schools?
Thesis statement:	Despite the pleas of citizen groups like Parochial School Parents United, using tax dollars to support church-affiliated schools directly violates the United States Constitution.
Evidence (deduction):	Explain general principle of separation of church and state in the Constitution.
Evidence (induction):	Present recent examples of court cases interpreting and applying this principle.
Evidence (deduction):	Explain how the Constitution and the court cases apply to your community's situation.
Opposition refuted:	Identify and respond to arguments used by Parochial School Parents United. Concede the point that parochial schools educate many children who would

otherwise have to be educated in public schools at taxpayers' expense.

Conclusion: Sum up the argument, restate the thesis, and end with a strong closing statement.

A STUDENT WRITER: ARGUMENTATION

The following editorial, written by Matt Daniels for his college newspaper, illustrates a number of the techniques discussed above.

AN ARGUMENT AGAINST THE
ANNA TODD JENNINGS SCHOLARSHIP*

Introduction   Recently, a dispute has arisen over the "Caucasian-   1
restricted" Anna Todd Jennings scholarship. Anna Jennings

Summary of   died in 1955, and her will established a trust that granted a
controversy
scholarship of up to $15,000 for a deserving student.
Unfortunately, Jennings, who had certain racist views,
limited her scholarship to "Caucasian students." After
much debate with family and friends, I, a white, well-
qualified, and definitely deserving student, have decided not
to apply for the scholarship. It is my view that despite

Thesis   arguments to the contrary, applying for the Anna Todd
statement   Jennings scholarship furthers the racist ideas that were held
by its founder.

Argument   Most people would agree that racism in any form is an   2
(deductive)
evil that should be opposed. The Anna Todd Jennings
scholarship is a subtle but nonetheless dangerous expression
of racism. It explicitly discriminates against African
Americans, Asians, Latinos, Native Americans, and
others. By providing a scholarship for whites only, Anna
Jennings frustrates the aspirations of groups who until
recently had been virtually kept out of the educational

*Eds Note—This essay discusses an actual situation; however, the name of the scholarship has been changed here.

mainstream. On this basis alone, students should refuse to apply and should actively work to encourage the school to challenge the racist provisions of Anna Todd Jennings's will. Such challenges have been upheld by the courts: The striking down of a similar clause in the will of the eighteenth-century financier Stephen Girard is one example.

Argument (inductive) The school itself must share some blame in this case. 3 Students who applied for the Anna Todd Jennings scholarship were unaware of its restrictions. The director of the financial aid office has acknowledged that he knew about the racial restrictions of the scholarship but thought **Evidence** that students should have the right to apply anyway. In addition, the materials distributed by the financial aid office gave no indication that the award was limited to Caucasians. Students were required to fill out forms, submit financial statements, and forward transcripts. In addition to this material, all students were told to attach a recent photograph to their application. Little did the applicants know that the sole purpose of this innocuous little picture was to separate whites from nonwhites. By keeping secret the restrictions of the scholarship, the school has put students, most of whom are not racists, in the position of unwittingly endorsing **Conclusion (based on evidence)** Anna Jennings's racism. Thus, the school has been in collusion with the administrators of the Anna Todd Jennings trust.

Refutation of opposing argument The problem that faces students is how best to deal with 4 the benefaction of a racist. A recent edition of the school paper contained several letters saying that students should accept Anna Jennings's scholarship money. One student said, "If we do not take that money and use our education to topple the barriers of prejudice, we are giving the money to those who will use the money in the opposite fashion." This argument, although attractive, is flawed. If an individual accepts a scholarship with racial restrictions, then he or she is actually endorsing the principles behind it. If a student does not want to appear to endorse racism, then he or she should reject the scholarship, even if this action causes hardship or gives adversaries a momentary advantage. To do otherwise is to further the cause of the individual who set up the scholarship. The best way to register a protest is to work to change the requirement for the scholarship and to encourage others not to apply as long as the racial restrictions exist.

Refutation of opposing argument

Another student letter made the point that a number of other restricted scholarships are available at the school and no one seems to question them. For example, one is for the children of veterans, another is for women, and yet another is earmarked for African Americans. Certainly all these scholarships do have restrictions, but to say that all restrictions are the same is to make a hasty generalization. Women, African Americans, and the children of veterans are groups whose special treatment is justified. Both women and African Americans have been discriminated against for years, and many educational opportunities have been denied them. Earmarking scholarships for them is simply a means of restoring some measure of equality. The children of veterans have been singled out because their parents have rendered extraordinary service to their country. Whites, however, do not fall into either of these categories. Special treatment for them is based solely on race and has nothing to do with any objective standard of need or merit.

Conclusion

I hope that by refusing to apply for the Anna Todd Jennings scholarship, I have encouraged other students to think about the issues involved in their own decisions. All of us have a responsibility to ourselves and to society. If we

Restatement of thesis

truly believe that racism in all its forms is evil, then we have

5

6

Concluding statement to make a choice between sacrifice and hypocrisy. Faced with these options, our decision should be clear: Accept the loss of funds as an opportunity to explore your values and to fight for principles in which you believe; if you do, this opportunity is worth far more than any scholarship.

Points for Special Attention

Gathering Evidence. Because of his involvement with his subject, Matt Daniels was able to provide examples from his own experience to make his point and did not have to do library research. This does not mean, however, that Matt did not spend a lot of time thinking about ideas and selecting evidence. He had to review the requirements for the scholarship and decide on the arguments he would make. In addition, he reviewed an article that appeared in the school newspaper and the letters students wrote in response to the article. He then chose facts that would help sustain interest and add authority to his points.

Certainly statistics, studies, and expert testimony, if they exist, would strengthen Matt's argument. But even without such evidence, an argument such as this one, based on strong logic and personal experience, can be quite compelling.

Refuting Opposing Arguments. Matt devotes two paragraphs to presenting and refuting arguments made by those who believe qualified students should apply for the scholarship despite its racial restrictions. He begins this section by asking a **rhetorical question**—a question asked not for information but to further the argument. He goes on to present what he considers to be the two strongest arguments against his thesis—that students should take the money and work to fight racism and that other scholarships at the school have restrictions. Matt counters these arguments by identifying a flaw in the logic of the first argument and by pointing to a fallacy, a hasty generalization, in the second.

Audience. Because his essay was an editorial for his college newspaper, Matt assumed an audience of general readers who were familiar with the issue he was discussing. Letters to the editor of the paper convinced him that his position was unusual, and he concluded that his readers, mostly students and instructors, would have to be persuaded that his points were valid. For this reason he is careful to present himself as a reasonable person, to explain issues that he believes are central to his case, and to avoid *ad hominem* attacks. In addition, he avoids sweeping generalizations and name-calling and goes into great detail to support his assertions and to convince his readers that his points are worth considering.

Organization.   Matt uses several strategies discussed earlier in the chapter. He begins his essay by introducing the issue he is going to discuss and then states his thesis: Applying for the Anna Todd Jennings scholarship furthers the racist ideas that were held by its founder.

Because Matt had given a good deal of thought to his subject, he was able to construct two fairly strong arguments to support his position. His first argument is deductive. He begins by stating a premise that he believes is self-evident. Most people agree that racism should be opposed. The rest of his argument follows a straightforward deductive pattern:

Major premise: Racism is an evil that should be opposed.
Minor premise: The Anna Todd Jennings scholarship is racist.
    Conclusion: Therefore, the Anna Todd Jennings scholarship should be opposed.

Matt ends his argument with a piece of factual evidence that reinforces his conclusion—the relatively recent successful challenge to the will of financier Stephen Girard, which limited admittance to Girard College in Philadelphia to white male orphans.

Matt's second argument is inductive, asserting that the school has put students in the position of unknowingly supporting racism. The argument begins with Matt's hypothesis and presents the fact that the school was actually aware of the racist restrictions of the scholarship and that it did nothing to make students aware of them. According to Matt, the school's knowledge and tacit approval of the situation leads to the conclusion that the school is in collusion with those who manage the scholarship.

In his fourth and fifth paragraphs, Matt refutes two criticisms of his argument. Although his conclusion is rather brief, it does effectively reinforce and support his main idea. Matt ends his essay by recommending a course of action to his fellow students.

Focus on Revision.   Matt constructed a solid argument that addresses the central issue very effectively. He could, however, add a section that gives more information about Anna Todd Jennings and her bequest. Of course the scholarship is the central issue of the essay, but more information about Anna Todd Jennings would help readers understand the implications of accepting her money. As it now stands, the essay dismisses Anna Todd Jennings as a racist, but biographical material and excerpts from the will—both of which appeared in the school paper—would enable readers to grasp the extent of her prejudice.

The essays that follow represent a wide variety of topical perspectives. Each, however, presents an argument to support a controversial thesis. In three cases, essays that take opposing stands on the same issue are paired in debates. In an additional debate, four essays on a single topic are included to present a greater variety of viewpoints. As you read each essay, try to identify the strategies that each author uses to convince readers.

THE DECLARATION OF INDEPENDENCE

Thomas Jefferson

Thomas Jefferson was born in 1743 at Shadwell, in what is now Albemarle County, Virginia. He attended the College of William and Mary and became a lawyer. Jefferson was elected to the House of Burgesses, Virginia's colonial legislature, in 1769 and began a distinguished political career. In 1774 he wrote a daring pamphlet titled A Summary View of the Rights of British America, *in which he denied all British parliamentary authority over America, and became known as a leading patriot. He was named a delegate to the second Continental Congress in Philadelphia, and on June 11, 1776, he was elected to join Benjamin Franklin, John Adams, Roger Sherman, and Robert Livingston in drafting a declaration of independence. The draft was written entirely by Jefferson, with suggestions from the other commission members. (Congress amended it to remove a passage containing a strong statement against slavery.) Jefferson also served as governor of Virginia; minister to France (serving with Benjamin Franklin on the commission that signed the Treaty of Paris, which ended the Revolutionary War); secretary of state in President George Washington's first cabinet; vice president under John Adams; and finally president—the first to be inaugurated in Washington—from 1801 to 1809. During his retirement, Jefferson founded the University of Virginia. He wrote only one book,* Notes on the State of Virginia, *but his published writings and correspondence fill sixty volumes. He died on July 4, 1826. The Declaration of Independence challenges a basic assumption of the age in which it was written—the divine right of kings. To accomplish his ends, Jefferson followed many of the principles of argumentative writing. Unlike many modern revolutionary manifestos, the Declaration of Independence is a model of clarity and precision that attempts to establish and support its thesis by means of irrefutable logic and reason.*

When in the course of human events, it becomes necessary for one 1
people to dissolve the political bands which have connected them
with another, and to assume among the powers of the earth, the
separate and equal station to which the Laws of Nature and of Nature's God entitle them, a decent respect to the opinions of mankind

requires that they should declare the causes which impel them to the separation.

We hold these truths to be self-evident, that all men are created   2
equal, that they are endowed by their Creator with certain unalienable rights, that among these are life, liberty and the pursuit of happiness. That to secure these rights, governments are instituted among men, deriving their just powers from the consent of the governed. That whenever any form of government becomes destructive of these ends, it is the right of the people to alter or to abolish it, and to institute new government, laying its foundation on such principles and organizing its powers in such form, as to them shall seem most likely to effect their safety and happiness. Prudence, indeed, will dictate that governments long established should not be changed for light and transient causes; and accordingly all experience hath shown, that mankind are more disposed to suffer, while evils are sufferable, than to right themselves by abolishing the forms to which they are accustomed. But when a long train of abuses and usurpations, pursuing invariably the same object, evinces a design to reduce them under absolute despotism, it is their right, it is their duty, to throw off such government, and to provide new guards for their future security. Such has been the patient sufferance of these Colonies; and such is now the necessity which constrains them to alter their former systems of government. This history of the present King of Great Britain is a history of repeated injuries and usurpations, all having in direct object the establishment of an absolute tyranny over these States. To prove this, let facts be submitted to a candid world.

He has refused his assent to laws, the most wholesome and neces-   3
sary for the public good.

He has forbidden his Governors to pass laws of immediate and   4
pressing importance, unless suspended in their operation till his assent should be obtained; and when so suspended, he has utterly neglected to attend to them.

He has refused to pass other laws for the accommodation of large   5
districts of people, unless those people would relinquish the right of representation in the legislature, a right inestimable to them and formidable to tyrants only.

He has called together legislative bodies at places unusual, un-   6
comfortable, and distant from the depository of their public records, for the sole purpose of fatiguing them into compliance with his measures.

He has dissolved representative houses repeatedly, for opposing 7 with manly firmness his invasions on the rights of people.

He has refused for a long time, after such dissolutions, to cause 8 others to be elected; whereby the legislative powers, incapable of annihilation, have returned to the people at large for their exercise; the State remaining in the meantime exposed to all the dangers of invasion from without and convulsions within.

He has endeavoured to prevent the population of these states; for 9 that purpose obstructing the laws for naturalization of foreigners; refusing to pass others to encourage their migration hither, and raising the conditions of new appropriations of lands.

He has obstructed the administration of justice, by refusing his 10 assent to laws for establishing judiciary powers.

He has made judges dependent on his will alone, for the tenure of 11 their offices, and the amount and payment of their salaries.

He has erected a multitude of new offices, and sent hither swarms 12 of officers to harass our people, and eat out their substance.

He has kept among us, in times of peace, standing armies without 13 the consent of our legislatures.

He has affected to render the military independent of and superior 14 to the civil power.

He has combined with others to subject us to a jurisdiction foreign 15 to our constitution, and unacknowledged by our laws; giving his assent to their acts of pretended legislation:

For quartering large bodies of troops among us: 16

For protecting them, by a mock trial, from punishment for any murders which they should commit on the inhabitants of these States: 17

For cutting off our trade with all parts of the world: 18

For imposing taxes on us without our consent: 19

For depriving us in many cases of the benefits of trial by jury: 20

For transporting us beyond seas to be tried for pretended offences: 21

For abolishing the free system of English laws in a neighbouring 22 Province, establishing therein an arbitrary government, and enlarging its boundaries so as to render it at once an example and fit instrument for introducing the same absolute rule into these Colonies:

For taking away our Charters, abolishing our most valuable laws, 23 and altering fundamentally the forms of our governments:

For suspending our own legislatures, and declaring themselves 24 invested with power to legislate for us in all cases whatsoever.

He has abdicated government here, by declaring us out of his protection and waging war against us. 25

He has plundered our seas, ravaged our coasts, burnt our towns, 26 and destroyed the lives of our people.

He is at this time transporting large armies of foreign mercenar- 27
ies to complete the works of death, desolation and tyranny, already
begun with circumstances of cruelty and perfidy scarcely paralleled
in the most barbarous ages, and totally unworthy the head of a
civilized nation.

He has constrained our fellow citizens taken captive on the high 28
seas to bear arms against their country, to become the executioners
of their friends and brethren, or to fall themselves by their hands.

He has excited domestic insurrections amongst us, and has en- 29
deavoured to bring on the inhabitants of our frontiers, the merciless
Indian savages, whose known rule of warfare, is an undistinguished
destruction of all ages, sexes, and conditions.

In every stage of these oppressions we have petitioned for redress 30
in the most humble terms: our repeated petitions have been answered only by repeated injury. A prince whose character is thus
marked by every act which may define a tyrant is unfit to be the
ruler of a free people.

Nor have we been wanting in attention to our British brethren. We 31
have warned them from time to time of attempts by their legislature
to extend an unwarrantable jurisdiction over us. We have reminded
them of the circumstances of our emigration and settlement here.
We have appealed to their native justice and magnanimity, and we
have conjured them by the ties of our common kindred to disavow
these usurpations, which would inevitably interrupt our connections
and correspondence. They too have been deaf to the voice of justice
and of consanguinity. We must, therefore, acquiesce in the necessity,
which denounces our separation, and hold them, as we hold the rest
of mankind, enemies in war, in peace friends.

We, therefore, the Representatives of the United States of Amer- 32
ica, in General Congress assembled, appealing to the Supreme
Judge of the world for the rectitude of our intentions, do, in the
name, and by authority of the good people of these Colonies, solemnly publish and declare, That these United Colonies are, and of
right ought to be, Free and Independent States; that they are ab-
solved from all allegiance to the British Crown, and that all political
connection between them and the state of Great Britain, is and
ought to be totally dissolved; and that as Free and Independent
States, they have full power to levy war, conclude peace, contract
alliances, establish commerce, and to do all other acts and things
which Independent States may of right do. And for the support of
this declaration, with a firm reliance on the protection of Divine
Providence, we mutually pledge to each other our lives, our fortunes,
and our sacred honor.

COMPREHENSION

1. What "truths" does Jefferson assert are "self-evident"?

2. What does Jefferson say is the source from which governments derive their powers?

3. What reasons does Jefferson give to support his premise that the United States should break away from Great Britain?

4. What conclusions about the British crown does Jefferson draw from the evidence he presents?

PURPOSE AND AUDIENCE

1. What is the major premise of Jefferson's argument? Should Jefferson have done more to establish the truth of this premise?

2. The Declaration of Independence was written during a period now referred to as the Age of Reason. In what ways has Jefferson tried to make his document appear reasonable?

3. For what audience is the document intended? Do you think all those in this audience would have been likely to accept it? Explain.

4. How effectively does Jefferson anticipate and refute the opposition?

5. In paragraph 31, following the list of grievances, why does Jefferson address his "British brethren"?

6. At what point does Jefferson state his thesis? Why does he state it where he does?

STYLE AND STRUCTURE

1. Does the Declaration of Independence rely primarily on inductive or deductive reasoning? Identify examples of each.

2. What techniques does Jefferson use to create smooth and logical transitions from one paragraph to another?

3. Why does Jefferson list all of his twenty-eight grievances? Why doesn't he just summarize them or mention a few representative grievances?

4. Jefferson begins the last paragraph of the Declaration of Independence with "We, therefore. . . ." How effective is this conclusion? Explain.

VOCABULARY PROJECTS

1. Define each of the following words as it is used in this selection.

station (1)	evinces (2)	tenure (11)
impel (1)	despotism (2)	jurisdiction (15)
self-evident (2)	sufferance (2)	arbitrary (22)
endowed (2)	candid (2)	insurrections (29)
deriving (2)	depository (6)	disavow (31)
prudence (2)	dissolutions (8)	consanguinity (31)
transient (2)	annihilation (8)	rectitude (32)
usurpations (2)	appropriations (9)	levy (32)

2. Underline ten words that have negative connotations. How does Jefferson use these words to help him make his point? How do you think words with more neutral connotations would affect his case?

3. What particular words does Jefferson use that are rarely used today? Would the Declaration of Independence be more meaningful today if it were updated, with more familiar words substituted? Try rewriting a paragraph or two, and assess your updated version.

JOURNAL ENTRY

Do you think Jefferson is being fair to the king? Do you think he should have been?

WRITING WORKSHOP

1. Following Jefferson's example, write a declaration of independence from your school, job, family, or any other institution with which you are associated.

2. Write an essay in which you state a grievance you share with other members of some group, and then argue for the best way to eliminate it.

3. In an argumentative essay written from the point of view of King George III, try to convince the colonists that they should not break away from Great Britain. If you can, refute some of the points Jefferson lists in the Declaration.

THEMATIC CONNECTIONS

- "On Seeing England for the First Time" (p. 146)
- "Grant and Lee: A Study in Contrasts" (p. 371)
- "Letter from Birmingham Jail" (p. 562)

LETTER
FROM BIRMINGHAM JAIL

Martin Luther King, Jr.

Martin Luther King, Jr., was born in 1929 in Atlanta, Georgia, and assassinated in 1968 in Memphis, Tennessee. He graduated from Morehouse College in 1948 and received his B.D. from the Crozer Theological Seminary in 1951. After receiving his doctorate in systematic theology from Boston University in 1955, King became pastor of the Dexter Avenue Baptist Church in Montgomery, Alabama. He led a 382-day bus boycott in Montgomery that led to the 1956 Supreme Court decision declaring the Alabama law requiring racial segregation on buses unconstitutional. In 1957, King was elected president of the newly formed Southern Christian Leadership Conference. During this time he developed a philosophy of nonviolent direct protest that would characterize his actions throughout the rest of his career. In 1963, King launched a campaign against segregation in Birmingham, Alabama, that met fierce opposition from police as well as from white moderates who saw him as dangerous. He was also a leader of the March on Washington in August of 1963, where he delivered his famous "I Have a Dream" speech. King was awarded the Nobel Peace Prize in 1964, becoming the youngest person ever to win the prize. His books include Stride Towards Freedom *(1958),* Why We Can't Wait *(1964), and* Where Do We Go From Here: Chaos or Community? *(1967). His shorter writings are collected in* A Testament of Hope *(1968), edited by James M. Washington, and* The Words of Martin Luther King *(1983), selected by Coretta Scott King. During the Birmingham demonstrations, King was arrested and jailed for eight days. He wrote his "Letter from Birmingham Jail" to white clergymen to explain his actions and to answer those who urged him to call off the demonstrations. Having much in common with the Declaration of Independence, "Letter from Birmingham Jail" is a well-reasoned defense of demonstrations and civil disobedience.*

April 16, 1963

My Dear Fellow Clergymen:

While confined here in the Birmingham city jail, I came across your recent statement calling my present activities "unwise and untimely." Seldom do I pause to answer criticism of my work and ideas. If I sought to answer all the criticisms that cross my desk, my secretaries would have little time for anything other than such correspondence in the course of the day, and I would have no time for constructive work. But since I feel that you are men of genuine good will and that your criticisms are sincerely set forth, I want to try to answer your statement in what I hope will be patient and reasonable terms.

I think I should indicate why I am here in Birmingham, since you have been influenced by the view which argues against "outsiders coming in." I have the honor of serving as president of the Southern Christian Leadership Conference, an organization operating in every southern state, with headquarters in Atlanta, Georgia. We have some eighty-five affiliated organizations across the South, and one of them is the Alabama Christian Movement for Human Rights. Frequently we share staff, educational, and financial resources with our affiliates. Several months ago the affiliate here in Birmingham asked us to be on call to engage in a nonviolent direct-action program if such were deemed necessary. We readily consented, and when the hour came we lived up to our promise. So I, along with several members of my staff, am here because I was invited here. I am here because I have organizational ties here.

But more basically, I am in Birmingham because injustice is here. Just as the prophets of the eighth century B.C. left their villages and carried their "thus saith the Lord" far beyond the boundaries of their home towns, and just as the Apostle Paul left his village of Tarsus and carried the gospel of Jesus Christ to the far corners of the Greco-Roman world, so am I compelled to carry the gospel of freedom beyond my own home town. Like Paul, I must constantly respond to the Macedonian call for aid.

Moreover, I am cognizant of the interrelatedness of all communities and states. I cannot sit idly by in Atlanta and not be concerned about what happens in Birmingham. Injustice anywhere is a threat to justice everywhere. We are caught in an inescapable network of mutuality, tied in a single garment of destiny. Whatever affects one directly, affects all indirectly. Never again can we afford to live with the narrow, provincial, "outside agitator" idea. Anyone who lives inside the United States can never be considered an outsider anywhere within its bounds.

You deplore the demonstrations taking place in Birmingham. But your statement, I am sorry to say, fails to express a similar concern for the conditions that brought about the demonstrations. I am sure that none of you would want to rest content with the superficial kind of social analysis that deals merely with effects and does not grapple with underlying causes. It is unfortunate that demonstrations are taking place in Birmingham, but it is even more unfortunate that the city's white power structure left the Negro community with no alternative.

In any nonviolent campaign there are four basic steps: collection of the facts to determine whether injustices exist; negotiation; self-purification; and direct action. We have gone through all these steps in Birmingham. There can be no gainsaying the fact that racial injustice engulfs this community. Birmingham is probably the most thoroughly segregated city in the United States. Its ugly record of brutality is widely known. Negroes have experienced grossly unjust treatment in courts. There have been more unsolved bombings of Negro homes and churches in Birmingham than in any other city in the nation. These are the hard, brutal facts of the case. On the basis of these conditions, Negro leaders sought to negotiate with the city fathers. But the latter consistently refused to engage in good-faith negotiation.

Then, last September, came the opportunity to talk with leaders of Birmingham's economic community. In the course of the negotiations, certain promises were made by the merchants—for example, to remove the stores' humiliating racial signs. On the basis of these promises, the Reverend Fred Shuttlesworth and the leaders of the Alabama Christian Movement for Human Rights agreed to a moratorium on all demonstrations. As the weeks and months went by, we realized that we were the victims of a broken promise. A few signs, briefly removed, returned; the others remained.

As in so many past experiences, our hopes had been blasted, and the shadow of deep disappointment settled upon us. We had no alternative except to prepare for direct action, whereby we would present our very bodies as means of laying our case before the conscience of the local and the national community. Mindful of the difficulties involved, we decided to undertake a process of self-purification. We began a series of workshops on nonviolence, and we repeatedly asked ourselves: "Are you able to accept blows without retaliating?" "Are you able to endure the ordeal of jail?" We decided to schedule our direct-action program for the Easter season, realizing that except for Christmas, this is the main shopping period of the year. Knowing that a strong economic-withdrawal program would be the by-product of direct action, we felt that this would be the best time to bring pressure to bear on the merchants for the needed change.

Then it occurred to us that Birmingham's mayoral election was coming up in March, and we speedily decided to postpone action until after election day. When we discovered that the Commissioner of Public Safety, Eugene "Bull" Connor, had piled up enough votes to be in the run-off, we decided again to postpone action until the day after the run-off so that the demonstrations could not be used to cloud the issues. Like many others, we waited to see Mr. Connor defeated, and to this end we endured postponement after postponement. Having aided in this community need, we felt that our direct-action program could be delayed no longer.

You may well ask, "Why direct action? Why sit-ins, marches, and so forth? Isn't negotiation a better path?" You are quite right in calling for negotiation. Indeed, this is the very purpose of direct action. Nonviolent direct action seeks to create such a crisis and foster such a tension that a community which has constantly refused to negotiate is forced to confront the issue. It seeks so to dramatize the issue that it can no longer be ignored. My citing the creation of tension as part of the work of the nonviolent-resistor may sound rather shocking. But I must confess that I am not afraid of the word "tension." I have earnestly opposed violent tension, but there is a type of constructive, nonviolent tension which is necessary for growth. Just as Socrates felt that it was necessary to create a tension in the mind so that individuals could rise from the bondage of myths and half-truths to the unfettered realm of creative analysis and objective appraisal, so must we see the need for nonviolent gadflies to create the kind of tension in society that will help men rise from the dark depths of prejudice and racism to the majestic heights of understanding and brotherhood.

The purpose of our direct-action program is to create a situation so crisis-packed that it will inevitably open the door to negotiation. I therefore concur with you in your call for negotiation. Too long has our beloved Southland been bogged down in a tragic effort to live in monologue rather than dialogue.

One of the basic points in your statement is that the action that I and my associates have taken in Birmingham is untimely. Some have asked: "Why didn't you give the new city administration time to act?" The only answer that I can give to this query is that the new Birmingham administration must be prodded about as much as the outgoing one, before it will act. We are sadly mistaken if we feel that the election of Albert Boutwell as mayor will bring the millennium to Birmingham. While Mr. Boutwell is a much more gentle person than Mr. Connor, they are both segregationists, dedicated to maintenance of the status quo. I have hoped that Mr. Boutwell will be reasonable enough to see the futility of massive resistance to desegregation. But he will not see this without pressure from devotees of civil rights. My friends, I must say to you that we have not made a single gain in civil rights without determined legal and nonviolent pressure. Lamentably, it is an historical fact that privileged groups seldom give up their privileges voluntarily. Individuals may see the moral light and voluntarily give up their unjust posture; but, as Reinhold Niebuhr* has reminded us, groups tend to be more immoral than individuals.

We know through painful experience that freedom is never voluntarily given by the oppressor; it must be demanded by the oppressed. Frankly, I have yet to engage in a direct-action campaign that was "well timed" in the view of those who have not suffered unduly from the disease of segregation. For years now I have heard the word "Wait!" It rings in the ear of every Negro with piercing familiarity. This "Wait" has almost always meant "Never." We must come to see, with one of our distinguished jurists, that "justice too long delayed is justice denied." 13

We have waited for more than 340 years for our constitutional and God-given rights. The nations of Asia and Africa are moving with jetlike speed toward gaining political independence, but we still creep at horse-and-buggy pace toward gaining a cup of coffee at a lunch counter. Perhaps it is easy for those who have never felt the stinging darts of segregation to say, "Wait." But when you have seen vicious mobs lynch your mothers and fathers at will and drown your sisters and brothers at whim; when you have seen hate-filled policemen curse, kick, and even kill your black brothers and sisters; when you see the vast majority of your twenty million Negro brothers smothering in an airtight cage of poverty in the midst of an affluent society; when you suddenly find your tongue twisted and your speech stammering as you seek to explain to your six-year-old daughter why she can't go to the public amusement park that has just been advertised on television, and see tears welling up in her eyes when she is told that Funtown is closed to colored children, and see ominous clouds of inferiority beginning to form in her little mental sky, and see her beginning to distort her personality by developing an unconscious bitterness toward white people; when you have to concoct an answer for a five-year-old son who is asking, "Daddy, why do white people treat colored people so mean?"; when you take a cross-country drive and find it necessary to sleep night after night in the uncomfortable corners of your automobile because no motel will accept you; when you are humiliated day in and day out by nagging signs reading "white" and "colored"; when your first name becomes "nigger," your middle name becomes "boy" (however old you 14

---

*EDS. NOTE—American religious and social thinker (1892–1971).

are) and your last name becomes "John," and your wife and mother are never given the respected title "Mrs."; when you are harried by day and haunted by night by the fact that you are a Negro, living constantly at tiptoe stance, never quite knowing what to expect next, and are plagued with inner fears and outer resentments; when you are forever fighting a degenerating sense of "nobodiness"—then you will understand why we find it difficult to wait. There comes a time when the cup of endurance runs over, and men are no longer willing to be plunged into the abyss of despair. I hope, sirs, you can understand our legitimate and unavoidable impatience.

You express a great deal of anxiety over our willingness to break laws. This is certainly a legitimate concern. Since we so diligently urge people to obey the Supreme Court's decision of 1954 outlawing segregation in the public schools, at first glance it may seem rather paradoxical for us consciously to break laws. One may well ask: "How can you advocate breaking some laws and obeying others?" The answer lies in the fact that there are two types of laws: just and unjust. I would be the first to advocate obeying just laws. One has not only a legal but a moral responsibility to obey just laws. Conversely, one has a moral responsibility to disobey unjust laws. I would agree with St. Augustine that "an unjust law is no law at all." 15

Now, what is the difference between the two? How does one determine whether a law is just or unjust? A just law is a man-made code that squares with the moral law or the law of God. An unjust law is a code that is out of harmony with the moral law. To put it in the terms of St. Thomas Aquinas*: An unjust law is a human law that is not rooted in eternal law and natural law. Any law that uplifts human personality is just. Any law that degrades human personality is unjust. All segregation statutes are unjust because segregation distorts the soul and damages the personality. It gives the segregator a false sense of superiority and the segregated a false sense of inferiority. Segregation, to use the terminology of the Jewish philosopher Martin Buber, substitutes an "I-it" relationship for an "I-thou" relationship and ends up relegating persons to the status of things. Hence segregation is not only politically, economically, and sociologically unsound, it is morally wrong and sinful. Paul Tillich** has said that sin is separation. Is not segregation an existential expression of man's tragic separation, his awful estrangement, his terrible sinfulness? Thus it is that I can urge men to obey the 1954 decision of the Supreme Court, for it is morally right; and I can 16

*EDS. NOTE—Italian philosopher and theologian (1225–1274)

**EDS. NOTE—American philosopher and theologian (1886–1965)

urge them to disobey segregation ordinances, for they are morally wrong.

Let us consider a more concrete example of just and unjust laws. An unjust law is a code that a numerical or power majority group compels a minority group to obey but does not make binding on itself. This is *difference* made legal. By the same token, a just law is a code that a majority compels a minority to follow and that it is willing to follow itself. This is *sameness* made legal.

Let me give another explanation. A law is unjust if it is inflicted on a minority that, as a result of being denied the right to vote, had no part in enacting or devising the law. Who can say that the legislature of Alabama which set up that state's segregation laws was democratically elected? Throughout Alabama all sorts of devious methods are used to prevent Negroes from becoming registered voters, and there are some counties in which, even though Negroes constitute a majority of the population, not a single Negro is registered. Can any law enacted under such circumstances be considered democratically structured?

Sometimes a law is just on its face and unjust in its application. For instance, I have been arrested on a charge of parading without a permit. Now, there is nothing wrong in having an ordinance which requires a permit for a parade. But such an ordinance becomes unjust when it is used to maintain segregation and to deny citizens the First-Amendment privilege of peaceful assembly and protest.

I hope you are able to see the distinction I am trying to point out. In no sense do I advocate evading or defying the law, as would the rabid segregationist. That would lead to anarchy. One who breaks an unjust law must do so openly, lovingly, and with a willingness to accept the penalty. I submit that an individual who breaks a law that conscience tells him is unjust, and who willingly accepts the penalty of imprisonment in order to arouse the conscience of the community over its injustice, is in reality expressing the highest respect for law.

Of course, there is nothing new about this kind of civil disobedience. It was evidenced sublimely in the refusal of Shadrach, Meshach, and Abednego to obey the laws of Nebuchadnezzar, on the ground that a higher moral law was at stake. It was practiced superbly by the early Christians, who were willing to face hungry lions and the excruciating pain of chopping blocks rather than submit to certain unjust laws of the Roman Empire. To a degree, academic freedom is a reality today because Socrates practiced civil disobedience. In our own nation, the Boston Tea Party represented a massive act of civil disobedience.

We should never forget that everything Adolph Hitler did in Germany was "legal" and everything the Hungarian freedom fighters did in Hungary was "illegal." It was "illegal" to aid and comfort a Jew in Hitler's Germany. Even so, I am sure that, had I lived in Germany at the time, I would have aided and comforted my Jewish brothers. If today I lived in a Communist country where certain principles dear to the Christian faith are suppressed, I would openly advocate disobeying that country's anti-religious laws. 22

I must make two honest confessions to you, my Christian and Jewish brothers. First, I must confess that over the past few years I have been gravely disappointed with the white moderate. I have almost reached the regrettable conclusion that the Negro's great stumbling block in his stride toward freedom is not the White Citizens Counciler or the Ku Klux Klanner, but the white moderate, who is more devoted to "order" than to justice; who prefers a negative peace which is the absence of tension to a positive peace which is the presence of justice; who constantly says, "I agree with you in the goal you seek, but I cannot agree with your methods of direct action"; who paternalistically believes he can set the timetable for another man's freedom; who lives by a mythical concept of time and who constantly advises the Negro to wait for a "more convenient season." Shallow understanding from people of good will is more frustrating than absolute misunderstanding from people of ill will. Lukewarm acceptance is much more bewildering than outright rejection. 23

I had hoped that the white moderate would understand that law and order exist for the purpose of establishing justice and that when they fail in this purpose they become the dangerously structured dams that block the flow of social progress. I had hoped that the white moderate would understand that the present tension in the South is a necessary phase of the transition from an obnoxious negative peace, in which the Negro passively accepted his unjust plight, to a substantive and positive peace, in which all men will respect the dignity and worth of human personality. Actually, we who engage in nonviolent direct action are not the creators of tension. We merely bring to the surface the hidden tension that is already alive. We bring it out in the open, where it can be seen and dealt with. Like a boil that can never be cured so long as it is covered up but must be opened with all its ugliness to the natural medicines of air and light, injustice must be exposed, with all the tension its exposure creates, to the light of human conscience and the air of national opinion, before it can be cured. 24

In your statement you assert that our actions, even though peaceful, must be condemned because they precipitate violence. But is 25 this a logical assertion? Isn't this like condemning a robbed man because his possession of money precipitated the evil act of robbery? Isn't this like condemning Socrates because his unswerving commitment to truth and his philosophical inquiries precipitated the act by the misguided populace in which they made him drink hemlock? Isn't this like condemning Jesus because his unique God-consciousness and never-ceasing devotion to God's will precipitated the evil act of crucifixion? We must come to see that, as the federal courts have consistently affirmed, it is wrong to urge an individual to cease his efforts to gain his basic constitutional rights because the quest may precipitate violence. Society must protect the robbed and punish the robber.

I had also hoped that the white moderate would reject the myth concerning time in relation to the struggle for freedom. I have just received a letter from a white brother in Texas. He writes: "All Christians know that the colored people will receive equal rights eventually, but it is possible that you are in too great a religious hurry. It has taken Christianity almost two thousand years to accomplish what it has. The teachings of Christ take time to come to earth." Such an attitude stems from a tragic misconception of time, from the strangely irrational notion that there is something in the very flow of time that will inevitably cure all ills. Actually, time itself is neutral; it can be used either destructively or constructively. More and more I feel that the people of ill will have used time much more effectively than have the people of good will. We will have to repent in this generation not merely for the hateful words and actions of the bad people, but for the appalling silence of the good people. Human progress never rolls in on wheels of inevitability; it comes through the tireless efforts of men willing to be co-workers with God, and without his hard work, time itself becomes an ally of the forces of social stagnation. We must use time creatively, in the knowledge that the time is always ripe to do right. Now is the time to make real the promise of democracy and transform our pending national elegy into a creative psalm of brotherhood. Now is the time to lift our national policy from the quicksand of racial injustice to the solid rock of human dignity.

You speak of our activity in Birmingham as extreme. At first I was rather disappointed that fellow clergymen would see my nonviolent efforts as those of an extremist. I began thinking about the fact that I stand in the middle of two opposing forces in the Negro community. One is a force of complacency, made up in part of Negroes who, as a result of long years of oppression, are so drained of self-respect and a sense of "somebodiness" that they have adjusted to segregation;

and in part of a few middle-class Negroes who, because of a degree of academic and economic security and because in some ways they profit by segregation, have become insensitive to the problems of the masses. The other force is one of bitterness and hatred, and it comes perilously close to advocating violence. It is expressed in the various black nationalist groups that are springing up across the nation, the largest and best-known being Elijah Muhammad's Muslim movement. Nourished by the Negro's frustration over the continued existence of racial discrimination, this movement is made up of people who have lost faith in America, who have absolutely repudiated Christianity, and who have concluded that the white man is an incorrigible "devil."

I have tried to stand between these two forces, saying that we 28 need emulate neither the "do-nothingism" of the complacent nor the hatred and despair of the black nationalist. For there is the more excellent way of love and nonviolent protest. I am grateful to God that, through the influence of the Negro church, the way of nonviolence became an integral part of our struggle.

If this philosophy had not emerged, by now many streets of the 29 South would, I am convinced, be flowing with blood. And I am further convinced that if our white brothers dismiss as "rabble-rousers" and "outside agitators" those of us who employ nonviolent direct action, and if they refuse to support our nonviolent efforts, millions of Negroes will, out of frustration and despair, seek solace and security in black-nationalist ideologies—a development that would inevitably lead to a frightening racial nightmare.

Oppressed people cannot remain oppressed forever. The yearning 30 for freedom eventually manifests itself, and that is what has happened to the American Negro. Something within has reminded him of his birthright of freedom, and something without has reminded him that it can be gained. Consciously or unconsciously, he has been caught up by the *Zeitgeist,* and with his black brothers of Africa and his brown and yellow brothers of Asia, South America, and the Caribbean, the United States Negro is moving with a sense of great urgency toward the promised land of racial justice. If one recognizes this vital urge that has engulfed the Negro community, one should readily understand why public demonstrations are taking place. The Negro has many pent-up resentments and latent frustrations, and he must release them. So let him march; let him make prayer pilgrimages to the city hall; let him go on freedom rides—and try to understand why he must do so. If his repressed emotions are not released in nonviolent ways, they will seek expression through violence; this is not a threat but a fact of history. So I have not said to my people, "Get rid of your discontent." Rather, I have tried to say that this normal and healthy discontent can be channeled into the creative outlet of nonviolent direct action. And now this approach is being termed extremist.

But though I was initially disappointed at being categorized as an extremist, as I continued to think about the matter I gradually gained a measure of satisfaction from the label. Was not Jesus an extremist for love: "Love your enemies, bless them that curse you, do good to them that hate you, and pray for them which despitefully use you, and persecute you." Was not Amos an extremist for justice: "Let justice roll down like waters and righteousness like an ever-flowing stream." Was not Paul an extremist for the Christian gospel: "I bear in my body the marks of the Lord Jesus." Was not Martin Luther an extremist: "Here I stand; I cannot do otherwise, so help me God." And John Bunyan: "I will stay in jail to the end of my days before I make a butchery of my conscience." And Abraham Lincoln: "This nation cannot survive half slave and half free." And Thomas Jefferson: "We hold these truths to be self-evident, that all men are created equal. . . ." So the question is not whether we will be extremists, but what kind of extremists we will be. Will we be extremists for hate or for love? Will we be extremists for the preservation of injustice or for the extension of justice? In that dramatic scene on Calvary's hill three men were crucified. We must never forget that all three were crucified for the same crime—the crime of extremism. Two were extremists for immorality, and thus fell below their environment. The other, Jesus Christ, was an extremist for love, truth, and goodness, and thereby rose above his environment. Perhaps the South, the nation, and the world are in dire need of creative extremists. 31

I had hoped that the white moderate would see this need. Perhaps I was too optimistic; perhaps I expected too much. I suppose I should have realized that few members of the oppressor race can understand the deep groans and passionate yearnings of the oppressed race, and still fewer have the vision to see that injustice must be rooted out by strong, persistent, and determined action. I am thankful, however, that some of our white brothers in the South have grasped the meaning of this social revolution and committed themselves to it. They are still all too few in quantity, but they are big in quality. Some—such as Ralph McGill, Lillian Smith, Harry Golden, James McBride Dabbs, Ann Braden, and Sarah Patton Boyle—have written about our struggle in eloquent and prophetic terms. Others have marched with us down nameless streets of the South. They have languished in filthy, roach-infested jails, suffering the abuse and 32 brutality of policemen who view them as "dirty nigger-lovers." Unlike so many of their moderate brothers and sisters, they have recognized the urgency of the moment and sensed the need for powerful "action" antidotes to combat the disease of segregation.

Let me take note of my other major disappointment. I have been 33 so greatly disappointed with the white church and its leadership. Of course, there are some notable exceptions. I am not unmindful of the fact that each of you has taken some significant stands on this issue. I commend you, Reverend Stallings, for your Christian stand on this past Sunday, in welcoming Negroes to your worship service on a nonsegregated basis. I commend the Catholic leaders of this state for integrating Spring Hill College several years ago.

But despite these notable exceptions, I must honestly reiterate 34 that I have been disappointed with the church. I do not say this as one of those negative critics who can always find something wrong with the church. I say this as a minister of the gospel, who loves the church; who was nurtured in its bosom; who has been sustained by its spiritual blessings and who will remain true to it as long as the cord of life shall lengthen.

When I was suddenly catapulted into the leadership of the bus 35 protest in Montgomery, Alabama, a few years ago, I felt we would be supported by the white church. I felt that the white ministers, priests, and rabbis of the South would be among our strongest allies. Instead, some have been outright opponents, refusing to understand the freedom movement and misrepresenting its leaders; all too many others have been more cautious than courageous and have remained silent behind the anesthetizing security of stained-glass windows.

In spite of my shattered dreams, I came to Birmingham with the 36 hope that the white religious leadership of this community would see the justice of our cause and, with deep moral concern, would serve as the channel through which our just grievances could reach the power structure. I had hoped that each of you would understand. But again I have been disappointed.

There was a time when the church was very powerful—in the time 37 when the early Christians rejoiced at being deemed worthy to suffer for what they believed. In those days the church was not merely a thermometer that recorded the ideas and principles of popular opinion; it was a thermostat that transformed the mores of society. Whenever the early Christians entered a town, the people in power became disturbed and immediately sought to convict the Christians for being "disturbers of the peace" and "outside agitators." But the Christians pressed on, in the conviction that they were "a colony of heaven," called to obey God rather than man. Small in number, they were big in commitment. They were too God-intoxicated to be "astronomically intimidated." By their effort and example they brought an end to such ancient evils as infanticide and gladiatorial contests.

Things are different now. So often the contemporary church is a weak, ineffectual voice with an uncertain sound. So often it is an archdefender of the status quo. Far from being disturbed by the presence of the church, the power structure of the average community is consoled by the church's silent—and often even vocal—sanction of things as they are. 38

But the judgment of God is upon the church as never before. If today's church does not recapture the sacrificial spirit of the early church, it will lose its authenticity, forfeit the loyalty of millions, and be dismissed as an irrelevant social club with no meaning for the twentieth century. Every day I meet young people whose disappointment with the church has turned into outright disgust. 39

Perhaps I have once again been too optimistic. Is organized religion too inextricably bound to the status quo to save our nation and the world? Perhaps I must turn my faith to the inner spiritual church, the church within the church, as the true *ekklesia** and the hope of the world. But again I am thankful to God that some noble souls from the ranks of organized religion have broken loose from the paralyzing chains of conformity and joined us as active partners in the struggle for freedom. They have left their secure congregations and walked the streets of Albany, Georgia, with us. They have gone down the highways of the South on torturous rides for freedom. Yes, they have gone to jail with us. Some have been dismissed from their churches, have lost the support of their bishops and fellow ministers. But they have acted in the faith that right defeated is stronger than evil triumphant. Their witness has been the spiritual salt that has preserved the true meaning of the gospel in these troubled times. They have carved a tunnel of hope through the dark mountain of disappointment. 40

I hope the church as a whole will meet the challenge of this decisive hour. But even if the church does not come to the aid of justice, I have no despair about the future. I have no fear about the outcome of our struggle in Birmingham, even if our motives are at present misunderstood. We will reach the goal of freedom in Birmingham and all over the nation, because the goal of America is freedom. 41

*EDS. NOTE—Greek word for the early Christian church.

Abused and scorned through we may be, our destiny is tied up with America's destiny. Before the pilgrims landed at Plymouth, we were here. Before the pen of Jefferson etched the majestic words of the Declaration of Independence across the pages of history, we were here. For more than two centuries our forebears labored in this country without wages; they made cotton king; they built the homes of their masters while suffering gross injustice and shameful humiliation—and yet out of a bottomless vitality they continued to thrive and develop. If the inexpressible cruelties of slavery could not stop us, the opposition we now face will surely fail. We will win our freedom because the sacred heritage of our nation and the eternal will of God are embodied in our echoing demands.

Before closing I feel impelled to mention one other point in your 42 statement that has troubled me profoundly. You warmly commended the Birmingham police for keeping "order" and "preventing violence." I doubt that you would have so warmly commended the police force if you had seen its dogs sinking their teeth into unarmed, nonviolent Negroes. I doubt that you would so quickly commend the policemen if you were to observe their ugly and inhumane treatment of Negroes here in the city jail; if you were to watch them push and curse old Negro women and young Negro girls; if you were to see them slap and kick old Negro men and young boys; if you were to observe them, as they did on two occasions, refuse to give us food because we wanted to sing our grace together. I cannot join you in your praise of the Birmingham police department.

It is true that the police have exercised a degree of discipline in 43 handling the demonstrators. In this sense they have conducted themselves rather "nonviolently" in public. But for what purpose? To preserve the evil system of segregation. Over the past few years I have consistently preached that nonviolence demands that the means we use must be as pure as the ends we seek. I have tried to make clear that it is wrong to use immoral means to attain moral ends. But now I must affirm that it is just as wrong, or perhaps even more so, to use moral means to preserve immoral ends. Perhaps Mr. Connor and his policemen have been rather nonviolent in public, as was Chief Pritchett in Albany, Georgia, but they have used the moral means of nonviolence to maintain the immoral end of racial injustice. As T. S. Eliot has said, "The last temptation is the greatest treason: To do the right deed for the wrong reason."

I wish you had commended the Negro sit-inners and demonstra- 44 tors of Birmingham for their sublime courage, their willingness to suffer, and their amazing discipline in the midst of great provocation. One day the South will recognize its real heroes. They will be the James Merediths,* with the noble sense of purpose that enables them to face jeering and hostile mobs, and with the agonizing loneliness that characterizes the life of the pioneer. They will be old, oppressed, battered Negro women, symbolized in a seventy-two-year-old woman in Montgomery, Alabama, who rose up with a sense of dignity and with her people decided not to ride segregated buses, and who responded with ungrammatical profundity to one who inquired about her weariness: "My feets is tired, but my soul is at rest." They will be the young high school and college students, the young ministers of the gospel and a host of their elders, courageously and nonviolently sitting in at lunch counters and willingly going to jail for conscience' sake. One day the South will know that when these disinherited children of God sat down at lunch counters, they were in reality standing up for what is best in the American dream and for the most sacred values in our Judaeo-Christian heritage, thereby bringing our nation back to those great wells of democracy which were dug deeply by the founding fathers in their formulation of the Constitution and the Declaration of Independence.

Never before have I written so long a letter. I'm afraid it is much too long to take your precious time. I can assure you that it would have been much shorter if I had been writing from a comfortable desk, but what else can one do when he is alone in a narrow jail cell, other than write long letters, think long thoughts, and pray long prayers? 45

If I have said anything in this letter that overstates the truth and indicates an unreasonable impatience, I beg you to forgive me. If I have said anything that understates the truth and indicates my having a patience that allows me to settle for anything less than brotherhood, I beg God to forgive me. 46

I hope this letter finds you strong in the faith. I also hope that circumstances will soon make it possible for me to meet each of you, not as an integrationist or a civil-rights leader but as a fellow clergyman and a Christian brother. Let us all hope that the dark clouds of racial prejudice will soon pass away and the deep fog of misunderstanding will be lifted from our fear-drenched communities, and in some not too distant tomorrow the radiant stars of love and brotherhood will shine over our great nation with all their scintillating beauty. 47

Yours for the cause of Peace and Brotherhood,
Martin Luther King, Jr.

*EDS. NOTE—James Meredith was the first African American to enroll at the University of Mississippi.

COMPREHENSION

1. Martin Luther King, Jr., says that he seldom answers criticism. Why, then, does he decide to do so in this instance?

2. Why do the other clergymen consider King's activities to be "unwise and untimely"?

3. What reasons does King give for the demonstrations? Why does he think it is too late for negotiations?

4. What does King say *wait* means to black people?

5. What are the two types of laws King defines? What is the difference between the two?

6. What does King find illogical about the claim that the actions of his followers precipitate violence?

7. Why is King disappointed in the white church?

PURPOSE AND AUDIENCE

1. Why, in the first paragraph, does King establish his setting (the Birmingham city jail) and define his intended audience?

2. Why does King begin his letter with a reference to his audience as "men of genuine good will"? Is this phrase ironic in light of his later criticism of them?

3. What indication is there that King is writing his letter to an audience other than his fellow clergymen?

4. What is the thesis of this letter? Is it stated or implied?

STYLE AND STRUCTURE

1. Where does King seek to establish that he is a reasonable person?

2. Where does King address the objections of his audience?

3. As in the Declaration of Independence, transitions are important in King's letter. Identify the transitional words and phrases that connect the different parts of his argument.

4. Why does King cite Jewish, Catholic, and Protestant philosophers to support his position?

5. King relies heavily on appeals to authority (Augustine, Aquinas, Buber, Tillich, etc.). Why does he use this strategy?

6. King uses both induction and deduction in his letter. Find an example of each, and explain how they function in the argument.

7. Throughout the body of his letter, King criticizes his audience of white moderates. In his conclusion, he seeks to reestablish a harmonious relationship with them. How does he do this?

VOCABULARY PROJECTS

1. Define each of the following words as it is used in this selection.

affiliates (2)	devotee (12)	reiterate (34)
cognizant (4)	estrangement (16)	intimidate (37)
mutuality (4)	ordinances (16)	infanticide (37)
provincial (4)	anarchy (20)	inextricably (40)
gainsay (6)	elegy (26)	scintillating (47)
unfettered (10)	incorrigible (27)	
millennium (12)	emulate (28)	

2. Locate five allusions to the Bible in this essay. How do these allusions help King express his ideas?

3. In paragraph 14 King refers to his "cup of endurance." To what is this a reference? How is the original phrase worded?

JOURNAL ENTRY

Do you believe King's remarks go too far or not far enough? Explain.

WRITING WORKSHOP

1. Write an argumentative essay in which you support a deeply held belief of your own. Assume that your audience, like King's, is not openly hostile to your position.

2. Assume that you are a militant political leader writing a letter to Martin Luther King, Jr. Argue that King's methods do not go far enough. Be sure to address potential objections to your position. You might want to go to the library and read some newspapers and magazines from the 1960s to help you prepare your argument.

3. Read the newspaper for several days, and collect articles about a controversial subject in which you are interested. Using the information from the articles, take a position on the issue, and write an essay supporting it.

THEMATIC CONNECTIONS

- "Finishing School" (p. 78)
- "The Civil Rights Movement: What Good Was It" (p. 315)
- "How the Pot Got to Call the Kettle Black" (p. 614)
- "A Negative Vote on Affirmative Action" (p. 625)

Debate: Multicultural Education

There once was a time when most American educators and scholars could agree on what constituted a good education. The list of authors and works that all educated people were supposed to have read was referred to as the *canon*. Recently, however, some have charged that the canon, as it is has traditionally been established, is like an exclusive club, with otherwise qualified members kept out for reasons of class, gender, and race. Indeed, when one examines the traditional canon, it is clear that with few exceptions the viewpoints represented are male, middle class, and white. For this reason, some educators have proposed a more inclusive, "multicultural" curriculum that would expose students to more works by women, people of color, and writers from different cultural backgrounds. The result has been that literature, history, and other courses at many high schools and colleges are now more culturally diverse than they were just a few years ago.

A fierce debate rages, however, around the issue of multicultural education. Critics charge that some teachers care less about the intellectual quality of the works on their reading list than they do about the variety of racial and ethnic groups represented. Others contend that multicultural courses are more concerned with making students feel good about themselves than they are about fostering critical thinking. Still others say the curriculum is being broadened at the expense of the great works of Western thought that reinforce our society's common values.

The two essays that follow reflect the ongoing debate about multicultural education. In "Multiculturalism Is Misguided," Trudy Rubin argues that multicultural education, which is hostile to the study of Western civilization, is "wrongfully misguided." In "Let's Tell the Story of All America's Cultures," Ji-Yeon Mary Yuhfill takes the opposite position, asserting that children should understand that the history of the United States is the story of people from many different cultures struggling to make a better life for themselves.

MULTICULTURALISM IS MISGUIDED

Trudy Rubin

*Trudy Rubin graduated from Smith College in 1965 and received
her master's degree from The London School of Economics in 1966.
Before joining the* Philadelphia Inquirer, *where she is a foreign
affairs columnist and a member of the newspaper's editorial board,
she worked for the British magazine* The Economist *as a staff writer
on American politics and for* The Christian Science Monitor *as a
national correspondent and then as a Middle East correspondent.
Rubin has lived in Prague (where, as a radio correspondent, she
reported on Czechoslovakia's short-lived effort to throw off Soviet
domination in 1968) as well as in London, Jerusalem, Cairo, and
Beirut, and she travels frequently in the Middle East, Russia,
Europe, and Asia. She has published articles in several newspapers
and magazines, including* The Atlantic Monthly, The New Republic, *and* The Nation. *"Multiculturalism Is Misguided," published in
the* Philadelphia Inquirer *in 1991, argues that while American universities are preoccupied with the virtues of multiculturalism and
the faults of Western civilization, the rest of the world is trying to
learn from the history and political theory of Western democracies.*

This week I traveled to my alma mater, Smith College, to take   1
part in an informal dialogue among alumnae, faculty and students
on the goals of a women's liberal arts college in uncertain times.

Smith, a small, elite women's college, is smack in the middle of   2
the raging national debate over multiculturalism. Smith's president, Mary Maples Dunn, has made "diversity" the college's premier
issue, including a major campaign to recruit minority students, faculty and staff and to introduce more "multicultural" material on
race and ethnicity into courses.

Many colleges and universities, such as Dartmouth, Wisconsin   3
and Mount Holyoke, now require students to take Third World or
ethnic studies courses but not courses in Western civilization. Smith
has no course requirements at all. But that may not continue to be
the case.

The Smith administration believes that a stronger multicultural   4
slant is necessary to enable students to cope with a more interde-

pendent world, in which nonwhite minorities will make up a bigger share of the U.S. population.

As someone who makes a living by traveling around the world, observing its staggering changes, I feel the hopes invested in "multiculturalism" are woefully misguided, especially since they are so often driven by a hostility toward the study of Western civilization. Many of the academic backers of multiculturalism seem to believe that Western liberal thought has spawned only imperialism, racism and sexism. They ignore the fact that much of the rest of the world is looking West for something very different.

All over the globe, in China, Africa, Southeast Asia, Soviet Asia, the Soviet Union, Eastern Europe, Latin America, elites and the public at large are struggling to find political formulas that give ordinary people a say in how they are governed and instill tolerance for different political views. In many of these places the most urgent need is to find a way for different ethnic groups to coexist without killing each other. In most of these struggles, women still play a painfully subordinate role.

From Korea to the Middle East, from Ukraine to Moscow to the Baltics, supporters of democracy are looking to the experience, history, literature and political theory of Western democracies for clues as to how to establish the tolerant systems that they seek.

In Moscow, politicians walk around carrying copies of the U.S. Constitution and James Madison's Federalist Papers, trying to grasp the idea of opposition politics and to learn how the American states managed to stay together with only one civil war. Little in their history or religion has prepared them for the give-and-take of democratic politics. And so they look West.

In the Middle East, young intellectuals have told me that democracy may not be possible because of Islamic beliefs that link mosque and state and because of the widespread belief in one Arab nation, which undermines respect for state democratic institutions. As for the rights of women, in Iran young women are beaten for letting bits of hair stick out of a head scarf, and in Saudi Arabia women can't even drive. In that region, the idea that the state must respect an individual's God-given human rights gets short shrift.

In Burma, China and elsewhere in Asia, leaders claim that the concept of inalienable human rights is antithetical to Asian culture. In Africa, I have seen the remnants of tribal slavery and the most brutal racism. In no Third World culture have I seen anything close to the respect—however imperfect—that women are accorded in Western societies. Some of my most horrible discussions have been with African women discussing the commonly accepted practice of clitoridectomy.

It is European culture, primarily the Anglo-Saxon tradition, that 11
has given the world the concepts of the rule of law, individual rights,
cultural freedom and pluralistic democracy. All over the world I have
had the American Declaration of Independence quoted to me. No one
was interested in Thomas Jefferson's history as a white male slave
owner. What they were concerned about was the argument that individuals were entitled to "life, liberty and the pursuit of happiness."

And so I find it bewildering to return home to the debate on multi- 12
culturalism, many of whose adherents seem to believe that a dilettantish dip into Third World studies will help American students
deal with America's and the world's ills. This is a deception, which
taken to extremes can polarize minority students, rather than making them aware of the unique cultural heritage that they are entitled
to share.

With all the immense mistakes made by the West, including the 13
overweening sin of slavery, it is still Western history and culture
that has given men and women the greatest possibility to fight for
change.

In today's world, one can't assume that students arrive at college 14
versed in European and American history or political theory. It is
these lessons that American students most need to study, to prevent
America from going the way of Yugoslavia or Lebanon.

It's fine to offer students the chance to study other cultures, so 15
long as those classes are taught without false illusions, laying out
the flaws of Third World cultures as well as their beauties. But if
required, those studies should be in conjunction with the study of
Western civilization. That tradition, white Anglo-Saxon though it
may be, belongs to all of us. Without it, the very idea of diversity
would be a joke.

COMPREHENSION

1. Why does the Smith College administration believe more multicultural education is necessary?

2. Why does Rubin make a point of saying that she is someone who
   makes her living traveling around the world?

3. According to Rubin, what misconception do the academic backers of
   multiculturalism have?

4. What does Rubin say that people from all over the world look for from
   the West?

5. According to Rubin, why should American students study Western civilization?

PURPOSE AND AUDIENCE

1. What attitudes does Rubin assume her readers have about her subject? Explain your conclusion.

2. At what point does Rubin state her thesis? What would she have gained or lost by stating it later?

3. What opposing point does Rubin concede? What does she hope to gain by doing so?

STYLE AND STRUCTURE

1. Rubin supports her thesis by presenting examples from all the major regions of the world. Why do you think she does this? Could she have used fewer examples?

2. Do Rubin's anecdotes adequately support her thesis? What other kinds of evidence could she have used?

3. Where does Rubin refute arguments against her position?

4. Is Rubin's argument primarily inductive or deductive?

5. How well does Rubin sum up her argument in her last paragraph? Could she have used a stronger closing statement?

VOCABULARY PROJECTS

1. Define each of the following words as it is used in this selection.

ethnicity (2)	mosque (9)	adherents (12)
imperialism (5)	clitoridectomy (10)	polarize (12)
subordinate (6)	Anglo-Saxon (11)	overweening (13)

2. In paragraph 12 Rubin clearly reveals her bias in the phrase "dilettantish dip." What other words and phrases show Rubin's attitude toward her subject? What would be the effect of substituting words that have more neutral connotations?

JOURNAL ENTRY

Do you think Rubin overstates her case? If so, do you think her overstatements are intentional? How do they affect you?

WRITING WORKSHOP

1. Write an argumentative essay in which you support Rubin's position that the white Anglo-Saxon tradition "belongs to all of us" (15). Use examples from your own experience to support your thesis.

2. Write an essay in which you refute Rubin's argument. The body of your essay should point out the weaknesses of Rubin's points, not make your own argument in favor of multicultural education.

3. Write an essay in which you argue whether or not your college or university courses would be strengthened by the addition of more multicultural material.

THEMATIC CONNECTIONS

- "Shooting an Elephant" (p. 96)
- "The Mystery of Mickey Mouse" (p. 136)
- "The Untouchable" (p. 494)

LET'S TELL THE STORY OF ALL AMERICA'S CULTURES

Ji-Yeon Mary Yuhfill

Ji-Yeon Mary Yuhfill was born in Seoul, South Korea, in 1965 and moved to the United States with her family in 1970. She received a master's degree in cognitive science from Stanford University in 1987 and is pursuing a doctorate in history at the University of Pennsylvania. Yuhfill has worked as an agricultural reporter for the Omaha World-Herald *and as a general assignment reporter for* New York Newsday. *She is currently living and working in South Korea. In "Let's Tell the Story of All America's Cultures," published in the* Philadelphia Inquirer *in 1991, Yuhfill argues for a multicultural curriculum that would give students a more inclusive view of history.*

I grew up hearing, seeing and almost believing that America was white—albeit with a little black tinged here and there—and that white was best. 1

The white people were everywhere in my 1970s Chicago childhood: Founding Fathers, Lewis and Clark, Lincoln, Daniel Boone, Carnegie,* presidents, explorers and industrialists galore. The only black people were slaves. The only Indians were scalpers. 2

I never heard one word about how Benjamin Franklin was so impressed by the Iroquois federation of nations that he adapted that model into our system of state and federal government. Or that the Indian tribes were systematically betrayed and massacred by a greedy young nation that stole their land and called it the United States. 3

I never heard one word about how Asian immigrants were among the first to turn California's desert into fields of plenty. Or about Chinese immigrant Ah Bing, who bred the cherry now on sale in groceries across the nation. Or that plantation owners in Hawaii imported labor from China, Japan, Korea and the Philippines to work the sugar cane fields. I never learned that Asian immigrants were the only immigrants denied U.S. citizenship, even though they served honorably in World War I. All the immigrants in my textbook were white. 4

*EDS. NOTE—Andrew Carnegie (1835–1919), American industrialist and philanthropist.

I never learned about Frederick Douglass, the runaway slave who ⁵ became a leading abolitionist and statesman, or about black scholar W. E. B. Du Bois. I never learned that black people rose up in arms against slavery. Nat Turner* wasn't one of the heroes in my childhood history class.

I never learned that the American Southwest and California ⁶ were already settled by Mexicans when they were annexed after the Mexican-American War. I never learned that Mexico once had a problem keeping land-hungry white men on the U.S. side of the border.

So when other children called me a slant-eyed chink and told me ⁷ to go back where I came from, I was ready to believe that I wasn't really an American because I wasn't white.

America's bittersweet legacy of struggling and failing and getting ⁸ another step closer to democratic ideals of liberty and equality and justice for all wasn't for the likes of me, an immigrant child from Korea. The history books said so.

Well, the history books were wrong. ⁹

Educators around the country are finally realizing what I realized ¹⁰ as a teenager in the library, looking up the history I wasn't getting in school. America is a multicultural nation, composed of many people with varying histories and varying traditions who have little in common except their humanity, a belief in democracy and a desire for freedom.

America changed them, but they changed America too. ¹¹

A committee of scholars and teachers gathered by the New ¹² York State Department of Education recognizes this in their recent report, "One Nation, Many Peoples: A Declaration of Cultural Interdependence."

They recommend that public schools provide a "multicultural edu- ¹³ cation, anchored to the shared principles of a liberal democracy."

What that means, according to the report, is recognizing that ¹⁴ America was shaped and continues to be shaped by people of diverse backgrounds. It calls for students to be taught that history is an ongoing process of discovery and interpretation of the past, and that there is more than one way of viewing the world.

Thus, the westward migration of white Americans is not just a ¹⁵ heroic settling of an untamed wild, but also the conquest of indigenous peoples. Immigrants were not just white, but Asian as well. Blacks were not merely passive slaves freed by northern whites, but active fighters for their own liberation.

---

*EDS. NOTE—leader of a slave rebellion in Virginia in 1831.

In particular, according to the report, the curriculum should help   16
children "to access critically the reasons for the inconsistencies between the ideals of the U.S. and social realities. It should provide
information and intellectual tools that can permit them to contribute to bringing reality closer to the ideals."

In other words, show children the good with the bad, and give them   17
the skills to help improve their country. What could be more patriotic?

Several dissenting members of the New York committee publicly   18
worry that America will splinter into ethnic fragments if this multicultural curriculum is adopted. They argue that the committee's report puts the focus on ethnicity at the expense of national unity.

But downplaying ethnicity will not bolster national unity. The his-   19
tory of America is the story of how and why people from all over the
world came to the United States, and how in struggling to make a
better life for themselves, they changed each other, they changed the
country, and they all came to call themselves Americans.

E pluribus unum. Out of many, one.   20

This is why I, with my Korean background, and my childhood tor-   21
mentors, with their lost-in-the-mist-of-time-European backgrounds,
are all Americans.

It is the unique beauty of this country. It is high time we let all our   22
children gaze upon it.

COMPREHENSION

1. What did Yuhfill grow up believing?

2. What was Yuhfill never taught? What was the result of her ignorance?

3. According to Yuhfill, what are educators all around the country finally
   realizing? What is the result of their change in thinking?

4. What does the committee formed by the New York State Department
   of Education mean when it says public schools should give students "a
   multicultural education, anchored to the shared principles of a liberal
   democracy" (13)?

5. According to Yuhfill, "downplaying ethnicity will not bolster national
   unity" (19). Why not?

PURPOSE AND AUDIENCE

1. What credentials does Yuhfill present to establish her expertise? Are
   they sufficient?

2. Where does Yuhfill state her thesis? Should she have stated it at the beginning of her essay?

3. Does Yuhfill assume her audience is friendly, hostile, or neutral? Explain.

STYLE AND STRUCTURE

1. Throughout the first part of her essay, Yuhfill repeats the phrase "I never heard." What is the effect of this repetition? How does this repetition help her make her point?

2. Yuhfill refers extensively to a New York State Department of Education report. Do these references adequately support her argument? Do you think she relies too much on a single source? Explain.

3. In paragraph 18 Yuhfill mentions the dissenting members of the committee that wrote the report. How effectively does she refute their objections? What else could she have said?

4. Yuhfill's essay contains a lot of one- and two-sentence paragraphs. How effective are these short paragraphs? Should they be combined with other paragraphs?

5. Yuhfill ends her essay with a one-sentence conclusion. How well does this conclusion reinforce her points? What other concluding strategy could she have used?

VOCABULARY PROJECTS

1. Define each of the following words as it is used in this selection.

albeit (1)	annexed (6)	inconsistencies (16)
federation (3)	legacy (8)	ethnicity (18)
abolitionist (5)	indigenous (15)	

2. Yuhfill uses many terms that have built-in value judgments. Identify several of these terms (*land-hungry* white men [6], for example), and substitute a term with more neutral connotations.

JOURNAL ENTRY

Paragraph 21 presents a conclusion ("This is why I . . ."). Do you think there is enough information in the essay to justify this conclusion?

WRITING WORKSHOP

1. Yuhfill gives a number of reasons why schools should adopt a multicultural curriculum. Write an essay in which you discuss the possible drawbacks of such a curriculum.

2. When the New York City Board of Education tried to mandate a multicultural curriculum, it was met with a good deal of resistance. Some people complained that the board was trying to impose its way of thinking on children. Others said the curriculum idealized many aspects of minority culture. Still others objected to some of the books students were required to read. Write a letter to the editor of the *New York Times* in which you outline the type of multicultural curriculum that you would like to see in a public elementary school. What kinds of material would you accept? What kinds would you reject?

THEMATIC CONNECTIONS

- "Grant and Lee: A Study in Contrasts" (p. 371)
- "Aria: A Memoir of a Bilingual Childhood" (p. 401)
- "An Argument against the Anna Todd Jennings Scholarship" (p. 550)

Debate: Speech Codes

What is more important in an academic community, an atmosphere in which anyone feels free to express any opinion or one in which no one feels persecuted or insulted? This dilemma has arisen as many colleges and universities have adopted speech codes, regulations that prohibit speech or other conduct that is abusive, threatening, or demeaning toward women, racial or ethnic minorities, or in some cases other groups as well. At the University of Pennsylvania, for example, a student had to appear before a disciplinary committee after using the term "water buffaloes" when shouting at several African-American women who were making noise on the street below his dorm room. At Oberlin College two Asian students brought charges against the editors of a campus humor magazine who had written a parody about Chinese food. Although both of these cases were subsequently dismissed, they illustrate the need for a clarification of what kind of speech is acceptable on a college campus and what kind, if any, is not.

Proponents of speech codes say that verbal or physical conduct that creates an intimidating or hostile environment has no place on a college campus, but strict civil libertarians argue that no limits, no matter how well meaning, should be put on speech, no matter how hurtful. Opponents have challenged speech codes in court, and a 1992 Supreme Court decision held that in public institutions racial slurs could not be prohibited as long as other kinds of slurs were allowed. Many schools, both public and private, have rewritten their speech codes in response to this decision. Even so, many students and faculty members are uncomfortable with vaguely worded prohibitions that they say can lead to prosecutions for being merely tasteless or rude. (One student, for example, was recently brought in front of a disciplinary committee for saying, "Amy is so stubborn sometimes I could strangle her.") Some also ask whether speech codes create an atmosphere on campus that inhibits rather than encourages the free exchange of ideas.

The two essays that follow illustrate two opinions concerning this issue. In "Civility and Its Discontents," Leslie Epstein argues that despite the many problems speech codes present, they are necessary

591

and desirable to ensure that learning can take place. In "The PC Speech Police," Barbara Dority says that in seeking to protect minorities and women, the advocates of such codes are becoming as intolerant as those they seek to suppress.

CIVILITY AND ITS DISCONTENTS

Leslie Epstein

Leslie Epstein, born in 1938 in Los Angeles, graduated from Yale University in 1960 and received his master's degree from the University of California at Los Angeles in 1963 and his doctorate in fine arts from Yale in 1967. Epstein also studied at Oxford University from 1960 to 1962 on a Rhodes scholarship. He taught English at Queens College of the City University of New York from 1965 to 1978, when he became director of the Creative Writing Program at Boston University. Epstein is the author of numerous novels and short stories, including the controversial King of the Jews: A Novel of the Holocaust *(1979). The book, about the leaders of a Polish ghetto who are forced to supply quotas of Jews for Nazi concentration camps or risk the annihilation of the entire ghetto, drew much praise as well as criticism and won several awards. Epstein's most recent books are a collection of short stories entitled* Goldkorn Tales *(1985) and the novel* Pinto and Sons *(1990). "Civility and Its Discontents," published in the academic journal* The American Prospect *in 1991, is Epstein's attempt to think through the complexities of free speech and its abuses on the one hand and "political correctness" and its excesses on the other.*

I have set myself a moral puzzle. What would I do if I were a college president and had to decide the fate of a student who had been caught writing racial and ethnic epithets—*niggers back to Africa, Hitler didn't finish the job*—on the doors of, respectively, a black and Jewish classmate, and was suspected of writing *gays suck*! in the entryway of an openly bisexual dorm? Hangdog or defiant, the miscreant is brought before me. In real life I expect my reactions would run something like this: righteousness, rage even, before the door opened, along with a fixed determination to expel the criminal from our midst; and a sudden surge of curiosity, zeal for reformation, and a form of fellow feeling, once the flesh-and-blood chap appeared on the other side of my desk. That's one good reason why the destiny of others should not be placed in my hands.

To expel or not expel? Even in the abstract, on paper, the question leaves me divided. My emotions boil at the prospect of having to

593

share a campus with such bad apples in it. But my mind, which has its instincts too, raises the flag of caution. I've lived in this democracy long enough to know that the First Amendment ought not to be monkeyed with and that the more absolute its protections the better off all of us are (well not *all:* not those libeled, or, more to the point, not those threatened on campus). I am a member of the ACLU. I am also a writer, with a writer's concern for minimizing the role of the censor in American life.

Wait a minute: the truth is, my view of censorship is more com- 3
plicated than that. The worst thing that can happen to any artist is to be shot dead by Stalin. The second worst is to be told that anything goes. I suppose the third worst is to be dragooned, by an NEA grant, into respecting the diversity of one's fellow citizens' beliefs. The point is, if there are no taboos in society, there will be few in the psyche. So much, then, for the disguises, the tricks and sleight of hand, that the public, which shares the magician's repressions, calls art.

How could I favor expulsion, moreover, when I had suffered that 4
fate myself, and more than once, in the fifties? The first occasion was at the Webb School, in California, when one of the preppies asked, "What's this?" as the turnips and gruel were plopped on his plate.

"The week's profit," quipped I. Papa Webb wasn't one to tolerate 5
teenage quipsters. Gone. Rusticated. Dismissed. Expelled.

A few years later the same wise guy was standing on York Street, 6
in New Haven, when the mayor came out of Phil's Barber Shop and stepped into Fenn-Feinstein next door. "What's the mayor doing?" asked my current straight man, as His Honor emerged from the doorway and ducked into the entrance of Barrie Shoes. "Wednesday. Two-thirty," I replied, just loud enough. "Time to collect." This was, remember, the fifties. The next thing I knew I had been thrust up against the side of a car, had handed over my wallet, and been ordered to be at the dean's office the next morning at ten. By eleven, I was no longer a Son of Eli.*

Hard to believe? Even those who lived through those days might 7
find it difficult to recall the atmosphere that lingered on campus well after Senator McCarthy's demise.** The master of my residen-

---

*EDS. NOTE—a term for a young man attending Yale University, which is named for its benefactor Elihu Yale.

**EDS. NOTE—In the early 1950s Joseph McCarthy (1908–1957), a Wisconsin Republican, made a series of speeches and conducted Senate hearings in which prominent people were accused of being Communists. The sensational accusations, which created a widespread climate of fear and destroyed numerous careers, were eventually discredited, and McCarthy was censured by the Senate.

tial college was a particularly despotic fellow. During my junior year a number of my pals secretly published a mimeographed newspaper, *The Trumbullian,* and at three in the morning shoved them under everyone's door. "Ape Rape in Trumbull Lounge" was the leading headline. Doc Nick, as he was known to his subjects, responded by calling in the FBI. For a week afterward we watched as a crack team of pale young men in dark suits went about dusting for fingerprints and testing our typewriters, as they had recently done for the Hiss trial,* for telltale keys.

To return to the tale, both my expulsions had been effected in order to remove from two bastions of Civilization, and Christendom, a threat to what is generally called, especially by those who do the expelling these days, civility. How can one learn, so goes the argument, in a boorish atmosphere, especially when one might be subjected to crude, offensive, even inflammatory remarks? The premise deserves explanation. My own feeling is that Miss Manners, and anyone else who thinks the university must be governed by a special code of decorum, have, slightly, but crucially, missed the point. Webb might be a finishing school, but Yale is not. At least not any longer. "When Jews and other scum beyond human ken make Yale fraternities . . ." The line is from the famed Yale *Record,* 1917 (and not, as you thought, from the *Dartmouth Review,* 1990**), and there was enough of that attitude left forty years later to make our class of '60, if not quite *Judenrein,**** then at least controlled by a quota so strict we could count the total number of blacks and Asians on the fingers of one hand, and which, of course, allowed for no women at all.

Many are the sins hidden behind the cloak of gentility; enough of them were revealed in the decade following my graduation to make me forever suspicious of those who invest much of their energy in attempting to make the tattered garment whole. Oddly enough, the worst of those sins was intellectual sloth. I saw this most clearly at Oxford, not long after my adventures in New Haven. Talk about finishing schools! I know of one student, an Englishman, whose tutor advised him to stay on an extra year, "because you haven't quite got

---

*Eds. Note—Alger Hiss (b. 1904) was a former U.S. State Department official accused in 1948 of spying for the Soviet Union. The FBI is believed by some to have tampered with evidence to secure his 1950 conviction for perjury.

**Eds. Note—a conservative student publication at Dartmouth College that printed a passage from Adolf Hitler's anti-Semitic book *Mein Kampf* during a Jewish religious holiday in 1990.

***Eds. Note—a Nazi term meaning "free of Jews" and referring to regions whose entire Jewish population had been deported to concentration camps.

the accent yet." My own tutor, a world-renowned figure, used to wave away my fears of Armageddon with the repeated mantra: "Epstein! You Americans and your atom bomb! Have another ale!" So frantic were the dons and dullards about their civilization being violated by a good hard thought that they had institutionalized the sconce as a means of ensuring that no one did much more than dally at tea or punt along the Isis.* This is how the OED defines the term:

> At Oxford, a fine of a tankard of ale or the like, imposed by under-graduates on one of their number for some breach of customary rule when dining in hall.

At Merton,** the customary rule forbade any conversation about   10
one's studies, about politics, or anything roughly resembling an idea. This left, as topics, the girls at St. Hilda's** and cricket.

I can't resist relating how, one night, an uncouth American,   11
Michael Fried, now a distinguished critic of art, thoughtlessly let slip a remark about Marx or Freud. An awful hush fell upon the hall. At high table, the dons froze, their asparagus savories hanging above their mouths. Down at the benches, the undergraduates let the peas roll off their knives. Behind the malefactor a waiter appeared, with the customary bloodshot cheeks and bushy mustache, holding a foam-ing chalice of ale. Fried, deep in discussion, paid no mind. The ruddy servant—in his white apron he looked the kosher butcher—tapped him on the shoulder and held up the tankard with a grin and a wink. Fried whirled round. "What am I supposed to do with this?" he asked, as if unaware that custom dictated he drink down the contents and order an equal portion for all those at table. "Shove it up your ass?" Thus, on the shores of England, did the sixties arrive.

Universities exist not to inculcate manners or teach propriety but   12
to foster inquiry, pass on the story of what has been best thought and done in the past, and to search for the truth. There is no proof that this teaching and this search can be done only when people are being polite to each other. Indeed, there is much evidence, beginning with Socrates, to suggest that it can be done best when people rub hard, and the wrong way, against each other, ruffling feathers, making sparks.

Does this mean, then, that one student may call another *fag* or   13
nigger or *kike*? As a college president I would have no trouble allow-

---

*EDS. NOTE—A popular activity at Oxford University, punting involves moving a flat boat along the Isis, the river that flows past many Oxford colleges, by pushing a long pole against the river bottom.

**EDS. NOTE—Merton is a men's college and St. Hilda's a women's college at Oxford.

ing anyone on campus who wished to argue that homosexuality was contrary to nature, that blacks were intellectually inferior to whites, or that the Holocaust never happened. Such visitations are far different than hurled epithets. To the awful arguments one may at least offer arguments of one's own, display one's charts and graphs and statistics, confident that the truth will out. But what argument can one make against a slur—even one that is not anonymous? If anything, an epithet is designed to short-circuit rationality, to inflame feelings, to draw a curtain, the color of boiling blood, across the life of the mind. Further, it is not just the life of the mind that is threatened: behind the word "nigger" hangs the noose, just as the ovens burn and smoke hovers behind the word "kike."

This distinction—between, if you will, inquiry and invective—   14
carries almost enough weight with me to force a decision: if anyone seeks to destroy another's ability to join the intellectual life of the university, that is, to reason freely, to search dispassionately, to think, he ought not to have any role in that community himself. Almost. The strongest voice against passing sentence comes not from civil libertarians (to whose arguments I hope to turn soon) but from a Yale Law School student, himself the recipient of an anonymous letter ("Now you know why we call you niggers"), who recently told the Yale *Herald,* "It infantilizes people of color to say we can't handle people saying mean things about us. . . . It's much better for people of color to know what people think of us. I'd feel much, much better if people said exactly what they think." Back, for the moment, on the fence.

I began the discussion of this moral puzzle by listing a number of   15
reasons why I am, through intellectual makeup and personal experience, drawn toward a merciful resolution of the dilemma. Not the least of these reasons has to do with the allies I would rather not have should I choose to expel. I am thinking, of course, of the movement whose members—though "movement" and "members" are clearly misnomers—have become the most censorious figures on college campuses. It is the politically correct who call for strict codes to define what is and is not permissible speech and who have exercised the will to enforce them.

Now I want to make it clear at once that if I have problems with   16
the PC crowd, I am no happier with what seems to be the orchestrated campaign of attack against them, a campaign whose sole purpose is to transform the last institution in American life not already controlled by the right. I'm caught, for friends, between people who call for the hide of others; or others, who have suddenly seen the

virtue of the Bill of Rights, like Representative Henry Hyde. (The congressman's bill states that "federally assisted institutions cannot discipline students if their spoken or printed views are found to be repugnant, offensive, or emotionally distressing to others on campus." This from a man who voted to force recipients of grants from the National Endowment for the Arts to consider their fellow citizens' beliefs!)

Everyone has a favorite example—at Michigan, for instance, a male student is officially proscribed from saying "women just aren't as good in this field as men"—of PC excess. Because I'm trying to keep these remarks as personal as possible, I'll turn to my own town, Brookline, which once had a first-rate school system. Nowadays it has embarked on a "hundred-year plan" to do away with what an assistant superintendent of curriculum calls the "traditional" white male perspective. Among the things this plan would eliminate is the "vertical" white male notion of excellence, along with disciplined thinking, logic, and what this same superintendent calls the "incredible abomination" of Black History Month, whose sin is to reinforce privileged ideas of excellence by pointing out "pinnacle people" who are "outstanding exceptions to their group."

A few weeks ago, a good thirty-two years after my undergraduate days, I took part in a panel on censorship at what is probably Yale's most prestigious, and certainly its most open-minded, senior society. The current delegation was there, class of '91, together with representatives of delegations going back almost to the days when the *Record* could speak of subhuman scum. The discussion, as you might imagine, was lively. At one point a contemporary of mine, an artist, told the story of how the curators of a Gauguin* exhibition had been lobbied to take down half the paintings because they demonstrated "an exploitative colonialist perspective." An appreciative chuckle went round the room. We codgers elbowed each other. Such an absurdity! Suddenly a member of the current delegation rose from his bench. "I'd like to point out," he said, in a voice that was only slightly shaking, "that no people of color are laughing." True enough. Nor was anyone much below the age of thirty-five.

I hope it isn't necessary for me to say how much I like these students. They are bright, sensitive, idealistic, and—at Yale, anyway—they work every bit as hard as I did in the fifties. They may be bamboozled, but these bits of zaniness are no more indicative of a

17

18

19

*Eds. Note—Paul Gauguin (1848–1903), French artist best known for his paintings of the native people of Polynesia.

totalitarian spirit than the knee-jerk liberalism I still feel a twitch of on rainy days. At the same time, there are elements of a kind of conformity that cannot be laughed away. To stick to my current campus, I've been present when a harassment officer browbeat my colleagues—who merely grinned and bore it—about how to notice sexist attitudes among its members and how to turn the offenders in to her office. And I know of a department that voted to offer a talented young assistant professor ("enchanting" was the word his students used to describe his teaching) the normal extension of his contract, then reversed itself twenty-four hours later, largely because of his supposed sexism (he had, as an example, observed a lousy performance by a graduate student and suggested that perhaps her advanced pregnancy had created a strain). Kaput career. There's more than a whiff of Peking in the air when professors are forced, as they have been, to recant, or apologize for their opinions, or sent to special classes for reeducation.

Yet even the thought police are not what worries me most about political correctness, or what tie these worries to the subject at hand. Perhaps I can best get at what I mean by reiterating what I told my daughter, who is struggling with these issues herself as a college junior, when she asked me for a one-sentence definition of PC. "Well," I said, perhaps less clumsily than this, "I guess this is a way of seeing society as a system of oppression, and that the interests of its victims ought to dictate our thinking and behavior, to the exclusion of pretty much any other consideration." What I didn't add was that the "other consideration" I had in mind was the very idea of objective reality, stubborn and recalcitrant as the law of gravity; and that it was this reality, with its laws, its truths, and—tricky, this—its values that the university was founded to discover, nurture, and pass on.   20

Which leads me to note that during that debate at Yale, the most engaged and vociferous students invariably turned out to be English majors. No surprise there. They were well versed in deconstruction and other reader-response theories, which together have provided the ideological underpinnings of political correctness. Here, from Jane Tompkins, a leading feminist scholar, is a nutshell version of how these students have been taught to approach a text: 21

> Critics deny that criticism has . . . an objective basis because they deny the existence of objective texts and indeed the possibility of objectivity altogether. . . . The net result of this epistemological revolution is to politicize literature and literary criticism. When discourse is responsible for reality and not merely a reflection of it, then whose discourse prevails makes all the difference.

Literary texts, then, have no inherent meaning or even a claim to   22
existence, apart from the baggage of the culture in which they were
written and now are read. Free speech? Value? Objective standards?
Timeless verities? Reality itself? Truth becomes simply an opinion,
whatever has been ferreted out as the reigning myth; and knowledge
is the triumph of one ideology over another. It is this academic version of might makes right, with its inherent nihilism, that has helped
me to solve the puzzle I set myself these many paragraphs back.

That is to say, there are *two* slopes that lead from the heights of   23
academe, one as slippery as the other. The first has, with good reason, preoccupied those concerned with civil liberties: once we begin
proscribing some speech, what other restrictions will follow? To
what end will we come? We already have the answer: to the harassment code at the University of Connecticut, which forbids "incon-
siderate jokes," "misdirected laughter," and "conspicuous exclusion
from conversation." Yet even these grotesqueries do not resolve our
dilemma. If the City College of New York were to prohibit Leonard
Jeffries of its Black Studies Department from saying that blacks are
superior to whites because of the melanin in their skins, or silence
Michael Levin, a professor of philosophy at the same institution,
who believes that blacks are inherently inferior, it would surely be
exercising a form of thought control. The trouble is, *not* censoring
the kind of racial epithet whose effect is to undermine the very processes of logic is a form of thought control as well.

Perhaps the solution, or at least a legal rationale for a solution, to   24
this dilemma lies as near to hand as my daily newspaper. On page
41 of today's *Boston Globe,* under the headline *Black workers at
Maine plant win in bias suit,* is the story of how three black men
from the South were recruited to work at the International Paper
Co. in Auburn, Maine. Once there they were harassed by "ugly oral
racial epithets and graffiti," and by co-workers "in Ku Klux Klan-
like garb 'prancing' around their work stations."

The United States District Court ruled that in creating "a hostile   25
and offensive workplace" and by substantially altering the plaintiffs'
working conditions, International Paper had violated Maine's human rights act. The three workers were awarded $55,000 each. Now
there is similar harassment legislation in every state of the union. Is
there any reason why, of all the institutions in America, only those
of higher education should be exempt from these statutes? The only
response is a truism: that a university, with its special mission and
need for forceful debate, and comprehensive points of view, is not a
paper mill. It is precisely the role of the university, its vulnerability,

and its fate in modern history, that leads me to look at the second, and steeper, of the slippery slopes.

The grease for this chute is applied by that same belief in the 26 relativity of all values that now prevails on so many campuses. Here are the words of one university president:

> Every people in every period must form its life according to its own law and fate, and to this law of its own, scholarship, with all other spheres of life, is also subject. . . . The idea of humanism, with the teaching of pure human reason and absolute spirit founded upon it, is a philosophical principle of the eighteenth century caused by the conditions of that time. It is in no sense binding upon us as we live under different conditions and under a different fate.

The speaker is Ernst Krick, rector of Frankfort University, and 27 the occasion was the 550th anniversary of the University of Heidelberg in 1936.*

At the bottom of this slope lies totalitarianism of one kind or another. 28 The movement of nihilism is both centrifugal and centripetal, moving outward from literary texts—which, since they have no enduring value, are all too easily burned—through discipline after discipline, in ever widening circles until even the obdurate laws of nature herself are subject to challenge. Hence, in the universities of the Third Reich, biology became "National Socialist biology," psychoanalysis become "mongrel psychology," and the theory of relativity was "Jewish physics."

If there are no lasting truths, nothing to be handed down from one 29 generation to another, then the only source of authority shrinks centripetally in narrower and narrower circles until one arrives at the fountainhead of truth, which in the German formula was the Fuehrer. What Hitler set out to destroy was Western culture and intelligence itself—and not in the name of diversity! On the contrary it was the Fuehrer, who became the only thinker, the sole author, the one biologist, legal expert, psychologist, and knower of nature's secrets.

The Weimar Republic** had as many laws against harassment as 30 has, these days, the state of Maine. Dueling societies were banned (and with them the practice of refusing to duel with Jews), as were all remarks tending to incite racial hatred or campus strife. The trouble was, the rules were not enforced—or worse, enforced selec-

---

*Eds. Note—By 1936 Frankfort and Heidelberg, along with other German universities, had allied themselves with the Nazi dictatorship established in 1933 by Hitler.
**Eds. Note—the democratic German government that held power from 1919 to 1933.

tively. The book has yet to be written as to why the right has always felt free ruthlessly to suppress the liberal left, and why the liberal left, and liberalism in general, has stood by, Hamlet-like, unable to repress the forces of the right. (The image of Hamlet is appropriate, since, according to the "mongrel science," the reason he cannot strike Claudius is that his uncle has enacted the very crimes—murdering his father and sleeping with his mother—that he wished, in the depths of his unconscious, to commit himself. The liberal may see, in the nationalist, the racist, and the fanatic, the embodiment of the passions he has smothered in his own breast.)

Hence Hitler, after the beer-hall putsch,* was put in a cell with a view and handed a paper and pencil. In the name of academic freedom, Weimar permitted every atrocity, even the assassinations it half-heartedly prosecuted and feebly punished. The result was that, well before Hitler took power, the universities had become such hotbeds of anti-Semitism and ultranationalism that the professorate, of all the classes in Germany, became the most devoted followers of his cause.   31

The fundamental mistake of Weimar Germany, and of liberalism in general, is the belief that, confronted by nihilistic fervor, one may yet count on a triumph of reason. Theodor Mommsen, the great German historian, wore himself out (and lost his job) in the attempt to defend what he called the "legacy of Lessing"** against "racial hatred and the fanaticism of the Middle Ages." In the end he came to realize: 32

> You are mistaken if you believe that anything at all could be achieved by reason. In years past I thought so myself and kept protesting against the monstrous infamy that is anti-Semitism. But it is useless, completely useless. Whatever I or anybody else could tell you are in the last analysis reasons, logical and ethical arguments which no anti-Semite will listen to. They listen only to their own envy and hatred, to the meanest instincts. Nothing else counts for them. They are deaf to reason, right morals. One cannot influence them.

Let us return to that Yale Law School student (his name is Anthony K. Jones) who faced with equanimity and no small amount of courage the prospect of a fellow student calling him nigger. What would he feel, I wonder, when faced by *two* screaming students? Or   33

---

*EDS. NOTE—an unsuccessful effort by Hitler and the Nazis to overthrow the Weimar Republic in 1923. For his part in the rebellion Hitler was imprisoned for nine months, during which he dictated *Mein Kampf* to Rudolf Hess.

**EDS. NOTE—Gotthold Ephraim Lessing (1729–1781), a philosopher, critic, and dramatist who was a leading proponent in Germany of the rationalist thought of the Enlightenment.

four? Eventually he would have to run, as others have before him, a gauntlet. Is there any prospect that, hounded by what Mommsen called "the mob of the streets or the parlors," anything resembling the free exchange of ideas could take place?

I cannot remain, even in my imagination, a university president if   34
I do not believe in certain things—chief among them the belief that reality can be known and its truths both taught and learned. Free speech, far from being an end in itself, is an instrument in a process of discovery. When it impedes or perverts that process—for instance by denying a student the exercise of his intellect or putting him in fear for his body—something must be done.

But what? About that I have come, through however tortuous a   35
route, to a decision. It is perhaps natural that, since my ideas have been divided against themselves, this conclusion should take the form of a paradox. Because the tactics of the civil libertarians, and liberalism in general, are unavailing against men and women seized by nihilistic fervor, I shall have to adopt those that belong to the fervent themselves. I do so not so much to circumscribe those who are politically correct, but to guard against those, like the young man about to be brought before me, who have been provoked to react—in what is always a deadly dance—against them.

Here he comes now. Of course he shall have due process. And we   36
shall have to go into every detail, each aspect of his case. But at bottom it is his unwillingness to engage others as free spirits, his attempt to extinguish reason within them, that dooms him. I shall not attempt to put ideas he does not feel into his head or words he does not feel into his mouth: no people's court here! Instead, I shall steel myself against my own nature and ask him to leave the university. Perhaps he might reapply and, if his self-knowledge has grown, be readmitted (as it happens, I got back into Webb and Yale, although the fifties might have been more forgiving than present times). And in passing this harsh sentence I shall turn, as college presidents like to do, to authority—this time, appropriately enough, to the man who above all others believed in the imperishability of ideas. Punishment, Plato said, is the most salutary thing one can do for a man who has done wrong.

COMPREHENSION

1. What moral puzzle has Epstein set for himself?

2. What two incidents caused Epstein to be expelled from prep school and college? What did he learn from these incidents?

3. According to Epstein, what is the difference between arguing that the Holocaust never happened and making a racial slur? Why would he permit one and not the other?

4. What problems does Epstein have with what he calls "the PC crowd"? What problems does he have concerning the attack against them?

5. Epstein identifies what he calls "two slippery slopes" (23): The first has to do with the consequences of proscribing free speech; the second has to do with the assertion that there are no lasting truths. What are the implications of these two methods of thinking? How do they relate to Epstein's dilemma concerning speech codes?

6. What conclusion does Epstein reach about speech codes and the need for civility on a college campus? How does he resolve his dilemma?

PURPOSE AND AUDIENCE

1. What preconceptions about his subject does Epstein think his readers have? How can you tell?

2. At the end of paragraph 2 Epstein lists some of his credentials. What does he expect to establish with this list? Is he successful?

3. Do you think Epstein is writing to students? To teachers? To the general public?

STYLE AND STRUCTURE

1. Epstein begins by imagining that he is a college president. Why does he do this?

2. Epstein shifts directions a number of times in his essay. How does he make sure his readers will be able to keep track of his discussion?

3. At what point in the essay does Epstein refute opposing arguments? What are the arguments? How effectively do you think he refutes them?

4. Throughout this essay, Epstein gives the impression that he is trying to make up his mind about the issue of speech codes. How does he give this impression? What does he gain by appearing to be undecided?

5. Epstein seems to digress a number of times in his essay. For example, he begins by outlining a moral puzzle, shifts to a discussion of expulsion, and then examines codes of civility. Why does he do so?

6. Does Epstein appeal primarily to logic or to the emotions? Explain.

VOCABULARY PROJECTS

1. Define each of the following words as it is used in this selection.

epithets (1)	infantilizes (14)	epithet (23)
zeal (1)	misnomers (15)	truism (25)
repressions (3)	abomination (17)	totalitarianism (28)
despotic (7)	dictate (20)	centrifugal (28)
decorum (8)	recalcitrant (20)	centripetal (28)
ken (8)	vociferous (21)	mongrel (28)
sloth (9)	ideological (21)	embodiment (30)
mantra (9)	epistemological (21)	fervor (32)
dons (9)	verities (22)	imperishability (36)
dullards (9)	ferreted (22)	salutary (36)
breach (9)	reigning (22)	
ruddy (11)	nihilism (22)	

2. At times Epstein sounds as if he is talking conversationally to his readers, and at other times he sounds as if he is preaching at them. List the words and phrases that convey each impression.

JOURNAL ENTRY

If you were a college president, how would you discipline a student found guilty of writing racial and ethnic epithets on the doors of an African-American and a Jewish student?

WRITING WORKSHOP

1. Write a response to Epstein in which you argue against his position. As you make your case, refute specific points that he makes.

2. Write your own version of a speech code. (Try to be as specific as you can to avoid the ambiguities that open you up to a charge of writing a code that is impossible to enforce.) Then, write a letter to your student newspaper in which you defend the code's provisions.

3. Write an essay in which you argue for or against a speech code at your college or university. Use examples from your own experience to support your position.

THEMATIC CONNECTIONS

- "The Same Difference" (p. 203)
- "Sex, Lies, and Conversation" (p. 393)
- "The Catbird Seat" (p. 522)

THE PC SPEECH POLICE

Barbara Dority

*Barbara Dority is president of the Humanists of Washington,
executive director of the Washington Coalition Against Censorship,
and cochair of the Northwest Feminist Anti-Censorship Taskforce.
She is also a board member of the Washington divisions of the
American Civil Liberties Union and the Hemlock Society. Dority
frequently writes articles on civil and human rights in the areas of
health care, education, poverty and homelessness, religion and politics, police brutality, and prisons. "The PC Speech Police" was published in her regular column for* The Humanist, *"Civil Liberties
Watch," in 1992. She argues here that restricting speech on campuses not only violates the freedom ensured by the First Amendment
but also avoids addressing the social causes of intolerance.*

> I have always been among those who believed that the freedom of
> speech was the greatest safety, because if a man is a fool, the best
> thing to do is to encourage him to advertise that fact by speaking.
> —Woodrow Wilson

The dogma of PCism advocates the suppression of anything that 1
might give offense "on the grounds of gender, sexual orientation,
race, ethnicity, religion, creed, national origin, ancestry, age, or handicap." Offense is determined by the affronted person; truth is no
defense. The aim is to protect minorities and women and enforce
awareness of their dignity and worth. This can include enforced
separatism—but only when blacks, gays, or women choose it.

When the form of language takes precedence over its meaning, 2
rationalists must take heed. Notwithstanding that the *intent* of PC
speech is usually humane and progressive, civil libertarians are jus-
tifiably concerned when universities (of all places) become enforcers
of imposed "tolerance" through speech-restrictive codes. What are
we teaching students about the guarantee of equal protection under
the law? Federal courts and the Supreme Court have consistently
held that restrictive speech codes are unconstitutional.

Certainly no one would argue that racist, sexist, ageist, and homo- 3
phobic beliefs do not persist in this country. But the way to ensure
that their toxic influence will multiply is to sweep them into a dark
corner and pretend they don't exist.

606

There is no question that certain non-European and feminist   4
views have been squeezed out of university studies for too long. But
now proponents have gone to the other extreme, censoring ideas
they dislike just as their own ideas were censored in the past. Surely
women and minorities should have learned that suppression is an
admission of weakness and fear—a diversion from dealing with the
real social issues at the root of intolerance.

The climate created by PC promoters has led to an appalling   5
level of academic self-censorship. For instance, many professors are
taping their lectures in case they have a future need to defend themselves from charges of sexism, racism, homophobia, and so on. Professors, most notably at Princeton University and Carleton College,
have dropped some courses entirely under pressure from PC forces.
Even Nadine Strossen, new president of the American Civil Liberties Union and a professor at New York University Law School, has
resorted to allowing students to make their "non-PC" feelings and
questions known through anonymous notes which she reads and
addresses in class—a culture of forbidden questions.

The Carnegie Foundation for the Advancement of Teaching, in its   6
report *Campus Life: In Search of Community,* states that "restrictive
codes, for practical as well as legal reasons, do not provide a satisfactory response to offensive language. They may be expedient, even
grounded in conviction, but the university cannot submit the cherished ideals of freedom and equality to the legal system and expect
them to be returned intact."

Benno Schmidt, president of Yale University, makes the same   7
point. "Universities cannot censor or suppress speech," he says, "no
matter how obnoxious in content, without violating their justification for existence. It is to elevate fear over the capacity for a liber-
ated and humane mind and will loose an utterly open-ended engine
of censorship." In other words, universities, above all, must not permit "sensitivity" to stifle the free discourse they are supposed to represent and encourage. The PC mindset is too rigid and reactionary
for careful thought or objective analysis.

A 1990 study by the American Council on Education and the Na-   8
tional Association of Student Personnel Administrators found that
60 percent of the colleges and universities they surveyed already
had written policies on bigotry and verbal intimidation, including
such schools as the University of Pennsylvania, the University of
California, Columbia, Tufts, Emory, and Stanford. Another 11 percent reported that such policies were being formulated.

The University of Connecticut's policy bans "inappropriately di-   9
rected laughter" and "conspicuous exclusion of students from con-

versations." The University of Wisconsin has become a model of PC decorum since the Wisconsin state legislature stiffened the student-conduct code to ban by state law "discriminatory comments, name calling, racial slurs, or 'jokes.'"

Numerous documented examples of the enforcement of such poli- 10 cies include an incident in which a University of Michigan student asserted in class that he felt homosexuality was treatable through therapy. The administration has charged him with violating the university's speech code and is seeking his expulsion. This student is black. So is another Michigan student who was punished under the same rules for using the term *white trash* in class.

In March 1991, the social-science department at Santa Monica 11 College censured economics professor Eugene Buchholz for arguing that ethnic- and gender-based studies "sidetrack students who could otherwise gain useful disciplines or skills."

At the University of Washington in early 1990, a student was re- 12 moved from a course with a nonpassing grade and threatened with expulsion because he questioned an assertion by a women's studies professor that lesbians make the best mothers.

Nina Wu, a sophomore at the University of Connecticut, was brought 13 up on charges of violating the student-behavior code, which prohibits "posting or advertising publicly offensive, indecent, or abusive matter concerning persons. . . ." She allegedly put a poster on her dorm-room door listing "people who should be shot on sight"—among them "preppies, bimboes, men without chest hair, and homos." Wu was ordered to move off campus and forbidden to set foot in any university dormitory or cafeteria. Under pressure from a federal lawsuit, the university administration allowed her to move back onto campus.

Certainly drunks shouting racial epithets in dormitory halls should 14 be disciplined for disturbing the peace, and people who spray-paint public or private property should be disciplined for vandalism regardless of the message. But when a Brown University student was expelled after a wee-hours drunken tirade, it was because he was found guilty not only of public inebriation and disruption but of violating the university's speech code prohibiting "racial, homophobic, and anti-Semitic slurs." (These slurs were not accompanied by verbal or physical threats.)

Linda Chavez, a Hispanic Reagan administration official, was 15 asked to speak at the University of Colorado. Upon learning that she opposed affirmative action and thought Hispanics should learn English as soon as possible, PC students protested and the university president, apologizing for his "gross insensitivity," withdrew his invitation to Chavez.

Students have been suspended not only for using "epithets" toward 16
blacks, gays, and other minorities in the classroom but also in dor-
mitories, at sporting events, and off-campus entirely.

Jean Bethke Elshtain, a political science professor at Vanderbilt, 17
says, "It's reached the point that, if you make any judgment or assessment as to the quality of a work, somehow you aren't being an
'intellectual egalitarian.'" At a recent conference, she referred to
Czeslaw Milosz's *The Captive Mind* as a "classic," to which another
female professor exclaimed in dismay that the word *classic* made
her "feel oppressed."

Some who should know better trivialize the problem, rationalizing 18
that incidents have been few and far between and that the accused
do have legal recourse. After all, they say, violators aren't shot or
sent to the gulag. Amazing. Are these to be the new standards by
which we measure the seriousness of First Amendment violations?

It has even been stated that Jewish organizations are "placating" 19
a bigot like David Duke when they uncategorically defend his right
to speak. It is suggested that they believe that, by doing this, they'll
"be spared."

Spared what? The suspension of their own free-speech rights? 20
Jewish organizations defend the rights of people like Duke because
they understand the First Amendment. They understand that, if one
wishes to preserve one's own freedom, one must be equally prepared
to defend the freedom of those who express views one abhors. They
know that no one was ever won over to a more inclusive view of life
via bullying and coercion, and that suppression merely allows insup-
portable views to become stronger. In short, they know the difference between genuine social change and enforced verbal purification.

In its publication *Bigotry on Campus: A Planned Response,* the 21
American Jewish Committee states:

> Universities work best when students and faculty are free to say what-
> ever they think. Whereas students should be aware that their words
> can hurt others, they should not be forced to weigh their thoughts
> against administration-imposed limits of political correctness. Higher
> education is at its best when the clash between ideas is heated, not
> chilled. . . . No lawyer can draft language precise enough to punish
> the person who says "nigger" only when he or she really means it. . . .
> Punishing a student for using bigoted words or printing bigoted arti-
> cles drapes the bigot, instead of the university, in the First Amend-
> ment. Thus, the bigot becomes the victim, even the martyr. . . .

What do the courts say? The Supreme Court ruled in *Near* v. 22
Minnesota that racist speech is protected by the First Amendment.

Last year, a federal court judge in Wisconsin ruled that a University of Wisconsin rule forbidding racist and sexist speech violated the First Amendment. The university's Board of Regents adopted the rule in 1989 after a series of incidents described as racist, including a fraternity's "Fiji Island" party which included some caricatures of blacks. The university has appealed.

Black students should remember that Malcolm X was censored on campuses 25 years ago. What is to save outspoken black rappers from the same fate today? How much better to expose hateful and bigoted ideas to the light of reason! 23

The underlying issues are much more complicated, and educational institutions are reluctant to tackle them. Some suggestions have been proposed: offering courses on racism; upgrading and expanding black studies; addressing the issues in orientation sessions; welcoming speakers and artists of every sort to contribute their perspective; and broadening the undergraduate curriculum so that no graduating student has failed to be exposed to other cultures and histories. 24

Truth cannot be determined by government fiat or popular opinion. It is particularly noxious to define truth according to those who are in political power at the moment. Bring on the neo-Nazis, the skinheads, the misogynists, the racists, the hateful, and the angry and let them speak. As always, the answer to a bad idea is a good idea; the answer to the "problem" of free speech is *more* speech. 25

Ray Bradbury, in a 1979 afterword to *Fahrenheit 451,* wrote: 26

> I have always maintained that there is more than one way to burn a book—and the world is full of people running about with lit matches. Every minority . . . feels it has the will, the right, and the duty to douse the kerosene and light the fuse. *Fahrenheit 451* describes how books were burned first by minorities, each ripping a page or a paragraph from this book, then that, until the day when the books were empty and the minds shut and the libraries closed forever.

Exaggeration? Alarmism? Not to those who understand the First Amendment. 27

COMPREHENSION

1. What does Dority say is "the dogma of PCism" (1)?

2. What, according to Dority, is the intent of PC speech?

3. By censoring ideas they do not like, what does Dority believe the proponents of speech codes have accomplished?

4. What kind of speech does Dority think should be controlled? What kind of speech does she think should be protected?

5. What reason does Dority give for defending the free-speech rights of others? According to her, what should those who would curtail the free speech of others remember?

PURPOSE AND AUDIENCE

1. Is Dority's purpose to educate readers? To suggest alternatives? Or does she want to achieve something else?

2. At what point does Dority state her thesis? What would she have gained or lost by withholding her thesis until the end of the essay?

3. How much information does Dority assume her readers know about her subject? How can you tell?

4. Is Dority's argument likely to appeal to those who support speech codes? Why, or why not?

STYLE AND STRUCTURE

1. How does the epigraph at the beginning of the essay set the tone for Dority's argument?

2. Where in the essay does Dority acknowledge the arguments against her position? How effectively does she deal with this opposition?

3. At the beginning of paragraph 12, Dority says that there are numerous examples of the negative effects of speech codes. Does she present enough examples to support this statement? Explain.

4. Does Dority rely primarily on inductive or deductive reasoning?

5. Dority ends her essay with a quotation. How compelling is this ending? What other strategies could she have used?

VOCABULARY PROJECTS

1. Define each of the following words as it is used in this selection.

affronted (1)	discourse (7)	vandalism (14)
precedence (2)	reactionary (7)	egalitarian (17)
appalling (5)	intimidation (8)	martyr (21)
homophobia (5)	decorum (9)	caricatures (22)
humane (7)	epithets (14)	fiat (25)

2. Dority refers to those who do not agree with her as *PC forces* and *PC promoters*. Find other examples of this type of language. What is the effect of these characterizations? Do they enhance or diminish the impact of Dority's argument?

JOURNAL ENTRY

Do you think Dority is being fair to proponents of speech codes?

WRITING WORKSHOP

1. Write an essay in which you support or refute Dority's assertion "The answer to a bad idea is a good idea; the answer to the 'problem' of free speech is *more* speech" (25).

2. Write an essay that defines the kinds of speech you think should be exempted from speech codes. Make sure you structure your essay as an argument and address possible objections to your position.

3. Write an argumentative essay in which you present alternatives to speech codes—required courses about minorities, for example. Use your own experiences and the materials in the essays you have read to support your ideas.

THEMATIC CONNECTIONS

- "Salvador" (p. 128)
- "The Civil Rights Movement: What Good Was It?" (p. 315)
- The Declaration of Independence (p. 556)

Debate: Affirmative Action

Affirmative action, the term generally used for programs that seek to redress past discrimination by granting members of minority groups (as well as women) preferential treatment in education, employment, and business, continues to provoke controversy more than a quarter century after it began in the late 1960s. As a result of these programs, many individuals have gained access to opportunities previously denied them. Some opponents, however, claim that affirmative action is "reverse discrimination"—that it deprives equally qualified whites (some of whom are poor and deserving) of the opportunities it gives to members of minority groups. Others—including some members of minority groups—say that affirmative action inevitably creates the impression, both among whites and in the beneficiaries' own minds, that they cannot qualify for good jobs and education on their own merits. In the long run, the critics say, affirmative action does as much harm as the original injustices that made this policy necessary. Recently, the courts have sent a mixed message concerning preferential treatment of minorities, upholding some specific affirmative action laws and ruling against others. These rulings virtually guarantee that affirmative action policies, such as the use of race as a factor in college admissions and the establishment of rules requiring banks to lend money to minority borrowers, will continue to be the cause of heated disputes and continuing litigation.

The two essays that follow summarize the debate that has swirled around affirmative action since its inception. In "How the Pot Got to Call the Kettle Black," Stanley Fish argues that the history and continuing power of racism in the United States more than justify efforts to remedy the effects of long-standing discrimination. In "A Negative Vote on Affirmative Action," Shelby Steele takes the position that not only does affirmative action not work, but it also has done more harm than good.

HOW THE POT GOT TO CALL
THE KETTLE BLACK

Stanley Fish

*Stanley Fish was born in 1938 in Providence, Rhode Island, grad-
uated from the University of Pennsylvania in 1959, and received his
doctorate from Yale University in 1962. He has taught at the University of California at Berkeley and at Johns Hopkins University
and is currently both chair of the English department and professor
of law at Duke University. Fish is the author of several books on
sixteenth- and seventeenth-century literature. More recently, he has
become widely known outside academic circles for his writing about
literary and legal theory and the experience of reading and interpretation, including* Is There a Text in This Class? The Authority of
Interpretive Communities *(1980),* Doing What Comes Naturally:
Change, Rhetoric, and the Practice of Theory in Literary and Legal
Studies *(1990), and* There's No Such Thing as Free Speech: And It's
a Good Thing, Too *(1993). In "How the Pot Got to Call the Kettle
Black," which appeared in the* Atlantic Monthly *in 1993, Fish defends affirmative action on the grounds that the need to redress
long-standing and continuing inequalities justifies current policies
that appear unfair only if abstracted from their historical context.*

I take my text from George Bush, who, in an address to the United   1
Nations on September 23, 1991, said this of the UN resolution equating Zionism with racism: "Zionism . . . is the idea that led to the creation of a home for the Jewish people. . . . And to equate Zionism
with the intolerable sin of racism is to twist history and forget the
terrible plight of Jews in World War II and indeed throughout history." What happened in the Second World War was that six million
Jews were exterminated by people who regarded them as racially
inferior and a danger to Aryan purity. What happened after the
Second World War was that the survivors of that Holocaust established a Jewish state—that is, a state centered on Jewish history,
Jewish values, and Jewish traditions: in short, a Jewocentric state.
What President Bush objected to was the logical sleight of hand by
which these two actions were declared equivalent because they were
both expressions of racial exclusiveness. Ignored, as Bush said, was
the *historical* difference between them—the difference between a
program of genocide and the determination of those who escaped it

to establish a community in which they would be the makers, not the victims, of the laws.

Only if racism is thought of as something that occurs principally in the mind, a falling-away from proper notions of universal equality, can the desire of a victimized and terrorized people to band together be declared morally identical to the actions of their would-be executioners. Only when the actions of the two groups are detached from the historical conditions of their emergence and given a purely abstract description can they be made interchangeable. Bush was saying to the United Nations, "Look, the Nazis' conviction of racial superiority generated a policy of systematic genocide; the Jews' experience of centuries of persecution in almost every country on earth generated a desire for a homeland of their own. If you manage somehow to convince yourself that these are the same, it is you, not the Zionists, who are morally confused, and the reason you are morally confused is that you have forgotten history."

A KEY DISTINCTION

What I want to say, following Bush's reasoning, is that a similar forgetting of history has in recent years allowed some people to argue, and argue persuasively, that affirmative action is reverse racism. The very phrase "reverse racism" contains the argument in exactly the form to which Bush objected: In this country whites once set themselves apart from blacks and claimed privileges for themselves while denying them to others. Now, on the basis of race, blacks are claiming special status and reserving for themselves privileges they deny to others. Isn't one as bad as the other? The answer is no. One can see why by imagining that it is not 1993 but 1955, and that we are in a town in the South with two more or less distinct communities, one white and one black. No doubt each community would have a ready store of dismissive epithets, ridiculing stories, self-serving folk myths, and expressions of plain hatred, all directed at the other community, and all based in racial hostility. Yet to regard their respective racisms—if that is the word—as equivalent would be bizarre, for the hostility of one group stems not from any wrong done to it but from its wish to protect its ability to deprive citizens of their voting rights, to limit access to educational institutions, to prevent entry into the economy except at the lowest and most menial levels, and to force members of the stigmatized group to ride in the back of the bus. The hostility of the other group is the result of these actions, and whereas hostility and racial anger are unhappy facts wherever they are found, a distinction must surely be made between the ideological hostility of the oppressors and the experience-based hostility of those who have been oppressed.

Not to make that distinction is, adapting George Bush's words, to twist history and forget the terrible plight of African Americans in the more than 200 years of this country's existence. Moreover, to equate the efforts to remedy that plight with the actions that produced it is to twist history even further. Those efforts, designed to redress the imbalances caused by long-standing discrimination, are called affirmative action; to argue that affirmative action, which gives preferential treatment to disadvantaged minorities as part of a plan to achieve social equality, is no different from the policies that created the disadvantages in the first place is a travesty of reasoning. "Reverse racism" is a cogent description of affirmative action only if one considers the cancer of racism to be morally and medically indistinguishable from the therapy we apply to it. A cancer is an invasion of the body's equilibrium, and so is chemotherapy; but we do not decline to fight the disease because the medicine we employ is also disruptive of normal functioning. Strong illness, strong remedy: the formula is as appropriate to the health of the body politic as it is to that of the body proper.

At this point someone will always say, "But two wrongs don't make a right; if it was wrong to treat blacks unfairly, it is wrong to give blacks preference and thereby treat whites unfairly." This objection is just another version of the forgetting and rewriting of history. The work is done by the adverb "unfairly," which suggests two more or less equal parties, one of whom has been unjustly penalized by an incompetent umpire. But blacks have not simply been treated unfairly; they have been subjected first to decades of slavery, and then to decades of second-class citizenship, widespread legalized discrimination, economic persecution, educational deprivation, and cultural stigmatization. They have been bought, sold, killed, beaten, raped, excluded, exploited, shamed, and scorned for a very long time. The word "unfair" is hardly an adequate description of their experience, and the belated gift of "fairness" in the form of a resolution no longer to discriminate against them legally is hardly an adequate remedy for the deep disadvantages that the prior discrimination has produced. When the deck is stacked against you in more ways than you can even count, it is small consolation to hear that you are now free to enter the game and take your chances.

A TILTED FIELD

The same insincerity and hollowness of promise infect another formula that is popular with the anti-affirmative-action crowd: the formula of the level playing field. Here the argument usually takes the form of saying "It is undemocratic to give one class of citizens advantages at the expense of other citizens; the truly democratic way is to have a level playing field to which everyone has access and where everyone has a fair and equal chance to succeed on the basis of his or her merit." Fine words—but they conceal the facts of the situation as it has been given to us by history: the playing field is already tilted in favor of those by whom and for whom it was constructed in the first place. If mastery of the requirements for entry depends upon immersion in the cultural experiences of the mainstream majority, if the skills that make for success are nurtured by institutions and cultural practices from which the disadvantaged minority has been systematically excluded, if the language and ways of comporting oneself that identify a player as "one of us" are alien to the lives minorities are forced to live, then words like "fair" and "equal" are cruel jokes, for what they promote and celebrate is an institutionalized unfairness and a perpetuated inequality. The playing field is already tilted, and the resistance to altering it by the mechanisms of affirmative action is in fact a determination to make sure that the present imbalances persist as long as possible.

One way of tilting the field is the Scholastic Aptitude Test. This test figures prominently in Dinesh D'Souza's book *Illiberal Education* (1991), in which one finds many examples of white or Asian students denied admission to colleges and universities even though their SAT scores were higher than the scores of some others—often African Americans—who were admitted to the same institution. This, D'Souza says, is evidence that as a result of affirmative-action policies colleges and universities tend "to depreciate the importance of merit criteria in admissions." D'Souza's assumption—and it is one that many would share—is that the test does in fact measure *merit,* with merit understood as a quality objectively determined in the same way that body temperature can be objectively determined.

In fact, however, the test is nothing of the kind. Statistical studies have suggested that test scores reflect income and socioeconomic status. It has been demonstrated again and again that scores vary in relation to cultural background; the test's questions assume a certain uniformity in educational experience and lifestyle and penalize those who, for whatever reason, have had a different experience and lived different kinds of lives. In short, what is being measured by the SAT is not absolutes like native ability and merit but accidents like birth, social position, access to libraries, and the opportunity to take vacations or to take SAT prep courses.

Furthermore, as David Owen notes in *None of the Above: Behind the Myth of Scholastic Aptitude* (1985), the "correlation between SAT scores and college grades . . . is lower than the correlation between weight and height; in other words you would have a better chance of predicting a person's height by looking at his weight than you would of predicting his freshman grades by looking only at his SAT scores." Everywhere you look in the SAT story, the claims of fairness, objectivity, and neutrality fall away, to be replaced by suspicions of specialized measures and unfair advantages.

Against this background a point that in isolation might have a   10 questionable force takes on a special and even explanatory resonance: the principal deviser of the test was an out-and-out racist. In 1923 Carl Campbell Brigham published a book called *A Study of American Intelligence*, in which, as Owen notes, he declared, among other things, that we faced in America "a possibility of racial admixture . . . infinitely worse than that faced by any European country today, for we are incorporating the Negro into our racial stock, while all of Europe is comparatively free of this taint." Brigham had earlier analyzed the Army Mental Tests using classifications drawn from another racist text, Madison Grant's *The Passing of the Great Race,* which divided American society into four distinct racial strains, with Nordic, blue-eyed, blond people at the pinnacle and the American Negro at the bottom. Nevertheless, in 1925 Brigham became a director of testing for the College Board, and developed the SAT. So here is the great SAT test, devised by a racist in order to confirm racist assumptions, measuring not native ability but cultural advantage, an uncertain indicator of performance, an indicator of very little except what money and social privilege can buy. And it is in the name of this mechanism that we are asked to reject affirmative action and reaffirm "the importance of merit criteria in admissions."

THE REALITY OF DISCRIMINATION

Nevertheless, there is at least one more card to play against affir-   11 mative action, and it is a strong one. Granted that the playing field is not level and that access to it is reserved for an already advantaged elite, the disadvantages suffered by others are less racial—at least in 1993—than socioeconomic. Therefore shouldn't, as D'Souza urges, "universities . . . retain their policies of preferential treatment, but alter their criteria of application from race to socioeconomic disadvantage," and thus avoid the unfairness of current policies that reward middle-class or affluent blacks at the expense of poor whites? One answer to this question is given by D'Souza himself when he acknowledges that the overlap between minority groups and the poor is very large—a point underscored by the former Secretary of Education Lamar Alexander, who said, in response to a question about funds targeted for black students, "Ninety-eight percent of race-specific scholarships do not involve constitutional problems." He meant, I take it, that 98 percent of race-specific scholarships were also scholarships to the economically disadvantaged.

Still, the other two percent—nonpoor, middle-class, economically 12 favored blacks—are receiving special attention on the basis of disadvantages they do not experience. What about them? The force of the question depends on the assumption that in this day and age race could not possibly be a serious disadvantage to those who are otherwise well positioned in the society. But the lie was given dramatically to this assumption in a 1991 broadcast of the ABC program *PrimeTime Live*. In a stunning fifteen-minute segment reporters and a camera crew followed two young men of equal education, cultural sophistication, level of apparent affluence, and so forth around St. Louis, a city where neither was known. The two differed in only a single respect: one was white, the other black. But that small difference turned out to mean everything. In a series of encounters with shoe salesmen, record-store employees, rental agents, landlords, employment agencies, taxicab drivers, and ordinary citizens, the black member of the pair was either ignored or given a special and suspicious attention. He was asked to pay more for the same goods or come up with a larger down payment for the same car, was turned away as a prospective tenant, was rejected as a prospective taxicab fare, was treated with contempt and irritation by clerks and bureaucrats, and in every way possible was made to feel inferior and unwanted.

The inescapable conclusion was that alike though they may have 13 been in almost all respects, one of these young men, because he was black, would lead a significantly lesser life than his white counterpart: he would be housed less well and at greater expense; he would pay more for services and products when and if he was given the opportunity to buy them; he would have difficulty establishing credit; the first emotions he would inspire on the part of many people he met would be distrust and fear; his abilities would be discounted even before he had a chance to display them; and, above all, the treatment he received from minute to minute would chip away at his self-esteem and self-confidence with consequences that most of us could not even imagine. As the young man in question said at the conclusion of the broadcast, "You walk down the street with a suit and tie and it doesn't matter. Someone will make determinations about you, determinations that affect the quality of your life."

Of course, the same determinations are being made quite early on   14
by kindergarten teachers, grade school principals, high school guidance counselors, and the like, with results that cut across socioeconomic lines and place young black men and women in the ranks of
the disadvantaged no matter what the bank accounts of their parents happen to show. Racism is a cultural fact, and although its effects may to some extent be diminished by socioeconomic variables,
those effects will still be sufficiently great to warrant the nation's
attention and thus the continuation of affirmative-action policies.
This is true even of the field thought to be dominated by blacks and
often cited as evidence of the equal opportunities society now affords
them. I refer, of course, to professional athletics. But national self-
congratulation on this score might pause in the face of a few facts:
A minuscule number of African Americans ever receive a paycheck
from a professional team. Even though nearly 1,600 daily newspapers report on the exploits of black athletes, they employ only seven
full-time black sports columnists. Despite repeated pledges and res-
olutions, major-league teams have managed to put only a handful of
blacks and Hispanics in executive positions.

WHY ME?

When all is said and done, however, one objection to affirmative   15
action is unanswerable on its own terms, and that is the objection of
the individual who says, "Why me? Sure, discrimination has persisted for many years, and I acknowledge that the damage done has
not been removed by changes in the law. But why me? I didn't own
slaves; I didn't vote to keep people on the back of the bus; I didn't
turn water hoses on civil-rights marchers. Why, then, should I be the
one who doesn't get the job or who doesn't get the scholarship or who
gets bumped back to the waiting list?"

I sympathize with this feeling, if only because in a small way I   16
have had the experience that produces it. I was recently nominated
for an administrative post at a large university. Early signs were
encouraging, but after an interval I received official notice that I
would not be included at the next level of consideration, and subsequently I was told unofficially that at some point a decision had
been made to look only in the direction of women and minorities.
Although I was disappointed, I did not conclude that the situation
was "unfair," because the policy was obviously not directed at me—
at no point in the proceedings did someone say, "Let's find a way to
rule out Stanley Fish." Nor was it directed even at persons of my
race and sex—the policy was not intended to disenfranchise white

males. Rather, the policy was driven by other considerations, and it was only as a by-product of those considerations—not as the main goal—that white males like me were rejected. Given that the institution in question has a high percentage of minority students, a very low percentage of minority faculty, and an even lower percentage of minority administrators, it made perfect sense to focus on women and minority candidates, and within that sense, not as the result of prejudice, my whiteness and maleness became disqualifications.

I can hear the objection in advance: "What's the difference? Unfair   17
is unfair: you didn't get the job; you didn't even get on the short list." The difference is not in the outcome but in the ways of thinking that led up to the outcome. It is the difference between an unfairness that befalls one as the unintended effect of a policy rationally conceived and an unfairness that is pursued as an end in itself. It is the difference between the awful unfairness of Nazi extermination camps and the unfairness to Palestinian Arabs that arose from, but was not the chief purpose of, the founding of a Jewish state.

THE NEW BIGOTRY

The point is not a difficult one, but it is difficult to see when the   18
unfairness scenarios are presented as simple contrasts between two decontextualized persons who emerge from nowhere to contend for a job or a place in a freshman class. Here is student A; he has a board score of 1,300. And here is student B; her board score is only 1,200, yet she is admitted and A is rejected. Is that fair? Given the minimal information provided, the answer is of course no. But if we expand our horizons and consider fairness in relation to the cultural and institutional histories that have brought the two students to this point, histories that weigh on them even if they are not the histories' authors, then both the question and the answer suddenly grow more complicated.

The sleight-of-hand logic that first abstracts events from history   19
and then assesses them from behind a veil of willed ignorance gains some of its plausibility from another key word in the anti-affirmative-action lexicon. That word is "individual," as in "The American way is to focus on the rights of individuals rather than groups." Now, "individual" and "individualism" have been honorable words in the American political vocabulary, and they have often been well employed in the fight against various tyrannies. But like any other word or concept, individualism can be perverted to serve ends the opposite of those it originally served, and this is what has happened when in the name of individual rights, millions of individuals are enjoined

from redressing historically documented wrongs. How is this managed? Largely in the same way that the invocation of fairness is used to legitimize an institutionalized inequality. First one says, in the most solemn of tones, that the protection of individual rights is the chief obligation of society. Then one defines individuals as souls sent into the world with equal entitlements as guaranteed either by their Creator or by the Constitution. Then one pretends that nothing has happened to them since they stepped onto the world's stage. And then one says of these carefully denatured souls that they will all be treated in the same way, irrespective of any of the differences that history has produced. Bizarre as it may seem, individualism in this argument turns out to mean that everyone is or should be the *same*. This dismissal of individual difference in the name of the individual would be funny were its consequences not so serious: it is the mechanism by which imbalances and inequities suffered by millions of people through no fault of their own can be sanitized and even celebrated as the natural workings of unfettered democracy.

"Individualism," "fairness," "merit"—these three words are continually misappropriated by bigots who have learned that they need not put on a white hood or bar access to the ballot box in order to secure their ends. Rather, they need only clothe themselves in a vocabulary plucked from its historical context and made into the justification for attitudes and policies they would not acknowledge if frankly named.   20

COMPREHENSION

1. What, according to Fish, allows people to argue that affirmative action is reverse racism?

2. According to Fish, what special conditions of the African-American experience justify affirmative action?

3. Why, according to Fish, do SAT scores not measure merit?

4. Does Fish think that race still creates disadvantages for individuals? Explain.

5. What does Fish mean in paragraph 19 when he says "This dismissal of individual difference in the name of the individual would be funny were its consequences not so serious . . ."?

PURPOSE AND AUDIENCE

1. What is Fish's thesis? Why does he state it where he does?

2. Does Fish assume his readers will be receptive or hostile to his ideas? How can you tell?

3. Do you think Fish respects his readers' intelligence, or does he seem to talk down to them? Explain.

STYLE AND STRUCTURE

1. Why does Fish begin his essay by referring to an address George Bush made in which he attacked a UN resolution equating Zionism with racism?

2. Fish devotes much of his essay to refuting opposing arguments. What arguments does he refute? How effective are his refutations?

3. Throughout his essay, Fish uses several hypothetical situations to make his point. Identify two of these situations, and comment on how effective you think they are.

4. Does Fish rely primarily on induction or deduction to construct his argument? Explain.

5. What points does Fish make in his concluding paragraph? Are these the points he should be reinforcing? Should he be making other points?

VOCABULARY PROJECTS

1. Define each of the following words as it is used in this selection.

plight (1)	chemotherapy (4)	bureaucrats (12)
sleight (1)	stigmatization (5)	minuscule (14)
genocide (1)	nurtured (6)	lexicon (19)
conviction (2)	perpetuated (6)	sanitized (19)
cogent (4)	admixture (10)	unfettered (19)
equilibrium (4)	affluent (11)	misappropriated (20)

2. Fish takes great pains to define certain terms—*affirmative action* and *reverse racism,* for example. Where does he define terms? How do these definitions help strengthen his argument?

JOURNAL ENTRY

In paragraph 16 Fish says that he was eliminated as a candidate for a job because he was neither a woman nor a minority. He explains that he does not consider this policy unfair because it was not directed at him. How would you react in his place?

WRITING WORKSHOP

1. A critic of this article might say that by giving African Americans special status, Fish is reinforcing their status as victims. Write an essay in which you support or refute this assessment.

2. Write an essay in which you support Fish's contention, "When the deck is stacked against you in more ways than you can even count, it is small consolation to hear that you are now free to enter the game and take your chances" (5). Use examples from your reading, observations, and experiences to support your thesis.

3. Consider Fish's point that the historical experience of a group—or of an individual—is enough to warrant special treatment. Write an essay in which you discuss whether you agree or disagree with Fish's position. If you agree with it, decide for how long a group's experience continues to justify such treatment. Use your own experience as a member of a ethnic or racial group to support your thesis.

THEMATIC CONNECTIONS

- "'What's in a Name?'" (p. 5)
- "Finishing School" (p. 78)
- "Just Walk On By" (p. 209)
- "The Civil Rights Movement: What Good Was It?" (p. 315)

A NEGATIVE VOTE ON AFFIRMATIVE ACTION

Shelby Steele

Born in Chicago in 1946, Shelby Steele earned his doctorate from the University of Utah in 1974 and is a professor of English at San Jose State University in California. He has written a series of essays criticizing affirmative action, which are collected in The Content of Our Character: A New Vision of Race in America *(1990). Steele's opinions also appear in* The Politics of Difference: Diversity or Separatism? *(1990), based on a roundtable discussion at George Washington University in which he participated. In "A Negative Vote on Affirmative Action," which appeared in the* New York Times Magazine *in 1990, Steele argues that the feelings of doubt and perceived incompetence engendered by racial preference are detrimental to establishing true racial equality.*

In a few short years, when my two children will be applying to college, the affirmative-action policies by which most universities offer black students some form of preferential treatment will present me with a dilemma. I am a middle-class black, a college professor, far from wealthy, but also well removed from the kind of deprivation that would qualify my children for the label "disadvantaged." Both of them have endured racial insensitivity from whites. They have been called names, have suffered slights and have experienced first hand the peculiar malevolence that racism brings out of people. Yet they have never experienced racial discrimination, have never been stopped by their race on any path they have chosen to follow. Still, their society now tells them that if they will only designate themselves as black on their college applications, they will probably do better in the college lottery than if they conceal this fact. I think there is something of a Faustian bargain in this.

Of course many blacks and a considerable number of whites would say that I was sanctimoniously making affirmative action into a test of character. They would say that this small preference is the meagerest recompense for centuries of unrelieved oppression. And to these arguments other very obvious facts must be added. In America, many marginally competent or flatly incompetent whites are hired every day—some because their white skin suits the conscious

625

or unconscious racial preference of their employers. The white children of alumni are often grandfathered into elite universities in what can only be seen as a residual benefit of historic white privilege. Worse, white incompetence is always an individual matter, but for blacks it is often confirmation of ugly stereotypes. Given that unfairness cuts both ways, doesn't it only balance the scales of history, doesn't this repay, in a small way, the systematic denial under which my children's grandfather lived out his days?

In theory, affirmative action certainly has all the moral symmetry   3
that fairness requires. It is reformist and corrective, even repentent and redemptive. And I would never sneer at these good intentions. Born in the late 1940's in Chicago, I started my education (a charitable term, in this case) in a segregated school, and suffered all the indignities that come to blacks in a segregated society. My father, born in the South, made it only to the third grade before the white man's fields took permanent priority over his formal education. And though he educated himself into an advanced reader with an almost professorial authority, he could only drive a truck for a living, and never earned more than $90 a week in his entire life. So yes, it is crucial to my sense of citizenship, to my ability to identify with the spirit and the interests of America, to know that this country, however imperfectly, recognizes its past sins and wishes to correct them.

Yet good intentions can blind us to the effects they generate when   4
implemented. In our society affirmative action is, among other things, a testament to white good will and to black power, and in the midst of these heavy investments its effects can be hard to see. But after 20 years of implementation I think that affirmative action has shown itself to be more bad than good and that blacks—whom I will focus on in this essay—now stand to lose more from it than they gain.

In talking with affirmative-action administrators and with blacks   5
and whites in general, I found that supporters of affirmative action focus on its good intentions and detractors emphasize its negative effects. It was virtually impossible to find people outside either camp. The closest I came was a white male manager at a large computer company who said, "I think it amounts to reverse discrimination, but I'll put up with a little of that for a little more diversity." But this only makes him a half-hearted supporter of affirmative action. I think many people who don't really like affirmative action support it to one degree or another anyway.

I believe they do this because of what happened to white and black   6
Americans in the crucible of the 1960's, when whites were confronted with their racial guilt and blacks tasted their first real power. In

that stormy time white absolution and black power coalesced into virtual mandates for society. Affirmative action became a meeting ground for those mandates in the law. At first, this meant insuring equal opportunity. The 1964 civil-rights bill was passed on the understanding that equal opportunity would not mean racial preference. But in the late 60's and early 70's, affirmative action underwent a remarkable escalation of its mission from simple anti-discrimination enforcement to social engineering by means of quotas, goals, timetables, set-asides and other forms of preferential treatment.

Legally, this was achieved through a series of executive orders and 7 Equal Employment Opportunity Commission guidelines that allowed racial imbalances in the workplace to stand as proof of racial discrimination. Once it could be assumed that discrimination explained racial imbalances, it became easy to justify group remedies to presumed discrimination rather than the normal case-by-case redress.

Even though blacks had made great advances during the 60's with- 8 out quotas, the white mandate to achieve a new racial innocence and the black mandate to gain power, which came to a head in the very late 60's, could no longer be satisfied by anything less than racial preferences. I don't think these mandates, in themselves, were wrong, because whites clearly needed to do better by blacks and blacks needed more real power in society. But as they came together in affirmative action, their effect was to distort our understanding of racial discrimination. By making black the color of preference, these mandates have reburdened society with the very marriage of color and preference (in reverse) that we set out to eradicate.

When affirmative action grew into social engineering, diversity 9 became a golden word. Diversity is a term that applies democratic principles to races and cultures rather than to citizens, despite the fact that there is nothing to indicate that real diversity is the same thing as proportionate representation. Too often the result of this, on campuses for example, has been a democracy of colors rather than of people, an artificial diversity that gives the appearance of an educational parity between black and white students that has not yet been achieved in reality. Here again, racial preferences allow society to leapfrog over the difficult problem of developing blacks to parity with whites and into a cosmetic diversity that covers the blemish of disparity—a full six years after admission, only 26 to 28 percent of blacks graduate from college.

Racial representation is not the same thing as racial development. 10 Representation can be manufactured; development is always hard earned. But it is the music of innocence and power that we hear in affirmative action that causes us to cling to it and to its distracting emphasis on representation. The fact is that after 20 years of racial preferences the gap between median incomes of black and white families is greater than it was in the 1970's. None of this is to say that blacks don't need policies that insure our right to equal opportunity, but what we need more of is the development that will let us take advantage of society's efforts to include us.

I think one of the most troubling effects of racial preferences for blacks is a kind of demoralization. Under affirmative action, the quality that earns us preferential treatment is an implied inferiority. However this inferiority is explained—and it is easily enough explained by the myriad deprivations that grew out of our oppression—it is still inferiority. There are explanations and then there is the fact. And the fact must be borne by the individual as a condition apart from the explanation, apart even from the fact that others like himself also bear this condition. In integrated situations in which blacks must compete with whites who may be better prepared, these explanations may quickly wear thin and expose the individual to racial as well as personal self-doubt. (Of course whites also feel doubt, but only personally, not racially.) 11

What this means in practical terms is that when blacks deliver themselves into integrated situations they encounter a nasty little reflex in whites, a mindless, atavistic reflex that responds to the color black with negative stereotypes, such as intellectual ineptness. I think this reflex embarrasses most whites today and thus it is usually quickly repressed. On an equally atavistic level, the black will be aware of the reflex his color triggers and will feel a stab of horror at seeing himself reflected in this way. He, too, will do a quick repression, but a lifetime of such stabbings is what constitutes his inner realm of racial doubt. Even when the black sees no implication of inferiority in racial preferences, he knows that whites do, so that—consciously or unconsciously—the result is virtually the same. The effect of preferential treatment—the lowering of normal standards to increase black representation—puts blacks at war with an expanded realm of debilitating doubt, so that the doubt itself becomes an unrecognized preoccupation that undermines their ability to perform, especially in integrated situations. 12

I believe another liability of affirmative action comes from the fact that it indirectly encourages blacks to exploit their own past victimization. Like implied inferiority, victimization is what justifies preference, so that to receive the benefits of preferential treatment one must, to some extent, become invested in the view of one's self as a victim. In this way, affirmative action nurtures a victim-focused 13 identity in blacks and sends us the message that there is more power in our past suffering than in our present achievements.

When power itself grows out of suffering, blacks are encouraged to 14 expand the boundaries of what qualifies as racial oppression, a situation that can lead us to paint our victimization in vivid colors even as we receive the benefits of preference. The same corporations and institutions that give us preference are also seen as our oppressors. At Stanford University, minority-group students—who receive at least the same financial aid as whites with the same need—recently took over the president's office demanding, among other things, more financial aid.

But I think one of the worst prices that blacks pay for preference 15 has to do with an illusion. I saw this illusion at work recently in the mother of a middle-class black student who was going off to his first semester of college: "They owe us this, so don't think for a minute that you don't belong there." This is the logic by which many blacks, and some whites, justify affirmative action—it is something "owed," a form of reparation. But this logic overlooks a much harder and less digestible reality, that it is impossible to repay blacks living today for the historic suffering of the race. If all blacks were given a million dollars tomorrow it would not amount to a dime on the dollar for three centuries of oppression, nor would it dissolve the residues of that oppression that we still carry today. The concept of historic reparation grows out of man's need to impose on the world a degree of justice that simply does not exist. Suffering can be endured and overcome, it cannot be repaid. To think otherwise is to prolong the suffering.

Several blacks I spoke with said they were still in favor of affir- 16 mative action because of the "subtle" discrimination blacks were subject to once they were on the job. One photojournalist said, "They have ways of ignoring you." A black female television producer said: "You can't file a lawsuit when your boss doesn't invite you to the insider meetings without ruining your career. So we still need affirmative action." Others mentioned the infamous "glass ceiling" through which blacks can see the top positions of authority but never reach them. But I don't think racial preferences are a protection against this subtle discrimination; I think they contribute to it.

In any workplace, racial preferences will always create two-tiered 17 populations composed of preferreds and unpreferred. In the case of blacks and whites, for instance, racial preferences imply that whites are superior just as they imply that blacks are inferior. They not only reinforce America's oldest racial myth but, for blacks, they have the effect of stigmatizing the already stigmatized.

I think that much of the "subtle" discrimination that blacks talk   18
about is often (not always) discrimination against the stigma of
questionable competence that affirmative action marks blacks with.
In this sense, preferences make scapegoats of the very people they
seek to help. And it may be that at a certain level employers impose
a glass ceiling, but this may not be against the race so much as
against the race's reputation for having advanced by color as much
as by competence. This ceiling is the point at which corporations
shift the emphasis from color to competency and stop playing the
affirmative-action game. Here preference backfires for blacks and
becomes a taint that holds them back. Of course one could argue
that this taint, which is after all in the minds of whites, becomes
nothing more than an excuse to discriminate against blacks. And
certainly the result is the same in either case—blacks don't get past
the glass ceiling. But this argument does not get around the fact
that racial preferences now taint this color with a new theme of
suspicion that makes blacks even more vulnerable to discrimination. In this crucial yet gray area of perceived competence, preferences make whites look better than they are and blacks worse,
while doing nothing whatever to stop the very real discrimination
that blacks may encounter. I don't wish to justify the glass ceiling
here, but only suggest the very subtle ways that affirmative action
revives rather than extinguishes the old rationalizations for racial
discrimination.

I believe affirmative action is problematic in our society because   19
we have demanded that it create parity between the races rather
than insure equal opportunity. Preferential treatment does not teach
skills, or educate, or instill motivation. It only passes out entitlement by color, a situation that in my profession has created an un-
realistically high demand for black professors. The social engineer's
assumption is that this high demand will inspire more blacks to
earn Ph.D's and join the profession. In fact, the number of blacks
earning Ph.D's has declined in recent years. Ph.D's must be developed from preschool on. They require family and community support. They must acquire an entire system of values that enables
them to work hard while delaying gratification.

It now seems clear that the Supreme Court, in a series of recent   20
decisions, is moving away from racial preferences. It has disallowed
preferences except in instances of "identified discrimination," eroded
the precedent that statistical racial imbalances are prima facie evidence of discrimination, and, in effect, granted white males the right
to challenge consent degrees that use preference to achieve racial bal-
ances in the workplace. Referring to this and other Supreme Court

decisions, one civil-rights leader said, "Night has fallen . . . as far as civil rights are concerned." But I am not so sure. The effect of these decisions is to protect the constitutional rights of everyone, rather than to take rights away from blacks. Night has fallen on racial preferences, not on the fundamental rights of black Americans. The reason for this shift, I believe, is that the white mandate for absolution from past racial sins has weakened considerably in the 1980's. Whites are now less willing to endure unfairness to themselves in order to grant special entitlements to blacks, even when those entitlements are justified in the name of past suffering. Yet the black mandate for more power in society has remained unchanged. And I think part of the anxiety many blacks feel over these decisions has to do with the loss of black power that they may signal.

But the power we've lost by these decisions is really only the   21
power that grows out of our victimization. This is not a very substantial or reliable power, and it is important that we know this so we can focus more exclusively on the kind of development that will bring enduring power. There is talk now that Congress may pass new legislation to compensate for these new limits on affirmative action. If this happens, I hope the focus will be on development and anti-discrimination, rather than entitlement, on achieving racial parity rather than jerry-building racial diversity.

But if not preferences, what? The impulse to discriminate *is* subtle   22
and cannot be ferreted out unless its many guises are made clear to people. I think we need social policies that are committed to two goals: the educational and economic development of disadvantaged people regardless of race and the eradication from our society— through close monitoring and severe sanctions—of racial, ethnic or gender discrimination. Preferences will not get us to either of these goals, because they tend to benefit those who are not disadvantaged—middle-class white women and middle-class blacks—and attack one form of discrimination with another. Preferences are inexpensive and carry the glamour of good intentions—change the numbers and the good deed is done. To be against them is to be unkind. But I think the unkindest cut is to bestow on children like my own an undeserved advantage while neglecting the development of those disadvantaged children in the poorer sections of my city who will most likely never be in a position to benefit from a preference. Give my children fairness; give disadvantaged children a better shot at development—better elementary and secondary schools, job training, safer neighborhoods, better financial assistance for college and so on. A smaller percentage of black high school graduates go to college today than 15 years ago; more black males are in prison, jail

or in some other way under the control of the criminal-justice system than in college. This despite racial preferences.

The mandates of black power and white absolution out of which preferences emerged were not wrong in themselves. What was wrong was that both races focused more on the goals of those mandates than on the means to the goals. Blacks can have no real power without taking responsibility for their own educational and economic development. Whites can have no racial innocence without earning it by eradicating discrimination and helping the disadvantaged to develop. Because we ignored the means, the goals have not been reached and the real work remains to be done.

23

COMPREHENSION

1. What dilemma do the affirmative action policies of most universities present to Steele? Is he able to resolve this dilemma?

2. What reasons does Steele give for the escalation of affirmative action in the 1960s and early 1970s?

3. In what way does Steele think affirmative action recreates the conditions it is calculated to eliminate?

4. What alternative does Steele suggest to affirmative action?

PURPOSE AND AUDIENCE

1. How does knowing Steele is a professor of English at San Jose State College affect your reaction to his argument? Should Steele have done more to establish his credentials in the area he is discussing?

2. At what point does Steele state his thesis? Why does he wait as long as he does?

3. To what audience is Steele addressing his remarks? Blacks? Whites? Those who support affirmative action? Those who oppose it? Explain.

4. What is Steele's purpose? To change attitudes? To bring about legislation? To change policy? Explain.

STYLE AND STRUCTURE

1. What opposing arguments does Steele refute? Does he ignore any important arguments against his position?

2. How much does Steele rely on personal experience? Does his use of personal examples strengthen or weaken his argument? Should he have relied more on studies and statistics? Explain.

3. Is Steele's argument primarily inductive or deductive?

4. What evidence does Steele offer to convince readers that racial preferences do not work? How convincing is this evidence?

VOCABULARY PROJECTS

1. Define each of the following words as it is used in this selection.

deprivation (1)	detractors (5)	debilitating (12)
malevolence (1)	mandates (6)	stigmatizing (17)
sanctimoniously (2)	coalesced (6)	gratification (19)
recompense (2)	demoralization (11)	absolution (20)
marginally (2)	atavistic (12)	eradicating (23)

2. What is the dictionary meaning of *diversity*? What additional meaning does Steele's essay imply that the word has acquired?

JOURNAL ENTRY

Do you think your school would benefit from recruiting more minority students and professors? Explain.

WRITING WORKSHOP

1. Write an essay in which you argue against Steele's position. Make sure that you specifically refute his points.

2. Assume you are an individual who could benefit from affirmative action programs. Write a letter to your student newspaper arguing that you do *not* need special treatment.

3. How do you think Fish would respond to Steele's essay? Choose a section of the essay and refute it using any of Fish's points that are relevant to the issue.

THEMATIC CONNECTIONS

- "My Mother Never Worked" (p. 85)
- "Aria: A Memoir of a Bilingual Childhood" (p. 401)
- "The Men We Carry in Our Minds" (p. 435)
- "Let's Tell the Story of All America's Cultures" (p. 586)

Debate: Date Rape

The phenomenon known as date rape has been going on for a long time, but recently it has become an important issue on many college campuses. The rise of feminism has called attention to the problem and has led to campus programs to train women students to avoid rape. Some colleges have even published behavior codes in an attempt to sensitize both men and women to this issue. (Antioch College, for example, has instituted a widely publicized code requiring students to ask a partner's permission at each stage of intimacy.)

Given the lack of controversy about the seriousness of rape, one might ask, "What is there to debate about date rape? Isn't rape rape?" But for many people the issue is not this simple. Some argue that many incidents characterized as date rape are not rape at all. What actually occurs in these situations, they say, is a miscommunication that results in sex, which the woman may not really want or may later regret but which cannot be fairly characterized as rape. Others say that drugs and alcohol frequently play a part in what are labeled date rapes. How can a woman cry rape, they ask, when she has contributed to the situation? And finally, some say that by applying the term *rape* to situations like these, date-rape activists risk diminishing the seriousness of "real" rape resulting from physical force or threats. In response to these arguments, activists say such excuses continue a long tradition of women's subjugation. The vast majority of men, they argue, manage to get through life bestowing their affections only on willing recipients, and the charge that large numbers of them are being falsely accused of rape by fickle or vindictive women not only ignores the facts but itself trivializes the severity of the crime.

The four writers in this section express a variety of opinions about date rape. In "It's a Jungle Out There," Camille Paglia asserts that the only solution to date rape is for a female to take responsibility for her own actions. In "Common Decency," Susan Jacoby argues that there should be no distinction between rape and date rape and that men can be expected to understand when "no" means "no." In "Date Rape Hysteria," Katie Roiphe argues that by portraying women as victims, the rhetoric that surrounds date rape emphasizes antiquated images of female behavior. Finally, in "Consent of a Woman," Cal Fussman considers the definition of date rape from a male perspective.

IT'S A JUNGLE OUT THERE

Camille Paglia

*Camille Paglia was born in 1947 in Endicott, New York, graduated
from the State University of New York at Binghamton in 1968, and
received her doctorate from Yale University in 1974. She has taught
at Bennington College, Wesleyan University, Yale, the University of
New Haven, and, since 1984, at the University of the Arts in Philadelphia. Paglia has published two books,* Sexual Personae: Art and
Decadence from Nefertiti to Emily Dickinson *(1990), a best-selling
scholarly work that examines pornographic elements in art and literature beginning in ancient Egypt and Greece, and* Sex, Art and
American Culture *(1992), a collection of provocative articles, interviews, book reviews, and lectures on popular culture, in which the
following piece appears. In "It's a Jungle Out There," which first
appeared in* New York Newsday *in 1991, Paglia argues that feminism misleads women by offering them a fantasy of sexual empow-
erment instead of warning them of the inevitability of male sexual
aggression.*

1   Rape is an outrage that cannot be tolerated in civilized society. Yet
feminism, which has waged a crusade for rape to be taken more seriously, has put young women in danger by hiding the truth about sex
from them.

2   In dramatizing the pervasiveness of rape, feminists have told
young women that before they have sex with a man, they must give
consent as explicit as a legal contract's. In this way, young women
have been convinced that they have been the victims of rape. On
elite campuses in the Northeast and on the West Coast, they have
held consciousness-raising sessions, petitioned administrations, demanded inquests. At Brown University, outraged, panicky "victims"
have scrawled the names of alleged attackers on the walls of wom-
en's rest rooms. What marital rape was to the '70s, "date rape" is to
the '90s.

3   The incidence and seriousness of rape do not require this kind of
exaggeration. Real acquaintance rape is nothing new. It has been a
horrible problem for women for all of recorded history. Once fathers
and brothers protected women from rape. Once the penalty for rape
was death. I come from a fierce Italian tradition where, not so long
ago in the motherland, a rapist would end up knifed, castrated, and
hung out to dry.

But the old clans and small rural communities have broken down. In our cities, on our campuses far from home, young women are vulnerable and defenseless. Feminism has not prepared them for this. Feminism keeps saying the sexes are the same. It keeps telling women they can do anything, go anywhere, say anything, wear anything. No, they can't. Women will always be in sexual danger.   4

One of my male students recently slept overnight with a friend in a passageway of the Great Pyramid in Egypt. He described the moon and sand, the ancient silence and eerie echoes. I will never experience that. I am a woman. I am not stupid enough to believe I could ever be safe there. There is a world of solitary adventure I will never have. Women have always known these somber truths. But feminism, with its pie-in-the-sky fantasies about the perfect world, keeps young women from seeing life as it is.   5

We must remedy social injustice whenever we can. But there are some things we cannot change. There are sexual differences that are based in biology. Academic feminism is lost in a fog of social constructionism. It believes we are totally the product of our environment. This idea was invented by Rousseau.* He was wrong. Emboldened by dumb French language theory, academic feminists repeat the same hollow slogans over and over to each other. Their view of sex is naive and prudish. Leaving sex to the feminists is like letting your dog vacation at the taxidermist's.   6

The sexes are at war. Men must struggle for identity against the overwhelming power of their mothers. Women have menstruation to tell them they are women. Men must do or risk something to be men. Men become masculine only when other men say they are. Having sex with a woman is one way a boy becomes a man.   7

College men are at their hormonal peak. They have just left their mothers and are questing for their male identity. In groups, they are dangerous. A woman going to a fraternity party is walking into Testosterone Flats, full of prickly cacti and blazing guns. If she goes, she should be armed with resolute alertness. She should arrive with girlfriends and leave with them. A girl who lets herself get dead drunk at a fraternity party is a fool. A girl who goes upstairs alone with a brother at a fraternity party is an idiot. Feminists call this "blaming the victim." I call it common sense.   8

For a decade, feminists have drilled their disciples to say, "Rape is a crime of violence but not of sex." This sugar-coated Shirley Temple nonsense has exposed young women to disaster. Misled by feminism,   9

*EDS. NOTE—Jean Jacques Rousseau (1712–1778), a French philosopher and political theorist.

they do not expect rape from the nice boys from good homes who sit next to them in class.

Aggression and eroticism are deeply intertwined. Hunt, pursuit, and capture are biologically programmed into male sexuality. Generation after generation, men must be educated, refined, and ethnically persuaded away from their tendency toward anarchy and brutishness. Society is not the enemy, as feminism ignorantly claims. Society is woman's protection against rape. Feminism, with its solemn Carry Nation* repressiveness, does not see what is for men the eroticism or fun element in rape, especially the wild, infectious delirium of gang rape. Women who do not understand rape cannot defend themselves against it.

The date-rape controversy shows feminism hitting the wall of its own broken promises. The women of my '60s generation were the first respectable girls in history to swear like sailors, get drunk, stay out all night—in short, to act like men. We sought total sexual freedom and equality. But as time passed, we woke up to cold reality. The old double standard protected women. When anything goes, it's women who lose.

Today's young women don't know what they want. They see that feminism has not brought sexual happiness. The theatrics of public rage over date rape are their way of restoring the old sexual rules that were shattered by my generation. Because nothing about the sexes has really changed. The comic film *Where the Boys Are* (1960), the ultimate expression of '50s man-chasing, still speaks directly to our time. It shows smart, lively women skillfully anticipating and fending off the dozens of strategies with which horny men try to get them into bed. The agonizing date-rape subplot and climax are brilliantly done. The victim, Yvette Mimieux, makes mistake after mistake, obvious to the other girls. She allows herself to be lured away from her girlfriends and into isolation with boys whose character and intentions she misreads. *Where the Boys Are* tells the truth. It shows courtship as a dangerous game in which the signals are not verbal but subliminal.

Neither militant feminism, which is obsessed with politically correct language, nor academic feminism, which believes that knowledge and experience are "constituted by" language, can understand preverbal or non-verbal communication. Feminism, focusing on sexual politics, cannot see that sex exists in and through the body. Sexual desire and arousal cannot be fully translated into verbal terms. This is why men and women misunderstand each other.

*Eds. Note—an American temperance leader and advocate of women's suffrage (1846–1911), who became legendary for her use of a hatchet to destroy liquor and other contents of saloons.

Trying to remake the future, feminism cut itself off from sexual   14
history. It discarded and suppressed the sexual myths of literature,
art, and religion. Those myths show us the turbulence, the mysteries
and passions of sex. In mythology we see men's sexual anxiety, their
fear of women's dominance. Much sexual violence is rooted in men's
sense of psychological weakness toward women. It takes many men
to deal with one woman. Woman's voracity is a persistent motif.
Clara Bow,* it was rumored, took on the USC football team on weekends. Marilyn Monroe, singing "Diamonds Are a Girl's Best Friend,"
rules a conga line of men in tuxes. Half-clad Cher, in the video for "If
I Could Turn Back Time," deranges a battleship of screaming sailors
and straddles a pink-lit cannon. Feminism, coveting social power, is
blind to woman's cosmic sexual power.

To understand rape, you must study the past. There never was   15
and never will be sexual harmony. Every woman must take personal
responsibility for her sexuality, which is nature's red flame. She
must be prudent and cautious about where she goes and with whom.
When she makes a mistake, she must accept the consequences and,
through self-criticism, resolve never to make that mistake again.
Running to Mommy and Daddy on the campus grievance committee
is unworthy of strong women. Posting lists of guilty men in the toilet
is cowardly, infantile stuff.

The Italian philosophy of life espouses high-energy confrontation.   16
A male student makes a vulgar remark about your breasts? Don't
slink off to whimper and simper with the campus shrinking violets.
Deal with it. On the spot. Say, "Shut up, you jerk! And crawl back
to the barnyard where you belong!" In general, women who project
this take-charge attitude toward life get harassed less often. I see
too many dopey, immature, self-pitying women walking around like
melting sticks of butter. It's the Yvette Mimieux syndrome: Make me
happy. And listen to me weep when I'm not.

The date-rape debate is already smothering in propaganda churned   17
out by the expensive Northeastern colleges and universities, with
their overconcentration of boring, uptight academic feminists and
spoiled, affluent students. Beware of the deep manipulativeness of
rich students who were neglected by their parents. They love to turn
the campus into hysterical psychodramas of sexual transgression,
followed by assertions of parental authority and concern. And don't
look for sexual enlightenment from academe, which spews out mountains of books but never looks at life directly.

As a fan of football and rock music, I see in the simple, swaggering   18
masculinity of the jock and in the noisy posturing of the heavy-metal

---

*EDS. NOTE—an American actress in silent movies (1905–1965).

guitarist certain fundamental, unchanging truths about sex. Masculinity is aggressive, unstable, combustible. It is also the most creative cultural force in history. Women must reorient themselves toward the elemental powers of sex, which can strengthen or destroy.

The only solution to date rape is female self-awareness and self-control. A woman's number one line of defense is herself. When a real rape occurs, she should report it to the police. Complaining to college committees because the courts "take too long" is ridiculous. College administrations are not a branch of the judiciary. They are not equipped or trained for legal inquiry. Colleges must alert incoming students to the problems and dangers of adulthood. Then colleges must stand back and get out of the sex game.   19

COMPREHENSION

1. According to Paglia, how does feminism mislead women?

2. How does Paglia explain the prevalence of date rape in our society?

3. According to Paglia, "Women who do not understand rape cannot defend themselves against it" (10). What does she say women must understand?

4. Why, according to Paglia, do men and women misunderstand each other?

5. What is Paglia's solution to the problem of rape?

PURPOSE AND AUDIENCE

1. Does Paglia assume her readers are hostile, friendly, or neutral? How can you tell?

2. Is Paglia primarily addressing men, women, or both?

3. Is Paglia's purpose to change people's ideas or to change their behavior? Explain.

STYLE AND STRUCTURE

1. Paglia makes no effort to hide her feelings toward those who disagree with her ideas. Underline the words that show her opinion of her opposition. How would you describe her tone? Reasonable? Angry? Sarcastic? Frustrated? Impatient?

2. Throughout her essay Paglia makes personal attacks against what she calls "academic feminists" and "militant feminists." Do these attacks strengthen or undercut her argument? Explain.

3. Is Paglia's argument primarily inductive or deductive? Explain.

4. How effectively does Paglia refute the arguments against her position?

5. What strategy does Paglia use to conclude her essay? Is this a wise choice? Explain your reasoning.

VOCABULARY PROJECTS

1. Define each of the following words as it is used in this selection.

pervasiveness (2)	eroticism (10)	motif (14)
incidence (3)	delirium (10)	conga (14)
solitary (5)	subliminal (12)	transgression (17)
taxidermist (6)	turbulence (14)	spews (17)
testosterone (8)	voracity (14)	combustible (18)

2. Find several examples of colloquial words and phrases Paglia uses in her essay. Do they help her make her point more clearly, or do they undermine her credibility?

JOURNAL ENTRY

Some of Paglia's critics have charged that she is more interested in shining the spotlight on herself than in addressing issues. After reading her essay, do you think this criticism is justified?

WRITING WORKSHOP

1. What do you think should be done to prevent date rape? Do you, like Paglia, think that the solution is in the hands of women? Or should other measures be taken?

2. Write an essay in which you take two of Paglia's points and refute them by either questioning their truth or identifying flaws in their logic.

3. Find out what your college's policy is concerning date rape. Write an essay in which you argue that the policy is sound—or that it should be modified.

THEMATIC CONNECTIONS

- "Just Walk On By" (p. 209)
- "Sex, Lies, and Conversation" (p. 393)
- "I Want a Wife" (p. 503)

COMMON DECENCY

Susan Jacoby

Susan Jacoby is a freelance writer. Fluent in Russian, she lived in the Soviet Union from 1969 to 1971 and wrote two books on her experiences and research there, Moscow Conversations *(1972) and* Inside Soviet Schools *(1974). Recently, Jacoby collaborated with Yelena Khanga on a biography of Khanga's family,* Soul to Soul: The Story of a Black Russian American Family 1865–1992 *(1992). Jacoby also has worked as an education reporter for* The Washington Post. *She is a regular contributor to* Cosmopolitan, Glamour, McCall's, *and* Woman's Day, *and she is the author of* Wild Justice: The Evolution of Revenge *(1983) and* The Possible She *(1979), a collection of essays from her research and magazine writings. In "Common Decency," published in 1991, Jacoby argues that excusing date rape on the grounds of "mixed signals" demeans men as well as women.*

She was deeply in love with a man who was treating her badly. To assuage her wounded ego (and to prove to herself that she could get along nicely without him), she invited another man, an old boyfriend, to a dinner *à deux* in her apartment. They were on their way to the bedroom when, having realized that she wanted only the man who wasn't there, she changed her mind. Her ex-boyfriend was understandably angry. He left her apartment with a not-so-politely phrased request that she leave him out of any future plans.

And that is the end of the story—except for the fact that he was eventually kind enough to accept her apology for what was surely a classic case of "mixed signals."

I often recall this incident, in which I was the embarrassed female participant, as the controversy over "date rape"—intensified by the assault that William Kennedy Smith has been accused of—heats up across the nation. What seems clear to me is that those who place acquaintance rape in a different category from "stranger rape"—those who excuse friendly social rapists on grounds that they are too dumb to understand when "no" means no—are being even more insulting to men than to women.

These apologists for date rape—and some of them are women— are really saying that the average man cannot be trusted to exercise any impulse control. Men are nasty and men are brutes—and a woman must be constantly on her guard to avoid giving a man any excuse to give way to his baser instincts.

If this view were accurate, few women would manage to get 5 through life without being raped, and few men would fail to commit rape. For the reality is that all of us, men as well as women, send and receive innumerable mixed signals in the course of our sexual lives— and that is as true in marital beds at age 50 as in the back seats of cars at age 15.

Most men somehow manage to decode these signals without using 6 superior physical strength to force themselves on their partners. And most women manage to handle conflicting male signals with- out, say, picking up carving knives to demonstrate their displeasure at sexual rejection. This is called civilization.

Civilized is exactly what my old boyfriend was being when he 7 didn't use my muddleheaded emotional distress as an excuse to rape me. But I don't owe him excessive gratitude for his decent behavior— any more than he would have owed me special thanks for not stab- bing him through the heart if our situations had been reversed. Most date rapes do not happen because a man honestly mistakes a woman's "no" for a "yes" or a "maybe." They occur because a minority of men—an ugly minority, to be sure—can't stand to take "no" for an answer.

This minority behavior—and a culture that excuses it on grounds 8 that boys will be boys—is the target of the movement against date rape that has surfaced on many campuses during the past year.

It's not surprising that date rape is an issue of particular impor- 9 tance to college-age women. The campus concentration of large num- bers of young people, in an unsupervised environment that encour- ages drinking and partying, tends to promote sexual aggression and discourage inhibition. Drunken young men who rape a woman at a party can always claim they didn't know what they were doing—and a great many people will blame the victim for having been there in the first place.

That is the line adopted by antifeminists like Camille Paglia, 10 author of the controversial *Sexual Personae: Art and Decadence from Nefertiti to Emily Dickinson.* Paglia, whose views strongly resemble those expounded 20 years ago by Norman Mailer in *The Prisoner of Sex,* argues that feminists have deluded women by telling them they can go anywhere and do anything without fear of rape. Feminism, in this view, is both naïve and antisexual because it ignores the power of women to incite uncontrollable male passions.

Just to make sure there is no doubt about a woman's place, Paglia 11 also links the male sexual aggression that leads to rape with the creative energy of art. "There is no female Mozart," she has declared, "because there is no female Jack the Ripper." According to this "logic," one might expect to discover the next generation of composers in fraternity houses and dorms that have been singled out as sites of brutal gang rapes.

This type of unsubtle analysis makes no distinction between sex as an expression of the will to power and sex as a source of pleasure. When domination is seen as an inevitable component of sex, the act of rape is defined not by a man's actions but by a woman's signals.

12

It is true, of course, that some women (especially the young) initially resist sex not out of real conviction but as part of the elaborate persuasion and seduction rituals accompanying what was once called courtship. And it is true that many men (again, especially the young) take pride in the ability to coax a woman a step further than she intended to go.

13

But these mating rituals do not justify or even explain date rape. Even the most callow youth is capable of understanding the difference between resistance and genuine fear; between a halfhearted "no, we shouldn't" and tears or screams; between a woman who is physically free to leave a room and one who is being physically restrained.

14

The immorality and absurdity of using mixed signals as an excuse for rape is cast in high relief when the assault involves one woman and a group of men. In cases of gang rape in a social setting (usually during or after a party), the defendants and their lawyers frequently claim that group sex took place but no force was involved. These upright young men, so the defense invariably contends, were confused because the girl had voluntarily gone to a party with them. Why, she may have even displayed sexual interest in *one* of them. How could they have been expected to understand that she didn't wish to have sex with the whole group?

15

The very existence of the term "date rape" attests to a slow change in women's consciousness that began with the feminist movement of the late 1960's. Implicit in this consciousness is the conviction that a woman has the right to say no at any point in the process leading to sexual intercourse—and that a man who fails to respect her wishes should incur serious legal and social consequences.

16

The other, equally important half of the equation is respect for men. If mixed signals are the real cause of sexual assault, it behooves every woman to regard every man as a potential rapist.

17

In such a benighted universe, it would be impossible for a woman (and, let us not forget, for a man) to engage in the tentative emotional and physical exploration that eventually produces a mature erotic life. She would have to make up her mind right from the start in order to prevent a rampaging male from misreading her intentions.

18

Fortunately for everyone, neither the character of men nor the general quality of relations between the sexes is that crude. By censuring the minority of men who use ordinary socializing as an excuse for rape, feminists insist on sex as a source of pure pleasure rather than as a means of social control. Real men want an eager sexual partner—not a woman who is quaking with fear or even one who is ambivalent. Real men don't rape. 19

COMPREHENSION

1. Why does Jacoby believe those who excuse "friendly social rapists" are being more insulting to men than to women?

2. According to Jacoby, why do most date rapes occur?

3. Why is date rape an issue that is particularly important to college-age women?

4. According to Jacoby, why does using mixed signals as an excuse for rape show a lack of respect for men?

5. What does Jacoby mean in paragraph 16 when she says, "The very existence of the term *date rape* attests to a slow change in women's consciousness that began with the feminist movement of the late 1960's"?

PURPOSE AND AUDIENCE

1. Does Jacoby seem to be addressing her remarks primarily to men, to women, or to both? Explain.

2. What steps does Jacoby take to establish her credentials in the area of date rape? Should she have done more?

3. What preconceptions does she think her readers have about her subject? Explain.

STYLE AND STRUCTURE

1. Jacoby begins her essay with a personal anecdote. How effective is this strategy? Would another strategy have been more effective?

2. How accurate is Jacoby's summary of Camille Paglia's position? How effectively does she refute Paglia's points?

3. What other arguments does Jacoby refute? How effective are these refutations?

4. What evidence does Jacoby use to support her points? Should she have used other kinds of evidence?

5. How well does Jacoby summarize her argument in her final paragraph? What new point does she introduce? Is this a wise strategy? Explain.

VOCABULARY PROJECTS

1. Define each of the following words as it is used in this selection.

   assuage (1)   elaborate (13)   rampaging (18)
   innumerable (5)   rituals (13)   ambivalent (19)

2. What does Jacoby mean by the phrase *common decency?* What connotations does it have?

JOURNAL ENTRY

Do you agree with Jacoby when she says apologists for date rape are even more insulting to men than they are to women?

WRITING WORKSHOP

1. Who makes a better argument, Paglia or Jacoby? Write an essay in which you summarize the positions of both writers and then support one or the other. Include the reasons why you prefer one argument over the other, and use material from both essays to support your points.

2. What do you think Camille Paglia would say about Jacoby's argument? Assuming you are Paglia, write a letter to Jacoby responding to the specific points she makes in her essay.

3. Write an essay in which you support Jacoby's point that "mating rituals do not justify or even explain date rape" (14). Use examples from personal experience (your own or someone else's) to support your thesis.

THEMATIC CONNECTIONS

- "38 Who Saw Murder Didn't Call the Police" (p. 91)
- "The Lottery" (p. 272)
- "Sex, Lies, and Conversation" (p. 393)

DATE RAPE HYSTERIA

Katie Roiphe

Katie Roiphe graduated from Harvard University in 1990 and is working on her doctorate in English literature at Princeton University. Her book The Morning After: Sex, Fear, and Feminism on Campus *(1993) focuses on current debates surrounding date rape and sexual harassment at colleges and universities. In "Date Rape Hysteria," which appeared on the Op-Ed page of the* New York Times *in 1991, Roiphe argues that feminist rhetoric about date rape only serves to reinforce traditional stereotypes of sexually aggressive men and passive, puritanical, defenseless women.*

In classrooms and journals, in lectures and coffee shops, academics everywhere are talking about rape. Although it wears a fashionable leftist mask, this is a neo-puritan preoccupation. While real women get battered, while real mothers need day care, certain feminists are busy turning rape into fiction. Every time one Henry James* character seizes the hand of another Henry James character, someone is calling it rape.

At a certain point the metaphor gets paranoid. An overused word, like an over-painted sunset, becomes a cliché, drained of specificity and meaning. With every new article on rape imagery, we threaten to confirm the vision of that 18th-century patriarch, Henry Fielding**, when he wrote, "These words of exclamation (murder! robbery! rape!) are used by ladies in a fright, as fa la la . . . are in music, only as vehicles of sound and without any fixed idea."

Only now the cry across campuses is "date rape." Those involved frame it as a liberal concern, cut and dry, beyond debate. But they don't stop to consider the fundamentally sexist images lurking beneath their rhetoric. The term "date rape" itself hints at its conservative bent. More than just a polemic against rape, it reveals a desire for dates.

Although not an explicit part of their movement, these feminists are responding, in this time of sexual suspicion, to the need for a more rigid courtship structure. The message represents, in part, a

---

*Eds. Note—American-born novelist (1843–1916) whose works generally portray upper-class, emotionally restrained characters.

**Eds. Note—English playwright and novelist (1707–1754).

nostalgia for 1950's-style dating. For Johnny picking Susie up for a movie and a Coke.

And the assumption embedded in this movement is our grandmother's assumption: men want sex, women don't. In emphasizing this struggle, him pushing, her resisting, the movement against date rape recycles and promotes an old model of sexuality.

One book, *Avoiding Rape On and Off Campus,* by Carol Pritchard, warns young women to "think carefully before you go to a male friend's apartment or dorm. . . . Do not expose yourself to any unnecessary risk." When did the possibility of sex become an "unnecessary risk"? Are we really such fragile creatures that we need such an extreme definition of safety? Should we really subject our male friends to scrutiny because after all men want one thing and one thing only?

The definition of date rape stretches beyond acts of physical force. According to pamphlets widely distributed on college campuses, even "verbal coercion" constitutes "date rape." With this expansive version of rape, then, these feminists invent a kinder, gentler sexuality. These pamphlets are clearly intended to protect innocent college women from the insatiable force of male desire. We have been hearing about this for centuries. He is still nearly uncontrollable; she is still the one drawing lines. This so-called feminist movement peddles an image of gender relations that denies female desire and infantilizes women. Once again, our bodies seem to be sacred vessels. We've come a long way, and now it seems, we are going back.

The date rape pamphlets begin to sound like Victorian guides to conduct. The most common date rape guide, published by the American College Health Association, advises its delicate readers to "communicate your limits clearly. If someone starts to offend you, tell them firmly and early."

Sharing these assumptions about female sensibilities, a manners guide from 1853 advises young women, "Do not suffer your hand to be held or squeezed without showing that it displeases you by instantly withdrawing it. . . . These and many other little points of refinement will operate as an almost invisible though a very impenetrable fence, keeping off vulgar familiarity, and that desecration of the person which has so often led to vice." And so ideals of female virtue and repression resonate through time.

Let's not chase the same stereotypes our mothers have spent so much energy running away from. Let's not reinforce the images that oppress us, that label us victims, and deny our own agency and intelligence, as strong and sensual, as autonomous, pleasure-seeking; sexual beings.

COMPREHENSION

1. Why does Roiphe think the word *rape* is becoming a cliché?

2. What are the "sexist images" (3) that Roiphe thinks lurk beneath the rhetoric of date rape?

3. According to Roiphe, in what ways do date rape pamphlets "begin to sound like Victorian guides to conduct" (8)?

4. Why does Roiphe believe certain feminists are attempting to impose a more rigid courtship structure?

5. What does Roiphe mean when she says, "Let's not chase the same stereotypes our mothers have spent so much time and energy running away from" (10)?

PURPOSE AND AUDIENCE

1. Is this essay aimed primarily at men or at women? Explain.

2. Does Roiphe assume her readers will be receptive or hostile to her thesis? Explain your conclusion.

STYLE AND STRUCTURE

1. Does Roiphe's introduction attract your attention? Would another strategy have been more effective?

2. Roiphe quotes passages from two nineteenth-century guides to manners to support her point that date rape pamphlets sound like Victorian guides to conduct. Should she have used more examples, or are these two sufficient?

3. At what point does Roiphe address the arguments against her thesis? Does she devote enough space to refuting these arguments?

4. In paragraph 7 Roiphe introduces an extended definition of date rape that some people would consider quite extreme. What point is she making with this definition? Is she being fair, or has she used an atypical example to support her point?

5. How effective is Roiphe's conclusion? In light of the seriousness of the rest of the essay, does it seem too abrupt? Too optimistic?

VOCABULARY PROJECTS

1. Define each of the following words as it is used in this selection.

cliché (2)   vessels (7)   virtue (9)
vehicles (2)   refinement (9)   autonomous (10)
rhetoric (3)   desecration (9)

2. Compare the two passages from the nineteenth-century books about female behavior with the rest of the essay. What words identify the passages as stodgy or old-fashioned? Rewrite the passages so that they sound more contemporary.

JOURNAL ENTRY

Some of Roiphe's critics have accused her of being antifeminist. After reading her essay, do you agree or disagree with their assessment?

WRITING WORKSHOP

1. Write an essay in which you argue for or against a more rigid "court-ship structure." What would such a structure be like? What would be its advantages and disadvantages?

2. Write an essay in which you argue for or against the desirability of the "old model of sexuality" (5). For example, is the older model viable or even preferable to today's standard of female behavior? Did it make things fairer, simpler, safer, or easier for women?

3. Many colleges have coed dorms; some even have coed bathrooms. Write an essay in which you argue either that these living situations promote male-female understanding or that they increase the likelihood of date rape.

THEMATIC CONNECTIONS

- "The Grave" (p. 168)
- "College Pressures" (p. 425)
- "Sexism in English: A 1990s Update" (p. 441)
- "A Negative Vote on Affirmative Action" (p. 625)

CONSENT OF A WOMAN

Cal Fussman

*Cal Fussman was born in Brooklyn, New York, and graduated from
the University of Missouri. He has worked as a sports writer and
more recently as a freelance writer, contributing articles to* Esquire,
Gentlemen's Quarterly, Harper's Bazaar, Life, *and* Lear's, *where
"Consent of a Woman" appeared in 1993. Fussman is currently
a general assignment writer for the feature section of* New York
Newsday. *In this essay, he warns against diluting the charge of
rape by including qualifications such as* date rape *and* verbal
coercion.

A woman tells you "Go ahead, try and rape me," and you never 1
forget it. Her words were misted with alcohol—and so was my brain.
All kinds of alcohol. The wine she'd poured into long-necked glasses
as she told me she was thinking about breaking up with her boyfriend. The beer that later had flowed from a keg near the hardwood
dance floor at the party. And then there was the Fog Cutter—that
vicious concoction that belies its name—we'd split just before last
call at the local watering hole.

Alcohol dissolved the tension between us, a 22-year-old man and 2
a 22-year-old woman who'd been looking at each other across the
campus from the corners of their eyes for years. It dissolved our in-
hibitions, so that we could press against each other in rhythm to the
music because, after all, it was only a dance. And it began to dissolve
my thoughts of a friend who still loved this woman joined to me at
the hips—though their involvement had ended a year before.

By the time we'd returned to her apartment, my friend and her 3
boyfriend had almost evaporated completely. *Almost.* So she un-
corked another bottle of wine, and as we clinked those long-necked
glasses I thought of how easy it would be if we hadn't known each
other so well.

But then, in a blurry instant, we didn't. 4

We kissed and felt, kissed and felt, but you can only kiss and feel 5
for so long. We paused.

"I learned a self-defense technique to stop a man from raping me," 6
she said.

"Huh?" 7

"You grab his hands, pull them to your shoulders, lock them in 8
place, and he can't do a thing. Then you can scream for help or kick
him into the Vienna Boys Choir."

I shook my head. "It'll never work." 9

"Bet you it would." Her eyes were defiant. Or maybe they hinted 10
mischief. "I'll prove it," she said. "Go ahead, try and rape me."

Slowly I turned toward her. In a blink her hands shot out and 11
snatched my wrists. On her back, she struggled to lock them in place.
"No, no, no" shot through her clenched teeth. Our arms wrestled, our
arms quivered. My legs wedged between hers so that she could no
longer kick. Her eyes were razor slits. Her grip on my wrists tight-
ened, but I no longer needed to struggle. I lowered my face just below
her collar and undid the top button with my teeth. Then the button
beneath, and the one under that. She squirmed, rocked from side to
side. Gusts of warm air burst from her nostrils. She'd lost control of
my hands, and suddenly I had her pinned down by the wrists and
her shirt was completely open and my lips were on her ribs and my
teeth were popping the snap of her jeans and I was at her navel. *"No,
no, no, no, no."*

For once in my life, I did something wise. I stopped—right at 12
the navel. Her eyes dimmed, her fingers slowly uncoiled—was she
disappointed?

Now it's 14 years later. Now processions of angry female students 13
march with lighted candles through darkness on college campuses,
chanting "Two-four-six-eight, no more date rape!" Now castration
lists—names of males accused of date rape—are scrawled in female
campus bathrooms. Now 13-year-old kids are led away from junior
high in handcuffs after running their hands over the clothed body
of a girl, held down in a schoolyard (in part by other girls) during a
game of "let's play rape." Now a New Jersey deputy public defender,
whose teenage client is convicted of date rape, says, "You not only
have to bring a condom on a date, you have to bring a consent form
as well." Now I sit here, thinking back 14 years, and I shudder. If I
hadn't stopped at the navel, how would I be judged today?

I can see myself on a witness stand in a courtroom, looking over at 14
the prosecutor, the judge, the jury. "You do understand the English
language, don't you?" The prosecutor strolls toward me. "You do
understand the meaning of the word *no*?"

"Yes, I understand English." I am prepared for this. "I understand 15
full well the sentence *Go ahead, try and rape me.*"

"Odd, how you could take those words literally. Yet when she 16
started to say 'No, no, no' you didn't seem to take those words lit-

erally, or seriously, at all." The prosecutor pauses damningly. "You'd been friends for so long. Didn't it occur to you that she might really want to try out a self-defense technique for her own safety? Or that she was merely playing a game?"

"What occurred to me was that she wanted to go past kisses but didn't feel right about it because she still had a boyfriend. By turning it into a game she could get what she wanted without having to take any responsibility for it."   17

"Oh, really. She could get *what she wanted.*"   18

I hadn't liked the way the words sounded when they left my lips.   19
They sounded far worse leaving the prosecutor's.

Maybe it's because of the disappointed look on the woman's face   20
when I halted at her navel, or maybe it's just because I'm a man, but the terms *date rape* and *acquaintance rape* have always puzzled me. So too the latest adjective in the violation vernacular: *emotional rape.* Every healthy society has taboos—unconscionable acts and words for them—that shake us to our core. To qualify the word *rape* is to diminish the jolt. Though progress is often measured by a society's ability to appreciate nuance, in this case the opposite is true. *Rape* is a word that has to be safeguarded so that its explosive charge never dissipates. The word must remain harsh. The punishment, too. No, we should not allow the word *rape,* the concept *rape,* to be violated.

But look at what is happening now. Intelligent people are saying   21
that a woman doesn't even have to say no to be date-raped, that she can be a victim if she doesn't articulate an explicit yes. Listen to the former leader of Columbia University's date-rape education program: "Every time you have intercourse there must be explicit consent, and if there's no explicit consent then it's rape." Others are putting forth the notion that verbal coercion falls under the definition of date rape. And I guess, to the Harvard student who wrote in a feminist magazine about what she considers emotional rape, a man can be presumed a rapist even if he doesn't attempt to penetrate. The more you try to grasp the subject, the slipperier it gets. Because the phrase *date rape* is equally misused at the other extreme. It's being applied in courtrooms to prosecute cases of barbaric behavior. Check out Chapters 11 and 12 of Linda A. Fairstein's recently published *Sexual Violence: Our War on Rape* and see if you don't agree. Fairstein, who has risen during 20 years in the New York district attorney's office to chief of the Sex Crimes Unit, and who is noted for her prosecutions of the Central Park jogger case and the "Preppy Murder" trial of Robert Chambers, tells a compelling story of crime

in the city. But her use of *date rape* and *acquaintance rape* left me bewildered.

One anecdote involves two 25-year-old ballet dancers, named   22
Cindy and Nick. They have known each other for several months by way of a dance studio when she gives him her phone number and he asks her to dinner. They share a joint at her apartment and a bottle of wine at the restaurant. They hold hands as they return to her apartment. Once inside, he refuses to leave and grabs Cindy in a hug. She tries to push him off. He throws her to the floor and straddles her. She yells. He covers her mouth and tells her to take off her clothes. She refuses. He slaps her face and says, "The pretty ones always say 'No.'" She fights. He tears off her clothes, then penetrates her vaginally and anally.

This is date rape? No. This is *rape*. The date has nothing to do   23
with it. There is no need to qualify here. She screams and pushes him away. He savagely attacks her. Nick gets 4 to 12 years, which, if he serves the minimum, with time off for good behavior, is not long enough. Not if he's walking on the same planet as my daughter.

If I had a daughter, that is. There would be no confusion in my   24
voice were I speaking to her right now. In an age when sex can mean death, in a world where dates can lead to rape, I would say: It is *your* responsibility to monitor what you drink. *Your* responsibility to choose whom you spend time with alone. *Your* responsibility to be clear with him before you step into the shadows. Because *your* life is *your* responsibility.

If my daughter needed to hear it in a woman's voice, I would hand   25
her a copy of *The Morning After: Sex, Fear and Feminism on Campus,* Katie Roiphe's thoughtful rejoinder to the politics of victimhood. Through it, she could see how unfair it is to vacillate in the shadows and then to finger the man after the act. She could see how all women suffer when the definition of *rape* is stretched like taffy so that now it even includes verbal coercion, a man talking a woman into the act. All that does, she would see, is make women see themselves as some men might: porcelain dolls who cannot fend off verbal manipulation, who remain silent and confused while they are being violated.

No, I don't want a porcelain daughter who sips sloe gin fizzes on   26
dates and lives 1950s morals. I would like her to be a black belt in tae kwon do and a traveler who enters remote villages with a pack on her back. A woman who knows that the world is not a safe place, that danger occurs randomly and you have to think and act clearly to be able to slide free. And if circumstances go beyond your control and you are raped on a date, you don't question your complicity.

You don't take your frustrations to the bathroom-stall door. You go straight to the police.

But what about my son, had I a son? It would be easy if all women 27 were sure about whether they wanted to have sex, but it has never been that way. Sex, between new partners especially, almost always occurs in that twilight zone that is part mystery, part fantasy, part vulnerability, and part conquest. It's almost always in the shadows.

I'm not exactly sure how to prepare my son for that excursion. 28 Yes, I can see a clear difference between a woman who fiercely fights against an unwanted advance and a woman who goes along with sex that she's really not sure she wants, and probably he could, too. But there are some people who can't. And it remains his responsibility to stay off the castration lists of his generation, to keep his name off a document in a courtroom.

The best I can say is this: Bring a condom. Stop at her navel. Take 29 the condom out. Tear open the wrapper. Put it in place. That gives her ample time to emphatically make the statement: *No!*

And it gives you ample time to digest it. That *"No!"* if it comes, is 30 final. The woman must convey it, in words or grunts or punches. And you must obey it—or there is rape. Not date rape—just because she ventured this far with you means nothing. Not emotional rape—just because you cajoled her this far means nothing. *Rape.* A violation; a crime for which you'll pay with years of your life.

And if a woman you don't know very well playfully suggests, "Go 31 ahead, try and rape me," back off. Find another woman. For there's only one sure way to avoid the dilemma of miscommunication. That is to know your partner so well that neither of you will ever need to say a word.

COMPREHENSION

1. What does Fussman think is wrong with qualifying the word *rape?*

2. According to Fussman, what is wrong with the way some people are expanding the definition of the term *date rape?*

3. What distinction does Fussman see between "rape" and "date rape"? Explain.

4. What does Fussman say he would tell his daughter about date rape? What advice does he say he would give his son?

5. According to Fussman, what is the difference between "sex play" and "sexual assault"?

PURPOSE AND AUDIENCE

1. Why does Fussman present a vision of himself on the witness stand in paragraph 14? How does he expect his readers to react?

2. Some of the examples Fussman uses to support his points are fairly explicit. What effect does he want these examples to have on his readers?

3. What image of himself do you think Fussman wants to project in his essay? That he is a reasonable person? A concerned parent? A sensitive male? Is he successful in this effort?

STYLE AND STRUCTURE

1. Fussman uses several anecdotes to support his points. Are they relevant? Sufficient? Representative? Should he have provided another kind of evidence?

2. In paragraph 24 Fussman defines Katie Roiphe's stand on date rape. How accurately does he summarize her position?

3. Is Fussman's argument primarily inductive or deductive?

4. What is the relationship between Fussman's introduction and conclusion? In what way do they frame the essay? Does the conclusion (the last three paragraphs) become weak after its strong beginning?

VOCABULARY PROJECTS

1. Define each of the following words as it is used in this selection.

   concoction (1)   dissipates (20)   rejoinder (25)
   taboos (20)   articulate (21)   coercion (25)
   nuance (20)   monitor (24)   excursion (28)

2. Fussman spends a great deal of time defining certain terms—*rape* and *date rape,* for example. Identify the terms he defines, and determine whether these definitions add to the argument or bog it down in technicalities.

JOURNAL ENTRY

What parts of Fussman's argument seem to have an explicitly male perspective? Does Fussman make any points that many women would find offensive?

WRITING WORKSHOP

1. Write an essay in which you agree or disagree with Fussman's point in paragraph 22: "This is date rape? No. This is *rape*. The date has nothing to do with it."

2. Write a letter to Fussman supporting the thesis that although he might not intend it, his essay has a distinct male bias. Identify some passages that could be seen as offensive, and explain why.

3. Would you expect Katie Roiphe to agree or disagree with Fussman's points? Write an essay in which you answer this question using material from both Roiphe's and Fussman's essays to support your thesis. (Make sure you include Fussman's summary of Roiphe's position in paragraph 24.)

THEMATIC CONNECTIONS

- "The Spider and the Wasp" (p. 251)
- "The Ways We Lie" (p. 455)
- "I Want a Wife" (p. 503)

WRITING ASSIGNMENTS FOR ARGUMENTATION

1. Write an essay in which you discuss a teacher's right to strike. Address the major arguments against your position and maintain an objective stance.

2. Assume that a library in your town has decided that certain books are objectionable and has removed them from the shelves. Write a letter to the local paper in which you argue for or against the library's actions. Make a list of the major arguments that you could refute, and address some of them in your essay. Remember to respect the rights of your audience and to address them in a respectful manner.

3. Write an essay in which you argue for or against the right of a woman to keep the baby after she has agreed to be a surrogate mother for another woman.

4. Write an essay in which you discuss under what circumstances, if any, animals should be used for scientific experimentation.

5. Write an essay in which you argue for or against the proposition that women soldiers should be able to serve in combat situations.

6. Go to the library and read the accounts of some criminal cases that resulted in the death penalty. Write an essay in which you use these accounts to support your arguments either in favor of or against the death penalty. Do not forget to give credit to your sources.

7. Write an argumentative essay in which you discuss whether there are any situations in which a person has an obligation to go or not to go to war.

8. Write an essay in which you discuss whether health care workers—doctors, nurses, and dentists, for example—should be required to be tested for the AIDS virus.

9. In the Declaration of Independence, Jefferson says that all individuals are entitled to "life, liberty, and the pursuit of happiness." Write an essay in which you argue that these rights are not absolute.

10. Write an argumentative essay on one of these topics: Should high school students be required to take sex education courses? Should fraternities/sororities be abolished? Should teachers be required to pass periodic competency tests? Should the legal drinking age be raised (or lowered)? Should any workers be required to submit to random drug testing?

COLLABORATIVE ACTIVITY FOR ARGUMENTATION

Working with three other students, select a controversial topic—one not covered in any of the debates in this chapter—that interests all of you. (You can look at the Writing Assignments for Argumentation on the previous page to get ideas.) When you choose a topic, state it the way a topic is stated in an actual formal debate:

Resolved: The United States should suspend all immigration quotas.

Then divide into two two-member teams, and decide which team will take the pro position and which will take the con. Each team should list the arguments on its side of the issue and then write two or three paragraphs summarizing its position. Finally, each group will stage a ten-minute debate—five minutes for each side—in front of the class. (The pro side presents its argument first.) At the end of each debate, the class should discuss which side has presented the stronger arguments.

Essays for Further Reading: Combining the Patterns

Few essays are pure "process essays" or "exemplification essays" or examples of any other single pattern of development; in fact, nearly every essay, including those in this text, combines a variety of different patterns. Even though an essay may be organized primarily as, say, a comparison and contrast, it is still likely to include sentences, paragraphs, and even groups of paragraphs whose structure is determined by other patterns of development. Combining patterns in this way gives you the flexibility and versatility you need to express your ideas most effectively.

The two essays that follow illustrate the ways in which a variety of different patterns of development may be combined in a single piece of writing. The first, by Michael Huu Truong, a student, relies primarily on narration and description to express the author's memories of childhood; the second, by Lars Eighner, combines sections of definition, exemplification, classification and division, cause and effect, and process—and as it does so, it tells the story (narration) and provides vivid details (description) of the author's life as a homeless person. It would be next to impossible (and, ultimately, not very useful) to identify and label every use (no matter how brief) of every pattern in the two essays. Instead, selective annotations identify extended examples of various patterns whose use is significant to the essays' development and explain how each is used.

A STUDENT WRITER: COMBINING THE PATTERNS

THE PARK

My childhood did not really begin until thirteen years   1
ago, when I first came to this country from the rural jungle
of Vietnam. I can't really remember much before this
period, and the things that I do remember are vague images
which I have no desire or intention to discuss. However, my

Thesis statement childhood in the States was a lot different, especially after I
met my friend James. While it lasted, it was paradise.

Narrative begins It was a cold wintry day in February after a big   2
Description: Effects of cold snowstorm--the first I'd ever seen. My lips were chapped,
my hands were frozen stiff, and my cheeks were burning
from the biting wind, and yet I loved it. I especially loved the
Comparison and contrast: U.S. vs. Vietnam snow. I had come from a country where the closest things to
snow were white paint and cotton balls. But now, I was in
America. On that frosty afternoon, I was determined to build
a snowman. I had seen them in books, and I had heard they
could talk. I knew they could come alive, and I couldn't wait.

"Eyryui roeow ierog," a voice said out of nowhere. I   3
Description: James turned around, and in my face was a short, red-faced
(probably from the cold wind) Korean kid with a dirty,
runny nose. I responded, "Wtefkjkr ruyjft gsdfr" in my own
tongue. We understood each other perfectly, and we
Narration: The first day expressed our understanding with a smile. Together, we
built our first snowman. We were disappointed that evening
when the snowman just stood there; however, I was happy
because I had made my first friend.

Analogy Ever since then we've been a team like Abbott and   4
Costello (or, when my cousin joined us, The Three
Stooges). The two of us were inseparable. We could've
made the greatest Krazy Glue commercial ever.

Narration:
What they did
that summer

The summer that followed the big snowstorm, from   5
what I can recall, was awesome. We were free like comets
in the heavens, and did whatever our hearts wanted. For the
most part, our desires were fulfilled in a little park across
the street. This park was ours; it was like our own planet
guarded by our own robot army (disguised as trees).
Together we fought against the bigger people who always
tried to invade and take over our world. The enemy could
never conquer our fortress because they would have to
destroy our robots, penetrate our force field, and then defeat
us; this last feat would be impossible.

Narrative
continues

Examples:
What they
banished
Examples:
Superhero
fantasies

The park was our fantasy land where everything we   6
wished for came true and everything we hated was banished
forever. We banished vegetables, cheese, bigger people,
and--of course--girls. The land was enchanted, and we
could be whatever we felt like. We were super ninjas one
day and millionaires the next; we became the heroes we
idolized and lived the lives we dreamed about. I had the
strength of Bruce Lee and Superman; James possessed the
power of Clint Eastwood and the Bionic Man. My weapons
were the skills of Bruce and a cape. James, however, needed
a real weapon for Clint, and the weapon he made was
awesome. The Death Ray could destroy a building with one
blast, and it even had a shield so James was always
protected. Even with all his mighty weapons and gadgets,
though, he was still no match for Superman and Bruce Lee.
Every day, we fought until death (or until our parents called
us for dinner).

Narrative
continues

When we became bored with our super powers, the   7
park became a giant spaceship. We traveled all over the
Universe, conquering and exploring strange new worlds and
mysterious planets. Our ship was a top secret, indestructible
space warship called the X–007. We went to Mars, Venus,

Pluto, and other alien planets, destroying all the monsters we could find. When necessary, our spacecraft was transformed into a submarine for deep-sea adventures. We found lost cities, unearthed treasures, and saved Earth by destroying all the sea monsters that were plotting against us. We became heroes--just like Superman, Bruce Lee, the Bionic Man, and Clint Eastwood.

Cause and effect: The prospect of school

James and I had the time of our lives in the park that summer. It was great--until we heard about the horror of starting school. Shocked and terrified, we ran to our fortress to escape. For some reason, though, our magic kingdom had lost its powers. We fought hard that evening, trying to keep the bigger people out of our planet, but the battle was soon lost. Bruce Lee, Superman, the Bionic Man, and Clint Eastwood had all lost their special powers.

8

Narrative continues

School wasn't as bad as we'd thought it would be. The first day, James and I sat there with our hands folded. We didn't talk or move, and we didn't dare look at each other (we would've cracked up because we always made these goofy faces). Even though we had pens that could be transformed into weapons, we were still scared.

9

Description: School

Everyone was darker or lighter than we were, and the teacher was speaking a strange language (English). James and I giggled as she talked. We giggled softly when everyone else talked, and they laughed out loud when it was our turn to speak.

10

Narrative continues

The day dragged on, and all we wanted to do was go home and rebuild our fortress. Finally, after an eternity, it was almost three o'clock. James and I sat at the edge of our seats as we counted under our breath: "10, 9, 8, 7, 6, 5, 4, 3, 2, 1." At last the bell sounded. We dashed for the door and raced home and across the street--and then we stopped. We stood still in the middle of the street with our hearts

11

pounding like the beats of a drum. The cold September wind began to pick up, and everything became silent. We stood

**Description:
The fence**

there and watched the metal of the fence reflect the beautiful colors of the sun. It was beautiful, and yet we hated everything about it. The metal fence separated us from our fortress, our planet, our spaceship, our submarine--and, most important of all, our heroes and our dreams.

We stood there for a long time. As the sun slowly turned red and sank beneath the ground, so did our dreams, heroes, and hearts. Darkness soon devoured the park, and after a while we walked home with only the memories of the summer that came after the big snowstorm.

12

ON DUMPSTER DIVING

Lars Eighner

Lars Eighner was born in 1948 and grew up in Houston, Texas. He attended the University of Texas at Austin for three years before dropping out and going to work in a state mental hospital. After leaving this job over a policy dispute in 1988 and falling behind in his rent payments, Eighner became homeless. He traveled for three years with his dog, Lizbeth, between Austin and Los Angeles, earning some money writing stories for magazines. Some of his fiction had already been collected in Bayou Boy and Other Stories *(1985). Eighner now lives in Austin. His most recent publications are* B.M.O.C. *(1993) and* American Prelude *(1994), both collections of short stories. Eighner's book of memoirs of his homelessness,* Travels with Lizbeth *(1993), was written on a personal computer found in a Dumpster, and portions of it were published serially in* The Utne Reader, Harper's Magazine, The Pushcart Prize XVII, *and* The Threepenny Review, *where this chapter first appeared in 1991. "On Dumpster Diving" details the practical dangers as well as the many possibilities of scavenging from Dumpsters.*

This chapter was composed while the author was homeless. The present tense has been preserved.

Definition: Dumpster

Long before I began Dumpster diving I was impressed with Dumpsters, enough so that I wrote the Merriam-Webster research service to discover what I could about the word *Dumpster.* I learned from them that it is a proprietary word belonging to the Dempster Dumpster company. Since then I have dutifully capitalized the word, although it was lowercased in almost all the citations Merriam-Webster photocopied for me. Dempster's word is too apt. I have never heard these things called anything but Dumpsters. I do not know anyone who knows the generic name for these objects. From time to time I have heard a wino or hobo give some corrupted credit to the original and call them Dipsy Dumpsters. 1

Narration: Eighner's story begins

I began Dumpster diving about a year before I became homeless. 2

664

Definition:
diving

I prefer the word *scavenging* and use the word 3
scrounging when I mean to be obscure. I have heard
people, evidently meaning to be polite, use the word
foraging, but I prefer to reserve that word for gathering nuts and berries and such, which I do also according to the season and the opportunity. *Dumpster
diving* seems to me to be a little too cute and, in my
case, inaccurate because I lack the athletic ability to
lower myself into the Dumpsters as the true divers
do, much to their increased profit.

I like the frankness of the word *scavenging,* which 4
I can hardly think of without picturing a big black
snail on an aquarium wall. I live from the refuse of
others. I am a scavenger. I think it a sound and honorable niche, although if I could I would naturally prefer to live the comfortable consumer life, perhaps—
and only perhaps—as a slightly less wasteful consumer, owing to what I have learned as a scavenger.

Narration:
**Story
continues**

While Lizbeth and I were still living in the shack 5
on Avenue B as my savings ran out, I put almost
all my sporadic income into rent. The necessities of
daily life I began to extract from Dumpsters. Yes, we
ate from them. Except for jeans, all my clothes came

Exemplification:
**Things found
in Dumpsters**

from Dumpsters. Boom boxes, candles, bedding, toilet paper, a virgin male love doll, medicine, books, a
typewriter, dishes, furnishings, and change, sometimes amounting to many dollars—I acquired many
things from the Dumpsters.

**Thesis
statement**

I have learned much as a scavenger. I mean to put 6
some of what I have learned down here, beginning
with the practical art of Dumpster diving and proceeding to the abstract.

What is safe to eat? 7

After all, the finding of objects is becoming some- 8
thing of an urban art. Even respectable employed
people will sometimes find something tempting
sticking out of a Dumpster or standing beside one.
Quite a number of people, not all of them of the bo-
hemian type, are willing to brag that they found this
or that piece in the trash. But eating from Dumpsters is what separates the dilettanti from the pro-

fessionals. Eating safely from the Dumpsters involves three principles: using the senses and common sense to evaluate the condition of the found materials, knowing the Dumpsters of a given area and checking them regularly, and seeking always to answer the question "Why was this discarded?"

Comparison and contrast: Dumpster divers vs. others

Perhaps everyone who has a kitchen and a regular   9
supply of groceries has, at one time or another, made a sandwich and eaten half of it before discovering mold on the bread or got a mouthful of milk before realizing the milk had turned. Nothing of the sort is likely to happen to a Dumpster diver because he is constantly reminded that most food is discarded for a reason. Yet a lot of perfectly good food can be found in Dumpsters.

Classification and division: Different kinds of food found in Dumpsters and their relative safety

Canned goods, for example, turn up fairly often in   10
the Dumpsters I frequent. All except the most phobic people would be willing to eat from a can, even if it came from a Dumpster. Canned goods are among the safest of foods to be found in Dumpsters but are not utterly foolproof.

Although very rare with modern canning meth-   11
ods, botulism is a possibility. Most other forms of food poisoning seldom do lasting harm to a healthy person, but botulism is almost certainly fatal and often the first symptom is death. Except for carbonated beverages, all canned goods should contain a slight vacuum and suck air when first punctured. Bulging, rusty, and dented cans and cans that spew when punctured should be avoided, especially when the contents are not very acidic or syrupy.

Heat can break down the botulin, but this requires   12
much more cooking than most people do to canned goods. To the extent that botulism occurs at all, of course, it can occur in cans on pantry shelves as well as in cans from Dumpsters. Need I say that home-canned goods are simply too risky to be recommended.

From time to time one of my companions, aware of   13
the source of my provisions, will ask, "Do you think these crackers are really safe to eat?" For some reason it is most often the crackers they ask about.

This question has always made me angry. Of   14
course I would not offer my companion anything I

had doubts about. But more than that, I wonder why he cannot evaluate the condition of the crackers for himself. I have no special knowledge and I have been wrong before. Since he knows where the food comes from, it seems to me he ought to assume some of the responsibility for deciding what he will put in his mouth. For myself I have few qualms about dry foods such as crackers, cookies, cereal, chips, and pasta if they are free of visible contaminates and still dry and crisp. Most often such things are found in the original packaging, which is not so much a positive sign as it is the absence of a negative one.

Raw fruits and vegetables with intact skins seem 15 perfectly safe to me, excluding of course the obviously rotten. Many are discarded for minor imperfections that can be pared away. Leafy vegetables, grapes, cauliflower, broccoli, and similar things may be contaminated by liquids and may be impractical to wash.

Candy, especially hard candy, is usually safe if it 16 has not drawn ants. Chocolate is often discarded only because it has become discolored as the cocoa butter de-emulsified. Candying, after all, is one method of food preservation because pathogens do not like very sugary substances.

All of these foods might be found in any Dumpster 17 and can be evaluated with some confidence largely on the basis of appearance. Beyond these are foods that cannot be correctly evaluated without additional information.

I began scavenging by pulling pizzas out of the 18 Dumpster behind a pizza delivery shop. In general, prepared food requires caution, but in this case I knew when the shop closed and went to the Dumpster as soon as the last of the help left.

Such shops often get prank orders; both the orders 19 and the products made to fill them are called *bogus.* Because help seldom stays long at these places, pizzas are often made with the wrong topping, refused on delivery for being cold, or baked incorrectly. The products to be discarded are boxed up because inventory is kept by counting boxes: A boxed pizza can be written off; an unboxed pizza does not exist.

I never placed a bogus order to increase the supply   20
of pizzas and I believe no one else was scavenging in
this Dumpster. But the people in the shop became
suspicious and began to retain their garbage in the
shop overnight. While it lasted I had a steady supply of fresh, sometimes warm pizza. Because I knew
the Dumpster I knew the source of the pizza, and
because I visited the Dumpster regularly I knew
what was fresh and what was yesterday's.

Cause and effect: Why Eighner visits certain Dumpsters; why students throw out food

The area I frequent is inhabited by many affluent   21
college students. I am not here by chance; the Dumpsters in this area are very rich. Students throw out
many good things, including food. In particular they
tend to throw everything out when they move at
the end of a semester, before and after breaks, and
around midterm, when many of them despair of college. So I find it advantageous to keep an eye on the
academic calendar.

Students throw food away around breaks because   22
they do not know whether it has spoiled or will spoil
before they return. A typical discard is a half jar of
peanut butter. In fact, nonorganic peanut butter
does not require refrigeration and is unlikely to spoil
in any reasonable time. The student does not know
that, and since it is Daddy's money, the student decides not to take a chance. Opened containers require caution and some attention to the question.
"Why was this discarded?" But in the case of dis-
cards from student apartments, the answer may be
that the item was thrown out through carelessness,
ignorance, or wastefulness. This can sometimes be
deduced when the item is found with many others,
including some that are obviously perfectly good.

Some students, and others, approach defrosting a   23
freezer by chucking out the whole lot. Not only do
the circumstances of such a find tell the story, but
also the mass of frozen goods stays cold for a long
time and items may be found still frozen or freshly
thawed.

Yogurt, cheese, and sour cream are items that are   24
often thrown out while they are still good. Occasionally I find a cheese with a spot of mold, which of
course I just pare off, and because it is obvious why

such a cheese was discarded, I treat it with less suspicion than an apparently perfect cheese found in similar circumstances. Yogurt is often discarded, still sealed, only because the expiration date on the carton had passed. This is one of my favorite finds because yogurt will keep for several days, even in warm weather.

Students throw out canned goods and staples at   25
the end of semesters and when they give up college at midterm. Drugs, pornography, spirits, and the like are often discarded when parents are expected— Dad's Day, for example. And spirits also turn up after big party weekends, presumably discarded by the newly reformed. Wine and spirits, of course, keep perfectly well even once opened, but the same cannot be said of beer.

My test for carbonated soft drinks is whether they   26
still fizz vigorously. Many juices or other beverages are too acidic or too syrupy to cause much concern, provided they are not visibly contaminated. I have discovered nasty molds in vegetable juices, even when the product was found under its original seal; I recommend that such products be decanted slowly into a clear glass. Liquids always require some care.

Example: A liquid that requires care One hot day I found a large jug of Pat O'Brien's Hurricane mix. The jug had been opened but was still ice cold. I drank three large glasses before it became apparent to me that someone had added the rum to the mix, and not a little rum. I never tasted the rum, and by the time I began to feel the effects I had already ingested a very large quantity of the beverage. Some divers would have considered this a boon, but being suddenly intoxicated in a public place in the early afternoon is not my idea of a good time.

I have heard of people maliciously contaminating   27
discarded food and even handouts, but mostly I have heard of this from people with vivid imaginations who have had no experience with the Dumpsters themselves. Just before the pizza shop stopped discarding its garbage at night, jalapeños began showing up on most of the thrown-out pizzas. If indeed this was meant to discourage me, it was a wasted effort because I am a native Texan.

For myself, I avoid game, poultry, pork, and egg-   28
based foods, whether I find them raw or cooked. I
seldom have the means to cook what I find, but
when I do I avail myself of plentiful supplies of beef,
which is often in very good condition. I suppose fish
becomes disagreeable before it becomes dangerous.
Lizbeth is happy to have any such thing that is past
its prime and, in fact, does not recognize fish as food
until it is quite strong.

Home leftovers, as opposed to surpluses from res-   29
taurants, are very often bad. Evidently, especially
among students, there is a common type of personality that carefully wraps up even the smallest leftover and shoves it into the back of the refrigerator
for six months or so before discarding it. Characteristic of this type are the reused jars and margarine
tubs to which the remains are committed. I avoid
ethnic foods I am unfamiliar with. If I do not know
what it is supposed to look like when it is good, I cannot be certain I will be able to tell if it is bad.

No matter how careful I am I still get dysentery at   30
least once a month, oftener in warm weather. I do
not want to paint too romantic a picture. Dumpster
diving has serious drawbacks as a way of life.

**Process: How
to scavenge**

I learned to scavenge gradually, on my own. Since   31
then I have initiated several companions into the
trade. I have learned that there is a predictable
series of stages a person goes through in learning to
scavenge.

At first the new scavenger is filled with disgust   32
and self-loathing. He is ashamed of being seen and
may lurk around, trying to duck behind things, or he
may try to dive at night. (In fact, most people instinctively look away from a scavenger. By skulking
around, the novice calls attention to himself and
arouses suspicion. Diving at night is ineffective and
needlessly messy.)

Every grain of rice seems to be a maggot. Every-   33
thing seems to stink. He can wipe the egg yolk off
the found can, but he cannot erase from his mind the
stigma of eating garbage.

That stage passes with experience. The scavenger 34
finds a pair of running shoes that fit and look and
smell brand-new. He finds a pocket calculator in perfect working order. He finds pristine ice cream, still
frozen, more than he can eat or keep. He begins to
understand: People throw away perfectly good stuff,
a lot of perfectly good stuff.

At this stage, Dumpster shyness begins to dissi- 35
pate. The diver, after all, has the last laugh. He is
finding all manner of good things that are his for the
taking. Those who disparage his profession are the
fools, not he.

He may begin to hang on to some perfectly good 36
things for which he has neither a use nor a market.
Then he begins to take note of the things that are
not perfectly good but are nearly so. He mates a
Walkman with broken earphones and one that is
missing a battery cover. He picks up things that he
can repair.

At this stage he may become lost and never re- 37
cover. Dumpsters are full of things of some potential
value to someone and also of things that never have
much intrinsic value but are interesting. All the
Dumpster divers I have known come to the point of
trying to acquire everything they touch. Why not
take it, they reason, since it is all free? This is, of
course, hopeless. Most divers come to realize that
they must restrict themselves to items of relatively
immediate utility. But in some cases the diver simply cannot control himself. I have met several of
these pack-rat types. Their ideas of the values of
various pieces of junk verge on the psychotic. Every
bit of glass may be a diamond, they think, and all
that glisters, gold.

Cause and   I tend to gain weight when I am scavenging. 38
effect: Why Partly this is because I always find far more pizza
Eighner gains and doughnuts than water-packed tuna, nonfat yo-
weight when gurt, and fresh vegetables. Also I have not developed
he scavenges much faith in the reliability of Dumpsters as a food
source, although it has been proven to me many
times. I tend to eat as if I have no idea where my
next meal is coming from. But mostly I just hate to

see food go to waste and so I eat much more than I should. Something like this drives the obsession to collect junk.

Cause and effect: Why Eighner collects junk

As for collecting objects, I usually restrict myself to collecting one kind of small object at a time, such as pocket calculators, sunglasses, or campaign buttons. To live on the street I must anticipate my needs to a certain extent: I must pick up and save warm bedding I find in August because it will not be found in Dumpsters in November. As I have no access to health care, I often hoard essential drugs, such as antibiotics and antihistamines. (This course can be recommended only to those with some grounding in pharmacology. Antibiotics, for example, even when indicated are worse than useless if taken in insufficient amounts.) But even if I had a home with extensive storage space, I could not save everything that might be valuable in some contingency.

39

I have proprietary feelings about my Dumpsters. As I have mentioned, it is no accident that I scavenge from ones where good finds are common. But my limited experience with Dumpsters in other areas suggests to me that even in poorer areas, Dumpsters, if attended with sufficient diligence, can be made to yield a livelihood. The rich students discard perfectly good kiwifruit; poorer people discard perfectly good apples. Slacks and Polo shirts are found in the one place; jeans and T-shirts in the other. The population of competitors rather than the affluence of the dumpers most affects the feasibility of survival by scavenging. The large number of competitors is what puts me off the idea of trying to scavenge in places like Los Angeles.

40

Comparison and contrast: Dumpsters in rich and poorer areas

Curiously, I do not mind my direct competition, other scavengers, so much as I hate the can scroungers.

41

People scrounge cans because they have to have a little cash. I have tried scrounging cans with an able-bodied companion. Afoot a can scrounger simply cannot make more than a few dollars a day. One can extract the necessities of life from the Dumpsters directly with far less effort than would be required to accumulate the equivalent value in cans.

42

(These observations may not hold in places with container redemption laws.)

Cause and effect: Why people scrounge cans

Can scroungers, then, are people who must have 43
small amounts of cash. These are drug addicts and
winos, mostly the latter because the amounts of cash
are so small. Spirits and drugs do, like all other
commodities, turn up in Dumpsters and the scavenger will from time to time have a half bottle of
a rather good wine with his dinner. But the wino
cannot survive on these occasional finds; he must
have his daily dose to stave off the DTs. All the cans
he can carry will buy about three bottles of Wild
Irish Rose.

I do not begrudge them the cans, but can scroungers tend to tear up the Dumpsters, mixing the contents and littering the area. They become so specialized that they can see only cans. They earn my
contempt by passing up change, canned goods, and
readily hockable items.

There are precious few courtesies among scavengers. But it is common practice to set aside surplus 45
items: pairs of shoes, clothing, canned goods, and

Comparison and contrast: Can scroungers vs. true scavengers

such. A true scavenger hates to see good stuff go to
waste, and what he cannot use he leaves in good condition in plain sight.

Can scroungers lay waste to everything in their 46
path and will stir one of a pair of good shoes to the
bottom of a Dumpster, to be lost or ruined in the
muck. Can scroungers will even go through individual garbage cans, something I have never seen a
scavenger do.

Individual garbage cans are set out on the public 47
easement only on garbage days. On other days going
through them requires trespassing close to a dwelling. Going through individual garbage cans without
scattering litter is almost impossible. Litter is likely
to reduce the public's tolerance of scavenging. Individual cans are simply not as productive as Dumpsters; people in houses and duplexes do not move so
often and for some reason do not tend to discard as
much useful material. Moreover, the time required
to go through one garbage can that serves one household is not much less than the time required to go

through a Dumpster that contains the refuse of twenty apartments.

But my strongest reservation about going through individual garbage cans is that this seems to me a very personal kind of invasion to which I would object if I were a householder. Although many things in Dumpsters are obviously meant never to come to light, a Dumpster is somehow less personal. 48

I avoid trying to draw conclusions about the people who dump in the Dumpsters I frequent. I think it would be unethical to do so, although I know many people will find the idea of scavenger ethics too funny for words. 49

Examples: Things found in Dumpsters

Dumpsters contain bank statements, correspondence, and other documents, just as anyone might expect. But there are also less obvious sources of information. Pill bottles, for example. The labels bear the name of the patient, the name of the doctor, and the name of the drug. AIDS drugs and antipsychotic medicines, to name but two groups, are specific and are seldom prescribed for any other disorders. The plastic compacts for birth-control pills usually have complete label information. 50

Despite all of this sensitive information, I have had only one apartment resident object to my going through the Dumpster. In that case it turned out the resident was a university athlete who was taking bets and who was afraid I would turn up his wager slips. 51

Occasionally a find tells a story. I once found a small paper bag containing some unused condoms, several partial tubes of flavored sexual lubricants, a partially used compact of birth-control pills, and the torn pieces of a picture of a young man. Clearly she was through with him and planning to give up sex altogether. 52

Dumpster things are often sad—abandoned teddy bears, shredded wedding books, despaired-of sales kits. I find many pets lying in state in Dumpsters. Although I hope to get off the streets so that Lizbeth can have a long and comfortable old age, I know this hope is not very realistic. So I suppose when her 53 time comes she too will go into a Dumpster. I will have no better place for her. And after all, it is fitting, since for most of her life her livelihood has come from the Dumpster. When she finds something I think is safe that has been spilled from a Dumpster, I let her have it. She already knows the route around the best ones. I like to think that if she survives me she will have a chance of evading the dog catcher and of finding her sustenance on the route.

Silly vanities also come to rest in the Dumpsters. I am a rather accomplished needleworker. I get a lot of material from the Dumpsters. Evidently sorority girls, hoping to impress someone, perhaps themselves, with their mastery of a womanly art, buy a lot of embroider-by-number kits, work a few stitches horribly, and eventually discard the whole mess. I pull out their stitches, turn the canvas over, and work an original design. Do not think I refrain from chuckling as I make gifts from these kits. 54

I find diaries and journals. I have often thought of compiling a book of literary found objects. And perhaps I will one day. But what I find is hopelessly commonplace and bad without being, even unconsciously, camp. College students also discard their papers. I am horrified to discover the kind of paper that now merits an A in an undergraduate course. I am grateful, however, for the number of good books and magazines the students throw out. 55

In the area I know best I have never discovered vermin in the Dumpsters, but there are two kinds of kitty surprise. One is alley cats whom I meet as they leap, claws first, out of Dumpsters. This is especially thrilling when I have Lizbeth in tow. The other kind of kitty surprise is a plastic garbage bag filled with some ponderous, amorphous mass. This always proves to be used cat litter. 56

City bees harvest doughnut glaze and this makes the Dumpster at the doughnut shop more interesting. My faith in the instinctive wisdom of animals is always shaken whenever I see Lizbeth attempt to catch a bee in her mouth, which she does whenever bees are present. Evidently some birds find Dump- 57 sters profitable, for birdie surprise is almost as common as kitty surprise of the first kind. In hunting season all kinds of small game turn up in Dumpsters, some of it, sadly, not entirely dead. Curiously, summer and winter, maggots are uncommon.

The worse of the living and near-living hazards of the Dumpsters are the fire ants. The food they claim is not much of a loss, but they are vicious and aggressive. It is very easy to brush against some surface of the Dumpster and pick up half a dozen or more fire ants, usually in some sensitive area such as the underarm. One advantage of bringing Lizbeth along as I make Dumpster rounds is that, for obvious reasons, she is very alert to ground-based fire ants. When Lizbeth recognizes a fire-ant infestation around our feet, she does the Dance of the Zillion Fire Ants. I have learned not to ignore this warning from Lizbeth, whether I perceive the tiny ants or not, but to remove ourselves at Lizbeth's first pas de bourée. All the more so because the ants are the worst in the summer months when I wear flip-flops if I have them. (Perhaps someone will misunderstand this. Lizbeth does the Dance of the Zillion Fire Ants when she recognizes more fire ants than she cares to eat, not when she is being bitten. Since I have learned to react promptly, she does not get bitten at all. It is the isolated patrol of fire ants that falls in Lizbeth's range that deserves pity. She finds them quite tasty.) 58

Process: How to go through a Dumpster

By far the best way to go through a Dumpster is to lower yourself into it. Most of the good stuff tends to settle at the bottom because it is usually weightier than the rubbish. My more athletic companions have often demonstrated to me that they can extract much good material from a Dumpster I have already been over. 59

To those psychologically or physically unprepared to enter a Dumpster, I recommend a stout stick, preferably with some barb or hook at one end. The hook can be used to grab plastic garbage bags. When I find canned goods or other objects loose at the bottom of a Dumpster, I lower a bag into it, roll the desired object into the bag, and then hoist the bag 60 out—a procedure more easily described than executed. Much Dumpster diving is a matter of experience for which nothing will do except practice.

Dumpster diving is outdoor work, often surprisingly pleasant. It is not entirely predictable; things of interest turn up every day and some days there are finds of great value. I am always very pleased when I can turn up exactly the thing I most wanted to find. Yet in spite of the element of chance, scavenging more than most other pursuits tends to yield returns in some proportion to the effort and intelligence brought to bear. It is very sweet to turn up a few dollars in change from a Dumpster that has just been gone over by a wino.

The land is now covered with cities. The cities are full of Dumpsters. If a member of the canine race is ever able to know what it is doing, then Lizbeth knows that when we go around to the Dumpsters, we are hunting. I think of scavenging as a modern form of self-reliance. In any event, after having survived nearly ten years of government service, where everything is geared to the lowest common denominator, I find it refreshing to have work that rewards initiative and effort. Certainly I would be happy to have a sinecure again, but I am no longer heartbroken that I left one.

Cause and effect: Results of his experiences as a scavenger

I find from the experience of scavenging two rather deep lessons. The first is to take what you can use and let the rest go by. I have come to think that there is no value in the abstract. A thing I cannot use or make useful, perhaps by trading, has no value however rare or fine it may be. I mean useful in a broad sense—some art I would find useful and some otherwise.

I was shocked to realize that some things are not worth acquiring, but now I think it is so. Some material things are white elephants that eat up the possessor's substance. The second lesson is the transience of material being. This has not quite converted me to a dualist, but it has made some headway in that direction. I do not suppose that ideas are immortal, but certainly mental things are longer lived than other material things.

61

62

63

64

Once I was the sort of person who invests objects   65
with sentimental value. Now I no longer have those
objects, but I have the sentiments yet.

Many times in our travels I have lost everything   66
but the clothes I was wearing and Lizbeth. The things
I find in Dumpsters, the love letters and rag dolls
of so many lives, remind me of this lesson. Now I
hardly pick up a thing without envisioning the time
I will cast it aside. This I think is a healthy state of
mind. Almost everything I have now has already
been cast out at least once, proving that what I own
is valueless to someone.

Anyway, I find my desire to grab for the gaudy   67
bauble has been largely sated. I think this is an attitude I share with the very wealthy—we both know
there is plenty more where what we have came from.
Between us are the rat-race millions who nightly
scavenge the cable channels looking for they know
not what.

I am sorry for them.   68

Glossary

Abstract/Concrete two kinds of language. Abstract words are names for concepts or qualities that cannot be directly seen or touched: *love, justice, emotion, concern, evil, anguish*. Concrete words vividly refer to objects or qualities that *can* be perceived by the senses: *green, fountain pen, ink-blot, leaky, overflowing, stain*. Concrete phrases that give the reader a complete and vivid visual picture are **images**. (See also **Imagery**.)

Abstract words are necessary at times to express ideas, but when used without concrete supporting detail they are very vague. The abstract phrase "The speaker was overcome with emotion" could mean almost anything, but the addition of concrete language clarifies the meaning: "He clenched his fist and shook it at the crowd" (anger); "He began to teeter and grabbed hold of the edge of the podium; at the same time his mouth went dry and no sound came out" (fear); "He wiped tears from his eyes with a blue cloth, shook his head, and stepped away from the microphone" (sadness).

Allusions brief references to people, objects, events, statements, or situations that readers are expected to recognize. Making an allusion is a way of evoking a vivid impression in very few words. "The gardener opened the gate and suddenly we found ourselves in Eden" suggests in one word (*Eden*) the stunning beauty of the garden that the writer visited. Allusions typically refer to literature ("The mayor is a Scrooge who will not even listen to our suggestions for a municipal sculpture garden.") or to historical or biblical figures or events.

Analogy a form of comparison that considers similarities between two essentially different items. By making an analogy, writers are able to explain one element by comparing it to another that is more familiar ("Money is like muck, not good unless it be spread."). Analogies can clarify abstract or technical information by presenting it to the reader in simpler, more concrete terms. *Analogous* means "very similar, parallel": "The effect of pollution on the environment is analogous to that of cancer on the body."

Annotating   a technique used by a reader to record responses to a reading selection by writing notes in the margins of the text; might involve asking questions, suggesting possible parallels with other reading selections or with the reader's own experience, arguing with or contradicting the writer's points, commenting on the writer's style, or defining unfamiliar terms or concepts. See Introduction: Reading to Write.

Antithesis   the name for a debatable viewpoint opposite from the one that is expressed in a **thesis**. The thesis of an argumentative essay must be debatable—that is, it should have one or more antitheses. One way a writer can test the strength of the thesis is to try to formulate an antithesis. If no antithesis exists, the writer's thesis is not debatable.

Antonym   a word opposite in meaning to another word. *Beautiful* is the antonym of *ugly*. A word may have several antonyms; other antonyms for *ugly* might be *pretty, handsome,* or *attractive.* **Synonym** is the antonym of *antonym.*

Argumentation   the form of writing that takes a stand on an issue and attempts to convince readers to agree by presenting a logical sequence of points supported by evidence. Argumentation may be reinforced by appeals to the readers' emotions. See Chapter 10.

Audience   the people "listening" to a writer's words. Writers who are sensitive to their audience will carefully choose a tone, examples, and allusions that their readers will understand and react to. Displaying such sensitivity is like making eye contact in a conversation; it engages the audience.

Even if a writer's thoughts are articulate and strong, they may seem weak if the writer has not written with the particular audience in mind. A work of writing for children would need to use relatively brief sentences and accessible language. A good article attempting to persuade high school students not to use drugs would use examples and allusions pertinent to a teenager's life. Different examples would need to be chosen if the writer were addressing middle-aged members of Alcoholics Anonymous.

Basis of Comparison   the term for the fundamental similarity between two or more things that allows a writer to compare them. In a comparison of how two different towns react to foreign immigrants, the basis of comparison might be that both towns have a rapidly expanding immigrant population. (If one of the towns did not have any immigrants, a comparison between the two dealing with immigrants would be impossible.) A basis for comparison may be thought of as justification: Could you defend the comparison in your paper if someone challenged the point of it? If so, you have a strong basis of comparison.

The lack of an obvious basis of comparison should not rule out creative comparisons, however. You may see a strong connection between two situations that have not previously been discussed together. Comparing two objects that appear vastly different can sometimes lead to an interesting and unique paper, as long as the two items have essential similarities. For example, you could compare a building with a tree because they share the same essential architectural pattern, or compare quantum mechanics with Buddhist philosophy because of the similar intuitive thought patterns they both require for understanding, as Fritjof Capra has done in *The Tao of Physics*. A paper's very lack of an obvious basis of comparison can provoke the reader's curiosity and disbelief at the outset, allowing the writer to present a strong defense in the pages that follow. Such an unexpected comparison is particularly effective for papers discussing abstract philosophical ideas or ideas that must be intuitively understood. The more diverse the elements of the comparison, however, the stronger the basis of comparison must be.

Brainstorming   See **Invention**

Causal Chain   the term for a sequence of events that are linked through a domino effect—one event causes another event that causes another event. Describing a causal chain can provide an essay with a simple, logical, and dynamic structure.

Cause and Effect   the pattern of development that discusses either the reasons for an occurrence or the observed or predicted consequences of an occurrence. Often both causes and effects are presented in the same essay. See Chapter 6.

Causes   the reasons for an event, situation, or phenomenon. An *immediate cause* is an obvious one; a *remote cause* is a more obscure, less easily perceived one. The *main cause* is the one that is the most important cause, whether immediate or remote. Other, less important causes that nevertheless encourage the effect in some way (for instance, by speeding it up or providing favorable circumstances for it) are called *contributory causes*.

Chronological Order   the time sequence in which events occur. Chronological order is a simple and common way to organize a narrative; it is also the structure that process essays follow.

Claim   in the method of structuring arguments advanced by Stephen Toulmin, the thesis or main point of an essay. Usually it is stated directly, but sometimes it is implied.

Classification and Division   related methods of organizing information. *Classification* involves searching for common characteristics among scattered items and grouping them accordingly, thereby giving order to previously random information. In contrast, *division* breaks up an entity into smaller groups or elements, providing for a more detailed and managable discussion. Classification generalizes; division specifies. See Chapter 8.

Cliché   See **Diction**

Clustering   See **Invention**

Coherence   the tight relationship between all the parts of a good piece of writing. Such a relationship ensures that the writing will make clear sense to readers. For a piece of writing to be coherent, it must be logical and orderly, with effective **transitions** making the movement between sentences and paragraphs clear.

Colloquialisms   expressions that are generally appropriate for conversation and informal writing but not for formal writing in college, business, or professional settings. For instance, you should write *center on,* not *center around; enthusiastic about,* not *enthused about;* and *very sorry,* not *good and sorry.* Words often have two types of meaning, a dictionary meaning (which is considered appropriate for formal writing in the way that a tuxedo would be appropriate for a diplomatic banquet) and a different, informal meaning that is used colloquially. For example, the formal definition of the word *aggravate* is "to make worse" ("Continual medical expenses aggravated their poverty"). Colloquially, however, *aggravate* means "to irritate" ("I get aggravated when I have to wait in a long line"). (See also **Diction**.)

Comparison and Contrast   two patterns of development, often found together. In a general sense, *comparison* shows how two or more subjects are alike; *contrast* shows how they are different. In a *subject-by-subject comparison*, the comparison is organized by subject rather than by the points on which the subjects are being compared. Although the subjects are compared in the thesis, they are discussed separately in similarly structured sections in the body of the essay. This kind of pattern works best for short, simple comparisons or for papers concerned with only a few points of comparison, where the reader can easily perceive the similarities between subjects. A *point-by-point comparison* is organized by points discussed rather than by subject. Typically, each paragraph in the essay raises a new issue and compares each subject in relation to the issue. This kind of pattern works well with complex, detailed comparisons. See Chapter 7.

Conclusion   the group of sentences or, in the case of a long paper, paragraphs that brings an essay to a close. To *conclude* means not only "to end" but also "to resolve." Although the purpose of the conclusion is not to resolve all the issues and questions raised in the essay, the conclusion is the place to show that they *have* been resolved, that all the points made have been supported by adequate evidence, and that the thesis of the paper is indeed reasonable. Conclusions should show that the writer is not just glad to be finished writing but also committed to what has been expressed. The conclusion is the writer's last chance to leave an impression with the readers, and the impression it leaves should be one of confidence.

Two commonly used weak endings should be avoided: 1) introducing new points or afterthoughts, suggesting that the writer has forgotten to discuss something in the body of the paper and is not ready to end the essay; and 2) apologizing or qualifying the thesis, leaving the impression that the essay is in charge of the writer rather than that the writer is in charge of the essay. Conclusions should give the whole essay a sense of completeness and unity.

Several possible ways of concluding an essay include the following:

1. Restating the thesis and/or giving a summary of the points made in the essay, perhaps also suggesting the implications or significance of the topic
2. Recommending a course of action or a solution to a problem that has been discussed in the essay
3. Making a prediction
4. Ending with an embellishment, such as a quotation, an anecdote, or a question, that indirectly supports and strengthens the thesis (and does not back away from it).

Several of these methods resemble methods that can be used in introducing essays. Sometimes during the **writing process** an original ending will be relocated to the beginning or a beginning will become an end. Although **introductions** and conclusions often convey similar information, an introduction generally focuses more on provoking the reader's interest and a conclusion on leaving the reader convinced that the thesis has been supported.

Concrete   See **Abstract/Concrete**

Connotation/Denotation   two terms that refer to the meanings of words. A word's denotation is its basic definition. Connotations are the word's associations, the meanings or feelings that are suggested beyond the word's literal meaning. The word *home* denotes one's place of residence, but it also connotes warmth and a sense of belonging.

Connotations are important in subjective writing; writers who are aware of connotations can carefully choose words that evoke the precise mood they want to convey. Connotations reveal a writer's attitude toward something and indicate how an audience should respond—if they should pity, sympathize with, or fear a person, for example.

English is such a rich language that many words have similar denotations; however, all words have at least slightly different connotations. The adjectives *thoughtful, reflective*, and *pensive* all denote the quality of thinking a lot, but they differ in degree and in association. *Thoughtful* implies "considerate, caring toward other people" as well as "full of thought." *Reflective* connotes "self-conscious" and sometimes "reminiscent." *Pensive* suggests deeper and more sober thought; it often suggests "withdrawn" and "melancholy."

Connotations may reveal or even conceal societal attitudes. Not being aware of connotations can sometimes be damaging. By using words with sexist or racist connotations, for example, a writer may unintentionally insult readers.

Contributory Cause See **Causes**

Deductive Reasoning the method of reasoning that presents a general premise and shows how it leads to a specific conclusion. (See also **Syllogism**.) The opposite of deductive reasoning is **inductive reasoning,** which begins with specific evidence and moves to a general conclusion. Deductive and inductive reasoning may be effectively used together. See Chapter 10.

Definition an explanation of a word's meaning. It may be a brief *formal definition* (as it appears in a dictionary) or a longer *extended definition* that elaborates on the formal definition through **exemplification, narration, classification,** or other rhetorical strategies, or that argues in favor of a particular meaning. An extended definition can be an effective pattern of development for an essay. See Chapter 9.

Denotation See **Connotation/Denotation**

Description a pattern of development that presents a word picture of a thing, a person, a situation, or a series of events through sensory details. See Chapter 3.

Diction the specific words and kinds of words that a writer chooses. The kind of diction a writer uses depends on the purpose of a piece of writing and on its audience. For instance, expressive writing might use poetic language, while business writing would avoid it in favor of the most direct words possible. A newsletter for computer engineers might use specialized technical words that would need defining in a textbook chapter for students learning computer engineering.

Many kinds of diction should be avoided in college writing as well as in business and professional writing:

- *Contractions* (write *will not* instead of *won't* and *they are* instead of *they're*)
- *Slang* (write *car*, not *wheels*; avoid words like *lousy, awesome, cool*)
- *Conversational fillers* (*I mean, you know*)
- *Unnecessary words and redundant phrases* (write *consensus*, not *consensus of opinion*, and *unique*, not *very unique*)
- *Bland words* (whenever possible, replace *good, nice, very, fine* with stronger, more specific and colorful words)
- *Colloquial uses of words* (write *enthusiastic*, not *enthused*, and *center on*, not *center around*)—See **Colloquialisms**
- *Pretentious words or jargon* (such as *disinformation* for *falsehood* or *lie; prioritize options* for *set priorities*)
- *Euphemisms* (write *died* rather than *passed on*)
- *Sexist language* (write *the writer . . . he or she* or *the writers . . . they*, not *the writer . . . he*; write *police officer* and *firefighter*, not *policeman* and *fireman*)
- *Clichés* (overused expressions such as *hustle and bustle; beauty is in the eye of the beholder; a picture is worth a thousand words; to make a long story short. . . .*)

In writing the first draft of an essay, try to use precise and colorful language. Then review word choices and eliminate or strengthen any weak phrases that you discover.

Digression a remark or series of remarks that wanders from the main point of a discussion. In the case of a personal narrative, a digression could prove entertaining because of its very irrelevance, but in other kinds of writing it interrupts and confuses the development of the essay. Writers should be especially careful when giving examples not to get so involved with developing the example that they fail to connect it to the idea they are illustrating.

Division See **Classification and Division**

Dominant Impression the mood or quality that is emphasized in a piece of writing.

Essay a short work of nonfiction writing on a single topic that usually expresses the author's impressions or opinions. The word *essay* also means "an attempt." In this sense, an essay as a piece of writing is never the last word on a subject but only the best attempt that the writer can make. An essay may be organized around one or several of the patterns of development presented in this book. A *formal essay* generally has a serious purpose and tone, formal diction (as opposed to colloquial language), and a tight structure based on a logical progression of ideas. An *informal essay* tends to offer a more entertaining viewpoint and therefore may employ colloquial expressions and a looser structure.

Evidence   statements composed of facts and opinions. *Facts*, which may include statistics, may be drawn from research or personal experience, and *opinions* may represent the conclusions of experts or your own ideas. Evidence for an analytical literature paper might include lines and passages from the work being discussed or quotations from literary critics; a historical research paper would probably draw on historical accounts, statistics, and the findings of scholars.

Example   a concrete, specific illustration used to support general points being made. An example may, among other things, be a brief historical account, a personal anecdote, or a summary of a passage from a work of literature.

Exemplification   the pattern of development that uses a single extended **example** or a series of shorter examples to support a thesis. See Chapter 4.

Fallacies   statements that resemble plausible arguments but are not. They are often persuasive, but they unfairly manipulate readers to win agreement. Fallacies include begging the question; argument from analogy; personal attack (*ad hominem*); hasty or sweeping generalization; false dilemma (the either/or fallacy); equivocation; red herring; you also (*tu quoque*); appeal to doubtful authority; and misleading statistics. See Chapter 10.

Figures of Speech (also **Figurative Language**)   imaginative comparisons that indirectly suggest to readers another meaning beyond their literal one. Three of the most common figures of speech are *similes, metaphors*, and *personification*.

A simile makes a comparison using *like* or *as* ("Hills Like White Elephants"—Ernest Hemingway). A metaphor compares two things without using *like* or *as* ("Not yet would they veer southward to the caldron of the land that lay below"—N. Scott Momaday). Personification describes animals or objects as if they were human ("the chair slouched"; "bees grumbled over the rose bush"; "the wind sighed outside the window"). Other figures of speech include **hyperbole** and **understatement.**

Freewriting   See **Invention**

Grounds   in the method of structuring arguments put forward by Stephen Toulmin, the material that a writer uses to support a claim. Grounds may be evidence (facts or expert opinion) or appeals to the emotions or values of an audience.

Highlighting   a technique used by a reader to record responses to a reading selection by marking the text with symbols; might involve underlining important ideas, boxing key terms, numbering a series of related points, circling unfamiliar words (or placing question marks next to them), drawing vertical lines alongside a particularly interesting or important passage, drawing arrows to connect related points, or placing asterisks next to discussions of the selection's central issues or themes. See Introduction: Reading to Write.

Hyperbole   deliberate exaggeration for emphasis or humorous effect: "I froze to death out in the storm"; "She has hundreds of boyfriends"; "Clothes these days seem to cost a million dollars"; "Last year passed by in a second." The opposite of hyperbole is understatement, which has similar intended effects: "The people who live near the power plant are not exactly looking forward to another Chernobyl in their backyards."

Imagery   a set of verbal pictures of sensory experiences. These pictures, conveyed through concrete details, make a description vivid and immediate to the reader. Some images are literal ("The cows were so white they almost glowed in the dark."), while some are more figurative ("The black and white cows looked like maps, with the continents in black and the seas in white."). A pattern of imagery (repeated images of, for example, shadows, forests, fire) in a work of writing may build up its own set of associations and become a **symbol** with a special meaning.

Immediate Cause   See **Causes**

Inductive Reasoning   the method of reasoning that first presents specific evidence and then draws a general conclusion based on this evidence. Inductive reasoning is the opposite of **deductive reasoning,** which moves from a general premise to a specific conclusion. The two forms of logic may be used together effectively in an essay. See Chapter 10.

Introduction   an essay's opening. Depending on the scope of the essay, it may be one paragraph or several paragraphs long—or even a few pages long in a lengthy research paper. In an introduction a writer wants to encourage the audience to read the essay that follows. This prompting involves carefully choosing a tone and diction that invite the readers and do not alienate them, as well as indicating either explicitly or implicitly what the paper is about and in what direction it will go. If an introduction is not interesting and lively, it may discourage readers.

Several possible ways of introducing an essay include the following:

1. Directly stating the thesis
2. Defining a relevant term or concept
3. Telling an anecdote or story that pertains to the thesis
4. Asking a provoking question
5. Beginning with a quotation

Invention (also **Prewriting**) the initial preparatory stage of writing in which a writer explores the writing assignment, focuses ideas, and ultimately decides on a thesis for an essay. A writer might begin by thinking through the requirements of the assignment—the purpose, the length of the essay, and the audience. Several of the following specific invention techniques can then help the writer to proceed.

Freewriting is an indirect method that allows the writer to back off from the subject and thus move beyond writer's block. Freewriting involves writing quickly, without stopping, for a fixed period of time on any subject. The goal of this strategy is to free-associate to discover ideas to write about.

Looping involves isolating one idea from a piece of freewriting and using this idea as a focus for a new piece of freewriting. Looping may be repeated if it is effective in generating new ideas.

Another invention technique uses *questions for probing* to explore a subject. These questions encourage a dialogue in the writer's mind; they allow the writer to delve deeper and deeper into the subject and also to think about which questions can most productively be explored in an essay.

Brainstorming is an invention technique that involves listing everything that comes to mind about the writing topic. It is a chance to be creative and to be drawn in new, even surprising directions.

Clustering is a method of grouping writing ideas visually by listing the main topic of the writing in the center of a page, circling it, surrounding it with words or phrases that identify major points to be addressed in the discussion of this topic, then circling these words or phrases and creating whole new clusters of ideas for each of them. This method allows the writer to divide and subdivide points, getting more specific with the movement out from the center of the page.

Journal Writing is a way of jotting down and exploring ideas that emerge from reading or from other experiences. Often writing recorded in a journal is a source from which longer and more complete writing pieces develop.

Using one or more of these methods, writers should be able to come up with a tentative thesis and then begin work on the essay itself. See Chapter 1.

Irony   language that points to a discrepancy between two different levels of meaning. *Verbal irony* is characterized by a gap between what is actually stated and what is really meant, which is often the opposite in meaning—for instance, "such a heavenly aroma" (referring to the smell from dirty socks); "his humble abode" (referring to a millionaire's estate), or "Let's go boating" (referring to a trickle of water that is supposed to be a river). Deliberately insincere and biting irony is called *sarcasm*—for example, "That's okay, I love it when you drop dishes on the floor and break them."

Another kind of irony is *situational* rather than verbal. It points to a discrepancy between what actually happens and what the situation leads readers to expect will happen. This kind of irony is present when a character, trying to scare away a rival, ends up being scared away himself.

Finally, *dramatic irony* occurs when the reader understands more about what is happening in a story than the rather naïve character who is telling the story does. For example, the narrator might tell an anecdote very simply and honestly and explain at the end how puzzled he was by other people's reactions, while it is obvious to the reader from the story's events that the narrator has made a fool of himself because of his gullibility.

Journal Writing   See **Invention**

Looping   See **Invention**

Main Cause   See **Causes**

Metaphor   See **Figures of Speech**

Narration   the pattern of development that tells a story. See Chapter 2.

Objective description/Subjective description   terms that refer to the degree to which an author's personal point of view is present in the writing. An *objective description* is a distanced, factual picture presented in as plain and direct a manner as possible. Objective description tries to avoid opinions and interpretations. Pure objectivity is difficult to achieve, however, because people's perceptions are often colored by their past experiences and their personal values and biases. Still, certain forms of writing—science papers, technical reports, and news articles, for example—strive for *objective language* that is plain, direct, and free of value judgments.

Descriptions that do contain value judgments (*a saintly woman,* for example) are subjective. Whereas objective language is distanced from an event or object, *subjective language* is involved. A subjective description focuses on the author's relationship to the event rather than on the event itself, conveying not just a factual record of details but also their significance. Subjective language, the language generally used in personal narratives and editorials, may include poetic words and impressionistic descriptions. It purposely avoids colorless, utilitarian language in favor of words that impart a judgment or emotional response to a description (*stride, limp, meander, pace, hobble, stroll, plod, glide,* or *shuffle* instead of *walk; snicker, snort, chuckle, titter, giggle,* or *guffaw* instead of *laugh*). Subjective language also includes **figures of speech.** See Chapter 3.

Paragraph the basic unit of an essay. A paragraph is composed of related sentences that together express one of the ideas in the essay. The **unifying idea** of a paragraph is often stated in a single **topic sentence**. Paragraphs are also graphic symbols on the page, mapping the progress of the ideas in the essay and also providing visual relief to the reader.

Parallelism the use of similar grammatical elements within a sentence or sentences. For a sentence to exhibit parallelism, any elements of equal importance—for example, paired elements or elements in a series—must be presented in the same form. "I like hiking, skiing, and to cook" is not parallel because *hiking* and *skiing* share the gerund form (*-ing*) of the verbs while *to cook* is the infinitive form. Revised for parallelism, the sentence could read either "I like hiking, skiing, and cooking" or "I like to hike, to ski, and to cook."

As a stylistic technique, parallelism can provide emphasis and cohesion, effectively linking elements in a sentence or a series of sentences through repetition of a grammatical form or a particular phrase—for example, "Walk groundly, talk profoundly, drink roundly, sleep soundly" (William Hazlitt). Parallelism is a powerful oratorical technique often employed by politicians and evangelists: "Until justice is blind to color, until education is unaware of race, until opportunity is unconcerned with the color of men's skins, emancipation will be a proclamation but not a fact" (Lyndon B. Johnson).

Paraphrase the restatement of another person's words in your own words. It is particularly necessary in a source-based paper where the purpose is to direct information gathered during research into pointed statements that support the ideas in the paper. Only information that is uniquely worded (for instance, Marie

Winn's labeling television a "plug-in-drug") or extremely difficult to paraphrase should be quoted directly. For example, Jonathan Kozol's "Illiterates cannot travel freely. When they attempt to do so, they encounter risks that few of us can dream of" (p. 219) might be paraphrased like this: "According to Jonathan Kozol, people who cannot read find travel extremely risky."

Personification See **Figures of Speech**

Persuasion a method of convincing an audience that relies on various appeals to win support of an opinion or to move readers to action. See "Argumentation and Persuasion," Chapter 10.

Plagiarism presenting the words or ideas of someone else as if they were your own. It should always be avoided.

***Post Hoc* Reasoning** the fallacy of looking back at two events that have occurred in chronological sequence and wrongly assuming that the first event caused the second.

Prewriting See **Invention**

Process the pattern of development that presents a series of steps in a procedure, such as a laboratory experiment, in chronological order. See Chapter 5.

Prose speech or writing as opposed to poetic verse.

Purpose a writer's reason for writing. A writer's purpose may, for example, be to entertain readers with an amusing story, inform them about a dangerous disease, move them to action by enraging them with an example of injustice, or change their perspective in some way by revealing a hidden dimension of a person or situation. To give an essay **coherence** and power, a writer should always keep its purpose or purposes in mind. One good way for a reader to become more deeply involved with a work of writing is to ask, "Why did this writer write this?" See Chapter 1.

Refutation the attempt to counter an opposing argument by revealing its weaknesses. Three of the most common weaknesses are logical flaws in the argument, inadequate evidence, and irrelevance. Refutation greatly strengthens an argument by showing that the writer is aware of the complexity of the issue and has considered opposing viewpoints.

Remote Cause See **Causes**

Rhetoric the study and art of effective communication through prose.

Rhetorical Question a question asked for effect and not meant to be answered.

Sarcasm See **Irony**

Satire writing that uses wit, irony, and ridicule to attack foolishness. Satire has a different purpose from comedy, which usually intends simply to entertain. For an example of ironic satire, see Judy Brady's "I Want a Wife," page 503.

Simile   See **Figures of Speech**

Subjective description   See **Objective description/Subjective description**

Syllogism   a basic form of deductive reasoning. Every syllogism includes three parts: 1) a major premise that makes a general statement ("Confinement is physically and psychologically damaging"); 2) a minor premise that makes a related but more specific statement ("Zoos confine animals"); and 3) a conclusion drawn from these two premises ("Therefore, zoos are physically and psychologically damaging to animals"). See Chapter 10.

Symbol   an occurrence, being, or thing that represents something more than its literal meaning.

Synonym   a word with the same denotative meaning as another word. A synonym for *loud* is *noisy*. Most words in the English language have several or many synonyms; however, each synonym has unique nuances or **connotations.** (See also **Connotation/ Denotation.**)

Thesis   the name for an essay's main idea, the idea that all the points made in the paragraphs of the essay support. Depending on the writer's purpose, a thesis may be *expressive, informative*, or *persuasive.* A thesis may be implied but is usually stated explicitly in the form of a **thesis statement.** In addition to conveying the essay's main idea, the thesis statement should indicate the writer's approach to the subject and express the writer's purpose (the reason for writing). It may also indicate the pattern of development that will structure the essay.

The thesis a writer develops in the early stages of the essay is usually a *tentative thesis,* one that serves as a guide while the writer thinks through the essay. Ultimately, however, the thesis should define a point of view that can be fully discussed in the body of the essay. A good thesis is much more than a statement of fact; it allows room for development. See Chapter 1. (See also **Antithesis.**)

Topic Sentence   a sentence stating the main idea of a paragraph. Often, but not always, the topic sentence opens the paragraph.

Transitions   links between ideas in a piece of writing. They may be words, sentences, or sometimes even paragraphs. The ideas themselves should be organized in a way that makes sense logically and sequentially, with each new sentence and paragraph building on the last. However, shifts in emphasis or subject matter can be unsettling to readers unless pivotal phrases and sentences guide them, reminding them where they have been and showing them the direction in which they are now moving.

Transitions between paragraphs bridge a larger gap than transitions between sentences; the last sentence of a paragraph might hint at what the next paragraph will discuss, and the first sentence of a new paragraph may echo a fragment of the preceding paragraph and indicate how that idea relates to a new idea. Transitional sentences often aid coherence by clarifying the relationship between thesis and support.

Within and between paragraphs, transition may be enhanced by the repetition of an essay's key words or concepts, by the use of pronouns to refer to nouns in previous sentences, and by the use of transitional expressions. Some of the more useful transitional expressions are listed below:

- To show chronological sequence: *simultaneously, meanwhile, afterward, then, subsequently, soon, at the same time, since, first (second, third . . .)*
- To indicate spatial relationships: *nearby, beside, facing, adjacent to, in front of, behind*
- To indicate results: *consequently, therefore, as a result, because*
- To indicate contrast: *in contrast, conversely, but, however, yet, on the other hand, still, nevertheless*
- To indicate similarity: *similarly, likewise, in the same way*
- To indicate addition: *first, second, third, also, in addition, furthermore, finally*
- To indicate movement from general to specific: *in fact, for example, for instance*

Unifying Idea the central point or concept expressed in a paragraph. This idea is often expressed in a topic sentence.

Unity the desirable attribute of a paragraph in which every sentence relates directly to the paragraph's main idea.

Warrant in the method of structuring arguments advanced by Stephen Toulmin, the inference that connects the claim to the grounds. The warrant can be a belief that is taken for granted or an assumption that underlies the argument.

Writing Process the name given to the sequence of tasks a writer undertakes when writing an essay. During *invention*, or *prewriting*, the writer gathers information and ideas and focuses them into a workable topic. During the *arrangement* stage, the writer organizes these ideas into a logical sequence. During *drafting and revision*, the essay is actually written and then reworked. Finally, during *editing*, the writer puts the finishing touches on the essay by correcting misspellings, checking punctuation, searching for grammatical inaccuracies, and so on.

These stages occur in no fixed order; many effective writers move back and forth among them. This process reveals that writing is not simply a way of expressing ideas that are clear in the writer's mind; it is actually a way of thinking and learning that can help writers to discover new ideas and new connections among ideas.

Leslie Epstein, "Civility and Its Discontents." From *The American Prospect,* Summer 1991. Copyright © 1991 by New Prospect, Inc. Reprinted with the permission of *The American Prospect.*

Stephanie Ericsson, "The Ways We Lie." From *Utne Reader,* November/December 1992. Notes for *Companion into the Dawn,* forthcoming from HarperCollins Publishers, 1995. Copyright © 1992 by Stephanie Ericsson. Reprinted with the permission of the Rhoda Weyr Agency.

Stanley Fish, "How the Pot Got to Call the Kettle Black." From *Atlantic Monthly,* November 1993. Reprinted with the permission of the author.

Cal Fussman, "Consent of a Woman." From *Lear's,* October 1993. Reprinted with the permission of the author.

Martin Gansberg, "38 Who Saw Murder Didn't Call the Police." From *The New York Times,* March 27, 1964. Copyright © 1964 by The New York Times Company. Reprinted with the permission of *The New York Times.*

Henry Louis Gates, Jr., "What's in a Name?" From *Dissent,* Fall 1989. Copyright © 1989 by Henry Louis Gates, Jr. Reprinted with the permission of Brandt & Brandt Literary Agents, Inc.

Ellen Goodman, "The Company Man." From *At Large.* Copyright © 1981 by the Washington Post Company. Reprinted with the permission of Summit Books, a division of Simon & Schuster, Inc.

Al Gore, "Ships in the Desert." From *Earth in the Balance.* Copyright © 1992 by Senator Al Gore. Reprinted with the permission of Houghton Mifflin Company. All rights reserved.

Edward T. Hall, "The Arab World." From *Hidden Differences* by Edward T. Hall and Mildred Reed Hall. Copyright © 1987 by Edward T. Hall and Mildred Reed Hall. Reprinted with the permission of Doubleday, a division of Bantam Doubleday Dell Publishing Group, Inc.

Alice Hoffman, "The Perfect Family." From *The New York Times Magazine,* November 1, 1992. Copyright © 1992 by The New York Times Company. Reprinted with the permission of *The New York Times.*

Shirley Jackson, "The Lottery." From *The Lottery.* Copyright 1948, 1949 by Shirley Jackson, renewed © 1976, 1977 by Laurence Hyman, Barry Hyman, Mrs. Sarah Webster, and Mrs. Joanne Schnurer. Reprinted with the permission of Farrar Straus & Giroux, Inc.

Susan Jacoby, "Common Decency." From *The New York Times Magazine,* May 9, 1991. Copyright © 1991 by Susan Jacoby. Reprinted with the permission of Georges Borchardt, Inc.

Jamaica Kincaid, "On Seeing England for the First Time." From *Transition* (1991). Reprinted with the permission of Wylie, Aitken & Stone, Inc.

Martin Luther King, Jr., "Letter from Birmingham Jail." From *Why We Can't Wait.* Copyright © 1963, 1964 by Martin Luther King, Jr., renewed 1991, 1992 by Coretta Scott King. Reprinted with the permission of Joan Daves Agency.

Jonathan Kozol, "The Human Cost of an Illiterate Society." From *Illiterate America.* Copyright © 1985 by Jonathan Kozol. Reprinted with the permission of Doubleday, a division of Bantam Doubleday Dell Publishing Group, Inc.

Janice Mirikitani, "Suicide Note." From *Shedding Silence.* Copyright © 1987 by Janice Mirikitani. Reprinted with the permission of the author and Celestial Arts, P.O. Box 7327, Berkeley, CA 94707.

Jessica Mitford, "The Embalming of Mr. Jones." From *The American Way of Death* (Simon & Schuster, 1963, 1978). Copyright © 1963, 1978 by Jessica Mitford. Reprinted with the permission of the author, c/o Renee Wayne Golden.

N. Scott Momaday, "The Way to Rainy Mountain." From *The Way to Rainy Mountain.* First published in *The Reporter,* January 26, 1967. Copyright © 1967, 1969 by The University of New Mexico Press. Reprinted with the permission of the publishers.

Alleen Pace Nilsen, "Sexism in English: A 1990s Update." From "Sexism in English: A Feminist View" from *Female Studies VI: Closer to the Ground: Women's Classes, Criticism, Programs– 1972,* edited by Nancy Hoffman, Cynthia Secor, Adrian Tinsley. Copyright © 1972 by Nancy Hoffman, Cynthia Secor, Adrian Tinsley. Updated by Alleen Pace Nilsen, English Department, Arizona State University, Tempe, AZ 85287-0302 and reprinted with her permission.

Flannery O'Connor, "Revelation." From *Everything That Rises Must Converge.* Copyright © 1964, 1965 by The Estate of Flannery O'Connor. Reprinted with the permission of Farrar Straus & Giroux, Inc.

George Orwell, "Shooting an Elephant." From *Shooting an Elephant and Other Essays.* Copyright by Sonia Brownell Orwell and renewed © 1974 by Sonia Orwell. Reprinted with the permission of Harcourt Brace and Company and The Estate of Sonia Brownell and Martin Secker & Warburg, Ltd.

Alice Walker, "The Civil Rights Movement: What Good Was It?" From *In Search of Our Mothers' Gardens.* Copyright © 1967 by Alice Walker. Reprinted with the permission of Harcourt Brace and Company.

Amy Wang, "The Same Difference." From *The Philadelphia Inquirer* magazine, December 12, 1993. Reprinted with the permission of the author.

E. B. White, "Once More to the Lake." From *Essays of E. B. White.* Copyright 1941 by E. B. White. Reprinted with the permission of HarperCollins Publishers, Inc.

Marie Winn, "Television: The Plug-In Drug." From *The Plug-In Drug.* Copyright 1967, 1985 by Marie Winn Miller. Reprinted with the permission of Viking Penguin, a division of Penguin Books USA, Inc.

Ji-Yeon Mary Yuhfill, "Let's Tell the Story of All America's Cultures." From *The Philadelphia Inquirer,* 1991. Reprinted with the permission of *The Philadelphia Inquirer.*

William Zinsser, "College Pressures." From *Blair & Ketchum's Country Journal,* Vol. VI, No. 4, April 1979. Copyright © 1979 by William K. Zinsser. Reprinted with the permission of the author and Carol Brissie.

Index of
Terms, Authors,
and Titles